# AGENCY
## Law and Principles

# AGENCY

## Law and Principles

### THIRD EDITION

RODERICK MUNDAY

# OXFORD
UNIVERSITY PRESS

# OXFORD
UNIVERSITY PRESS

Great Clarendon Street, Oxford, OX2 6DP,
United Kingdom

Oxford University Press is a department of the University of Oxford.
It furthers the University's objective of excellence in research, scholarship,
and education by publishing worldwide. Oxford is a registered trade mark of
Oxford University Press in the UK and in certain other countries

Second Edition published in 2013
Third Edition published in 2016

Impression: 1

Published in the United States of America by Oxford University Press
198 Madison Avenue, New York, NY 10016, United States of America

British Library Cataloguing in Publication Data

Data available

Library of Congress Control Number: 2016950211

ISBN 978-0-19-878468-5

Printed and bound by
CPI Group (UK) Ltd, Croydon, CR0 4YY

# PREFACE TO THE THIRD EDITION

The French have a more or less counter-intuitive adage: *jamais deux sans trois*. Its roots are claimed to lie in mediaeval procedure: *tierce fois c'est droit*. Whatever the truth, the encouraging reception accorded to its predecessors lent a certain inevitability to the appearance of a third edition of *Agency: Law and Principles*.

The text of the present volume has been updated, revised and expanded. Most considerately, soon after the proofs of the book hit my desk, the Supreme Court handed down judgment in *Bailey and another v Angove's Pty Ltd* [2016] UKSC 47, treating of the unaccustomed subject of irrevocable agencies. At the eleventh hour the case has been integrated into the text, which is intended to represent the law as at August 2016.

In an address, delivered on the occasion of the call to the Bar and Bench of the Inner Temple of the Prince of Wales, Lord Coleridge declared himself fully satisfied that His Royal Highness had "assimilated all those gay and giddy text-books which add such zest to the perusal of the law" (*This for Remembrance*, 1925, London: T Fisher Unwin, p. 241). The present work may not rise to that dizzying level of authorship. I have tried nonetheless to ease the reader's burden and to make the text of the third edition as readable as possible.

The number three carries many connotations. Hoping that it will not evoke the opening of the witches' spell, "Thrice the brindled cat hath mew'd," I prefer to imagine that readers may make out just the very faintest echo of Ulysses' words to Ajax:

"Famed be thy tutor, and thy parts of nature
Thrice-famed, beyond all erudition."
   (*Troilus and Cressida*, act ii, sc. 3, l. 253.)

Manosque, Alpes de Haute-Provence
9 August 2016

# PREFACE TO THE SECOND EDITION

In a celebrated interview reported in *The Paris Review* in 1956 Ernest Hemingway was asked why, according to his own account, he had re-written the final section of *A Farewell to Arms* thirty-nine times. 'Was there some technical problem there? What was it that had stumped you?' the interviewer probed. With malign simplicity, Hemingway responded: 'Getting the words right'. If getting the words right first time round is tough, returning to the task for a fresh edition is not appreciably easier. Following the kind reception accorded to its predecessor, this second edition pursues an objective identical to that which propelled the first: namely, to supply a text setting forth the principles of the law of agency in as clear, rational and orderly a manner as can be managed.

No chapter has escaped amendment. Some have indeed undergone considerable reconstruction. Amongst the major new material, one could highlight two decisions of English judges sitting in cases litigated before foreign courts—Lord Neuberger of Abbotbury's judgment in the Singapore Court of Appeal in *Skandinaviska Enskilda Banken AB (Publ) v Asia Pacific Breweries (Singapore) Pte Ltd* [2009] SGCA 22 and Lord Sumption's opinion in the Judicial Committee in an appeal from Jamaica in *Kelly v Fraser* [2012] 3 WLR 1008—that go a considerable way towards clarifying the notion of apparent authority and, more particularly, the caliginous decision delivered by the Court of Appeal in *First Energy (UK) Ltd v Hungarian International Bank Ltd* [1993] 2 Lloyd's LR 194. In a similar way, *Knight Frank LLP v du Haney* [2011] EWCA Civ 404 might be said to have identified more exactly the extent of an agent's warranty of authority. The text also takes account of what the author, along with others, would consider the retrograde decision of the Court of Appeal in *Sinclair Investments (UK) Ltd v Versailles Trade Finance Ltd* [2012] Ch 453. *Sinclair Investments* has unexpectedly given *Lister v Stubbs* (1890) LR 45 ChD 1 a fresh lease of life, supporting the proposition that a beneficiary can have no proprietary interest in a bribe or secret commission unless it is, or has been, beneficially the property of the beneficiary or unless the fiduciary acquired the asset by taking advantage of an opportunity or right which was properly that of the beneficiary (see further *Cadogan Petroleum plc v Tolley* [2012] 1 P & CR DG5).

Revision of this text took place under difficult circumstances. I would like to express my appreciation to Rachel Alban and Rachel Mullaly for their understanding and patience. However, to my wife, Jasmine, go my greatest thanks.

Roderick Munday
Cambridge, 22 July 2013

# CONTENTS—SUMMARY

# CONTENTS

## 9. Legal Relations Between Principal and Agent: Rights of the Agent against the Principal

## 10. Legal Relations Between Principal and Third Party

## 11. The Tortious Liabilities of Principal and Agent

## 12. Legal Relations Between Agent and Third Party

## 13. Termination of Agency

# Contents

# TABLE OF CASES

# TABLE OF EUROPEAN LEGISLATION

## DIRECTIVES

# TABLE OF STATUTES

# STATUTORY INSTRUMENTS

# 1

# THE NATURE OF 'AGENCY'

## Usage of the Term 'Agent'

The American Law Institute's *Restatement of the Law—Agency* defines agency as 'the **1.01** fiduciary relationship that arises when one person (a "principal") manifests assent to another person (an "agent") that the agent shall act on the principal's behalf and subject to the principal's control, and the agent manifests assent or otherwise consents so to act'.[1] Although issue could be taken with the detail, this does bring

---

[1] See §1.01 'Agency Defined'.

out the following distinctive legal traits of agency: that agency is a fiduciary relationship; that in most instances the relationship between principal and agent will be consensual, very often contractual; and that the agent's role is to act on behalf of the principal.

### The term 'agency' is frequently employed imprecisely in commerce

**1.02** The concept of agency is notoriously slippery, and difficult to define. In part, this is because agency can take on a multitude of different forms, and in part because the word 'agent' is often used indiscriminately to describe individuals and entities whose activities, in strict legal terms, are not actually governed by the law of agency. Just as a Bombay duck would not be expected to quack, so too a 'motor factor' is unlikely to be a 'factor' in a conventional agency sense of a selling agent, a 'sole agent' is more probably a distributor than an 'agent', and even an 'estate agent' will not normally fulfil the classical criteria of agency when selling properties for clients as he will rarely be empowered, without more, to bring his principal into direct contractual relations with a third party purchaser.[2]

**1.03** The problem of distinguishing between true cases of agency and other legal relationships is far from new. Lord Herschell perceived it clearly in *Kennedy v De Trafford*:

> No word is more commonly and constantly abused than the word 'agent'. A person may be spoken of as an 'agent', and no doubt in the popular sense of the word may properly be said to be an 'agent', although when it is attempted to suggest that he is an 'agent' under such circumstances as create the legal obligations attaching to agency that use of the word is only misleading.[3]

In *WT Lamb and Sons v Goring Brick Co Ltd*,[4] too, where a manufacturer of bricks appointed a merchant who purchased his bricks and re-sold them to builders and contractors as 'sole selling agents', Greer, LJ felt impelled to remark:

> It is somewhat remarkable that, notwithstanding the numerous cases in which the difference between a buyer and an agent has been pointed out, there are still

---

[2] To mention a few further commercial examples, an 'escrow agent'—*aliter*, an 'escrow officer'—simply signifies a legal arrangement whereby money, or intellectual or other property is handed over to a neutral third party who holds that money or property in trust pending the fulfilment of a contract: eg *Dyer v Piclux SA* [2004] EWHC 1266 (Comm). Nor is a 'company formation agent' an agent in the true sense: *Aerostar Maintenance Int'l Ltd v Wilson* [2010] EWHC 2032 (Ch) at [73] *per* Morgan, J, any more than is a 'calculation agent': *WestLB AG v Nomura Bank International plc* [2012] EWCA Civ 495. Nomenclature, then, can deceive. Indeed, a contract may import substance to the term, distinct from its conventional legal sense: *NYK Bulkship (Atlantic) NV v Cargill International SA* [2016] 1 WLR 1853, esp at [14].

[3] [1897] AC 180, 188. This passage was recently cited by the High Court of Australia in *Cassegrain v Gerard Cassegrain & Co Pty Ltd* [2015] HCA 2 at [37]: 'as has been said (in *Sweeney v Boylan Nominees Pty Ltd* (2006) 226 CLR 161 at [29]) ... in a closely related context, using a word like "agent" is to begin, not end, the relevant inquiry.'

[4] [1932] 1 KB 710.

innumerable persons engaged in business who do not understand the simple and logical distinction between a buyer and agent for sale, but are content to treat the two words as synonymous.[5]

Subsequently, in *Potter v Customs & Excise Commissioners*,[6] Sir John Donaldson, MR noted:

> The use of the word 'agent' in any mercantile transaction is, of itself, wholly un-informative of the legal relationship between the parties, and the use of the words 'independent agent' takes the matter no further. Either is consistent with a self-employed person acting either as a true agent who puts his principal into a con-tractual relationship with a third party or with such a person acting as a principal.[7]

To compound the difficulties, some commercial actors who regularly style them-selves 'agents'—such as 'forwarding agents', who are responsible for organizing ship-ments of goods—will not necessarily be acting in that capacity: 'forwarding agents act in many capacities, sometimes as agents and sometimes as principals.'[8] It has been said that determining in which capacity a forwarding agent is acting is 'very much a matter of impression'.[9]

At other times, the term 'agent' is not necessarily employed even where there exists **1.04** a principal-and-agent relationship. Although, broadly, company law falls outside the present book's remit, a significant proportion of the cases to which reference will be made concern the actions of company directors. As Cairns, LJ remarked in *Ferguson v Wilson*:

> What is the position of directors of a public company? They are merely agents of a company. The company itself cannot act in its own person, for it has no person; it can only act through directors, and the case is, as regards those directors, merely the ordinary case of principal and agent. Wherever an agent is liable those directors would be liable; where the liability would attach to the principal, and the principal only, the liability is the liability of the company. This being a contract alleged to be made by the company, I own that I have not been able to see how it can be maintained that an agent can be brought into this court, or into any other court, upon a proceeding which simply alleges that his principal has violated a contract that he has entered into. In that state of things, not the agent, but the principal, would be the person liable.[10]

Usage of the term 'agent', then, may be legally uninformative. However, it would be **1.05** an error to assume that, even when used in a correct legal sense, the rules affecting agents are uniform. As we shall discover throughout this book, specific rules and

---

[5] *Ibid* at 720.
[6] [1985] STC 45.
[7] *Ibid* at 51.
[8] *Mar-Train Heavy Haulage Ltd. v Shipping.DK Chartering A/S* [2014] EWHC 355 (Comm) at [28].
[9] *Tetroc Ltd v Cross-Con (International) Ltd* [1981] 1 Lloyd's Rep 192, 198. See further *Aqualon (UK) Ltd v Vallana Shipping Corporation* [1994] 1 Lloyd's Rep 669, 674 *per* Mance, J.
[10] (1866) LR 2 Ch App 77, 89 90.

customs may apply to different species of agent. Additionally, from time to time both domestic and European legislation have created new forms of agency. In order to foster uniformity of practice within the Union, European legislation also requires courts to adopt a mode of interpreting texts distinct from that employed in the domestic context.

## Varieties of Agency

**1.06**  A law of agency first emerged as a largely unitary body of common law. However, particular customs, many of which later hardened into rules, came to be recognized to apply to particular classes of intermediary. By the eighteenth century, for instance, it was fully accepted that those agents known as 'factors' had the right to sell their principals' goods in their own names; brokers, in contrast, did not.[11] But whereas the fundamental notion of an agent, as a fiduciary, acting on behalf of a principal and altering the latter's legal relations with third parties has endured, the terminology of the subject has not always remained constant over time. Confusingly, whilst some traditional 'factors' still exist selling goods in their own names, today one direct descendant of the factor—the factoring company—is actually a species of financier, specializing in the acquisition of accounts receivable, and no longer an agent at all.[12]

### The degree of liability undertaken by the agent

**1.07**  The extent of the liability an agent undertakes on behalf of his principal, too, can vary considerably. In the classical form of agency the agent will act very much as a facilitator: the agent will bring principal and third party into direct relations with one another but will incur neither rights nor liabilities under the resulting contract. As Lord Denning, MR said in *Phonogram Ltd v Lane*:

> The general principle is, of course, that a person who makes a contract ostensibly as an agent cannot afterwards sue or be sued upon it.[13]

---

[11] *George v Claggett* (1797) 7 TR 359; (1797) 2 Esp 557. In relation to specialized classes of agent, too, nomenclature must be viewed with suspicion. As Sir Andrew Park noted in *Re Global Trader Europe Ltd* [2010] BCC 729 at [17], 'Global Trader was commonly described as a broker. It carried on business with persons whom it described as clients and who wished to enter into either or both of two kinds of financial transaction, referred to as contracts for differences and spread bet trades. The terms "broker" and "client" were regularly used, but in the context of Global Trader's business they did not carry their more usual meanings of one person, the broker, acting on behalf of another, the client, and arranging for the client to enter into a transaction with a third party. Usually a person described as a broker is an agent of some sort for the client. In the present case, however, Global Trader was not an agent for its "clients". If a client wanted to enter into, say, a contract for differences he concluded the contract with Global Trader: Global Trader was not the client's agent; it was itself the counterparty to the contract.'

[12] See, eg, R Munday, *A Legal History of the Factor* (1977) 6 Anglo-American LR 221.

[13] [1982] 3 CMLR 615 at [23].

In contrast, however, an agent may act in such a manner as to engage his personal liability on his principal's contract. The agent who acts for an undisclosed principal, in the first instance, will be party to the contract with the third party and normally will remain so until such time as the principal chooses to disclose himself.[14] Also, as we shall see, an agent may contract with the third party so as to engage his personal liability, either by an express term of the contract, perhaps by trade custom,[15] or by the character in which he signs the contract on behalf of his principal.[16] Some agencies even incorporate an element of credit insurance. Notably, *del credere* agency occurs when an agent, for a specially agreed commission (often, a double commission) undertakes to act as surety in respect of the due performance of contracts he has entered into on behalf of his principal. Because this variety of agency involves the agent's undertaking unusually extensive liability to the principal—normally, with the agent guaranteeing the creditworthiness of third parties,[17] although such an arrangement may be inferred from the parties' previous business dealings—*del credere* agency will almost always be specifically negotiated between principal and agent. *Del credere* agency has a long history,[18] but is nowadays said to be something of a rarity. In view of the range of alternative credit mechanisms available to principals—documentary credits, export credit guarantees, etc—'*del credere* agency would often in modern conditions involve liabilities which an ordinary commercial agent acting for commission would be reluctant to undertake.'[19] Buxton, LJ, in *Blything v BVV/ HFA Dekker*, added the further reflection 'that that must necessarily be the case when the parties concerned are all within the European Union.'[20] Nevertheless, the practice endures.[21]

The law of agency has gained in complexity largely thanks to legislation, which **1.08** has intervened both to create new species of agent outright and to provide specifically for duties and privileges to attach to particular categories of agent, either by the enactment of settled trade customs or by the introduction of fresh rules.

---

[14] See **chapter 10**.

[15] *Hutchinson v Tatham* (1873) LR 8 CP 482.

[16] See paras **12.05–12.15**.

[17] 'A *del credere* agent is one who guarantees the price of goods purchased by a third party': *Mercantile International Group plc v Chuan Soon Huat Industrial Group Ltd* [2002] 1 All ER (Comm) 788 at [40] *per* Rix, LJ.

[18] Eg, *Associated British Ports v Ferryways NV* [2008] 2 Lloyd's Rep 353 at [63] *per* Field, J.

[19] *Bowstead & Reynolds on Agency* (2014: London, Sweet & Maxwell) 20th ed, by Watts, para 1.038.

[20] (1999) 27 April, unreported, transcript no QBENF 1997/1630/1.

[21] Eg, *Gabem Management Ltd v Commissioners for Revenue and Customs*, 2007 WL 919446; *Bank Negara Indonesia 1946 v Taylor* [1995] CLC 255; *Mercury Publicity Ltd v Wolfgang Loerke GmbH* [1993] ILPr 142.

### 'Mercantile agents' under the Factors Act 1889

**1.09**  A significant statutory invention has been the creation of a class of 'mercantile agents' under the Factors Act 1889. The current statute followed a succession of earlier Acts passed during the course of the nineteenth century to regulate the powers of factors. Over the centuries, 'factor' has meant several different things. Cotton, LJ, in *Stevens v Biller*, famously defined the factor at common law as a mercantile agent who has goods in his possession for the purpose of sale.[22] The 1889 Act, which repealed and replaced the Factors Acts 1823–1877—those earlier 'treasuries of perplexing pomposity'[23]—curiously only uses the word 'factor' in its long and short titles, substituting instead in the body of the statute the term 'mercantile agent'.[24] Section 1(1) defines a 'mercantile agent', somewhat tautologously, as:

> ... a mercantile agent having in the customary course of his business as such agent authority either to sell goods, or to consign goods for the purpose of sale, or to buy goods, or to raise money on the security of goods.

The statutory definition reaches far beyond the traditional factor, the selling agent, to a very wide range of persons indeed. The mercantile agent need no longer belong to any recognized class of agent, such as factors and brokers.[25] The definition may encompass those acting as agents in a single transaction, provided that they were acting in the course of business.[26] It has even been held to apply in certain circumstances to the owner of goods.[27] The effect of the 1889 Act has been to create an entirely new class of agent, of which the traditional factor of the common law was just one part.

**1.10**  The Factors Act 1889 endows a 'mercantile agent' with wide powers to pass title to goods belonging to his principal which are in the agent's possession. As Lord Goff of Chieveley explained in *National Employers' Mutual General Insurance Association Ltd v Jones*,[28] successive Factors Acts have sought to provide protection for those dealing in good faith with factors or mercantile agents to whom goods or documents of title had been entrusted by the true owner to the extent that their rights overrode those of the true owner.[29] The Acts were not intended, however, to enable a *bona fide*

---

[22] (1883) 25 ChD 31, 37.

[23] AR Butterworth, *Bankers' Advances and Mercantile Securities* (1902: London) p 43.

[24] See *Triffit Nurseries v Salads Etcetera Ltd* [2000] 2 Lloyd's Rep 74, 79 *per* Robert Walker, LJ. See also H Gutteridge, *Contract and Commercial Law* (1935) 51 LQR at p 140.

[25] See *Lowther v Harris* [1927] 1 KB 393.

[26] Eg, *Budberg v Jerwood and Ward* (1934) 51 TLR 99.

[27] Eg, *Lloyd's Bank Ltd v Bank of America National Trust & Savings Association* [1937] 2 KB 147. Cp *Belvoir Finance Co Ltd v Harold G Cole & Co Ltd* [1969] 1 WLR 1877.

[28] [1990] 1 AC 24.

[29] The declared aim was 'to protect bankers who made advances to mercantile agents ... by means of an inroad on the common law rule that no one could give better title to goods than he himself had': *Official Assignee of Madras v Mercantile Bank of India Ltd* [1935] AC 53, 60 *per* Lord Wright. However, as Scrutton, LJ pointed out, this was a concept that the courts were slow to embrace: 'The

purchaser for value to override the true owner's title where the mercantile agent had been entrusted with the documents or goods by a thief or a purchaser from a thief.

Perhaps suffice it to say for the time being, whilst the Law of Agency can still be **1.11** claimed with some justice to exhibit a common core of principles, it is also a subject that in its detail grows ever more fragmentary.

### Sole agencies and contracts in restraint of trade

*Contracts in restraint of trade.* Both during the course of the agency and, more espe- **1.12** cially, after termination of the relationship, a principal may wish to protect his com-mercial position by means of restraint of trade clauses that seek to restrict the agent's freedom to engage in commercial activities that risk competing with those in which the principal engages. English law holds that, irrespective of whether they apply during the operation of the contract or after its termination, contractual terms that operate in unreasonable restraint of trade are unlawful and unenforceable.[30] The law on restrictive practices embodies a proposition, enunciated with authority by Lord McNaghten in *Nordenfelt v Maxim Nordenfelt Guns & Ammunition Co Ltd*, that:

> The public have an interest in every person's carrying on his trade freely: so has the individual. All interference with individual liberty of action in trading, and all restraints of trade of themselves, if there is nothing more, are contrary to public policy …[31]

Broadly speaking,[32] a principal seeking to uphold an agreement that restricts the activities of his agent must show[33] that he has a legitimate interest to protect, that the restraint the contract imposes is reasonable in the context of protecting that interest,[34] and that the restraint does not otherwise operate in a manner contrary to the public interest.[35] The scope of the restraint will be examined by the court. If it

---

history of the Factors Acts is restriction of their language by the Courts in favour of the true owner, followed by reversal of the Courts' decisions by the Legislature': *Folkes v King* [1923] 1 KB 282, 306.

[30] *A. Schroeder Music Publishing Co Ltd v Macaulay* [1974] 1 W.L.R. 1308.

[31] [1894] AC 535, 564.

[32] Detailed treatment of this subject is beyond the scope of an introductory book. For further information, see, *Chitty on Contracts* (2015) 32nd ed, by Beale, §§16-085–16-151.

[33] *Herbert Morris Ltd v Saxelby* [1916] 1 AC 688, 700 *per* Lord Atkinson, and 707 *per* Lord Parker of Waddington.

[34] 'Now the better opinion is that the Court ought not to hold the contract void unless the defendant "made it plainly and obviously clear that the plaintiff's interest did not require the de-fendant's exclusion or that the public interest would be sacrificed" if the proposed restraint were upheld: *Tallis v Tallis* (1853) 1 El&Bl 391': quoted in *Nordenfelt v Maxim Nordenfelt*, at p 565 *per* Lord Macnaghten.

[35] 'What is the doctrine's purpose and scope? It arises from the deep concern of our common law with the personal liberty of the citizen. So innate is personal liberty to us as a people and thus to our common law that our common law has identified it with public policy': *Texaco Ltd v Mulberry Filling Station Ltd* [1972] 1 WLR 814, 827 *per* Ungoed-Thomas, J. As DD Prentice has noted, '[T]he requirement of public interest adds nothing to the requirement that the restraint be reasonable in the interests of the parties' (*Chitty on Contracts*, §16-106.)

extends over too great a length of time, over too wide a geographical area, or over an excessive range of commercial activities, the restraint will not be upheld.[36]

**1.13** *Sole agency agreements.* At first sight, it might appear that sole agency agreements, under which an agent is bound to work exclusively for one principal, are liable to fall foul of this principle. The law, however, recognizes that sole agencies are a common, and potentially beneficial, feature of modern commerce.[37] For this reason, in such cases something especially restrictive is required before the restraint of trade principle will bite. In the words of Lord Pearce:

> Sole agencies are a normal and necessary incident of commerce and those who desire the benefits of a sole agency must deny themselves the opportunities of other agencies.[38]

Thus, his Lordship declared:

> When a contract only ties the parties during the continuance of the contract, and the negative ties are only those which are incidental and normal to the positive commercial arrangements at which the contract aims, even though those ties exclude all dealings with others, there is no restraint of trade within the meaning of the doctrine and no question of reasonableness arises.[39]

If, in contrast, a contract ties the trading activities of either party after the termination of the contract, it is a restraint of trade, and the question of reasonableness will arise. Equally, if during the contract one of the parties is unilaterally fettered to an excessive degree and the contract, as a result, loses its character of a contract for the regulation and promotion of trade and acquires instead the predominant character of a contract in restraint of trade, it will be assumed to be an unlawful restraint of trade unless the restrictions can be shown to be reasonable.

**1.14** In *One Money Mail Ltd v Ria Financial* Services,[40] for example, an agent, W, was granted a sole agency by OMM, a firm that specialized in the Polish money remittance business. Under his contract, W had agreed not to operate as a principal or as an agent for another money transfer organization and also agreed certain post-termination restrictions. In breach of these undertakings, after three years W began to work for the respondent company, R. OMM appealed against the first-instance judge's ruling that both sets of restrictions on W were in restraint of trade and unenforceable. The judge's ruling had been determined by a lack of reciprocity in the parties' agreement, which permitted OMM to appoint another agent in the area if it so wished as well as a comparatively short notice period for termination of the agency

---

[36] For a fuller list of elements that might render such an agreement reasonable, see *Cavendish Square Holdings BV v Makdessi* [2013] 1 All ER (Comm) 787 at [15] *per* Burton, J.

[37] In *Esso Petroleum Co Ltd v Harper's Garage (Stourport) Ltd* [1968] A.C. 269, at p 336 Lord Wilberforce observed that the law had come to accept that in the case of sole agencies restrictions on trade were accepted because they served to encourage and strengthen, rather than limit, trade.

[38] *Ibid* at 328.

[39] *Ibid* at 328.

[40] [2015] EWCA Civ 1084.

available to OMM but not to W. On appeal, Longmore, LJ was not persuaded that OMM's ability under the contract to appoint another agent under the contract was decisive.[41] 'The key', it was said, was 'the question of sterilisation', a concept derived from Lord Pearce's speech in *Esso Petroleum Co Ltd v Harper's Garage (Stourport) Ltd*, in which he had said:

> The [restraint of trade] doctrine does not apply to ordinary commercial contracts for the regulation and promotion of trade during the existence of the contract, provided that any prevention of work outside the contract, viewed as a whole, is directed towards the absorption of the parties' services and not their sterilisation ... When a contract only ties the parties during the continuance of the contract, and the negative ties are only those which are incidental and normal to the positive commercial arrangements at which the contract aims, even though those ties exclude all dealings with others, there is no restraint of trade within the meaning of the doctrine and no question of reasonableness arises. If, however, the contract ties the trading activities of either party after its determination, it is a restraint of trade, and the question of reasonableness arises. So, too, if during the contract one of the parties is too unilaterally fettered so that the contract loses its character of a contract for the regulation and promotion of trade and acquires the predominant character of a contract in restraint of trade. In that case ... the question whether it is reasonable arises.[42]

In *One Money Mail* it was held that W's activities were not 'sterilised' and nothing prevented W from earning commission on transfers he effected on behalf of OMM. In any case, there might be legitimate reasons for OMM wishing to appoint another agent—for instance, if the volume of business within the relevant area rose unexpectedly or if W proved ineffectual in persuading Polish nationals to avail themselves of OMM's services.[43]

## Agency and European Union Law

In recent years European law has excited considerable impact on the English law of agency. It both affects the way in which certain bodies of rules require to be interpreted, and also via the Commercial Agents (Council Directive) Regulations 1993 has created an entirely new and commercially significant form of agency, whose enacted principles are at variance with traditional common-law agency rules. **1.15**

When determining the purpose of a European Directive, courts may have to consult a range of sources, relatively unfamiliar to English lawyers. They may refer to the instrument's preamble[44] or to the explanatory notes that accompany the Directive.[45] **1.16**

---

[41] *Ibid* at [11].
[42] [1968] AC 269, 328.
[43] [2015] EWCA Civ 1084, [11].
[44] *P Conradsen A/S v Ministeriet for Skatter og Afgifter* [1979] ECR 2221 at [1] (Case 161/78).
[45] *East (t/a Margetts and Addenbrooke) v Cuddy* [1988] ECR 625 at [11] (Case 143/86). The use of explanatory notes as an aid to the interpretation of English statutes is contested: R Munday, *Explanatory Notes and Statutory Interpretation* (2006) 170 JPJo 124.

Equally, in order to tease out the legislative intention it is not unheard of for a court to invoke draft legislative proposals that may have preceded the final version of the Directive.[46] Since the European Union is a multi-lingual legal endeavour, in the interests of uniform application reference to other language versions of the enactment may be necessary in order to arrive at the authoritative interpretation.[47] Expressions found in the enactment must, so far as possible, be construed consistently with the EU Treaties as well as with 'general principles of Community law'.[48] Courts are duty-bound to promote the effectiveness (the so-called *effet utile*) of EU norms.[49] And, in the absence of any express reference to the laws of individual Member States, terms employed in EU legislation should receive 'an independent and uniform interpretation throughout the European Union'.[50] More generally, English courts must conform to the principle of consistent interpretation,[51] which may result in their giving legislation a meaning different to that which it would have received had English canons of statutory construction applied.

---

[46] Eg, *Bellone v Yokohama SpA* [1998] ECR I-2191 at [16] (Case C-215/97): 'That interpretation of the Directive is borne out by the fact that, as already mentioned, the question of registration of agents had already been addressed during the preparatory work, but was not taken up, since it was not considered necessary for agents to be registered in order to enjoy rights under the Directive.'

[47] *Ferrière Nord SpA v Commission of the European Communities* [1997] ECR I-4411 at [15] (Case C219/95): 'In fact, ... it is settled case-law that Community provisions must be interpreted and applied uniformly in the light of the versions existing in the other Community languages (*Van der Vecht and CILFIT v Ministry of Health* [1967] ECR 345 at [18]). This is unaffected by the fact that, as it happens, the Italian version of Article 85, considered on its own, is clear and unambiguous, since all the other language versions expressly render the condition set out in Article 85(1) of the Treaty in the form of an alternative.'

[48] *Ordre des barreaux francophones et germanophones v Conseil des ministres* [2007] ECR I-5305 (C-305/05) at [28]: '[T]he Court has consistently held that, if the wording of secondary Community law is open to more than one interpretation, preference should be given to the interpretation which renders the provision consistent with the EC Treaty rather than to the interpretation which leads to its being incompatible with the Treaty (see *Commission v Council* [1983] ECR 4063 (Case 218/82) at [15], and *Spain v Commission* [1995] ECR I-1651 (Case C-135/93) at [37]). Member States must not only interpret their national law in a manner consistent with Community law but also make sure they do not rely on an interpretation of wording of secondary legislation which would be in conflict with the fundamental rights protected by the Community legal order or with the other general principles of Community law (Case C-101/01 *Lindqvist* [2003] ECR I-12971 at [87]).'

[49] Eg, *Grad v Finanzamt Traunstein* [1970] ECR 825 (Case 9/70) esp at [5].

[50] *Brüstle v Greenpeace eV* [2011] ECR (Case C-34/10) at [25]: 'It must be borne in mind that, according to settled case-law, the need for a uniform application of European Union law and the principle of equality require that the terms of a provision of European Union law which makes no express reference to the law of the Member States for the purpose of determining its meaning and scope must normally be given an independent and uniform interpretation throughout the European Union (see, in particular, *Ekro* [1984] ECR 107 (Case 327/82) at [11]; *Linster* [2000] ECR I-6917 (Case C-287/98) at [43]; *Infopaq International* [2009] ECR I-6569 (Case C-5/08) at [27]; and *Padawan* [2010] ECR I-0000 (Case C-467/08) at [32]).'

[51] *Bernhard Pfeiffer v Deutsches Rotes Kreuz, Kreisverband Waldshut eV* [2004] ECR I-8835, Cases C-397/01-C-403/01 at [118]: '[T]he principle of interpretation in conformity with Community law thus requires the referring court to do whatever lies within its jurisdiction, having regard to the whole body of rules of national law, to ensure that Directive ... is fully effective, ... (see, to that effect, [Case C-106/89 *Marleasing* [1990] ECR I-4135], at [7] and [13]).'

## European Union law: the Customs Code

The notion of 'agency' and the expression 'agent' may therefore require to be dif- **1.17** ferently interpreted in different contexts. In the realm of taxation, for instance, when interpreting the Customs Code, which involves construing matters according to principles of European Community law, courts are enjoined to avoid applying the technical agency concepts of domestic law. The reason is that, when answering a question by reference to Community law, the court should interpret the situation according to a broad 'notion of acting in the name and for the account of another and not by reference to civil law provisions concerning agency and mandate which vary from one legal system to another'.[52] *Ex hypothesi* technical common-law concepts, too, are to be eschewed.

To take an example, in *Umbro International Ltd v Revenue and Customs* **1.18** *Commissioners*,[53] U, which used P to import football team shirts manufactured in China, sought to argue that P was its buying agent and that the Commissioners had wrongly assessed U for customs duty not only for the price of the goods but also for its agent's commission which for a number of years had been incorporated into the overall price stated on P's invoices to U. P did not manufacture goods itself, but placed orders for U only with companies on an approved list produced by U. U furnished P with detailed specifications, indicating the quality and quantity of products it required as well as setting target prices that it was prepared to pay for them. P was responsible, at its own expense, for visiting manufacturers, negotiating prices with them, obtaining samples, scheduling delivery dates, performing quality control functions, ensuring that the products fell within EC customs duty quotas and ensuring that the goods could be supplied within the requisite timescale. P was also responsible for insurance and payment for transport, storage and delivery of the goods. In agreeing a contract price with U, P took into account the manufacturing costs, its costs of providing the above services, and its own profit. U did not enquire about P's margin of profit, which might vary from order to order, and sometimes even within a single order. A written purchase order, containing terms and conditions describing P as 'supplier', was submitted by U to P once a contract price had been agreed. P was free to place orders with any approved manufacturer of its choice without reference to U. On delivery of the goods, the Chinese manufacturer invoiced P for them and P then invoiced U in a higher sum, the difference being P's gross profit. U would then pay P. P's invoices to U did not specify P's commission; it was not possible to calculate the amount of its profit from the information stated in the invoices. The invoices, raised 'for account U', did not describe P as U's agent. In the invoices from the manufacturer to P, P was described

---

[52] Advocate-General Kokott in *De Danske Bilimpotorer v Skatteministeriet* (Case C-98/05, judgment 16 March 2006), with whose argument the European Court of Justice agreed.
[53] [2009] EWHC 438 (Ch); [2009] STC 1345.

as 'purchaser' and there was no mention of U. There was no written agreement between P and U purporting to define the commercial relationship between them.

1.19    The VAT and Duties Tribunal (Manchester) had concluded[54] that all in all there was insufficient evidence of a buying agency and declined to order repayment of duty. It laid particular emphasis on the parties' documentation—the standard terms and conditions printed on the back of each purchase order. This not only described P as 'the supplier', with no mention of agency, but also imposed obligations pointing towards a liability as principal (eg, the incidence of risk, warranty as to quality and provision as to refunds for unsatisfactory goods) and rendered P liable, at its own cost, to provide product liability insurance for the goods. This was said to tie in with the fact that all invoices from the manufacturer were addressed to P, which in turn invoiced Umbro, and the fact that all payments were made by P and all debit notes were issued by U to P. Admittedly, these circumstances were not necessarily inconsistent with U acting as undisclosed principal.[55] Nevertheless, the Tribunal considered that there was no, or insufficient, evidence that P was merely facilitating a contract between the Chinese manufacturer and U or otherwise to support a finding of agency.

1.20    On appeal, Proudman, J derived assistance from the Explanatory Notes and the Commentary accompanying Article 8 of the WTO's GATT Agreement,[56] which stress such matters as the need for an agent always to act for the account of a principal, to take a commission that is normally expressed as a percentage of the cost of goods bought or sold, to be paid by the importer, etc. Also, those Explanatory Notes stress that whether or not a particular individual is actually an 'agent' will turn 'in the final analysis, on the role played by the intermediary and not on the term ("agent" or "broker") by which he is known.' Drawing a further analogy with the way in which one identifies which 'commercial agents' fall within that designation under the European Directive on Commercial Agents,[57] and adopting Rix, LJ's view of that Directive expressed in *Mercantile International Group plc v Chuan Soon Huat Industrial Group Ltd*[58] that the test is one of substance rather than form, Proudman, J concluded that although the Tribunal did not indicate how they thought that the Customs Code ought to be construed, nevertheless one could infer that they correctly believed that the expressions used in the definition of 'buying commission' in the Code had to be ascribed their natural meaning as understood by an English court, bearing in mind

---

[54] See *Umbro International Ltd v Revenue and Customs Commissioners* [2009] EWHC 438 (Ch).
[55] On undisclosed agency, see paras **10.27ff**.
[56] See also Case C-486/06 *BVBA Van Landeghem*, judgment 6 December 2007, para 25.
[57] See, eg, discussion of *AMB Imballaggi Plastici SRL v Pacflex Ltd* [1999] 2 All ER (Comm) 249, at para **1.43**.
[58] [2002] 1 All ER (Comm) 788.

the Explanatory Note and Commentary. Proudman, J, therefore, upheld the Tribunal's decision that U had not discharged the burden of proving that P was its buying agent, agreeing incidentally that the variable commission was a neutral circumstance.[59]

### European Union law: the Commercial Agents (Council Directive) Regulations

In a similar way, we shall discover presently that, in the context of 'commercial **1.21** agents' operating under the Commercial Agents (Council Directive) Regulations 1993, it remains a moot question whether certain well-understood concepts of the English law of agency, which appear to figure in the definition of 'commercial agent' in reg 2(1) of the Directive—notably, the words 'conclude the sale or purchase of goods on behalf of and in the name of that principal'—are actually intended to wear the same meaning under the Directive.[60] Nor has this difficult question necessarily been clarified by Lord Hoffmann's speech in *Lonsdale (t/a Lonsdale Agencies) v Howard & Hallam Ltd (Winemakers' Federation of Australia Inc intervening)*,[61] where his Lordship justified different national interpretations of the Directive's rules on compensation of commercial agents applying in different jurisdictions because the agents in question, whilst trading within a single market, in another sense could be said to be operating in different markets. Since it is unlikely that the Directive's draughtsmen had in mind English law's particular perspective on what actually constitutes agency—and what generic forms are legally permissible—when they framed the Directive, and bearing in mind the harmonizing objectives of the Directive,[62] it is not self-evident that 'commercial agent' was intended to have diverse meanings within the Member States.[63]

## Seeking the Essence of Agency

In orthodox parlance, in English law agency is a legal relationship that involves three **1.22** parties: a 'principal', on whose behalf the agent acts; an 'agent', who acts on behalf of the principal; and 'third parties' whom the agent brings into legal relations with

---

[59] *Ex p Bright re Smith* (1879) 10 Ch D 566, 570 *per* Sir George Jessel, MR.
[60] See paras **13.48–13.49**.
[61] [2007] 1 WLR 2055, esp at [18].
[62] See *Tamarind International Ltd v Eastern Natural Gas (Retail) Ltd* [2000] CLC 1397, esp at [10] *per* Morison, J.
[63] Nor are matters helped when a report mistakenly refers to a commercial agent under the Directive as a 'mercantile agent', a term that properly refers to agents under the Factors Act 1889 and the Sale of Goods Act 1979: *Mercantile International Group plc v Chuan Soon Huat Industrial Group Ltd* [2003] ECC 28, at H5.

the principal. That said, the question is frequently posed, what distinctive element or elements lie at the heart of agency?

### The agent creates or alters legal relations between a principal and a third party

**1.23**  One thing, which is beyond dispute, is that the agent enjoys the power to alter the legal relations of his principal *vis-à-vis* a third party. Having first rehearsed Lord Hershell's concerns over how loosely the term 'agent' is used,[64] Justice Gummow, in the Australian High Court in *Scott v Davis*, supplied a helpful working definition of the archetypal form of agency:

> There is considerable terminological confusion in this area. The term 'agency' is best used, in the words of the joint judgment of this Court in *International Harvester Co. of Australia Pty Ltd. v. Carrigan's Hazeldene Pastoral Co*,[65] 'to connote an authority or capacity in one person to create legal relations between a person occupying the position of principal and third parties.'[66]

As Justice Gummow went on to explain:

> Usually the legal relations so created will be contractual in nature. In all these cases, the principal's liability will not be vicarious. The resultant contract is formed directly between the principal and the third party and there is no contract between the agent and the third party which is attributed to the principal.[67]

We shall see that this outline does not cover every variant of agency, but it does serve to emphasize that agency is primarily concerned to create or alter legal relations between principals and third parties, and that those resulting relations are almost invariably contractual.

### The agent as fiduciary

**1.24**  Another indisputable fact is that agency is a fiduciary relationship. Because a principal places the agent in a position of trust, empowering the latter to act for him and to alter his legal relations with third parties, the agent owes his principal 'single-minded loyalty'.[68] In short, the agent is a fiduciary and, alongside any obligations the agent may owe the principal in contract or otherwise, the agent is also subject to the conventional, strict equitable duties owed by fiduciaries: a duty not to allow his interests to conflict with those of the principal, a duty to make disclosure, a duty not to take advantage of his position, a duty not to take bribes or a secret commission, a duty not to delegate his office, and a duty to account.

---

[64] See para **1.03**.
[65] (1958) 100 CLR 644, 652 at [12].
[66] (2000) 204 CLR 333 at [227].
[67] Ibid at [228].
[68] *Bristol & West BS v Mothew* [1998] Ch 1, 18 *per* Millett, LJ.

## Agency and consent

Many would claim that consent lies at the heart of agency. As we have seen, the   **1.25**
*US Restatement* defines agency as a relationship to which both principal and agent
manifest assent. Similarly, Article 1 of *Bowstead & Reynolds on Agency*, the classical English work on the subject, states that agency founds in the notion that the
principal:

> expressly or impliedly manifests assent that the other should act on his behalf so as
> to affect his relations with third parties, and the other of whom similarly manifests
> assent so to act or so acts pursuant to the manifestation.[69]

Certain case law, too, has adopted a similar approach. In *Garnac Grain Co Inc v
HMF Faure and Fairclough Ltd*[70] Lord Pearson famously declared:

> The relationship of principal and agent can only be established by the consent
> of the principal and the agent. They will be held to have consented if they had
> agreed to what amounts in law to such a relationship, even if they do not rec-
> ognise it themselves and even if they have professed to disclaim it, as in *ex parte
> Delhasse*.[71] But the consent must have been given by each of them, either ex-
> pressly or by implication from their words and conduct. Primarily one looks to
> what they said and did at the time of the alleged creation of the agency. Earlier
> words and conduct may afford evidence of a course of dealing in existence at that
> time and may be taken into account more generally as historical background.
> Later words and conduct may have some bearing, though likely to be less im-
> portant. As to the content of the relationship, the question to be asked is: 'What
> is it that the supposed agent is alleged to have done on behalf of the supposed
> principal?'[72]

Of course, it is comparatively easy to state that consent lies at the root of agency.   **1.26**
In practice, matters may be very different when it comes to fixing the exact
nature of the various parties' relationships. For example, Rix, J, who was willing to adopt Lord Pearson's approach, admitted that the facts with which the
case presented him in *Nueva Fortuna Corporation v Tata Ltd. The 'Nea Tyhi'* occasioned 'considerable difficulties of exegesis and analysis'. These were caused by
the court's inability to penetrate the relations between the putative agent and
third party, the absence of a material witness whose written declarations in any
case were unreliable, confused documentation, claimants who were unable to
decide how to qualify the defaulting party's conduct, incomplete accounts of the
parties' elaborate dealings, witness evidence of dubious credibility, as well as the
fact that 'the legal tests contain their own difficulties of objective perception in

---

[69] (2014: London, Sweet & Maxwell) 20th ed, by Watts, para 1.001.
[70] [1968] AC 1130.
[71] See *In re Megevand, ex p Delhasse* (1878) LR 7 ChD 511.
[72] [1968] AC 1130, 1137.

circumstances where the terms "agent" or "partner" maybe used or misused more or less freely.'[73]

**1.27**  In any case, it does not do to rely too heavily on assent/consent to explain agency. Consent does not lie at the heart of every agency. When the apparent authority of the agent is engaged, and the principal is effectively estopped from denying the authority of his agent, the resulting relationship is not exactly consensual.[74] When the law either imposes an agency relationship on the parties or extends an existing agency, as a matter of necessity, in order to enable the 'agent' to confront some emergency and protect the principal's interests, the relationship is scarcely consensual. Further, as the passage from Lord Pearson's speech in *Garnac Grain* reminds us, detecting agency is not merely a matter of looking mechanically for assent on the part of the putative principal and agent. Agency is a legal, rather than simply a factual, question. In Lord Pearson's words, the parties 'will be held to have consented if they had agreed to what amounts in law to such a relationship, even if they do not recognise it themselves and even if they have professed to disclaim it.'[75]

### Agency and authority

**1.28**  Another way of viewing the agency relationship has been in terms of the agent's possessing the authority to bind his principal. Although agency cases and texts repeatedly speak in terms of the agent's authority, again this affords an incomplete account of agency. In a number of situations an agent, who clearly lacks authority—either because the principal never granted authority to the agent to act for him in the first place or because the agent exceeded what limited authority the principal did confer upon him—can affect the legal relations of the principal. *Lloyd v Grace Smith & Co*[76] provides a celebrated example. A widow owned two cottages and a sum of money secured on a mortgage. She consulted a firm of solicitors about maximizing the yield on these assets. She saw the managing clerk, who conducted the firm's conveyancing business unsupervised. She was induced to give him instructions to sell the cottages and to call in the mortgage money. To that end, she handed over her title deeds and signed two documents, which she neither read nor had explained to her. She believed that she had to sign them in order to effect the sale of the cottages. In fact, they served to convey the cottages to the clerk and also transferred the mortgage to him. The clerk dishonestly disposed of the property for his own benefit. The House of Lords held

---

[73] [1999] 2 Lloyd's Rep 497, 500 *per* Rix, J.
[74] See **chapter 4**.
[75] [1968] AC 1130, 1137. See also *National Trust for Places of Historic Interest v Birden* [2009] EWHC 2023 (Ch) at [150]–[151] *per* HHJ Toulmin, QC.
[76] [1912] AC 716.

that the clerk's principal, the firm of solicitors, was liable for the fraud committed by its agent in the course of his employment or authority. The House thereby dispatched any notion that earlier authorities[77] supported the proposition that a principal is not liable for the fraud of his agent unless committed for the benefit of the principal. Quite simply, a principal will be liable for the fraud of his agent, if acting within the scope of his authority, irrespective of whether or not the fraud was committed for the benefit of the principal.[78] As Lord Woolf, MR subsequently explained in *Crédit Lyonnais Bank Nederland NV v ECGD*,[79] the guiding principle is:

> The wrong of the servant or agent for which the master or principal is liable is one committed in the case of a servant in the course of his employment, and in the case of an agent in the course of his authority. It is fundamental to the whole approach to vicarious liability that an employer or principal should not be liable for acts of the servant or agent which are not performed within this limitation. In many cases, particularly cases of fraud, the question arises as to whether the particular conduct complained of is an unauthorised mode of performing what the servant or agent is engaged to do.[80]

By no stretch of the imagination could the agent in *Lloyd v Grace Smith* realistically have been said to have had true authority to act, even though the principal was held legally responsible for its errant managing clerk's acts.

### A power-liability relation

The key relationship, between principal and agent, is often stated in a more abstract **1.29** form, being described simply as a power-liability relationship. This 'nucleus of the relation of principal and agent'[81] consists in the agent possessing the power to affect the principal's legal position and the principal being under a correlative liability to see his legal position altered by his agent. In Dowrick's words:

> The distinctive feature of the agency power-liability relation is that the power of the one party to alter the legal relations of the other party is a reproduction of the power possessed by the latter to alter his own legal position. In other words, the power conferred by law on the agent is *a facsimile of the principal's own power*.[82]

---

[77] Notably, *Barwick v English Joint Stock Bank* (1867) LR 2 Ex 259. Cp *Hamlyn v Houston & Co* [1903] 1 KB 81, 85 *per* Collins, MR.

[78] See also *Armagas Ltd v Mundogas Ltd* [1986] AC 717, 782 *per* Lord Keith of Kinkel: 'In the end of the day the question is whether the circumstances under which a servant has made the fraudulent misrepresentation which has caused loss to an innocent party contracting with him are such as to make it just for the employer to bear the loss.' The *Armagas* case is discussed at paras **4.22–4.23**.

[79] [2000] 1 AC 486.

[80] *Ibid* at 494.

[81] Dowrick, *The Relationship of Principal and Agent* (1954) 17 MLR 24, 37. The 'power-liability' relationship derives from Hohfeld's analysis of jural relations in *Fundamental Legal Conceptions as Applied in Judicial Reasoning* (1946: New Haven, Yale University Press).

[82] Dowrick (1954) (emphasis added).

Dowrick's phrase evokes one of Pollock's remarks, that 'by agency the individual's legal personality is multiplied in space'.[83] That the relationship is one of power-liability, Dowrick maintains, is to be inferred from the following leading principles of the law of agency:

> [W]hen the agent acts on behalf of his principal in a legal transaction and uses the principal's name, the result in law is that the principal's legal position is altered but the agent drops out of the transaction; persons who are not themselves *sui juris* may nevertheless have the power to act as agents for persons who are; the power of the agent to bind his principal is limited to the power of the principal to bind himself; if the powers of the principal to alter his own legal relations are ended by death, insanity or bankruptcy, the agent's powers are terminated automatically.[84]

A natural corollary of the agent's power replicating that of the principal is that 'the contract is the contract of the principal, not that of the agent, and, *prima facie*, at common law the only person who may sue is the principal, and the only person who can be sued is the principal.'[85] However, this principle is subject to a number of exceptions:

> *First*, the agent may be added as the party to the contract if he has so contracted ... *Secondly*, the principal may be excluded in several other cases. He may be excluded if the contract is made by a deed *inter partes*, to which the principal is no party ... Another exception is ... if a person who is an agent makes himself a party in writing to a bill or note, by the law merchant a principal cannot be added. Another exception is that by usage, ... where there is a foreign principal, generally speaking the agent in England is the party to the contract, and not the foreign principal ... Again, where the principal is an undisclosed principal, he must, if he sues, accept the facts as he finds them at the date of his disclosure, so far as those facts are consistent with reasonable and proper conduct on the part of the other party ... Also, ... in all cases the parties can by their express contract provide that the agent shall be the person liable either concurrently with or to the exclusion of the principal, or that the agent shall be the party to sue either concurrently with or to the exclusion of the principal.[86]

**1.30**  This relatively abstract account of the role of the agent serves to emphasize that the agent's power to alter his principal's relations reflects a legal concept and not simply a factual reality. As Montrose explained:

> The power of an agent is not strictly conferred by the principal *but by the law*: the principal and agent do the acts which bring the rule into operation, as a result of which the agent acquires a power.[87]

---

[83] Winfield, *Principles of Contract* (1950: London, Stevens & Sons) 13th ed, p 45.
[84] (1954) 17 MLR 24, 37.
[85] *Montgomerie v United Kingdom Mutual SS Association Ltd* [1891] 1 QB 370, 371 *per* Wright, J.
[86] *Montgomerie* [1891] 1 QB 370 at 371–2, *per* Wright, J.
[87] *The Basis of the Power of an Agent in Cases of Actual and Apparent Authority*, 16 Can Bar Rev 756, 761 (1938) (emphasis added).

Whether a particular transaction is one of agency or, say, one of sale and resale remains a matter of proof.

*Establishing agency on the facts*

Even if one has satisfactorily teased out the essential legal attributes of the relation-  **1.31**
ship between principal and agent, actually determining whether a particular transaction is one of agency *stricto sensu*, where the agent is representing the principal and bringing a third party into relations with that principal, or a situation in which, say, a party is independently purchasing and reselling goods without bringing 'principal' and third party into direct legal relations, remains a matter of proof; and sometimes a question of some difficulty. Take Buxton, LJ's judgment in *Blything v BVV/HFA Dekker, Wright-Manley (a firm)*:[88]

> [T]he question was whether W-M was an agent at all. If, as here, the objective facts indicate that he is not, it is a matter of evidence and common sense, not of legal rule, that that analysis must prevail, unless one or other of the parties makes it clear that the facts are different.

The evidence may not all point one way. The parties will not necessarily have given the precise nature of their legal relationship detailed thought. In *Blything* itself, W-M, which was a firm of auctioneers and agricultural agents, had assisted a Cheshire farming couple in the purchase of a herd of pedigree Holstein heifers from a breeder in Holland. The Court of Appeal accepted that W-M was acting outside its normal sphere in the transaction, that W-M appeared prepared to act *ad hoc* as principal, had failed to make clear what its terms of business were, and had given the farmers no reason to think that it was acting as an agent; that no meaningful contractual discussions ever took place between the farmers and the Dutch supplier; and that the Dutch supplier regarded W-M as its customer and the farmers regarded W-M as their vendor. The documentation, too, indicated that W-M accepted financial responsibility to the Dutch supplier as it was W-M which had invoiced the farmers and received payment from them. The relationship, then, was one of sale and resale, not of agency—although Buxton, LJ also admitted, confusingly, that 'it might have been open to [the first-instance judge] to come to a different conclusion.'

The inquiry may prove far from easy. In *A1 Lofts Ltd v IIM Revenue & Customs*,[89]  **1.32**
for instance, in order to determine whether a loft conversion company had supplied a homeowner with a finished loft conversion, thereby becoming liable to account

---

[88] (1999) 27 April, unreported, transcript no QBENF 1997/1630/1. See also *Katrina Shipping Company Ltd v Adesloye* [2015] EWHC 1442 (Comm) at [15] where, despite describing himself as a forwarding agent, the court held that the defendant was a carrier offering 'a door-to-door service to the claimants for an all-in fee': 'It is a question of fact in every case where someone who is responsible for the shipping of goods is himself a shipper or an agent or a freight forwarder.'
[89] [2010] STC 214.

for VAT, or whether it acted only as an agent and project manager in respect of supplies of building services offered by independent contractors, Lewison, J was obliged to pass in review a series of complex cases in which courts had previously analysed parties' relationships to determine whether or not they were in a principal-agent relationship for purposes of liability for the Value Added Tax Act 1994, ss 4(1) and 2(1).[90] In *Benourad v Compass Group plc*,[91] too, the first-instance judge had a particularly difficult task in determining whether or not there was an agency relationship between the parties.[92] The evidence in the case was predominantly oral. Much of it was so conflicting that Beatson, J was prompted to quote HHJ Jack, QC's words in *Loosemoore v Financial Concepts*:

> Memory, where it is unsupported by documents, must inevitably be suspect. Things which occurred can be forgotten. Things can apparently be remembered which did not in fact occur. What did occur can be remembered with a false slant to it. All of that can happen without dishonesty. So, unless the documents are clear, the court's task is difficult.[93]

But this is scarcely unique to matters of agency.

**1.33**  The manner in which the agent is remunerated for his services may contribute to the confusion. Whilst agents more usually are paid a commission, fixed as a percentage of the value of the business they conduct on behalf of the principal, nothing prevents the adoption of other arrangements that may make an agency resemble in some sort a sale and resale. As Lord Jessel, MR observed in *exp Bright re Smith*:

> There is nothing to prevent the principal from remunerating the agent by a commission varying according to the amount of profit obtained by the sale. At present there is nothing to prevent his paying a commission depending on the surplus which the agent can obtain over and above the price which will satisfy the principal. The amount of commission does not turn the agent into a purchaser.[94]

Illustrating again that the manner in which an agent is paid will not always be determinative of whether the relationship is one of true agency or not, Christopher Clarke, J more recently observed of cargo recovery agents, such agents 'are often paid by way of commission on the recoveries which they take by way of deduction from the monies recovered. They then pass on the balance to the principal on whose behalf they have acted.'[95] The fact that the commission is deducted from sums recovered by no means necessarily excludes the agency relationship. Similarly,

---

[90]  At [47] Lewison, J includes a helpful summary, in which he distils nine propositions from the case law.

[91]  [2010] EWHC 1882 (QB).

[92]  See *ibid* esp at [8]–[73].

[93]  [2001] Lloyd's Rep PN 235, 237.

[94]  (1879) 10 ChD 566, 570.

[95]  *Dolphin Maritime & Aviation Services Ltd v Sveriges Angartygs Assurans Forening* [2009] 2 Lloyd's Rep 123 at [6].

in *Commissioners for HM Revenue and Customs v Secret Hotels2 Limited (formerly Med Hotels Limited)*[96] the Supreme Court held that a company that marketed holiday accommodation around the world, which received gross sum payments for hotel bookings from clients (both travel agents and individuals) and then passed on smaller net sum payments to hoteliers after deduction of a 'commission' were acting as 'intermediaries' and therefore were not liable for VAT in the UK under EU Directive 2006/112, art 306(1)(b). First, the parties' legal documentation showed clearly that the company was intended to be the hotelier's agent for the purpose of marketing rooms in the hotel, and that 'clients' would book rooms through the agency of the company directly with the hotelier. The company's website also emphasized that the company 'acts as agent only', as did the booking conditions, which explained that the company bore no liability for the accommodation arrangements. Secondly, this analysis was said to coincide entirely with the 'economic reality'; it was not a 'purely artificial arrangement'.[97]

Occasionally the parties' negotiations will make clear that what, to outward appearances, might resemble an agency relationship, with an 'agent' seemingly representing a 'principal', is in fact nothing of the sort. In *Becerra and Page v Close Bros Corporate Finance Ltd*,[98] having learned that Close Bros were to conduct the sale of William Hill's betting shops, P, acting with B, contacted Close Bros offering to contact potential buyers in the Far East and at Nomura. Close Bros made clear that B could do so, but that if he did, he would be 'acting off his own bat'. B contacted an acquaintance in Nomura whom he introduced to Close Bros. Following completion of the sale, B claimed a commission. As Thomas, J held,     **1.34**

> As I have come to the conclusion of fact that the plaintiffs were not requested by Close Bros to perform any service for them and their overwhelmingly dominant motivation was their own self-interest if not their sole motivation, then it is clear they cannot recover.

## 'Commercial Agents' under the Commercial Agents (Council Directive) Regulations 1993

Since the passing of the Commercial Agents (Council Directive) Regulations 1993,[99]     **1.35** a further distinct species of agent, the 'commercial agent', exists alongside English law's traditional forms of agent.[100] The Regulations were enacted in December 1993

---

[96] [2014] 2 All ER 685.

[97] *Ibid* at [57]–[58] *per* Lord Neuberger.

[98] [1999] EWHC 289 (Comm), discussed in Floyd LJ's judgment in *TFL Management Services v Lloyds TSB Bank* [2014] 1 WLR 2006 at [40].

[99] SI 1993/3053.

[100] For detailed treatment of this form of commercial agency, see S Saintier and J Scholes, *Commercial Agents and the Law* (2005: London, LLP); S Singleton, *Commercial Agency Agreements: Law and*

pursuant to s 2(2) of the European Communities Act 1972. They give effect to a Council Directive of 18 December 1986 on the co-ordination of the law of the Member States relating to self-employed commercial agents.[101] The Directive, in turn, grew out of an explanatory memorandum of December 1976 and a proposal first submitted to the Commission in January 1977.

**1.36** The 1993 Regulations were lightly amended in 1998.[102] Apart from correcting a misprint in reg 17(2), the 1998 draft of the Regulations responded to EC Commission representations that the 1993 version omitted to deal with cases where principal and commercial agent had expressly agreed that UK law was to apply to their contract and that, although the activities of the agent were to be carried out elsewhere in the Community, a court in the UK was to have jurisdiction. The 1998 Regulations put that matter beyond doubt. In such cases a UK court or tribunal is required to apply the Regulations, provided that the law of the other relevant Member State so permits. The 1993 Regulations had already made provision for the converse case, thereby permitting commercial agents in the UK to agree to the application of the law of another member State.

### Construction of the Regulations

**1.37** When construing and applying the Regulations, the duty of English courts is to give effect to the manifest purpose of the Directive under which the Regulations are made. As Lord Templeman made clear in *Lister v Forth Dry Dock and Engineering Co Ltd*:

> [T]he courts of the United Kingdom are under a duty to follow the practice of the European Court by giving a purposive construction to directives and to regulations issued for the purpose of complying with directives.[103]

The underlying objective of the Regulations therefore has always to be borne in mind. Morison, J reflected upon the European and domestic legislative history of the Directive and the Regulations in *Tamarind International Ltd v Eastern Natural Gas (Retail) Ltd*:

> The Directive has as an essential function, the co-ordination of laws relating to self-employed commercial agents. The rights of nationals from one member state to set up agencies, branches or subsidiaries in another member state (the right of establishment) lies at the heart of the Community. The Directive was made partly so as to

---

Practice (2010: London, Bloomsbury Professional) 4th ed; F Randolph and J Davey, *The European Law of Commercial Agency* (2010: Oxford, Hart Publishing) 3rd ed; M Hesselink, JW Rutgers, O Bueno Diaz, M Scotton, and M Veldman, *Principles of European Law: Commercial Agency, Franchise, and Distribution Contracts* (2006: Oxford, Oxford University Press).

[101] Directive 86/6 5 3/EEC.
[102] See Commercial Agents (Council Directive) (Amendment) Regulations 1998, SI 1998/2868.
[103] [1990] 1 AC 546, 558.

give effect to the right of establishment and to the correlative obligation upon the Council and the Commission to effect, progressively, the abolition of restrictions on freedom of establishment (Arts. 43 and 44). It was also made pursuant to Art. 47 'to make it easier for persons to take up and pursue activities as self-employed persons' and to harmonise laws so as to enhance fundamental social rights including the promotion of employment and working conditions (Art. 136).[104]

The Regulations therefore must be construed in accordance with their purpose: namely, the promotion of freedom of establishment. With this in mind, Morison, J went on to contemplate the outlook courts should adopt in construing the Regulations:

**1.38**

> [T]he court is invited to look at the nature of the commercial bargain between the principal and the agent. Was it in the principal's commercial interests that this agent should be appointed to develop the market in the particular goods by the agent's expenditure of time, money and his own resources? It seems to me that by adopting this approach Parliament has properly reflected the purpose of the Directive. What the Directive is aimed at is the protection of agents by giving them a share of the goodwill which they have generated for the principal and from which the principal derives benefit after the agency agreement has been terminated … Essentially … the Regulations are asking whether this agent has been engaged in such circumstances as he can be said to have been engaged to develop goodwill in the principal's business.[105]

Viewed in this way, the principal concern becomes one of determining whether the agent's primary role is to develop goodwill in his principal's business—virtually developing a form of partnership with the principal in the market within which they operate.[106]

### The definition of 'commercial agent'

Regulation 2(1) defines 'commercial agent' as follows:

**1.39**

> '[C]ommercial agent' means a self-employed intermediary who has continuing authority to negotiate the sale or purchase of goods on behalf of another person

---

[104] [2000] CLC 1397. See L Vogel (ed), *Les agents commerciaux en Europe, échec de l'harmonisation?* (2012: Paris, Editions Panthéon-Assas) for a study that sets out to analyse how successful the harmonisation of commercial agents' activities has been under the Directive.

[105] [2000] CLC 1397 at [28]. It is an inevitable consequence that basic terms that have a settled meaning in English law may have a wider, autonomous meaning under the Regulations. Thus, whilst not having actually to decide the point, Mann, J in *Fern Computer Consultancy Ltd v Intergraph Cadworx & Analysis Solutions Inc* [2015] 1 Lloyd's Rep 1 at [93] acknowledged that it was arguable that the terms 'sale' and 'purchase' in the Regulations 'should have an autonomous meaning and should not be confined to the concepts of transfer of property which underpin the Sale of Goods Act and would be capable of applying to a transaction based on a licence'. (See also *Usedsoft GmbH v Oracle International Corp* [2012] 3 CMLR 44, albeit a decision wrestling with a different Directive.)

[106] This is confirmed by para 16 of the Law Commission report on the draft European Directive which noted that the term 'commercial agent', as employed in the Directive, is clearly based on the German *Handelsvertreter* or *Handelsagent*. The latter performs certain functions on a permanent basis for a standing client (Law Com No 84).

('the principal'), or to negotiate and conclude the sale or purchase of goods on behalf of and in the name of that principal ...

The Regulations will only govern the relationship of the parties if the activities of an agent comply with this definition, subject to what will be said presently regarding agents who 'act as commercial agents but by way of secondary activity only'. As Rix, LJ remarked in *Mercantile International Group plc v Chuan Soon Huat Industrial Group Ltd*, 'It is common ground that the word "agent" can be carelessly and indiscriminately used, and that the test is ultimately one of substance rather than form.'[107] HHJ Mackie expanded upon this point in a subsequent case, noting that:

> Many claims under the Regulations are brought by and against relatively modest businesses ... and the court should try to ensure that they are resolved as quickly and as cheaply as possible. Business people habitually use expressions like 'agent' and 'distributor' in a variety of loose ways. Moreover relationships which are in law agencies or [distributorships] as such take a wide variety of forms. Evidence from the parties or from their witnesses of what they understand the words to mean and how they characterise a particular commercial relationship will rarely assist.[108]

### The agent must be a 'self-employed intermediary'

**1.40**  Regulation 2(1) requires that the agent be the equivalent of an independent contractor, as opposed to an employee of the principal. In the majority of cases the agent's self-employed status will be self-evident from the facts.[109]

### The agent must be engaged in 'the sale or purchase of goods'

**1.41**  Although the Regulations provide no definition of 'goods',[110] it is clear that they do not apply to agents whose principal occupation is, say, the provision of services.

> Nor do they govern the activities of estate agents because they negotiate the sale and purchase of land, not goods. If part of the agent's activities consists in the provision of services, provided that the sale or purchase of goods is not 'by way of secondary activity only',[111] he may still qualify as a commercial agent under the Regulations.

---

107  [2002] EWCA Civ 288 at [6].

108  *Raoul Sagal (t/a Bunz UK) v Atelier Bunz Gmbh* [2008] 2 Lloyd's Rep 158 at [11].

109  Eg, *Marjandi Ltd v Bon Accord Glass Ltd* (2007) 15 October, 2007 WL 4947410 at [15].

110  It may be recalled that in *St Albans City and District Council v International Computers Ltd* [1997] FSR 251, 264–5 Sir Iain Glidewell mused, 'Is software goods?', and hazarded *obiter* that under s 18 of the Sale of Goods Act 1979 and s 61 of the Supply of Goods and Services Act 1982 computer disks, as tangible media, qualified as 'goods', but computer programs, as intangible software, did not so qualify. Similar questions could readily arise under the Regulations. But see *London Borough of Southwark v IBM UK Ltd* (2011) 135 Con LR 136; *Fern Computer Consultancy Ltd v Intergraph Cadworx & Analysis Solutions Inc* [2015] 1 Lloyd's Rep 1 at [76]–[86] *per* Mann, J.

111  See paras **1.54–1.63**.

**The agent must act 'on behalf of and in the name of that principal'**

The meaning of this expression, in the context of English law, is far from clear. **1.42**
One can be confident that the activities of an agent who acts for an undisclosed
principal will fall outside the Regulations because clearly he cannot be said to
be negotiating the sale or purchase of goods 'in the name of that principal'.
However, in other situations it is argued that what is intended by the expression
is that the agent should act 'on behalf of and in the name of that principal' in the
sense that a civilian lawyer would understand: namely, the agent will drop out of
the transaction and will acquire neither rights nor personal liability in respect of
the sales and purchases he negotiates on behalf of his principal.[112] Under English
law, either by express provision or by construction of the agency agreement, an
agent acting for a named principal,[113] and more frequently an agent acting for
an unnamed principal,[114] can engage his personal liability. In civilian terms, such
an agent would not be described as acting 'on behalf of and in the name of that
principal'.[115]

**A person who buys and sells as principal is not a 'commercial agent'**

Regulation 2(1) requires that a commercial agent must act 'on behalf of another  **1.43**
person'. Thus, as Waller, LJ explained in *AMB Imballaggi Plastici SRL v Pacflex Ltd*:

> If a person buys or sells himself as principal he is outside the ambit of the regula-
> tions. This is so because in negotiating that sale or purchase he is acting on his own
> behalf and not on behalf of another. All the regulations point in the direction of
> the words 'on behalf of' meaning what an English Court would naturally construe
> them as meaning. The other person on whose behalf the intermediary has authority
> to negotiate the sale or purchase of goods is called the 'principal'; the duties are con-
> sistent with true agency and not with buying and reselling; 'remuneration' is quite
> inconsistent with 'mark-up', particularly 'mark-up' within the total discretion of the
> re-seller.[116]

In *Pacflex*, P dealt with the products in England of AMB, an Italian manufacturer.
There was little documentation other than a letter in which AMB offered P the
choice either to operate on commission on the basis that contracts would be arranged directly between end-users and AMB or to operate on a mark-up on the basis
of a purchase from AMB and a resale to end-users. P selected the second option,
but a formal agreement was never executed and the parties' reciprocal rights and

---

[112] See, eg, *Bowstead & Reynolds on Agency* (2014: London, Sweet & Maxwell) 20th ed, by Watts, para 11-019. See now *Sagal (t/a Bunz UK) v Atelier Bunz GmbH* [2009] 2 Lloyd's Rep 303, discussed at para **1.44**.

[113] See paras **12.05–12.15**.

[114] See paras **12.16–12.17**.

[115] See further *Sagal (Trading as Bunz UK) v Atelier Bunz GmbH* [2008] 2 Lloyd's Rep 158 esp at [35] and [41].

[116] [1999] 2 All ER (Comm) 249, 252.

obligations were never fully clarified. The Court of Appeal found that the evidence showed that all business was in fact done on the basis of sale and resale—P endeavouring to conceal the extent of its mark-up from AMB, albeit that P carried no stock and that AMB delivered directly to the end-users.[117]

**1.44**  Peter Gibson, LJ, in the same case, added:

> The plain implication of the language of the Directive and of the Regulations is that if the sale or purchase of goods is negotiated by the intermediary in its own interest rather than on behalf of the principal, the intermediary is not a commercial agent. The paradigm example of an intermediary so negotiating is as a distributor purchasing goods from the manufacturer but reselling the goods for a profit on the mark-up.[118]

This distinction came to the fore in *Raoul Sagal (t/a Bunz UK) v Atelier Bunz Gmbh*.[119] Under an oral contract, for some three-and-a-half years, S sold in the UK jewellery manufactured by a German company, B. S had a retail shop in St Albans and formerly had a jewellery business in Tel Aviv. He held no stock, but placed orders with B whenever he had customers. In his accounts S set out purchases from B and sales to customers separately for VAT purposes. S bought most of the jewellery from B at a 20 per cent discount on the wholesale price and when he failed to pay on time B's accounts department would send 'dunning notices' seeking payment. When S, in turn, had to chase up his customers for payment, he did so in his own trading name. The relationship between S and B broke down, and S claimed compensation under the Regulations. Since the evidence clearly showed that this commercial relationship involved purchase of goods by S from B for the purpose of re-selling to his customers, and that S had no authority from B to negotiate or contract on its behalf, S was merely a distributor who bought and sold on his own account as principal and not a 'commercial agent' within the meaning of the Regulations.

**1.45**  The *Raoul Sagal* case invites comparison with the nineteenth-century Court of Appeal decision, *Re Nevill*.[120] T & Co habitually sent goods for sale to N, a partner in the firm of N & Co. N received them on his private account. The goods were accompanied by a price list, and N sold the goods on whatever terms he pleased, each month sending T & Co an account of the goods he had sold, debiting himself with the prices named for them in the price list, and at the expiration of another month paying the amount due in cash without any regard to the prices at which he had sold the goods, or the length of credit he had extended to his customers. N,

---

[117] See also *Mercantile International Group plc v Chuan Soon Huat Industrial Group Ltd* [2002] EWCA Civ 288. 'Mark-up is not … conclusive against commercial agency': *Sagal (t/a Bunz UK) v Atelier Bunz GmbH* [2009] 2 Lloyd's Rep 303 at [15] *per* Longmore, LJ.

[118] [1999] 2 All ER (Comm) 249, 255.

[119] [2008] 2 Lloyd's Rep 158 (aff'd by Court of Appeal at [2009] 2 Lloyd's Rep 303).

[120] (1870–71) LR 6 Ch App 397.

however, paid the monies he received from these sales into the general account of his firm, and made his payments to T & Co through his firm, with whom he did keep a separate account covering transactions unconnected with N & Co, including those involving T & Co. N & Co having executed a deed of arrangement with its creditors, T & Co sought to prove against the joint estate for the amount standing to N's credit with his firm, arguing that it derived from monies belonging to T & Co. The Court of Appeal held that the course of dealing indicated that, whilst both parties might very well have looked upon their arrangements as in the nature of an agency, N did not in fact sell the goods as agent for T & Co. He sold them on his own account, upon the terms of his paying T & Co for them at a fixed rate if he sold them. The monies he received for them were therefore his own monies, which T & Co had no right to follow:

> [I]f the consignee is at liberty, according to the contract between him and his consignor, to sell at any price he likes, and receive payment at any time he likes, but is to be bound, if he sells the goods, to pay the consignor for them at a fixed price and a fixed time ... whatever the parties may think, their relation is not that of principal and agent.[121]

**Can agents who conclude contracts in their own names be 'commercial agents' within the terms of the Directive?**

On appeal in *Sagal (t/a Bunz UK) v Atelier Bunz GmbH*,[122] S contended that, con-  **1.46**
trary to the first-instance judge's finding, the prices he charged for jewellery were mandatory, not advisory. S, it was said, had no discretion as to what he charged UK retailers, the prices being related mathematically to those B charged its German customers. In response to B's suggestion that because S made contracts with purchasers in his own name, albeit under the trade name 'Bunz UK', S fell outside the definition of a commercial agent, S argued that the mere fact that the mechanism chosen for implementing S' authority to negotiate the sale of jewellery was to make contracts under which he became personally liable to customers as 'Bunz UK' rather than making a contract in the name of the German company 'Bunz GmbH' was irrelevant. Longmore, LJ, looking to the terms of the Commercial Agents Council Directive[123] in preference to the English Regulations, considered that this raised 'an important question of construction',[124] with which 'the English authorities have not had to grapple directly',[125] namely, whether the Directive applies only to agents

---

[121] *Ibid* at 403 *per* Mellish, LJ.
[122] [2009] 2 Lloyd's Rep 303.
[123] Article 1(2) of the Directive reads: 'For the purposes of this Directive "commercial agent" shall mean a self-employed intermediary who has continuing authority to negotiate the sale or the purchase of goods on behalf of another person, hereinafter called the "principal", or to negotiate and conclude such transactions on behalf of and in the name of the principal.'
[124] [2009] 2 Lloyd's Rep 303 at [10].
[125] *Ibid* at [14].

who bring their principals into direct contractual relationship with their customers or whether it can also apply to agents who make their own contracts with customers. He concluded that the terms of the definition precluded an agent who makes contracts in his own name and on his own behalf from being treated as a 'commercial agent' under the Directive. More specifically, if such agents were 'commercial agents', the second limb of the definition would thereby be rendered redundant:

> If someone is an agent for another he will invariably have authority to negotiate (namely, to find out the terms on which a third party wishes to contract) on behalf of his principal; the question may then arise whether he has authority to contract on behalf of his principal. The first limb of the definition envisages that the agent does not have authority to contract on his principal's behalf but only has authority to negotiate terms on behalf of his principal and then refer back to him to see whether he wants to make a contract on certain terms with a third party customer. To my mind, the definition further envisages that, if the principal does want to make a contract with the customer, he will then do so and there will then be a contract made directly between the customer and the principal which will be made in the name of the principal. It does not envisage that, after the agent refers back to the principal and obtains the go-ahead for making a contract, the agent will enter into a contract in his own name with the customer; the reason for that is that, although he will then have authority to conclude a contract which is not in the principal's name, he will not come within the second limb of the definition which is the limb dealing with authority to contract.[126]

Longmore, LJ, therefore, concluded that agents with authority to contract (as opposed to authority to negotiate) only constitute 'commercial agents', for the purposes of the Directive, if they have authority to contract (and do contract) in the name of the principal as well as on his behalf.

### 'Commercial agents' and the question of proof

**1.47** In *Sagal (t/a Bunz UK) v Atelier Bunz GmbH* Longmore, LJ advanced a further practical reason for construing the Directive in such a way as to exclude agents contracting in their own names: such a construction dispensed with the need for courts to receive possibly complex and conflicting evidence in order to determine whether a particular party was contracting in his own name on behalf of a principal and thus qualified as a 'commercial agent':

> [I]f the Directive only applies where the principal's name appears on the face of the contracts made with the third parties, the inquiry can be a quick and straightforward inquiry, only requiring disclosure of the parties' contractual documentation.[127]

**1.48** The latter consideration led Longmore, LJ to reflect more generally on the degree to which a court should have to consider evidence in contested cases. He counselled

---

[126] *Ibid* at [12].
[127] *Ibid* at [13].

that even if documentation is equivocal, 'judges should be cautious about allowing the question whether commercial agency exists to develop into an extended trial with extensive oral evidence.'[128]

### The agent must have 'continuing authority to negotiate the sale or purchase of goods'

In determining what is meant by a 'continuing authority to negotiate the sale or purchase of goods' in reg 2(1), Guidance Notes issued by the Department of Trade and Industry in September 1994 commented: **1.49**

> Some agents only effect introductions between their principals and third parties. The question arises as to whether such agents are commercial agents for the purposes of the Regulations. Such agents are sometimes known as 'canvassing' or 'introducing' agents. As such, they generally lack the power to bind their principals and are not really agents in the true sense of the word. However, to the extent that such an agent 'has continuing authority to negotiate the sale or purchase of goods' on behalf of his principal, even though, as a matter of fact, he merely effects introductions, it seems that he would fall within the definition of 'commercial agent' in reg 2(1). It is clear that an 'introducing' agent who lacks such authority falls outside the scope of the definition of 'commercial agent'. It may be that the courts would give a wide interpretation to the word 'negotiate' and that, as a result, 'introducing' agents will, in general, have the benefit of the Regulations.

In *Parks v Esso Petroleum Co Ltd*,[129] Morritt, LJ gave the term 'to negotiate' a wide construction. *Parks* concerned a person who occupied a service station under a motor fuels agency agreement. Morritt, LJ adopted one of the *Oxford English Dictionary*'s definitions of negotiation: '(2) *Trans.* To deal with, manage, or conduct (a matter, affair etc., requiring some skill or consideration)'—observing that this definition did not require a process of bargaining in the sense of invitation to treat, offer, counter-offer and finally acceptance, more colloquially known as a haggling. Therefore, adopting this approach, in order to determine whether someone was a 'commercial agent' it was necessary to consider, *inter alia*:

(i) whether the suggested agent dealt with, managed or conducted the relevant transaction, and

(ii) whether a material process of negotiation was involved.

Subsequently, in *PJ Pipe & Valve Co Ltd v Audco India Ltd*[130] it was argued that the particular definition which Morritt, LJ had adopted in *Parks* was unduly **1.50**

---

[128] 'Bunz GmbH is, of course, German; most German businessmen would be surprised that it should take four days of trial to determine the question whether somebody is a "commercial agent" within the meaning of the Directive and appalled at the resulting cost ... We were told that Bunz GmbH is now in liquidation or administration; one can only hope that that is not because of the expense of these English proceedings': *ibid* at [17].

[129] (1999) 18 TrLR 232.

[130] [2005] EWHC 1904 (QB); [2006] Eur LR 368.

wide and that other 'primary' definitions to be found in the *OED* were to be preferred. These were variously to 'try to reach an agreement or compromise by discussion with others' and 'to hold communication or conference (with another) for the purpose of arranging some matter by mutual agreement; to discuss a matter with a view to some settlement or compromise'. Fulford, J, however, rejected this argument. Whilst accepting that an agent's authority to negotiate the sale of relevant products was one of a number of factors that might demonstrate the existence of a commercial agency, he found that these definitions placed too narrow an interpretation on the word 'negotiate'. He was fortified in this view by *Tigana Ltd v Decoro Ltd*.[131] In *Tigana* it had been held, without argument, that an agent whose primary role was to effect introductions of potential customers interested in leather upholstery produced by the principal was a 'commercial agent' within the meaning of the Regulations. The agent typically introduced the importer, and its goods, to prospective substantial retailers in the UK with a view to securing the placing of orders. Thereafter he acted as a point of contact and liaison, trying to secure further orders, administering the relationship, overseeing delivery of goods and helping to deal with any service and specification problems that might arise.[132] As Davis, J explained, to a considerable extent the agent's role was 'front loaded', although he also performed functions designed to cement the relationship between his principal and their clientele.[133] In *PJ Pipe & Valve Co Ltd v Audco India Ltd*[134] the agent performed broadly analogous functions. It partly managed discussions and transactions—notably, effecting introductions and engaging contractors' interest—when contractors were in the process of selecting a manufacturer. It also helped to put its client on the approved list of vendors and ensured that the client received the invitations to tender, in part by putting in an appropriate bid. It assisted with quotations and queries as well as providing feedback and advising on how a quotation might be improved. In Fulford, J's view, this showed that the agent was 'retained, *inter alia*, to develop goodwill on the part of [the principal]'. Because the purpose of the Directive was to provide protection to agents by giving them a stake in the goodwill which they had generated for the principal:

> the courts should avoid a limited or restricted interpretation of the word 'negotiate' that would exclude agents who have been engaged to develop the principal's business in this way, and who successfully generated goodwill for the manufacturer, to the latter's benefit after the agency terminated.[135]

---

[131] [2003] EWHC 23 (QB); [2003] ECC 23.
[132] *Ibid* at [4].
[133] *Ibid* at [58].
[134] [2005] EWHC 1904 (QB); [2006] Eur LR 368.
[135] *Ibid* at [155].

In consequence, Fulford, J concluded that the agent in this case was a 'commercial agent', as defined by the Regulations, notwithstanding the fact that it lacked authority to progress agreement on commercial terms or prices.

As Patten, J has pointed out in *Nigel Fryer Joiner Services Ltd v Ian Firth Hardware*   **1.51** *Ltd*, 'the word "negotiate" is not defined in the Regulations'.[136] In *PJ Pipe Valve Co Ltd v Audio India Ltd*, however, Fulford, J did treat 'negotiate' as meaning, 'to deal with, manage or conduct'.[137] In *Nigel Fryer* the agent, F, had no authority to conclude sales of doors and hardware on behalf of IFH, but F could suggest contract prices, which were sometimes approved by IFH's head office and sometimes adjusted. F's role was to interest customers in a product, to quote an indicative price and request a price from head office, and in some cases—following receipt of the quotation from head office—to relay customers' queries about the price and to encourage the customer to place an order with IFH. F's authority was limited to introducing goods to clients and suggesting what prices might be charged. Although it was argued that Fulford, J had adopted too broad an interpretation of 'to negotiate' in *PJ Pipe*, Patten, J concluded that the inclusion in reg 2(1) of two definitions of commercial agent ('negotiate the sale' or 'negotiate and conclude the sale') indicated that the first could include the wider meaning which Fulford, J attributed to the term 'negotiate' in the first of the two definitions. Thus, the activities of an agent like F came 'well within the ordinary meaning of "negotiate"'.[138]

The European Court of Justice, too, has had to consider the meaning of 'continuing   **1.52** authority'—and, more specifically, whether 'continuing authority' refers only to an agent who performs multiple transactions or whether it also extends to a case where a self-employed intermediary has authority to conclude a single contract, but the principal has conferred authority on that intermediary to negotiate successive extensions to the contract over several years. This question arose in *Poseidon Chartering BV v Marianne Zeeschip VOF*,[139] where a company had acted as intermediary in concluding the charter of a ship and in subsequent years negotiated extensions of the charter, which were recorded in addenda to the charter party. The company received a commission for securing extensions of the charter party. Whilst acknowledging that '[t]he number of transactions concluded by the intermediary for and on behalf of the principal is normally an indicator of that continuing authority',[140] the ECJ held that this is not the sole determining factor. It concluded that, provided that

---

[136] [2008] 2 Lloyd's Rep 108 at [17].
[137] [2005] EWHC 1904 (QB); [2006] Eur LR 368. See also *Parks v Esso Petroleum Co Ltd* (1999) 18 TrLR 232 *per* Morritt, LJ.
[138] [2008] 2 Lloyd's Rep 108 at [20].
[139] [2006] 2 Lloyd's Rep 105.
[140] *Ibid* at [25].

the national court makes the requisite findings of fact, continuing authority for the purposes of the Directive could relate to a single mandated transaction:

> [W]here a self-employed intermediary had authority to conclude a single contract, subsequently extended over several years, the condition laid down by that provision that the authority be continuing requires that the principal should have conferred continuing authority on that intermediary to negotiate successive extensions to that contract.[141]

### Specific exemptions

**1.53** Regulation 2 explicitly excludes from the application of the Regulations certain classes of persons who might otherwise be considered to act as intermediaries in the sense of reg 2(1). Thus:

> ['Commercial agent'] shall be understood as not including in particular:
> (i) a person who, in his capacity as an officer of a company or association, is empowered to enter into commitments binding on that company or association;
> (ii) a partner who is lawfully authorised to enter into commitments binding on his partners;
> (iii) a person who acts as an insolvency practitioner (as that expression is defined in s 388 of the Insolvency Act 1986) or the equivalent in any other jurisdiction;[142]

Equally, the Regulations have no application to commercial agents who act gratuitously, to commercial agents when they operate on commodity exchanges or in the commodity market, or to Crown Agents.[143] Most curiously for an English lawyer, however, the Regulations have no application to those 'persons whose activities as commercial agents are to be considered secondary'.[144]

### Persons whose activities as commercial agents are 'secondary'

**1.54** The concept of 'persons whose activities as commercial agents are to be considered secondary' was bound to appear alien to an English lawyer. Owing to the fact that, prior to 1993, English law did not possess a concept of commercial agency *tout court*, the idea of agents whose activities as commercial agents were 'secondary' would make little sense. Nevertheless, the distinction between the agent's primary and secondary activities is important because art 4 of the Directive provides that in their domestic legislation implementing the Directive, Member States are at liberty not to apply certain portions of the Directive 'to persons who act as commercial agents but by way of secondary activity only'.[145] Just to add to the mystery,

---

141 *Ibid* at [27].
142 Commercial Agents (Council Directive) Regulations 1993, reg 2(1).
143 Commercial Agents (Council Directive) Regulations 1993, reg 2(2).
144 Commercial Agents (Council Directive) Regulations 1993, reg 2(3) and (4).
145 As Waller, LJ observed in *AMB Imballaggi Plastici SRL v Pacflex Ltd* [1999] 2 All ER (Comm) 249, the United Kingdom 'took advantage of that provision, and by an almost impenetrable piece of drafting sought by Regulation 2(3) and (4), together with a Schedule, to exercise that right' (p 250).

as originally drafted, art 4(1) went on to state that 'the question whether the activity is carried on in that way being determined in accordance with commercial usage in the State whose law governs the relations between principal and agent.' There were moves to delete this provision. It was retained, however, even though the Legal Affairs Committee admitted that it was 'impossible to lay down suitable criteria for every possible case'.[146] The final version, incorporated into art 2(2) of the Directive, read:

> Each of the Member States shall have the right to provide that the Directive shall not apply to those persons whose activities as commercial agents are considered secondary by the law of that Member State.

Article 2(2) leaves it open to Member States to derogate from whatever provisions of the Directive it wishes in the case of those practising the activities of a commercial agent in a secondary capacity. It also now declares that it is the law of each Member State that will regulate which agents fall into this 'secondary' category. Since English common law—unlike the laws of virtually all other Member States—possessed no such concepts prior to implementation of the Directive,[147] the Regulations contain a provision intended to enable English law to distinguish between agents who act as commercial agents in a primary and a secondary capacity.[148]    **1.55**

To this end, reg 2 fills this lacuna in English law by providing:    **1.56**

(3)  The provisions of the Schedule to these Regulations have effect for the purpose of determining the persons whose activities as commercial agents are to be considered secondary.

(4)  These Regulations shall not apply to the persons referred to in paragraph (3) above.

In essence, the Schedule does not define secondary activities but employs a formula that defines activities with a specified primary purpose. The Regulations then assume that anyone performing any other activities falling outside these defined areas is likely to be considered to be performing them in a secondary capacity. The Schedule provides as follows:

1.  The activities of a person as a commercial agent are to be considered secondary where it may reasonably be taken that the primary purpose of the arrangement with his principal is other than as set out in para 2 below.

---

[146]  Report of Mr P de Keersmaeker of July 27, 1978, para 25.

[147]  The Law Commission laid stress on this inconvenient fact in its report on the proposed Directive in 1977 (Law Com 84).

[148]  This would explain why the Directive's recital states, 'Whereas additional transitional periods should be allowed for certain Member States which have to make a particular effort to adapt their regulations, especially those concerning indemnity for termination of contract between the principal and the commercial agent, to the requirements of the Directive.' To this end, the United Kingdom and Eire were allowed four extra years to comply with the Directive (art 22(3)).

2. An arrangement falls within this paragraph if—
    (a) the business of the principal is the sale, or as the case may be the purchase, of goods of a particular kind; and
    (b) the goods concerned are such that—
        (i) transactions are normally individually negotiated and concluded on a commercial basis, and
        (ii) procuring a transaction on one occasion is likely to lead to further transactions on those goods with that customer on future occasions, or to transactions in those goods with other customers in the same geographical area or among the same group of customers, and that accordingly it is in the commercial interests of the principal in developing the market in those goods to appoint a representative to such customers with a view to the representative devoting effort, skill and expenditure from his own resources to that end.
3. The following are indications that an arrangement falls within para 2 above, and the absence of any of them is an indication to the contrary—the principal is the manufacturer, importer or distributor of the goods;
    (a) the goods are specifically identified with the principal in the market in question rather than, or to a greater extent than, with any other person;
    (b) the agent devotes substantially the whole of his time to representative activities (whether for one principal or for a number of principals whose interests are not conflicting);
    (c) the goods are normally available in the market in question other than by means of the agent;
    (d) the arrangement is described as one of commercial agency.
4. The following are not normally indications that an arrangement does not fall within para 2 above—
    (a) promotional material is supplied direct to potential customers;
    (b) persons are granted agencies without reference to existing agents in a particular area or in relation to a particular group;
    (c) customers normally select the goods for themselves and merely place their orders through the agent.

**1.57** Contemplating these provisions in *Edwards v International Connection (UK) Ltd*,[149] Moore-Bick, LJ suggested:

> [T]he purpose of Regulation 2(4) and of paras 2, 3 and 4 of the Schedule is to distinguish between those persons falling within the definition of a commercial agent in reg 2(1) who are engaged primarily to carry out the functions of a commercial agent, that is, generating customers, obtaining repeat orders, and creating and developing a market for their principal's goods, and those who are primarily engaged for some other purpose but who incidentally provide some or all of those services. In the latter case their activities can properly be described as 'secondary'. One essential criterion

---

[149] [2006] EWCA Civ 662.

in para 2 of the circumstances under which a person is engaged for the primary purpose of acting as a commercial agent is that to be found in the final lines of that paragraph, namely:

> ... that accordingly it is in the commercial interests of the principal in developing the market in those goods to appoint a representative to such customers with a view to the representative devoting effort, skill and expenditure from his own resources to that end.

In most cases the arrangement will fall within para 2, and the agent's activities will not be considered secondary, if its primary purpose is to achieve those ends.[150]

### The burden of proving whether the agent's activities are secondary

Because the Schedule defines 'secondary' in terms of what is not 'primary', in deter-   **1.58**
mining whether or not a commercial agent's activities are to be considered secondary, the agent will normally bear the burden of showing that his arrangement with the principal falls within para 2 of the Schedule—which is to say that it is an arrangement whose primary purpose is as described in para 2. This analysis, however, may not fit every situation.[151] As Briggs, J observed in *Crane v Sky-In-Home Ltd and Secretary of State for Trade and Industry*:

> There may ... be cases ... where two purposes of the relevant arrangement can be identified, but with equal status, so that neither can be described as primary. In such a case, para 1 will not apply, there being no single primary purpose, and the activities of the agent will not be secondary.[152]

The test laid down in para 2 looks almost exclusively to the purpose of the principal:

> The claimant has to show that it is in the commercial interests of the principal in developing the market for the particular kind of goods which are the subject of the arrangement to appoint a representative to the defined customers of his with a view to the representative devoting effort, skill and expenditure from his own resources to the development of the market.[153]

The court has to be convinced that the commercial interests of the principal are furthered in the ways set out in para 2(a) and (b). Whilst it may well be that the principal's interests are served in other ways by the appointment of a representative, these will entail that the representative is a commercial agent for the purposes of the Regulations.[154]

---

[150] *Ibid* at [17]. See also *Tamarind International v Eastern Natural Gas (Retail) Ltd* [2000] Eu LR 708 at [28] *per* Morison, J; *Fern Computer Consultancy Ltd v Intergraph Cadworx & Analysis Solutions Inc* [2015] 1 Lloyd's Rep 1 at [97]–[103] *per* Mann J.

[151] In *Edwards v International Connection (UK) Ltd* [2006] EWCA Civ 662 at [15]. Moore-Bick, LJ expressed some uncertainty on the incidence of this burden of proof.

[152] [2007] 2 All ER (Comm) 599 at [54].

[153] *Crane v Sky-In-Home Ltd and Secretary of State for Trade and Industry* [2007] 2 All ER (Comm) 599 at [55].

[154] [2007] 2 All ER (Comm) 599 at [56].

**1.59** Although in *AMB Imballaggi Plastici SRL v Pacflex Ltd*[155] the matter did not strictly arise for decision, Waller, LJ set out the difficulties the drafting of the English Regulations poses, contending that 'the right answer must be to clarify the matter as soon as possible.'[156] In essence, the problem is that whilst the Directive permits Member States to disapply the Directive where the activities of the agent *qua* agent are secondary as compared with the rest of the agent's business, the English Schedule appears to contemplate an assessment not of the activities of the agent as 'a commercial agent' as compared with his other business, but an assessment of the agent's arrangement with the principal.[157] Paragraph 1 of the Schedule states that a person's activities as a commercial agent are to be considered secondary 'where it may reasonably be taken that the primary purpose of the arrangement with his principal is other than as set out in para 2.' Inconveniently, para 2 does not set out any purpose but focuses upon aspects of the arrangement with a particular principal. As Waller, LJ explained:

> Paragraphs 3 and 4 suggest pointers are being supplied as to whether an arrangement is within para. 2, but provide no assistance as to what is being compared with what for the purpose of deciding what might be secondary as compared with what might be primary, nor any assistance as to whether other factors are excluded.[158]

Waller, LJ saw 'much force' in the argument that, contrary to what seemed to be required under the Directive, if an agent has entered into an arrangement with:

> the principal which falls within para 2, using the indications under paras 3 and 4 purely for the purpose of making that assessment, 'then it must be taken that that business is not secondary.'[159]

**1.60** The very validity of the notion of commercial agency as a secondary activity has been called into question. In *Crane v Sky-In-Home Ltd and Secretary of State for Trade and Industry*[160] counsel sought unsuccessfully to argue that reg 2(3) and (4) was *ultra vires*, being outwith the authority to make secondary legislation conferred by s 2(2) of the European Communities Act 1972. This argument exploited the fact that, unlike other European jurisdictions, prior to the enactment of the Directive, English law had no concept of commercial agency and thus no need to set apart those agents whose commercial agency activities were secondary. The relevant Article of the Directive, it was contended, was meant for those States which already provided for commercial agents in their national law and was not intended as an option to

---

[155] [1999] 2 All ER (Comm) 249.
[156] Both the other members of the Court, Peter Gibson and Judge, LJJ associated themselves with Waller, LJ's remarks.
[157] Waller, LJ suggested that in likelihood this had not been the intention, as indicated by the Guidance Notes issued by the DTI.
[158] [1999] 2 All ER (Comm) 249 at [4].
[159] *Ibid* at [23].
[160] [2007] 2 All ER (Comm) 599.

decide precisely to how wide a class the benefit of the Directive should apply. The Regulations were, in counsel's submission, an exercise in national legislation, which the Directive neither required nor authorized. Briggs, J held that:

> The rational and common-sense interpretation of art 2(2) in relation to Member States with no such existing national law is that to enable them to exercise the right to derogate expressly conferred, they were expected if necessary to create national rules defining secondary activities by whatever means they thought fit.[161]

There is no requirement under para 2(a) of the Schedule that the sale or purchase of **1.61** the relevant goods was the sole or main business of the principal. Since the purpose of the Regulations is to protect the interests of a particular class of self-employed intermediaries, it has been suggested:

> The same agent may be appointed for the development of the same market in the same particular goods by, on the one hand, a large unitary corporation with many different businesses, including the sale of those goods, and on the other hand by a group of companies in which each different business is carried on by a different group company.[162]

Such a view makes sense as it would be odd if the relevant group company was liable to pay compensation on termination, but the large unitary corporation was not because sale or purchase of those goods was not its sole or main business. Paragraph 2(a) of the Schedule focuses the analysis upon the commercial interests served by the development of a market for goods of the relevant kind, rather than, for instance, a market for related services.

In making a determination whether an agent is a commercial agent for these pur- **1.62** poses the 'indications' for and against making such a finding enumerated in paras 3 and 4 are not to be 'used in some slavish numerical way'.[163] They do not constitute an exclusive list or relevant considerations; others might be relevant. Moreover, they may possess different weight in different proceedings:

> Viewed in the aggregate they do provide some assistance towards an understanding of the elusive concept of secondary activities which the Schedule seeks to define by its identification of the opposite. Taken as a whole they appear ... to be directed at distinguishing between a relationship where the agent develops goodwill (in rela- tion to the market for the particular goods) which passes to the principal, and one where that does not happen, either because the agent's activities are not typically generative of such goodwill, or because the principal generates goodwill mainly by other means.[164]

---

[161] [1999] 2 All ER (Comm) 249 at [41]. The matter was not discussed in the Court of Appeal: [2008] EWCA Civ 978 at [8] *per* Arden, LJ, when the appellant applied unsuccessfully to raise issues not investigated at trial.

[162] [1999] 2 All ER (Comm) 249 at [58].

[163] *Ibid* at [59]. See *McQuillan v McCormick* [2010] EWHC 1112 (QB); [2011] ECC 18 at [129(1)].

[164] [1999] 2 All ER (Comm) 249 at [59].

Thus in *Crane*, Briggs, J held that under para 2(a) it was irrelevant that the principal conducted other sales (and service business) alongside the selling of box packages, which was the subject of the agency agreement. As regards para 2(b), para 2(b)(i) was satisfied because the box packages were normally sold one-to-one to customers in retail transactions on a commercial basis. Paragraph 2(b)(ii), however, was not satisfied as it would have been 'unreal' to describe the sale of box packages as playing a significant part in generating goodwill in the sale of further box packages: whatever commercial interests may have led to the agent's appointment, 'they were not derived from a likelihood that sales of box packages would lead in any causative sense to further such sales.'[165] In consequence, the agent's arrangement with the principal had a primary purpose different from that described in para 2, and had therefore to be considered 'secondary' within the meaning of para 1.[166]

**1.63** In *Crane*, Briggs, J also held that in the requirement in para 3(c) that 'the agent devotes substantially the whole of his time to representative activities', 'representative activities' were not confined to activities in relation to goods rather than services. Paragraph 3(c) is focused on the question, for what primary purpose was the agent appointed? If his agency is ancillary to other non-representative activities, then it is unlikely that he was appointed for the exploitation of his skills as an agent. The question is simply whether the person in question is a full-time agent (ie, sales or purchase representative). Since the question addresses the purpose of the appointment, it is best answered at the time of the appointment. Otherwise he might drift in and out of qualifying commercial agency during the currency of the arrangement.[167]

### The question, who qualifies as a 'commercial agent' under the Directive, is of considerable practical importance

**1.64** As the fecund case law shows, numerous agents either fall, or would seek to fall, within the terms of the 1993 Regulations. The Directive makes generous provision for agents upon termination of their agency;[168] and, unlike the common law, it gives the agent a general right to remuneration, the right to demand a written statement of the terms of the agency agreement, statutorily delineated rights and duties, and a regime stipulating periods of notice of termination. Owing to their growing commercial significance, the special features of the law affecting commercial agents

---

[165] *Ibid* at [67].

[166] In *Crane* it was not thought to be an insuperable obstacle that the principal's commercial objective was the development of a distinct market for Box Packages and that it actually sold them at a loss as an incentive to customers to subscribe to Sky Digital, a service provided by the principal's sister company. 'The commercial interests of a group may satisfy the commercial interests test in para 2 without having to show that the purely separate interests of the principal are served, viewed in isolation' (at [72]).

[167] [2007] 2 All ER (Comm) 599 at [77].

[168] See **chapter 13**.

under the Directive will be discussed separately from the relevant elements of the general law of agency in ensuing chapters.

### Contracting in

Whilst identifying whether or not a particular individual is a 'commercial agent' **1.65** under the 1993 Regulations may involve nice points of interpretation, parties are at liberty simply to incorporate the Regulations into their contract regardless of their standing under reg 2(1). Although in *McQuillan v McCormick*[169] HHJ Behrens would have held on the facts that the parties' relationship in any case fell within the definition in reg 2(1), he determined that there was no need to pursue this analysis as the parties had expressly incorporated the Regulations into their agency agreement, as witnessed initially in correspondence prior to formation of their contract as well as in the principal's subsequent acceptance that the agents' contract had been subject to the protection of those Regulations.[170]

---

[169] [2010] EWHC 1112 (QB); [2011] ECC 18.
[170] *Ibid* at [125] and [127].

# 2

# CREATION OF AGENCY

## Contractual and Gratuitous Agencies

### Agency invariably arises out of an agreement between principal and agent

**2.01** The agreement between a principal and his agent may be either express or implied.[1] The great majority of agency agreements will in fact be contractual. Yet, even in the commercial setting, this is not exclusively the case. As Colman, J pointed out in *Yasuda Fire & Marine Insurance Co of Europe Ltd v Orion Marine Insurance Underwriting Agency Ltd*:[2]

> Although in modern commercial transactions agencies are almost invariably founded upon a contract between principal and agent, there is no necessity for such a contract to exist. It is sufficient if there is consent by the principal to the exercise by the agent of authority and consent by the agent to his exercising such authority on behalf of the principal.[3]

---

[1] Agreement, of a sort, may also occur retrospectively if a 'principal' on whose behalf an agent has purportedly acted subsequently ratifies the unauthorized acts of his agent: see further, **chapter 6**.

[2] [1995] QB 174.

[3] *Ibid* at 185.

For this reason, Colman, J held that non-contractual duties borne by an agent, such as the fiduciary duty to account to the principal,[4] may continue to bind the agent even after the agency contract has been terminated or bind even if the agency is gratuitous *ab initio*. What is required, however, is that the parties should have consented to the agency.

### There are differences between contractual and non-contractual agencies

**2.02**  In the case of contractual agencies, (i) consideration must be present, and (ii) the agent will be under an enforceable obligation to do what he has promised and, in likelihood, the principal will be under an accompanying obligation to pay the agent remuneration. This is not to say, however, that gratuitous agents have no rights and obligations. As we shall see, gratuitous agents may incur liability for faulty performance of their agency.[5] Equally, they may possess rights against their principals, notably the right to be indemnified for losses and expenses incurred in the course of their agency. The right to an indemnity is a normal incident of agency and exists independently of any contract between principal and agent. As Lord Wright, MR explained in *Brook's Wharf and Bull Wharf Ltd v Goodman Bros*:

> The obligation is imposed by the Court simply under the circumstances of the case and on what the Court decides is just and reasonable, having regard to the relationship of the parties. It is a debt or obligation constituted by the act of the law, apart from any consent or intention of the parties or any privity of contract.[6]

## Agency that arises as a Matter of Law

### The existence of an agency is a matter of law

**2.03**  If the parties have entered into a contract, the terms of the contract will govern their relationship. However, the fact that the parties have described themselves as 'principal' and 'agent' in that contract does not necessarily mean that the court will treat them as principal and agent if this is not the reality of their relationship.[7] Similarly, the parties' omission to use these terms will not preclude a court from holding that in law they are in fact principal and agent. As Lord Pearson emphasized in *Garnac Grain Company Inc v HMF Faure & Fairclough Ltd*:

---

[4] See paras **8.68–8.74**.
[5] See paras **8.13–8.14**.
[6] [1937] 1 KB 534, 545. See further, paras **9.41–9.51**.
[7] Just as the courts will not treat a term of the contract as a 'condition' merely because the parties have chosen to use that term in their agreement: see *Schuler AG v Wickman Machine Tool Sales Ltd* [1974] AC 235.

[The parties] will be held to have consented if they have agreed to what amounts in law to such a relationship, *even if they do not recognise it themselves and even if they have professed to disclaim it.*[8]

In *Garnac Grain* Lord Pearson considered what evidence a court might look at **2.04** in order to determine whether the parties could be taken to have consented to an agency. In the main, it will be a matter of looking to what the parties have said and done at the time of the alleged creation of the agency. Earlier words and conduct can afford evidence of a course of dealing in existence at the relevant time. They also furnish an historical background. The parties' subsequent words and conduct may have a bearing on the question, too, although these are likely to be of less significance.[9]

### An agency agreement may be implied from the circumstances

A two-man Court of Appeal, in *Targe Towing Ltd v Marine Blast Ltd*,[10] consid- **2.05** ered the appropriate test for determining whether an agency agreement had arisen by implication. Adopting *Bowstead*'s analysis, Mance, LJ accepted that the correct approach is to imply an agreement only 'where one party has conducted himself towards another in such a way that it is reasonable for that other to infer from that conduct consent to the agency relationship.'[11] This principle applies to both contractual and non-contractual agencies. Mance, LJ quoted *verbatim*, with approval, Lord Wilberforce's comment that:

> While agency must ultimately derive from consent, the consent need not necessarily be to the relationship of principal and agent itself (indeed the existence of it may be denied) but it may be to a state of fact upon which the law imposes the consequences which result from agency.[12]

In *Targe Towing* itself the Court had to decide whether N was, by implication, a party to a towage contract. It analysed the terms of the relevant charterparty, and examined the external, objective circumstances—notably, communications that had passed between the parties and their respective conduct—and emphasized that, in the absence of other indications, no inference of an agency having been agreed could be drawn from N's silence in response to the offer of a towage contract.[13] The Court concluded that the circumstances 'simply [did] not support a conclusion that N ever or in any way consented to the creation of an agency relationship, or consented to MB making all or any part of the towage contract with T on its behalf.'[14]

---

[8] [1968] AC 1130, 1137 (emphasis added).
[9] *Ibid* at 1137.
[10] [2004] 1 Lloyd's Rep 721.
[11] *Ibid* at [21].
[12] *Branwhite v Worcester Works Finance Ltd* [1969] 1 AC 552, 587 (dissenting).
[13] N's 'silence and conduct is equally, if not more, consistent with ignorance of or indifference to the precise terms of the towage contract, and fulfilment of the charter-party terms': [2004] 1 Lloyd's Rep 721 at [26].
[14] [2004] 1 Lloyd's Rep 721 at [31].

## Legal Capacity of the Parties

**The principal must possess the legal capacity to perform the act that the agent performs on his behalf**

**2.06**   Broadly speaking, whatever a party may himself do, he may do through the intermediary of an agent. The key element, therefore, is the capacity of the principal. For this reason a person of full capacity can appoint as his agent a minor who would not himself be capable of performing the mandate. By the same token, a minor can appoint an agent to perform an act for him, provided that the minor himself could have performed that act. As Lord Denning, MR explained in *G(A) v G(T)*:

> Whenever a minor can lawfully do an act on his own behalf, so as to bind himself, he can instead appoint an agent to do it for him. Thus, if a minor can lawfully bind himself by a particular contract because it is for his benefit, he can lawfully appoint an agent to enter into it for him.[15]

**2.07**   More generally, it might be thought that a principal who lacks capacity cannot create an agency. In the Supreme Court in *Dunhill v Burgin (Nos 1 and 2)*,[16] in which the point was raised, Lady Hale alluded to, but declined to treat, the argument that since intervening incapacity automatically terminates an agency, whether or not known to the agent,[17] then logically a contract of agency cannot be created if the principal is incapable. Were this argument to be accepted, the rule in *Imperial Loan Co Ltd v Stone*,[18] to the effect that a contract made by someone who lacked capacity is not void, but can be avoided provided that the other party to the contract knew (or ought to have known) of the incapacity, does not apply to a contract made by an agent on behalf of a principal who lacks capacity. (Similarly, apparent authority cannot apply if the principal lacked capacity at the time of making the initial representation as to the agent's authority, again regardless of whether the other party knew of this.)

> Reliance is placed, in particular, upon a passage in *Bowstead & Reynolds on Agency* (19th ed, (2010) para 2-009). This argument has led the current editor of that work, Professor Peter Watts, to reconsider and disavow what is there stated. The authorities are indeed in a state of some confusion, as is amply demonstrated by A.H. Hudson at (1959) 37 Can Bar Rev 497. It would be most unwise for this court to express any opinion, one way or another, as to the present state of the law. Fortunately, the issue does not arise.[19]

---

[15]  [1970] 2 QB 643, 652.
[16]  [2014] 1 WLR 933.
[17]  *Yonge v Toynbee* [1910] 1 KB 215.
[18]  [1892] 1 QB 599.
[19]  [2014] 1 WLR 933 at [31] *per* Lady Hale. On this topic, see Watts, *Contracts made by Agents on Behalf of Principals with Latent Mental Incapacity: The Common Law Position* [2015] CLJ 140. The author argues that, generally speaking, such a principal ought to be able to confer actual authority

### In order to act on behalf of a principal, an agent must be of sound mind

Since the focus is placed upon the capacity of the principal, it is agreed that an agent   **2.08**
need not have capacity to perform the acts that he performs on his principal's behalf
and that, generally speaking, the basic requirement that the agent needs to fulfil is
to be of sound mind. Thus, minors and those who lack contractual capacity may
act as agents. In *Norwich and Peterborough Building Society v Steed* Scott, LJ invoked
this principle in a case where the donor of a power of attorney sought to escape the
consequences of having appointed as his donee his mother, who may have lacked
ordinary competence and capacity when she was tricked into transferring his house
to his sister and her husband:

> The donor of a power of attorney who appoints as his attorney a person incapable
> of understanding the import of a simple transfer can hardly be allowed, if the
> donee signs a transfer without any understanding of what he or she is doing, to
> repudiate the transfer on the ground of a lack of understanding on the part of the
> donee.[20]

### Capacity, incapacity, and the burden of proof

On the other hand, as we shall see, it is open to an agent to contract in such a   **2.09**
manner as to acquire rights and to engage his personal liability, alongside that of the
principal, on the contract he has concluded on the principal's behalf. If the agent
lacks capacity to contract on his own behalf, *ex hypothesi* he cannot acquire rights or
incur personal liability on such contracts.

In the case of natural persons, the law presumes *prima facie* that everyone enjoys the   **2.10**
capacity to contract. For this reason, the burden of establishing lack of capacity will
fall upon the party who claims it: 'where exemption from liability to fulfil an obligation is claimed by reason of want of capacity, this fact must be strictly established
on the part of the person who claims the exemption.'[21] The position, however, is
altered where the question is whether a transaction or other act is within the objects
of a legal person. As Andrew Smith, J noted in *Crédit Suisse International v Stichting
Vestia Groep*,[22] whereas a contract is generally voidable at common law if it is made
by a natural person without capacity, 'at common law, if a corporation purports
to make a contract that is outside its capacity, it is void *ab initio*, and cannot be
ratified.'[23] Viewed as no more than the application of the maxim *ei qui affirmat non
ei qui negat incumbit probatio*, in cases involving the capacity of legal persons the

---

to contract on an agent so long as the latter reasonably is, and remains, unaware of the principal's
incapacity. On the same basis, an *incapax* principal can tell a third party that such an appointment
has been made, thereby creating apparent authority in the agent.

[20] [1993] Ch 116, 128.
[21] *Chitty on Contracts* (2015, 32nd ed), vol 1, para 9-001.
[22] [2015] Bus LR D5.
[23] *York Corp v Henry Leetham & Sons* [1924] 1 Ch 557, 573.

onus of proof will rest upon the party asserting the positive case.[24] Such an approach is said to be in line with the position where an agent's authority is challenged[25] and, additionally, tallies with the old rules of pleading.[26]

# Formalities

### An agency may normally be created without formality

2.11   Subject to certain limited exceptions, even if an agent is to perform an act on behalf of a principal that is required by law to be in writing or evidenced by writing, there is no requirement that the agency itself must have been created in any particular manner. Notably, appointments of agents by corporations follow precisely the same rules as apply to individuals. Thus, s 43(2) of the Companies Act 2006 provides:

> Any formalities required by law in the case of a contract made by an individual also apply, unless a contrary intention appears, to a contract made by or on behalf of a company.

An agency, therefore, may be created by deed, by writing, or orally; it is entirely as the parties wish. In *Heard v Pilley*,[27] for example, it was held that a contract for the purchase of land made on behalf of a principal by an agent would be enforced even though the agent had been appointed orally. The agent's attempt in this case to take the personal benefit of the principal's contract therefore failed.

2.12   There are two important statutory exceptions to the general principle of informality. Under the Law of Property Act 1925 interests in land may be created or disposed of by an agent, and dispositions of equitable interests may be effected by an agent, only if that agent has been authorized to do so in writing.[28] Under the Trustee Act 1925, s 25, a trustee wishing to delegate the execution or exercise of all or any of the trusts, powers and discretions vested in him may only do so by executing a power of attorney.[29]

2.13   Regarding real property, the creation and disposal of interests has to be distinguished from contracts to sell or dispose of real property, which are governed by s 2 of the Law of Property (Miscellaneous Provisions) Act 1989. The need for a written appointment in the case of transactions involving the creation and disposal of interests in real property was considered in *McLaughlin v Duffill*.[30] The

---

[24] *Joseph Constantine SS Ltd v Imperial Smelting Corp Ltd* [1942] AC 154, 174 *per* Viscount Maugham.

[25] See *Hely-Hutchinson v Brayhead Ltd* [1968] 1 QB 549, 593 *per* Lord Pearson.

[26] See *Governor and Company of the Copper Miners of England v Fox* (1851) 16 QB 229, 235 *per* Lord Campbell, CJ. See [2015] Bus LR D5 esp at [185]–[187].

[27] (1869) LR 4 Ch App 548.

[28] Law of Property Act 1925, ss 53(1)(a) and (c), and 54(1).

[29] This provision was substituted by the Trustee Delegation Act 1999, s 5(1).

[30] [2010] Ch 1.

trial judge having found that the vendor had orally authorized her estate agent to sell her house, the Court of Appeal determined that there is nothing in s 2(1) and (3) of the Law of Property (Miscellaneous Provisions) Act 1989 to suggest that the authority to conclude a *contract* for the sale or other disposition of an interest in land, which 'can only be made in writing', can only be performed by an agent if the latter's authority, too, is conferred in writing.[31] Contracts for the disposition of an interest in land under the 1989 Act have to be distinguished from actual dispositions of interests in land under s 53(1)(a) of the Law of Property Act 1925. The 1925 Act specifically stipulates that 'no interest in land can be created or disposed of except by writing signed by the person creating or conveying the same, *or by his agent thereunto lawfully authorised in writing* ...[32] As Sir Andrew Morritt, C explained, historically:

> the normal law of agency applies to transactions within s 2 of the 1989 Act. By that law the authority may be conferred orally as well as in writing.[33]

Whilst for most practical purposes such a contract, coupled with an order for specific performance, may resemble a conveyance in that it confers on the purchaser an immediate equitable interest in the property and effectively functions as a disposition of an interest in land, which would be governed by s 53(1)(a) of the 1925 Act, Sir Andrew Morritt, C stressed:

> The existence of the contract is a necessary precondition for an order of specific performance, but it is not itself and without more a disposition of the land, the subject-matter of the contract, or of an interest in it.[34]

It is also well established that if an agent is required to execute a deed on behalf of his **2.14** principal, the agent's authority must also have been conferred by deed.[35] As Abbot, CJ remarked in *Berkeley v Hardy*, a case in which the agent's authority had been granted in a writing not under seal:

> those strict technical rules of law applicable to deeds under seal, which, I believe, are peculiar to the law of England ... have been laid down and recognised in so many

---

[31] Section 2 of the 1989 Act, so far as relevant provides:

    (1) A contract for the sale or other disposition of an interest in land can only be made in writing and only by incorporating all the terms which the parties have expressly agreed in one document or, where contracts are exchanged, in each.

    ...

    (3) The document incorporating the terms ... must be signed by or on behalf of each party to the contract.

[32] Law of Property Act 1925, s 53(1)(a) (emphasis supplied).

[33] [2010] Ch 1 at [24].

[34] *Ibid* at [26].

[35] 'It is well-known law that an agent cannot execute a deed, or do any part of the execution which makes it a deed, unless he is appointed under seal': *Powell v London and Provincial Bank* [1893] 2 Ch 555, 563 *per* Bowen, LJ. This is subject to the Law of Property (Miscellaneous Provisions) Act 1989, s 1(3).

cases, that I think we are bound to say no action can be maintained by [B] upon the deed in question.[36]

If an agent is appointed by deed, in likelihood the agency will have been created by execution of a power of attorney. Section 1(1) of the Powers of Attorney Act 1971, as amended, provides:

> An instrument creating a power of attorney shall be executed as a deed by the donor of the power.[37]

---

[36] (1826) 5 B&C 355, 359.
[37] As Lewison, J observed, 'At common law a power of attorney is an agency created by deed': *In re J (Enduring Power of Attorney)* [2010] 1 WLR 210 at [4]. Section 1(1) has to be read subject to s 1(3).

# 3

# THE ACTUAL AUTHORITY OF THE AGENT

As the term would suggest, 'actual authority' refers to authority the agent pos- **3.01** sesses either because the principal has expressly conferred that authority upon him ('express actual authority') or because the law regards the authority as having been conferred upon the agent by necessary implication ('implied actual authority').

'Actual authority' was famously defined by Diplock, LJ in *Freeman & Lockyer (a* **3.02** *Firm) v Buckhurst Park Properties (Mangal) Ltd* as follows:

> An 'actual' authority is a legal relationship between principal and agent created by a consensual agreement to which they alone are parties. Its scope is to be ascertained by applying ordinary principles of construction of contracts, including any proper implications from the express words used, the usages of the trade, or the course of business between the parties. To this agreement the [third party] is a stranger; he may be totally ignorant of the existence of any authority on the part of the agent. Nevertheless, if the agent does enter into a contract pursuant to the 'actual' authority, it does create contractual rights and liabilities between the principal and the [third party].[1]

As a practical matter, the 'actual authority' of an agent is customarily contrasted **3.03** with an agent's 'apparent authority'—that is to say, the legal relationship as between principal and third party created by a representation, made by the principal to the

---

[1] [1964] 2 QB 480, 502–3.

third party, intended to be and in fact acted upon by the latter. Such representation is to the effect that the agent possesses the necessary authority to enter into a contract of a given kind on the principal's behalf, so as to render the principal liable to perform any obligations imposed upon him under that contract.[2] As Diplock, LJ went on to explain in *Freeman & Lockyer*, 'it is upon the apparent authority of the agent that the contractor normally relies in the ordinary course of business when entering into contracts.' This is because:

> in ordinary business dealings the [third party] at the time of entering into the contract can in the nature of things hardly ever rely on the 'actual' authority of the agent. His information as to the authority must be derived either from the principal or from the agent or from both, for they alone know what the agent's actual authority is. All that the contractor can know is what they tell him, which may or may not be true. In the ultimate analysis he relies either upon the representation of the principal, that is, apparent authority, or upon the representation of the agent, that is, warranty of authority.[3]

Although there is a strong element of truth in this, it remains important to define the scope of an agent's actual authority both when determining the agent's liability to the principal, if it is suggested that the agent has acted outside the terms of his authority as fixed by the principal, and also in settling the bounds of the agent's authority in cases where other varieties of authority—notably, apparent authority—do not come into play.

## Express Actual Authority

**3.04** The precise extent of an agent's actual authority will turn on the true construction of the words of his appointment. If the agreement between principal and agent is oral, its terms may involve contested evidence and, incidentally, difficulty of proof. Thus, in *Ramsay v Love*,[4] a celebrity chef contested his father-in-law's authority to append the chef's signature to a personal guarantee, using a 'Ghostwriter' signature writing machine. Although the removal and deletion of many documents following the father-in-law's dismissal had not simplified matters, it was said that 'the court has to do the best it can with the evidence it has been given and it has to decide the case on that evidence'.[5] The chef was found on the evidence to have conferred extensive authority on his father-in-law to bind him contractually in commercial matters and, significantly, to have been in the habit of providing personal guarantees when acquiring restaurants without being expressly asked to do so and without attaching great importance to the matter. He therefore failed to show on a balance of

---

[2] On the apparent authority of the agent, see **chapter 4**.
[3] [1964] 2 QB 480, 503.
[4] [2015] EWHC 65 (Ch).
[5] *Ibid* at [12].

probabilities that he was unaware of the personal guarantee contracted on his behalf and that, in providing it, his father-in-law had been acting within a wide general authority conferred on him. If the agency has been reduced to writing, as will normally be the case in a commercial setting, the relevant document or documents will need to be construed in the customary manner. This is to say, the ambit of the agent's authority will be ascertained by applying the normal principles of interpretation of contracts, including any proper implications from the express words used, any relevant trade customs, and the previous course of business between the parties, where appropriate.

### Construing authority conferred by deed

If the agent has been appointed by deed, interpretation of that instrument will **3.05** follow the strict rules of construction that apply to deeds generally. Although it is by no means necessary for an agency to be created by formal grant,[6] it is not uncommon for an agent to be appointed under a power of attorney. Section 1 of the Powers of Attorney Act 1971 requires that powers of attorney be executed under seal. In determining the authority of an agent operating under a power of attorney, the written instrument will be construed in conformity with the strict interpretative rules that apply to the construction of deeds.

#### *A power of attorney will be strictly construed*

The first principle of construction of deeds is that a deed will be construed strictly. **3.06** This is taken to mean that:

> where an act purporting to be done under a power of attorney is challenged as being in excess of the authority conferred by the power, it is necessary to shew that on a fair construction of the whole instrument the authority in question is to be found within the four corners of the instrument, either in express terms or by necessary implication.[7]

Scrutton, LJ set out the leading principles succinctly in *Reckitt v Barnett, Pembroke and Slater Ltd*:

> A power of attorney is to be construed strictly. The recitals show its objects and control its meaning, and general words only refer to the special powers. Such a power gives only such authority as it expressly or by necessary implication confers.[8]

Adopting a passage from *Bowstead and Reynolds*, in *Brown v InnovatorOne plc* **3.07** Hamblen, J enumerated the most important rules of construction affecting deeds:

(1) The operative part of a deed is controlled by the recitals where there is ambiguity;

---

[6] See para **2.14**.
[7] *Bryant, Powis, and Bryant Ltd v La Banque du Peuple* [1893] AC 170, 177 *per* Lord Macnaghten.
[8] [1928] 2 KB 244, 265.

(2) Where authority is given to do particular acts, followed by general words, the general words are restricted to what is necessary for the proper performance of the particular acts;

(3) General words do not confer general powers, but are limited to the purpose for which the authority is given, and are construed as enlarging the special powers only when necessary for that purpose;

(4) A deed must be construed so as to include all incidental powers necessary for the effective execution of the power it confers.[9]

The judge was at pains to add that whilst deeds, and powers of attorney in particular, must be strictly construed, this must be done 'having regard to the purpose for which the authority is conferred.' This will demand consideration of the relevant context. In *Brown v InnovatorOne plc*, a dispute arising out of a failed tax scheme, this meant that the court had to construe the power of attorney against the backdrop of the information memoranda sent to investors inviting them to apply to invest and even submit subscription monies in order to join the partnership as well as the tax relief and/or business opportunity the scheme afforded: 'This was not a freestanding power of attorney.'[10]

### The effect of general words in deeds

**3.08** If the deed confers upon the donee of the power authority to perform particular acts, and that authority is followed by general words, the general words do not confer any general authority but are confined to what is necessary to perform the particular acts. Thus, in *Jacobs v Morris*[11] an English agent was authorized by his Australian principal, a tobacco merchant, 'to purchase and to make any contract for the purchase of any goods in connection with the business carried on by [the principal] as aforesaid', and to make, draw, sign, accept, or indorse any bills of exchange or promissory notes which should be requisite or proper in the premises, and to sign the plaintiff's name or his trading name to any cheques on his bank account in London. The agent, purporting to act under the power of attorney, borrowed £4,000 on the security of some bills of exchange and then applied the money to his own use. The court held that the power of attorney gave the agent no particular power to borrow money and that the general words regarding bills and promissory notes did not render the principal liable for his agent's unauthorized act. Similarly, in *Midland Bank Ltd v Reckitt*[12] a solicitor was authorized by a power of attorney to draw cheques on a client's bank account and to apply the monies for the purposes of that client. The solicitor fraudulently drew cheques on the account

---

9 [2012] EWHC 1321 (Comm) at [808].
10 [2012] EWHC 1321 (Comm) at [809].
11 [1902] 1 Ch 816.
12 [1933] AC 1.

and applied the money to settling his personal overdraft at another bank. The power of attorney incorporated a ratification clause under which the donor 'confirms and agrees to ratify and confirm whatsoever the attorney or any such person as aforesaid acting as the agent of or substitute for or in place of the attorney shall do or purports to do by virtue of these presents ...' Lord Atkin, with whom the other four members of the court concurred, considered that the ratification clause could not be construed as extending the actual authority given by the power of attorney, not least because 'such a construction would make powers of attorney a danger instead of a business facility and would certainly defeat the intention of any reasonable principal.'[13]

*If the terms of the deed are ambiguous, the ambiguity may be resolved
by consideration of the recitals*

The generality of the operative part of a power of attorney therefore is controlled by **3.09** the expression in the recitals of the object for which the power has been granted. In *Danby v Coutts & Co*,[14] for example, D, an Australian resident, had appointed two solicitors ('the notorious Parkers') as his agents under a power of attorney without, in terms, limiting the duration of their powers in the operative part of the deed. Both during D's absence from England, and again after his return, the agents, without D's knowledge, purported to act under the power (which authorized them to borrow money on mortgage) and borrowed monies from a bank upon the security of charges on D's property, which monies they afterwards misappropriated. Because the deed was preceded by a recital in which D stated that he was going abroad, and was desirous of appointing attorneys to act for him during his absence, the court concluded that the recital controlled the generality of the operative part of the instrument, and limited the exercise of the powers of the attorneys to the period of D's absence from this country:

> A power of attorney ... seems to me precisely the kind of instrument which may be limited by a recital. And the only question upon which it appears to me there can be any reasonable doubt is whether that is the true effect of the recital in this power.[15]

*Authority will be limited to the purpose for which it was given under the deed*

Even if the deed is framed in general words, these will not be construed to confer **3.10** general powers. They will be confined to the purpose for which the power was given and their meaning will only be extended when it is necessary in order to fulfil that purpose. In *Jonmenjoy Coondoo v Watson*[16] an agent was authorized under a power of attorney 'from time to time to negotiate, make sale, dispose of, assign, and

---

[13] *Ibid* at 18.
[14] (1885) LR 29 ChD 500.
[15] (1885) LR 29 ChD 500, 515 *per* Kay, J.
[16] (1884) LR 9 App Cas 561.

transfer' government promissory notes, and 'to contract for, purchase, and accept the transfer' of the same. The agent proceeded to pledge a government promissory note as security for a loan. The Privy Council held that, upon its true construction, the holders of this power of attorney were authorized to sell or purchase such notes, but not to pledge them.

*Ministerial powers*

**3.11**  Finally, although not expressly referred to in the body of the deed, the instrument must be construed as conferring upon the donee any ministerial powers necessary for accomplishment of the agency. Thus, in *Henley v Soper the Elder*[17] a partner gave his son a power of attorney 'to act on his behalf in dissolving the partnership, with authority to appoint any other person as he might see fit'. It was held that this authority also necessarily conferred on the son the power to submit the partnership accounts to arbitration.

## Construing authority not conferred by deed

**3.12**  If the agent has been appointed in a document not under seal, or has been appointed orally, the applicable rules of interpretation are more liberal. As Lord Reid observed in *Ashford Shire Council v Dependable Motors Pty Ltd*,[18] a case in which the extent of the authority granted to an agent in the course of a telephone conversation was disputed, the meaning of the words used had to be considered in the light of the circumstances known to both parties. His Lordship added:

> The extent of an agent's authority, if in doubt, must be determined by inference from the whole circumstances.[19]

Thus, in *Foxtons Ltd v Puri*[20] a client instructed an estate agent to sell a property. The agent's standard contract referred to the 'sale of the property'. Since both estate agent and client knew at the time of formation of the contract that the property was the only asset of an offshore company, 'the parties must have contemplated including simply transferring the property by transferring the shares in the company ... no other view makes any sense whatever.'[21]

*Authority given in general terms is construed to mean authority to act in the usual way*

**3.13**  This principle flows from the general notion that an appointment made otherwise than by deed will be given a liberal interpretation. In *Wiltshire v Sims*,[22]

---

[17]  (1828) 8 B&C 16.

[18]  [1961] AC 336.

[19]  *Ibid* at 349. For an example of this process, see *Aviva Life & Pensions UK Ltd v Strand Street Properties Ltd* [2010] EWCA Civ 444 at [53]–[66] *per* Lloyd, LJ.

[20]  [2010] EWCA Civ 925.

[21]  *Ibid* at [3] and [4] *per* Jacob, LJ.

[22]  (1808) 1 Camp 258.

a case that also illustrates the converse, a broker was authorized to sell a principal's stock. As the transfer could not be made before the expiry of a fortnight, acting *bona fide* the broker sold the stock on credit taking a promissory note. The principal refused to transfer the stock, because he had not received any purchase money. Lord Ellenborough, CJ held that the transaction was not binding on the principal:

> When the defendant employed the broker to sell the stock, he employed him to sell it in the usual manner. He made him his agent for common purposes in a transaction of this sort ... The broker here sold the stock in an unusual manner; and unless he was expressly authorised to do so, his principal is not bound by his acts.[23]

Similarly, in *Guerreiro v Peile*,[24] where a factor employed to sell twenty-five pipes of 1815 vintage port sought to combine a sale of the port with a purchase of rum, it was held that since in the ordinary course of trade a factor has no right to barter, the principal was not bound by the transaction. In the words of Bayley, J:

> [The agent] had authority only to sell, and that for money, to be forthcoming to the plaintiffs. But in this case not one farthing of money would ever be forthcoming to the plaintiffs; for the amount due for the rums exceeded the value of the wine.[25]

More broadly, the fiduciary obligations owed by an agent to his principal, when enshrined in legislation, can place restraints upon an agent's actual authority. To take an important example, under s 170(1) of the Companies Act 2006 directors owe to their companies the general duties set out in ss 171–177—duties which derive originally from common law and equitable sources.[26] This has been held to mean that 'a director owes to his company a fiduciary duty to exercise his powers ... in what he (not the court) honestly believes to be the company's best interests.'[27] Because s 170 imposes this *subjective* requirement, it follows that 'a director cannot have actual authority to act in a way which he does not consider in good faith to be in his company's interest.'[28]

---

[23] *Ibid* at 259.

[24] (1820) 3 B&Ald 616.

[25] *Ibid* at 618.

[26] See Companies Act 2006, s 170(3) and (4).

[27] *Extrasure Travel Insurances Ltd v Scattergood* [2003] 1 BCLC 598 at [87].

[28] *LNOC Ltd v Watford AFC Ltd* [2013] EWHC 3615 (Comm) at [64] *per* HHJ Mackie. The judge, it might be noted, rejected the more ambitious argument that a passage in Lightman, J's judgment in *Hopkins v Dallas Group Limited* [2004] EWHC 1379 (Ch) at [88] represented the general law (at [66]). This was to the following effect: 'The grant of actual authority should be implied as being subject to a condition that it is to be exercised honestly and on behalf of the principal: *Lysaght Bros & Co Ltd v Falk* (1905) 2 CLR 421. It follows that, if an act is carried out by an agent which is not in the interests of his principal, for example signing onerous unconditional undertakings, then the act will not be within the scope of the express or implied grant of actual authority.'

*What if the principal's instructions are expressed ambiguously?*

**3.14**  The instructions of the principal may not always be clearly expressed. Indeed, they may be capable of more than one reasonable interpretation. How is the agent placed if it is later claimed that he misinterpreted the instructions and failed to perform the agency in the manner actually intended by the principal? The House of Lords considered this question in *Ireland v Livingston*.[29] Livingston wrote to Ireland, his commission agent in Mauritius, requesting that Ireland ship him 500 tons of sugar at a fixed price, indicating that to the nearest 50 tons made no difference. Livingston's instruction ran, 'if it enables you to get a suitable vessel. I should prefer the option of sending vessel to London, Liverpool, or the Clyde; but if that is not compassable, you may ship to either Liverpool or London.' In the Mauritius market it was often impossible to obtain so large a quantity of sugar as 500 tons from one house, or to find one vessel to take it. With difficulty, Ireland procured fewer than 400 tons at the price set by Livingston, and had to acquire that from fourteen different sellers. Ireland shipped the sugar in one vessel to Liverpool, where Livingston refused to take delivery of the 5788 bags of sugar. Livingston's instructions were capable of being read in two ways. Livingston's first preference was to have a vessel at Ireland's disposal as regards its destination, which meant that the whole cargo would have had to belong to Ireland since Ireland could not give a destination to a vessel containing other people's cargo. The alternative of shipping to one of two designated ports, London or Liverpool, allowed other people's cargo to be carried along with that of Livingston. Because it was impossible for Ireland to adopt the first course, the question was, whether, though Ireland's cargo did not need to occupy the whole ship, it was essential that it should form a single shipment on board one ship? Lord Chelmsford held that Livingston was bound to accept the cargo:

> If a principal gives an order to an agent in such uncertain terms as to be susceptible of two different meanings, and the agent *bonâ fide* adopts one of them and acts upon it, it is not competent to the principal to repudiate the act as unauthorized because he meant the order to be read in the other sense of which it is equally capable. It is a fair answer to such an attempt to disown the agents' authority to tell the principal that the departure from his intention was occasioned by his own fault, and that he should have given his order in clear and unambiguous terms.[30]

**3.15**  This notion, that unless instructions are clearly given, the instructing party should bear the consequences, has been applied in other contexts—notably, by Devlin, J in *Midland Bank Ltd v Seymour*,[31] in relation to instructions given to a banker who paid a letter of credit. Devlin, J stated matters thus:

> The true view of the matter … is that when an agent acts upon ambiguous instructions he is not in default if he can show that he adopted what is a reasonable meaning.

---

[29] (1871) LR 5 HL 395.
[30] *Ibid* at 416. See also *Loring v Davis* (1886) 32 Ch D 625, 631 *per* Chitty, J; *Weigall & Co v Runciman & Co* (1916) 85 LJKB 1187.
[31] [1955] 2 Lloyd's Rep 147.

It is not enough to say afterwards that if he had construed the documents properly he would on the whole have arrived at the conclusion that in an ambiguous document the meaning which he did not give to it could be better supported than the meaning which he did give to it.[32]

However, as Robert Goff, LJ subsequently emphasized in *European Asian Bank AG v Punjab & Sind Bank (No 2)*,[33] some limit must be put on the operation of this principle. The agent who relies upon his own interpretation of an instruction must have acted reasonably in all the circumstances in so doing. This may impose on the agent a duty to seek clarification of ambiguous instructions which obviously, or which the agent ought to have realized, are ambiguous. In the case of patent ambiguity, 'it may well be right (especially with the facilities of modern communications available to him) to have his instructions clarified by his principal, if time permits, before acting upon them.'[34] Toulson, J summarized matters succinctly in *Patel v Standard Chartered Bank*: '[36] the critical question is not limited to whether the agent's interpretation was reasonable; it is whether he behaved reasonably in acting upon that interpretation.'[35]

## Implied Actual Authority

### Actual authority implied by the parties' conduct, the circumstances of the case, or trade custom

Whilst an agent's authority may have been conferred upon him by express **3.16** agreement with the principal—in short, his authority may be real, additionally the agent may possess implied authority which is to be inferred from the way in which the parties have conducted themselves and from the objective circumstances of the case. As Lord Denning, MR explained in *Hely-Hutchinson v Brayhead Ltd*:[36]

> [A]ctual authority may be express or implied. It is express when it is given by express words, such as when a board of directors pass a resolution which authorises two of their number to sign cheques. It is implied when it is inferred from the conduct of the parties and the circumstances of the case, such as when the board of directors appoint one of their number to be managing director. They thereby

---

[32] [1955] 2 Lloyd's Rep 147, 153.

[33] [1983] 1 WLR 642.

[34] *Ibid* at 656. See also Salmon, LJ's judgment in *Woodhouse AC Israel Cocoa Ltd SA v Nigerian Produce Marketing Co Ltd* [1972] AC 741. Although he concluded that *Ireland v Livingston* was not in point, his Lordship did observe that 'in 1872 there were no means by which an agent, at the other end of the world, receiving ambiguous instructions, could communicate with his principal in London to clear up any doubt about their meaning before carrying out his duty to act upon them promptly' (p 772).

[35] [2001] Lloyd's Rep Bank 229 at [36]. See also *Cooper v National Westminster Bank plc* [2010] 1 Lloyd's Rep 490 at [62]–[63] *per* HHJ Richard Seymour, QC.

[36] [1968] 1 QB 549.

impliedly authorise him to do all such things as fall within the usual scope of that office.[37]

Thus, implied authority is a matter of inference from the circumstances of the case or, if appropriate, from the course of dealing between the parties.

**3.17**   In *Hely-Hutchinson v Brayhead Ltd* Brayhead's (B's) chairman, R, acted as B's *de facto* managing director with the acquiescence of B's board. H-H, the chairman and managing director of another company, Perdio Electronics Ltd (P), gave a personal guarantee to bankers for a loan of £50,000 to P. P was sustaining trading losses and needed financial assistance. B was willing to help, although his intention was eventually to gain control of P. In due course B purchased shares from H-H and proposed injecting a further £150,000 into P. At roughly the same time, H-H became a director of B. After attending his first board meeting, R and H-H held a discussion, and H-H agreed to put more money into P provided that B agreed to secure his position. To that end R, as chairman of B, signed two letters on B's notepaper addressed to H-H purporting to indemnify H-H against loss on his personal guarantee of £50,000 and guaranteeing to repay money lent by H-H personally to P. H-H advanced £45,000 to P in reliance on those letters. The Court of Appeal held that B was bound by the actions of its *de facto* managing director, R, because the latter had implied authority to act in the way in which he did. In the view of Lord Denning, MR:

> It is plain that [R] had no express authority to enter into these two contracts on behalf of [B]: nor had he any such authority implied from the nature of his office. He had been duly appointed chairman of the company but that office in itself did not carry with it authority to enter into these contracts without the sanction of the board. But I think he had authority implied from the conduct of the parties and the circumstances of the case … such authority being implied from the circumstance that the board by their conduct over many months had acquiesced in his acting as their chief executive and committing [B] to contracts without the necessity of sanction from the board.[38]

*The overlap between implied actual authority and apparent authority*

**3.18**   Even when authority is implied by the parties' conduct and by the circumstances, as in *Hely-Hutchinson*, not infrequently 'actual authority and ostensible authority are not mutually exclusive.'[39] At first instance, Roskill, J had held that B was

---

[37]   *Ibid* at 583.

[38]   [1968] 1 QB 549, 584–5. As Sir Bernard Eder remarked in *Sino Channel Asia Ltd v Dana Shipping and Trading Pte Singapore, Dana Shipping and Trading SA* [2016] EWHC 1118 (Comm) at [46], 'Although the broad test in *Hely-Hutchinson* is easy to state, it is often far from straightforward to reach a conclusion in practice as to the circumstances in which an … agent may have an implied actual authority to perform some particular act on behalf of another.'

[39]   *Ibid* at 593 *per* Lord Pearson. On apparent authority, see **chapter 4**.

liable under the undertakings R had purportedly given on B's behalf on the ground that R possessed apparent authority. B had made a representation holding R out as having authority to commit it to such transactions. Although Lord Denning, MR preferred to rely upon the concept of R having implied authority to act for B, he did not disagree that R also had apparent authority. Indeed, the Master of the Rolls proceeded to explore the relationship between apparent authority and actual authority, stating:

> [A]pparent authority … often coincides with actual authority. Thus, when the board appoint one of their number to be managing director, they invest him not only with implied authority, but also with ostensible authority to do all such things as fall within the usual scope of that office. Other people who see him acting as managing director are entitled to assume that he has the usual authority of a managing director.[40]

Apparent and actual authority, however, are not necessarily co-extensive: 'sometimes ostensible authority exceeds actual authority.' This will be the case, for instance, where the company's board/principal expressly restricts the powers of its managing director/agent. In such a case the managing director's actual authority will be subject to the limitation, but 'his ostensible authority includes all the usual authority of a managing director'[41] and the company will be bound by his ostensible authority in his dealings with those who are ignorant of the restriction on his authority.

Brightman, LJ also considered the relationship between the two forms of author- **3.19** ity in *Waugh v HB Clifford & Sons Ltd*,[42] a case concerned with solicitors' implied authority to compromise their clients' suits. Brightman, LJ insisted:

> [I]t is … necessary to bear in mind the distinction between on the one hand the implied authority of a solicitor to compromise an action without prior reference to his client for consent: and on the other hand the ostensible or apparent authority of a solicitor to compromise an action on behalf of his client without the opposing litigant being required for his own protection either (1) to scrutinise the authority of the solicitor of the other party, or (2) to demand that the other party (if an individual) himself signs the terms of compromise or (if a corporation) affixes its seal or signs by a director or other agent possessing the requisite power under the articles of association or other constitution of the corporation.[43]

Not only may the agent's implied authority be less extensive than the agent's apparent authority, as Brightman, LJ explained, the purpose underlying the two concepts may also be rather different. Whereas actual implied authority has particular relevance to legal relations as between principal and agent, an agent's apparent authority

---

[40]  *Ibid* at 583.
[41]  *Ibid* at 583.
[42]  [1982] Ch 374.
[43]  *Ibid* at 383.

is more directed at protecting the expectations of third parties who have been induced to assume that the agent was acting within his actual authority:

> Suppose that a defamation action is on foot; that terms of compromise are discussed; and that the defendant's solicitor writes to the plaintiff's solicitor offering to compromise at a figure of £100,000, which the plaintiff desires to accept. It would ... be officious on the part of the plaintiff's solicitor to demand to be satisfied as to the authority of the defendant's solicitor to make the offer. It is perfectly clear that the defendant's solicitor has ostensible authority to compromise on behalf of his client, notwithstanding the large sum involved ...

> But it does not follow that the defendant's solicitor would have implied authority to agree damages on that scale without the agreement of his client. In the light of the solicitor's knowledge of his client's cash position it might be quite unreasonable and indeed grossly negligent for the solicitor to commit his client to such a burden without first inquiring if it were acceptable. But that does not affect the ostensible authority of the solicitor to compromise, so as to place the plaintiff at risk if he fails to satisfy himself that the defendant's solicitor has sought the agreement of his client. Such a limitation on the ostensible authority of the solicitor would be unworkable ...

> It follows ... that a solicitor (or counsel) may in a particular case have ostensible authority *vis-à-vis* the opposing litigant where he has no implied authority *vis-à-vis* his client.[44]

### Implied authority deriving from the usual incidents of the agent's professional activities

**3.20** An agent possesses implied authority to perform his agency in the usual manner in which an agent of that particular type would normally be expected to act. It will be recalled that in *Hely-Hutchinson v Brayhead Ltd* Lord Denning, MR stated that when a board of directors appoint someone to be their managing director, 'they thereby impliedly authorise him to do all such things as fall within the usual scope of that office.'[45] For this reason, Brayhead's *de facto* managing director's undertaking to indemnify Hely-Hutchinson, even though it was not specifically authorized, committed Brayhead: it was within the conventional sphere of activity of a company's managing director to enter into such transactions.

**3.21** Pursuing the theme of the implied authority of managing directors, in *Dey v Pullinger Engineering Co*,[46] where a managing director had drawn a bill without his board's authority, the court held that a person taking the bill in due course was entitled to assume that he had authority in fact:

> A holder in due course cannot as a rule be expected to know what goes on in the company's board room, and if he has to take the risk of its turning out that the persons

---

[44] *Ibid* at 387.
[45] [1968] 1 QB 549, 583. See para **3.16**.
[46] [1921] 1 KB 77.

signing had no authority, and much more so if he has to prove that they had authority, people in business would be very shy in dealing with such bills.[47]

Not surprisingly, a managing director has been held not usually to have authority to bribe the representative of another company in order to obtain work for his principal.[48]

This source of authority, which is sometimes referred to as usual authority, is broadly applicable to agents at large. In each individual case it will be a matter of looking to the *milieu* within which the particular agent operates and then of determining what incidental activities are normally conducted by that type of agent. If the activity, which has not been expressly authorized by the principal, is one that would not usually constitute part of that type of agent's duties or employment, then it will fall outside the agent's implied authority. If the activity is usually incidental to the conduct of a particular species of agent's business, it will fall within the agent's implied authority. For this reason, in *Howard v Sheward*[49] it was held that a horse-dealer with authority to sell a horse was also impliedly authorized to warrant the soundness of the horse. By the same token, in *Mardorf Peach & Co Ltd v Attica Sea Carriers Corporation of Liberia*[50] it was determined that 'it was not within the banker's express or implied authority to make commercial decisions on behalf of their customers by accepting or rejecting late payments of hire without taking instructions.'[51] In each case it is a matter of deciding what is usually to be expected. **3.22**

In *The Unique Mariner*,[52] the master of a ship that had run aground on a reef mistakenly signed a contract on standard Lloyd's terms with a salvage tug that happened by rather than with the tug which the owners had instructed to steam to the assistance of their stricken vessel. The shipowners sought to avoid liability under the contract signed by their master. Brandon, J enunciated the guiding principle: **3.23**

> [T]he implied actual authority of a master, unless restricted by such instructions lawfully given, extends to doing whatever is incidental to, or necessary for, the successful prosecution of the voyage and the safety and preservation of the ship.[53]

The judge then decided that the implied actual authority of the master of a stranded ship to accept the services of a suitable tug was not limited to his accepting them subject to the ordinary maritime law of salvage but extended to accepting such services on the terms of any reasonable contract.[54] In this case, there had been nothing

---

[47] *Ibid* at 79 *per* Bray, J.
[48] *E Hannibal & Co Ltd v Frost* (1988) 4 BCC 3.
[49] (1866) LR 2 CP 148.
[50] [1977] AC 850.
[51] *Ibid* at 880 *per* Lord Salmon.
[52] [1978] 1 Lloyd's Rep 438.
[53] *Ibid* at 449.
[54] *Ibid* at 450.

unusual in the master accepting the services of the passing tug on the terms of the Lloyd's form without first seeking to communicate with his principal. Moreover, there was no good reason to have expected the tugboat captain to ask the master whether he had communicated with the owners. The tugboat's captain was unaware, and ought not to have been taken to be aware, of any restriction on the implied actual authority of the master. Because 'the ostensible authority of a master is the same as his implied actual authority, unless the latter has been restricted by express instructions from his owners or their representatives, and the third party concerned is, or should be taken to be, aware of such restriction',[55] Brandon, J concluded that the contract fell within both the implied actual authority and the apparent authority of the master, and that the owners were contractually bound by the contract into which their master had mistakenly entered.

**3.24** What a particular species of agent is usually empowered to do may be a matter of evidence in each case. However, some agents' usual powers are firmly established by case law. In the case of estate agents, for instance, in the absence of express authority to sell,[56] it is settled law that even when the vendor has told the agent the price at which he is prepared to part with his property an estate agent has no implied authority to sell the principal's land.[57] Similarly, in the absence of contrary agreement,[58] it is accepted that an auctioneer is usually entitled to do a number of things without his principal's express authority, such as to describe the property he is charged to sell[59] and, in the case of personal property, to receive payment of the whole price.[60] It is equally well understood that in the absence of express authority an auctioneer does not usually have the authority to engage in certain activities, such as warranting the property he is selling without the vendor's consent[61] or negotiating the sale of property by private contract if the auction chances to have proved abortive.[62]

**3.25** Yet, no matter how entrenched such findings may appear to be in the case law, these are not rules of law so much as observations of general practice. Over time, practice can change; new business methods and technological advances can transform the situation. To take a common example, the Court of Appeal in *Waugh v HB Clifford & Sons Ltd*[63] affirmed the proposition that a solicitor has authority, as between himself and an opposing litigant, to compromise his

---

[55] See paras **3.18–3.19**.
[56] *Rosenbaum v Belson* [1900] 2 Ch 267.
[57] See *Hamer v Sharp* (1874) LR 19 Eq 108.
[58] *Overbrooke Estates Ltd v Glencombe Properties Ltd* [1974] 1 WLR 1335.
[59] *Smith v Land and House Property Corp* (1885) LR 28 ChD 7.
[60] *Chelmsford Auctions Ltd v Poole* [1973] QB 542.
[61] *Payne v Lord Leconfield* (1882) 51 LJQB 642.
[62] *Marsh v Jelf* (1862) 3 F & F 234.
[63] [1982] Ch 374. Also *In re Newen* [1903] 1 Ch 812, 817 *per* Farwell, J.

client's suit, provided that the compromise does not involve matters collateral to the action.[64] In practice, in view of their potential liability in negligence, solicitors—and, for that matter, barristers, who also enjoy implied authority to compromise suits[65]—are most unlikely to conclude a compromise without first seeking their clients' instructions. One of the primary reasons for implying this authority in the first place was said to be that it might be considered 'officious on the part of the plaintiff's solicitor to demand to be satisfied as to the authority of the defendant's solicitor to make the offer'.[66] The dominant view today, however, is that, given developments in communications over the past quarter of a century, it is doubtful whether a solicitor today would choose to exercise such authority and, more particularly, whether such inquiries would be considered unduly importunate.[67]

### Implied authority deriving from customs and trade usages

An agent's implied authority may derive from customs and trade usages that apply **3.26** in the market within which the agent operates. The rule is that a party to a contract is bound by usages applicable to that contract provided that they are certain, notorious, and reasonable. This is so, even if the usages are not known to the party in question. As will be seen, a custom may sometimes be held to be unreasonable. That being so, the usage will not be binding upon a principal unless it can be shown that the latter knew of such a practice and agreed to it.[68] Thus in *Robinson v Mollett*,[69] a tallow broker, who had sent his principal a bought note stating 'Bought of A. on your account', claimed that it was a custom of the London tallow market for brokers to purchase tallow in bulk and then allocate it amongst their principals, rather than fulfilling each principal's order individually. As Lord Chelmsford explained:

> [T]he usage is of such a peculiar character, and is so completely at variance with the relation between the parties, converting a broker employed to buy, into a principal selling for himself, and thereby giving him an interest wholly opposed to his duty, that I think no person who is ignorant of such an usage can be held to have agreed to submit to its conditions, merely by employing the services of a broker, to whom the usage is known, to perform the ordinary and accustomed duties belonging to such employment.[70]

---

[64] What is collateral to the action is not to be interpreted too restrictively: *Waugh v HB Clifford Sons Ltd* [1982] Ch 374, 388.

[65] See *Arthur JS Hall v Simons* [2002] 1 AC 615.

[66] [1982] Ch 374, 387 *per* Brightman, LJ.

[67] See notably Foskett, *Law and Practice of Compromise* (2015: London, Sweet & Maxwell) 8th ed, para 21-11.

[68] *Cunliffe-Owen v Teather & Greenwood* [1967] 1 WLR 1421, 1439 *per* Ungoed-Thomas, J.

[69] (1875) LR7HL 802.

[70] *Ibid* at 838.

*If a custom of the trade is invoked, its existence must be proved*

**3.27**   If the existence or content of a custom is contested, precise proof is required that the custom binds people operating within that particular commercial setting. As Devlin, J explained in *Stag Line Ltd v Board of Trade*:

> [I]t is a bold task to endeavour to establish custom by means purely of affidavit evidence, for this reason. There are very few topics upon which witnesses are likely to depart more widely under cross-examination from their original evidence than on the question of custom. I think anyone who is familiar with endeavouring to prove custom would probably recognize the truth of that observation, and that is because witnesses so rarely appreciate exactly what a custom is for the purposes of the law. They think that if only they can say what the way is in which they think a particular problem ought to be dealt with, that is sufficient to establish custom.[71]

Staughton, J endorsed Devlin, J's approach in *Drexel Burnham Lambert International NV v El Nasr*,[72] where, in a memorable passage, he stressed the fact that 'custom' in this context is not simply to be equated with what is customarily done within a particular market. A custom means a practice that is binding on persons transacting business within a given market or locality:

> Evidence of what always happens in a particular market is not by itself enough to show a binding practice. For example, it may be the universal practice in some markets for contracts to be typed on A4 paper with double spacing in black ink. It does not follow that a contract typed on some other size of paper with single spacing in red ink is invalid. What has to be shown by evidence is that the practice is recognized as imposing a binding obligation. The evidence does not come near to establishing that in the present case.[73]

**3.28**   A party relying upon a custom must be able to show three things: certainty, notoriety, and reasonableness. As Ungoed-Thomas, J explained in *Cunliffe-Owen v Teather & Greenwood*:

> 'Usage' is apt to be used confusingly in the authorities, in two senses, (1) a practice, and (2) a practice which the court will recognise. 'Usage' as a practice which the court will recognise is a mixed question of fact and law. For the practice to amount to such a recognised usage, it must be *certain*, in the sense that the practice is clearly established; it must be *notorious*, in the sense that it is so well known, in the market in which it is alleged to exist, that those who conduct business in that market contract with the usage as an implied term; and it must be *reasonable*.[74]

---

[71] (1949–50) 83 Ll L Rep 356, 360. In *Nelson v Dahl* (1879) 12 ChD 568, 575 Sir George Jessel suggested that a custom 'must be so notorious that everybody in the trade enters into a contract with that usage as an implied term. It must be uniform as well as reasonable, and it must have quite as much certainty as the written contract itself.'

[72] [1986] 1 Lloyd's Rep 356.

[73] *Ibid* at 365.

[74] [1967] 1 WLR 1421, 1438 (emphasis added).

*The reasonableness of the custom*

In *Tucker v Linger*[75] a landlord leased out his farm, reserving to himself 'all **3.29** mines and minerals, sand, quarries of stone ...' A recent local custom was said to allow tenants, operating under similarly worded leases, to take away any flints turned up in the ordinary course of good husbandry and to sell them for their own benefit. One issue was whether the custom was reasonable. In the words of Lord O'Hagan, the removal of the flints was reasonable simply because it was 'a necessity for the proper management of the agricultural operations'.[76] The House of Lords also concluded that the custom was not inconsistent with the other terms of the contract between landlord and tenant, reserving mines and minerals.[77]

In *Anglo-African Merchants Ltd and Another v Bayley*[78] it was argued that the un- **3.30** derwriters' practice followed at Lloyd's at the time—and, in likelihood, elsewhere in the insurance market—was unreasonable. When a dispute arose between underwriter and assured, brokers, who in law had always been considered to operate as the agents of the insured parties who employed them,[79] made their files available to the underwriters (the third parties). They would even refuse to make their files, which contained copies of assessors' reports obtained by them on the instructions of the underwriters, available to the assured on the ground that, despite their position as agents for the assured, that document was the property of the underwriters. Megaw, J drew attention to the sacrosanct principle that 'no agent who has accepted an employment from one principal can in law accept an engagement inconsistent with his duty to the first principal ... unless he makes the fullest disclosure to each principal of his interest, and obtains the consent of each principal to the double employment',[80] before observing that the custom for which the agents argued would '[invite] suspicion that the broker is hunting with the hounds whilst running with the hare.'[81] Counsel had contended that the practice was common knowledge at Lloyd's, and even represented general practice throughout the insurance market. In addition to expressing scepticism at this bold claim, Megaw, J held that even if it could be established by evidence that such a custom obtained:

> I should hold the view ... that a custom will not be upheld by the courts of this country if it contradicts the vital principle that an agent may not at the same time serve ...

---

[75] (1883) LR 8 App Cas 508.

[76] *Ibid* at 510.

[77] (1883) LR 8 App Cas 508, 516 *per* Lord Fitzgerald.

[78] [1970] 1 QB 311.

[79] Eg, *Rozanes v Bowen* (1928) 32 Ll L Rep 98, 101 *per* Scrutton, LJ: '[I]n the case of marine insurance there is not the slightest doubt, and never has been the slightest doubt, that the broker is not the agent of the underwriter.'

[80] *Fullwood v Hurley* [1928] 1 KB 498, 502 *per* Scrutton, LJ.

[81] [1970] 1 QB 311, 323.

two principals ... in actual or potential opposition to one another: unless, indeed, he has the explicit, informed, consent of both principals. An insurance broker is in no privileged position in this respect.[82]

**3.31** In similar vein, in the absence of clear evidence, in *Accidia Foundation v Simon C Dickinson Ltd*[83] Vos, J declined to recognize that in the international art market it was the common practice of art dealers to agree with their principals for a return price on the basis that the dealer might sell the piece at any price without informing the principal of that ultimate price or of the level of commission the dealer thereby received after passing on only the return price:

> Such arrangements may exceptionally have occurred, but they cannot be described on the evidence I have heard as usual practice or the way in which valuable paintings are usually sold ... in the London art market. Moreover, such arrangements would be objectionable as being unreasonable and unlawful, unless they were concluded with the fully informed consent of the principal seller or the dealer accounted to that principal for the secret profit secured.[84]

*Unlawful customs and customs excluded by the parties' contract*

**3.32** It should be noted that a custom, no matter how pervasive, will not be recognized by the court if it is unlawful.[85] Thus, in what Lord Thomas of Cwmgiedd, CJ described as a 'vivid contemporary illustration',[86] in his study of secret commissions and bribes, Albert Crew relates the following typically brisk exchange in a case heard before Sir George Jessel, MR:

> In 1877, Jessel, MR tried an action brought by a firm of merchants at Bombay which complained that their shipping agent in Lancashire had systematically been receiving two invoices, one which he sent out to India, the other, the real invoice, which he retained. He asked if there were any answer to the charge, and the reply was that the practice was universal throughout the whole shipping trade in Lancashire, and prevalent elsewhere. 'I have a mass of evidence', counsel said. 'There are a large number of most respectable people in court to give evidence in proof that the practice is universal.' Sir George Jessel replied: 'You can send those respectable people

---

[82] *Ibid* at 323–4. To Donaldson, J's evident surprise, the issue arose again in *North and South Trust Co v Berkeley* [1971] 1 WLR 470. He concluded: 'If a usage is to have effect in law it must at least be notorious, certain and reasonable. On the evidence before me, it may be certain, ... I entertain doubts whether it is sufficiently notorious, ... It is sufficient for present purposes to say that I regard the practice as wholly unreasonable and therefore incapable of being a legal usage' (p 482).

[83] [2010] EWHC 3058 (Ch).

[84] *Ibid* at [75].

[85] There is a complex case law, mainly concerned with one particular statute, since repealed, dealing with whether a principal can assent to an unlawful custom if he is aware of it. The preferred view is probably that, generally speaking, an agent's implied authority ought not to derive from an unlawful custom. See further *Bowstead & Reynolds on Agency* (2014: London, Sweet & Maxwell) 20th ed, by Watts, para 3-036.

[86] *R v J(P)* [2014] 1 WLR 1857 at [16].

home; they have come to prove an iniquitous practice, and the sooner they leave the court the better.'[87]

Finally, it remains to add that a custom will only be recognized provided that it has **3.33** neither been expressly excluded by terms of the parties' contract nor is otherwise inconsistent with the terms of their contract.

---

[87] Albert Crew, *The Law Relating to Secret Commissions and Bribes (Christmas Boxes, Gratuities etc): the Prevention of Corruption Act 1906* (1913: Pitman).

# 4

# APPARENT AUTHORITY

## What is 'Apparent Authority'?

### Apparent authority and actual authority distinguished

As its name suggests, 'apparent authority'—or 'ostensible authority', as it is other-    **4.01**
wise known—arises where a third party is induced to enter into a transaction with
a principal by a party who appears to have authority to act but who in fact lacks
such authority. As Diplock, LJ explained in *Freeman & Lockyer (a firm) v Buckhurst
Park Properties (Mangal) Ltd*, actual authority and apparent authority are quite independent of one another. Although they generally co-exist and coincide, either
may exist without the other; and their respective scopes may be different.[1] Actual
authority, as we saw, is a legal relationship between principal and agent created by
a consensual agreement to which they alone are parties. In contrast, Diplock, LJ
defined apparent authority in *Freeman & Lockyer* in the following terms:

> [A] legal relationship between the principal and the contractor created by a rep-
> resentation, made by the principal to the contractor, intended to be and in fact

---

[1] [1964] 2 QB 480, 502.

acted upon by the contractor, that the agent has authority to enter on behalf of the principal into a contract of a kind within the scope of the 'apparent' authority, so as to render the principal liable to perform any obligations imposed upon him by such contract. To the relationship so created the agent is a stranger. He need not be (although he generally is) aware of the existence of the representation but he must not purport to make the agreement as principal himself. The representation, when acted upon by the contractor by entering into a contract with the agent, operates as an estoppel, preventing the principal from asserting that he is not bound by the contract. It is irrelevant whether the agent had actual authority to enter into the contract.[2]

Hence, as Toulson, J observed more recently in *ING Re (UK) Ltd v R & V Versicherung AG*:

> The doctrine of apparent or ostensible authority is based on estoppel by representation. Where a principal (P) represents or causes it to be represented to a third party (T) that an agent (A) has authority to act on P's behalf, and T deals with A as P's agent on the faith of that representation, P is bound by A's acts to the same extent as if A had the authority which he was represented as having.[3]

Toulson, J added that this general principle was 'too well established to need citation of authority'.[4]

**4.02**  Apparent authority, then, is not authority as such. Rather, the law gives effect to the illusion of authority. In the oft-quoted words of Professor Montrose:

> Apparent authority is really equivalent to the phrase 'appearance of authority'. There may be an appearance of authority whether in fact or not there is authority.[5]

The illusion may be created by the principal's specifically misrepresenting to third parties that the agent enjoys authority to perform certain acts or by the principal's allowing third parties to infer that the agent has the authority that such an agent would usually possess.

*Theoretical underpinnings*

**4.03**  It is not easy to settle the legal foundation of apparent authority. As the courts admit, not all the cases are easy to reconcile in every respect.[6] The courts

---

[2]  *Ibid* at 503.

[3]  [2006] 2 All ER (Comm) 870 at [99]. The notion—that apparent authority rests upon an estoppel, whereby, by his representation to a third party that the agent enjoys authority, the principal is prevented from denying that authority—was said by Buxton, LJ in *AMB Generali Holding AG v SEB Trygg Liv Holding Aktiebolag* [2006] 1 WLR 2276 at [31] to '[go] back at least as far as the speech of Lord Selborne LC in *Scarf v Jardine* (1882) 7 App. Cas. 345.'

[4]  [2006] 2 All ER (Comm) 870 at [99].

[5]  *The Basis of the Power of the Agent in Cases of Actual and Apparent Authority* (1932) 16 Can Bar Rev 756, 764.

[6]  *Thanakharn Kasikorn Thai Chamkat (Mahachon) v Akai Holdings Ltd (in liquidation)* [2010] HKCFA 64 at [42] *per* Lord Neuberger of Abbotsbury NPJ.

consistently associate apparent authority with the concept of estoppel by representation. As Slade, J observed in *Rama Corporation Ltd v Proved Tin and General Investments Ltd*:

> Ostensible or apparent authority ... is merely a form of estoppel, indeed, it has been termed agency by estoppel, and you cannot call in aid an estoppel unless you have three ingredients:
> (i)   a representation,
> (ii)  a reliance on the representation, and
> (iii) an alteration of your position resulting from such reliance.[7]

Although this analysis is widely accepted,[8] it has been pointed out that in the context of agency estoppel wears a meaning different from its customary common-law usage: in particular, it is noted, the representation upon which the third party relies can be 'very general indeed' and the detriment suffered by the latter 'may be small'.[9] The writer accepts that the objective analysis applicable to the formation of contract 'has much to commend it' in this context as it would avoid the conceptual difficulties just mentioned as well as allowing certain true cases of agency by estoppel to be distinctly hived off from the general run of cases of apparent authority.[10] Although the theoretical underpinning admittedly is 'shaky', on balance the conventional analysis of apparent authority as a variety of estoppel by representation should be retained; but it should be treated as 'invoking a special (and weak) type of estoppel relevant only in the agency context'.[11] In any case, as Colman, J pointed out in *The Starsin*, responding to earlier objections that the notion of representation in the context of apparent agency can appear a little 'artificial' and that the connection with estoppel is therefore 'more difficult to maintain',[12] substantially similar public policy considerations apply both to this kind of apparent authority and to estoppel by representation. In both cases:

> it would be unconscionable for a principal to deny that he was bound by a transaction which had been entered into apparently on his behalf by someone whom he had permitted to represent to third parties that he had the principal's authority to bind the principal to transactions of the kind in question. To permit the principal to rely on lack of actual authority in such circumstances to the prejudice of the third party would be to permit a similarly prejudicial inconsistency of conduct to that against which the law of estoppel is directed.[13]

---

[7]  [1952] 2 QB 147, 149–50 *per* Slade, J.

[8]  Eg, *Northside Developments Pty Ltd v Registrar-General* (1989–90) 179 CLR 146, 173–4 *per* Brennan, J.

[9]  *Bowstead & Reynolds on Agency* (2014: London, Sweet & Maxwell) 20th ed, by Watts, para 8-028, p 393.

[10]  *Bowstead & Reynolds* (2014) 20th ed, para 8-029, p 394. See discussion of *Spiro v Lintern* at paras **4.56–4.58**.

[11]  *Bowstead & Reynolds* (2014) 20th ed, para 8-029, p 395.

[12]  *Bowstead & Reynolds* (1996) 16th ed, para 8-018.

[13]  *Homburg Houtimport BV v Agrosin Private Ltd. The Starsin* [2000] 1 Lloyd's Rep 85 at [95].

## When does Apparent Authority arise?

**4.04**  Apparent authority can arise in a variety of circumstances. For analytical purposes, it is suggested that an agent may come to have apparent authority in several broad categories of situation.

### A person may allow another to appear to third parties to be his agent when in fact he is not

**4.05**  A 'principal', by his conduct, may represent to third parties that someone, who in fact has no authority to act as agent at all, is authorized to act as that principal's agent. In the well-known case of *Barrett v Deere*[14] a third party sought to settle a debt he owed to a merchant by making payment at the merchant's counting house. He paid someone who, to all intents, appeared to be authorized to receive monies—the person concerned was sitting inside the counting house with account books near him and gave a receipt on behalf of the principal. Although the person who received the payment had no authority whatever to do so, Lord Tenterden, CJ held that the payment was effective to discharge the third party's debt:

> The debtor has a right to suppose that the tradesman has the control of his own premises, and that he will not allow persons to come there and intermeddle in his business without his authority.[15]

**4.06**  Similarly, in *Gurtner v Beaton*,[16] following an accident in which people were killed or injured, it transpired that an aviation firm had allowed its part-time aviation manager to use its name for the purpose of running a private flying club and had represented to third parties that he had control of suitable aircraft and could make contracts in his managerial capacity. In these circumstances, the manager was found to have apparent authority as those dealing with the flying club would reasonably have thought that they were dealing with the aviation firm. More recently, in *OBG Ltd v Allan*, Mance, LJ suggested as another example of someone who might become endowed with apparent authority, even though not employed as an agent by the 'principal', 'an intended agent whose appointment has been announced in the trade press, but prematurely so, since his contract has never in fact been finalised.'[17] In both these situations, the words or conduct of the principal induce third parties reasonably to believe that the purported agent has authority to bind the principal. The courts simply give effect to the impression created by the words or conduct of the principal.

---

[14]  (1828) Mood&M 200.
[15]  *Ibid* at 202.
[16]  [1992] 2 Lloyd's Rep 369.
[17]  [2005] QB 762 at [88].

**A principal may allow his agent to continue to appear as his agent after the agency has terminated**

An agency can terminate automatically in a variety of circumstances. Whenever the **4.07** principal ceases to be competent to act for himself, the agency will automatically terminate and the agent will cease to have actual authority to act for the principal. This will occur, for example, if the principal dies or becomes insane. In the context of company law it has been consistently held that the appointment of a provisional liquidator automatically revokes the authority of agents appointed to act on behalf of the company by or under the authority of its directors—reflecting the general tenet that an agent's authority ceases when his principal becomes incapable of acting on his own behalf.[18] In *Drew v Nunn*, a case in which Brett, LJ reserved judgment for over six months pondering the conceptual problems of revocation by incapacity,[19] a tradesman sued to recover the price of boots and shoes supplied to the defendant's wife whilst the defendant was insane. Prior to his insanity, the defendant had given his wife 'absolute authority to act for him' and had held her out to the tradesman as clothed with that authority. Upon recovering his sanity following his bout of mental derangement, the husband argued that he did not owe the price of the footwear as his wife's authority had automatically terminated from the moment that he became insane. The majority of the court accepted that the wife's agency terminated automatically upon the intervening insanity of her spouse. Nevertheless the court also held that a person who deals with the agent, without knowledge of the principal's insanity, has a right to enter into a contract with him, and the principal, although a lunatic, is bound so that he cannot repudiate the contract assumed to be made upon his behalf. If a principal has held out another person as his agent, the principal cannot withdraw the agent's authority *vis-à-vis* third persons without giving them notice of the withdrawal. If a third party has no notice that the agent's authority has been retracted, even though both principal and third party are innocent of any wrongdoing, the person who made the representation which, as between the two, was the original cause of the mischief, ought to bear the loss.

**A principal may allow the impression to be given that his agent has greater authority than is in fact the case**

This may occur, for instance, if the principal has restricted the actual or implied **4.08** authority of his agent but omitted to inform third parties of the agent's limited authority. In *Todd v Robinson*[20] an agent, resident in London, on six prior occasions had purchased linen from a local wholesaler on behalf of his principal, a Yorkshire

---

[18] See *Pacific and General Insurance Co Ltd v Hazell* [1997] BCC 400.
[19] See *In re K (Enduring Powers of Attorney)* [1988] Ch 310, 314 *per* Hoffmann, J.
[20] (1825) Ry&M 217.

shopkeeper. The agent then proceeded to order further goods from the London wholesaler to a value of £45. The agent appropriated these goods to his own use. The principal had in fact restricted the purchasing authority of the agent to £31. It was found nevertheless that the principal was liable to the third party for the whole sum. As Abbott, LCJ explained to the jury:

> The liability of the [principal] to the only disputed part of this demand [*scilicet* £14] depends on the question, whether the [principal] has by his own acts and conduct constituted W his general agent to order goods. The authority actually given in each particular instance to [the agent] can only be known to the [principal] himself; the [third party] can only look to the appearances held out by him.[21]

In *The Unique Mariner*,[22] mistakenly believing that a tugboat which offered to salve his ship, which had run aground, was the one sent by his ship's owners, the master of 'The Unique Mariner' signed a Lloyd's Standard Form salvage agreement engaging the defendant's tugboat. Subsequently, upon learning that the tugboat which had actually been engaged by the owners was still on its way, the master purported to terminate the agreement he had signed. Brandon, J held that since a captain has authority which extends to acceptance of any reasonable contract for services, even though his instructions restricted his actual authority the master still possessed apparent authority to sign the Lloyd's Standard Form given that the captain of the first tugboat on the scene had no notice of any restriction on the master's authority. Secret restrictions on an agent's authority, therefore, will not bind third parties who are unaware of them and who might reasonably conclude from circumstances such as previous dealings that the agent has a general, or at least a greater, authority to act on behalf of the principal than is in fact the case.

**4.09**   A principal, then, may confer authority upon his agent, but restrict its scope. If third parties are unaware of the limitations imposed by the principal on the agent's authority but could reasonably infer that the agent possessed a wider authority than is in fact the case, the principal will become liable for acts performed within what appears to be the agent's authority. In *Manchester Trust v Furness*,[23] although they had been appointed and paid by the owners, unusually a charterparty contained a proviso whereby the ship's master and crew were to be the servants of the charterers. Additionally, the charterparty stated that in signing bills of lading the captain might only do so as the agent of the charterers, who would indemnify the owners against all liabilities arising from the captain signing the bills of lading. The master signed a bill of lading for delivery of coal

---

[21] *Ibid* at 217–18.
[22] [1978] 1 Lloyd's Rep 438.
[23] [1895] 2 QB 539.

to Rio de Janeiro. Having fallen prey to a deception, the master misdelivered the coal to Buenos Aires, where it was stolen. The holders of the bills of lading in Rio sued the shipowners for their losses. In a decision which contains oft-cited pronouncements as to the undesirability of importing notions of constructive notice into commercial transactions,[24] the Court of Appeal held that the special clause inserted into the charterparty was binding only as between the owners and the charterers, and did not affect the liability of the owners to the holders of the bills of lading, who were entitled to consider that the normal situation obtained and that the master was the agent of the owners. In the absence of an explicit indication that the master was acting for the charterers, 'the holders of the bill of lading ... would naturally believe and imagine that the master when he signed the bill of lading was exercising the ordinary authority which attaches to him in his capacity of master.'[25]

Lord Denning, MR, in *Hely-Hutchinson v Brayhead Ltd*, supplied a further common example of apparent authority created by the principal's failure to make third parties aware of restrictions on an agent's authority:  **4.10**

> [W]hen the board [of directors of a company] appoint the managing director, they may expressly limit his authority by saying he is not to order goods worth more than £500 without the sanction of the board. In that case his actual authority is subject to the £500 limitation, but his ostensible authority includes all the usual authority of a managing director. The company is bound by his ostensible authority in his dealings with those who do not know of the limitation.[26]

## The Requirements of Apparent Authority

As Slade, J pointed out in *Rama Corporation*,[27] in the context of agency an estoppel by representation requires three elements:  **4.11**

(i) a representation,

(ii) a reliance on the representation, and

(iii) an alteration of position resulting from such reliance.

---

[24] '[A]s regards the extension of the equitable doctrines of constructive notice to commercial transactions, the Courts have always set their faces resolutely against it. The equitable doctrines of constructive notice are common enough in dealing with land and estates ... but there have been repeated protests against the introduction into commercial transactions of anything like an extension of those doctrines, and the protest is founded on perfect good sense. In dealing with estates in land title is everything, and it can be leisurely investigated; in commercial transactions possession is everything, and there is no time to investigate title; and if we were to extend the doctrine of constructive notice to commercial transactions we should be doing infinite mischief and paralysing the trade of the country': [1895] 2 QB 539, 545 *per* Lindley, LJ.

[25] [1895] 2 QB 539, 547 *per* Lopes, LJ.

[26] [1968] 1 QB 549, 583.

[27] See para **4.03**.

### Representation

*It must have been represented to third parties that the agent had authority to act on behalf of the principal*

**4.12** This proposition raises a number of questions. How may the representation be made? Who is authorized to make it? To whom must the representation have been directed? What is the content of the relevant representation? Must a representation have been made deliberately?

*A representation may be made by words or by conduct*

**4.13** If a principal represents to a third party that an identified person has authority to act on his behalf or if a principal so conducts himself as to permit it to be represented that that person has authority to act on his behalf, the principal will be bound by the acts of the agent *vis-à-vis* any third party who acts in reliance upon the representation just as though that agent possessed actual authority. The representation may be contained in a written instrument. In *ex p Harrison*,[28] for example, H had handed a signed underwriting letter to the agent of a company promoter, L, which stated that L had authority to agree to subscribe for 300 shares in a brewery company. According to the letter, if H failed to apply for the shares on a particular day, L was authorized to apply for them in H's name. H did not apply for the shares, and the acceptance of the offer appeared from L's signed acceptance on the document itself. In a separate document, of which the brewery company knew nothing, H had stipulated that the acceptance of his offer by L had to be communicated to him by a particular day. This was not done. The first H knew of L's having acted on his behalf was when the shares were allotted to him. The Court of Appeal held that, because the brewery company was unaware of the private restriction on L's authority, the company could rely upon the writing of which they had knowledge and that H was estopped from denying that L had unrestricted authority to apply for 300 shares in his name.

*The representation may be implied by previous dealing between the parties*

**4.14** If there has been a previous course of dealings between the parties, until notified to the contrary, the third party may be entitled to assume that the agent, who previously was authorized to act for the principal, continues to have authority to act on behalf of the principal. In *Summers v Solomon*[29] the defendant employed his nephew to manage his jeweller's shop at Lewes. The nephew, who had authority to order goods for the shop, had several times ordered jewellery from the plaintiff, in London, which the defendant had accepted. The nephew left the shop, thereby terminating the agency, came to London, and purported to order jewellery from the

---

[28] (1893) 69 LT 204.
[29] (1857) 7 El&Bl 879.

plaintiff on behalf of his uncle. The nephew then absconded with the jewellery. In holding the defendant liable to the plaintiff, Crompton, J stated:

> [O]ne instance of authorizing an agent to pledge the employer's credit was enough to justify a party dealing with the employer in assuming that the authority continued. It is no answer, that the employer here would find it difficult to give notice of withdrawing the agency. As soon as you have given the agent authority to pledge your credit, you render yourself liable to parties who have acted upon notice of such authority until you find the means of giving them notice that the authority is determined.[30]

As Coleridge, J explained:

> The question is, not what was the actual relation between the defendant and his nephew, but whether the defendant had not so conducted himself as to make the plaintiff suppose the nephew to be the defendant's general agent. What passes between the defendant and his nephew cannot limit the defendant's liability to the plaintiff.[31]

It is however to be borne in mind that a court will not too readily infer from a prior **4.15** course of dealings that a principal has represented that a putative agent has authority to enter into future contracts on its behalf.[32] Romer, LJ made this point in *Slingsby v District Bank Ltd (Manchester)*:

> ... the fact that the [employer of the putative agent] had, even on numerous occasions, employed [the putative agent] to prepare cheques for signature cannot amount to a holding out by them of [him] as their general agent for that purpose.[33]

Romer LJ's reasoning was subsequently endorsed by Robert Goff, LJ in *Armagas Ltd v Mundogas SA*,[34] where, in determining whether a broker whom the defendants had employed on previous occasions had apparent authority to enter into a charterparty, it was pointed out:

> Simply by using the broker as his channel of communication ... the principal makes no representation that the broker has authority to make any such communication in relation to future transactions, so as to bind the principal. It is well settled that mere repetition of this kind does not of itself constitute a representation necessary to found ostensible authority ... All that a third party can derive from what has happened is that the principal regularly transacts business through the broker in question, and that when he does so he uses the broker to communicate his approval of transactions when he has in fact given such approval.[35]

---

[30] *Ibid* at 884–5.
[31] *Ibid* at 884.
[32] *PEC Ltd v Asia Rice Co Ltd* [2014] EWHC 1583 (Comm) at [67] *per* Andrew Smith, J.
[33] [1932] 1 KB 544, 566.
[34] [1986] AC 717.
[35] *Ibid* at p 733.

A previous course of dealing will not, without more, bind the principal to subsequent transactions which he has not authorised the agent to transact on his behalf. No doubt it can be said that, in a sense, a third party may rely on the fact that the broker is the principal's regular broker; but that is not enough, for there has been no representation by the principal necessary to give rise to ostensible authority.[36]

*The representation may be implied from the principal's conduct*

**4.16**  The representation may be implied from the principal's conduct, notably in placing the agent in a position that carries with it a 'usual authority'. Delivering judgment in the Western Australian Court of Appeal in *Auxil Pty Ltd v Terrannova*, Newnes, JA observed: 'the most common form of representation by a principal is by conduct, that is, by permitting the agent to act in the management or conduct of the principal's business.'[37] As Lord Keith of Kinkel explained in *Armagas Ltd v Mundogas Ltd*, in the commonly encountered case an agent's apparent authority will be general in character, and will arise when the principal has placed the agent in a position that, in the outside world, is generally regarded as carrying authority to enter into transactions of the kind in question.[38]

*What falls within the 'usual authority' of a particular species of agent is a question of fact*

**4.17**  In *United Bank of Kuwait Ltd v Hammoud*,[39] in 1983, a solicitor, E, acting without authority, undertook to transfer monies to a certain account when they came under his firm's control. The plaintiffs advanced a loan to the first defendant on the security of this undertaking, later claiming that as E had apparent authority they could enforce the undertaking against the partners of E's firm. In a conjoined appeal, *City Trust Ltd v Levy*, in 1986, E was employed by the defendant as an assistant solicitor with authority to give undertakings on behalf of the firm, L & Co. Without L & Co's knowledge, E falsely represented to the plaintiffs that the firm controlled offshore funds belonging to a non-resident client, part of which was to be applied to the discharge of a debt owing to a third party, J. With no actual authority, E undertook to transfer the funds to J's account with the plaintiffs, and on such security the plaintiffs advanced a loan to J, which was not repaid. The plaintiffs sought to enforce this undertaking. The Court of Appeal was required to determine whether the solicitor's unauthorized acts fell within his apparent authority.

**4.18**  The Court of Appeal held that in each case it was a matter of deciding whether the giving of the undertaking by E was an act for carrying on, in the usual way, business of the kind conducted by a firm of solicitors. Evidence was called on

---

[36]  *Ibid* at p 733. See also *PEC Ltd v Asia Rice Co Ltd, cit supra* at [69].
[37]  (2009) 260 ALR 164 at [176].
[38]  [1986] AC 717, 777.
[39]  [1988] 1 WLR 1051.

this issue. In the case of undertakings to pay money it was found that solicitors do not pledge their own credit on behalf of clients unless they are can be fairly confident that money will be available out of which they can reimburse themselves. Therefore, a fund to draw on must be in the hands of, or under the control of, the firm; or at any rate there must be a reasonable expectation that it will come into the firm's hands. Also, the actual or anticipated fund must come into the firm's hands in the course of some ulterior transaction which is itself the sort of work that solicitors undertake. In the ordinary course of business solicitors do not receive money or a promise from their client in order that, without more, they can give an undertaking to a third party. Some other service must be involved.[40] Having reviewed the expert evidence on the operations of solicitors, the Court concluded that in *United Bank of Kuwait*, on the information that E (who had authority to represent himself as what he was—a partner in the defendants' firm) gave to the bank, a reasonably careful and competent bank would most probably have concluded that there was an underlying transaction of a kind forming part of a solicitor's business, and thus that the undertaking was an act for the carrying on of such business. The partners were therefore liable as E had been acting within his apparent authority. Similarly in *City Trust Ltd v Levy* the Court upheld the first-instance judge's finding that E's undertaking, given in the circumstances which E stated—albeit falsely—to exist, was one which could properly be given by a solicitor acting as such. E had actual authority to represent himself as a qualified solicitor in the employment of the defendants. On the evidence, the undertaking E gave to the plaintiffs fell within the ordinary course of a solicitor's business. Since the plaintiffs had relied on it in granting the loan to J and thereby acted to their detriment, E had been acting within the scope of his apparent authority when he purported to give the undertaking on behalf of the defendant solicitor.

The role played by solicitors when acting as agents within the financial and commercial spheres has probably altered more over the decades than that of any other profession. In *Dubai Aluminium Co Ltd v Salaam*,[41] when construing the meaning of s 10 of the Partnership Act 1890, Aldous, LJ reflected on the extent to which the role of solicitors had mutated since the passage of that Act:    **4.19**

> Decisions of judges as to what was in the ordinary business of a particular partnership may not be of guidance as to what was the ordinary business of another partnership. For example, solicitors in 1890 did not provide a full range of financial services whereas some do today. Thus, the buying and selling of shares would not in 1890 be held to be in the ordinary course of the business of a firm of solicitors. The contrary could be true today, but the answer would depend on the facts.[42]

---

[40] See esp at p 1063 *per* Staughton, LJ.
[41] [2001] QB 113.
[42] *Ibid* at 142.

This echoed Lord Donaldson of Lymington, MR in *United Bank of Kuwait*,[43] who had been concerned that a somewhat narrow view might mistakenly be taken of the role of solicitors in society. In determining whether a representation has been made as to a solicitor's authority, provided that third parties know that the agent is a solicitor, as he claims to be, they are entitled to assume that that solicitor is of good character and someone whose statements 'do not require that degree of confirmation and cross-checking which might well be appropriate in the case of statements by others who are not members of so respected a profession'.[44] In deciding exactly which services qualify as 'solicitorial', Lord Donaldson emphasized, first, that a solicitor's work is highly personal and confidential, which means that third parties—even banks—have only limited ability to investigate what lies behind whatever transactions a solicitor is performing for a client. Secondly, it needs to be recognized that 'the ordinary course of the professional work of a solicitor extends far beyond giving legal advice and assistance.'[45] In short, solicitors are, 'to use an old-fashioned expression, "men of affairs." '[46] Moreover, owing to their peculiar status—they offer clients 'total independence, total integrity, total confidentiality, total dedication to the interests of the client, competent legal advice and competent other more general advice based on a wide experience of people and their problems, both in a personal and in a business context'—in assessing any representation emanating from their employment in both these cases 'the banks, knowing that E was a practising solicitor with established firms, were entitled to assume the truth of what he stated unless alerted to the fact that the contrary might be the case. There was nothing to alert them.'[47]

**4.20** More generally, taking into account the fact that agents' roles in commerce may develop, shift and metamorphose over time, transactions that fall outside what those agents might normally be expected to do will fall outside the scope of their apparent authority. In *Freeman & Lockyer (a firm) v Buckhurst Park Properties (Mangal) Ltd*[48] Willmer, LJ provided three examples of unusual transactions that fell outside what ordinarily would be expected to be the scope of the authority of the agent in question. In *Houghton & Co v Nothard, Lowe & Wills*[49] a director, acting without authority, entered into an agreement with the plaintiff fruit brokers on behalf of his company whereby the brokers would sell on commission all fruit imported by the defendant company and whereby they would also be entitled to retain the proceeds

---

[43] [1988] 1 WLR 1051.
[44] *Ibid* at 1065.
[45] *Ibid* at 1066.
[46] [1988] 1 WLR 1051, 1066.
[47] *Ibid* at 1066. As Mr Donaldson, QC pointed out in *Ruparel v Awan* [2001] Lloyd's Rep PN 258, 'The essential question is therefore: what activities are and what are not "solicitorial"?' See, eg, Neuberger, J's judgment in *Antonelli v Allen* [2001] Lloyd's Rep PN 487, esp at [65]–[77].
[48] [1964] 2 QB 480, 494.
[49] [1927] 1 KB 246.

of sale as security for a debt owed by another company. In *Kreditbank Cassel GmbH v Schenkers*,[50] the branch manager of the defendant forwarding agents, without authority, fraudulently drew seven bills to the order of that company, purporting to do so on the company's behalf. Another company in which the branch manager had an interest accepted the bills, and indorsed them on behalf of the defendants. The acceptors dishonoured the bills, and the plaintiffs, who were holders in due course, sued the defendants as drawers. Finally, in *Rama Corporation Ltd v Proved Tin and General Investments Ltd*,[51] W, the plaintiff company's director, who had known the defendant's director T for some time but had never heard of T's company, entered into a joint venture with T's company. At no time did T inform his fellow directors of the transaction which he had purported to make on their company's behalf with W on behalf of the plaintiff company. Although the deal was *intra vires*, T had no actual authority to bind the defendant company to the joint venture. The plaintiff company sought an account of monies allegedly paid to the defendant company, arguing that T's fraudulent actions fell within the scope of T's ostensible authority. As Willmer, LJ pointed out, in none of these cases could the plaintiffs reasonably allege that the person with whom they contracted was acting within the scope of such authority as one in his position would be expected to possess. Accordingly, the relevant agents could not be claimed to have been held out by their respective companies as having authority to perform the acts relied on:

> The plaintiffs ... had nothing to go on beyond the fact that in each case power to do the acts relied on might, under the articles of association, have been delegated to the person with whom they contracted. But in none of the cases did the plaintiffs have any knowledge of the articles of association.[52]

In short, third parties seeking to set up an estoppel must be able to demonstrate that they did in fact rely upon the representation.

In contrast, in *Freeman & Lockyer (a firm) v Buckhurst Park Properties (Mangal) Ltd*[53] itself, although the board of a development company never made a formal appointment, they knowingly acquiesced in K's acting in the capacity of managing director. K, purporting to act on behalf the company, instructed the plaintiff architects to apply for planning permission to develop an estate and to perform various other tasks in connection with it. After the work was done, the company refused to pay the architects' fees arguing that K had no authority to commission the works. The Court of Appeal held that what K had done fell within the ordinary ambit of the authority of a managing director. Moreover, the Court of Appeal held that the plaintiffs did not therefore have to inquire whether K had been properly appointed. **4.21**

---

[50] [1927] 1 KB 826.
[51] [1952] 2 QB 147.
[52] [1964] 2 QB 480, 494 *per* Willmer, LJ.
[53] [1964] 2 QB 480.

It was sufficient for them that under the articles there was in fact power to appoint him as such.[54]

**4.22**  May a third party, who is aware that the agent has no general authority to act for the principal, claim to have relied upon a representation that the agent enjoyed a specific authority to act in a particular transaction? In *Armagas Ltd v Mundogas SA*[55] M, who was the defendants' vice-president (transportation) and chartering manager, acting in collusion with a shipbroker, fraudulently informed the claimants' representative that he had authority to complete an agreement for the sale of a ship with a three-year charter back to the defendants. The claimants were told that for internal reasons the defendants needed a charterparty for a period of twelve months only. In consequence, documents purporting to relate to a three-year and a twelve-month charter-party came into existence. The fraud, which created a spurious three-year charterparty, was meant to deceive the defendants into agreeing to the purchase of the vessel. M only had authority from the defendants to agree to a straightforward sale of the vessel. M had no authority to agree to a three-year charter back of the vessel. M also knew that it would be impossible for him to obtain such authority. The defendants only received the twelve-month charterparty. Having been induced to believe that they had sold their ship and had entered into a twelve-month charterparty, the defendants duly redelivered the vessel at the end of the year. The House of Lords had to decide whether the defendants were bound by their corrupt agent's acts on the basis that M had apparent authority to bind them to a three-year charterparty.

**4.23**  It is well established that apparent authority cannot arise if the third party is aware that the agent's authority is limited so as to exclude his entering into transactions of the type in question.[56] In *Armagas v Mundogas*, however, it was argued that even if the third party knows that an agent does not have general authority to act, the principal might have represented that the agent had specific authority to perform a particular act. Lord of Keith of Kinkel, delivering judgment on behalf of the House of Lords, was prepared to concede such a possibility:

> The principal might conceivably inform the contractor that, in relation to a transaction which to the contractor's knowledge required the specific approval of the principal, he could rely on the agent to enter into the transaction only if such approval had been given. In such a situation, if the agent entered into the transaction without

---

[54]  See also *Biggerstaff v Rowatt's Wharf Ltd* [1896] 2 Ch 93, 104, where, again, a third party transacted business with someone who was acting with his board's knowledge as *de facto* managing director, and where Lopes, LJ said, 'a company is bound by the acts of persons who take upon themselves, with the knowledge of the directors, to act for the company, provided such persons act within the limits of their apparent authority; and that strangers dealing *bona fide* with such persons, have a right to assume that they have been duly appointed.'

[55]  [1986] AC 717.

[56]  Eg, *Russo-Chinese Bank v Li Yau Sam* [1910] AC 174.

approval, the principal might be estopped from denying that it had been given. But it is very difficult to envisage circumstances in which the estoppel could arise from conduct only in relation to a one-off transaction ...[57]

In *Armagas v Mundogas*, however, it was held that even though the defendants had appointed M vice-president and chartering manager, M was known not to have any general authority to enter into a three-year charterparty. In the absence of any contradictory representation by the defendants as to his authority, M could not reasonably be believed by the claimants to have had specific authority to notify the other contracting party that the defendants' consent had been obtained and thereafter to complete the agreement:

> [N]o representation by [M] can help [the claimants]. They must be in a position to found upon some relevant representation by the responsible management of [the defendants] as to [M's] authority: *Freeman & Lockyer v Buckhurst Park Properties (Mangal) Ltd.* [1964] 2 QB 480, 505 *per* Diplock LJ.[58]

*The scope of an agent's apparent authority will be a matter of proof in each individual case*

In *Sea Emerald SA v Prominvestbank Joint Stockpoint Commercial Industrial and Investment Bank*[59] a shipping company sought to claim under a refund guarantee which had been signed by the employee of a bank in respect of a ship construction contract between a shipyard (which was a client of the bank) and the shipping company. The shipping company unsuccessfully claimed that the bank had held out its employees as having authority to enter into such financial transactions as would ordinarily fall within the scope of the authority of the main regional office of a major commercial bank, or at least that of a major commercial bank in the business of providing services to the shipbuilding industry. It said that it relied upon that holding-out in accepting the terms of the guarantee. It was argued that the provision of commercial guarantees was within the ordinary scope of the authority of the main regional office of a major commercial bank, that the guarantee was of an ordinary commercial type—at least in the context of a shipbuilding or comparable construction project, and that the buyer itself, or through the yard, relied upon the fact that the bank, being a major commercial bank, had set up the main regional office and appointed its head. Andrew Smith, J held that it was not sufficient for the buyer to contend that it was within the ordinary scope of the authority of the main regional office of a major commercial bank, and so of the appointed head of the main regional office, to provide commercial guarantees. Something more specific was required: namely, the buyer had to establish—in this case, by specialized

**4.24**

---

[57] [1986] AC 717, 778.

[58] *Ibid* at 778. See further Watts, 'Some Wear and Tear on *Armagas v Mundogas*: The Tension between Having and Wanting in the Law of Agency' [2015] LMCLQ 36.

[59] [2008] EWHC 1979 (Comm).

expert evidence—that it was within the ordinary scope of their authority to provide a refund guarantee to cover potential liability by the supplier to the customer for money paid to him. The judge found, on the evidence, that the common form of provision conferring authority upon regional offices of banks did not include general authority to provide guarantees; nor was there evidence either that it was usual for officials to be given specific authority to issue guarantees or that it was usual for officials at regional offices to give guarantees when they were not properly authorized to do so. The buyer had therefore failed to show that it was within the ordinary scope of the authority of the main regional office of a major commercial bank to provide commercial guarantees.[60]

*Orthodox doctrine*

**4.25**  Orthodox doctrine holds that the representation upon which a third party relies must have been made either by the principal himself or by a person acting in accordance with the law of agency. Normally, the representation cannot be made by the agent himself. Were it otherwise and the third party allowed to rely upon statements made by the agent without the authority of the principal, in the words of Lord Neuberger of Abbotsbury, NPJ, 'it would seems precious close to pulling up oneself by one's own bootstraps.'[61] The classical exposition of the law on this matter is to be found in *Freeman & Lockyer v Buckhurst Park Properties Ltd*, where Diplock, LJ stated:

> [I]n order to create an estoppel between the corporation and the contractor, the representation as to the authority of the agent which creates his 'apparent' authority must be made by some person or persons who have 'actual' authority from the corporation to make the representation. Such 'actual' authority may be conferred by the constitution of the corporation itself, as, for example, in the case of a company, upon the board of directors, or it may be conferred by those who under its constitution have the powers of management upon some other person to whom the constitution permits them to delegate authority to make representations of this kind. It follows that where the agent upon whose 'apparent' authority the contractor relies has no 'actual' authority from the corporation to enter into a particular kind of contract with the contractor on behalf of the corporation, the contractor cannot rely upon the agent's own representation as to his actual authority. He can rely only upon a representation by a person or persons who have actual authority to manage or conduct that part of the business of the corporation to which the contract relates.[62]

In *Freeman & Lockyer* itself, the second defendant, K, who was a director of the first defendant company, instructed architects to apply for planning permission to

---

[60] *Ibid* esp at [106]–[109].

[61] *Thanakharn Kasikorn Thai Chamkat (Mahachon) v Akai Holdings Ltd (in liquidation)* [2010] HKCFA 64 at [64].

[62] [1964] 2 QB 480, 504–5. See also *Credit Suisse International v Stichting Vestia Groep* [2014] EWHC 3103 (Comm); [2015] Bus LR D5 at [278] *per* Andrew Smith, J.

develop the estate the parties had purchased. The architects did as instructed. But when they sued for their fee the first defendant objected that since its articles of association contained a power to appoint a managing director that had never been exercised, K had no authority to bind the first defendant to the contract. K, who in the meantime had disappeared, was therefore personally liable to settle the fee. The court found, however, that the other directors of the company were aware of K's activities and had acquiesced in his acting as *de facto* managing director of the first defendant company. The Court of Appeal therefore determined that K's act, in engaging the architects to obtain planning permission, fell within the normal ambit of authority of a managing director. Under the company's constitution the directors enjoyed actual authority to manage its business. By allowing one of their number to run the company, the other directors had represented to the world that he had authority to transact the ordinary business that an agent of his type would characteristically have authority to transact on the company's behalf. Because the act of engaging architects to secure planning permission for the estate owned by the company fell within the ordinary ambit of the authority of a managing director, K had authority to bind the company. K's apparent authority derived from the actual authority of his fellow directors to appoint a managing director. More particularly, the architects did not have to inquire whether K had been properly appointed; it was sufficient for them that under the articles of association there was in fact power to appoint him as such.

The essential component is that the agent's authority can be traced back either to the principal himself or at least to someone who had actual authority deriving from the principal, to make such a representation. Although he admitted that authorities in support of this proposition are thin on the ground,[63] Toulson, J, in *ING Re (UK) Ltd v R & V Versicherung AG*, articulated the principle in the following manner: **4.26**

> [W]here P represents or causes it to be represented to T that A1 has authority to represent to T that A2 has authority to act on P's behalf, and T deals with A2 as P's agent on the faith of such representations, P is bound by A2's acts to the same extent as if he had the authority which he was represented as having. The critical requirement is that A2's authority must be able to be traced back to the principal by a representation or chain of representations upon which T acted and whose authenticity P is estopped from denying by his representation through words or conduct.[64]

It might seem that on occasion the courts have strayed beyond the strict proposition that an agent cannot confer authority upon himself. In *United Bank of Kuwait v Hammoud*,[65] for example, third parties were allowed to rely upon a solicitor's **4.27**

---

[63] The principle was recognized, for example, in *British Bank of the Middle East v Sun Life Assurance Co of Canada (UK) Ltd* [1983] 2 Lloyd's Rep 9, 16, but was held not to apply on the facts of that case.
[64] [2006] 2 All ER (Comm) 870 at [100].
[65] [1988] 1 WLR 1051.

false representations that certain background facts directly relating to the scope of his authority obtained.[66] Staughton, LJ found that once it was established that an agent had actual authority to represent himself as an agent (*in specie*, as a solicitor), it could no longer be objected that what the agent himself said about the transactions in which he was engaged could not by itself demonstrate that they were part of the ordinary business of solicitors, and thus within the authority which he was held out as having:

> [A] third party is only concerned as to whether a transaction appears to be of a kind that is within the ordinary authority that the agent is held out as having, not whether it is in fact a transaction of that kind. To depart from that doctrine would gravely weaken the credit which is given to solicitors' undertakings; it would also do much to destroy the rule that any agent can be held out as having general ostensible authority to bind his principal.[67]

Lord Donaldson of Lymington, MR added a supplementary observation, particular to solicitors—for whom Masters of the Rolls have a particular responsibility. In his view, solicitors were 'not to be regarded as potential fraudsters or accomplices to fraud' but '*prima facie* ... are to be taken to be men and women of good character whose word is their bond and whose statements do not require that degree of confirmation and cross-checking which might well be appropriate in the case of statements by others who are not members of so respected a profession.'[68] For this reason, provided that there was nothing to alert them that something was amiss, third-party banks which knew that the agent was a practising solicitor 'were entitled to assume the truth of what he stated unless alerted to the fact that the contrary might be the case.'[69] In essence, to the extent that a solicitor correctly informs third parties that he has actual authority to act on behalf of his principals, thereby holding himself out as having the authority which customarily goes with being a solicitor, these representations bind his partners or employers in respect of any acts that such a solicitor might usually perform. This line of authority, however, was not thought to extend to cases where third parties actually knew that the agent lacked authority to perform the transaction for which he claimed to have the necessary authority.

### Departure from orthodox doctrine

**4.28** Occasionally, the courts may have seemed prepared to depart from the orthodox doctrine that apparent authority may not derive from the representations of the agent. In *First Energy (UK) Ltd v Hungarian International Bank Ltd*[70] the Court of Appeal took matters further. The client of a bank, whilst awaiting the opening of a

---

[66] See *ante*, paras **4.17–4.18**.
[67] [1988] 1 WLR 1051, 1064.
[68] *Ibid* at 1065.
[69] *Ibid* at 1066.
[70] [1993] 2 Lloyd's Rep 194.

more permanent financial facility, arranged *ad hoc* finance through one of the bank's senior managers. The client had dealt with the bank in the past and was aware that this particular manager did not have authority to agree a financial arrangement. The client also knew that any decision the bank made would be communicated to it by a letter bearing two signatures. The bank manager wrote and signed a letter to the client informing it that the bank had approved the temporary facility. This was not true. The bank subsequently sought to repudiate the arrangement to which its manager had purported to commit it. Despite the fact that the third party/client had notice that the manager lacked authority, the Court of Appeal held that the manager did possess apparent authority to inform the client that the bank had approved the grant of the *ad hoc* facility. At first, this decision would appear to undermine the traditional principle that an agent cannot confer authority upon himself simply by misrepresenting his powers, particularly when the third party has notice of the true state of affairs.[71] Steyn, LJ, however, in *First Energy*, openly stated: 'the law does not recognise, in the context of apparent authority, the idea of a self-authorizing agent.'[72] What, then, is the significance of the *First Energy* decision?

*First Energy* has been described by one leading commentator as 'exceptional on its **4.29** facts',[73] and the judgments of Steyn and Nourse, LJJ have been said to 'illustrate how the law struggles to reconcile principle and predictability with commercial reality and fairness', underlining the 'inadvisability of seeking to lay down any rigid principles in this area.'[74]

Other judges, too, have experienced difficulty in identifying the precise principle **4.30** upon which the decision reposes. The tendency has been to see *First Energy* as a case in which 'the bank manager was held out as having authority to *communicate* to the customer decisions of the bank's head office.'[75] Potter, LJ, in *Sun Life Assurance Co of*

---

[71] 'I would only say that the *First Energy* decision will plainly be apposite in cases where, as in that case, the third party knew of a limitation on the agent's authority': *Pharmed Medicare Private Ltd v Univar Ltd* [2002] EWCA Civ 1569 at [15] *per* Longmore, LJ.

[72] [1993] 2 Lloyds Rep 194, 201. See, eg, *GPN Ltd v O2 (UK) Ltd* [2004] EWHC 2494 (TCC).

[73] Reynolds, *The Ultimate Apparent Authority* (1994) 110 LQR 21, 24.

[74] *Thanakharn Kasikorn Thai Chamkat (Mahachon) v Akai Holdings Ltd (in liquidation)* [2010] HKCFA 64 at [70] *per* Lord Neuberger of Abbotsbury, NPJ.

[75] Eg, *Petromec Inc v Petroleo Brasileiro SA Petrobras, Braspetro Oil Services Co* [2004] EWHC 127 (Comm) at [117] *per* Moore-Bick, J; *Vodafone Ltd v GNT Holdings (UK) Ltd* [2004] EWHC 1526 (QB) at [106] *per* Christopher Moger, QC; *Sea Emerald SA v Prominvestbank-Joint Stockpoint Commercial Industrial and Investment Bank* [2008] EWHC 1979 (Comm) at [107] *per* Andrew Smith, J; *Gallaher International Ltd v Tlais Enterprises Ltd* [2008] EWHC 804 (Comm) at [1193] *per* Christopher Clarke, J; *Golden Ocean Group Ltd v Salgaocar Industries Pvt Ltd* [2011] 1 WLR 2575 at [121] *per* Christopher Clarke, J. It should be noted that in *First Energy* the branch manager's relatively senior position within the corporate structure was significant. In *Skandinaviska Enskilda Banken AB (Publ) v Asia Pacific Breweries (Singapore) Pte Ltd* [2009] SGCA 22, in contrast, the Singapore Court of Appeal held that the position of Asia Pacific's 'finance manager'—'a title which does not connote the possession of any specific authority'—was too lowly to carry with it authority to communicate to various banks his company's board's approvals of loans he had dishonestly negotiated on the company's behalf.

*Canada v CX Reinsurance Co Ltd*, stated matters succinctly when he described *First Energy* as a case involving an agent's usual authority, in which:

> a manager, who, lacking actual authority to authorise and offer a particular loan facility to the plaintiff, nonetheless did so by sending him a letter of offer which he accepted. In that case the court held that, albeit the manager lacked actual authority to make the loan and that no other person in the bank had held him out as having such authority, by reason of his very position he was a person who would ordinarily have authority to communicate the decision of more senior members of the bank who were authorised to make and/or approve such a loan and that the plaintiff was accordingly entitled to rely upon the offer which he had received.[76]

**4.31**    Subsequently, in *Lovett v Carson Country Homes Ltd*,[77] Davis, J characterized *First Energy* as a case that shows that the realities of modern commerce sometimes require that 'an officer or employee of a company can in any event be authorised actually or ostensibly by the company to warrant that procedures have been properly complied with and that documents are genuine.'[78] In *Lovett* a bank, B, worried at the level of S's unsecured indebtedness, tried to secure its position in respect of money S had lent to CCH, by exercising a guarantee and a debenture in its favour over CCH's assets. C and J, CCH's directors, had divided up administration of the company between themselves: J dealt with finance, whereas C managed the practical opera-tion of the company's activities. Occasionally, J would replicate C's signature on financial documents. C condoned this practice so long as he was informed to what his signature was being put. B drafted the debenture and guarantee and sent it to the CCH's office. The documents were returned to B bearing both C's and J's signa-tures. When the pair's professional relationship disintegrated, B exercised its right under the debenture to appoint administrators. C challenged the appointments on the ground that he had been unaware of the existence of either a debenture or a guarantee in B's favour, and that he had not put his signature to either document. J admitted forging C's signature, but claimed that he had properly explained the documents and their effects to C. One issue which Davis, J was required to deter-mine was whether J had authority to sign on C's behalf and to bind the company to the documents. Davis, J held that since C and J had not discussed the execution of a debenture and guarantee, J did not have express or implied authority to sign C's name on the documents. A company, however, could be estopped from contest-ing the validity of forged documents. More particularly, as *Lloyd v Grace Smith & Co*[79] and *First Energy*[80] demonstrate, a principal could be bound by the fraudulent acts of an agent if the agent was acting with ostensible authority. Here, therefore,

---

[76] [2003] EWCA Civ 283 at [39].
[77] [2009] 2 BCLC 196.
[78] *Ibid* at [94].
[79] [1912] AC 716.
[80] [1993] 2 Lloyd's Rep 194.

J, who over the years had handled all CCH's financial agreements with B with C's knowledge and approval, had been clothed by the company with apparent authority. On this account, B was entitled to rely upon the document as one that had been executed in accordance with the correct procedures and equally entitled to treat the signatures thereto as being genuine. The bank had therefore validly appointed the administrators. Such a rule, Davis, J stressed, had the benefit of legal certainty and fairly represented commercial reality where third parties, such as banks, faced inherent difficulties in securing information about the validity and enforceability of binding documents.

*The agent clothed with apparent authority to make representations of fact*

To this extent, *First Energy* falls within a broader notion that in each individual case **4.32** it is a matter of identifying what precisely the agent has apparent authority to do on the principal's behalf. Thus, in *Primus Telecommunications plc v MCI WorldCom International Inc*[81] Mance, LJ accepted Steyn, LJ's proposition in *First Energy*[82] that the law recognizes that in modern commerce an agent who has no apparent authority to conclude a particular transaction may sometimes be clothed with apparent authority to make representations of fact. Nevertheless, as Lord Neuberger of Abbotsbury, NPJ noted in an influential decision of the Hong Kong Final Court of Appeal, *Thanakharn Kasikorn Thai Chamkat (Mahachon) v Akai Holdings Ltd (in liquidation)*:

> I find it very hard indeed to conceive of any circumstances in which an alleged agent, who does not have actual or apparent authority to bind the principal, can nevertheless acquire apparent authority to do so, simply by representing to the third party that he has such authority ... [B]efore any representation by the agent could be relied on to assist the contention that he had apparent authority, the court would have to be satisfied that the principal had given the alleged agent apparent authority to make the representation in question    [A]ny such representation would have to be 'clear and unequivocal.'[83]

*First Energy* fell to be considered by the Privy Council in *Kelly v Fraser*.[84] In this case **4.33** the transfer value of a member of a pension plan had been transferred to a new pension plan when the member, F, changed employment. Owing to the fact that the transfer was conducted by M, a senior employee of the human resources department of the employer who sponsored the pension plan, the pension plan's trustees had not been involved in the process and were oblivious both to the transfer request and to the receipt and investment of the transfer funds. The Privy Council was required

---

[81] [2004] 2 All ER (Comm) 833 at [25].
[82] [1993] 2 Lloyd's Rep 194, 204.
[83] [2010] HKEC 927 at [70]–[71].
[84] [2012] 3 WLR 1008. Discussed by Yap, *Apparent Authority: Doctrinal Underpinnings and Competing Policy Considerations* [2014] JBL 72.

to rule whether, under these circumstances, the transfer value had been properly received and held to the account of the relevant pension plan. More specifically, since the transfer had boosted F's funds in the pension plan, was F entitled to a commensurate share in the distribution of the surplus when the scheme was eventually wound up? Without disputing that they could have lawfully approved the transaction had they known of it, the trustees sought to take advantage of their own oversight and applied for a declaration that they were entitled to distribute the fund without taking into account this additional transfer effected by M, which they had not endorsed. The question was whether the representations made by M, a senior employee of the sponsoring company's occupational pension scheme, informing F that whatever steps needed to be taken to carry out this transaction regularly had been duly performed, fell within the apparent authority of an agent acting such as to bind the principal—*in specie* the trustees.

**4.34**   Lord Sumption referred extensively to *Armagas v Mundogas*, pointing out in particular that that decision was not authority for the proposition that a person without authority of any kind to enter into a transaction cannot as a matter of law occupy a position in which he has ostensible authority to tell a third party that the proper person has authorized it:[85]

> [T]he ordinary authority to communicate a company's authorisation of a transaction will generally be more widely distributed than that, especially in a bureaucratically complex organisation and in the case of routine transactions. It is not at all uncommon for the authority to approve transactions to be limited to a handful of very senior officers, but for their approval to be communicated in the ordinary course of the company's administration by others whose function it is to do that.[86]

Referring to *First Energy*, a case in which it will be recalled the Court of Appeal had regarded its approach as wholly consistent with the law as stated by Lord Keith in *Armagas v Mundogas*, Lord Sumption stressed, 'Every case calls for a careful examination of its particular facts.'[87] Since it is perfectly possible for a company, or indeed any principal, to so organize its affairs that subordinates who would not have authority to approve a transaction are nevertheless held out by those authorities as the persons who are to communicate to outsiders the fact that it has been approved by those who are authorized to approve it or that some particular agent has been

---

[85] [2012] 3 WLR 1008 at [12].

[86] *Ibid* at [13]. As Browne-Wilkinson, LJ inquired in *The Raffaella* [1985] 2 Lloyds Rep 36, 42–3, '[I]f a company confers actual or apparent authority on A to make representations on the company's behalf but no actual authority on A to enter into the specific transaction, why should a representation made by A as to his authority not be capable of being relied on as one of the acts of holding out?' See also *Hudson Bay Apparel Brands LLP v Umbro International Ltd* [2011] 1 BCLC 259 at [55] *per* Lord Neuberger, MR.

[87] [2012] 3 WLR 1008 at [15].

duly authorized to approve it, in this case the trustees were bound by representations purportedly made on their behalf by M. Pension fund trustees will perform some of their functions personally, but others they will delegate. Pension fund trustees very rarely communicate personally with contributories and beneficiaries. Rather, they make decisions which are then communicated and applied by professional managers, often in the pensions department of the sponsoring employer. Here, the trustees delegated to the company administrative functions which must have included communicating with contributors and confirming the entitlements which resulted from their contributions and from the trustees' decisions. M, the senior officer of the relevant department of the company:

> never professed to have authorised the acceptance of the transfer funds himself, but the plan could hardly have been operated if he did not have authority to write letters informing contributors that they had been duly accepted and in respect of what contributions. Moreover, with or without the trustees' approval, the transfer funds were in fact accepted, and accruals to the transfer funds notified in successive benefit statements.[88]

The trustees could only disclaim this and treat the transfer funds for some purposes as if they had been received and for other purposes as if they had not if it appeared that F had not relied to his detriment upon the agent's representations. This contention was not open to the trustees as it could be inferred that F was worse off by having been led to believe that his transfer fund had been duly invested than he would have been if he had not been told this and had raised the issue at the time.[89]

*First Energy* has not proven to be quite such a revolutionary decision as may at first **4.35** have been anticipated. Nevertheless, it has been argued that Steyn, LJ's judgment offers the potential for a fundamental re-appraisal of the entire doctrine of apparent authority. Although the courts have not fully espoused this approach, the argument runs that *First Energy* might enable the courts to re-jig the entire notion of apparent authority in a manner that better acknowledges the practicalities of modern commerce.[90] Modern business is impersonal and complex. The reality is that it is difficult, embarrassing, and sometimes commercially unwise for third parties to launch inquiries into the actual scope of an individual agent's authority. Because intrusive investigation will not always be a realistic option, an approach to apparent authority more favourable to third parties is justified. This, as Steyn, LJ observed in *First Energy*, would fulfil 'the objective which has been and still is the principal moulding force of our law of contract', namely, 'the reasonable

---

[88] *Ibid* at [16].

[89] For consideration of *First Energy* and *Kelly v Fraser* in the legal context of Singapore, see Pey-Woan Lee, *The Apparent Authority of the Unauthorised Agent* (2014) 26 SAcLJ 258.

[90] See further Brown, *The Agent's Apparent Authority: Paradigm or Paradox?* [1995] JBL 360.

expectations of honest men'.[91] Hitherto, the courts may have been over-protective of the interests of principals. Hence, in *British Bank of the Middle East v Sun Life Assurance Co of Canada (UK) Ltd* the House of Lords upheld the principle that an agent can have apparent authority to make representations as to the authority of other agents, provided that his own authority can finally be traced back to a representation by the principal or to a person with actual authority from the principal to make it.[92] Besides, the courts' customary characterization of the agent as a mere passive conduit between principal and third party is an 'outmoded paradigm' in contemporary commerce:

> [I]n most instances the agent's apparent authority emanates from joint actions of principal and agent; the principal's appointing an agent to a position thereby frequently enabling or necessitating the latter's ability to bolster his authority in dealings with the third party.[93]

*First Energy* could be said to elevate the protection afforded to a third party by assessing the authority of the agent according to the way in which a third party would have apprehended the situation. Primary responsibility rests with the principal, who chose to place the agent in a position within his organization where he could appear to third parties to have usual authority to perform certain acts and to give certain undertakings which could not reasonably or easily be questioned. Read in this way, the law places emphasis not on the precise nature of the representation made by the principal (as has been the case hitherto), but on a third party's perception of the conduct of the agent.

**4.36**   It is conceivable that the extension of the agent's apparent authority, in the cases discussed above, to cover situations where it is the agent himself who makes the relevant representation, and even to situations where effectively the third party has notice that the agent may lack the relevant authority, is an intimation that in the future a climate may develop that is more benevolent to third parties, who often are more or less helpless in the modern corporate environment to discover the true scope of an agent's authority, no matter how thorough their inquiries may have been. Such an approach is underscored by Steyn, LJ's reference in *First Energy* to one of the enduring objectives of the law of contract being the need to meet the reasonable expectations of third parties:

> A theme that runs through our law of contract is that the reasonable expectations of honest men must be protected. It is not a rule or a principle of law. It is the

---

[91] [1993] 2 Lloyd's Rep 196. This passage is often cited with approval: eg, *ING Re (UK) Ltd v R&V Versicherung AG* [2006] 2 All ER (Comm) 870 at [155] *per* Toulson, J; *General Trading Company (Holdings) Ltd v Richmond Corporation Ltd* [2008] 2 Lloyd's Rep 475 at [96] *per* Beatson, J.

[92] [1983] 2 Lloyd's Rep 9, 16, quoting with approval *Bowstead & Reynolds on Agency* (2001) 17th ed, para 8-021.

[93] [1995] JBL 360, 368.

objective which has been and still is the principal moulding force of our law of contract. It affords no licence to a judge to depart from binding precedent. On the other hand, if the *prima facie* solution to a problem runs counter to the reasonable expectations of honest men, this criterion sometimes requires a rigorous re-examination of the problem to ascertain whether the law does indeed compel demonstrable unfairness.[94]

Toulson, J adopted a not dissimilar line in *ING Re (UK) Ltd v R&V Versicherung AG*.[95] He expressed concern at the risks to which those dealing with agents are exposed whenever an agent lacks the authority he claims to possess. The judge felt that if a third party has dealt honestly with an agent whose principal goes ahead with the transaction with knowledge of what the agent has ostensibly done on the principal's behalf, the third party's reasonable expectation would be that the principal would be bound by the transaction. Therefore, 'if the principal knows what the agent has done, but does not know that the agent lacked authority to do it because of a lack of adequate records or internal organisation, I do not see why in justice that should operate to the detriment of the third party.' Any growing inclination to place greater emphasis on the viewpoint and interests of the third party, however, is yet to be fully worked out. It remains the case that such developments seemingly run counter to traditional accounts of apparent authority, which has rested on a strict requirement that a representation concerning the agent's authority emanated from the principal or from someone having the latter's authority to make such a representation.

### A representation may be fact or of law

It used to be maintained that apparent authority could only found on a representa·  **1.37** tion of fact. However, since the House of Lords in *Kleinwort Benson Ltd v Lincoln City Council*[96] determined that the traditional distinction between mistakes of fact and mistakes of law no longer holds for restitutionary claims made for money paid under a mistake—and since this ruling has also been applied to claims in contractual mistake,[97] estoppels by representation,[98] and misrepresentation,[99] the courts can scarcely maintain that apparent authority may not result from a pure representation of law.

---

[94] [1993] 2 Lloyd's Rep 194, 196. See also *G Percy Trentham Ltd v Archital Luxfer* [1993] 1 Lloyd's Rep 25, 27 *per* Lord Steyn: '[I]n practice our law generally ignores the subjective expectations and the unexpressed mental reservations of the parties. Instead the governing criterion is the reasonable expectations of honest men and in the present case that means that the yardstick is the reasonable expectations of sensible businessmen.'

[95] See also *General Trading Company (Holdings) Ltd v Richmond Corporation Ltd* [2008] 2 Lloyd's Rep 475 at [96] *per* Beatson, J.

[96] [1999] 2 AC 349.

[97] See *Brennan v Bolt Burdon* [2004] 3 WLR 321.

[98] *Briggs v Gleeds (Head Office)* [2014] 3 WLR 1469.

[99] See *Pankhania v Hackney LBC* [2002] EWHC 2441 (Ch); [2002] NPC 123.

**Reliance**

**4.38** As will now be evident, apparent authority requires both (i) that a representation must have been made to a third party, and (ii) that the third party can be shown to have relied upon that representation.

**4.39** As regards (i), Lord Lindley made clear in *Farquharson Bros & Co v King & Co* that 'the "holding out" must be to the particular individual who says he relied on it, or under such circumstances of publicity as to justify the inference that he knew of it and acted upon it.'[100]

*A causal link must be shown between the representation and the third party's actions*

**4.40** As regards (ii), a third party can only rely upon the agent's apparent authority provided that a causal link can be shown between the representation and the third party's actions. This causal relation may need to be proved. In *Bedford Insurance Co Ltd v Instituto de Resseguros do Brasil*,[101] for example, a Hong Kong-based insurance company authorized their agents to write marine insurance risks in the UK with defined financial limits. Neither principal nor agent was authorized by law to transact marine insurance business within the UK. The relevant legislation declared any such transactions void *ab initio* and unenforceable. The agent entered into such agreements and exceeded the financial restrictions imposed by the principal. Claims were made under the policies and the principal purported to ratify these contracts. Having satisfied these claims, the principal sought an indemnity under an agreement with the defendant reinsurers. Parker, J had little difficulty in holding that a principal cannot ratify an act void *ab initio*. However, in addressing what proved to be the defendant's secondary argument, namely, that the principal had not conferred authority on the agent to act on its behalf, Parker, J did remark:

> A person relying on ostensible authority has … to show that he relied on the representation of the principal, and none of the insured or their brokers was called to testify to this effect. [Counsel for the insurance company] asks me to infer that they did so rely. The documents certainly suggest that they could very well have done so, but I am not prepared to hold that they did so … In the circumstances of this case, where a number of documents were clearly shown to have created, and deliberately to have created, a false impression, oral evidence was, in my judgment, required.[102]

**4.41** Therefore, apparent authority cannot apply if the third party had no legitimate belief that the agent had authority to act for the principal. In *Armagas Ltd v Mundogas SA*,[103] it will be noted, the third party was unable to demonstrate

---

[100] [1902] AC 325, 341.
[101] [1985] QB 966.
[102] [1985] QB 966, 985.
[103] [1987] AC 156. See para **4.22**.

that the principal had represented that the agent had authority to enter into a three-year charterparty. It was known that the agent lacked actual authority to do so and the third party could only show that it had entered into the transaction through misguided reliance on what the agent himself had represented. Similarly, in *Overbrooke Estates Ltd v Glencombe Properties Ltd*[104] the plaintiffs sought specific performance of a contract for the sale of land into which the defendants had entered. The sale had been by auction. Before the auction the defendants received a copy of the general conditions of sale, one of which was that the auctioneer had no authority to give any representation or warranty relating to the property. The defendants had asked the auctioneer prior to the auction whether the Greater London Council had any plans or schemes, including compulsory purchase, for the land. The auctioneer had told them that the Council had no such plans and was not interested in compulsorily purchasing it. On making further inquiry of the local authority, the defendants learned that whereas the council had approved no schemes that would involve acquisition of the property, it was 'within an area where the age and condition of some of the properties are such that they may shortly be included in a slum clearance programme'. In light of this information, the defendants stopped payment of their cheque and refused to complete the contract. Brightman, J held that since the defendants knew, or ought to have known, from the general conditions of sale that the auctioneer's representation was beyond the scope of his authority, they could not claim to have relied upon it. They were therefore ordered to complete the purchase of the land:

> [I]n the case before me it is not ... possible for the defendants to assert that [the auctioneer] had ostensible authority to make the representations said to have been made by them, for these reasons—before any contract was made and, indeed before any representation was made, the defendants were obviously in possession of a document which in terms, negatived any such authority.[105]

The suggestion that it was sufficient in *Overbrooke Estates* to show that the third party ought to have known of the auctioneer's lack of authority introduces an allied question: whether a third party ever owes a duty to inquire into the agent's authority. This will depend upon the circumstances. As we have seen, notably where an agent is transacting business that an agent of his type would not normally transact, a third party may find himself put upon inquiry to ascertain whether the agent does in fact possess the necessary authority.[106] Where no suspicion is aroused as the agent appears to be doing what someone in his position would usually do, no duty to inquire is likely to arise. **4.42**

---

[104] [1974] 1 WLR 1335.
[105] *Ibid* at 1341.
[106] Eg, *Midland Bank Ltd v Reckitt* [1933] AC 1; para **4.53**.

*In the absence of dishonesty or irrationality, reliance will normally be presumed*

**4.43**  It would seem that comparatively little evidence will be demanded of a third party seeking to establish that he relied on an agent's apparent authority. As Lord Neuberger of Abbotsbury, NPJ said in *Thanakharn Kasikorn Thai Chamkat (Mahachon) v Akai Holdings Ltd (in liquidation)*:

> [O]nce a third party has established that the alleged agent had apparent authority, … and that the third party has entered into a contract with the alleged agent on behalf of the principal, then, in the absence of any evidence or indication to the contrary, it would be an unusual case where reliance was not presumed.[107]

This statement, delivered in the Hong Kong Final Court of Appeal, related to a bank's entitlement to trust to an agent's apparent authority. On the facts apparent authority was not actually established since the relevant transaction which involved the execution of securities by company A that were to cover the substantial liabilities of company B—not being for the purpose of company A's business nor otherwise for its benefit—looked suspicious and would not ordinarily fall within the authority of company A's directors.

**4.44**  The Final Court of Appeal nevertheless held as a general proposition that a third party could rely on an agent's appearance of authority unless its 'belief in that connection was dishonest or irrational (which includes turning a blind eye and being reckless)'.[108] Dishonesty and irrationality therefore comprise what Lord Blackburn in *Jones v Gordon* famously described as 'blind eye knowledge':

> [I]f the facts and circumstances are such that … whoever has to try the question … came to the conclusion that he was not honestly blundering and careless, but that he must have had a suspicion that there was something wrong, and that he refrained from asking questions, not because he was an honest blunderer or a stupid man, but because he thought in his own secret mind—I suspect there is something wrong, and if I ask questions and make farther inquiry, it will no longer be my suspecting it, but my knowing it, and then I shall not be able to recover—I think that is dishonesty.[109]

Third parties are not to be fixed with constructive notice of the agent's lack of authority.[110]

**4.45**  Lord Neuberger's test was adopted by Proudman, J in *Newcastle International Airport Ltd v Eversheds LLP* in relation to a firm of solicitors which had accepted instructions from the executive director of a company to draft a service contract under which the latter would receive a substantial bonus.[111] In the *Newcastle* case apparent

---

[107]  [2010] HKCFA 64 at [75].
[108]  *Ibid* at [62].
[109]  (1877) 2 App Cas 616, 629.
[110]  [2010] HKCFA 64 at [52].
[111]  [2012] EWHC 2648 (Ch); [2013] PNLR 5 at [109]. See also *Quinn v CC Automotive Group Ltd (t/a Carcraft)* [2011] 2 All ER (Comm) 584 at [23] *per* Gross, LJ, *Gaydamak v Leviev* [2012]

authority was found to exist as it was commonplace for remuneration committees to instruct solicitors through their executive directors, even as to the detail of their own contracts. Echoing the words of Lord Neuberger, Proudman, J added: 'Life would be very difficult for commercial solicitors if they were required to check the word of apparently authorised agents against the minutiae of all the documents in the case.'[112]

### The rules governing apparent authority in the context of companies

Time was when the rules governing the apparent authority of agents acting on behalf **4.46** of companies followed a different legal regime from that of other agents. This was a consequence of the *ultra vires* rule and of a doctrine of constructive notice, both of which have now been abolished by legislation. The provision, now set out in s 40(1) of the Companies Act 2006,[113] altered the rules regarding the power of directors to enter into binding agreements on behalf of their companies by laying down:

> [i]n favour of a person dealing with a company in good faith, the power of the directors to bind the company, or authorise others to do so, is deemed to be free of any limitation under the company's constitution.

This provision owes its origins to the EC First Directive on Company Law (68/151/EEC),[114] whose art 9 required Member States to do away with the *ultra vires* doctrine according to which a company was not bound by acts—and notably contracts—entered into on its behalf contrary to the terms of its memorandum of association. Alongside the *ultra vires* doctrine, under the pre-Directive law a party dealing with a company was also considered to be fixed with constructive notice of the contents of the company's memorandum. To all intents this meant that a party dealing with the agents of a company could not rely upon the doctrine of apparent authority. Section 40 henceforth prevents future recourse to constructive notice by laying down that a person 'dealing with the company' is under no obligation to inquire into the powers of the directors; that such a person is initially presumed to have acted in good faith; and that he 'is not to be regarded as acting in bad faith by reason only of his knowing that an act is beyond the powers of the directors under the company's constitution.'[115] In these circumstances, an agent's power to bind the company 'is deemed to be free of any limitation under the company's constitution'.

---

EWHC 1740 (Ch) at [249] *per* Vos, J, and *LNOC Ltd v Watford AFC Ltd* [2013] EWHC 3615 (Comm) at [92] *per* HHJ Mackie.

[112] [2012] EWHC 2648 (Ch); [2013] PNLR 5 at [115]. In *Thanakharn* Lord Neuberger had said: 'in a commercial context, absent dishonesty or irrationality, a person should be entitled to rely on what he is told: this may occasionally produce harsh results, but it enables people engaged in business to know where they stand': [2010] HKCFA 64 at [52]. See further Lee and Ho, 'Reluctant Bedfellows: Want of Authority and Knowing Receipt' (2012) 75 MLR 91, 92–4.

[113] Formerly, the Companies Act 1885, s 35A, as amended by the Companies Act 1989, s 108.

[114] It was first implemented in the European Communities Act 1972, s 9(1).

[115] Companies Act 2006, s 40(2)(b)(iii).

Moreover, under the terms of the Act 'limitation[s] under the company's constitution', referred to in s 40(1), include those deriving from a resolution of the company or of any class of shareholders or from any agreement between the members of the company or of any class of shareholders[116] as well as such things as quorum requirements.[117] By doing away with the *ultra vires* rule and a doctrine of constructive notice that had shown itself capable of inflicting real hardship on third parties, the current legislation places agents acting on behalf of companies on a similar footing to agents acting beyond the scope of their authority in other domains.

### Alteration of position

**4.47**   In *Rama Corporation Ltd v Proved Tin and General Investments Ltd*,[118] it will be recalled, Slade, J stated that the third requirement of apparent authority was that there had to have been an alteration of position on the part of the third party. If it is accepted that apparent authority sounds in an estoppel, the general law has sometimes required that the party seeking to rely upon an estoppel must not only have acted upon the other party's representation but also have acted to his detriment. As Lord Robertson declared in *George Whitechurch Ltd v Cavanagh*:

> My Lords, the case of the respondent is one of estoppel, and it is an essential element in such cases (as is clearly expressed in the case of *Carr v London and North Western Rly Co* (1875) LR 10 CP 317, cited by the Master of the Rolls) that the person to whom the representation was made has suffered loss by acting upon it; or, to put it in another way, has altered his position to his detriment by acting on the representation.[119]

**4.48**   This reasoning has been applied in some agency cases. For instance, in *Norfolk CC v Secretary of State for the Environment*[120] a planning officer, who had authority to inform parties of the outcome of their planning applications, mistakenly wrote to a company that it had been granted permission to build a factory extension. The planning authority had in fact refused the application. In reliance on the planning officer's letter, the company immediately ordered machinery. Two days later it was informed that the letter had been sent in error and a correct notice of refusal was issued. The company insisted that it had been issued with a valid planning permission and began digging a foundation trench for the extension. The authority served an enforcement notice requiring the trench to be filled in. In the meantime, the company succeeded in cancelling its order for machinery without penalty. A three-man High Court held that before the local planning authority could be estopped

---

[116] Companies Act 2006, s 40(3).
[117] See *Smith v Henniker-Major & Co* [2003] Ch 182.
[118] [1952] 2 QB 147, 149–50.
[119] [1902] AC 117, 135.
[120] [1973] 1 WLR 1400.

from denying the validity of the original notice, the applicant had to show that it had been induced by the representation of the local authority to act to its detriment. In this particular case, Lord Widgery, CJ considered that by making a token start on extension work and placing an order that could be cancelled without incurring a penalty, the applicant had not done sufficient to show that it had acted to its detriment. Detriment was found to be 'an essential feature of any claim [it] can make to stand upon [its] planning permission, and it is a feature now established beyond doubt not to be present in this case.'[121] Since the applicants had not acted effectively to their detriment, the local planning authority was not bound by the original notice.

Nevertheless, in very many agency cases the courts require only an alteration of position, not evidence of a detriment suffered. Indeed, in *Rama Corporation* itself, the court merely refers to an alteration of position.[122] The alteration of position may only consist in the third party entering into the contract with the principal. Thus, in *Freeman & Lockyer (A Firm) v Buckhurst Park Properties (Mangal) Ltd* Diplock, LJ declared: **4.49**

> The representation, *when acted upon by the contractor by entering into a contract with the agent, operates as an estoppel*, preventing the principal from asserting that he is not bound by the contract.[123]

In light of such statements, it is legitimate to wonder whether alteration of position in fact constitutes a separate requirement from reliance.

## The Effects of Apparent Authority

### The third party may look to the principal

The obvious consequence of a finding that, when transacting business with the third party, the agent was acting within the scope of his apparent authority is that the third party will be held to be in direct relations with the principal and may look to the latter. Such being the case, the principal may put forward defences and advance counterclaims against the third party. However, it might be asked whether the principal may also sue on a contract which has been made by his agent, acting without actual authority but within the scope of his apparent authority? Since, according to conventional wisdom, apparent authority sounds in the doctrine of estoppel, whereby a principal is prevented from denying the authority of his agent which he has represented to the third party to be genuine, the principal does not **4.50**

---

[121] *Ibid* at 1405.
[122] [1952] 2 QB 147, 171 *per* Slade, J.
[123] [1964] 2 QB 480, 503 (emphasis added).

acquire a right to sue on the contract on which he is held liable to the third party. Nevertheless, since in very many circumstances it will be open to the principal to ratify his agent's unauthorized transactions,[124] this is unlikely to prove a significant restriction on the principal.

## Apparent Authority and the Agent's Fraudulent and Disloyal Acts

**4.51** Do an agent's fraudulent or disloyal acts bind the principal if they fall within his apparent authority? Because there will always be an implication that an agent's actual authority is subject to a condition that the agency will be exercised honestly and in the interests of the principal,[125] any act the agent performs in the name of but not in the interests of the principal—eg, signing onerous unconditional undertakings[126]—may fall outside the agent's actual express or actual implied authority. Any such transactions will therefore be void, unless the third party can invoke the agent's apparent authority. To quote Millett, J in *Macmillan Inc v Bishopgate Investment Trust (No 3)*, 'English law ... recognises the distinction between want of authority and abuse of authority.'[127] The courts nevertheless hold that if an agent's acts fall within his apparent authority, his principal will be bound by the actions of the agent, even if the latter acts fraudulently or contrary to the principal's interests.[128]

**4.52** Thus, in *Armagas v Mundogas*, the House of Lords accepted that, if an employee's fraudulent representation caused loss to an innocent party contracting with him, an employer could be held liable to bear the loss provided that the latter's words or conduct had induced the innocent party to believe that the employee was acting in the course of the employer's business. However, where, as in *Armagas*, such belief was induced through misguided reliance on the employee himself, when the servant was not authorized to do what he was purporting to do, when what he was purporting to do was not within the class of acts that an employee in his position was usually authorized to do, and when the employer had done nothing to represent that he was authorized to do it, the employer would not be liable:

> At the end of the day the question is whether the circumstances under which a servant has made the fraudulent misrepresentation which has caused loss to an innocent party contracting with him are such as to make it just for the employer to bear the

---

[124] See **chapter 6**.

[125] *Lysaght Bros & Co Ltd v Falk* (1905) 2 CLR 421.

[126] *Hopkins v TL Dallas Group Ltd* [2005] 1 BCLC 543 at [88] *per* Lightman, J; *Lexi Holdings (in administration) v Pannone & Partners* [2009] EWHC 2590 (Ch).

[127] [1995] 1 WLR 978, 984.

[128] *Hopkins v TL Dallas Group Ltd* [2005] 1 BCLC 543 at [89].

loss. Such circumstances exist where the employer by words or conduct has induced the injured party to believe that the servant was acting in the lawful course of the employer's business. They do not exist where such belief, although it is present, has been brought about through misguided reliance on the servant himself, when the servant is not authorised to do what he is purporting to do, when what he is purporting to do is not within the class of acts that an employee in his position is usually authorised to do, and when the employer has done nothing to represent that he is authorised to do it.[129]

The nature of an agent's acts may serve to put a third party on notice of the agent's **4.53** want of authority, thereby excluding the possibility that the agent's act fell within his apparent authority. As Denning, J noted in *Nelson v Larholt*:

All the cases that occur in the books, of trustees or agents who draw cheques on the trust account or the principal's account for their own private purposes, or of directors who apply their company's cheques for their own account, fall within this one principle. The rightful owner can recover the amount from anyone who takes the money with notice, subject, of course, to the limitation that he cannot recover twice over ... If, therefore, [the third party] knew or is to be taken to have known of the want of authority, as, for instance, if the circumstances were such as to put a reasonable man on inquiry, and he made none, or if he was put off by an answer that would not have satisfied a reasonable man, or, in other words, if he was negligent in not perceiving the want of authority, then he is taken to have notice of it.[130]

In the well-known case of *Midland Bank Ltd v Reckitt*,[131] a solicitor, who had authority under a power of attorney to draw cheques on his client's bank account and to apply the monies for the purposes of his client, fraudulently drew fifteen cheques on his client's account with a bank, contriving to sign them as attorney for the client.[132] The solicitor next paid the cheques into his own account with the Midland Bank, with whom he had an overdraft. Upon discovering what had occurred, the client sued the Midland Bank for conversion of the cheques. The bank sought to rely on the defence provided by s 82 of the Bills of Exchange Act 1882, alleging that they had received the crossed cheques in good faith and without negligence. Whilst it was admitted that the bank had acted in good faith, the House of Lords held that the bank could not bring itself within s 82 owing to the fact that, since the form of the cheques put the bank upon notice that the money was not the solicitor's money, it was negligent in making no inquiry as to the solicitor's authority to make these payments into his own account to reduce his personal overdraft

---

[129] [1986] AC 717, 782–3 *per* Lord Keith of Kinkel.

[130] [1948] 1 KB 339, 343.

[131] [1933] AC 1.

[132] He signed the cheques on an impression made by a rubber stamp containing in the upper line 'Harold G. Reckitt by' and on the lower line 'his attorney' and placed his own signature between the lines, so that the completed signature on each cheque ran 'Harold G. Reckitt by Terrington, his attorney'.

## Duration of Apparent Authority

**4.54** How should one calculate the duration of apparent authority? One can see that where a representation emanating from a principal induces a third party to believe that the 'agent' has authority, the time from which authority exists can be fixed with comparative ease. The duration of that authority—or, more specifically, the point at which that authority ceases to bind the principal—has sometimes been claimed to be more difficult to fix, not least because the great majority of decided cases concern the extent rather than the duration of the agent's apparent authority. In *SEB Trygg Liv Holding AB v Manches*[133] Buxton, LJ addressed the question whether a doctrine of apparent authority had been 'fully worked out' in cases where the issue is termination of authority. He pointed out that the leading case, *Scarf v Jardine*,[134] which involved the authority enjoyed by members of a partnership, concerned termination. *Willis Faber & Co v Joyce*,[135] too, where an underwriter employed an agent to underwrite for him under a written agreement that terminated on 31 December 1909, was concerned with the duration of the agent's continuing apparent authority. Buxton, LJ concluded that, despite the relative paucity of case law, 'Once the underlying principle of estoppel is established, there is no logical reason why, subject of course to the facts of each particular case, the doctrine should not operate in cases falling into each category',[136] whether the issue be one of the extent or the duration of the agent's powers.

## Authority arising out of Estoppel by Representation

**4.55** Although the agency could be said to devolve from a different principle altogether, it should be added that the courts occasionally recognize a type of agency which resembles agency arising out of apparent authority, but which is a product of estoppel by representation. This situation arises when a 'principal' displays inertia, omitting to correct a false impression by denying his 'agent's' appearance of authority, thereby leading a third party to infer that the 'agent' possesses authority. The first English case of this type originated in the context of estate agency, but the principle has since been accepted to apply in the general commercial context, too.

**4.56** In *Spiro v Lintern*[137] L1, who was separating from his wife, left it to his wife, L2, to arrange with estate agents to find a purchaser for their house, but gave her no

---

[133] [2006] 1 WLR 2276.
[134] (1882) 7 App Cas 345.
[135] (1911) LT 576.
[136] *Ibid* at [31].
[137] [1973] 1 WLR 1002.

authority to sell. Through estate agents the wife agreed to the sale of the property and a written agreement was executed according to which L2 agreed to sell the house to S. L1 neither accepted nor denied his wife's authority to sell, but permitted S's gardener to work in the garden, a builder to do work in the house on S's behalf, and S's solicitor to assure S that he would not enter into any dealings with the property without first informing S of his intention to do so. Before setting off for India, L1 executed a full power of attorney in L2's favour, empowering her to complete the sale, and signed a transfer of the house in S's favour, which was never handed over. L2 proceeded to sell the property to another lady, A. S obtained specific performance of L2's agreement to transfer the house to him, and A was ordered to deliver up possession. The Court of Appeal held that S had been under a mistaken belief that L1 was under an obligation to sell the house to him and had acted in a manner consistent only with the existence of such an obligation. In these circumstances, L1 had been under a duty to disclose to S that L2 had acted without his authority. His failure to do so amounted to a representation by conduct that she had his authority. Since it could be shown that S had acted on that representation to his detriment, L1 was estopped from asserting that the contract was entered into without his authority. Buckley, LJ, delivering the judgment of the court, extrapolated from the orthodox principle of estoppel to the effect that A cannot stand by and watch B act in a manner inconsistent with a right which would be to B's disadvantage if the right were later asserted against him. He expressed the principle upon which the decision in *Spiro v Lintern* reposes thus:

> [I]f A sees B acting in the mistaken belief that A is under some binding obligation to him and in a manner consistent only with the existence of such an obligation, which would be to B's disadvantage if A were thereafter to deny the obligation, A is under a duty to B to disclose the non-existence of the supposed obligation.[138]

**4.57** A's duty to speak arises whenever a reasonable man could expect the person against whom the estoppel is raised, acting honestly and reasonably, to bring the true facts to the attention of the other party known by him to be under a mistake as to their respective rights and obligations.[139] For this reason, the Court was able to conclude in *Spiro v Lintern* that all the necessary incidents of a valid estoppel by representation were present.

**4.58** The courts have occasionally referred to *Spiro v Lintern*. In *The Stolt Loyalty*, for example, Clarke, J stressed that 'before a person can be held to be estopped as a result of mere inaction he must be shown to be under a legal duty to take action of some kind.'[140] In a later case, Moore-Bick, J declined to extend the principle set

---

[138] *Ibid* at 1011. Without relying upon the case, Buckley, LJ pointed out that the Court of Appeal's decision was consistent with a similar ruling delivered in *West v Dillicar* [1920] NZLR 139; [1921] NZLR 617.

[139] See, eg, *Pacol Ltd v Trade Lines Ltd, The Henrik Sif* [1982] 1 Lloyd's Rep 456.

[140] [1993] 2 Lloyd's Rep 281, 289.

forth in *Spiro v Lintern* to create a broad duty on someone who had played no part in encouraging another party to rely upon it, to alert that person of an unauthorized act.[141] However, in *Baird Textiles Holdings Ltd v Marks & Spencer plc* Mance, LJ did recognize that:

> A may ... estop himself after the event from denying that B was acting as his agent in contracting with C ... But in these situations there is either a purported or an actual legal relationship created by the conduct of B and C, to which A is estopped from denying that he is party ... [A] is estopped from denying that B was acting as his undisclosed agent in making an actual contract.[142]

---

[141] *Yona International Ltd v La Réunion Française Société Anonyme d'Assurances et de Réassurances* [1996] 2 Lloyd's Rep 84.

[142] [2002] 1 All ER (Comm) 737. This principle does not mean that one can 'create a legally binding agreement when there never was one and never any intention to create one. That an estoppel cannot do': *Smithkline Beecham Plc v Apotex Europe Ltd* [2006] CP Rep 39 at [112] *per* Jacob, LJ.

# 5

# AUTHORITY DERIVING FROM AGENCY OF NECESSITY

## Agency of Necessity

There exist a number of situations in which the law will impose the incidents of **5.01** agency where one party has acted on behalf of another in the course of an emergency. This occurs when one party (the 'agent') is confronted with an emergency that poses such an imminent threat to the property or other interests of another person (the 'principal') that there is insufficient time for the former to seek the latter's authority or instructions before acting. The 'agent' elects to act for the benefit of the 'principal', without prior authority, in order to preserve or protect that property or those interests.

The authority deriving from this form of agency differs from those considered thus **5.02** far. First, the 'principal' will not have assented to the creation of an agency—although it is arguable in some situations that the principal would impliedly have assented to the agent's intervention. Thus, if a party saves a vessel in distress, in some sense the salvor might be said to have the owner's consent to do so. Secondly, in these cases the 'principal' will not have represented to third parties that his 'agent' possesses authority to act. For these reasons, on the whole, it may be best to view these cases as instances where an agency springs up because, for a range of policy reasons, the law imposes such a relationship upon the parties.

That category of cases that traditionally falls within the designation 'agency of ne- **5.03** cessity' poses a further problem. By no means are all of them true cases of agency. In some instances, an emergency will confer on an existing agent more extensive authority to bind his principal to transactions. In a smaller, and more striking, group of cases the emergency will serve to create an agency relationship where none existed previously. But in other cases—possibly, the majority—no agency relationship *stricto sensu* will arise. The intervening 'agent' will not bring the 'principal' into direct legal relations with a third party; the issue will simply be whether the 'agent' who has intervened on another's behalf in order to safeguard the latter's property or other interests is entitled to reimbursement of his expenses. Although all these situations share in common the necessity for the actor to respond to some pressing emergency, it is preferable not to conflate what are very different legal relationships. Lord Diplock made this point forcibly in *China-Pacific SA v Food Corporation of India. The Winson*,[1] a case concerning a salvage agreement:

> Whether one person is entitled to act as agent of necessity for another person is relevant to the question whether circumstances exist which in law have the effect of conferring on him authority to create contractual rights and obligations between that other person and a third party that are directly enforceable by each against the other. It would ... be an aid to clarity of legal thinking if the use of the expression 'agent of necessity' were confined to contexts in which this was the question to be determined and not extended, as it often is, to cases where the only relevant question is whether a person who without obtaining instructions from the owner of goods incurs expense in taking steps that are reasonably necessary for their preservation is in law entitled to recover from the owner of the goods the reasonable expenses incurred by him in taking those steps. Its use in this wider sense may ... have led to some confusion in the instant case, since where reimbursement is the only relevant question all of those conditions that must be fulfilled in order to entitle one person to act on behalf of another in creating direct contractual relationships between that other person and a third party may not necessarily apply.[2]

The present account will apply this distinction, treating separately what might be termed true cases of agency of necessity, where all the normal incidents of agency will arise, and what will be termed necessitous interventions, which do not give rise to conventional incidents of agency and where the intervening party simply seeks to recoup from the beneficiary expenses (and in the case of salvage, an element of reward, too) which he has incurred by his actions.

### True cases of agency of necessity

**5.04**   In those situations that fall within this first category, apart from the fact that the agency arises by operation of law, without either the assent of the principal or any representation on his part, the normal incidents of agency are to be found: as well as binding the principal to a transaction which the agent has purportedly entered into on his behalf, the agent will have a defence if sued by the principal for acting without authority, and the agent will in many circumstances be entitled to be reimbursed by the principal for expenses incurred in the course of the

---

[1] [1982] AC 939.
[2] *Ibid* at 958.

agency. Sometimes, it has been suggested—for example, by Scrutton, LJ in *Jebara v Ottoman Bank*[3]—that a further distinction ought to be drawn between cases of pre-existing agency where an emergency necessitates an extension of an agent's existing authority and cases where, through an emergency, the 'agent' acquires authority where none was previously possessed.[4] However, provided that these two separate scenarios are borne in mind, probably little is to be gained from drawing such a distinction.

The doctrine of necessity owes its origins to early practices of mercantile law, and to shipping law in particular. It can even be retraced to the Roman-law doctrine of *negotiorum gestio*, which was concerned with rights and liabilities arising out of the unrequested management of another's affairs.[5] In fact, it is no accident that the three principal, exceptional situations in which English law has for long recognized that unsolicited work performed or unsolicited services rendered for another can give rise to an enforceable right to remuneration—agency of necessity, salvage, and the acceptance of a bill of exchange for honour *supra protest*—all originated in the same jurisdiction, the Court of Admiralty. This Court was staffed by the lawyers of Doctors' Commons, who were imbued with the traditions of the civil law, and who, in this respect, possessed a more open outlook than many of their common-law counterparts. Thus, many of the early cases of agency of necessity concern masters of ships who variously were held entitled to jettison goods to lighten their ship if such a course was necessary to preserve the ship or the remaining cargo;[6] to sell[7] or to hypothecate[8] part or all of the ship in order to raise money to pay for repairs necessary to enable the vessel to prosecute her voyage; or to incur expenses on behalf of cargo-owners in order to preserve their cargo—for instance, unloading and drying out cargo or employing people to save it from wreck.[9] In one of its most recent incarnations, *The Choko Star*,[10] although it did not find that an agency of necessity existed, the Court of Appeal did recognize that had the requisite conditions been met, the master of a ship stranded at the mouth of the Paraná river could have signed a salvage agreement binding on the cargo-owner.

**5.05**

---

[3] [1927] 2 KB 254.

[4] Scrutton, LJ, it is true, sought to employ this distinction in gauging the appropriateness of McCardie, J's proposal in *Prager v Blatspiel, Stamp & Heacock Ltd* [1924] 1 KB 566 that agencies of necessity ought to extend beyond marine cases to certain non-marine situations.

[5] See generally J Kortmann, *Altruism in Private Law: Liability for Nonfeasance and Negotiorum Gestio* (2005: Oxford, Oxford University Press) pp 99ff.

[6] *The Gratitudine* (1801) 3 C Rob 240, 256 *per* Lord Stowell.

[7] *Gunn v Roberts* (1874) LR 9 CP 331, 337 *per* Brett, J.

[8] *The Gratitudine* (1801) 3 C Rob 240, 257 *per* Lord Stowell.

[9] *Notara v Henderson* (1872) LR 7 QB 225, 230–1 *per* Willes, J; *Brown v Gaudet* (1873) LR 5 PC 134, 165–6 *per* Sir Montague Smith; *Hingston v Wendt* (1876) 1 QBD 367.

[10] *Industrie Chimiche Italia v Alexander G Tvarliris & Sone Maritime Co. The Choko Star* [1990] 1 Lloyd's Rep 516.

*The criteria of an agency of necessity*

**5.06**   In *The Choko Star*,[11] where a ship's master had purported to enter into a salvage agreement on behalf of the ship and its solitary cargo-owner, Slade, LJ set out the four criteria of an agency of necessity. An agency of necessity would only be considered to have arisen if, in all the circumstances:

(1) it is necessary to take salvage assistance; and

(2) it is not reasonably practicable to communicate with the cargo-owners or to obtain their instructions; and

(3) the master or shipowners act *bona fide* in the interests of the cargo; and

(4) it is reasonable for the master or shipowner to enter into the particular contract.[12]

In the event, these conditions were not met in *The Choko Star*. Notably, it was not shown to have been impractical for the captain to consult with the cargo-owner before entering into a salvage agreement with Greek salvors in preference to the local, and presumably more economical, Argentine salvors.

**5.07**   English salvage law, in fact, has altered since *The Choko Star*. Whereas that case ordained that in order to bind cargo-owners, an agency of necessity had to be established where the owners' prior consent to the entry into a salvage contract had neither been sought nor given,[13] following adherence to the International Salvage Convention 1989—art 6.2 of which provides that '... the master or the owner of the vessel shall have the authority to conclude ... [contracts for salvage operations] ... on behalf of the owner of the property on board the vessel'—the ruling in the *The Choko Star* has effectively been reversed.[14] By giving effect to the 1989 Convention, s 224 of the Merchant Shipping Act 1995 endows both the master and the owner of a ship with express authority in a wide range of circumstances to conclude salvage contracts on behalf of the owners of cargo.

**5.08**   **(i) The agent's intervention must be necessary**   The first requirement of an agency of necessity is that the agent's intervention must have been necessary. As Longmore, LJ recently remarked in *ENE 1 Kos Ltd v Petroleo Brasileiro SA*, 'As a general principle English law does not, in the absence of an agency of necessity, impose any obligation on a party, on whom a benefit has been

---

[11] *Industrie Chimiche Italia* [1990] 1 Lloyd's Rep 516. See further Munday, *The Curious Case of the Master's Ostensible Authority* (1986) 136 NLJ 508; Reynolds [1990] JBL 505.

[12] *Industrie Chimiche Italia* [1990] 1 Lloyd's Rep 516, 525.

[13] Eg, *Galaxy Special Maritime Enterprise v Prima Ceylon Ltd* [2005] All ER (D) 213 (Jul) at [30] *per* Arthur Marriott, QC.

[14] Eg, *Ministry of Trade of the Republic of Iraq v Tsavliris Salvage (International) Ltd* [2008] 2 Lloyd's Rep 90 at [42] *per* Gross, J.

conferred, to pay for that benefit.'[15] Necessity, then, lies at the heart of this species of agency.

What will constitute 'necessity' in the mercantile context? In *Australasian Steam Navigation Company v Morse*[16] Sir Montague Smith proposed a definition of what will amount to 'necessity' in a commercial setting:

**5.09**

> [T]he word 'necessity', when applied to mercantile affairs, where the judgment must, in the nature of things, be exercised, cannot of course mean an irresistible compelling power—what is meant by it in such cases is, the force of circumstances which determine the course a man ought to take. Thus, when by the force of circumstances a man has the duty cast upon him of taking some action for another, and under that obligation adopts the course which, to the judgment of a wise and prudent man, is apparently the best for the interest of the persons for whom he acts in a given emergency, it may properly be said of the course so taken, that it was, in a mercantile sense, necessary to take it.[17]

In a subsequent case, *Tsavliris Salvage (International) Ltd v Guangdong Shantou Overseas Chinese Materials Marketing Co*[18] Clarke, J reflected further on this question in the setting of salvage. He quoted with approval a passage from Brice's *Maritime Law of Salvage*, which appeared 'to be common sense and to reflect commercial reality',[19] in which the author stated:

**5.10**

> There are of course countless situations which may arise so as to require that salvage assistance be provided to a ship and her cargo. It is probable that, at least in most cases, where the danger to the vessel is such that the services rendered would, in accordance with the ordinary principles of law be categorised as salvage services, that the degree of danger to which the ship and cargo are exposed will be such as to amount to an 'emergency' giving rise to a 'necessity' for taking action to protect ship and cargo in the form of engaging a salvor to perform salvage services.

At least in the context of salvage the authorities suggest that a ship's master and, where appropriate, the ship's owner too[20] ought to be allowed considerable latitude:

> It is not necessary ... that the distress should be actual or immediate, or that the danger should be imminent and absolute; it will be sufficient if, at the time the assistance is rendered, the ship has encountered any damage or misfortune which might possibly expose her to destruction if the services were not rendered.[21]

---

[15] [2010] 2 Lloyd's Rep 409 at [24].

[16] (1872) LR4 PC 222.

[17] *Ibid* at 230.

[18] [1999] 1 Lloyd's Rep 338.

[19] *Ibid* at [6].

[20] Clarke, J considered that the need to afford shipowners latitude was implicit in the decision in *The Troilus* [1951] AC 280: [1999] 1 Lloyd's Rep 338 at [8].

[21] *The Charlotte* (1848) 3 WRob 68, 71 *per* Dr Lushington. See also *The Strathnaver* (1875) 1 App Cas 58, 65 *per* Sir Robert Phillimore. In *The Phantom* (1866) LR 1 A&E 58, 60, Dr Lushington declared: 'It is not necessary there should be absolute danger in order to constitute a salvage service; it is sufficient if there is a state of difficulty, and reasonable apprehension.'

What is clear is that agency of necessity requires demonstration of the fact that there was an urgent necessity to act,[22] and that 'it is not sufficient to prove that the master thought that he was doing the best for all concerned, or even that the course adopted was, so far as can be ascertained, the best for all concerned.'[23]

**5.11** **(ii) It is not reasonably practicable to communicate with the principal to seek instructions**   This requirement is expressed in several different ways. McCardie, J, for instance, stated: 'agency of necessity does not arise if the agent can communicate with his principal.'[24] More attuned to commercial realities, perhaps, is the test formulated by McCardie, J's nemesis, Scrutton, LJ, who suggested that communication with the principal must be 'commercially impossible'.[25] Certainly, as the cases often have shown, if it would have been realistic for the agent to obtain instructions from the principal, or principals, before acting, the courts will not find that an agency of necessity has been established. Sir Montague Smith stressed this factor in *Brown v Gaudet*:

> The authority of the master being founded on necessity would not have arisen, if he could have obtained instructions from the defendant or his assignees. But under the circumstances this was not possible.[26]

**5.12** **(iii) The court must be satisfied that the agent acted in the interests of the principal and in a *bona fide* manner**   This requirement is often stated, and occasionally a court will find that a purported agent of necessity's actions were not performed *bona fide* in the principal's interests.[27] However, parties' motives are often mixed. As Lord Diplock pointed out in *The Winson*:

> The law does not seem to have determined in this context what ensues where interests are manifold or motives mixed: it may well be that the court will look to the interest mainly served or to the dominant motive.[28]

It is not clear whether Lord Diplock would have favoured as the relevant test, 'the interest mainly served' or 'the dominant motive'. Whilst the law, in unravelling such

---

[22] Eg, *Acatos v Burns* (1878) 3 ExD 282, 290 *per* Brett, LJ.

[23] *Atlantic Mutual Insurance Co v Huth* (1880) 16 ChD 474, 481 *per* Cotton, LJ.

[24] *Prager v Blatspiel, Stamp & Heacock Ltd* [1924] 1 KB 566, 571.

[25] *Springer v Great Western Railway* Co [1921] 1 KB 257, 265, a case McCardie, J cited in *Prager*. See also *Tetley & Co v British Trade Corp* (1922) 10 Ll L Rep 678, 680 *per* Bailhache, J: 'Whether [the defendants] were agents of necessity depends on whether it would have been *reasonably proper* on their part to have cabled at some time or other to the plaintiffs for instructions as to what they were to do with the goods in the event of this evacuation becoming an accomplished fact, and in order to ascertain if it was reasonable that they should do this.'

[26] (1873) LR 5 PC 134, 165–6.

[27] Eg, *Prager v Blatspiel* [1924] 1 KB 566, 572ff *per* McCardie, J ('I decided, without hesitation, that the defendants did not act *bona fide*').

[28] [1982] AC 939, 966.

questions, in some contexts adopts as its yardstick the dominant motive,[29] 'the interest mainly served' may be the more fitting test in the context of agency of necessity. If the interests of the principal have been protected by the actions of the agent, it is suggested that it is only right that the agent should be reimbursed for his pains. The question, however, awaits an authoritative answer.

**(iv) It must be shown that the action taken by the agent was reasonable and prudent in the circumstances**   Not only does this requirement link up with the idea that the agent must have acted in the interests of the principal, and consulted the latter if it was commercially practicable, but also it incorporates the idea that the agent's acts were not expressly or impliedly forbidden by the principal.   **5.13**

**(v) The principal must have been competent at the time that the agent acted**   Finally, as with other forms of agency, there is authority that the principal on whose behalf the agent acts must have been competent at the relevant time. Notably, Scrutton, LJ, in *Jebara v Ottoman Bank*,[30] when called upon to extend agencies of necessity beyond the traditional case of the master of a ship coping with an emergency, expressed the view that extension of the doctrine was:   **5.14**

> ... still more difficult when there is a pre-existing agency, but it has become illegal and void by reason of war, and the same reason will apply to invalidate any implied agency of necessity. How can one imply a duty in an enemy to protect the property of his enemy? Will he not be violating his duty to his own country if he takes active steps to preserve an enemy's property? I do not feel strong enough to expand the common law to this extent.[31]

*Does the doctrine of agency of necessity extend beyond the maritime realm?*

As Sir Christopher Staughton observed in *Surrey Breakdown Ltd v Knight*:[32]   **5.15**

> The doctrine of agency of necessity is not wholly settled in English law. It is well established in maritime cases that there may be what is called officious intervention creating, as it were, an agency. Whether the same is the case on land is not settled.[33]

---

[29] As Lord Sumption, JSC remarked in *Hayes v Willoughby* [2013] 1 WLR 935 at [17], in the context of a tortious claim arising out of the Protection from Harrassment Act 1997: 'A person's purposes are almost always to some extent mixed, and the ordinary principle is that the relevant purpose is the dominant one.' See also *R v Crown Court at Southwark, ex p Bowles* [1998] 2 All ER 193, where this self-same concept, borrowed from administrative law, was applied to the issuance of court orders in criminal cases requiring the disclosure of material in the hands of third parties.

[30] [1927] 2 KB 254.

[31] [1927] 2 KB 254, 271. Scrutton, LJ underlined the point later in his judgment, questioning how in *Ananiadi v Ottoman Bank* (1923) March 12, unreported, Greer, J could have reached what appeared to be a contrary conclusion on broadly similar facts: 'if all prior obligations were invalidated by the outbreak of war, how could an implied obligation arise between enemies? How could the bank be "bound" to an enemy to do anything? How is an enemy bound to take steps to preserve the property of his enemy? So far as I understand the facts in this case, I doubt whether the latter part of the judgment of Greer, J can be supported' (p 272).

[32] [1999] RTR 84.

[33] *Ibid* at 88.

On several occasions the courts have been invited to extend agency of necessity to a wider class of cases. They have declined to do so.[34] Notably, McCardie, J, in *Prager v Blatspiel, Stamp & Heacock Ltd*,[35] argued that 'judges should expand the common law to meet the needs of expanding society, and ... expand the doctrine of agent of necessity without clearly defining the limits, if any, of its expansion.'[36] Although it could be pointed out, with some justice, that 'an agent may be faced with the same necessity to act whether he finds himself on foreign waters or on land',[37] a rescuer of a parcel of timber was held not to enjoy similar rights to a maritime salvor—his actions, it was said, 'should depend altogether for their reward upon the moral duty of gratitude.'[38] In *Falcke v Scottish Imperial Insurance Co*, too, Bowen, LJ was adamant that 'no similar doctrine [to maritime salvage] applies to things lost upon land, nor to anything except ships or goods in peril at sea.'[39] In *Jebara v Ottoman Bank*, Scrutton, LJ did however concede that the extension for which McCardie, J argued in *Prager*:

> becomes less difficult when the agent of necessity develops from an original and subsisting agency, and only applies itself to unforeseen events not provided for in the original contract, which is usually the case where a shipmaster is agent of necessity. But the position seems quite different when there is no pre-existing agency.[40]

**5.16** Whilst the bulk of English cases reject the extension of agency of necessity to non-maritime contexts, there is a small group of cases, dealing in the main with the conservation of perishable goods, which lends further uncertainty to this subject. In *Sims & Co v Midland Railway Co*,[41] for example, butter was consigned for delivery by rail. Owing to a general strike, the railway company found itself unable to forward the butter to its destination. In the hot weather, the butter began to deteriorate, oozing through the joints of the boxes. The stationmaster, therefore, acting on the instructions of the railway company, sold the consignment. Scrutton, LJ desired to say that 'the law as to the power of sale and the duty to take care of the goods which is laid down in the case of a carrier by sea applies to a carrier by land where the necessary conditions giving rise to such a power and duty exist.'[42]

---

[34] Eg, *Hawtayne v Bourne* (1841) 7 M&W 595, 599 *per* Parke, B; *Gwilliam v Twist* [1895] 2 QB 84, 87 *per* Lord Esher, MR: 'I am very much inclined to agree with the view taken by Eyre, CJ in the case of *Nicholson v Chapman*, and by Parke, B in the case of *Hawtayne v Bourne*, to the effect that this doctrine of authority by reason of necessity is confined to certain well-known exceptional cases, such as those of the master of a ship or the acceptor of a bill of exchange for the honour of the drawer.'

[35] [1924] 1 KB 566.

[36] *Jebara v Ottoman Bank* [1927] 2 KB 254, 270 *per* Scrutton, LJ.

[37] Stoljar, *Law of Agency* (1961: London, Sweet & Maxwell) p 154.

[38] *Nicholson v Chapman* (1793) 2 HBl 254, 257 *per* Eyre, CJ.

[39] (1886) 34 ChD 234, 248.

[40] [1927] 2 KB 254, 271.

[41] [1913] 1 KB 103.

[42] *Ibid* at 112.

Scrutton, LJ derived support for this view from the judgment of Pollock B in *Great Northern Railway Co v Swaffield*,[43] where a horse was handed over to a livery stable to be cared for when its consignee failed to turn up at the railway station to collect it and the stable keeper was held entitled to recover the cost of stabling from the owner.

### Matrimonial law and agency of necessity

For the sake of completeness, it might be mentioned that over the centuries the **5.17** law has recognized other agencies of necessity. In the case of husband and wife, whilst a wife cohabiting with her husband was held to have apparent authority to contract as his agent for the expenses of the household, if they were living apart the common law recognized her agency of necessity, the right to pledge her husband's credit for necessaries according to her station in life.[44] This rule was complicated, not least because the agency of necessity subsisted only if the wife was justified in living apart from her husband.[45] Moreover, once the law allowed a wife to gain custody of a child, even against the father's will, the law recognized that her agency of necessity extended to necessaries for a child in her custody as well as for herself.[46]

### Necessitous interventions

Primarily owing to the fact that it did not inherit the quasi-contractual institu- **5.18** tion of *negotiorum gestio* from the Roman law, English law has never developed a general doctrine of necessitous intervention. In a few isolated instances an English *gestor* may be permitted to recover expenses incurred when intervening on behalf of another. If the *gestor* was 'a proper person to interfere', he has been held entitled to recover the cost of burying[47] or of arranging the funeral of another,[48] of caring for the sick,[49] of discharging certain debts,[50] or possibly of acting in relief of paupers.[51] There are also the more significant cases of the salvor, in the case of maritime salvage,

---

[43] (1874) LR 9 Ex 132, 138.

[44] See *R (Kehoe) v Secretary of State for Work and Pensions* [2006] 1 AC 42, 70–1 *per* Baroness Hale of Richmond. 'The statutory power to order periodic sums by way of maintenance first appeared in the Matrimonial Causes Act 1866. At that date a wife was incapable of property ownership, the corollary being that her husband was ordinarily liable for her debts, since she contracted as his agent of necessity': *McFarlane v McFarlane* [2005] Fam 171 at [87] *per* Thorpe, LJ.

[45] Thus, the agency of necessity ceased if the wife committed adultery, regardless of how despicably the husband might previously have behaved towards her: *Govier v Hancock* (1796) 6 TR 603.

[46] *Bazeley v Forder* (1868) LR 3 QB 559.

[47] *Jenkins v Tucker* (1788) 1 HBl 90.

[48] *Rogers v Price* (1829) 3 Y&J 28.

[49] *In re Rhodes* (1890) 44 ChD 94.

[50] *Owen v Tate* [1976] QB 402, 409 *per* Scarman, LJ; *The Zukal K and Selin* [1987] 1 Lloyd's Rep 151.

[51] A Burrows, *The Law of Restitution* (2005: Oxford, Oxford University Press) p 311.

and of the acceptor of a bill of exchange for honour. Otherwise, as Lord Diplock noted in *The Winson*:

> It is, of course, true in English law a mere stranger cannot compel an owner of goods to pay for a benefit bestowed on him against his will.[52]

**5.19**  The classical statement of the English law on the subject of necessitous intervention is to be found in Bowen, LJ's judgment in *Falcke v Scottish Imperial Insurance Co*:

> The general principle is, beyond all question, that work and labour done or money expended by one man to preserve or benefit the property of another do not according to English law create any lien upon the property saved or benefited, nor, even if standing alone, create any obligation to repay the expenditure. Liabilities are not to be forced upon people behind their backs any more than you can confer a benefit upon a man against his will.[53]

This refusal to recognize the rights of those who confer unrequested benefits on others is well illustrated by *Hawtayne v Bourne*.[54] Labourers in a mine had obtained warrants of distress upon the materials belonging to the mine in order to satisfy arrears of wages owed to them by the mine. Finding that these warrants were about to be put into execution, the mine manager applied to a bank in the company's name, but without the knowledge of the shareholders, for a loan of £400 for three months out of which he paid what was due to the labourers. Having saved the situation for the company, the manager was held not to be entitled to an indemnity from the company in respect of the unauthorized loan he had taken out: the court held he had neither implied authority to do so nor could he claim reimbursement on grounds of necessity. As Parke, B explained:

> [I]t appears that the ... Judge told the jury that they might infer an authority in the agent, not only to conduct the general business of the mine, but also, in cases of necessity, to raise money for that purpose. I am not aware that any authority is to be found in our law to support this proposition. No such power exists, except in the cases ... of the master of a ship, and of the acceptor of a bill of exchange for the honour of the drawer ... I am ... of opinion that the agent of this mine had not the authority contended for.[55]

**5.20**  English courts have justified their reluctance to reimburse those who incur expense in acting in the interests of others in a number of ways—as well as positing that the law ought not to encourage unscrupulous intermeddlers to confer benefits on other parties against their will,[56] the courts have also subscribed to the idea that

---

[52]  [1982] AC 936, 961.
[53]  (1887) LR 34 ChD 234, 248.
[54]  (1841)7 M&W 595.
[55]  *Ibid* at 599–600.
[56]  *Bradshaw v Beard* (1862) 12 CB (NS) 344, 349 *per* Erle, CJ.

charitable acts are more properly a matter of gratitude than the cause for reward.[57] This apart, vastly improved methods of communication, and the advent of a national public health system, have greatly reduced the need for necessitous intervention by well-meaning individuals who are unable to seek instructions from the party to be benefited prior to acting. *Cessat ratio, cessat lex.*

As Lord Diplock pointed out in *The Winson*,[58] it can lead to confusion to conflate these instances of necessitous intervention with the cases of true agency discussed above:

> [W]here reimbursement is the only relevant question all of those conditions that must be fulfilled in order to entitle one person to act on behalf of another in creating direct contractual relationships between that other person and a third party may not necessarily apply.[59]

**5.21**

Nevertheless, for the sake of completeness—and because it has been the custom to treat of these matters alongside true cases of agency of necessity—acceptance of bills of exchange for honour and of salvage will be briefly outlined.

### The acceptor of a bill of exchange for honour

Sections 65–68 of the Bills of Exchange Act 1882 provide that a party who accepts a bill of exchange for honour *supra protest* is entitled to be reimbursed by the acceptor whose honour has been saved. Notably, s 65(1) lays down:

**5.22**

> Where a bill of exchange has been protested for dishonour by non-acceptance, or protested for better security, and is not overdue, any person, not being a party already liable thereon, may, with the consent of the holder, intervene and accept the bill *supra protest*, for the honour of any party liable thereon, or for the honour of the person for whose account the bill is drawn.

The payer for honour who intervenes and accepts a bill in such circumstances succeeds to the rights of the holder against the person from whom he accepts. Thus, according to s 68(5):

> [T]he payer for honour is subrogated for, and succeeds to both the rights and duties of, the holder as regards the party for whose honour he pays, and all parties liable to that party.

This device, which is claimed to derive originally from the law merchant,[60] scarcely resembles a case of agency. It is more obviously a case of an intervening party becoming entitled to be reimbursed the sums expended in preserving the acceptor's honour.

---

[57] *Nicholson v Chapman* (1793) 2 HBl 254, 259 *per* Eyre, LCJ.
[58] See para **5.03**.
[59] [1982] AC 939, 958.
[60] *Hawtayne v Bourne* (1841) 7 M&W 595, 599 *per* Parke, B.

*Maritime salvage*

**5.23**  In cases where the parties have not agreed a contract of salvage,[61] a salvor will wish to be compensated for expense incurred in saving life or property.[62] The salvor is entitled to compensation provided that a number of conditions have been met:

(i) There must be a situation of necessity, meaning a situation of real danger to life or property such that 'no reasonable, prudent and skilful person in charge of the venture would refuse a salvor's help if it were offered to him upon the condition of his paying a salvor's reward'.[63]

(ii) The salvor must not have been acting within the scope of a pre-existing legal duty to the owner of the salvaged property; nor must the salvor have been acting solely to save himself.

(iii) The salvage must have successfully contributed to saving life or property.

Various rules also regulate the quantum of remuneration to which the salvor becomes entitled:

(i) In order to encourage mariners to perform hazardous services, as well as reimbursement of expenses the salvor's compensation must include an element of reward.[64]

(ii) The salvor's award may not exceed the value of the property saved.[65]

(iii) The salvor may forfeit his award if he commits serious misconduct.

(iv) The salvor is entitled to a maritime lien over the property saved.

(v) If in the course of saving a vessel the salvor negligently damages cargo, he can be held liable to the cargo-owners.[66]

---

[61] 'Today, in the latter half of the twentieth century, most salvage services … are performed by professional salvors under a salvage agreement in Lloyd's Standard Form. Under it the salvage contractor undertakes a continuing obligation, until the ship is lost or brought to a safe port, to use his best endeavours to salve her and to provide the equipment and labour which in the circumstances it would be reasonable for him to use for this purpose': *The Tojo Maru* [1972] AC 242, 292 *per* Lord Pearson.

[62] The doctrine applies to ships, provided they are in tidal waters (*The Goring* [1988] AC 831) and to aircraft.

[63] *Kennedy and Rose on the Law of Salvage* (2013: London, Sweet & Maxwell) 8th ed, by F Rose, para 330. See, eg, *The Hamtun and The St. John* [1999] 1 Lloyd's Rep 883, 889ff.

[64] The measure of the shipowner's liability to a successful salvor is not necessarily equivalent to the value of the benefit he has gained from the salvor's services: *The Tojo Maru* [1972] AC 242, 293 *per* Lord Diplock.

[65] This rule can be explained by the fact that, at least until the beginning of the nineteenth century, the salvor's only remedy to recover his remuneration was a remedy *in rem* against the property saved, which disabled him from recovering more than its value: *The Tojo Maru* [1972] AC 242, 293 *per* Lord Diplock.

[66] See generally *Marc Rich & Co AG v Bishop Rock Marine Co Ltd ('The Nicholas H')* [1996] AC 211.

# 6

# RATIFICATION

## Ratification of Unauthorized Acts

The doctrine of ratification is concerned with acts performed without authority **6.01** by an agent in the name of a principal. If someone acts without the authority of a principal, either (i) because he exceeds the bounds of his actual authority, his apparent authority or any authority conferred by operation of law or (ii) because he was never employed as the principal's agent in the first place, the would-be principal may nevertheless be entitled to ratify a transaction effected in his name by the agent. It is for the principal to decide whether or not to ratify such transactions. But if the principal does so, he thereby adopts the agent's unauthorized acts and it is as though he had authorized them *ab initio*. As Lord Sterndale, MR explained in *Koenigsblatt v Sweet*:

> Ratification ... is equivalent to an antecedent authority ... and when there has been ratification the act that is done is put in the same position as if it had been antecedently authorised.[1]

Tindal, CJ, in *Wilson v Tumman*, defined ratification in the following manner:

> That an act done, for another, by a person, not assuming to act for himself, but for such other person, though without any precedent authority whatever, becomes the act of the principal, if subsequently ratified by him, is the known and well-established rule of law. In that case the principal is bound by the act, whether it be for his detriment or his advantage, and whether it be founded on a tort or on a contract, to the same effect as by, and with all the consequences which follow from, the same act done by his previous authority.[2]

**6.02** Whilst 'ratification may be regarded as a species of election by which the supposed principal for whom the supposed agent did not have authority (or did not have it to the extent claimed) chooses between disavowing the transaction and ratifying it,'[3] the doctrine of ratification is not entirely anomalous. It can be justified on the basis that it gives effect to what the agent and the third party originally intended. From the outset the third party intended to enter into contractual relations with the principal, who subsequently ratifies the transaction, whilst it was the agent's expressed intention to act on the latter's behalf. Although the principal may be presented with an opportunity, even a windfall, not of his making, the important consideration is that the third party ought not to feel himself disadvantaged by the principal's ratification. This situation may be contrasted with that of undisclosed agency.[4] In the case of undisclosed agency the third party will have been ignorant of the very existence of a principal, who, in most circumstances, is permitted to intervene on his agent's contract. Undisclosed agency is more readily seen to be anomalous because it was never the third party's intention to contract with the principal. Ratification, however, presents the converse situation as the third party will find himself bound to the very person with whom he always intended to contract. The third party's expectations are fulfilled by the ratifying principal.[5]

**6.03** By way of illustration of the doctrine, in *Williams v North China Insurance Co*[6] an 'agent' effected an insurance on behalf another party without the latter's authority.

---

[1] [1923] 2 Ch 314, 325.
[2] (1843) 6 M&G 236, 242.
[3] *Demco Investment & Commercial SA v Interamerican Life Insurance (International) Ltd* [2012] EWHC 2053 (Comm) at [106] *per* Christopher Clarke, J.
[4] See **chapter 10**.
[5] For a comparative study exploring some of the imbalances produced by the doctrine, see DeMott, *Ratification: Useful but Uneven* (2009) 17 Eur Rev Priv L 987.
[6] (1876) 1 CPD 757.

Even after a loss had occurred, the professed principal was held to have been entitled to ratify the transaction entered into nominally on his behalf. In *Buron v Denman*,[7] in the course of his duty a naval commander who was entrusted to assist in suppressing the slave trade freed the plaintiff's slaves and destroyed the plaintiff's ship which had been used to transport slaves. The defendant's actions were communicated to the Lords of the Admiralty in London, who later adopted and ratified them. The plaintiff brought an action for trespass against the naval commander. It was held, however, that the minister of state's ratification of the defendant's actions 'was equivalent to prior command and rendered it an act of state'[8] and therefore conferred upon the commander immunity from suit under the doctrine of act of state.

At first sight, ratification would seem to permit the signature of documents in a  **6.04** form not originally agreed by the principal to be effective provided that ratification has taken place. In the leading case of *Koenigsblatt v Sweet*,[9] for example, the defendant agreed to sell two properties to the plaintiff and his wife. When the parties' solicitors met to exchange duplicate parts of the contract, the plaintiff's part contained only his name as sole purchaser, whereas the defendant's part contained the names of both the plaintiff and his wife. Without authority, the defendant's solicitor struck out the name of the plaintiff's wife from the defendant's part. The defendant later ratified this action and ordered the solicitor to proceed with the transaction. Subsequently, wishing not to complete, the defendant attempted to resist specific performance on the ground that the requirements of the Statute of Frauds had not been satisfied. The Court of Appeal held that since ratification is 'equivalent to an antecedent authority', it was as if the solicitor had had in his possession a document with alterations, signed by the defendant after they had been made, and with authority to hand it over as part of an operative agreement in return for a similar document signed by the plaintiff. There was no need for the document to have been in its final authorized form at the moment of signature. Ratification could therefore retrospectively validate an otherwise defective transaction.

However, this may not be the rule for all signed documents. The question of ratifi-  **6.05** cation of deeds was highlighted a few years ago when Underhill, J, in *R (on the application of Mercury Tax Group Ltd) v HM Commissioners of Revenue & Customs*,[10] delivered a judgment on the execution of documents that caused some ripples in

---

[7] (1848) 2 Exch 167.

[8] The decision is expressed thus in the headnote. Parke, B, in fact, had slight reservations but declined to dissent from his brethren. He felt that this case was not on all-fours with ratification that took place between private individuals because 'if the Crown ratifies an act, the character of the act becomes altered' insofar as it deprives the third party of the double option of suing the agent and the principal, only allowing the former to a remedy '(such as it is)' against the Crown: (1848) 2 Exch 167, 188–9.

[9] [1923] 2 Ch 314.

[10] [2008] EWHC 2721 (Admin); [2009] STC 743.

the City. During the course of an inquiry into tax avoidance schemes, HMRC discovered that relevant deeds had apparently not been duly executed by the claimant's clients. The practice had been for the deeds to be executed whilst they were still in draft form; the all-important signature pages were then transferred and appended to the finalized versions, which often varied significantly from the executed drafts. The claimants suggested that this was standard practice and that, to the extent that the final version of deeds simply filled in the blanks left in the preliminary version, such changes were implicitly authorized. After all, anyone signing a document containing blank spaces must envisage that they will be completed, and such person will be bound so long as the words inserted fall within the scope of what he could reasonably have expected. Underhill, J, however, did not accept this interpretation. Not only was he unsure 'that the evidence establishes that … clients implicitly authorised (or ratified) the change in the identity of the strip as between the draft and final versions of the Option Agreement and Sale and Purchase Agreement.'[11] More importantly, he pointed out that in ratification cases, such as *Koenigsblatt v Sweet*, the document, altered after signature, was the selfsame document as that which the party had originally signed. No decided authority endorsed the practice of taking a signature page from one document and recycling it for use in another. Rather:

> [t]he parties … must be taken to have regarded signature as an essential element in the effectiveness of the documents: that is to be inferred from their form. In such a case I believe that the common understanding is that the document to be signed exists as *a discrete physical entity* (whether in a single version or in a series of counterparts) at the moment of signing. The significance of this is not entirely talismanic (though it would not affect my view even if it were): the requirement that a party sign *an actual existing authoritative version* of the contractual document gives some, albeit not total, *protection against fraud or mistake*.[12]

**6.06** The *Mercury* case, with its insistence on the necessity that the signed deed must be a discrete physical entity, constituting an actual existing authoritative version of the contractual document, and that signature and attestation must be integrated into that same physical document, has perturbed the City. It may predicate a fundamental distinction between the signature of contracts and the execution of deeds. Whether *Mercury* will stand the test of time, or whether counsel's arguments that the instruments of modern technology and the advent of electronic completion demand a more flexible regime, remains to be seen.[13]

---

[11] *Ibid* at [38].

[12] *Ibid* at [39] (emphasis added). Underhill, J additionally pointed out that execution of a deed in this form might not conform with the requirements of the Law of Property (Miscellaneous Provisions) Act 1989, s 1(3).

[13] The *Mercury* case was cited before Vos, J in *Chapman (t/a Chapman & Co Solicitors) v Wilson* [2010] EWHC 1746 (Ch), but distinguished on the facts. It has subsequently been cited, but not applied, in a number of cases.

**A unilateral act of will**

Ratification is a unilateral act of will. There is no requirement that the princi- **6.07** pal notify the agent, or indeed anyone else, that ratification has taken place. As Rowlatt, J explained in *Harrison & Crossfield Ltd v London & North-Western Railway Co*:

> Now, ratification does not rest on estoppel. It need not be communicated to the party alleging it. Ratification is a unilateral act of the will, namely, the approval after the event of the assumption of authority which did not exist at the time. It may be expressed in words or be implied from or involved in acts. It is implied from or involved in acts when you cannot logically analyse the act without imputing such approval to the party, whether his mind in fact approved or disapproved or wholly disregarded the question.[14]

Moore-Bick, J subsequently amplified this point in *Yona International Ltd v La Réunion Française SA*, emphasizing that ratification can sometimes be inferred from the silence or inactivity of the ratifying party:

> The essence of ratification is a decision by the principal to adopt the unauthorized act as his own ... It does not therefore depend on communication with or representation to the third party and is thus in principle distinct from estoppel, but since the intention to ratify must be manifested in some way it will in practice often be communicated to and relied upon by the other party to the transaction. Ratification can no doubt be inferred without difficulty from silence or inactivity in cases where the principal, by failing to disown the transaction, allows a state of affairs to come about which is inconsistent with treating the transaction as unauthorized. That is probably no more than a form of ratification by conduct. Where there is nothing of that kind, however, the position is more difficult since silence or inaction may simply reflect an unwillingness or inability on the part of the principal to commit himself. For that reason it will not usually be sufficient to evidence ratification, nor will it amount to an unequivocal representation sufficient to give rise to an estoppel.[15]

It deserves mention that powers of attorney frequently incorporate so-called **6.08** 'ratification clauses' under which the donor agrees to ratify in advance various acts that the donee of the power may perform. Because the stipulation anticipates the actions of the donee, such clauses do not operate as true cases of ratification. Rather, they will often serve to confer antecedent authority, actual or apparent, on the agent to perform the acts enumerated in the instrument on behalf of the donor.

---

[14] [1917] 2 KB 755, 758.
[15] [1996] 2 Lloyd's Rep 84, 106. It is possible that Christopher Clarke, J has cast doubt on the proposition that ratification need not be communicated to the third party in *Demco Investment & Commercial SA v Interamerican Life Insurance (International) Ltd* [2012] EWHC 2053 (Comm) at [106]: 'It would appear—see *Bowstead on Agency* 2-074—that the ratification does not need to be communicated to the third party. It is not, however, necessary to decide this.'

# Who May Ratify

**Only the person in whose name and on whose behalf the 'agent' has purported to act may ratify**

**6.09** It is of the essence of ratification that at the time when he carried out the transaction the 'agent' purported to act on behalf of the principal who subsequently seeks to ratify the unauthorized transaction. In *Keighley, Maxted & Co v Durant*,[16] R, acting outside the scope of his authority, purchased wheat from D. Although R contracted in his own name, R actually intended to make the purchase in the joint names of KM and himself. The following day KM's manager agreed with R to take the wheat on joint account. KM and R subsequently failed to take delivery of the wheat and D was forced to resell it at a loss. D sued KM and R for the loss he had suffered. The House of Lords held that KM had not been entitled to ratify the contract since the agent did not profess to be acting on his behalf at the time of the contract. Civil obligations in English law, as Lord Macnaghten explained in *Keighley, Maxted*, 'are not to be created by, or founded upon, undisclosed intentions'.[17] It is therefore axiomatic that an undisclosed principal may not ratify the unauthorized actions of his agent.[18]

**6.10** In contrast, if an agent falsely declares that he is acting on behalf of a principal, the person named as principal is entitled to ratify the contract into which the agent has purported to enter on his behalf. In *Re Tiedermann and Ledermann Frères*[19] V, acting as an agent under a power of attorney, sold some wheat on behalf of P. However, when V saw the price of wheat begin to rise V bought it back and re-sold it the selfsame day at a profit, purporting to act for P but in reality speculating on his own behalf. Third parties became suspicious of V's activities. The price of wheat began to fall and the third parties repudiated their contracts. At this point P, the nominal 'principal', sought to ratify V's unauthorized transactions. Channell, J held that P was entitled to do so. The fact that the buyers had repudiated their contracts before ratification took place was not to the point.[20] Nor was the fact that the agent had acted fraudulently in falsely asserting that he was selling the wheat on P's behalf. V had assumed to act for P, and from a third party's viewpoint the contract, from the outset, had been concluded with P. It could be said that even if P did receive a windfall, third parties were not actually disadvantaged. Channell, J's only reservation was that, had it

---

[16] [1901] AC 240.
[17] *Ibid* at 247.
[18] See further, **chapter 10**. Cp Rochvarg, *Ratification and Undisclosed Principals* (1989) 34 McGill LJ 286.
[19] [1899] 2 QB 66.
[20] *Bolton v Lambert* (1889) 41 ChD 295.

been shown that the principal had been fraudulent too, he might have held that ratification was not permissible.

The only person entitled to ratify is the named party upon whose behalf the agent **6.11** purported to act.[21] Brett, LJ expressed this principle forcibly in *Jones v Hope*:

> If there is one legal principle better established than another it is this, that nobody can ratify a contract purporting to be made by an agent except the party on whose behalf the agent purported to act.[22]

Thus the ratifying principal will be put to proof that the agent 'purported to act' on his behalf, in a representative capacity.[23]

### The principal must have been in existence at the time when the agent purportedly acted on his behalf

This requirement relates to agents acting on behalf of companies. If an agent pur- **6.12** ports to enter into a transaction on behalf of a company prior to its formation, the company may not ratify that transaction once it is incorporated. This rule, formerly set out in the Companies Act 1985, s 36C (as substituted by the Companies Act 1989, s 130(4)), has been retained in s 51(1) of the Companies Act 2006, which similarly provides:

> A contract that purports to be made by or on behalf of a company at a time when the company has not been formed has effect, subject to any agreement to the contrary, as one made with the person purporting to act for the company or as agent for it, and he is personally liable on the contract accordingly.

Section 51(2) adds that the same rules apply to the execution of deeds on behalf of a company pre-incorporation. The agent cannot escape personal liability by the usual expedient of signing 'as agent'. He must actually show that it has been explicitly agreed that his personal liability is not to be engaged. Alternatively, if a company wishes to endorse an unauthorized transaction purportedly effected on its behalf prior to its formation, it is always open to the company to enter into a fresh contract with the third party on the same terms as the original unauthorized deal.[24]

The legislation refers only to the agent incurring personal liability under contracts **6.13** entered into on behalf of a company prior to its incorporation. Does an agent also

---

[21] *Heath v Chilton* (1844) 12 M&W 632.

[22] (1880) 3 TLR 247n, 251.

[23] A situation in which ratification may take place cannot therefore be inferred from the simple fact that the agent is the agent of a particular principal. As Hildyard, J said in *Edenwest Ltd v CMS Cameron McKenna (a firm)* [2012] EWHC 1258 (Ch); [2013] BCC 152 at [128], 'It is a fallacy to assume that everything that a person who happens to be an agent does is done in the capacity of agent and with the intention and effect of binding his principal.'

[24] *In re Empress Engineering Co* (1880) 16 ChD 125, 128 *per* Sir George Jessel, MR; *Howard v Patent Ivory Manufacturing Co* (1888) 38 ChD 156, 164 *per* Kay, J.

acquire rights under such a contract? Although the Companies Act 2006, like its predecessor, is silent on this point, it has been held in *Braymist Ltd v Wise Finance Ltd* [25] that under the 1985 Act not only does the agent incur personal liability if he acts on behalf of a company before it has been formed, but by implication the Act also confers upon the agent a right to enforce such a contract. The statute was originally introduced in order to implement the 1968 Company Law Directive and thereby to protect third parties. Allowing the agent to enforce unauthorized transactions is simply an extension of this policy, and is neither unworkable nor unfair. [26]

**6.14** The rule only applies to companies prior to their incorporation. Therefore, s 51 has no application in a situation where an agent has acted on behalf of a company which formerly existed but which has been dissolved prior to the agent's purporting to enter into a transaction on its behalf. In such a case the agent cannot be said to have been acting on behalf of a company that has not been formed. The company has been incorporated, but simply ceased to exist. [27]

**6.15** The Companies Act 2006 applies only to non-existent companies, *stricto sensu*. Therefore, the principle under which an agent's personal liability is engaged has no application in cases where the agent acts on behalf of an existing but misnamed company. In *Coral (UK) Ltd v Rechtman and Altro Mozart Food Handels Gmbh*, [28] for example, following corporate restructuring the director of a German trading subsidiary innocently used the German company group's old name when contracting for the sale of a quantity of sugar on behalf of the subsidiary. The court declined to impose personal liability on the director after the subsidiary failed to perform the contract. Potter, J held that on the facts, even though the company group had been misnamed, there was ample evidence to show that the contract was intended exclusively to bind the third party and the subsidiary company, and the latter was declared liable as principal upon the contract. [29]

### The principal must have been competent to perform at the time that the agent purportedly acted on his behalf

**6.16** Because ratification relates back to the time when the agent purported to act on the principal's behalf, it is a requirement that the principal would have been

---

[25] [2002] Ch 273.

[26] As Etheridge, J explained at first instance, 'there is nothing objectionable, from a European perspective, in a construction of s 36C(1) which both gives effect to the purpose of the Directive by protecting third parties dealing with persons acting on behalf of a non-existent company, but also confers corresponding obligations on those third parties … [W]here the wording of a statute fairly permits an interpretation which is consistent with mutuality, and is not otherwise unworkable, that would be a consideration in favour of such an interpretation': (2001) 2 March, LexisNexis transcript, at [25].

[27] *Cotronic (UK) Ltd v Dezonie* [1991] BCLC 721.

[28] [1996] 1 Lloyd's Rep 235.

[29] See also *Oshkosh B'gosh Inc v Dan Marbel Inc Ltd* [1989] BCLC 507.

competent to perform that act himself at that time.[30] A clear example of this principle at work is furnished by the case of an agent acting on behalf of an alien enemy. In *Boston Deep Sea Fishing & Ice Co Ltd v Farnham (Inspector of Taxes)*[31] an English company which owned trawlers took control of a trawler belonging to a French company in which the English company owned a share. The trawler in question happened to be in an English port at the moment when France fell to Germany during the Second World War. After the conclusion of hostilities the French company purported to ratify all the English company's actions. Harman, J held that since, at the time when the English company acted, the French company was an alien enemy at common law, it was not a competent principal. As such, the French company could not have performed the acts carried out by the agent and the French company's subsequent ratification was neither valid nor operative. A similar outcome would arise if an unauthorized agent purported to act on behalf of someone who, at the relevant time, lacked the necessary mental capacity to perform the act himself.

It will now be seen that, as Wright, J made clear in *Firth v Staines*: **6.17**

> To constitute a valid ratification three conditions must be satisfied: first, the agent whose act is sought to be ratified must have purported to act for the principal; second, at the time the act was done the agent must have had a competent principal; and, thirdly, at the time of the ratification the principal must have been legally capable of doing the act himself.[32]

### The principal must have been capable of being ascertained at the time when the act was done

An agent may sometimes act without prior authority on behalf of unnamed principals. As Willes, J explained in *Watson v Swann*, in these circumstances: **6.18**

> To entitle a person to sue upon a contract, it must clearly be shown that he himself made it, or that it was made on his behalf by an agent authorised to act for him at the time, or whose act has subsequently been ratified and adopted by him. The law obviously requires that the person for whom the agent professes to act must be a person capable of being ascertained at the time. It is not necessary that he should be

---

[30] Although of limited relevance in the commercial domain, infants used to furnish a typical example of this principle at work. If the infant possessed the capacity to perform an act at the time the agent unauthorizedly acted on his behalf—for example, a contract for necessaries—the infant might ratify. If the agent's act fell foul of the Infants Relief Act 1874, ratification was no longer possible. The Minors' Contracts Act 1987 has altered the situation. Whilst an infant has capacity to enter into contracts for necessaries, contracts of employment and other contracts adjudged beneficial, as well as contracts for marriage, company shares and partnerships, other contracts are not binding upon the infant unless they are ratified upon his reaching his majority. Whilst an adult cannot enforce a contract against an infant, the latter is entitled to enforce his contracts against adult contracting parties, who are not permitted to plead the infant's incapacity.

[31] [1957] 3 All ER 204.

[32] [1897] 2 QB 70, 75.

named; but there must be such a description of him as shall amount to a reasonable designation of the person intended to be bound by the contract.[33]

From this declaration it would appear that ratification is restricted to situations where it can be shown that the third party's expectations are met, in the sense that the third party either knew or had the means of knowing with whom the agent was drawing him into contractual relations. In *Watson v Swann* itself an insurance broker received instructions to effect an open policy for £5,000 for the plaintiff against jettison only, 'subject to declaration thereafter'. Because he was unable to do so, the broker declared certain deck cargo shipped for Ostend on board one of the plaintiff's vessels on the back of a general policy which he had previously effected for himself 'upon any kind of goods and merchandise, as interest might appear.' The policy was initialled by the underwriters. A loss having occurred, it was held that the plaintiff could not maintain an action against the underwriters upon the policy owing to the fact that the contract had not been made by him or on his behalf at the relevant time. At the time that the agent had made the contract the plaintiff was not even known to him.

**6.19** This case might suggest that as a general rule a valid ratification is dependent upon the principal having been capable of ascertainment at the time when the unauthorized agent performed the act the principal is seeking to ratify. The position, however, may not be so clear-cut. As was pointed out in *Southern Water Authority v Carey*, the remarks of Erle, J 'may be *obiter dicta* but they have been accepted for 100 years as expressing the basic principle. To such principle there may well be limited exceptions in the law of marine insurance ... and no doubt where there is a fiduciary relationship.'[34]

**6.20** It is not unusual for agents to enter into agreements on behalf of unnamed principals. Sometimes, as a matter of evidence, it can be demonstrated that these unnamed principals were the intended beneficiaries of unauthorized transactions entered into on their behalf by the agent. Marine insurance policies have regularly been taken out on such terms as 'for the benefit of all those to whom they may appertain.' In *Hagedorn v Oliverson*,[35] for example, it was held that where the plaintiff had taken out an insurance on a ship in his own name as well as for and in the name of all and every person interested in it, etc, in the usual form, any such person could subsequently ratify the policy and sue the underwriters. As Lord Ellenborough, CJ explained, the policy explicitly stated that the plaintiff had a right to effect an insurance, on the chance of its being adopted, for the

---

[33] (1862) 11CBNS 756, 771.
[34] [1985] 2 All ER 1077, 1084 *per* HHJ David Smout, QC. For an example of the principal being permitted to ratify the unauthorized acts of a trustee, see *Lyell v Kennedy* (1889) 14 App Cas 437.
[35] (1814) 2 M&S 485.

benefit of all those to whom it might appertain. The plaintiff, therefore, might insure for those who were actually interested, and possibly for those who might be interested. Nor did it matter that the ratification took place after the loss had occurred for, as was later explained, 'where an agent effects an insurance subject to ratification, the loss insured against is very likely to happen before ratification, and it must be taken that the insurance so effected involves that possibility as the basis of the contract.'[36]

These principles have since been extended to other forms of insurance. In **6.21** *National Oilwells (UK) Ltd v Davy Offshore Ltd*,[37] Colman, J stated the rule in the following form:

> Where at the time when the contract of insurance was made the principal assured or other contracting party had no actual authority to bind the other party to the contract of insurance, but the policy is expressed to insure not only the principal assured but also a class of others who are not identified in that policy, a party who at the time when the policy was effected could have been ascertained to qualify as a member of that class can ratify and sue on the policy as co-assured if at that time it was intended by the principal assured or other contracting party to create privity of contract with the insurers on behalf of that particular party.[38]

It will be a question of proof in each individual case. As Colman, J proceeded to explain, 'evidence as to whether in any particular case the principal assured or other contracting party did have the requisite intention may be provided by the terms of the policy itself, by the terms of any contract between the principal assured or other contracting party and the alleged co-assured or by any other admissible material showing what was subjectively intended by the principal assured.'[39] This necessarily means that if the ratifying party is someone who qualifies as a beneficiary after the agent has entered into the transaction, that party will not be permitted to ratify. In an Australian case where an insurance policy was taken out on behalf of a named party and 'all its subsidiary associate and related companies, all contractors and subcontractors and/or suppliers', a subcontractor who was appointed a year later was held not to be entitled to ratify and sue on that policy.[40]

---

[36] *Jardine v Leathley* (1863) 3 B&S 700, 764-5. See also *Williams v North China Insurance Co* (1876) 1 CPD 757. This rule, it seems, applies to non-marine insurance, too: *National Oilwells (UK) Ltd v Davy Offshore Ltd* [1993] 2 Lloyd's Rep 582, 608 *per* Colman, J: 'It is undesirable that different rules should apply to [different] classes of insurance and that in the absence of binding or compelling authority to the contrary the English Courts should take a different view on a question of principle in insurance law from the views already established in other common law jurisdictions.'

[37] [1993] 2 Lloyd's Rep 582.

[38] *Ibid* at 596–7.

[39] *Ibid* at 597.

[40] *Trident General Insurance Co Ltd v McNiece Bros Pty Ltd* (1987) 8 NSWLR 270.

## Full Knowledge of All Material Circumstances

### Apparently ratificatory conduct can be vitiated by want of knowledge

**6.22**  What might otherwise appear to be conduct amounting to ratification of an agent's unauthorized act may be vitiated by want of knowledge. There is a requirement that the principal must have ratified in full knowledge of all the material circumstances in which the act was done. Waller, J stated this requirement crisply in *Suncorp Insurance and Finance v Milano Assicurazioni SpA*:

> In order that a person may be held to have ratified an act done without his authority, it is necessary that at the time of the ratification, he should have full knowledge of all the material circumstances in which the act was done, unless he intended to ratify and take the risk whatever the circumstances may have been.[41]

Endorsing a passage in *Bowstead*, Waller, J went on to state that this principle, which is designed to protect the principal from being held too readily to have ratified his agent's unauthorized acts, is less strictly applied in the contractual context than it is in the tortious context.[42] This is said to be the case because both the courts' objective approach to the interpretation of contractual situations and the underlying notion that one can be taken to know matters of which one might be anticipated to be aware operate in the contractual context, permitting ratification to be inferred in situations where such would not be the case in the law of tort.[43]

**6.23**  The key question is: how much does the principal actually need to know? In *SEB Trygg Holding Aktiebolag v Manches Sprecher Grier Halberstam* Gloster, J characterized this as 'a fact-specific inquiry, which is necessarily dependent upon the specific circumstances of any case.'[44] Sometimes it will be sufficient to look to the principal's actual state of knowledge; in other cases, it may be appropriate to consider what could, or should, have been known to him. Generally speaking, Toulson, J declared in *ING Re (UK) Ltd v R&V Versicherung AG*:

> If a principal knows the essentials of what happened as between the agent and the third party, … I find it difficult to see as a matter of justice and principle why that should not be sufficient knowledge for the purposes of ratification of the agent's conduct *vis-à-vis* the third party.[45]

**6.24**  This requirement may pose certain difficulties. Sometimes the principal may not actually know or even be in a position to discover speedily whether the

---

[41] [1993] 2 Lloyd's Rep 225, 234.
[42] *Ibid* at 234.
[43] See *Bowstead & Reynolds on Agency* (2014: London, Sweet & Maxwell) 20th ed, by Watts, para 2-070.
[44] [2005] 2 Lloyd's Rep 129 at [133].
[45] [2006] 2 All ER (Comm) 870 at [153].

agent acted without authority and, therefore, whether ratification is necessary to validate the transaction. In most cases, of course, this will not be a problem. Difficulties may arise where an unauthorized act has been performed on behalf of a complex organization, or where the agent has acted fraudulently and covered his tracks, or where there is an inadequate documentary record of the transaction, or where files have gone missing, or where the principal cannot quickly work out who in the organization handled the transaction in question. In such situations, where the principal is aware of what his purported agent has done but does not know whether the act was authorized, Toulson, J could not see that such circumstances should operate to the detriment of the third party. Adopting the general approach advocated by Steyn, LJ in *First Energy (UK) Ltd v Hungarian International Bank Ltd* that the 'moulding force' of the English law of contract is 'that the reasonable expectations of reasonable men must be protected',[46] Toulson, J noted that:

> Dealing with an agent carries risks, because the agent may not have the authority which he claims, but where a party deals honestly with an agent whose principal goes ahead with the transaction with knowledge of what the agent has ostensibly done on the principal's behalf, his reasonable expectation would surely be that the principal would be bound by the transaction.[47]

He added: 'Entirely different considerations would apply if the party dealing with the agent was not acting honestly but was involved in fraudulent conduct by the agent.'[48]

In *SEB Trygg Holding Aktiebolag v Manches Sprecher Grier Halberstam*[49] the princi-  **6.25**
pal was aware that the agent had entered into a quota share treaty on behalf of the principal with the third party and, in Gloster, J's view in this particular case, that was sufficient knowledge of the transaction for the purposes of ratification. In contrast, in *Sea Emerald SA v Prominvestbank—Joint Stockpoint Commercial Industrial and Investment Bank*, where a shipping company unsuccessfully claimed under a refund guarantee which had been signed by the employee of a bank in respect of a ship construction contract between a shipyard (which was a client of the bank) and the shipping company, Andrew Smith, J held that whereas there was evidence that the bank's head office in Kiev was aware of the lending to the bank and of the contracts between the group and the shipyard, it had not been shown that the chairman and the board of management actually knew of the terms of those contracts and, more particularly, were content to adopt the guarantee, whatever its terms.[50]

---

[46] [1993] 2 Lloyd's Rep 194, 196.
[47] *ING Re (UK) Ltd v R&V Versicherung AG* [2006] 2 All ER (Comm) 870 at [156].
[48] *Ibid* at [156].
[49] [2005] 2 Lloyd's Rep 129.
[50] [2008] EWHC 1979 (Comm) esp at [104].

## What Constitutes Ratification

### Ratification may be express or implied, and may be by words or conduct

**6.26** Ratification occurs whenever the ratifying party clearly manifests that he has adopted the unauthorized transaction effected by the agent purportedly on his behalf. There is no requirement that this intention must be communicated either to the third party or to the agent. Express ratification is self-explanatory.[51] Implied ratification, however, will take place where either the conduct of the principal or the surrounding circumstances invite the inference that the principal has endorsed the agent's conduct. Thus, in *The Bonita, The Charlotte*,[52] Lushington, J suggested *obiter* that if a master sold his vessel without the owner's authority, but the latter pocketed the proceeds of sale in full knowledge of the circumstances in which the ship was sold, such receipt could constitute ratification of the master's unauthorized act. In *Hogan v London Irish RFC Trading Ltd* [53] the defendant rugby club's chief coach and director of rugby, who had been expressly informed that he had no authority to enter into binding agreements with players without the agreement of the club's board, was held not only to have had apparent authority to enter into oral agreements on the club's behalf with players as to the basic terms of their contracts but also to have had his actions ratified since the club had then allowed the claimants to represent the club and to turn up for training sessions, and had continued to pay them at the rate agreed with the chief coach.

**6.27** Whether ratification can be inferred from the conduct of the putative principal will be fact-sensitive in each individual case. In *English v English*,[54] for example, the claimant's son entered into various loan agreements and a charge on his mother's house, purportedly acting on behalf of the latter. Although the son had done this by forging his mother's signature, the court held that the mother's conduct, once she became aware of these transactions, amounted to acceptance that the loans and charge were binding upon her. The mother had wished to help her son and to conceal his forgeries from her other children. In conversation she had promised a payment and asked to amend the payment date, and later had made arrangements to make a payment of £900 towards the arrears as well as discussing the application of the proceeds of a claim which her son had made under a PPI policy, all in the context of avoiding an order for possession.

---

[51] Whether ratification has actually occurred will still be a question of construction: *Bao Xiang International Garment Centre v British Airways plc* [2015] EWHC 3071 (Ch); [2016] CP Rep 8 at [22]–[25] *per* Rose J.

[52] (1861) 1 Lush 252.

[53] (1999) 20 December (QBD).

[54] [2010] EWHC 2058 (Ch).

These circumstances offered some indication that the claimant regarded the loans as binding on her. On their own, however, they might not have sufficed. But, when coupled with the fact that the claimant had instructed her conveyancing solicitors about the existence of the loans and the fact that they were secured on the property, and had caused those solicitors to pay the amount necessary to redeem the charge on sale, without protest and without even seeking their advice on whether she was actually liable to pay, her conduct went 'beyond acquiescence and [amounted] to a positive acceptance of the binding effect of the charge and loan agreements on the claimant'.[55] To take one further example, in *OPM Property Services Ltd v Venner*[56] a vendor refused to execute a sale of his house on the ground that his agent had acted without authority and that the contract was therefore unenforceable. The court, however, held that the defendant had, on the evidence, clearly and unequivocally approved the exchange of contracts and had been in possession of all the material facts when he ratified the contract. One item of evidence which weighed with the court was that after the property had remained unsold for a long period, *inter alia* on hearing news that his estate agent had sold it at last, the vendor went round to the agent's office with a bottle of champagne.

### Is acquiescence or inactivity on the part of the 'principal' sufficient?

Normally, the principal will need to do something positive which will allow the **6.28** court to conclude that either expressly or impliedly he has ratified the contract entered into by the agent. Sometimes, however, the principal's silence or acquiescence may be sufficient to imply ratification on the part of the principal. A party's silence or acquiescence may be ambivalent, signalling either a willingness to adopt the agent's unauthorized act or a reluctance to do so. As a Canadian judge once remarked:

> Silence and inactivity are not evidence of approval and adoption of the contract but rather of disquiet, disapproval and ignorance of rights, and in the case of one of [the three children involved in the case], lack of knowledge that a contract has been made.[57]

However, Waller, J made clear in *Suncorp Insurance & Finance v Milano Assicurazioni SpA*, when determining whether ratification has occurred 'mere acquiescence or

---

[55] *Ibid* at [54] *per* HHJ David Cooke, QC. In contrast, in *Swotbooks.com Ltd v Royal Bank of Scotland plc* [2011] EWHC 2025 (QB) the court found that ratification had not taken place precisely because certain accounting entries did not supply unequivocal evidence of Swotbook's intention to ratify. Adopting Rowlatt, J's test in *Harrisons & Crossfield Ltd v London & North-Western Rly Co* [1917] 2 KB 755, 758, the court stated that ratification will only be held to have occurred 'when you cannot logically analyse the act without imputing ... approval'.

[56] [2003] EWHC 427 (Ch).

[57] *713860 Ontario Ltd v Royal Trust Corporation of Canada* (1996) 22 January *per* Wilson J, unreported (Ontario).

inactivity may be sufficient.'[58] It will be a question in each individual case of determining whether the only reasonable inference to draw in all the circumstances is that the principal ratified his agent's transaction. As Waller, J went on to explain:[59]

> It seems to me that it should not be open to a principal, who to the outside world by his conduct, or that of his duly authorized agents, appears to have adopted a transaction to be able to prove subjectively that in fact he had not, any more than such a principal would be able to prove subjectively that he did not intend to adopt a transaction when he does an act, eg accepts the payment of money, which objectively adopts the transaction.[59]

In this sense, although not identical thereto, ratification is not entirely dissimilar from estoppel. It is a matter of construing the objective character of the principal's conduct as it appears to the outside world, and a principal cannot defeat the inference by stating that, contrary to outward appearances, he did not intend to adopt the transaction.[60] If, therefore, the principal had reservations about a transaction purportedly effected in his name by the unauthorized agent but he did not communicate them to the third party, ratification will nevertheless be inferred where that is the objective appearance to the outside world of the principal's conduct:

> A time must come when whatever reservations a principal is making internally, it is just too late to take issue as to the extent of an agent's authority. It is not an estoppel case, but where it is known to the principal that the other contracting party is acting on the basis and incurring expenditure on the basis that the extent of the principal's authority is as being stated by the agent, and he does nothing to correct that impression, ratification will be inferred.[61]

**6.29** If an outsider ought to have attributed the principal's silence or apparent acquiescence to causes other than an intention to adopt the transaction, ratification will not be held to have taken place. In *SEB Trygg Holding Aktiebolag v Manches Sprecher Grier Halberstam*, for instance, Gloster, J concluded that silence on the part of the defendant did not signify ratification but more realistically could be ascribed to its uncertainty. The parties' relationship was one of considerable complexity. In these circumstances, 'if in such a state of unsureness [the defendant] had done any positive act by way of performance of the treaty without expressly reserving its position, it would have ratified the treaty, but it did nothing.'[62] Similarly, in *Sea Emerald SA v Prominvestbank-Joint Stockpoint Commercial Industrial and Investment Bank* Andrew Smith, J could not discern an unequivocal manifestation of an intention to ratify and concluded that a bank's inactivity could not be interpreted as ratification

---

58 [1993] 2 Lloyd's Rep 225, 234.
59 *Ibid* at 235.
60 *Ibid* at 235.
61 *Suncorp Insurance & Finance v Milano Assicurazioni SpA* [1993] 2 Lloyd's Rep 225, 241.
62 [2005] EWHC 35 (Comm) at [162].

of a refund guarantee in respect of a ship construction contract signed by one of the bank's employees because this was:

> not a case in which the purported principal remained silent in the context of continuing dealings or exchanges with the other contracting party ... [S]ilence about the guarantee is in the circumstances no less explicable by a belief that the buyer was unlikely to call upon it, not least perhaps in light of government assurances of support for the [shipyard] and for the group's contracts with it, and that it could only cause unnecessary difficulty to renounce the guarantee than by a decision tacitly to adopt it.[63]

### A principal may be permitted to ratify even though at first he declined to do so

Sometimes a principal initially will refuse to ratify unauthorized acts performed **6.30** nominally on his behalf, but later may change his mind and seek to ratify. The principal is allowed to do so and to take the benefit of the contract, provided that it does not operate unfairly to the third party. Assuming that ratification takes place within a reasonable time,[64] if the third party is unaware of the principal's initial refusal to ratify, the principal may acquire rights under the contract with the third party.[65] On the other hand, if the principal has at first led the third party to believe that he will not ratify and the latter has acted to his prejudice, then the principal will not later be allowed to ratify. In contrast, in cases where the third party is seeking to hold the principal liable on the transaction, since prejudice to the third party will be absent subsequent ratification by the principal is permissible.

### A principal may ratify through an agent

In the same manner that a principal may authorize an agent to perform other acts **6.31** on his behalf, he may also authorize an agent to ratify on his behalf an act that previously was unauthorized. The agent may have express authority to ratify, or actual implied authority, or just apparent authority to do so.[66]

### Factors to which courts will have regard

The case law reveals that the courts identify several factors as important when deter- **6.32** mining whether or not ratification has actually taken place.

- Ratification of part of the transaction may be held to constitute ratification of the entire transaction. Although ratification will typically be an all-or-nothing

---

[63] [2008] EWHC 1979 (Comm) esp at [105].

[64] See discussion of the rule in *Bolton v Lambert* at para **6.35**.

[65] *Simpson v Eggington* (1855) 10 Exch 845.

[66] *SEB Trygg Holding Aktiebolag v Manches Sprecher Grier Halberstam* [2005] 2 Lloyd's Rep 129 at [97(viii)] *per* Gloster, J.

decision on the part of the principal,[67] sometimes ratification of part only of a transaction may be held to amount to ratification of the whole transaction. In *Re Mawcon Ltd* a provisional liquidator did not authorize directors to hire lorries for the company's earth-moving business. He did however bring into his accounts money earned by use of the lorries. Pennycuick, J held:

> It is well established that a ratification may be implied from conduct. It is further well established that the adoption of part of a transaction operates as ratification of the whole transaction. A principal cannot pick out of a transaction those acts which are to his advantage. If he ratifies at all he must ratify *cum onere*.[68]

- Once the principal has adopted his agent's unauthorized transaction, he may not change his mind and resile from the ratification.[69]
- In the case of silence or acquiescence on the part of the principal, ratification will be more readily inferred where there is a pre-existing relationship of principal and agent. This is because a principal who authorizes an agent (to any extent) puts himself at risk as to that agent's acts and will be bound by them.[70]
- The principal is not allowed to wait and see whether the transaction is actually advantageous to him before deciding whether to approve it.[71]
- Lapse of time is relevant to whether an inference may be drawn that ratification has occurred. The longer the principal simply stands by and does nothing, while action is taken by the contracting third party (and indeed by others) under a false impression as to the agent's authority, the more compelling the inference of ratification becomes. And this is irrespective of whether the principal came under any positive duty to speak.[72]

*Ratification of deeds*

**6.33** Generally speaking, a party seeking to ratify a deed does not have to observe any formality. Just as a principal may give oral authority to an agent to execute a written contract, so too even ratification of a written contract does not need to be in writing. Transactions that must be effected by deed, it would seem, constitute the sole exception. Just as a principal's authority to execute a deed is required to be in the form of a deed, ratification of an unauthorized deed must also be executed by deed. If the transaction did not actually need to be executed by deed, however, there is old authority indicating that the deed will be treated

---

[67] 'A party wishing to ratify a transaction must adopt it in its entirety': *Smith v Henniker-Major & Co (a firm)* [2003] Ch 182 at [56] *per* Robert Walker, LJ.

[68] [1969] 1 WLR 78, 83.

[69] *SEB Trygg Holding Aktiebolag v Manches Sprecher Grier Halberstam* [2005] 2 Lloyd's Rep 129 at [97(ix)(b)] *per* Gloster, J.

[70] [2005] 2 Lloyd's Rep 129 at [97(ix)(c)] *per* Gloster, J.

[71] *Ibid* at [97(ix)(d)] *per* Gloster, J.

[72] *Suncorp Insurance & Finance v Milano Assicurazion SpA* [1993] 2 Lloyd's Rep 225, 235.

as an ordinary written instrument and that parol ratification may be treated as valid.[73]

## No Unfair Prejudice to Third Party

Ratification operates retrospectively, enabling a principal to 'so extend his rights **6.34** by seeking an advantage for himself beyond any that he would have in the absence of ratification'[74] that, were ratification to be applied to its logical limits, it could unduly prejudice third parties. To take a straightforward case, if A purports to accept on P's behalf a contractual offer made by T, is T at liberty to revoke his offer at any time before P ratifies the unauthorized transaction? Under the general principles of the law of contract an offeror is normally free to revoke his offer at any time prior to acceptance by the offeree. In the case of transactions effected by unauthorized agents, however, T may not do so although the agent's act may not ultimately be ratified. A is not the offeree as T always intended to contract with P. P is not the offeree until he ratifies the transaction because initially he will know nothing about it. But once P does ratify, because ratification has retrospective effect the legal effect is to make it appear that the contract was entered into with P from the outset. It can thus be seen that conventional contractual principles do not apply in this situation: T is bound and cannot revoke his offer, whereas P is not bound until such time as he elects to ratify. If P does ratify, then there is held to be a contract between P and T, which will operate as though the parties had been agreed from the moment that A accepted T's offer, ostensibly on P's behalf. P will be entitled to sue and be sued on this contract. On the other hand, if P chooses not to ratify A's action, T has no remedy save to sue A for breach of his warranty of authority.[75]

### The supposed rule in *Bolton v Lambert*

This situation arose in the celebrated case of *Bolton Partners v Lambert*.[76] The de- **6.35** fendant submitted an offer to acquire a lease to the plaintiffs' agent, S. S, who had no authority to do so, purported to accept the defendant's offer on the plaintiffs' behalf. The defendant then withdrew his offer. Only after the defendant's attempted withdrawal from the sale did the plaintiffs seek to ratify what S had agreed to in their name. The Court of Appeal granted the plaintiffs specific performance on the ground that their ratification related back to S's acceptance of the defendant's

---

[73] *Hunter v Parker* (1840) 7 M&W 322, 343–4 *per* Parke, B.
[74] *Kaupthing Singer & Friedlander Ltd (in administration) v UBS AG* [2014] EWHC 2450 (Comm) at [72] *per* Andrew Smith, J.
[75] See **chapter** 7.
[76] (1889) LR 41 ChD 295.

offer. The defendant's attempted withdrawal from the transaction, therefore, was inoperative.

**6.36**  It had been pointed out in the past, in *Hagedorn v Oliverson*, how favourable such a rule could be to the principal who, unlike the third party, until ratification occurs is not bound but still retains the option whether or not to adopt what had been done in his name.[77] In *Bolton Partners v Lambert* Cotton, LJ reasoned:

> Of course the [defendant's] withdrawal could not be effective, if it were made after the contract had become complete … The rule as to ratification by a principal of acts done by an assumed agent is that the ratification is thrown back to the date of the act done, and that the agent is put in the same position as if he had had authority to do the act at the time the act was done by him.[78]

Lindley, LJ expressed the point even more forcibly:

> It is not a question whether a mere offer can be withdrawn, but the question is whether, when there has been in fact an acceptance which is in form an acceptance by a principal through his agent, though the person assuming to act as agent has not then been so authorized, there can or cannot be a withdrawal of the offer before the ratification of the acceptance? I can find no authority in the books to warrant the contention that an offer made, and in fact accepted by a principal through an agent or otherwise, can be withdrawn. The true view on the contrary appears to be that the doctrine as to the retrospective action of ratification is applicable.[79]

**6.37**  Because it is perceived that ratification can operate unfairly to third parties, the putative principal's right to ratify has been restricted in a number of ways. The case law is complex, even contradictory, and has generated a considerable literature.[80] Of late, however, the Court of Appeal has sought to clarify matters. Most significantly, it has taken to declaring that 'ratification is not effective where to permit it would unfairly prejudice a third party'.[81] This general principle, that third parties are not to be unduly prejudiced, manifests itself in a number of recognized exceptions and propositions.

---

[77]  (1814) 2 M&S 485, 490 *per* Lord Ellenborough, CJ; *Ancona v Marks* (1862) 7 H&N 686.

[78]  (1889) LR 41 ChD 295, 306.

[79]  *Ibid* at 308–9. Lopes, LJ also remarked, 'To hold otherwise would be to deprive the doctrine of ratification of its retrospective effect. To use the words of Martin, B in *Brook v Hook* (1871) LR 6 Ex 89, the ratification would not be "dragged back as it were, and made equipollent to a prior command".'

[80]  Eg, Tan, '*The Principle in* Bird v Brown *Revisited*' (2001) 117 LQR 626.

[81]  *The Owners of the 'Borvigilant'* [2003] 2 Lloyd's Rep 520 at [70] *per* Clarke, LJ. This general principle, borrowed from *Bowstead & Reynolds*, had previously been adopted by Robert Walker, LJ in *Smith v Henniker-Major & Co* [2003] Ch 182 at [71]: 'In my view, the right approach would be to regard the deprivation of an accrued right as an important example of the general rationale identified in *Bowstead and Reynolds'* Article 19—that is, unfair prejudice.'

### Ratification must take place within a reasonable time

A general principle that is often invoked is that, if it is to take effect, ratification **6.38** must take place within a reasonable time. The longer a third party's rights are held in suspense, the greater the likelihood of injustice. In *Re Portuguese Consolidated Copper Mines Ltd*[82] the board of a company made an invalid allotment of shares at a meeting on 24 October 1888. Although one allottee failed to pay for his shares and another paid under protest, neither took action to withdraw their applications or to repudiate the transaction. Exactly two months later the company sued the first allottee for monies owed, and at subsequent meetings in January and March 1889 confirmed the allotments informally (by signature of the minutes of the original meeting), and then formally. A powerful Court held that the ratification of the original invalid transaction had been made within a reasonable time. Bowen, LJ stated the principle with customary clarity:

> [A]s it is an election, it must take place within a reasonable time, and the standard of reasonableness must depend upon the circumstances of the case.[83]

Cotton, LJ accepted that, had it been made out by the allottee, any 'considerable alteration in the position and prospects of the company' would potentially have been a relevant consideration in determining whether or not ratification had taken place within a reasonable time.

The self-same principle was invoked in *Metropolitan Asylums Board Managers v* **6.39** *Kingham & Sons*.[84] On 18 September the defendants tendered to supply eggs at a given price over a period of months in response to an advertisement placed by a manager of the asylum. The supply contract was to commence on 30 September. On 22 September, at a meeting of the board of the asylum, the defendants' offer was accepted but, through inadvertence, the corporation's seal was not affixed. A clerk nevertheless wrote on the same day informing the defendants that their offer had been accepted. On 24 September the defendants wrote to the asylum withdrawing their offer on the grounds that they had miscalculated and stated the wrong price in their tender. Only on 6 October did the asylum board meet again and ratify the transaction and affix the corporate seal. It was held that the plaintiff in this case could not rely upon *Bolton v Lambert* as ratification had not taken place within a reasonable time:

> If ratification is to bind, it must be made within a reasonable time after acceptance by an unauthorised person.[85]

---

[82] (1890) 45 ChD 16. This has been described as 'the most important English authority in support of this statement of principle': *Smith v Henniker-Major & Co* [2003] Ch 182 at [63] *per* Robert Walker, LJ.

[83] (1890) 45 ChD 16, 34. See also p 37 *per* Cotton, LJ and p 31 *per* Lindley, LJ.

[84] (1890) 6 TLR 217.

[85] *Ibid* at 218. In *Re Portuguese Consolidated Copper Mines Ltd* (1890) LR 45 ChD 16, at p 31 Lindley, LJ made the additional point: 'Of course the principal cannot by his agent ratify what that

### Agreements subject to ratification by the principal

**6.40**  *Bolton Partners v Lambert* has no application if the agent's offer is made expressly
subject to ratification by the principal. If an agent makes clear that the contractual
offer he is extending to the third party on behalf of the principal is conditional
upon ratification by the latter, *Bolton Partners v Lambert* will have no application.
Thus, in *Watson v Davies*[86] D wrote to the board of a charity offering to sell certain
property to the board for £6,500. The board arranged to inspect the property and
sent a deputation to do so. D was told that all members of the board present had
resolved to buy the property, and that they could carry the necessary resolution,
and they purported to accept the defendant's offer subject to a formal meeting.
The secretary of the charity, however, pointed out the deputation was not quorate
and could not act as a properly constituted board. The secretary duly notified
members of the board of a special meeting to be held two days later 'to receive
the report and recommendation of the deputation'. On the day of the meeting D
telegraphed to the secretary cancelling all negotiations. The meeting nevertheless
passed resolutions ratifying the deputation's acceptance of D's offer. The chairman of the board unsuccessfully sought specific performance of the agreement.
Maugham, J held that on the facts the deputation's acceptance of D's offer to sell
was subject to ratification by the board and in such circumstances there is no contract or contractual relation until ratification; the offer may be withdrawn at any
time before ratification. Distinguishing the situation in *Bolton Partners v Lambert*,
Maugham, J stated:

> An acceptance by an agent subject in express terms to ratification by his principal is
> legally a nullity until ratification, and is no more binding on the other party than an
> unaccepted offer which can, of course, be withdrawn before acceptance.[87]

The Privy Council followed this ruling in *Warehousing & Forwarding Company
of East Africa Ltd v Jafferali & Sons Ltd*,[88] where, having found that there was no
concluded agreement as to whether the parties' contract was for a one-year or
a three-year lease, the Board determined that before ratification it was open to
the third party to withdraw. In Lord Guest's words, when the third 'party to the
contract has intimation of the limitation of the agent's authority neither party can
be bound until ratification has been duly intimated to the other [third] party to
the contract'.[89]

---

agent has done; but I never heard, nor do I think it is sound law to say, that a principal cannot employ
one agent to do one thing and another agent to ratify what the other has done.' See also *Suncorp
Insurance and Finance v Milano Assicurazioni SpA* [1993] 2 Lloyd's Rep 225, 235 *per* Waller, J.

[86] [1931] 1 Ch 455.
[87] *Ibid* at 469.
[88] [1964] AC 1.
[89] *Ibid* at 9–10.

### Ratification after expiry of a time limit

**6.41** If the validity of an act is dependent upon its being accomplished within a certain time, ratification taking place outside that period will be ineffective. Clearly, if, for any reason, an assumed principal is required to do something within a fixed period of time, to allow him to ratify an unauthorized transaction outside that period is likely to operate unjustly to the third party. A number of authorities may be said to illustrate the proposition that a third party cannot be disadvantaged in this way. *Bird v Brown*[90] is normally taken to be the leading authority. In that case the defendants had ordered the stoppage *in transitu* of some goods. They purported to act on behalf of the consignor, but possessed no authority to do so. At the time when they ordered the stoppage, had it not been for the master of the ship's wrongful refusal to deliver them up as requested by those acting on behalf of the consignee, the goods would already have been in the hands of the consignee or his trustee in bankruptcy. The consignor proceeded to ratify the agent's unauthorized action. It was held that the ratification was ineffective in this case and could not serve to divest the trustee of his right to possession of the goods: quite simply, at the time of ratification the consignor no longer had the right to ratify the acts of his assumed agent. The exact meaning of the case is contested. It has been claimed to stand for the proposition that the act of ratification must take place at a time, and under circumstances, when the ratifying party might himself have lawfully done the act which he ratifies.[91]

**6.42** *Dibbins v Dibbins*[92] presents a broadly similar factual pattern. Articles of partnership stated that, on the death of either partner, the survivor would have an option to purchase the deceased partner's share. However, he could only do so if he gave notice of such intention within three months of the partner's death. One partner died. The survivor was of unsound mind. Notice of his intention to purchase nevertheless was given on his behalf by his solicitor within three months of the death. Subsequently, an order was made under the Lunacy Acts authorizing a notice to be given on his behalf, and a second notice was given accordingly, but after the three months had expired. On the strength of *Bolton Partners v Lambert* it was argued that under the doctrine of ratification, an option, which had normally to be finally exercised within a limited time, could be properly exercised after that time. Rejecting this contention, Chitty, J held that since the option had not been exercised within the time specified in the articles, there was no contract capable of being confirmed by the second notice. The option, therefore, had not been validly exercised:

> It makes no difference that the person to exercise it was of unsound mind. It is impossible to hold that an unauthorized agent could exercise such

---

[90] (1850) 4 Exch 786.
[91] Eg, *Smith v Henniker-Major & Co (A Firm)* [2003] Ch 182 at [67] *per* Robert Walker, LJ.
[92] [1896] 2 Ch 348.

an option as this so as to bind a person incompetent to exercise the option himself.[93]

These cases might support the view that ratification will not be permitted to take place outside any allotted time limits.

**6.43**   *Bird v Brown*, however, has sometimes been taken to support a slightly different proposition: namely, that 'an estate once vested cannot be divested'—meaning that ratification cannot divest a party of a vested proprietary right. Cotton, LJ had stated matters thus in *Bolton Partners v Lambert*.[94] However, as Clarke, LJ subsequently indicated in *The Owners of the Ship 'Borvigilant'*, Cotton, LJ's view is at odds with the explanation of the rule given by Dillon, LJ in *Presentaciones Musicales SA v Secunda*,[95] which Clarke, LJ preferred.[96] The rival interpretations were discussed in the Court of Appeal in the latter case. In *Presentaciones Musicales* solicitors who were under the mistaken illusion that they enjoyed the requisite authority, issued a writ on behalf of a Panamanian company in April 1988 for breach of agency contracts and breach of copyright in respect of certain recordings of Jimi Hendrix concerts. The breaches related to events as far back as November 1981. In March 1991 the defendant learned that the Panamanian company was in fact in liquidation, having been dissolved in June 1987. The defendant therefore applied to have the action struck out. In May 1991 the Panamanian company's administrators ratified the solicitors' issue of the writ. The Court of Appeal determined that the administrators could validly ratify the solicitors' unauthorized act after the expiry of the three-year limitation period applicable to the cause of action under Panamanian company law.[97] Dillon, LJ reviewed the authorities and suggested that:

> [I]f a time is fixed for doing an act, whether by statute or by agreement, the doctrine of ratification cannot be allowed to apply if it would have the effect of extending that time.[98]

The ratification question in *Presentaciones Musicales* was complicated by the fact that the court held that, because adoption or ratification do not require that a fresh application be made to the court, a writ issued without authority is not a complete

---

[93] *Ibid* at 353. Chitty, J also referred to *Doe d Lyster v Goldwin* (1841) 2 QB 143, which concerned a notice to quit that would have operated at common law to terminate a tenancy. There, the court had held that because a tenant must be able to rely safely upon a notice to quit, a notice given by an unauthorized agent cannot be made good by an adoption of it by the principal after the proper time for giving it.

[94] (1889) LR 41 ChD 295, 307.

[95] [1994] Ch 271.

[96] [2003] 2 Lloyd's Rep 520 at [84].

[97] See also *Nottinghamshire Healthcare NHS Trust v Prison Officers' Association* [2003] ICR 1192.

[98] [1994] Ch 271, 279. See also *Owners of the ship 'Borvigilant' v Owners of the ship 'Romina G'* [2003] EWCA Civ 935; [2004] 1 CLC 41 at [73] *per* Clarke, LJ.

nullity.[99] It was decided that the assumed principal was entitled to ratify after the limitation period provided that the effect was not to extend the period for doing any relevant thing. Such was not the case in *Presentaciones Musicales*. This case might suggest that, at least if the vesting of property rights is not in issue, where a time limit has been imposed for the accomplishment of a particular act—for instance, the acceptance of a contractual offer—the court will consider the purpose of the time limit and will only deny the assumed principal the right to ratify after expiry of that period of time if expiry of that time limit is intended to affect the validity of the transaction.

It is often said that in *Presentaciones Musicales* Roch, LJ adopted a narrower view **6.44** of the scope of this exception to the principle in *Bolton Partners v Lambert*[100] than Dillon and Nolan, LJJ.[101] Roch, LJ quoted a passage from Cotton, LJ's judgment in *Bolton Partners v Lambert* in which the latter said, 'The rule as to ratification is of course subject to some exceptions. An estate once vested cannot be divested, nor can an act lawful at the time of its performance be rendered unlawful, by the application of the doctrine of ratification.'[102] Significantly, Roch, LJ went on to suggest that Cotton, LJ was merely giving examples of exceptions and was not attempting to set out an exhaustive list of exceptions to the rule in *Bolton Partners v Lambert*.[103] Roch, LJ concluded:

> I would suggest that that exception ought to be stated in these terms: that the putative principal will not be allowed to ratify the acts of his assumed agent, if such ratification will affect adversely rights of property in either real or personal property including intellectual property, which have arisen in favour of the third party or others claiming through him since the unauthorised act of the assumed agent. The expiry of the limitation period in the present case does not create any such right in the defendants; if applicable it would merely bar the plaintiff company's remedies. I would not extend this exception to cases such as the present where a defendant would receive a windfall defence in a case where the vice against which the Limitation Acts are designed to protect defendants, namely the bringing of claims at a time so far after the occurrence of the cause of action that a defendant is put at a disadvantage in defending the claim, does not exist.[104]

---

[99] See [1994] Ch 271, 280: 'Where a writ is issued without authority, the cases show that the writ is not a nullity. For the nominal plaintiff to adopt the writ, or ratify its issue, does not require any application to the court. Accordingly, on the same general principle that justifies *Pontin v Wood* [1962] 1 QB 594, the plaintiff, in the simple example of an action raising a single cause of action which has been begun by solicitors without authority, must be entitled to adopt the action notwithstanding the expiration of the limitation period applicable to that cause of action' (*per* Dillon, LJ).

[100] See notably *Bowstead & Reynolds on Agency* (2014: London, Sweet & Maxwell) 20th ed, by Watts, para 2-089.

[101] [1994] Ch 271, 280.

[102] (1889) LR 41 ChD 295, 307.

[103] [1994] Ch 271, 285.

[104] *Ibid* at 285–6.

**6.45** Discussion of the precise scope of the exception/exceptions to *Bolton Partners v Lambert* can appear somewhat rarefied, even sterile. As Robert Walker, LJ remarked in *Smith v Henniker-Major & Co (a firm)*, 'I am inclined to think that this debate (as to whether the exception is limited to ratification affecting property rights) may not be particularly profitable ... In my view the right approach would be to regard the deprivation of an accrued right as an important example of the general rationale identified in *Bowstead & Reynolds's* Art. 19, that is, unfair prejudice.'[105] Commenting on Robert Walker, LJ's judgment in *Smith v Henniker-Major*, Lewison, J later concluded:

> The general *rationale*, therefore, of the limits on the ability to ratify is the prevention of unfair prejudice to the other party to the putative contract. Whether unfair prejudice would be caused by allowing ratification is, as Robert Walker LJ said, 'a judgmental application of principle.'[106]

**6.46** Robert Walker, LJ's judgment in *Smith v Henniker-Major* would appear to represent the current thinking in this confusing area: namely, that unfair prejudice to the third party is the watchword whenever a court has to determine whether ratification is permissible and, furthermore, that prejudice may arise in a variety of ways.[107] The following emerges from the case law:

- unfair prejudice may result from the assumed principal not ratifying within a reasonable time;
- unfair prejudice may result from the principal ratifying a transaction after the expiry of an ordained time limit;
- unfair prejudice, it would seem, is always present if the effect of a purported principal's ratification would be to divest a third party of vested proprietary rights.

The notion of unfair prejudice may also explain the cases noted above,[108] which would once have been counted exceptional, where in marine insurance—and, more recently, in other forms of insurance, too—it is held that a policy may be ratified even following loss.

### Ratification cannot take place if nothing remains to be ratified

**6.47** Ratification cannot take place where nothing remains to be ratified. In *Walter v James*[109] the defendant's attorney, S, whose authority had been revoked, paid the claimant £60 in discharge of a disputed claim on behalf of the defendant. Before the latter could ratify S's action, the claimant learned that S had acted without authority

---

[105] [2003] Ch 182 at [71].
[106] *Kilcarne Holdings Ltd v Targetfollow (Birmingham) Ltd* [2005] 2 P&CR8 at [185].
[107] See [2003] Ch 182 at [71].
[108] See paras **6.20–6.21**.
[109] (1871) LR 6 Ex 124.

and therefore repaid S. The claimant thereupon initiated an action directly against the defendant. The court resolved that whilst it was open to the defendant to ratify the agent's unauthorized act, he could not do so if the claimant had been entitled to cancel the transaction. Kelly, CB considered that since this was money paid in mistake, the claimant could cancel the transaction and ratification could no longer take place. Martin, B stated the proposition with even greater confidence:

> The rule which I conceive to be the correct one may be stated as follows. When a payment is not made by way of gift for the benefit of the debtor, but by an agent who intended that he should be reimbursed by the debtor, but who had not the debtor's authority to pay, it is competent for the creditor and the person paying to rescind the transaction at any time before the debtor has affirmed the payment, and repay the money, and thereupon the payment is at an end, and the debtor again responsible.[110]

## Effects of Ratification

### Ratification is tantamount to antecedent authority

As a general rule, ratification is considered 'equivalent to an antecedent authority'.[111]    **6.48**
This means that the principal and the third party will be deemed to have entered into their contract from the moment that the agent, acting without authority, purported to conclude the transaction with the third party. In consequence:

- Principal and third party will each become entitled to enforce the contract one against another.
- Normally, the agent will no longer be liable to the principal for having acted outside his authority. In the majority of instances, when the principal adopts the agent's transaction the effect will be to exonerate the agent because the transaction, although unauthorized, is perceived to be in the principal's interests. This, however, will not always be the case.[112]
- Technically, even after ratification the agent may be liable to the third party. He may either (i) be liable under the terms of the ratified contract if it provided for joint rights and liabilities, or (ii) he may be liable for breach of his warranty of authority.[113] In the first case, if the unauthorized agent initially purported to contract both on his own behalf as well on that of his the principal,[114] he will be in contractual relations with the third party. Otherwise, provided that the third party can show that he has suffered damage, the agent may be liable under his warranty of authority. Since the effect of ratification is to realize the third party's

---

[110] *Ibid* at 128.
[111] *Koenigsblatt v Sweet* [1923] 2 Ch 314, 325 *per* Lord Sterndale, MR.
[112] See para **6.49**.
[113] On warranty of authority, see further **chapter 7**.
[114] On situations where the agent incurs rights and liabilities under the contract, see **chapter 12**.

expectations—namely, a contract concluded with the principal—actionable damage will rarely be present. However, if the third party has incurred costs as a consequence of the agent's unauthorized actions, these may be recoverable under the agent's warranty of authority.

Following ratification, the agent may acquire rights against his principal, notably (i) a right to commission and (ii) a right to be indemnified for expenses incurred in performance of the now legitimized agency.

*(i) Commission.* In *Keay v Fenwick*[115] the managing owner of a ship sold a ship, through the claimant shipbrokers, to the Turkish government without the express authority of his co-owners. The latter did in fact know that a sale was contemplated. After the event, the co-owners executed a power of attorney, reciting that they had agreed to the sale, and had received the purchase-money, and empowering the transfer of their respective shares and the delivery of the vessel to the purchasers. They later received their shares of the purchase price. Subsequently, they sought to resist the shipbrokers' claim to retain commission on the ratified sale. Lindley, LJ, delivering the judgment of the court, found:

> [T]he defendants knew that [the managing owner] was in England, and that the ship was sold in Constantinople, and that, in the ordinary course of business, she could only be sold by some agent, and that agent would require to be paid. A ratification of the sale was a ratification of a sale in the ordinary course of business; and it is not competent for the defendants to ratify part of the transaction and repudiate the rest.[116]

*(ii) Indemnity.* In *Bristow v Whitmore*,[117] acting without authority, the master of a ship entered into a charterparty under seal to carry troops from the Mauritius to England. The charterparty stipulated, on the master's own responsibility, that the ship would be modified to enable her to carry the troops. At the Cape of Good Hope he entered into a further charterparty, not under seal, to similar effect. The master made the agreed alterations, and met the expenses. The voyage was performed. Following the owner's adoption of the transaction, the House of Lords held that if sued by the owner for the freight as money had and received, the master would have had a right at law to deduct the money so advanced, and that he had a right in equity to be reimbursed out of the freight so earned.

### Waiver of the principal's rights against the agent

**6.49** Does ratification by the assumed principal necessarily operate as waiver of any rights the principal might otherwise have against the agent? A principal may ratify an

---

[115] (1876) LR 1 CPD 745.
[116] *Ibid* at 752–3.
[117] (1861) 9 HL Cas 391.

unauthorized transaction entered into on his behalf for many reasons. Very often it will be because the principal perceives commercial advantage in adopting the contract as his own. However, sometimes the principal may feel constrained to ratify for other reasons, not actuated by self-interest. For example, a principal may wish to ratify a transaction for sound commercial reasons in order to preserve his commercial reputation. In such cases, is it open to the principal to reserve his position, adopting the contract concluded in his name with the third party but not waiving any breach of duty committed by the agent when he acted without authority on the principal's behalf? Waller, J considered this question in *Suncorp Insurance and Finance v Milano Assicurazioni SpA*.[118] Waller, J could see no reason why the principal should not be able to make his position clear in this regard, in that there are two distinct but connected contractual relations: namely, the principal's contract with the third party, and the principal's contract with the agent. It is true that ratification is normally assumed to relieve the agent of all personal liability to the principal. It is also the case that the authorities prior to *Suncorp*—notably, Lloyd, J's judgment in *Great Atlantic Insurance Co v Home Insurance Co*[119]—could not be said to have settled this point. In Waller, J's view, however, a principal may retain his rights against his agent in cases where the former, for commercial reasons, makes clear that albeit he is ratifying, he is not intending to exonerate the agent. The court simply has to approach the matter in two stages:

> First is there ratification of the contract which the agent has purported to make. Second has the principal waived the breach of duty if any *vis-à-vis* the agent. Often the facts will lead to both ratification and exoneration, but not always.[120]

---

[118] [1993] 2 Lloyd's Rep 225.
[119] [1981] 2 Lloyd's Rep 219.
[120] [1993] 2 Lloyd's Rep 225, 235.

# 7

# THE AGENT'S LIABILITY FOR BREACH
# OF WARRANTY OF AUTHORITY

## Warranty of Authority

### When does an agent's warranty of authority arise?

If an agent acts without authority—that is, acts without the express, implied or **7.01** apparent authority of the principal or without authority conferred by operation of law—and if the principal fails to ratify the agent's unauthorized transaction, the agent may incur personal liability to the third party. The agent's liability may arise in more than one way. If the agent has acted fraudulently, an action for deceit will lie. Alternatively, if both negligence and the requisite relationship can be established, the agent may be held liable under the principle laid down in *Hedley Byrne & Co Ltd v Heller & Partners Ltd*.[1] More generally, if the agent has contracted in

---

[1] [1964] AC 46 5. The decision whether to seek to hold the agent liable under *Hedley Byrne* or on breach of the agent's warranty of authority may turn on the anticipated measure of damages. As Lord

such a way as to engage his personal alternative liability on the contract with the third party additionally to purporting to engage the liability of the principal,[2] the third party may sue the agent on the latter's personal contractual undertaking. However, if, as is more likely, the agent has not attempted to contract personally alongside the principal, but has simply contracted on the principal's behalf without authority, the agent's liability to the third party may arise under his warranty of authority. In the oft-quoted words of Lord Esher, MR in *Firbank's Executors v Humphreys*:

> Where a person by asserting that he has the authority of the principal induces another person to enter into any transaction which he would not have entered into but for that assertion, and the assertion turns out to be untrue, to the injury of the person to whom it is made, it must be taken that the person making it undertook that it was true, and he is liable personally for the damage that has occurred.[3]

### When an action for breach of warranty of authority will lie

**7.02**  An action for breach of warranty of authority will lie whenever the 'agent', no matter how innocently, represents to a third party that he has authority to act on behalf of a principal and the third party, relying upon that representation, acts in a manner in which he would not otherwise have done had the representation not been made.[4] The agent will be taken to have warranted the truth of his assertion and will be liable for the loss occasioned to the third party by his misrepresentation of authority. The agent may be acting under an existing agency agreement and misrepresent the extent of his authority. Alternatively, the representation may be made by someone who is not an agent, or who has ceased to be an agent,[5] but falsely or mistakenly represents to a third party that he in fact is. Strictly speaking, an agent who has apparent authority to act may still be held liable on his warranty of authority as he is still falsely promising that he has actual authority. Some cases have suggested otherwise.[6] However, the better view is that, technically, such an agent may still be held liable for breach of warranty of authority—although, in practice, because the principal will be bound by his agent's undertakings *vis-à-vis*

---

Hoffmann pointed out in *South Australia Asset Management Corp v York Montague Ltd* [1997] AC 191, 216, the methods of calculation are quite distinct: see below, para **7.18**.

[2] See further **chapter 12**.

[3] (1887) LR 18 QBD 54, 60. As Mocatta, J explained in *V/O Rasnoimport v Guthrie & Co Ltd* [1966] 1 Lloyd's Rep 1, 10: 'It is only when the agent has no actual or ostensible authority that the third party need look for his remedy to the agent and rely, if he can, on breach by that agent of his implied warranty of authority.'

[4] A claim will therefore fail if reliance cannot be demonstrated: *Everton Football Club Co Ltd v Sail Group Ltd and Alexander Ross Ltd* [2011] EWHC 126 (QB) at [45]–[47].

[5] *Yonge v Toynbee* [1910] 1 KB 215, 226 *per* Buckley, LJ: 'I can see no difference of principle between the case in which the authority never existed at all and the case in which the authority once existed and has ceased to exist.'

[6] Eg, *Rainbow v Howkins* [1904] 2 KB 322, *326 per* Kennedy, J.

the third party, the latter will have suffered no loss and will recover little or no damages from the agent.

### Liability for breach of warranty of authority is strict

It is of no significance that the agent acted throughout in good faith and was **7.03** honestly mistaken in representing that he had the principal's authority to act on the latter's behalf. Breach of warranty of authority can occur irrespective of whether the agent was at fault in maintaining that he had authority to act. In *Firbank's Executors v Humphreys*, for example, directors of a company issued debenture stock and security in satisfaction of the balance due under a contract for the construction of a railway line. Unknown to the directors, the company had already issued the entire debenture stock it could then lawfully issue. As Lindley, LJ made clear:

> The fact that the directors were themselves deceived and did not know or suspect that they had not the power to do what they did is immaterial in cases of this description. Speaking generally an action for damages will not lie against a person who honestly makes a misrepresentation which misleads another. But to this general rule there is at least one well established exception, *viz*, where an agent assumes an authority which he does not possess, and induces another to deal with him upon the faith that he has the authority which he assumes.[7]

Similarly, in *Suart v Haigh*[8] a shipbroker, who possessed no authority to enter into a charterparty on his principal's behalf, signed such a contract adding the words 'by telegraphic authority of Noonan & Dewjee, of Bombay'. Even though the broker had acted in good faith, honestly believing that the telegram from his employers conferred the requisite authority upon him to act for the purported charterers, he was held liable because, in the words of Lord Watson, 'a contract professing to bind B as a principal executed on his behalf by A in the character of his agent conveys to the other contracting party an implied, but very distinct, assertion by A that he has full authority from B to make the contract.'[9]

### Warranty of authority extends to all transactions

An agent's warranty of authority is not confined to contracts but extends to all **7.04** transactions. Although the doctrine of warranty of authority will normally apply in cases where an agent has purported to bring a principal and a third party into direct contractual relations, in fact the doctrine is not restricted to contracts but, in Lord Esher, MR's words in *Firbank's Executors v Humphreys*, applies whenever

---

[7] (1887) LR 18 QBD 54, 62.
[8] (1893) 9 TLR 488.
[9] *Ibid* at 489. See also *AO Lindvig v Furness, Withy & Co Ltd* (1922) 12 Ll L Rep 495.

'a person by asserting that he has the authority of the principal induces another person to enter into *any transaction* which he would not have entered into but for that assertion.'[10]

### Warranty of authority and misrepresentations of law

**7.05**  It used to be held that an 'agent' would only incur liability on his warranty of authority if the representation upon which the other party relied was a representation of fact. Representations of law did not give rise to this liability. Thus in *Rashdall v Ford*[11] the plaintiff had advanced money to a company, receiving in return a Lloyd's bond, signed by its secretary, whereby the company purported to acknowledge the debt and to covenant to pay interest on it at 6 per cent. Subsequently, when the company could no longer pay its way, the plaintiff learned that because the company was in breach of its own borrowing requirements the so-called bond was wholly void. It had been falsely misrepresented to him that the company had the power to enter into this transaction. Sir W Page Wood, V-C considered that it was 'impossible to extend the principle of relief arising out of misrepresentation, to a statement of law which turns out to be an incorrect statement. The plaintiff must be taken to have been well informed of the state of the law ...'[12] Following the decision of the House of Lords *in Kleinwort Benson Ltd v Lincoln CC*,[13] however, which in the context of the law of restitution reversed the old rule that money paid under a mistake of law is not recoverable, and following subsequent decisions doing away with the distinction between matters of fact and matters of law in the context of contractual mistake[14] and misrepresentation,[15] it is suggested that this restriction on an injured party's right to sue an agent who has falsely warranted his authority can no longer be maintained.

### Warranting the authority of another party

**7.06**  The doctrine of warranty of authority can also apply in cases where the defendant (D) has misrepresented to a third party (T) that another (A) has authority to act on behalf of the principal (P). In such circumstances, if A does not possess the authority, as represented, D may be held liable to T for breach of warranty of authority. In *Chapleo v Brunswick Permanent Benefit Building Society*,[16] company directors informed a third party that the company secretary had power to borrow money. It later emerged that the secretary was borrowing sums in excess of those permitted

---

[10] (1887) LR 18 QBD 54, 60.
[11] (1866) LR 2 Eq 750.
[12] *Ibid* at 754.
[13] [1998] 3 WLR 1095.
[14] *Brennan v Bolt Burdon* [2004] 3 WLR 321.
[15] *Pankhania v Hackney LBC* [2002] EWHC (Ch) 2441; [2002] NPC 123.
[16] (1881) 6 QBD 696.

under the rules of the company. The court held that the directors, albeit they had acted innocently throughout, were liable to the third party having warranted the authority of the secretary to act on behalf of and to bind the company.

**Warranty not made directly to the party seeking to rely upon it**

Whilst many cases speak in terms of the agent having to give the warranty to the third party and the transaction into which the third party was led to enter having to be some form of dealing with the purported principal, the doctrine is not so narrowly circumscribed. The third party does not need to be the person to whom the warranty was in fact addressed, provided that it can be shown that he relied upon the agent's warranty and that the agent could have anticipated that such a person might have relied upon his warranty. In *VIO Rasnoimport v Guthrie & Co Ltd* the court held that it was open to the indorsee of a bill of lading to rely upon a warranty of authority innocently given to the original shipper on behalf of the owner of goods when the agents signed for more goods than were actually shipped. Likening the situation to that found in *Carlill v Carbolic Smoke Ball Co*,[17] Mocatta, J considered that the agents, when they signed the bill of lading, had to be taken to know that in the ordinary course of commerce, in likelihood, the document would pass from hand to hand and that one or more indorsees from the original shipper would receive the bill, would rely upon the statements in it and would pay money for the goods represented in it to have been shipped which he or they would not otherwise have paid. For this reason, the judge could see: **7.07**

> nothing extravagant or heterodox in holding that the implied warranty of author-
> ity ... was given by the [agents] to all whom they could reasonably foresee would
> become ... indorsees and became actionable by such persons on proof of their having
> acted in reliance upon the warranty and having suffered damage thereby. Common
> sense and principle alike seem to require this conclusion.[18]

Although it is difficult to contemplate similar situations arising beyond the realms of negotiable instruments and bills of lading,[19] as a matter of general principle *Rasnoimport* establishes that what must be proved in each case is simply a contract under which a promise has been made either expressly or by implication to the promisee, for which promise the promisee has in turn provided consideration.

Consideration for the agent's promise may be supplied by the third party entering into a transaction with a party other than the supposed principal. In *Penn v Bristol & West Building Society*[20] a solicitor, B, was instructed by a husband to sell a house **7.08**

---

[17] [1892] 2 QB 484.
[18] [1966] 1 Lloyd's Rep 1, 13.
[19] See remarks of Waller, L J in *Penn v Bristol & West Building Society* [1997] 1 WLR 1356, 1363.
[20] [1997] 1 WLR 1356.

but mistakenly believed that he was acting for both husband and wife in the sale. B purported to negotiate on the couple's behalf with another solicitor who, B knew, acted for both the prospective purchaser and the building society which, it was hoped, would lend money to make the purchase. In due course the Court of Appeal held that B's warranty that he had authority to act for both vendors was given to both the purchaser and to the building society that had lent the money on the strength of the assurance B had given to the purchaser. It is therefore sufficient that the party to whom a warranty is given provides consideration by acting in reliance on that promise. As Waller, LJ explained:

> [C]onsideration can be supplied by the promisee entering into some transaction with a third party in a warranty of authority case just as it can in any other collateral warranty case. Furthermore, the promise can be made to a wide number of people or simply to one person, again all depending on the facts.[21]

## The Legal Character of the Third Party's Claim

### The agent's liability is strict and arises out of a collateral contract

**7.09** Although an agent may now in appropriate circumstances be held liable in negligence under the *Hedley Byrne* doctrine, historically the agent's liability emerged from contract. This serves to explain why liability is strict and an agent virtually guarantees his authority *vis-à-vis* other parties.

**7.10** Two cases, *Collen v Wright*[22] and *Yonge v Toynbee*,[23] have settled that the agent's liability is strict and arises out of a collateral contract. In *Collen v Wright* W, who had acted as G's land agent, purported to lease G's land to C for a period of twelve-and-a-half years. G proved that W did not have authority to grant such a long lease. C at first sought specific performance of the lease against G, but when this suit failed sought to hold W's estate personally liable for costs and damages. Willes, J, delivering the judgment of Court of Exchequer Chamber, stated:

> [A] person who induces another to contract with him, as the agent of a third party, by an unqualified assertion of his being authorized to act as such agent, is answerable to the person who so contracts for any damages which he may sustain by reason of the assertion of authority being untrue ... The fact that the professed agent honestly thinks that he has authority affects the moral character of his act; but his moral innocence, so far as the person whom he has induced to contract is concerned, in no way aids such person or alleviates the inconvenience and damage which he sustains. The obligation arising in such a case is well expressed by saying that a person professing to contract as agent for another, impliedly, if not expressly, undertakes to or promises

---

[21] *Ibid* at 1363.
[22] (1857) 8 E&B 647.
[23] [1910] 1 KB 215.

the person who enters into such contract, upon the faith of the professed agent being duly authorized, that the authority which he professes to have does in point of fact exist. *The fact of entering into the transaction with the professed agent, as such, is good consideration for the promise.*[24]

The Court of Appeal endorsed this approach in *Yonge v Toynbee*.[25] Solicitors had **7.11** been instructed to conduct the defence of a client. Before the action was commenced, the client was certified insane. In ignorance of this, the solicitors entered an appearance for him, delivered a defence, to which the plaintiff replied, and various other interlocutory proceedings took place in the action. The action did not proceed to trial, but upon learning of the client's mental state the plaintiff's solicitor successfully sought an order that the appearance and all subsequent proceedings in the action should be struck out, and that the solicitors who had assumed to act for the defendant should be ordered personally to pay the plaintiff's costs of the action up to date, on the ground that they had so acted without authority. The Court of Appeal held that the agent's liability arises out of an implied undertaking or promise made by him that the authority which he professes to have does in point of fact exist. In the words of Swinfen Eady, J:

> Where an agent represents that he has authority to do a particular act, and he has not such authority, and another person is misled to his prejudice, the ground upon which the agent is held liable in damages is that there is an implied contract or warranty that he had the authority which he professed to have.[26]

Buckley, LJ, too, expressed the principle in broad terms:

> [T]he liability of the person who professes to act as agent arises *(a)* if he has been fraudulent, *(b)* if he has without fraud untruly represented that he had authority when he had not, and *(c)* also where he innocently misrepresents that he has authority where the fact is either (1) that he never had authority or (2) that his original authority has ceased by reason of facts of which he has not knowledge or means of knowledge. Such last-mentioned liability arises from the fact that by professing to act as agent he impliedly contracts that he has authority, and it is immaterial whether he knew of the defect of his authority or not.[27]

At one time it was suggested that *Collen v Wright* operated as an exception to the **7.12** general rule that no action was maintainable for a false statement unless the maker was aware that it was untrue. In *Dickson v Reuter's Telegram Co Ltd*,[28] however, Bramwell, LJ repudiated this analysis:

> *Collen v Wright* establishes a separate and independent rule, which, without using language rigorously accurate, may be thus stated: if a person requests and, by

---

[24] (1857) 8 E&B 647, 657–8 (emphasis added).
[25] [1910] 1 KB 215.
[26] *Ibid* at 231.
[27] *Ibid* at 227.
[28] (1877) LR 3 CPD 1.

asserting that he is clothed with the necessary authority, induces another to enter into a negotiation with himself and a transaction with the person whose authority he represents that he has, in that case there is a contract by him that he has the authority of the person with whom he requests the other to enter into the transaction.[29]

Bramwell, LJ's view, that liability for warranty of authority arises under an independent rule, has since been adopted by Mocatta, J in *V/O Rasnoimport v Guthrie & Co Ltd*,[30] who held that the contract on which the agent may be held liable is a separate contract involving an implied warranty that the agent possesses authority to make a contract on behalf of his alleged principal, and subsequently has been followed by the Court of Appeal in *The Piraeus*[31] and by Clarke, J in *The Kurnia Dewi*.[32]

### The extent of an agent's warranty of authority

**7.13** It is beyond question, since *Yonge v Toynbee*,[33] that a solicitor who, for whatever reason, acts without his client's authority, may be held liable for breach of his warranty of authority. Although the analysis is acknowledged to present 'some conceptual problems in the case of a solicitor conducting litigation',[34] it is now firmly established that liability in such cases reposes on a collateral contract.[35] It is also generally accepted that the justification for holding solicitors strictly liable in such circumstances is that this avoids the potential injustice that the person for whom the unauthorized solicitor purports to act cannot himself be made responsible for the opposing party's costs. However, whilst a solicitor will be taken to warrant that he has authority to act on his client's behalf, can this warranty be further particularized? For instance, if the solicitor—or, for that matter, any other variety of agent— misnames his client, does he also thereby place himself in breach of his warranty of authority?

**7.14** In *Knight Frank LLP v du Haney*[36] the Court of Appeal had to consider whether an estate agent, who in the course of making a contract with a third party misrepresented the name of his principal, attracted liability for breach of warranty of authority in circumstances where the principal was nonetheless identified and his correct name capable of being established. The agent had stated that he was acting

---

[29] (1877) LR 3 CPD 1, 5.
[30] [1966] 1 Lloyd's Rep 1.
[31] [1974] 2 Lloyd's Rep 266.
[32] See *Smit International Singapore Pte Ltd v Kurnia Dewi Shipping SA Ocean Marine Mutual Protection and Indemnity Association* [1997] 1 Lloyd's Rep 552, 562.
[33] [1910] 1 KB 215.
[34] *SEB Trygg Liv Holding AB v Manches* [2006] 1 WLR 2276 at [61] *per* Buxton, LJ.
[35] See *Collen v Wright* (1857) 8 E&B 647, 656 *per* Willes, J.
[36] [2011] EWCA Civ 404; [2011] 16 EG 78 (CS). Cf. *Cheshire Mortgage Corporation Ltd v Grandison* [2012] CSIH 66; [2013] SC 160 (IH (Ex Div)); McGregor, *The Agent's Warranty of Authority: Thus Far but no Further* [2013] 17 Edin LR 398.

for 'Morecombe Investments Ltd' when in fact his true principal was 'Morecambe Investment Ltd'. Tomlinson, LJ concluded that as the agent had not specifically warranted that his principal was 'Morecombe Investments Ltd', he was not in breach of his warranty of authority:

> The [agent] made it very clear that he was acting as agent only. The [agent] did not contract as a principal in his own right. The [agent] warranted that he was acting on behalf of the entity that was negotiating to purchase the site.... [H]e was, or at any rate there is no reason to believe that he was not. It has not therefore been demonstrated that the respondent was in breach of his warranty of authority.[37]

Whilst acknowledging that the agent had indeed represented that his principal's name was, firstly, 'Morecambe Investment Ltd' and, secondly, 'Morecombe Investments Ltd', the agent:

> did not on either occasion warrant the accuracy of the name given in the sense that he effectively guaranteed that it was correct ... The warranty which the respondent gave was as to the fact of his agency, not as to the precise accuracy of the name which he attributed to his principal.[38]

The Court of Appeal had considered a similar question in *SEB Trygg Liv Holding AB* **7.15**
*v Manches*.[39] Four corporate owners had sold an insurance company to SEB. Later, when a dispute arose, they employed an insurance professional, M, to administer the dispute. The owners claimed payment of the remainder of the purchase price, whilst SEB counterclaimed alleging the misselling of pensions by the insurance company under its previous ownership. Arbitration proceedings commenced but were interrupted when SEB queried whether the company against whom they thought they were counterclaiming actually existed and requested confirmation of the entity for which the vendors' solicitors claimed to act. The corporate history was complicated,[40] but in essence a point of warranty of authority arose in the case because M had not been informed that a company merger had taken place and the solicitors then acting for the vendors had stated that one of their clients was a company known in the case as 'Old Aachener Re'. The solicitors were unaware that 'Old Aachener Re' had been dissolved following its merger with a company called AMB. SEB issued proceedings against the solicitors for damages for breach of warranty of authority. At first instance Gloster, J held that because on the judge's findings the solicitors were authorized to act by 'Old Aachener Re', alternatively by AMB, they were not in breach of their warranty of authority, but they were in breach of a more limited warranty, that the client for whom they acted bore the

---

[37] [2011] EWCA Civ 404; [2011] 16 EG 78 (CS) at [13].
[38] *Ibid* at [13].
[39] [2006] 1 WLR 2276.
[40] It was set out in Gloster, J's judgment at first instance: see [2005] EWHC 35 (Comm) at [3].

name in which they pursued the proceedings. Buxton, LJ stated the issue crisply on behalf of the Court:

> It is common ground that a solicitor who starts, defends or continues litigation or arbitration on behalf of a client warrants that he has authority to do so. Such a warranty necessarily involves the solicitor representing that he has a client who exists. The question is whether he also represents that he has named his client correctly ... [T]he question is whether [the solicitors] were in breach of warranty by mistakenly naming or continuing to represent that their client was Old Aachener Re.[41]

**7.16** There had possibly been a suggestion in McCowan, LJ's judgment in *Nelson v Nelson* that a solicitor might be taken to warrant more than the general fact that he had authority to act for his client and that additionally he warranted that 'the client bears the name of the party to the proceedings'.[42] Peter Gibson, LJ, on the other hand, in the same case could 'not see that [the solicitor] warrants more than that he has a retainer from the client who exists and has authorised proceedings and against whom a costs order can be made',[43] whilst Waller, LJ did not feel that, if a solicitor acts for a party who is defunct or who lacks capacity (as in *Nelson*, where, unknown to the solicitors, the client was an undischarged bankrupt), the court was 'concerned to make a solicitor strictly liable simply because the person who instructs him turns out not to be the right plaintiff, as opposed to ensuring that there is a party against whom the opposing party can obtain an order for costs.'[44] In *SEB Trygg Liv Holding AB v Manches* the Court concluded that, as a matter of principle, it would be wrong to impose strict liability upon a solicitor for incorrectly naming his client.[45] This determination dovetails neatly into other existing rules governing solicitors' liability: generally, solicitors conducting proceedings do not warrant what they say or do on behalf of their clients; solicitors do not warrant that a client, the named party to proceedings, has title to sue, is solvent, has a good cause of action or defence, or has any other attribute asserted on his behalf; solicitors rely upon their clients' instructions for all these things, as they will normally do for naming their clients correctly. As solicitors give no warranty as to the accuracy of their instructions generally, the Court of Appeal could see no reason to hold that the naming of a client should be treated as an exception.

**7.17** Tomlinson, LJ, in *Knight Frank LLP v du Haney*, summarized matters in the following manner:

> There is an obvious distinction between matters upon which the solicitor must simply rely on his client's instructions without having independent knowledge and matters within his own knowledge, such as his authority to act.[46]

---

[41] [2006] 1 WLR 2276 at [57].
[42] [1997] 1 WLR 233, 235.
[43] *Ibid* at 237.
[44] *Ibid* at 240.
[45] [2006] 1 WLR 2276 at [67] *per* Buxton, LJ.
[46] [2011] EWCA Civ 404 at [14]. In *SEB Trygg* the court also noted that the sort of loss that would be incurred where a solicitor misnamed his client would in likelihood be small.

The situation, he added, is not different in the case of other breeds of agent:

> [S]imilar considerations militate here against the imposition of strict liability for the accuracy of the name attributed by the respondent to his principal ... [H]ere the [agent] identified and named his principal in a manner which was entirely adequate for all practical purposes and it is neither a sensible nor a necessary analysis that the [agent] is to be regarded as having warranted, in the sense of having guaranteed, the precise accuracy of the name supplied. The [agent] could if necessary have made independent enquiries as to the correct title of the principal identified by the [agent].[47]

## The Measure of Damages

### What is the appropriate measure of damages for breach of warranty of authority?

Lord Esher, MR stated the principle governing the measure of damages payable **7.18** for an agent's breach of warranty of authority in *Firbank's Executors v Humphreys* as follows:

> The damages under the general rule are arrived at by considering the difference in the position [the person acting in reliance on the warranty] would have been in had the representation been true and the position he is actually in in consequence of its being untrue.[48]

In the most common case of breach of warranty of authority, therefore, where an agent falsely warrants that he possesses authority to contract on the principal's behalf, the basis of the damages is the amount that the claimant has lost by being unable, by reason of falsity of the warranty, to sue the alleged principal.

In case of breach of warranty the court has regard to what the position would have **7.19** been had the information furnished by the agent been accurate. The general principle applicable to the measure of damages for breach of warranty of authority was considered in *Singh v Sardar Investments*.[49] Aldous, LJ invoked Lord Hoffmann's speech in *South Australia Asset Management Corp v York Montague Ltd*,[50] in which his Lordship distinguished between the measure of damages for breach of a duty to take care to provide accurate information and the measure of damages for breach of a warranty that information is accurate:

> In the case of breach of a duty of care, the measure of damages is the loss attributable to the inaccuracy of the information which the plaintiff has suffered by reason of having entered into the transaction on the assumption that the information was

---

[47] [2011] EWCA Civ 404 at [15].
[48] (1886) 18 QBD 54, 60.
[49] [2002] EWCA Civ 1706 at [50]; [2002] NPC 134.
[50] [1997] AC 191 (on appeal from *Banque Bruxelles Lambert SA v Eagle Star Insurance Co Ltd* [1995] QB 375).

correct. One therefore compares the loss he has actually suffered with what his position would have been if he had not entered into the transaction and asks what element of this loss is attributable to the inaccuracy of the information. In the case of a warranty, one compares the plaintiff's position as a result of entering into the transaction with what it would have been if the information had been accurate. Both measures are concerned with the consequences of the inaccuracy of the information but the tort measure is the extent to which the plaintiff is worse off because the information was wrong whereas the warranty measure is the extent to which he would have been better off if the information had been right.[51]

Reprising a statement in *Bowstead & Reynolds*, Dyson, LJ too accepted that because the cause of action for breach of warranty of authority has been classified as contractual:

the damages are those required to put the plaintiff in the position in which he would have been had the warranty been good *viz.* had the representation of authority been true.[52]

**7.20**  In *Singh* S, a lessee, agreed with A, one of two brothers who jointly owned Sardar, to the purchase of premises whose lease was coming to an end. S was unaware that A and his brother were at one another's throats. The brother opposed the sale and claimed that A had no authority to conclude a sale on behalf of Sardar. The question for the Court of Appeal was, if A had breached his warranty of authority, did such breach give rise to a recoverable loss? It was argued that in the particular circumstances of this case, because the claimants would not have been able to complete and the contract would have been rescinded in any event, even if it had been duly authorized, the claimants suffered only nominal loss as a result of the breach of warranty. Counsel for the claimants vainly argued that in this case a number of eventualities ought to be assumed—namely, that A ought to be taken to have specifically warranted that the contract had been properly authorized by the arbitral committee; that, of necessity, the option to purchase would have been removed as part of its ruling; that such being the case, there would have been nothing to stop the claimants obtaining the necessary finance to complete the transaction; and that the claimants could therefore be said to have suffered substantial damages as a result of the breach of warranty. Disregarding the fact that this exact series of eventual happenings was debatable on the evidence,[53] Dyson, LJ was able to point out that all

---

[51] [1997] AC 191, 216. The distinction is not always that clear-cut. Costs incurred by a third party in consequence of making a claim against the principal following an agent's misrepresenting his authority have been held recoverable. In *Farley Health Products Ltd v Babylon Trading Co* (1987) *The Times*, 29 July Sir Neil Lawson held that where an agent had misrepresented that he had authority to act on behalf of B, a company that had ceased trading more than three years earlier, the correct basis for the assessment of damages was an award that compensated the promisee for both the money wasted in manufacturing, packing and shipping the goods which were not paid for and the costs thrown away by the promisee claiming against the non-existent principal.

[52] *Bowstead & Reynolds on Agency* (2001: London, Sweet & Maxwell) 17th ed, para 9-072.

[53] [2002] EWCA Civ 1706 at [55].

that has to be established is that an agent has warranted the fact that he had authority, not the circumstances whereby he came by it. Devlin, J made this point crisply in *Heskell v Continental Express Ltd*:

> An agent who warrants that he has authority need warrant no more than the bare fact. In the absence of special circumstances, he makes no warranty or representation about how he got his authority, whether it is express or implied, specific or general. Still less does he warrant that an event, on which the proper exercise of a general authority may depend, has in fact taken place.[54]

A claim for breach of warranty of authority cannot be deployed to put the promisee **7.21** in a better position than if the warranty had been true. Thus, substantial damages will not normally be recoverable for breach of a solicitor's warranty of authority if a supposed client is insolvent because the promisee would not have been able to recover costs against the client even if the solicitor had possessed authority to act.[55]

What is the measure of damages when the promisee, believing in the reality of the **7.22** agent's authority, seeks to enforce the contract and suffers loss thereby? In most cases in which a third party is deceived by the agent's promise that he possesses authority on a principal's behalf, upon discovering the truth the former will seek to escape from the bargain. Thus, if the third party is induced to sell a chattel in the belief that the contract has been concluded with the principal, upon discovering the agent's lack of authority it is not unlikely that the former may have to sell the goods in the market at a loss. In such cases, it is settled that the appropriate measure of damages is the difference between the contract price and the market value of the chattel, if any, at the relevant time. Thus, in *Simons v Patchett* an the agent agreed to purchase a ship without the principal's authority to do so. The vendor was held entitled to recover from the agent the contract price less the lower price at which the former had resold, this being taken as the best price obtainable.[56] Similarly, in *Re National Coffee Palace Co; ex p Panmure*,[57] where brokers falsely warranted a principal's authority to buy shares, the court applied the difference between the contract price and the market value as the measure of damages, eventually awarding the full value of the shares only because it had been shown that the shares were in fact unsaleable in the market.

Sometimes, however, the party to whom the agent has misrepresented his authority **7.23** will be unaware of the latter's lack of authority and will continue to try to enforce the contract. How are damages to be calculated in such cases, particularly if the chattel contracted for loses its value? In *Habton Farms v Nimmo*[58] N, purporting to act on behalf of W, on 12 October 1998 agreed to purchase a racehorse from HF

---

[54] [1950] 1 All ER 1033, 1043.
[55] Eg, *Skylight Maritime SA v Ascot Underwriting Ltd* [2005] PNLR 25 at [20] *per* Colman, J.
[56] (1857) 7 E&B 568.
[57] (1883) 24 ChD 367.
[58] [2004] QB 1.

for £70,000. N did not have authority to conclude such a contract for W. HF did not sell the horse to anyone else. In November the horse contracted peritonitis and was destroyed in early December. The Court of Appeal was required to determine the extent of N's liability under his warranty of authority. Whilst the three members of the Court agreed as to the relevant principle, they disagreed as to how to apply it. Acknowledging that the ordinary measure of damages for an agent's breach of warranty would be the difference between the contract price and the market value of the chattel, if any, at the relevant time, the majority (Auld and Clarke, LJJ) acknowledged that, were this measure applied in *Habton Farms*, HF would only be entitled to nominal damages:

> because at any relevant time the contract price was the same as the market value, namely £70,000. As already stated, no one has suggested that the market value of [the racehorse] was less than that at any time until it contracted peritonitis at the end of November. The question therefore arises whether the normal measure of damages should be applied and, if not, why not.[59]

**7.24**  In *Habton Farms*, the majority emphasized that HF had refrained from selling the racehorse to anyone else owing to N's breach of warranty: HF had relied on N's warranty and regarded the horse as sold. In these circumstances, it was not appropriate to deduct the market value of the horse from the purchase price when calculating damages. N was therefore liable for the whole of the contract price. In contrast, the dissenting judge, Jonathan Parker, LJ, took the view that the operative date for deducting the market value of the animal from its contract price was the date of the breach of warranty, ie 12 October 1998. He considered that HF was therefore entitled to no damages, as on the date of breach the horse's market value would have been identical to his contract price. Clarke and Auld, LJJ, on the other hand, thought that a distinction needed to be drawn between two categories of case:

> Where a seller ... has accepted the notional buyer's repudiation and sold elsewhere at a lower market price, as in *Simons v Patchett*, the measure of damages will, of course, be the price less the market value normally identified at that sale price. But where, as here, the claimant has not accepted repudiation and is seeking to enforce it, the position is different.[60]

As Auld, LJ argued by analogy,[61] HB's financial loss deriving from the death of the racehorse, namely the loss of a valuable contract, needed to be treated as 'an ordinary and natural consequence of [N's] breach of warranty of authority, just as might have been a loss resulting from a general fall or collapse in the market price for horses of

---

[59]  *Ibid* at [61] *per* Clarke, LJ.

[60]  *Ibid* at [127].

[61]  Clarke, LJ underwent a change of heart in the course of the case and eventually allied himself with Auld, LJ (at [89]), to Jonathan Parker, LJ's evident sorrow: 'I think Clarke LJ was right first time' (at [108]).

this calibre during that period ... For those reasons, the claimant's decision not immediately to attempt to sell the horse elsewhere and its death were *not independent of the breach of warranty.*'[62]

## Exceptional Situations in which the Agent will not be held Liable

An agent who has acted without authority may escape liability on his implied warranty of authority in a number of situations. **7.25**

### Ratification by the principal

The agent's liability to a third party may be extinguished if the principal ratifies **7.26** the agent's previously unauthorized acts. To the extent that ratification is treated as 'equivalent to an antecedent authority',[63] it is as though the agent had been fully authorized to act on the principal's behalf from the outset and had never misrepresented his authority.

### Where the party seeking to rely on the warranty knew or ought to have known of the agent's lack of authority

Warranty of authority requires that the third party has actually placed reliance upon **7.27** the agent's promise that he possesses authority to act for the principal. In *Yonge v Toynbee* Buckley, LJ indicated that in certain circumstances an agent could escape liability for breach of his warranty of authority. The implied contract, he suggested, may be excluded:

> [i]f, for instance, the agent proved that at the relevant time he told the party with whom he was contracting that he did not know whether the warrant of attorney under which he was acting was genuine or not, and would not warrant its validity, or that his principal was abroad and he did not know whether he was still living, there will have been no representation upon which the implied contract will arise.[64]

Thus, if the third party is aware that the agent has misrepresented his authority or expressed doubts about it, he cannot maintain that he has relied on the agent's

---

[62] [2004] QB 1 at [128]–[130] (emphasis added). See also *Suleman v Shahsavari* [1988] 1 WLR 1181, where it was held that although the normal measure of damages for a breach of warranty would be the difference between the contract price and the market value at the date of completion, this was not an absolute rule and damages may be assessed by reference to the value at some other date if it is more just to do so. Such was particularly the case where 'the innocent party reasonably continues to try to have the contract completed: in such a case it is logical and just to assess damages as at the date when (otherwise than by his default) the contract is lost' (at p 1183 *per* Andrew Park, QC).

[63] *Koenigsblatt v Sweet* [1923] 2 Ch 314, 325.

[64] [1910] 1 KB 215, 227.

promise and the latter will therefore not be held liable. In *Halbot v Lens*[65] the agent established not only that the third party knew that he had no authority to sign a memorandum as agent for the purported principals, but also that the third party knew that one of them had actually declined to give the requested release. Kekewich, J did concede that:

> [a] man, of course, might say, 'I have no authority, and probably cannot obtain such authority, but yet I will contract to obtain it, and run the risk of damages.' Such a contract is conceivable, and would be good in law, but ought not ... to be inferred except from facts leading directly to that conclusion ...[66]

**7.28**  In the normal situation, however, a third party's knowledge of the true position will debar his right to recover damages for breach of warranty. This may result from the agent expressing misgivings or, it would seem, from an inference drawn from the manner in which the agent signed on the principal's behalf. In *Lilly, Wilson & Co v Smales, Eeles & Co*[67] Denman, J was prepared to find that the form in which shipbrokers had signed a charterparty on behalf of the charterer ('by telegraphic authority' of the charterer 'as agent') was well understood in the trade 'to negative the implication of a warranty by the charterer's agent, at all events, to a greater extent than warranting that he has had a telegram which, if correct, authorizes such a charter as that which he is signing.'[68] In *Lilly, Wilson & Co* telegraphic officials had bungled transmission of the principal's message to his agent, communicating the incorrect rate of freight. Because the evidence showed that this form of signature was commonly adopted in order to negative any implication of any further warranty by the agent than that he had received a telegram, which, if correct, authorized such a charter as that which he was signing, the defendant shipbrokers were held not liable. Third parties ought to have been aware of what the qualified form of signature meant within the industry.

### Powers of attorney executed under the Powers of Attorney Act 1971

**7.29**  If the power of an agent acting under a power of attorney is revoked, the agent is afforded protection under s 5(1) of the Powers of Attorney Act 1971 which provides:

> A donee of a power of attorney who acts in pursuance of the power at a time when it has been revoked shall not, by reason of the revocation, incur any liability (either to the donor or to any other person) if at that time he did not know that the power had been revoked.

The donee of a power of attorney who innocently misrepresents his authority will not be liable for breach of warranty of authority.

---

[65] [1901] 1 Ch 344.
[66] *Ibid* at 351.
[67] [1892] 1 QB 456.
[68] *Ibid* at 458.

# Summary

To recapitulate, in order to engage an agent's liability on his warranty of authority, **7.30** the following matters need to be established:

(1) That the agent purported to act as agent. Normally, this will occur when the agent has indicated that he was acting for a specified individual or that he was acting for an unnamed principal. If this proves not to be the case—or if he has misrepresented the extent of his authority—the agent will incur liability. The agent's personal liability will also be engaged if he has represented that he was acting on behalf of a certain named individual but was in fact acting on behalf of another party who was not named in the transaction. In *Savills v Scott* Sir Douglas Frank, QC declared:

> It does not seem to me to need authority for the proposition that where a person holds himself out as an agent for a named person but is in fact acting as agent for an unnamed person then the agent is personally liable.[69]

(2) That the agent lacked the principal's authority to act. The agent may lack this authority:
   (a) because he had no authority from the outset to act on the principal's behalf, owing to the fact either that he never possessed authority or because his authority had been revoked or otherwise terminated; or
   (b) because the agent acted beyond the scope of whatever authority he did enjoy.
(3) That the agent has neither informed the third party that he lacks authority or that he has misgivings concerning his authority.
(4) That the third party relied on the agent's representation that he possessed authority to act on the principal's behalf.

---

[69] [1988] 1 EGLR 20.

# 8

# LEGAL RELATIONS BETWEEN PRINCIPAL AND AGENT: DUTIES THE AGENT OWES TO HIS PRINCIPAL

The duties an agent owes to his principal fall into two broad categories. On the one **8.01** hand, because the majority of agencies will arise out of a contract between principal and agent, the latter will owe well recognized duties at common law—most notably, a duty to perform his mandate with reasonable skill and care. On the other hand, however, equity has also wielded strong influence over the development of agents' duties. In an oft-quoted passage in *Armstrong v Jackson*, in which he drew a distinction between the respective rights and duties of buyer and seller and of principal and agent, McCardie, J stated:

> The position of principal and agent gives rise to particular and onerous duties on the part of the agent, and the high standard of conduct required from him springs from the fiduciary relationship between his employer and himself. His position is confidential. It readily lends itself to abuse. A strict and salutary rule is required to meet the special situation. The rules of English law as they now exist spring from the strictness originally required by Courts of Equity in cases where the fiduciary relationship exists. Those requirements are superadded to the common law obligations of diligence and skill.[1]

---

[1] [1917] 2 KB 822, 826.

In *Armstrong v Jackson*, instead of acquiring shares in the market as instructed, a broker had sold his own shares to a client without the latter's knowledge. McCardie, J's judgment illustrates just how strict these equitable principles are. Not only could the broker not sell his own shares unless he made full and accurate disclosure to his principal of what he proposed doing, but equity would also not countenance the transaction unless, in full knowledge of those facts, the principal gave his assent to the changed position of the broker. Because the rule is one 'not merely of law but of obvious morality' and is designed to deter the agent from allowing his interests to conflict with those of his principal, McCardie added:

> It matters not that the broker sells at the market price, or that he acts without intent to defraud … The prohibition of the law is absolute. It will not allow an agent to place himself in a situation which, under ordinary circumstances, would tempt a man to do that which is not the best for his principal … The Court will not enter into discussion as to the propriety of the price charged by the broker, nor is it material to inquire whether the principal has or has not suffered a loss. If the breach of duty by the broker be shown, the Court will set aside the transaction …[2]

**8.02** The agent, therefore, has often to be considered both as a contracting party, under customary contractual duties to his principal, and also as a fiduciary, owing strict equitable obligations to the principal arising out of the special position of trust in which the law of agency places him.[3] These two species of obligation will be considered separately.

## The Agent's Duty to Perform his Agency

### Contractual agencies

*An agent is under a general duty to carry out the contractual instructions of his principal*

**8.03** Whenever an agent enters into a contract with his principal, he is bound to act in accordance with the terms of that contract, and the agent must personally carry out the principal's instructions with reasonable care and diligence. As Hamblen, J pointed out in *Dunlop Haywards (DHL) Ltd v Barbon Ins Group Ltd*, 'It is a fundamental duty of any agent to exercise reasonable skill and care in the performance of the functions which he has undertaken.'[4] This general duty can then be particularized

---

[2] *Ibid* at 825.

[3] Eg, *Rothschild v Brookman* (1831) 5 Bli (NS) 165, 197 *per* Lord Wynford: 'If any man who is to be trusted places himself in a condition in which he has an opportunity of taking advantage of his employer, by placing himself in such a situation, whether acting fairly or not, he must suffer the consequence of his situation. Such is the jealousy which the law of England entertains against any such transactions.' Quoted with approval by Dunn, LJ in *O'Sullivan v Management Agency and Music Ltd* [1985] QB 428, 451.

[4] [2010] Lloyd's Rep IR 149 at [156].

to individual professions. Thus, in *Youell v Bland Welch & Co Ltd (The 'Superhull's Cover' case)* Phillips, J explained:

> When a Lloyd's broker accepts instructions from a client he implicitly undertakes to exercise reasonable skill and care in relation to his client's interests in accordance with the practice at Lloyd's. That general duty will normally require the broker to perform a number of different activities on behalf of the client, but the performance of those activities constitutes no more than the discharge of the duty to exercise reasonable skill and care.[5]

What that core duty requires in the context of a particular client/broker relationship will therefore depend on all the circumstances.[6] Furthermore, the terms of the individual contract may expressly incorporate, modify or even exclude certain of the normal incidents of agency. The general principle, however, is that the agent is bound to carry out the instructions of the principal.

*Commercial agents operating under the Regulations must 'act dutifully and in good faith'*

In the case of commercial agents under the Commercial Agents (Council Directive) **8.04** Regulations 1993,[7] reg 3(1) decrees that a commercial agent must 'in performing his activities look after the interests of his principal and act dutifully and in good faith'. More specifically, this obligation to act dutifully and in good faith includes a non-derogable duty under reg 3(2)(c) to 'comply with reasonable instructions given by his principal'.[8]

*An agent must comply with his principal's lawful instructions*

The agent must do what he has contracted to do. Thus, in *Turpin v Bilton*, where **8.05** an agent breached his principal's instructions to arrange insurance for the latter's ship, when the uninsured vessel was lost the agent was held liable to his principal.[9] Similarly, in *Dufresne v Hutchinson* it was held that an action would lie against a broker who, having advanced money to a principal on the security of certain cloths with express instructions not to sell goods at even ¼ per cent below their invoice price, grew impatient and sold them at a far inferior price.[10] Again, in *Williams v Evans*[11] an auctioneer, who had been instructed to insist that purchasers of malt that he was entrusted to sell paid 25 per cent of the value of the malt in advance and settled the remainder of the price prior to delivery, was held not to have had authority to receive payment by way of a bill of exchange

---

[5] [1990] 2 Lloyd's Rep 431, 458.
[6] [2010] Lloyd's Rep IR 149 at [158].
[7] On who qualifies as a 'commercial agent' under the Regulations, see paras **1.35–1.65**.
[8] See *infra*, paras **8.76ff**.
[9] (1843) 5 Man&G 455.
[10] (1810) 3 Taunt 117.
[11] (1866) LR 1 QB 352.

and was therefore liable to the principal for failing to comply with his instructions. Obviously, an agent's authority will be governed by the exact terms of the agreement with the principal. Thus, in *Leeds City Council v Waco UK Ltd*,[12] the question arose whether the principal to a JCT Design and Build Contract was bound after practical completion to accept applications for interim payments which had not been made on the dates specified in the contract. There was evidence of an established course of dealing between the parties under which the council's agent would certify all such applications, despite their having been made irregularly, three or four days after the prescribed dates. There was no evidence of any express agreement to vary the application dates. Nevertheless, although the contract specified that after practical completion applications were to be made at two-monthly intervals, it also added the caveat 'unless otherwise agreed'. Since agreeing other dates was merely to implement a mechanism permitted by the contract, in so doing the council's agent could be said to be acting 'for the employer under a condition' within the meaning of the contract, and it had both ostensible and actual authority to do so.

*An agent is not obliged to perform an illegal or void act on behalf of the principal*

**8.06** The agent cannot be expected to carry out instructions that would be null and void at common law or under statute. In *Cohen v Kittell*,[13] a turf commissioner had been asked to place bets on horses on commission at Sandown Park and Newmarket races. When sued by the principal for failing to do so, because the agent was being asked to perform an illegal wagering transaction, he was not liable to the principal for omitting to carry out his mandate. Similarly, in *Thomas Cheshire & Co v Vaughan Bros & Co*,[14] a powerful Court of Appeal held that breach of a contract by an insurance broker to enter into a PPI policy (ie, to enter into a gaming policy declared to be null and void by s 4 of the Marine Insurance Act 1906) was one for breach of which damages could not be recovered. As the court pointed out:

> Where the employment [of the agent] is to make a contract which is null and void, if the agent breaks the contract of employment his principal has no right to damages, whether nominal or substantial ...[15]

*An agent must not exceed his authority*

**8.07** Even if actuated by the highest motives, an agent must not exceed the authority conferred by the principal. To take an established and straightforward example, if

---

[12] [2015] EWHC 1400 (TCC); [2015] TCLR 5 at [26–27]. Cp *Hurst Stores v ML Property Europe Ltd* [2004] BLR 249.

[13] (1889) 22 QBD 680.

[14] [1920] 3 KB 240.

[15] *Ibid* at 258. See also *Fraser v BN Furman (Productions) Ltd* [1967] 3 All ER 57, 63 *per* Diplock, LJ.

contrary to a client's instructions a solicitor compromises an action in which the client is engaged, the solicitor will be held contractually liable to the client, even if he considered that in compromising the action he was acting in the client's best interests. As Lord Campbell, CJ explained:

> An attorney retained to conduct a case is entitled, in the exercise of his discretion, to enter into a compromise, if he does so skilfully and bona fide ... provided always that his client has given him no express directions to the contrary.[16]

Is the agent obliged to carry out the principal's instructions, even if they are com-    **8.08**
mercially imprudent? If he acts in accordance with his principal's instructions, an agent may not be held liable for carrying out those express instructions, even if the agency proves calamitous. In *Overend & Gurney Co v Gibb*,[17] for example, although the transaction proved a 'disastrous concern', the directors of a company, formed with the express purpose of acquiring another business that had sustained heavy losses, were sued for having acquired the company as they had been instructed to do. The principal ought to have appreciated the imprudence of the transaction and that it ought not to have been authorized. Moreover, the House of Lords assumed that the directors were aware that the business's liabilities exceeded its assets before they put the seal of the company to the deeds in question. All the same, because they had been employed expressly to undertake the transaction on the principal's behalf, the agents were not held responsible for the consequences of doing what they had been instructed to do. As Lord Chelmsford explained, musing on the proposition that:

> an agent ... being authorized to do an act, which act is in itself an imprudent one, and which the principal ought never to have authorized to be done, is when the loss is occasioned by his having done the act, to be made liable for it. That certainly is rather a startling proposition, and one which it would require a great deal of argument to lead me to adopt.[18]

In similar vein, in *Redmayne Bentley Stockbrokers v Isaacs* it has been held that a stockbroker does not owe an implied duty to prevent excessive risk-taking by his principal; the stockbroker's duty is purely advisory:

> The investment decision remains that of the client. Provided that proper advice has been given I do not accept that the broker would be under an implied obliga-tion to go further and prevent any investment being made contrary to the advice

---

[16] *Fray v Voules* (1859) 1 E&F 839, 847.

[17] (1871–72) LR 5 HL 480.

[18] *Ibid* at 502. In *Luffeorm Ltd v Kitsons LLP* [2015] PNLR 30 the court reviewed the case law ac-cording to which the starting point is that a solicitor 'unless instructed expressly ... does not normally have a duty to advise on the commercial wisdom of a transaction particularly where ... the client is an experienced businessman' (*Gabriel v Little* [2013] EWCA Civ 1513; [2013] 16 ITELR 567 at [51] *per* Gloster, LJ). There is considerable authority holding that a solicitor's duty is to be measured against his retainer: eg, *Midland Bank Trust Co v Hett Stubbs & Kemp* [1979] Ch 384; *Clark Boyce v Mouat* [1994] 1 AC 428, 437 *per* Lord Jauncey; *Pickersgill v Riley* [2004] PNLR 31 at [8] *per* Lord Scott of Foscote; *Swain Mason v Mills & Reeve* [2011] STC 1177 at [143]–[156] *per* Arnold, J.

given. That is not a necessary obligation for the working of the advisory relationship. It is also contrary to the broker's duty as an agent to follow his principal's instructions.[19]

### Ambiguous instructions

**8.09**  How ought the agent to deal with instructions that are ambiguous? Is there an obligation to seek further instructions? As was seen when we considered the agent's actual authority,[20] according to *Ireland v Livingston*,[21] an agent who has received instructions that may bear several meanings but who fairly and honestly acts according to one of those interpretations will not be held liable to his principal for breach of their contract of agency. In *Ireland*, it should be stressed, where the principal's instructions were so badly framed that their meaning was obscure and the judges who tried the case were deeply divided over their true meaning,[22] the agent was also required to act promptly. There was no time for him to seek further instructions. As Robert Goff, LJ pointed out in *European Asian Bank AG v Punjab & Sind Bank (No 2)*, however, it cannot be left open to every contracting party to act upon a *bona fide*, but mistaken, interpretation of a contractual document, and to hold the other party to that interpretation. Even when the instructions are ambiguous and genuinely capable of two alternative readings, the agent must have acted reasonably in all the circumstances. This means that if there is a patent ambiguity in the agent's instructions, 'it may well be right (especially with the facilities of modern communications available to him) to have his instructions clarified by his principal, if time permits, before acting upon them.'[23]

### Time limit for carrying out instructions

**8.10**  An agent must carry out his principal's instructions either within the period specified in the agency agreement or, if no time limit has been prescribed, within a reasonable time. If a period for performance has been agreed, obviously the agent must comply with that requirement. If no time limit has been specified in their agreement, the agent must carry out his principal's instructions within a reasonable time. By way of example, in *Barber v Taylor*[24] a principal wrote asking an agent to

---

[19] [2010] EWHC 1504 (Comm) at [100] *per* Hamblen, J.

[20] See para **3.13**.

[21] (1872) LR 5 HL 395.

[22] See *Woodhouse AC Israel Cocoa Ltd SA v Nigerian Produce Marketing Co Ltd* [1972] AC 741, 772 *per* Lord Salmon of Sandwich.

[23] [1983] 1 WLR 642, 656. Robert Goff, LJ took his cue from Devlin, J's judgment in *Midland Bank Ltd v Seymour* [1955] 2 Lloyd's Rep 147, 153 who had said: 'Perhaps it is putting it too high for this purpose to say that it is a duty cast upon [the agent]. The true view of the matter ... is that when an agent acts upon ambiguous instructions he is not in default if he can show that he adopted what is a reasonable meaning. It is not enough to say afterwards that if he had construed the documents properly he would on the whole have arrived at the conclusion that in an ambiguous document the meaning which he did not give to it could be better supported than the meaning which he did give to it.'

[24] (1839) 5 M&W 527.

buy 150 bales of cotton on his behalf. The letter stated that 'upon executing the above and forwarding a bill of lading' the principal would accept the agent's draft at 60 days' sight after receipt of the bill of lading. The court held that the agent was in breach of his contract in failing to pass the bill of lading on to the principal within a reasonable time, which the court determined meant within 24 hours of the goods' arrival. However, not only must the agent adhere to any time limits prescribed or implied for performance of his task, if the agent is unable to perform his mandate as instructed or within a reasonable time, he may be under a further duty to inform the principal of his inability to comply. As Phillips, J said in *Youell v Bland Welch & Co Ltd (The 'Superhulls Cover' case) (No 2)*, where brokers had been instructed to place various insurance policies:

> [T] the brokers were at fault in failing to inform the insurers of the 48-month cut-off when inviting them to write the original insurance and to order reinsurance. The brokers then proceeded to obtain for the insurers reinsurance which was … not in accordance with the reinsurance cover ordered. Having done this they were … subject to the further duty to inform the insurers of what they had done—in effect to draw attention to their prior shortcomings.[25]

### An agent must exercise due care and skill in the performance of the agency

Every agent, acting under a contract of agency, is expected to exercise the degree of **8.11** care, skill and diligence that is to be anticipated of an agent employed in that particular role. Naturally enough, this form of inquiry is fact-specific. Thus, brokers charged with selling goods have been held to have failed to exercise due care and diligence when they did not ensure that they obtained the best price for the principal.[26] Similarly, a mercantile agent who, having failed to comply with the principal's specific and urgent request to sell a cargo of groundnuts immediately in order not to lose a market, was in breach of this duty when, much later, he was compelled to sell at a considerable loss after a strike broke out at Marseilles and the market collapsed.[27] In the *The 'Superhulls Cover' case (No 2)*, Phillips, J held that agents were responsible for ensuring that documents were carefully drafted: 'The brokers were bound to exercise reasonable skill and care in drafting [the] documents so as to ensure that they gave clear expression to the terms that had been agreed. They failed to do so.'[28] Solicitors have been held 'bound to bring a fair and reasonable amount of skill to the performance of [their] professional duty';[29] forwarding agents have been held not liable for failing to warn customers that goods were uninsured when the latter led them to understand that the goods were already insured;[30] and so on.

---

[25] [1990] 2 Lloyd's Rep 431, 446–7.
[26] *Solomon v Barker* (1862) 2 F&F 726.
[27] *William Alexander and Stewart Allan Arthur (t/a Alexander & Co) v Wilson, Holgate & Co Ltd* (1923) 14 Ll L Rep 538.
[28] [1990] 2 Lloyd's Rep 431, 446.
[29] *Parker v Rolls* (1854) 14 CB 691, 695 *per* Talfourd, J.
[30] *Club Speciality (Overseas) Inc v United Marine (1939) Ltd* [1971] 1 Lloyd's Rep 482.

**8.12**  In order to assist in determining whether an agent has measured up to the accepted standards of his profession in a particular transaction, expert evidence may be received under s 3 of the Civil Evidence Act 1972. Section 3 states that expert evidence may be admitted 'on any relevant matter', 'relevant' in this context being taken to mean 'helpful' to the court. In *Barings plc v Coopers & Lybrand*,[31] for example, a case arising out of what at the time were thought to be mind-boggling losses registered by Barings when their employee, L, engaged in increasingly crazed derivatives trading, which eventually led to the collapse of that bank. In admitting expert testimony addressing the question, whether a competent derivatives manager, examining the size and profitability of L's reported trading, should have realized that the patterns of risk and reward observed were incredible or, at the very least, so unusual as to merit extensive and detailed examination, Evans-Lombe, J found that there did exist a body of expertise with recognized standards in relation to the managers of investment banks conducting or administering the highly technical and specialized business of futures and derivatives trading. His decision was heavily influenced by the fact that traders in futures and derivatives are required to be licensed by a regulator and may be made answerable before a disciplinary tribunal for failure to comply with ordained professional standards of conduct.

### Gratuitous agencies

*The liability undertaken by the gratuitous agent*

**8.13**  Gratuitous agency may be rare in the commercial sphere. But as Colman, J reminded us in *Yasuda Fire & Marine Insurance Co of Europe Ltd v Orion Marine Insurance Underwriting Agency Ltd*:

> Although in modern commercial transactions agencies are almost invariably founded upon a contract between principal and agent, there is no necessity for such a contract to exist. It is sufficient if there is consent by the principal to the exercise by the agent of authority and consent by the agent to his exercising such authority on behalf of the principal.[32]

In the absence of an enforceable contract, a principal cannot compel a gratuitous agent to perform what he has promised to do on behalf of the principal. More generally, there is little or no authority holding that a gratuitous agent may be liable to his principal for nonfeasance. Misfeasance, however, is another matter. If a gratuitous agent commences what he has undertaken to do or carries it out negligently, he will be tortiously liable to the principal according to standard principles of the law of tort.

---

[31] [2001] PNLR 22, esp at [47].
[32] [1995] QB 174, 185. See also *Garnac Grain Co Inc v HMF Faure & Fairclough Ltd* [1968] AC 1130, 1137 *per* Lord Pearson.

*What level of duty does the law impose on gratuitous agents?*

There may once have been a tendency to hold, in line with the rules governing the **8.14** liability of bailees,[33] that different levels of duty applied according to whether the relationship between principal and agent was gratuitous or for reward—and, more particularly, that the gratuitous agent was only required to display that level of care that he would have exercised in the conduct of his own affairs.[34] However, in *Chaudhry v Prabakhar*,[35] where a close friend lent assistance to a newly quali-fied driver who was searching for a suitable car to purchase and carelessly recom-mended one that had been badly damaged in an accident and was unroadworthy, the Court of Appeal laid down the level of duty to be observed by gratuitous agents. Whilst May, LJ may have doubted the correctness of counsel's concession in *Chaudhry* that the friend owed a duty of care to the purchaser of the car at all,[36] Stocker and Stuart-Smith, LJJ declared that a gratuitous agent owes his principal a duty to take that care which might reasonably be expected of him in all the circumstances, judged objectively. This means that account must be taken either of the agent's actual degree of skill and experience or of the skill and experience to which he has himself laid claim. The existence of friendship between principal and agent is relevant only to the standard of care owed, not to the existence of the duty to take care. The majority of the court said that the very fact of agency, albeit gratuitous, is powerful evidence of the existence of a business connection between the principal and the agent which, even if they are friends, gives rise to a duty of care in respect of statements made by the agent to the principal with regard to the subject matter of the agency whenever the agent knows that the principal is relying on his skill and judgement, the standard of care being the same as that required of a gratuitous agent.

## Fiduciary Duties owed by the Agent

Alongside his duties relating to the performance of his agency according to the **8.15** terms agreed with the principal, an agent is also treated as a fiduciary. Millett, LJ has defined a fiduciary as 'someone who has undertaken to act for or on behalf of another in a particular matter or circumstances which give rise to a relationship of trust and confidence.' In his fiduciary capacity, whether he acts on behalf of the principal for reward or gratuitously, an agent owes his principal a number of

---

[33] *Coggs v Bernard* (1703) 2 Ld Raym 909. See *JP Morgan Chase Bank v Springwell Navigation Corp* [2008] EWHC 1793 (Comm), esp at [194]–[196] *per* Gloster, J.

[34] *Gomer & Co v Pitt & Scott Ltd* (1922) 12 Ll L Rep 115, 116 *per* Warrington, J.

[35] [1989] 1 WLR 9.

[36] *Ibid* at 38–9: 'I do not find the conclusion that one must impose upon a family friend looking out for a first car for a girl of 26 a *Donoghue v Stevenson* duty of care in and about his quest, enforce-able with all the formalities of the law of tort, entirely attractive ... To do so in this and similar cases will make social relations and responsibilities between friends unnecessarily hazardous.'

strict duties in equity. Millett, LJ proceeded to amplify what a fiduciary relationship entails:

> The distinguishing obligation of a fiduciary is the obligation of loyalty. The principal is entitled to the single-minded loyalty of the fiduciary. This core liability has several facets. A fiduciary must act in good faith; he must not make a profit out of his trust; he must not place himself in a position where his duty and his interest may conflict; he may not act for his own benefit or for the benefit of a third person without the informed consent of his principal. This is not intended to be an exhaustive list, ... They are the defining characteristics of the fiduciary.[37]

More recently Lord Millett has written:

> The [no-conflict and no-profit] rules are prophylactic or deterrent, not compensatory or restitutionary. They are based on a pessimistic but realistic appraisal of human nature, and are directed to the avoidance of temptation.[38]

Fiduciary obligations, then, do not derive from the agreement of the parties,[39] but attach to the position of trust in which the agent has been placed by being empowered to act for and to alter the legal relations of the principal.

**8.16** More generally, it has been said that a fiduciary is 'a person who undertakes to act in the interest of another person. It is immaterial whether the undertaking is in the form of a contract. It is immaterial that the undertaking is gratuitous.'[40] As McLachlin, J pointed out in *Norberg v Wynrib*, whilst fiduciary relationships can be properly recognized in the absence of consent by the beneficiary, 'they are more typically the product of voluntary agreement of the parties that the beneficiary will cede to the fiduciary some power and are always dependent on the fiduciary's undertaking to act in the beneficiary's interests.'[41] Nor should it be assumed that all fiduciaries owe identical duties.[42] It has been forcefully argued of late that one should think of fiduciary duties not as arising out of status but as being based upon consent. Moreover, 'the recognition of fiduciary duties and the implications of contractual terms[43] involve an identical process ... [F]iduciary duties arise when they are expressed or implied into voluntary relationships.' The exercise of identifying which

---

[37] *Bristol & West BS v Mothew* [1998] Ch 1, 18. For recent discussion of fiduciary duties, see L Smith, *Fiduciary Relationships: Ensuring the Loyal Exercise of Judgment on Behalf of Another* (2014) 130 LQR 608.

[38] *Bribes and Secret Commissions Again* [2012] CLJ 583, 590.

[39] *E contra, Kelly v Cooper* [1993] AC 205, 213–14 *per* Lord Browne-Wilkinson.

[40] A Scott, *The Fiduciary Principle*, 37 Calif L Rev 539, 544 (1949).

[41] [1992] 2 SCR 226, 272. A fiduciary relationship 'may arise from what one party undertakes or appears to undertake ... for the other; from what actually is agreed between the parties; or, for reasons of public policy, from legal prescription': P Finn, 'Fiduciary Law and the Modern Commercial World', in E McKendrick (ed), *Commercial Aspects of Trusts and Fiduciary Obligations* (1992: Oxford, Oxford University Press) p 9, n 18.

[42] See *Henderson v Merrett Syndicates Ltd* [1995] 2 AC 145, 206 *per* Lord Browne-Wilkinson.

[43] See notably, Lord Hoffmann's opinion in *Attorney General of Belize v Belize Telecom Ltd* [2009] 1 WLR 1988.

particular duties attach to a particular fiduciary is therefore performed applying 'the standard principles of construction and implication':

> In England ... the common emphasis is therefore upon all particular circumstances of the undertaking, especially circumstances of trust, confidence, power, vulnerability and/or discretion. The essential question being asked when those circumstances are examined is exactly the same as the test for implication of terms as enunciated by Lord Hoffmann in the *Belize* case: did the party, by his words or conduct, give rise to an understanding or expectation in a reasonable person that he would behave in a particular way? ... The greater the degree of trust, vulnerability, power and confidence reposed in the fiduciary then the more likely that a reasonable person would have such an expectation.[44]

Even if fiduciary duties cannot be said to derive as such from the agency contract, **8.17** they are unquestionably shaped by that contract. As Lord Browne-Wilkinson warned in *Henderson v Merrett Syndicates Ltd*, 'the phrase "fiduciary duties" is a dangerous one, giving rise to a mistaken assumption that all fiduciaries owe the same duties in all circumstances':

> [T]he extent and nature of the fiduciary duties owed in any particular case fall to be determined by reference to any underlying contractual relationship between the parties. Thus, in the case of an agent employed under a contract, the scope of his fiduciary duties is determined by the terms of the underlying contract. Although an agent is, in the absence of contractual provision, in breach of his fiduciary duties if he acts for another who is in competition with his principal, if the contract under which he is acting authorises him so to do, the normal fiduciary duties are modified accordingly: see *Kelly v Cooper*[45] ... [T]he contract can ... modify the extent and nature of the general duty that would otherwise arise.[46]

As Lewison, J has put it, 'it is the wrong approach to label someone a fiduciary and then reach for a "one size fits all" package of supposed fiduciary duties. The contract is the starting point.'[47]

In *Bristol & West BS v Mothew* Millett, LJ considered how one can identify a breach **8.18** of fiduciary duty. 'The nature of the obligation', he said, 'determines the nature of the breach.' This means that the obligations imposed by the law on fiduciaries merely reflect different aspects of their core duties of loyalty and fidelity.

> Breach of fiduciary obligation, therefore, connotes disloyalty or infidelity. Mere incompetence is not enough. A servant who loyally does his incompetent best for his master is not unfaithful and is not guilty of a breach of a fiduciary duty ...[48]

---

[44] J Edelman, *When Do Fiduciary Duties Arise?* (2010) 126 LQR 302, 317.

[45] [1993] AC 205.

[46] [1995] 2 AC 145, 206. See *Acer Investment Management Ltd v Mansion Group Ltd* [2014] EWHC 3011 (QB), esp at [90]–[104].

[47] *Fattal v Wallbrook Trustees (Jersey) Ltd* [2010] EWHC 2767 (Ch); [2012] Bus LR D7 at [113].

[48] [1998] Ch 1, 18. Cp Stephen A Smith, 'The Deed, not the Motive: Fiduciary Law without Loyalty' in Miller & Gold (eds), *Contract, Status, and Fiduciary Law* (2016: Oxford), taking issue

A fiduciary's conduct need not be dishonest, but must be intentional and involve some element of disloyalty. For this reason, whilst an unconscious omission on the part of a fiduciary may amount to a breach of his duty to exercise reasonable skill and care, it will not amount to breach of fiduciary duty. As Lord Scott explained in *Cave v Robinson Jarvis & Rolf*:

> If the claimant can show that the defendant knew he was committing a breach of duty, or intended to commit the breach of duty—I can discern no difference between the two formulations; each would constitute ... a deliberate commission of the breach ...[49]

Thus, in *Mortgage Express v Abensons*,[50] where a mortgage lender sued solicitors alleging a failure on their part to report various matters relating to two sets of transactions entered into by their borrower client, it was held that if the lender could show that the solicitors 'were conscious of an obligation owed to the [lender] to do something (or refrain from doing something), but felt, rightly or wrongly, that they were inhibited in complying with that obligation by reason that they were also acting for the borrower', that would fall within Lord Scott's formulation in *Cave*. In contrast, it would not suffice if the lender could only show that the solicitors had acted 'in ignorance, even negligent ignorance', of any obligation owed to the lender: 'Acting in ignorance, even negligent ignorance, of any obligation owed to the claimant would not be enough.'[51]

**8.19**  As will become apparent below, the fiduciary duties an agent owes to the principal primarily relate to performance of the agency. However, just as the agent's strict duty of loyalty to the principal informs performance of the agency, it can also exert an impact on termination of agency. In *Temple Legal Protection Ltd v QBE Insurance (Europe) Ltd*,[52] for instance, after the principal terminated a legal expenses insurance agency, the agent claimed to be entitled to continue to handle the principal's run-off business. Moore-Bick, LJ not only observed that such a claim by the agent 'might appear a little surprising at first sight',[53] but also concluded that in view of the duty of loyalty owed by the agent, as well as the essentially 'uncommercial' nature of the claim, in the absence of clear language, it made no sense for any principal who had employed an agent to manage some aspect of his business to be obliged to allow that agent to continue to act on his behalf once the necessary degree of trust and confidence reposed in the agent had, for whatever reason, been lost.[54]

---

with Lionel Smith, 'The Motive, not the Deed' in Getzler (ed), *Rationalising Property, Equity and Trusts: Essays in Honour of Edward Burn* (2003: Oxford).

[49] [2003] 1 AC 384, 403.
[50] [2012] EWHC 1000 (Ch); [2012] 2 EGLR 83.
[51] *Ibid* at [16].
[52] [2009] 1 CLC 553; [2009] Lloyd's Rep IR 544.
[53] *Ibid* at [13].
[54] *Ibid* at [65].

## Duty not to allow his interests to conflict with those of the principal

It is trite law that an agent owes a fiduciary duty of loyalty, including a duty to act **8.20**
*bona fide* for the principal's benefit.[55] More particularly, it is his duty not to allow his
personal interests to conflict with those of the principal. As Lord Cairns, LC put it
in *Parker v McKenna*:

> Now the rule of this court ... as to agents is not a technical or arbitrary rule. It is a
> rule founded on the highest and truest principles of morality. No man can in this
> court, acting as an agent, be allowed to put himself in a position in which his interest
> and his duty will be in conflict.[56]

The reason for the rule is not far to seek. It is obvious that a principal is entitled to
expect that his agent will exercise 'a disinterested skill, diligence, and zeal'[57] for the
exclusive benefit of the principal. The latter reposes confidence in the agent to act
with a sole regard to the interests of the principal. Were such a duty not imposed on
agents, the agent might be unable to resist 'a temptation not faithfully to perform
his duty to his employer'.[58] Moreover, the agent's duty is stern in order to encourage
proper conduct amongst that class of commercial men and women. As Scrutton, LJ
urged in *Rhodes v Macalister*:

> The more that principle is enforced the better for the honesty of commercial transac-
> tions ... [I]t cannot be repeated too often to commercial men—that in matters of
> agency they must act with strict honesty.[59]

Many cases illustrate the operation of this principle.[60]

---

[55] 'Every authority conferred upon an agent, whether express or implied, must be taken to
be subject to a condition that the authority is to be exercised honestly and on behalf of the
principal. That is a condition precedent to the right of exercising it, and, if that condition is
not fulfilled, then there is no authority, and any act purporting to have been done under it
unless in dealing with innocent parties, is void': *Lysaght Bros & Co Ltd v Falk* (1905) 2 CLR
421, 439 *per* O'Connor, J; 'All the cases show that an agent must not put himself in a position where there is a conflict between his interest in getting a commission and his duties to
his principal': *Meadow Schama & Co v C Mitchell & Co* (1973) 228 EG 1511, 1512 *per* Lord
Denning, MR.

[56] (1874) LR 10 Ch App 96, 118. 'The fundamental principle in all these cases is that one contracting party shall not be allowed to put the agent of the other in a position which gives him an
interest against his duty. The result to the agent's principal is the same whatever the motive which
induced the other principal to promise the commission. The former is deprived of the services of
an agent free from the bias of an influence conflicting with his duty, for which he had contracted
and to which he was entitled': *Barry v The Stoney Point Canning Co* (1917) 55 SCR 51, 73 *per*
Justice Anglin.

[57] *Story on Agency*, Joseph Story, *Commentaries on the Law of Agency* (1851: Boston, Little, Browne
& Co) 4th ed, § 210, p 262.

[58] *Boston Deep Sea Fishing v Ansell* (1888) 39 ChD 339, 357 *per* Cotton, LJ.

[59] (1923) 29 Com Cas 19, 28.

[60] The principle may also be embodied in professional bodies' codes. Rule 15-04 of the Law
Society Rules, for example, reads: 'A solicitor must not act where his or her own interests conflict with
the interest of a client or a potential client.'

**8.21**  In *Boston Deep Sea Fishing v Ansell*[61] the managing director of a company secretly agreed to receive a commission from the shipbuilders with whom he was placing orders for vessels on behalf of his own company. Cotton, LJ said of these goings-on, 'If people have got an idea that such transactions can be properly entered into by an agent, the sooner they are disabused of that idea the better.' In taking a secret commission, an agent puts himself in such a position that he has 'a temptation not faithfully to perform his duty to his employer.'[62] Fearful that such side deals were becoming a commonplace of commerce, Bowen, LJ felt that 'there never … was a time in the history of our law when it was more essential that Courts of Justice should draw with precision and firmness the line of demarcation which prevails between commissions which may be honestly received and kept, and commissions taken behind the master's back, and in fraud of the master.'[63] Bowen, LJ went on to state the underlying principle thus:

> [T]here can be no question that an agent employed by a principal or master to do business with another, who, unknown to that principal or master, takes from that other person a profit arising out of the business which he is employed to transact, is doing a wrongful act inconsistent with his duty towards his master, and the continuance of confidence between them. He does the wrongful act whether such profit be given to him in return for services which he actually performs for the third party, or whether it be given to him for his supposed influence, or whether it be given to him on any other ground at all; if it is a profit which arises out of the transaction, it belongs to his master, and the agent or servant has no right to take it, or keep it, or bargain for it, or to receive it without bargain, *unless his master knows it.*[64]

Fry, LJ, the third member of the court in *Boston Deep Sea Fishing*, saw matters in terms of 'the simple dictates of conscience, and according to the broad principles of morality and law.'[65] Whether or not the agent was in breach of this duty was to be judged accordingly. Thus, the managing director had to account for the commissions received and he was held not to be entitled to outstanding salary which otherwise would have been due.

**8.22**  Similar questions arose in *Andrews v Ramsay*.[66] A principal had instructed an estate agent to sell his house for £2,500. The agent found a purchaser willing to pay £2,100, who paid over a £100 deposit. The agent handed over £50 to the vendor, and with the latter's assent retained the other £50 for himself. The agent, it later transpired, had also received a further side commission of £20 from the purchaser.

---

[61]  (1888) 39 ChD 339.
[62]  *Ibid* at 357.
[63]  *Ibid* at 362.
[64]  *Ibid* at 363 (emphasis added).
[65]  *Ibid* at 368.
[66]  [1903] 2 KB 635.

In an action brought by the vendor to recover the £50 commission from the agent, Lord Alverstone, CJ said:

> A principal is entitled to have an honest agent, and it is only the honest agent who is entitled to any commission. In my opinion, if an agent directly or indirectly colludes with the other side, and so acts in opposition to the interest of his principal, he is not entitled to any commission. That is ... supported both by authority and on principle; but if, as is suggested, there is no authority directly bearing on the question, I think that the sooner such an authority is made the better.[67]

Again, in *Rhodes v Macalister*[68] an agent, who was acting to find someone willing to sell mineral rights to his principal, informed the latter that appropriate properties could be purchased for between £8,000 and £10,000. The parties thereupon agreed that if the agent could find someone prepared to sell at below £9,000, the agent would be entitled to the difference between the actual price and £9,000. Having found a seller at £6,625 the agent claimed the difference, viz. £2,375. It later emerged that the agent had also secretly negotiated with the seller to be paid an additional commission on the sale. The agent's claim for commission from his principal failed. Scrutton, LJ set out the relevant principle with customary decisiveness:

> The law I take to be this: that an agent must not take remuneration from the other side without both disclosure to and consent from his principal. If he does take such remuneration he acts so adversely to this employer that he forfeits all remuneration from the employer, although the employer takes the benefit and has not suffered a loss by it.[69]

If an agent wishes to receive a commission from the third party as well as from the **8.23** principal, such a proceeding must be cleared with the principal. As Atkin, LJ explained in *Rhodes v Macalister*:

> The complete remedy is disclosure, and if an agent wishes to receive any kind of remuneration from the other side and wishes to test whether it is honest or not, he has simply to disclose the matter to his own employer and rest upon the consequences of that. If his employer consents to it, then he has performed everything that is required of an upright and responsible agent.[70]

Lightman, J made the same point in *Hopkins v TL Dallas Group Ltd*, where he declared that, 'The grant of actual authority to an agent will not normally include authority to act for the agent's benefit rather than that of his principal and therefore, without agreement, the scope of actual authority will not include this.'[71] Moreover, the principal's consent must be fully informed. In *Hurstanger Ltd v Wilson*,[72]

---

[67] [1903] 2 KB 635, 642.
[68] (1923) 29 Com Cas 19.
[69] *Ibid* at 23.
[70] *Ibid* at 29.
[71] [2005] 1 BCLC 543 at [88].
[72] [2007] 1 WLR 2351.

a finance broker put himself in a position of conflict of interest in obtaining a commission from the lender additional to that paid by his client. Whilst the broker could show that the client had signed a document that contained a term acknowledging that in some circumstances the broker was to be paid commission by the lender, the Court of Appeal held that in these circumstances the principal's consent was not fully informed and that the broker was in breach of fiduciary duty. Delivering the leading judgment, Tuckey LJ held that consent could only be given with full knowledge of all the material circumstances and of the nature and extent of the broker's interest.[73]

**8.24** More recently, in *Imageview Management Ltd v Jack*,[74] Jacob, LJ both applied these principles and articulated the agent's duty of fidelity with particular force. A football agent had entered into a two-year contract with J, Trinidad's international goalkeeper, under which the agent undertook to find J employment with a UK club, to provide the player with advice and representation, and to 'use its reasonable endeavours to promote [J] and act in his best interests.' The agent later entered into an agreement with Dundee United FC whereby the latter would pay the agent a £3,000 fee to secure a work permit for J. J signed for Dundee, but after a year learned of the agent's side deal with Dundee. The Court of Appeal had little trouble in finding that the side deal had been agreed, that the football agent had breached his duty of fidelity, that it was immaterial whether or not the agent realized that what he was doing was wrong, and that J was entitled to the return of commission he had paid the agent under their agency agreement. The agent had taken a secret profit from the third party, and this amounted to a breach of fiduciary duty owing to the existence of a real conflict of interest. As has often been laid down, once a conflict of interest is shown, all right to remuneration is automatically forfeit.[75]

**8.25** The reason for depriving the agent of his commission, even in cases where his breach of duty has not occasioned the principal any loss, is simple. It is because the law is:

> concerned not with merely damages such as those for a tort or breach of contract but with what the remedy should be when the agent has betrayed the trust reposed in him—notions of equity and conscience are brought into play. Necessarily such a betrayal may not come to light. If all the agent has to pay if and when he is found out are damages the temptation to betray the trust reposed in him is all the greater. *So the strict rule is there as a real deterrent to betrayal.*[76]

Very occasionally, a court may allow a deduction to reflect the value of work done by the unfaithful agent. It may do so if 'it would be inequitable now for the beneficiaries to step in and take the profit without paying for the skill and labour which has

---

[73] *Ibid* at [34].
[74] [2009] 1 Lloyd's Rep 436.
[75] *Keppel v Wheeler* [1925] 1 KB 577, 592 *per* Atkin, LJ.
[76] [2009] 1 Lloyd's Rep 436 at [50] (emphasis added).

produced it'.[77] However, this power is exercised very sparingly so as not to encourage fiduciaries to act in breach of fiduciary duty.[78]

Admitting that the courts find it necessary to reiterate this rule from time to time, **8.26** Jacob, LJ summarized the position as follows:

> The law imposes on agents' high standards. Footballers' agents are not exempt from these. An agent's own personal interests come entirely second to the interest of his client. If you undertake to act for a man you must act 100%, body and soul, for him. You must act as if you were him. You must not allow your own interest to get in the way without telling him. An undisclosed but realistic possibility of a conflict of interest is a breach of your duty of good faith to your client.[79]

In fact, the standards the law imposes are even more extensive because a conflict of **8.27** interest will be assumed to exist even if it can be shown that in the given case there was no conflict of interest. Lord Cranworth, LC stated the position in *Aberdeen Railway Co v Blaikie Bros*:

> It is a rule of universal application, that no-one, having such duties to discharge, shall be allowed to enter into engagements in which he has, or can have, personal interests conflicting, or which possibly may conflict, with the interests of those whom he is bound to protect.[80]

Thus, in the leading case of *Boardman v Phipps* the House of Lords held that agents for trustees who acquired extra shares in a company, thereby benefiting both the trust and themselves, were obliged to account for the profit they made because there existed a possibility of a conflict of interest—'even if the possibility of conflict is present between personal interest and the fiduciary position, the rule of equity must be applied.'[81] As was indicated above, the fiduciary can only defeat the principal's claim by showing that he made profits with the knowledge and assent of the principal.[82]

One particular situation in which an agent's duty to his principal may most readily **8.28** be compromised arises where the agent acts for more than one competing principal. This situation frequently arises in the context of estate agency.[83] The leading

---

[77] *Phipps v Boardman* [1964] 1 WLR 993, 1018 *per* Wilberforce, J.

[78] In *Guinness plc v Saunders* [1990] 2 AC 663, 700–1 Lord Goff added: 'the exercise of the jurisdiction is restricted to those cases where it cannot have the effect of encouraging trustees in any way to put themselves in a position where their interests conflict with their duties as trustees.' See *Cobbetts LLP v Hodge* [2010] 1 BCLC 30, esp at [115]–[118] *per* Floyd, J.

[79] [2009] 1 Lloyd's Rep 436 at [6]. Mummery, LJ, at [64], paid homage to the courts that had delivered the judgments mentioned above in the following terms: 'The stringent agency duties so brilliantly expounded in *Boston Deep Sea Fishing v Ansell* by the greatest constitution of the Court of Appeal in the 19th century and in *Rhodes v Macalister* by the greatest constitution of the Court of Appeal in the 20th century apply to the facts of this case. It is inspiring to read their judgments. I would not qualify them in any respect. I cannot improve upon them in any way.'

[80] (1854) 1 Macq 461, 471.

[81] [1967] 2 AC 46, 111 *per* Lord Hodson.

[82] *Ibid* at 105.

[83] But not necessarily in all estate agency contexts. See *Northampton Regional Livestock Centre Co Ltd v Cowling* [2014] EWHC 30 (QB) at [187], where an agent who acted for vendor and purchaser

authority is *Kelly v Cooper*.[84] A client sued his Bermudan estate agent for damages for breach of duty in failing to disclose this material information to him and for thereby placing himself in a position where his duty and his self-interest conflicted. The Judicial Committee held that, in view of the highly peculiar position occupied by estate agents, it was appropriate in this case to imply a term into the contract between client and agent to the effect that the latter was entitled to act for other principals selling competing properties provided that he kept confidential the information obtained from each of those principals, even though that information might well have been material to the client:

> In a case where a principal instructs as selling agent for his property or goods a person who to his knowledge acts and intends to act for other principals selling property or goods of the same description, the terms to be implied into such agency contract must differ from those where an agent is not carrying on such general agency business. In the case of estate agents, it is their business to act for numerous principals: where properties are of a similar description, there will be a conflict of interest between the principals each of whom will be concerned to attract potential purchasers to their property rather than that of another. Yet, despite this conflict of interest, estate agents must be free to act for several competing principals otherwise they will be unable to perform their function ... The scope of the fiduciary duties owed by the [estate agent] to the [client] (in particular the alleged duty not to put themselves in a position where their duty and their interest conflicted) are to be defined by the terms of the contract of agency.[85]

Following the Court of Appeal's decision in *Rossetti Marketing Ltd v Diamond Sofa Co Ltd*,[86] it is doubtful whether these principles will apply to other species of agents.[87]

### Duty to make full disclosure

**8.29** Pursuing the latter point, a common theme that runs through the various fiduciary duties considered in this chapter is that an agent may only act contrary to his duty of loyalty to the principal with the latter's full knowledge. Nor will it be sufficient for the agent to show that had permission been sought of the principal, it would have

---

in the sale of a former livestock auction site was found in breach of his fiduciary duty. Green, J drew a distinction between estate agents involved in residential and in commercial property transactions.

[84] [1993] AC 205.
[85] *Ibid* at 214 and 215.
[86] [2013] 1 All ER (Comm) 308.
[87] Without determining the point, in *Rossetti*, a case involving a commercial agent under the Commercial Agents Regulations, the Court of Appeal gave no encouragement to the view that such an agent could act for competing principals. An agent can only act for two or more principals with conflicting interests where all those principals had given their fully informed consent and, as in *Kelly v Cooper*, where the principals must have appreciated that the nature of the agent's business was such as to require the agent 'to act for numerous principals' in order to perform his function. Clearly, in *Rossetti* there was no need to extend the reasoning in *Kelly v Cooper* to a commercial agent who was employed to promote, place and sell foreign-manufactured furniture in the United Kingdom.

been granted.[88] As Lord Wilberforce explained in *New Zealand Netherlands Society 'Oranje' Inc v Kuys*, this means that:

> [I]f an arrangement is to stand, whereby a particular transaction, which would otherwise come within a person's fiduciary duty, is to be exempted from it, there must be full and frank disclosure of all material facts.[89]

The agent's obligation to make full disclosure to the principal is exacting. The agent **8.30** bears the burden of proving that he did so, for if the agent, say, is selling his principal's property, 'nothing is better settled than that an agent, purchasing for himself, must tell his principal he is the purchaser, or one of the purchasers.'[90] An agent is required to deal with his principal at arm's length, and may only do so after disclosure of everything material that he knows with respect to such property.[91] It is not sufficient for the agent simply to intimate to the principal that he has an interest in the transaction or to claim to have communicated sufficient information to the principal to put the latter upon inquiry. Disclosure is not an empty formality.[92] As Sir George Jessel declared in *Dunne v English*:

> [E]ven a statement which would in other cases be constructive notice sufficient to put the party on inquiry will not be sufficient in the case of principal and agent—that for reasons of policy he must not only put the principal on inquiry, but must give him full information and make full disclosure.[93]

Trade customs that purportedly permit an agent to act as principal, to acquire an **8.31** interest in transactions carried out on behalf of the principal or to act potentially in opposition to the interests of the principal,[94] will be treated as unreasonable unless they are brought to the principal's attention and the latter agrees to be bound by them. Nor will it avail the agent to claim that, if the principal had been aware of what was afoot, he would surely have agreed to the agent's transaction or even to show that the principal benefited from the impugned transaction. As Clarke, LJ made clear in *Murad v Al-Saraj*:

> [T]he fiduciary must disgorge the profit that he makes as a fiduciary without the informed consent of his principal and the fact that if the principal had been asked

---

[88] *Crown Dilmun v Sutton* [2004] 1 BCLC 468 at [137] and [179]–[180]; *Bristol & West BS v Mothew* [1998] Ch 1, 18.

[89] [1973] 1 WLR 1126, 1131–2.

[90] *Dunne v English* (1874) LR 18 Eq 524, 533 *per* Sir George Jessel, MR.

[91] See *Murphy v O'Shea* (1845) 2 J&Lat 422, 425 *per* Lord St Leonards.

[92] Eg, *Gluckstein v Barnes* [1900] AC 240, 249 *per* Lord Macnaghten: 'With all deference to the learned counsel for the appellant, that seems to me to be absurd. "Disclosure" is not the most appropriate word to use when a person who plays many parts announces to himself in one character what he has done and is doing in another. To talk of disclosure to the thing called the company, when as yet there were no shareholders, is a mere farce. To the intended shareholders there was no disclosure at all. On them was practised an elaborate system of deception.'

[93] (1874) LR 18 Eq 524, 535.

[94] Eg, *Anglo African Merchants Ltd v Bayley* [1970] 1 QB 311; *North & South Trust Co v Berkeley* [1971] 1 WLR 470.

he would have agreed is irrelevant. So too is the fact that the principal is making a profit which he would not otherwise have made or that he would otherwise have made a loss.[95]

**8.32**  The duty of disclosure extends to transactions where the agent seeks to act on behalf of more than one principal. In *Fullwood v Hurley* a hotel broker, acting on commission on behalf of a vendor, also sought to claim commission under an agreement with the purchaser. The Court of Appeal declined to permit the broker to receive a double commission. As Scrutton, LJ said:

> No agent who has accepted an employment from one principal can in law accept an engagement inconsistent with his duty to the first principal from a second principal, unless he makes the fullest disclosure to each principal of his interest, and obtains the consent of each principal to the double employment … [A]n agent who wants to make two contracts for double commission must do so in the clearest possible terms and with the clearest possible information to each of his principals what he is doing, otherwise he cannot sue under an alleged agreement.[96]

Megaw, LJ addressed this selfsame question at the end of his judgment in *Eagle Star Insurance Co Ltd v Spratt*.[97] Having initially acted for Eagle Star in obtaining reinsurance, brokers subsequently allowed themselves to be used as agents of the underwriters. Although it was perfectly possible that, had they asked, assent would have been readily forthcoming in the special circumstances obtaining in this case, the brokers did not seek the consent of their original principals. This undisclosed dual role produced difficulties, and the parties disputed their knowledge, actual or constructive, in relation to one or the other of the two capacities in which they were acting for different principals. In Megaw, LJ's view:

> It is a matter which ought to be mentioned in order that such questions may be considered to try and avoid the recurrence of difficulties and embarrassments in future. An agent for one party should not act for the opposite party in connection with the same transaction without the latter's informed consent.[98]

### Duty not to take advantage of his position

**8.33**  Just as an agent must not allow his own interests to come into conflict with those of his principal, so too an agent may neither make use of the principal's property nor exploit any confidential information that has come into his possession during the course of the agency. Thus, it has for long been held that profits derived by a fiduciary from an opportunity, obtained as a result of acting as a fiduciary, which

---

[95]  [2005] EWCA Civ 959 at [129]; [2005] WTLR 1573.
[96]  [1928] 1 KB 498, 502, and 504.
[97]  [1971] 2 Lloyd's Rep 116.
[98]  *Ibid* at 133.

he is otherwise bound to use (if at all) only for the benefit of his principal, are regarded as profits for which the false fiduciary is accountable.[99] Moreover, the fiduciary cannot retain the benefit of such a transaction for himself, but will be regarded as holding the profits on behalf of the principal.[100] The agent will only be allowed to make a profit from his agency if he has the principal's fully informed consent.

The strictness of these equitable principles is observable in *Keech v Sandford*. Upon **8.34** its expiry, a trustee renewed in his own name a lease previously held by the trust. The court held that the trustee could not renew the lease for his own benefit, but henceforth held the lease for the benefit of the *cestui que trust*. The trustee was forbidden to renew, even though the landlord had already refused to renew the lease for the benefit of the *cestui que trust*. The rule is severe for a reason:

> I very well see, if a trustee, on the refusal to renew, might have a lease to himself, few trust estates would be renewed to *cestui que* use; though I do not say there is a fraud in this case, yet he should rather have let it run out, than to have had the lease to himself. This may seem hard, that the trustee is the only person of all mankind who might not have the lease: but it is very proper that rule should be strictly pursued, and not in the least relaxed; for it is very obvious what would be the consequence of letting trustees have the lease, on refusal to renew to *cestui que* use.[101]

### The agent who takes advantage of his position as agent or who makes a profit out of the principal

In *Ritchie v Cooper*[102] the defendant was a co-owner of a ship. He was also a provi- **8.35** sions merchant. The defendant supplied the vessel with goods at the market price. The plaintiff, who was the other co-owner, claimed that the defendant ought only to have charged for goods at cost price. The court upheld the plaintiff's claim, declaring that the provisions merchant would only have been entitled to charge market prices if the other co-owner had expressly consented to pay such prices. By way of further example of agents exploiting their position, in *Turnbull v Garden* a principal requested an agent to purchase a cavalry uniform for his son. The agent succeeded in acquiring the apparel at a discount. The agent was held not to be entitled to charge the principal the full sum.[103] In the same way a stockbroker who managed to acquire shares at a lower price than had been agreed with the principal was not entitled to keep the difference.[104] Again, in *Diplock v Blackburn*, where, thanks to the exchange rate, the master of a ship in a foreign port received a premium for a bill drawn

---

[99] *Boardman v Phipps* [1967] 2 AC 46.
[100] See *Cook v Deeks* [1916] AC 554.
[101] (1726) Select Cases Temp King 61, 62.
[102] (1860) 28 Beav 344.
[103] (1869) 20 LT 218.
[104] *Thompson v Meade* (1891) 7 TLR 698.

upon in England on account of the ship, it was held that the premium belonged to the shipowner. As Lord Ellenborough, CJ riposted when it was suggested that by custom the master was permitted to retain these sums:

> If a contrary usage has prevailed, it has been a usage of fraud and plunder. What pretence can there be for an agent to make a profit by a bill upon his principal? This would be to give the agent an interest against his duty.[105]

**8.36** Perhaps one of the best-known cases on this topic is *Reid Newfoundland Co v Anglo-American Telegraph Co Ltd*.[106] The appellants, who leased their railway subject to a subsisting contract with the respondents, were allowed to use a special wire erected and maintained by the latter in and about their railway as defined in the contract. The appellants, however, were enjoined by the contract 'not to pass or transmit any commercial messages over the said special wire except for the benefit and account of' the respondents. The appellants nevertheless used the special wire for all the purposes of their business, which encompassed a host of different undertakings. The Judicial Committee held that the appellants were accountable as trustees for the profits so made:

> [W]hen ... the appellants used the special wire for the transmission of unprivileged messages an obligation in the nature of a trust arose on their part, and it became their duty to keep an account of the profits accruing from such use of the wire, and to set those profits aside as moneys belonging to the respondents.[107]

The appellants had sought to argue that they were not obliged to account owing to the expiry of the relevant statutory limitation period. However, the court endorsed the words of Giffard, LJ in *Burdick v Garrick*, who had said:

> I do not hesitate to say that where the duty of persons is to receive property and to hold it for another and to keep it until it is called for, they cannot discharge themselves from that trust by appealing to the lapse of time. They can only discharge themselves by handing over that property to somebody entitled to it.[108]

*Taking advantage of confidential information*

**8.37** The obligations of the agent extend to the misuse of confidential information acquired during the course of his agency. *Lamb v Evans*[109] provides an example of agents who sought to make use of such confidential information. Canvassers, who had been employed on commission to collect advertisements from traders for exclusive publication in the claimant's business directory, were held not to be entitled to

---

[105] (1811) 3 Camp 43, 44.
[106] [1910] AC 555.
[107] [1910] AC 555, 559.
[108] (1870) LR 5 Ch 233. See also *Lyell v Kennedy* (1889) 14 App Cas 437, 463 *per* Lord Macnaghten.
[109] [1893] 1 Ch 218.

hand them on to a rival publication when their employment terminated and they joined another similar outfit. As Lindley, LJ explained:

> Such a use is contrary to the relation which exists between principal and agent. It is contrary to the good faith of the employment, and good faith underlies the whole of an agent's obligations to his principal. No case ... can I believe be found which is contrary to the general principle upon which this injunction is framed, *viz.*, that an agent has no right to employ as against his principal materials which that agent has obtained only for his principal and in the course of his agency. They are the property of the principal. The principal has ... such an interest in them as entitles him to restrain the agent from the use of them except for the purpose for which they were got.[110]

Although this may well be incorporated as a term of the agent's contract, this duty is quite distinct from contractual obligations. Lord Denning, MR famously declared in *Seager v Copydex Ltd (No 1)* the rule that an agent may not derive a profit from use of such confidential information 'depends on the broad principle of equity that he who has received information in confidence shall not take unfair advantage of it. He must not make use of it to the prejudice of him who gave it without obtaining his consent.'[111]

*Remedies*

When an agent has taken advantage of his position to make a personal benefit, the principal disposes of a range of remedies. As in *Lamb v Evans*,[112] an injunction may afford an appropriate remedy. Obviously, if the agent is in breach of his contract with the principal, the latter may obtain contractual damages in respect of that breach. If a contractual action is unavailable, however, the court may award damages in equity. In *Dowson & Mason Ltd v Potter*,[113] for example, where an employee had revealed confidential information about the manufacture of artificial limbs to a would-be competitor, the court declared that the general purpose of such damages must be to compensate the claimant for the loss which he has suffered. This will vary from case to case. Thus, if the claimant would have licensed the use of his confidential information, then almost invariably the measure of damages is going to reflect the price that the claimant could have commanded for that information; and no question of loss of profits will arise precisely because the claimant was always ready to allow someone else to manufacture at a price. If, on the other hand, the claimant manufacturer would not have licensed its use, then he would not have been exposed to competition at the time when he was exposed because of the defendant's wrongdoing, and the loss of profits becomes relevant. As Slade, J's ruling in *English*

**8.38**

---

[110] *Ibid* at 226.
[111] [1967] 1 WLR 923, 931.
[112] [1893] 1 Ch 218.
[113] [1986] 1 WLR 1419.

*v Dedham Vale Properties Ltd* shows, the right to damages in equity is separate from, and may be additional to, a party's right to damages in lieu of an injunction.[114]

**8.39** Finally, a principal is also entitled to an account from his agent of any profits the latter may have made in breach of confidence. In *Peter Pan Manufacturing Corp v Corsets Silhouette Ltd*,[115] for instance, the claimants sought injunctions restraining the defendants from manufacturing or selling brassières of the styles known as 'U15' and 'U25' (and also a fabric known as 'striped fabric') which the claimants had designed, patented, and marketed under a variety of alluring brand names. The defendants, an English company, who for eight years had sold one of the claimants' earlier products under licence, were given a preview in confidence of the new 'U15' and 'U25' designs when their designer visited the claimants' American factory. The defendants subsequently exploited this confidential information and manufactured similar foundation garments to the claimants. Having been adjudged to have acted in breach of confidence, Pennycuick, J ordered both an injunction forbidding further manufacture of products deriving from use of the confidential information and that the defendants account to the claimants for all profits made from sales of the articles in question. It might finally be added, a fiduciary who has made a profit from use of his principal's confidential information holds those profits on trust for the principal.

### Duty not to take bribes or secret commissions

**8.40** It is obvious that an agent who, in the course of his agency, takes a bribe or agrees to take a bribe or receives a secret commission from any third party who is either seeking to enter into legal relations with the principal or who is already transacting business with the principal will be in breach of his fiduciary duty to that principal. If an agent takes a bribe or secret commission, he must account for it to the principal. Thus, the agent is liable, jointly and severally along with the briber, to the principal for the sum of the bribe or secret commission. Any bribe that has actually been paid will be held by the agent on trust for his principal.[116] Additionally, the principal may be entitled to bring an action in tort against the agent for losses he has incurred as a result of entering into a transaction in which a bribe was either offered or taken.[117]

---

[114] [1978] 1 WLR 93, 111–12.

[115] [1964] 1 WLR 96.

[116] *Att-Gen for Hong Kong v Reid* [1994] 1 AC 324; *FHR European Ventures LLP v Mankarious* [2013] 1 Lloyd's Rep 416.

[117] *Mahesan v Malaysia Government Officers Co-operative Housing Society Ltd* [1979] AC 374. In *National Grid Electricity Transmission plc v McKenzie* [2009] EWHC 1817 (Ch), for instance, the claimant company was awarded damages or an account of profits against one of its corrupt or dishonest project managers, M, who had conspired with a contractor, R. M had accepted bribes in return for approving fraudulent time sheets and expense claims, and granting contracts for the provision of labour. The relief granted included an order that M account for bribes or, alternatively,

*What constitutes a bribe or secret commission?*

In *Industries & General Mortgage Co Ltd v Lewis* Slade, J stated:  **8.41**

> [A] bribe means the payment of a secret commission, which only means (i) that the person making the payment makes it to the agent of the other person with whom he is dealing; (ii) that he makes it to that person knowing that that person is acting as the agent of the other person with whom he is dealing; and (iii) that he fails to disclose to the other person with whom he is dealing that he has made that payment to the person whom he knows to be the other person's agent. Those three are the only elements necessary to constitute the payment of a secret commission or bribe for civil purposes.[118]

Slade, J added that for purposes of civil law 'proof of corruptness or corrupt motive is unnecessary'.[119] On the contrary, once the bribe is established,[120] it is presumed that it was given with an intention to induce the agent to act favourably to the payer and, thereafter, unfavourably to the principal. Indeed, as Romer, LJ emphasized in *Hovenden and Sons v Millhoff*, the law does not require proof that the bribe had any influence on the behaviour of the agent:

> [T]he court will presume in favour of the principal, and as against the briber and the agent bribed, that the agent was influenced by the bribe; and this presumption is irrebuttable.[121]

As Christopher Clarke, J explained in *Novoship (UK) Ltd v Mikhaylyuk*, 'The underlying rationale for the strict approach taken by the cases is that a principal is entitled to be confident that an agent will act wholly in his interests.'[122]

---

pay damages in respect of overcharges on labour contracts, for which R was jointly liable in part; an order that M pay damages in respect of wrongly allowed fuel charges; an order that M pay damages in respect of wrongly procured goods, including vehicles; an order for payment in respect of N's costs of the investigation, for which M and R were jointly liable; and, finally, interest upon those sums.

[110] [1949] 2 All ER 573, 575. 'Bribe' was succinctly defined by Leggatt J, as he then was, in *Anangel Atlas Compania Naviera SA v Ishikawajima-Harima Heavy Industries* [1990] 1 Lloyd's Rep 167 at 171, as: 'A commission or other inducement which is given by a third party to an agent as such, and which is secret from his principal.'

[119] [1949] 2 All ER 573, 575. See *Hovenden and Sons v Millhoff* (1900) 83 LT 41 *per* Romer, LJ: 'If a bribe be once established to the court's satisfaction, then certain rules apply. Amongst them the following are now established, and, in my opinion, rightly established, in the interests of morality with the view of discouraging the practice of bribery. First, the court will not inquire into the donor's motive in giving the bribe, nor allow evidence to be gone into as to the motive.'

[120] To constitute a bribe, the payment or gift to the agent must amount to more than 'a little present' (*The Parkdale* [1897] P 53, 58–9 *per* Gorell Barnes, J). This is taken to mean that it must be sufficient to create a real possibility of a conflict between interest and duty: *Imageview Management Ltd v Jack* [2009] 1 Lloyd's Rep 436 at [6] *per* Jacob, LJ; *Fiona Trust & Holding Corp v Privalov* [2010] EWHC 3199 (Comm) at [73(ii)] *per* Andrew Smith, J.

[121] [1949] 2 All ER 573, 575. Subsequently, in *Petrograde Inc v Smith* (2000) 29 February, unreported, David Steel, J held that it was not necessary to show that the bribe induced a contract between the principal of the recipient of the payment and the donor; the law, it was said, focuses on the conflict of interest which any bribe is presumed to induce in the agent.

[122] [2012] EWHC 3586 (Comm) at [110].

Consequently, if a third party bribes an agent, the principal is not required to prove that the briber acted with a corrupt motive or intention to persuade or influence the agent; it will be presumed. Nor need the principal show that the agent was in fact influenced by the bribe. The principal does not have to show that he actually suffered loss as a consequence of his agent having received a bribe.[123] Nor does it need to be shown that the briber knew, or even suspected, that the agent would conceal the bribe from the principal: the briber cannot be heard to say that he believed that the agent would disclose the existence of the bribe to his principal.[124] Finally, the principal does not have to show that the bribe was given in connection with a particular transaction or series of transactions: the possibility of a conflict between duty and interest may be created by a bribe paid to an agent in order to influence him generally and not directed to any particular matter or intended to influence him in relation to a particular transaction.[125]

**8.42**  Bribes are commonly differentiated from secret commissions according to their motive. If the third party's motive in making a payment to the agent is corrupt, the sums involved are referred to as 'bribes', whereas 'secret commissions' are payments that are not actuated by corrupt motives. Neither bribes nor secret commissions need take the form of payments.

### What if the principal becomes aware of the bribe or secret commission?

**8.43**  The principal will be unable to recover from either his agent or a third party a payment made by the third party to the agent if the principal knows of the payment, or would have known of it, if he had thought about it. Knowledge of, and consent to, the fact of payment is sufficient to legitimate it, without it being necessary to prove that the principal knew the exact amounts paid, provided that they were reasonable.[126]

### The principal's restitutionary claim against the agent

**8.44**  In *Att-Gen for Hong Kong v Reid* a strong Privy Council rejected the earlier view, represented by *Lister & Co v Stubbs*,[127] according to which an agent who received a secret commission was not held to hold those sums on trust for his principals but only as the principals' debtor. Preferring the extra-judicial opinion of Sir Peter

---

[123] See *Hovenden & Sons v Millhoff* (1900) 83 LT 41; *Tesco Stores Ltd v Pook* [2003] EWHC 823 (Ch) at [39]–[45].

[124] *Grant v Gold Exploration and Development Syndicate Ltd* [1900] 1 QB 233, 249 *per* Collins, LJ.

[125] *Fiona Trust & Holding Corp v Privalov* [2010] EWHC 3199 (Comm) at [73] *per* Andrew Smith, J. See generally, *Otkritie Int'l Investment Management Ltd v Urumov* [2014] EWHC 191 (Comm) at [68] *per* Eder, J.

[126] *Anangel Atlas Compania Naviera SA v Ishikawajima-Harima Heavy Industries Co Ltd* [1990] 1 Lloyd's Rep 167, 171 *per* Leggatt, J.

[127] (1890) LR 45 ChD 1.

Millett[128] to a veritable host of academic writers, in *Att-Gen for Hong Kong v Reid* the Judicial Committee, accepted that:

> *Lister & Co v Stubbs* is not consistent with the principles that a fiduciary must not be allowed to benefit from his own breach of duty, that the fiduciary should account for the bribe as soon as he receives it and that equity regards as done that which ought to be done. From these principles it would appear to follow that the bribe and the property from time to time representing the bribe are held on a constructive trust for the person injured.[129]

Lord Templeman opined that if a fiduciary receives a bribe, or as occurred in *Reid*, where a corrupt prosecutor had acquired properties with the proceeds of bribes in New Zealand, has converted it into other property, the corrupt party holds the property on trust for the beneficiary. The Privy Council's decision to grant the principal such a powerful equitable interest in bribes and secret commissions received by his agent did occasion considerable surprise at the time. For no especially good reason it is argued that *Reid* reinforces the position of the principal as against other parties who may lodge claims in the event of an agent's insolvency.[130]

Despite the problems of precedent raised by a Privy Council decision displacing the **8.45** earlier decision of the Court of Appeal in *Lister & Co v Stubbs*, in *Daraydan Holdings Ltd v Solland International Ltd*[131] Lawrence Collins, J sided with the view that if an agent accepts a bribe, equity insists on treating it as a legitimate payment intended for the benefit of the principal; he will not be allowed to say that it was a bribe. In *Daraydan Holdings* a high-ranking government official in Qatar, and corporate vehicles through which he held property in England, were granted a restitutionary remedy against a corrupt employee/agent, because there was a proprietary basis for the claim and the bribes derived directly from the claimants' property. Since the contract price was actually increased by the amount of the bribe and the bribe was paid out of the money paid by the claimants for what they thought was the contract price, the claim was truly one for the restitution of money extracted from the claimants. This was reinforced by the fact that the employee was a party to a conspiracy to defraud the claimants. As Lawrence Collins, J also made clear:

> There are powerful policy reasons for ensuring that a fiduciary does not retain gains acquired in violation of fiduciary duty, and I do not consider that it should make any difference whether the fiduciary is insolvent. There is no injustice to the creditors in their not sharing in an asset for which the fiduciary has not given value, and which the fiduciary should not have had.[132]

---

[128] See *Bribes and Secret Commissions* [1993] Restitution LR 7, 20.

[129] [1994] 1 AC 324, 336.

[130] See, eg, K Uff, 'The Remedies of the Defrauded Principal after *Att-Gen for Hong Kong v. Reid*', in D Feldman and F Meisel (eds), *Corporate and Commercial Law: Modern Developments* (1996: London, LLP Professional Publishing) pp 239–45.

[131] [2005] Ch 119.

[132] *Ibid* at [86].

**8.46** The principal is entitled to retain the bribe or secret commission even if he decides to set aside the tainted transaction. In *Logicrose Ltd v South end United Football Club Ltd*[133] Millett, J held that a principal is entitled to recover a bribe from the agent regardless of whether the principal elects to affirm or rescind the tainted transaction. Moreover, in recovering the money there is no implication that the principal has adopted the transaction for the money is equally his whether he adopts the transaction or not.

**8.47** The Court of Appeal, in 2012, in *Sinclair Investments (UK) Ltd v Versailles Trade Finance Ltd*,[134] re-ignited the debate over whether an agent holds any bribe he receives on trust for his principal, by declaring that *Lister & Co v Stubbs* was in fact correctly decided. Lord Millett published a devastating critique on the Court of Appeal's decision in *Sinclair Investments*.[135] Finn, J, too, writing for a Full Federal Court of Australia, which rejected outright the resurrection of *Lister & Co v Stubbs*, with characteristic self-restraint described that decision as 'an anomalous limitation ... upon the reach of the ... constructive trust in English law'.[136] Speaking of the *Sinclair* decision, Finn, J archly observed: 'English law may have its own reasons for so contriving the limits to proprietary relief. We need not speculate about them.'[137] English courts were once again constrained to follow *Lister & Co v Stubbs*. As Newey, J noted in *Cadogan Petroleum plc v Tolley*:

> [I]t seems to me that the Court of Appeal's decision in *Sinclair* was based on (and I am therefore bound by) the proposition that 'a beneficiary of a fiduciary's duties cannot claim a proprietary interest ... in respect of any money or asset acquired by a fiduciary in breach of his duties to the beneficiary, unless the asset or money is or has been beneficially the property of the beneficiary or the trustee acquired the asset or money by taking advantage of an opportunity or right which was properly that of the beneficiary.' While the significance of that proposition doubtless extends beyond bribes and secret commissions, it means, I think, that I must proceed on the footing that a beneficiary will have no proprietary interest in a bribe or secret commission unless it can be said that it 'is or has been beneficially the property of the beneficiary or the [fiduciary] acquired the asset or money by taking advantage of an opportunity or right which was properly that of the beneficiary.' Further, I do not think it is open to me (or would be open to any other judge at trial) to choose to follow *Reid* instead of *Lister & Co v Stubbs*.[138]

It may well have been the law for a time, but as Lord Millett has noted, the sorry result was that:

> *Lister v Stubbs* and *Sinclair v Versailles* are contrary to principle and authority, fail to give effect to the policy of the law, reduce English law to a state of

---

[133] [1988] 1 WLR 1256, 1263.
[134] [2012] Ch 453.
[135] *Bribes and Secret Commissions Again* [2012] CLJ 583.
[136] *Grimaldi v Chameleon Mining NL (No 2)* [2012] FCAFC 6 at [569].
[137] *Ibid* at [574].
[138] [2012] 1 P&CR DG5 at [27].

incoherence, and leave this country in the uncomfortable position of being the only common law jurisdiction where a dishonest fiduciary is allowed to retain a profit he has made by profitably investing a bribe or otherwise exploiting the fiduciary relationship for his own benefit without the fully informed consent of his principal.[139]

English courts were briefly constrained, albeit in some cases reluctantly,[140] to follow **8.48** *Lister & Co v Stubbs*. In *European Ventures LLP v Cedar Capital Partners LLC*,[141] however, the Supreme Court reconsidered the question. FHR, having established that their agent, Cedar Capital, in the course of negotiating on FHR's behalf the purchase of the issued share capital in the company that owned a long lease on a swish hotel in the Principality of Monaco, had without FHR's informed consent accepted a €10 million commission from the vendor, contested the trial judge's refusal to grant FHR a proprietary remedy in respect of these monies. Lord Neuberger, who had delivered judgment in *Sinclair Investments Ltd* two years earlier upholding the proposition in *Lister & Co v Stubbs* that the relationship between agent and principal in cases where the agent has received a wrongful benefit is one of debtor and creditor, also delivered the judgment of the seven-man Supreme Court in *FHR European Ventures*. The Supreme Court was required to pronounce upon the rule whereby an agent who receives a bribe or secret commission is to be treated as having acquired the benefit on behalf of the principal so that the benefit is beneficially owned by the principal. As Lord Neuberger admitted, '[i]n the end, it is not possible to identify any plainly right or wrong answer to the issue of the extent of the Rule, as a matter of pure legal authority.'[142] Despite powerful academic writing to the contrary,[143] Lord Neuberger preferred the view that whether it concerned a bribe, secret commission, or other benefit received by the agent or simply the agent taking advantage of an opportunity that came his way as a result of the agency, the principal was entitled not merely to an equitable account in respect of the benefit,[144] but also to the beneficial ownership of the benefit: 'a bribe or secret commission accepted by an agent is held on trust for his principal.'[145] Such a rule, it was claimed, is consistent with the fundamental principle of the law of agency that commands

---

[139] [2012] CLJ 583, 614.
[140] Eg, *Cadogan Petroleum plc v Tolley* [2012] 1 P & CR DG5 at [27] *per* Newey, J.
[141] [2014] 3 WLR 535.
[142] *Ibid* at [32].
[143] Eg, Goode, 'Proprietary Restitutionary Claims' in Cornish (ed), *Restitution: Past, Present and Future* (1998) p. 69; Goode, *Proprietary Liability for Secret Profits—A Reply* (2011) 127 LQR 493; Worthington, *Fiduciary Duties and Proprietary Remedies: Addressing the Failure of Equitable Formulae* [2013] CLJ 720. See further, literature cited by Lord Neuberger at [2014] 3 WLR 535 at [29], a literature said to reveal 'passions of a force uncommon in the legal world' ([2014] Ch 1 at [61] *per* Pill, LJ).
[144] *Regal (Hastings) Ltd v Gulliver (Note)* [1967] 2 AC 134, 145 *per* Lord Russell: 'The liability [to account] arises from the mere fact of a profit having ... been made. The profiteer, however honest and well intentioned, cannot escape the risk of being called upon to account.'
[145] [2014] 3 WLR 535 at [46].

the agent's undivided loyalty to the principal,[146] has 'the merit of simplicity', since it applies uniformly in all situations,[147] serves to align 'the circumstances in which an agent is obliged to account for any benefit received in breach of his fiduciary duty and those in which his principal can claim the beneficial ownership of the benefit',[148] and conforms with elementary economics in as much as there is normally a strong possibility that the bribe or secret commission will have disadvantaged the principal.[149] Lord Neuberger claimed that the Court's decision that bribes and secret commissions were held on trust for the principal also conformed with wider policy considerations: it served to recognize that bribery, in particular, was an evil practice that undermined trust in the commercial world[150] whilst also drawing English law into alignment with the rule that prevails in a number of other common-law jurisdictions.[151]

### The tortious liability of the agent

**8.49**   If an agent receives a bribe or secret commission and his principal incurs loss as a result of the agent's dishonest conduct, the principal may hold the agent (and, indeed, the briber too) liable in the tort of deceit for any losses he incurs. Given that the principal is already entitled to claim the amount of the bribe from his agent, the question arises as to whether the principal's remedy in tort is additional to, or alternative to, his restitutionary claim against the agent for the sum of the bribe. The Privy Council addressed this issue in *Mahesan S/O Thambiah v Malaysia Government Officers' Co-operative Housing Society Ltd*.[152] In *Mahesan* a housing society brought an action against its corrupt agent who, in exchange for a bribe, had connived with another individual to make a profit from a land transaction at the expense of the society. The society claimed both the amount of the bribe and the loss it had suffered as a result of entering into the tainted transaction. The Federal Court of Malaysia had held that both sums were recoverable. Reversing this decision, the Privy Council stated that at common law a principal can recover from his bribed agent (or from the briber) *either the* amount of the bribe as money had and received *or*, alternatively, compensation for the actual loss sustained through entry into the tainted transaction as damages for fraud. The housing society was not entitled to make double recovery from the agent but was bound to elect, at the time when

---

[146]   *Bristol & West Building Society v Mothew* [1998] Ch 1.
[147]   [2014] 3 WLR 535 at [35].
[148]   *Ibid* at [36].
[149]   As the Court suggested, since the vendor in *FHR European Ventures* was prepared to pay €10m to the agent in respect of a deal worth €211.5m, it must have been 'quite likely' that the vendor would have been willing to sell for less, 'possibly €201.5 m': *ibid* at [37].
[150]   See esp *Att Gen for Hong Kong v Reid* [1994] 1 AC 324, 330 *per* Lord Templeman.
[151]   '[I]t seems to us highly desirable for all those jurisdictions to learn from each other, and at least to lean in favour of harmonising the development of the common law round the world': [2014] 3 WLR 535 at [45].
[152]   [1979] AC 374.

judgment was to be entered, between its claim for the amount of the bribe and its claim for damages.[153] As Lord Diplock observed:

> This extension to the briber of liability to account to the principal for the amount of the bribe as money had and received, whatever conceptual difficulties it may raise, is now and was by 1956 too well established in English law to be questioned. So both as against the briber and the agent bribed the principal has these alternative remedies: (1) for money had and received under which he can recover the amount of the bribe as money had and received or, (2) for damages for fraud, under which he can recover the amount of the actual loss sustained in consequence of his entering into the transaction in respect of which the bribe was given, but he cannot recover both.[154]

Although some commentators have argued that dual recovery ought to have been permitted because the interest in discouraging secret profits overrides the interest in preventing people from receiving an unlooked-for windfall, others consider that the rule endorsed in *Mahesan* is adequate: it allows the principal to opt for whichever form of relief offers the fuller compensation, may serve to punish the agent in cases where the tortious damages exceed the value of the bribe, and avoids the incongruity of the principal receiving a conspicuous windfall.

### Further consequences

Other consequences may flow from the agent receiving a bribe or secret commission. **8.50**
As *Andrews v Ramsay & Co*[155] shows, where an agent employed to sell a property sold it but received a secret profit from the purchaser, the agent was held not only to be obliged to account to his principal for that profit, but was also not entitled to claim any commission on the transaction from his principal. In the words of Lord Alverstone, CJ:

> A principal is entitled to have an honest agent, and it is only the honest agent who is entitled to any commission. In my opinion, if an agent directly or indirectly colludes with the other side, and so acts in opposition to the interest of his principal, he is not entitled to any commission. That is, I think, supported both by authority and on principle; but if, as is suggested, there is no authority directly bearing on the question, I think that the sooner such an authority is made the better.[156]

If the transactions are severable, however, the agent will only forfeit commission on those dealings in which he has been dishonest. In *Nitedals Taendstikfabrik v Bruster* Nevill, J held that:

> [T]he doctrine ... laid down [in *Andrews v Ramsay & Co*] does not apply to the case of an agency where the transactions in question are separable ... and does not entitle

---

[153] See also *United Australia Ltd v Barclays Bank Ltd* [1941] AC 1.

[154] [1979] AC 374, 383. Toulson, J, in *Fyffes Group Ltd v Templeman* [2000] 2 Lloyd's Rep 643, 672, emphasized that there were 'cogent grounds, in principle and in practical justice, for ... holding that the briber of an agent may be required to account to the principal for benefits obtained from the corruption of the agent. The law ought not to assist a party to retain the profits of such a vice.'

[155] [1903] 2 KB 635.

[156] *Ibid* at 638.

the principal to refuse to pay commission to his agent in cases where he has acted honestly because there are other cases in which the agent, acting under the same agreement, has acted improperly and dishonestly.[157]

An agent who receives a bribe may also incur criminal liability, as may the third party who has corruptly offered the bribe.[158]

### Duty not to delegate his office; sub-agency

*An agent may only delegate his authority with the express or implied authority of the principal*

8.51 Owing to the fiduciary nature of the parties' relationship, and the personal trust the principal reposes in his agent, an agent may not normally delegate his authority or employ a sub-agent to accomplish part, or all, of the task he has been employed to perform. *Delegatus non potest delegare.* According to Thesiger, LJ, in *de Bussche v Alt*, this tag:

> when analysed, merely imports that an agent cannot, without authority from his principal, devolve upon another obligations to the principal which he has himself undertaken to personally fulfil; and that, inasmuch as confidence in the particular person employed is at the root of the contract of agency, such authority cannot be implied as an ordinary incident in the contract.[159]

8.52 If an agent does delegate his mandate without authority, the sub-agent's acts will be invalid and will not be binding upon the principal, unless the latter chooses to ratify the delegation. Thus, in *John McCann & Co v Pow* the vendor of a leasehold flat was held not liable to pay commission to an estate agent who, while claiming to be 'sole agent', had delegated his personal functions and duties to a sub-agent without the express authority of his principal.[160] Similarly, in *Catlin v Bell*, the claimant entrusted the master of a ship trading with the West Indies with the task of selling a quantity of her millinery goods there. When the master found himself unable to find a purchaser in the West Indies, without authority he consigned the goods to another party in Caracas, where they were destroyed in an earthquake. Lord Ellenborough, CJ held that, since special confidence had been reposed in the ship's master with respect to the sale of the millinery goods, the master had no right to

---

[157] [1906] 2 Ch 671, 674–5.
[158] Bribery Act 2010, ss 1 and 2.
[159] (1878) LR 8 ChD 286, 310. Although the parallel ought not to be pressed too far, in the realm of tort law a contractor will not normally be held vicariously liable for the tortious acts of his subcontractor's employees. Only if the agreement between contractor and subcontractor can be seen to confer upon the former the power to control the way in which the subcontracted work is executed can vicarious liability be transferred from subcontractor to contractor: eg, *Biffa Waste Services Ltd v Maschinenfabrik Ernst Hese GmbH* [2009] 3 WLR 324 at [55]–[61].
[160] [1974] 1 WLR 1643.

hand them over to another person, and to give them a new destination.[161] If the delegation is unauthorized, the agent will also be liable to the principal for breach of his duty not to delegate.

Although the general underlying principle is that an agent may not delegate perfor- **8.53** mance of his agency to another, nevertheless there exist a number of situations in which delegation is permissible.

*(i) An agent may delegate his authority if, at the time of his appointment, the principal* **8.54** *was aware and agreed to the agent delegating his authority.* Clearly, if delegation is expressly or impliedly authorized by the principal—or, indeed, if an agent's unauthorized delegation is subsequently ratified by the principal—there is no reason not to uphold the parties' wishes.

*(ii) An agent may delegate his authority if it is usual practice in the trade or profession to* **8.55** *which the agent belongs to delegate authority, and it is neither an unreasonable practice nor inconsistent with the terms of the agent's contract with the principal.* In the old case of *Solley v Wood*,[162] where the validity of the issue of proceedings by a London solicitor was contested on the ground that the claimant had only granted authority to her attorney in Canterbury, the court accepted that it was the ordinary and recognized practice of country solicitors to employ a London agent. Such a practice was considered to have been eminently reasonable. For, were it otherwise, it was said that a client would not be able to employ a country solicitor in a suit, unless such solicitor himself went up to London to conduct the litigation in person.

*(iii) An agent may delegate his authority if the nature of the agency requires that it be* **8.56** *wholly or partly performed by a sub-agent.* In *Quebec & Richmond Railway v Quinn*, where the principals conferred powers on persons whom they knew would exercise them only by deputy, the court concluded: 'When the power given by a person is of such a nature as to require its execution by a deputy, the attorney may appoint such deputy ...'[163]

*(iv) An agent may delegate his authority where it can be presumed from the circum-* **8.57** *stances of the case and from the conduct of the parties that the agent was intended to have power to delegate his authority.*[164]

*(v) An agent may delegate his authority where the act is purely ministerial and does* **8.58** *not require particular confidence and discretion.* In *Allam & Co Ltd v Europa Poster Services Ltd*,[165] a case in which a sub-delegation of an agency was held to have been

---

161 (1815) 4 Camp 183.
162 (1852) 16 Beav 370.
163 (1858) 12 Moo PCC 232, 265.
164 *de Bussche v Alt* (1878) LR 8 ChD 286.
165 [1968] 1 WLR 638.

permissible, a firm of outdoor advertising contractors had obtained licences from various site owners permitting them to display advertisements on hoardings placed on those sites. The firm persuaded some site owners to allow them to display advertisements on sites on which their competitor, the claimant, had hitherto possessed licences to do so. It also acquired from the latter owners authority to give notice on behalf of the site owners, terminating their competitor's existing licences 'so soon as may be legally possible'. The defendant employed its solicitors to deliver the relevant notices. One question raised in the case was whether the defendant had been entitled to delegate this task to the solicitor, acting as sub-agent. In determining that the delegation had been permissible, Buckley, J explained the rationale underlying this exception to the general principle that an agent may not delegate the performance of his agency to another:

> The relation of an agent to his principal is, normally at least, one which is of a confidential character and the application of the maxim *delegatus non potest delegare* to such relationships is founded on the confidential nature of the relationship. Where the principal reposes no personal confidence in the agent the maxim has no application, but where the principal does place confidence in the agent, that in respect of which the principal does so must be done by the agent personally, unless, either expressly or inferentially, he is authorised to employ a sub-agent or to delegate the function to another. If the agent personally performs all that part of his function which involves any confidence conferred upon him or reposed in him by the principal, it is ... immaterial that he employs another person to carry out some purely ministerial act on his behalf, in completing the transaction.[166]

Again, in *The Berkshire* Brandon, J ruled that charterers, who possessed authority to sign the bills of lading on behalf of shipowners, were entitled to appoint another company as agents to do this for them, who were then entitled to appoint another concern as sub-agents to do it for them:

> The signing of a bill of lading is a ministerial act and I do not consider for this and other reasons that the principle *delegatus non potest delegare* applies to such an act.[167]

**8.59** *(vi) An agent may delegate his authority where delegation is necessitated by unforeseen circumstances.* Thesiger, LJ, in *de Bussche v Alt*, recognized that whilst delegation could not normally be implied as an incident of any contract between principal and agent, the exigencies of business do from time to time render necessary the carrying out of the instructions of a principal by a person other than the agent originally instructed for the purpose. Delegation is permissible in a number of circumstances, including 'where, in the course of the employment, unforeseen emergencies arise which impose upon the agent the necessity of employing a substitute.'[168] In *de*

---

[166] *Ibid* at 642.
[167] [1974] 1 Lloyd's Rep 185, 188.
[168] (1878) LR 8 ChD 286, 310–11.

*Bussche v Alt* itself a shipowner employed an agent to sell a yacht at any port at which the ship might happen to be from time to time in the course of its employment under charter. This arrangement, Thesiger, LJ stated, 'is pre-eminently one in which the appointment of substitutes at ports other than those where the agent himself carries on business is a necessity, and must reasonably be presumed to be in the contemplation of the parties.'[169] The sub-agent whom the agent appointed had sold the yacht, but taken an enormous secret profit. The shipowner sued the sub-agent to recover that secret profit, and succeeded. In *Gwilliam v Twist*,[170] on the other hand, an employment case in which it was held that there was no necessity to authorize a former bus conductor who happened to be standing by a bus, whose driver had been adjudged to be inebriated by a passing police officer, to drive the bus a quarter of mile to its depot without first consulting the employer, the Court of Appeal left open whether the employer would have been vicariously liable for the negligent driving of the erstwhile conductor if there had existed a situation of necessity.

*(vii) Apparent authority.* Technically, if a principal, who has not conferred upon his **8.60** agent an authority to delegate, was considered to have represented that the agent did possess authority to delegate his authority, a party who relied upon that representation and agreed to act as sub-agent to the principal would be validly appointed. From this, one would conclude that any third party dealing with the sub-agent could then rely upon the latter's authority to act on behalf of the agent.

Although the exceptions to *delegatus non potest delegare* have been set out discretely, **8.61** they will sometimes overlap. In *Amoutzas v Tattersalls Ltd*,[171] a case arising out of a payment made in the course of the sale of some racehorses, Robin Spencer, QC held that the agent had power to delegate his authority to the sub-agents both because (i) by necessary implication the authority carried with it power to do anything necessary to effect the parties' intention, and (ii) because they were purely ministerial acts.[172]

### What legal relations are created between principal and sub-agent in cases where the delegation was authorized?

If delegation by the agent was authorized, the principal is bound by acts performed **8.62** by the sub-agent as though the agent had performed them himself. However, this

---

[169] *Ibid* at 311. For good measure, in *de Bussche v Alt* there was also express authority to appoint a substitute as well as 'a complete ratification' of the sub-agent's appointment.

[170] [1895] 2 QB 84.

[171] [2010] EWHC 1696 (QB) at [123]–[128].

[172] 'It must be remembered that [the agent] speaks virtually no English and was heavily reliant upon [the sub-agents] to interpret for him, and to speak and write on his behalf. [The principal] must have been well aware of this': [2010] EWHC 1696 (QB) at [128].

does not necessarily mean that direct contractual relations will have been created between principal and sub-agent. Whether direct privity has been established between principal and sub-agent will depend upon the intentions of the parties. Privity will be held to be established if the principal has expressly or impliedly authorized the delegation of the agent's duties, or has ratified his agent's unauthorized delegation, and it was the parties' intention that privity was to be established. As Rix, J remarked in *Prentis Donegan & Partners Ltd v Leeds & Leeds Co Inc*, 'it has to be the intention of all three parties, principal, agent and sub-agent, to effect a direct contractual relationship between principal and sub-agent.'[173] Thus, it is a matter of construing what the intention of the parties actually was. Although it may be a relevant factor, the mere fact that the principal has authorized the appointment of a sub-agent by the agent is by no means determinative of this question. As Rix, J explained, the fact that:

> in every case of agency and sub-agency, the ultimate principal and the ultimate third party will be brought into direct contractual relations … does not prevent the general rule that a principal and a sub-agent are not in privity of contract with one another: and that shows that the fact that the agent who appoints a sub-agent is an agent is not determinative of his ability to disclaim any liability to the sub-agent he appoints.[174]

**8.63** The point has often been made in case law. In *New Zealand and Australian Land Co Ltd v Watson*, for example, Bramwell, LJ made clear that the principal's authority to make a contract of agency between himself and the sub-agent did not necessarily follow from the fact that he had conferred authority upon the agent to appoint a sub-agent through whom the principal might be brought into privity of contract with a third party. Even though the principal had expressly authorized a factor to delegate the task of selling the principal's goods to a broker, when the factor became bankrupt it was determined that no privity of contract existed between principal and sub-agent and that the broker was not liable to account to the principal for the proceeds of sale.[175] Similarly, in *Powell & Thomas v Evan Jones & Co*,[176] where a principal brought a claim against a sub-agent both for breach of fiduciary duty and for breach of contract in relation to a secret profit, two of the three members of the Court of Appeal displayed reluctance to place reliance on the contractual link between the parties, preferring to uphold the sub-agent's liability on the grounds that he was in a fiduciary position.[177] Wright, J surveyed the authorities in *Calico*

---

[173] [1998] 2 Lloyd's Rep 326, 327.

[174] *Ibid* at 330.

[175] (1881) 7 QBD 374, 381–2.

[176] [1905] 1 KB 11.

[177] *Ibid* at 18 *per* Henn Collins, MR and pp 20–1 *per* Stirling, LJ. The liability of sub-agents as fiduciaries is sometimes questioned: see most recently, comments of Teare, J in *Markel International Insurance Co Ltd v Surety Guarantee Consultants Ltd* [2009] Lloyd's Rep IR 77 at [225].

*Printers Association v Barclays Bank Ltd*[178] and concluded that the general position in English law was thus:

> English law ... has in general applied the rule that even where the sub-agent is prop-
> erly employed, there is still no privity between him and the principal: the latter is
> entitled to hold the agent liable for breach of the mandate, which he has accepted,
> and cannot in general claim against the sub-agent for negligence or breach of duty.
> I know of no English case in which a principal has recovered against a sub-agent
> for negligence. The agent does not as a rule escape liability to the principal merely
> because employment of the sub-agent is contemplated. To create privity it must be
> established not only that the principal contemplated that a sub-agent would perform
> part of the contract, but also that the principal authorised the agent to create privity
> of contract between the principal and the sub-agent, which is a very different matter
> requiring precise proof. In general where a principal employs an agent to carry out a
> particular employment, the agent undertakes responsibility for the whole transaction
> and is responsible for any negligence in carrying it out, even if the negligence be that
> of the sub-agent properly or necessarily engaged to perform some part; because there
> is no privity between the principal and the sub-agent.[179]

As we shall see, it may be possible sometimes for the principal to sue the sub-agent in negligence[180]—although, as Rix, J has pointed out, this alternative route to holding the sub-agent liable to the principal 'makes it easier, rather than more difficult, to maintain the classical position of absence of direct privity in contract.'[181]

In *Prentis Donegan & Partners Ltd v Leeds & Leeds Co Inc*, Rix, J noted Lord Goff's    **8.64**
remarks in *Henderson v Merrett Syndicates Ltd*,[182] in which he endorsed the following statement in *Bowstead and Reynolds*:

> But there is no privity of contract between a principal and a sub-agent as such, merely
> because the delegation was effected with the authority of the principal; and in the
> absence of such privity the rights and duties arising out of any contracts between the
> principal and the agent, and between the agent and the sub-agent, respectively, are
> only enforceable by and against the immediate parties to those contracts. However,
> the sub-agent may be liable to the principal as a fiduciary, and possibly in other
> respects.[183]

Taking his cue from this declaration, Rix, J went on to claim, 'the influence of *de
Bussche v Alt* would seem to have waned', and to note that it seemed only once to
have been applied in a decision of the courts since 1878. Thus, in *Prentis Donegan*
itself, where a placing broker sought summary judgment against a producing broker

---

[178] (1930) 36 Com Cas 71.
[179] *Ibid* at 77–8.
[180] See paras **8.66–8.67**, and discussion of *Henderson v Merrett Syndicates Ltd* [1995] 2 AC 145.
[181] *Prentis Donegan & Partners Ltd v Leeds & Leeds Co Inc* [1998] 2 Lloyd's Rep 326, 331.
[182] See [1995] 2 AC 145, 202.
[183] This text, lightly modified to include tortious liability, and possibly a duty to account, may
be found in *Bowstead & Reynolds on Agency* (2006: London, Sweet & Maxwell) 18th ed, art 35(3).

in order to be reimbursed for insurance premiums which the former had itself paid to underwriters, Rix, J insisted that what was required was not merely evidence that the involvement of the placing broker was authorized by the principal but that it was intended by both principal, agent and sub-agent to create contractual relations directly between principal and sub-agent.

*A sub-agent may be liable to the principal under the law of tort*

**8.65**  Even if the courts prove generally reluctant to admit a contractual relationship between principal and sub-agent, a sub-agent may nevertheless be liable to the principal in tort under the principle in *Hedley Byrne & Co v Heller & Partners*.[184] This situation arose in *Henderson v Merrett Syndicates Ltd (No 1)*,[185] where Lloyd's direct and indirect names sought to recover catastrophic losses they had suffered as a consequence of the alleged negligence of those managing their syndicates. Apart from holding that the existence of a contract does not preclude a concurrent liability in tort, the House of Lords decided that in appropriate circumstances managing agents, who were technically sub-agents appointed by the syndicates' agents, might owe a tortious duty of care to the principals if the requisite conditions under *Hedley Byrne* could be established. According to Lord Goff of Chieveley, this was in tune with the incremental approach to negligence liability adopted by the House in *Caparo Industries plc v Dickman*.[186] More specifically, where it could be shown that one party had assumed responsibility towards another to exercise some particular skill (broadly understood), whether this assumption of responsibility involved the provision of information and advice or the performance of other services, irrespective of whether their relationship was contractual or not, a duty of care would be owed. In these circumstances, Lord Goff said that 'there is no reason in principle why a tortious duty should not coexist with a contractual duty in the case of the broad duty of care now recognised following the generalisation of the tort of negligence in the 20th century.'[187] Nor is there said to be any reason why in such cases the law of tort should impose identical duties to those owed in contract.[188]

**8.66**  As Jackson, LJ pointed out in *Robinson v PE Jones (Contractors) Ltd*, where R unsuccessfully claimed tortious damages for economic loss occasioned by shoddy construction of a gas flue under a building contract, in *Henderson* Lord Goff was by no means saying every contractual obligation to do something carried with it a parallel

---

[184]  [1964] AC 265.

[185]  [1995] 2 AC 145.

[186]  [1990] 2 AC 605, adopting the approach of Brennan, J in *Sutherland Shire Council v Heyman* (1985) 60 ALR 1, 43–4.

[187]  [1995] 2 AC 145, 192. Lord Goff's analysis was founded in great part on Oliver, J's judgment in *Midland Bank Trust Co Ltd v Hett Stubbs & Kemp* [1979] Ch 384.

[188]  *Robinson v PE Jones (Contractors) Ltd* [2011] 3 WLR 815 at [79] *per* Jackson, LJ. See also at [94] *per* Stanley Burnton, LJ.

tortious duty to the same effect.[189] He was simply indicating that the existence of a contract does not prevent a tortious duty from arising. The result might well be untidy; but, given that the tortious duty is imposed by the general law, and the contractual duty is attributable to the will of the parties, in Lord Goff's view, there was no objection to a claimant taking advantage of whichever remedy happened to be most advantageous to him. The only caveat was that it would be necessary to ascertain whether the tortious duty was so inconsistent with the applicable contract that, in accordance with ordinary principle, the parties must be taken to have agreed that the tortious remedy was thereby limited or excluded. Applied to the facts of *Henderson*, in which no such inconsistency was detected—in part, one would suspect, owing to the unusually close relations existing between the principals and sub-agents in this particular case[190]—this meant that 'there must be implied into the sub-agency agreements a duty upon the managing agents to exercise due skill and care.'[191] Nevertheless, Lord Goff also stressed that this litigation was 'most unusual' and that 'it cannot therefore be inferred from the present case that other sub-agents will be held directly liable to the agent's principal in tort.'[192]

**8.67** Lord Goff's cautionary words regarding the rarity of sub-agents' tortious liability to the agent's principal, and an absence of subsequent authority on the point, do suggest that one need not place too great store by Rix, J's observations in *Prentis Donegan & Partners Ltd v Leeds & Leeds Co Inc* to the effect that the availability to the principal of a tortious remedy against the sub-agent 'makes it easier, rather than more difficult, to maintain the classical position of absence of direct privity in contract.'[193]

### Duty to account

**8.68** The general position is that an agent who receives monies or goods from his principal or on behalf of his principal is bound to account to the principal for those monies or goods. This obligation may arise by virtue of the agent's fiduciary position. However,

---

[189] [2011] 3 WLR 815 at [77].

[190] [1995] 2 AC 145, 196.

[191] *Ibid* at 194.

[192] *Ibid* at 195. 'See further *Riyad Bank v AHLI United Bank (UK) plc* [2007] PNLR 1 at [36]–[47] *per* Neuberger, LJ: '[T]he law of tort should not be invoked in a commercial context, at least where there are no gaps, where the parties have contractually provided for a duty, or a chain of duties.' 'Gap-filling', Neuberger, LJ suggested, means that 'there are cases involving contractual duties, where, if the law of tort cannot be invoked, as a matter of policy, there would be a "liability gap" which would be unacceptable'. (The liability gap was something mentioned in Lord Steyn's judgment in *Williams v Natural Life* [1998] AC 830, 837: 'the law of tort, as the general law, has to fill an essential gap-filling role'.) However, Neuberger, LJ also said: 'the fact that the law of tort can be invoked where there is a "liability gap" in certain exceptional cases does not mean that it can never be invoked in a case where there is no "liability gap".'

[193] [1998] 2 Lloyd's Rep 326, 331

this is far from being so in every case. As La Forest, J once noted, 'not every legal claim arising out of a relationship with fiduciary incidents will give rise to a claim for a breach of fiduciary duty.'[194] Millett, LJ echoed this point in *Bristol & West BS v Mothew*, stressing that this is 'not just a matter of semantics' but is something that 'goes to the very heart of the concept of breach of fiduciary duty and the availability of equitable remedies.'[195] The fact that the agent is a fiduciary does not mean that all his duties, central and important as they may be, are therefore fiduciary duties. Thus, on another occasion, in *Coulthard v Disco Mix Club Ltd*, Jules Sher, QC declared that 'the simple duty to account, central though it is, is not a fiduciary duty.'[196] In each case, therefore, it will be a matter of determining whether the agent's duty to account arises at common law or is meant to wear a fiduciary character.

**8.69**   If there is a contract between principal and agent, the parties may either have specified in what legal capacity monies are to be held by the agent for the principal or the court may deduce what their relations were by objectively construing their intentions.[197] More generally, if it can be shown that the principal has acceded to the agent's mixing the principal's monies with his own, the agent will not be required to account as a fiduciary but as a simple debtor at common law.[198] Although the tradition has been to state that the agent owes a fiduciary duty either (a) where the principal specifically entrusts money or property to be held by the agent for the principal's benefit, or (b) where the third party confides money or property into the safekeeping of the agent to be held for the principal's benefit, the modern tendency appears to be to ask the more functional question: is a trust relationship, with its accompanying fiduciary incidents, appropriate to the type of commercial relationship existing between the parties?[199] In *Kingscroft Insurance Co Ltd v HS Weavers (Underwriting) Agencies Ltd*, for instance, where an underwriting agent operated the business of a number of principals by receiving premiums, paying claims and holding monies on deposit in its own name, Harman, J dealt with the nature of claims concerning monies held on deposit in banks by declaring:

> [T]his agreement constitutes a perfectly normal agency relationship. The agent ... is entitled to carry on the principal's insurance and reinsurance business, to receive all premiums due to the principal in that business; to pay out all monies due from the principal as a result of carrying on that business and pay expenses incurred on behalf

---

[194]   *Lac Minerals Ltd v International Corona Ltd* (1989) 61 DLR (4th) 14, 28.

[195]   [1998] 1 Ch 1, 18.

[196]   [2000] 1 WLR 707, 728.

[197]   Very occasionally, a statute may state in which capacity an agent holds his principal's monies: eg, Solicitors Act 1974, s 32 (as amended).

[198]   *Wilsons and Furness-Leyland Line Ltd v British and Continental Shipping Co Ltd* (1907) 23 TLR 397; *John Youngs Insurance Services Ltd v Aviva Insurance Service UK Ltd* [2012] 1 All ER (Comm) 1045 at [94] *per* Ramsey, J.

[199]   See notably the discussion in *Bowstead & Reynolds on Agency* (2014: London, Sweet & Maxwell) 20th ed, para 6.040.

of the principal in carrying on the business. [Almost] the whole of the principal's business is in the hands of this agent ... [N]o 'Trust' relationship is constituted by a normal principal and agent relationship, nor in my judgment is a trust relationship created by this particular agency agreement. The agent is a commercial agent, it is entitled to collect the principal's money into one account of its own, it is entitled to mix its own monies and the principal's monies with other principals' monies in one account. The agent can dispose of monies in its account as it thinks fit and is not bound, as a trustee would be to invest the monies on its principal's behalf ...[200]

Millett, LJ underlined this point in *Paragon Finance plc v DB Thakerar & Co*, where leave was sought to amend a claim to allege fraud, conspiracy to defraud, fraudulent breach of trust and intentional breach of fiduciary duty, owing to expiry of the limitation period for the common-law claim for breach of contract, etc:

The law on this subject has been settled for more than a hundred years. An action for an account brought by a principal against his agent is barred by the statutes of limitation unless the agent is more than a mere agent but is a trustee of the money which he received ... A claim for an account in equity, absent any trust, has no equitable element; it is based on legal, not equitable rights.[201]

However, where the indications are that something more than a debtor–creditor **8.70** relationship was contemplated—possibly, it was made clear that the principal's monies were to be kept separate from those of the agent;[202] or that the agent was to invest or manage the funds in particular ways;[203] or that the agency concerned only a single transaction, rather than a continuing course of business with a general account operating between principal and agent—the duty to account will wear a fiduciary character. In *Henry v Hammond*, a case involving shipping agents, Channell, J stated:

It is clear that if the terms upon which the person receives the money are that he is bound to keep it separate, either in a bank or elsewhere, and to hand that money so kept as a separate fund to the person entitled to it, then he is a trustee of that money and must hand it over to the person who is his *cestui que trust*. If on the other hand he is not bound to keep the money separate, but is entitled to mix it with his own money and deal with it as he pleases, and when called upon to hand over an equivalent sum of money, then, in my opinion, he is not a trustee of the money, but merely a debtor.[204]

This statement was bound up with the wider consideration that it would be unfortunate to see the intricacies and doctrines connected with trusts introduced into commercial transactions.[205] Shipping agents, Channell, J insisted, carry on a

---

[200] [1993] 1 Lloyd's Rep 187, 191.
[201] [1999] 1 All ER 400, 415.
[202] See, eg, *Lyell v Kennedy* (1889) 14 App Cas 437. See also *Re Nanwa Gold Mines Ltd* [1955] 1 WLR 1080; *Re Kayford Ltd (In Liquidation)* [1975] 1 WLR 279.
[203] Eg, *Burdick v Garrick* (1870) LR 5 Ch App 233.
[204] [1913] 2 KB 515, 521.
[205] *New Zealand and Australian Land Co v Watson* (1880–81) LR 7 QBD 374.

well-understood business, and it could not possibly be said that they were bound to keep separate the money of each of the persons by whom they were employed in the course of that business.

**8.71** Nevertheless, where the law imposes the higher fiduciary duty on the agent, the stern duties that ordinarily bind trustees will then apply. If the agent mixes the principal's property or monies with his own, the latter may be entitled to hold a charge over the mixed property unless the agent is able to show which is his own.[206] And if the agent converts the principal's property into money or goods and mixes it with his own, the principal may trace the property in the hands of the agent so long as it is identifiable.[207] As is well known, in *Re Hallett's Estate* it was held that if money held by a person in a fiduciary character, though not as trustee, is paid by him to his account at his bankers, the person for whom he held the money can follow it, and has a charge on the balance in the bankers' hands.

*The agent's duty to maintain and deliver up accurate accounts*

**8.72** The agent is additionally under a duty to keep accurate accounts and to produce them on request. As Lord Chelmsford, LC put it in *Turner v Burkinshaw*:

> It is the first duty of an agent ... to be constantly ready with his accounts ... [T]his must mean that the agent must be ready to render his accounts when they are demanded.[208]

In *Dadswell v Jacobs* principals residing overseas requested their agent to present accounts to the principals' nominated representative. Although the court accepted that the representative had to be a proper person to receive those accounts, Cotton, LJ also recognized:

> [O]f course it was the duty of the ... agent ... to produce to the principals any accounts that were kept for them; and where the principal is abroad, in my opinion the agent is bound to produce to any properly appointed agent of the principal any books of account kept for the principal.[209]

**8.73** As *Yasuda Fire & Marine Insurance Co of Europe Ltd v Orion Marine Insurance Underwriting Agency Ltd*[210] shows, the duty to account may endure after termination of the contract between principal and agent. In *Yasuda* a principal terminated its contracts with two agents whose activities had aroused its suspicions. The contract contained a clause expressly authorizing the principal to inspect the agents' books. The agents refused to allow the principal to do so, arguing that the clause

---

[206] *Lupton v White* (1808) 15 Ves 432, 436–7 *per* Lord Eldon, LC.
[207] *Re Hallett's Estate, Knatchbull v Hallett* (1880) 13 ChD 696.
[208] (1867) LR 2 Ch App 488, 481–2. See also *Pearse v Green* (1819) 1 Jac&W 135.
[209] (1887) 34 ChD 278, 281.
[210] [1995] QB 174.

perished when the contract was terminated. Nevertheless, the principal obtained a declaration granting it access to large quantities of records held by the agents concerning the reinsurance of the principal's interests. This was achieved in part on the strength of the agents' fiduciary duty to account. This duty subsisted independently of the contract and of the contractual clause that additionally gave the principal access to the data during the life of the contracts.[211]

A failure to keep accounts is a serious matter. Everything will be presumed against **8.74** an agent who fails to keep proper accounts.[212] Thus if the accounts show that he has credited the principal with a certain sum, it will be assumed that he has received that sum and will be liable to the principal accordingly,[213] unless the agent can adduce clear proof that the money has not been received.[214] If an agent wrongly withholds monies belonging to the principal, interest accruing on those sums will belong to the principal to whom the agent must account; and if an agent receives or holds monies in breach of his fiduciary duty, he will be obliged to pay interest from the date of that breach.[215]

*Conveyancing transactions in which the agent may be held to be a trustee*

In one category of situation an agent will actually be held to have acted as a trustee. **8.75** Owing to the peculiarities of the rules governing conveyancing, and more especially to the fact that a conveyance made to the agent of a principal, whether disclosed or undisclosed, does not convey a title to the principal, if an agent purchases land or takes a lease in his own name, the courts will hold that he holds that land or lease on trust for his principal.

---

[211] Survival of the principal's right to inspect his agent's books and commercial records following the agent's repudiatory breach of the agency agreement in *Yasuda* is reminiscent of the survival of the arbitration clause in *Heyman v Darwins Ltd* [1942] AC 356. In the latter case, it was held that such a clause may continue to bind the parties to submit to arbitration even after discharge of a party's liability under the contract following acceptance of a repudiatory breach (or, for that matter, following frustration of the contract). In the words of Lord Porter, 'Strictly speaking, to say that on acceptance of the renunciation of a contract the contract is rescinded is incorrect ... By that acceptance [the injured party] is discharged from further performance and may bring an action for damages, but the contract itself is not rescinded' (p 399). In each case it will be a matter of construing whether expressly or by necessary implication the contractual clause in question is intended to survive the 'termination' of the contract. Typically, clauses that may survive 'termination' include liquidated damages clauses, clauses which impose restrictive covenants or obligations of confidentiality post-termination (*Involnert Management Inc v Aprilgrange Ltd* [2015] 2 Lloyd's Rep 289 at [173] *per* Leggatt, J), as well as investigatory provisions in contracts (*Yasuda, supra*). As Colman, J explained in *Strive Shipping Corp v Hellenic Mutual War Risks Ass'n (Bermuda) Ltd. The Grecia Express* [2002] 1 CLC 401, 534: 'such investigatory provisions are separate from the contract to which they are ancillary to the effect that they survive avoidance of the contract for repudiatory breach.'
[212] *Gray v Haig* (1855) 20 Beav 219, 226 *per* Romilly, MR.
[213] *Smith v Woodcock* (1827) 7 B&C 73.
[214] *Shaw v Dartnall* (1826) 6 B&C 56, 65 *per* Abbot, CJ.
[215] See, however, Supreme Court Act 1981, s 35A.

## Duties owed by Commercial Agents

### Commercial agent's obligation to 'act dutifully and in good faith'

**8.76**  Regulation 3 of the Commercial Agents (Council Directive) Regulations 1993, SI 1993/3053, sets out the particular duties a self-employed commercial agent owes to his principal under the Directive. Notably, paragraph 1 states as a general requirement that:

> In performing his activities a commercial agent must look after the interests of his principal and act dutifully and in good faith.

Although the concept of a commercial agent's duty to 'act dutifully' has not received the same attention as has that of good faith—and strictly speaking, is a concept of European law with an autonomous meaning—it has been said to connote the obligation to act loyally, resembling the fiduciary duty of an agent at common law.[216]

**8.77**  The ensuing paragraph of the Regulations sets out more fully the duties owed under reg 3 to the extent that, in particular, a commercial agent must:

(a)  make proper efforts to negotiate and, where appropriate, conclude the transactions he is instructed to take care of;

(b)  communicate to his principal all the necessary information available to him;

(c)  comply with reasonable instructions given by his principal.

Although certain of the terminology may be unfamiliar, it will be seen that to a degree these provisions mirror common-law and equitable duties owed by agents under English law. The biggest difference between them, however, is that under the Regulations parties are forbidden to derogate from these stated duties.[217]

**8.78**  It has been forcibly argued by one scholar that English fiduciary duties afford, at best, an imperfect analogy to the Directive's obligation to 'act dutifully and in good faith'.[218] Since English courts are bound to construe the Regulations 'as far as possible, in the light of the wording and purpose of the Directive',[219] in order to interpret the 'hendiadys that generates the single obligation' to act 'dutifully and in good faith', it therefore behoves a court to have close regard to European law. Analysis of European law reveals the following distinctive features, all embedded in the concept of 'good faith' in EU private law:

(i)  'Good faith' has an autonomous meaning that should be applied consistently across Member States

---

[216]  *Rossetti Marketing Ltd v Diamond Sofa Co Ltd* [2012] 1 All ER (Comm) 18 at [41] *per* Cranston, J.

[217]  Commercial Agents (Council Directive) 1993, reg 5(1).

[218]  Tosato, *Commercial Agency and the Duty to Act in Good Faith* (2016) OJLS 1. See also Tosato, *An Exploration of the European Dimension of the Commercial Agents Regulations* [2013] LMCLQ 544.

[219]  Eg, *Marleasing SA v La Comercial Internacional de Alimentacion SA* (1990) C-106/89.

(ii) 'Good faith' is an abstraction that requires to be reduced to principles and guidelines that can be applied to individual cases by national courts

(iii) Although 'good faith' cannot easily be reduced to a single clear definition, in recent years EU 'soft law instruments', such as the Draft Common Frame of Reference and the Principles of European Contract Law, as well as some EU legislation, have treated it as comprising notions like honesty, openness and regard for the interests of the other party

(iv) There are recurring themes in the EU texts in which 'good faith' appears, such as avoidance of market failures, prevention of the abuse of asymmetries, consideration for the intentions of the parties as objectively attested in their agreement, and attention to the relevant commercial context.[220]

From this, it is contended that the obligation to act dutifully and in good faith 'bears all these features and thus requires parties to act with honesty, openness and regard for the interests for the other party to the transaction'.[221] In the performance of commercial agency, this will require principal and agent to co-operate fully with one another and to avoid exploiting asymmetries in their relationship so as to frustrate the other party's legitimate expectations. For this reason, the author concludes that Cranston, J's acceptance in *Rossetti Marketing Ltd v Diamond Sofa Co Ltd* of the suggestion that the duty to act 'dutifully and in good faith' 'reflects the fiduciary duty of an agent at common law [*sic*]' is 'unconvincing' and even 'incompatible with the Directive' in so far as it overlooks the European dimension of the Directive and the EU principle of consistent interpretation.[222] In fact, 'while performance duties and fiduciary obligations may overlap with the [duty to act dutifully and in good faith], they never completely obscure it'.[223]

### Applicable law in case of breach

Regulation 5(2) states that 'The law applicable to the contract shall govern the consequence of breach of the rights and obligations' set out in reg 3. Although the parties are at liberty to agree that their contract will be governed by the law of another Member State,[224] in all other cases it may be assumed that the applicable law is English law.[225]  **8.79**

---

[220] *Ibid* at p 14.

[221] (2016) OJLS 1, 14.

[222] Similarly, the suggestion in *Vick v Vogle-Gapes Ltd* [2006] EWHC 1665 (QB) and *Crocs Europe BV v Anderson* [2013] 1 Lloyd's Rep 1 that the obligation to act dutifully and in good faith was akin to the implied obligation of trust in an English master and servant relationship.

[223] (2016) OJLS 1, 18.

[224] Commercial Agents (Council Directive) 1993, reg 1(3)(a).

[225] In 1998 the Regulations were amended at the instance of the EC Commission in order to make clear that where parties had expressly agreed that UK law was to apply to their contract but the commercial agent was to carry on his activities elsewhere in the Community, a court was required to apply the UK Regulations provided that this was permissible under the law of the other Member State: see Commercial Agents (Council Directive) (Amendment) Regulations 1998, SI 1998/2868.

# 9

# LEGAL RELATIONS BETWEEN PRINCIPAL AND AGENT: RIGHTS OF THE AGENT AGAINST THE PRINCIPAL

Whereas we have seen that an agent may owe a veritable constellation of duties **9.01** towards the principal, the principal's corresponding duties towards his agent are more restricted. Three principal rights enjoyed by the agent, specific to the principal–agent relationship, need to be considered.

(i) *Remuneration:* if it is a term of the contract, the agent will be entitled to remuneration in accordance with what the parties have expressly or impliedly agreed in their contract. Alternatively, the agent may be entitled to recover from the principal on the basis of a *quantum meruit.* A commercial agent, under the Commercial Agents (Council Directive) Regulations 1993, however, operates under a different regime.[1]

(ii) *Indemnity:* regardless of whether or not there is a contract, an agent is entitled to be indemnified for expenses incurred by him and losses occasioned to him in the performance of his agency. Finally,

(iii) *Lien:* the agent may enjoy a possessory lien over his principal's property.

---

[1] See paras **9.25–9.40**.

Each of these rights will be considered in turn.

## The Agent's Entitlement to Remuneration

**An agent's remuneration will be governed by the express or implied terms of his contract with the principal**

**9.02**  Invariably, the agent's right to be remunerated will be determined by the express terms of the contract between principal and agent. Such terms are to be interpreted as they would have been understood by a reasonable person in possession of all the background knowledge reasonably available to the parties at the time when the agreement was concluded.[2] Only rarely will a court be prepared to imply a term according remuneration to an agent if the contract is silent. Provided that the agent has complied with the terms of his contract, or the principal has subsequently ratified an unauthorized transaction effected by the agent, the latter will become entitled to commission according to the terms of the contract. However, if the agent has acted outside the scope of his authority and the principal has not ratified the agent's acts,[3] no commission will be due. Similarly, commission will not be due if the agent has so breached his duty to his principal as to entitle the latter to repudiate the contract of agency, or if he became an agent by operation of law.[4]

**If the parties' contract has stipulated the rate of commission, the terms of the contract will govern**

**9.03**  Although principal and agent, in their contract, may have set out in some detail what commission is to be paid upon accomplishment of the agency, as with any other contractual agreement disputes may still arise as to the precise meaning of those agreed terms.[5] However, the scope for disagreement is likely to be greater where the agreement deliberately leaves matters open. In *KofiSunkersette Obu v A Strauss & Co Ltd*[6] a company's agent, who was responsible for acquiring rubber in West Africa, under his contract was paid an agreed monthly sum and 'a commission ... which I have agreed to leave to the discretion of the company'. Following termination of his agency, the agent asked the court to settle upon a rate of commission to be paid in respect of work he had performed on the company's behalf.

---

[2]  *Unite the Union v Liverpool Victoria Banking Services Ltd.* [2014] EWHC 19 (Comm) at [16] *per* Teare, J. (rev'd on appeal: [2015] EWCA Civ 285).

[3]  Eg, in *Mason v Clifton* (1863) 3 F&F 899, where an agent was instructed to obtain a loan for his principal 'on the usual terms'. The agent delegated his authority without his principal's consent to a sub-agent, who procured the loan on quite different terms. See also *March v Jelf* (1862) 3 F&F 234, where an agent instructed to sell a property by auction sold it by private treaty.

[4]  See **chapter 5**.

[5]  Eg, *Cavendish Corporate Finance LLP v GIL Investments Ltd* [2009] EWCA Civ 368.

[6]  [1951] AC 243.

The Privy Council declined to do so as the parties' contract had expressly left the matter of commission at the entire discretion of the principal:

> [P]ayment of commission based on rubber purchased or shipped, is beyond the competence of any court to grant. The court cannot determine the basis and rate of the commission. To do so would involve not only making a new agreement for the parties but varying the existing agreement by transferring to the court the exercise of a discretion vested in the respondents.[7]

A similar situation faced Plowman, J in *Re Richmond Gate Property Co Ltd*, where a company's articles of association provided that the managing director's remuneration was to be 'such amount as the directors may determine'. Plowman, J commented:

> In the present case there was an express contract which relates to payment of remuneration, and the only question with which I am concerned is: according to the terms of that express contract, is any sum payable for remuneration? When one finds that the express contract is that the remuneration payable is such sum as the directors may determine that the managing director shall have, and that the directors have not determined that any sum is to be payable to the managing director, it seems to me to follow as a necessary consequence that no remuneration can be claimed.[8]

Just as the courts will not order payment of remuneration if it is not demanded by the contract, so too they will not interfere if it is claimed that a particular agreed rate of commission is derisory or unfair.

If the contract provides that a reasonable rate of commission is payable, or if the **9.04** agent claims that a particular rate of commission is payable by custom, a court will determine what sums it considers reasonable. The method of calculation will vary from case to case. It may derive from customary scales of commission charged by a particular profession. However, a court is not bound by such scales of charges if they are deemed unreasonable. In *Wilkie v Scottish Aviation Ltd*, for example, it was held that a chartered surveyor was entitled to remuneration at the customary rate only if he could prove the existence of a custom which was 'reasonable, certain and notorious'. The Court of Session declared that, unless satisfied that the resulting fee was reasonable in the circumstances, it was not bound rigidly to apply a schedule of professional charges drawn up by the Royal Institution of Chartered Surveyors.[9] Alternatively, the rate of reasonable commission may be deduced from the parties' previous dealings.[10] Sometimes, however, it will be difficult to discern on what exact basis a rate of remuneration has been calculated.[11]

---

[7] *Ibid* at 250 *per* Sir John Beaumont.
[8] [1965] 1 WLR 335, 338.
[9] 1956 SC 198. See also *Davidson, Syme v Liquidator of Highland Engineering* 1972 SC 1.
[10] Eg, *Baring v Stanton* (1876) LR 3 ChD 502.
[11] Eg, *Hugh V Allen & Co Ltd v A Homes Ltd* [1969] 1 Lloyd's Rep 348. More generally, if a court concludes that the parties did not actually agree upon any particular rate of commission, it must then resolve from the evidence, the nature of the business, and so on what would constitute a

**9.05**  A contract may provide that commission is only to become payable upon the happening of some event. If it specifies that payment is conditional upon the performance of certain acts or the successful accomplishment of a designated result, commission will only become due upon the occurrence of that event. McCardie, J stated the matter crisply in *Howard Houlder & Partners Ltd v Manx Isles SS Co Ltd*:

> It is a settled rule for the construction of ... documents which refer to the remuneration of an agent that a plaintiff cannot recover unless he shows that the conditions of the written bargain have been fulfilled. If he proves fulfilment he recovers. If not, he fails. There appears to be no halfway house, and it matters not that the plaintiff proves expenditure of time, money and skill.[12]

In *Estafnous v London & Leeds Business Centres Ltd*[13] an estate agent was held not to be entitled to recover remuneration under an agreement providing for payment of commission upon the sale of a property. Negotiations between the would-be buyer and seller went cold, but later revived leading to the projected sale becoming restructured as a share sale agreement. Under this agreement the purchaser acquired shares in the seller's holding company, the property's ultimate owner. By this means the purchaser acquired effective control of the property, but not legal or beneficial title to it. As Warren, J observed, 'This is one of those cases where those involved did not think about what was to happen in certain circumstances, namely if the property sale were restructured as a share sale.'[14]

**9.06**  If the specified task is not accomplished, it will only be open to an agent to seek to recover on a *quantum meruit* for his time and trouble, provided that has been expressly (or, most unlikely, impliedly) agreed in the contract.

**If the contract is silent, a court may imply a term into an agency contract entitling the agent to earn commission**

**9.07**  If the contract makes no provision for payment of commission, a court will only rarely be prepared to imply a term entitling the agent to remuneration. As the Judicial Committee made clear in its recent discussion of implied terms, in *Att-Gen*

---

reasonable commission: eg, *Berezovsky v Edmiston & Co Ltd* [2011] 1 Lloyd's Rep 419 at [54]–[63] *per* Field, J.

[12] [1923] 1 KB 110, 113–14. Determining whether commission has become payable will be a matter of construing the relevant agreement. In *Crema v Cenkos Securities plc* [2011] 1 WLR 2066 a sub-broker claimed that under the terms of his contract with the broker he was entitled to claim commission from the broker before the latter had been paid his commission by the principal. The Court of Appeal held that in ascertaining and interpreting the express and implied terms of an agreement, since this will have been part of the factual context known to both parties, the court is entitled to have regard to market practices falling short of trade usage or custom to assist in gaining a full understanding of the factual background. Unsurprisingly perhaps, no evidence of such a market practice was forthcoming.

[13] [2012] 1 P&CR DG4.

[14] *Ibid* at [29].

*of Belize v Belize Telecom Ltd*, a court cannot introduce terms just to make a contract fairer or more reasonable. Thus, in *JWB Group Ltd v Westminster CC*, because the contract already possessed business efficacy, Jack, J declined to imply a term even though it would have allowed the contract to operate more fairly.[15] As Lord Hoffmann explained in the *Belize* case:

> [A court] is concerned only to discover what the instrument means ... [T]hat meaning is not necessarily or always what the authors or parties to the document would have intended. It is the meaning which the instrument would convey to a reasonable person having all the background knowledge which would reasonably be available to the audience to whom the instrument is addressed.[16]

Ominously, Lord Hoffmann's account continued:

> The question of implication arises when the [contract] does not expressly provide for what is to happen when some event occurs. *The most usual inference in such a case is that nothing is to happen.* If the parties had intended something to happen, the instrument would have said so. Otherwise, the express provisions of the instrument are to continue to operate undisturbed. If the event has caused loss to one or other of the parties, the loss lies where it falls.[17]

What this means is that a court will only imply a term because it is necessary to do so in order to give that contract business efficacy[18] under whichever alternative formulation of the implied term test a court adopts: either the 'officious bystander' test;[19] or the five requirements enumerated by Lord Simon of Glaisdale in *BP Refinery (Westernport) Pty Ltd v Shire of Hastings*.[20] No matter which test is employed, however, a term will only be applied if 'such a provision would spell out in express words what the instrument, read against the relevant background, would reasonably be understood to mean.'[21]

The courts will imply a term into the contract if it is obvious from the circum-  **9.08**
stances that the parties must have intended that commission would be paid to the agent. In *Way v Latilla*,[22] for example, the agent alleged that there was

---

[15] [2009] EWHC 2697 (QB), esp at [21].

[16] [2009] 1 WLR 1988 at [16], citing his earlier remarks in *Investors Compensation Scheme Ltd v West Bromwich BS* [1998] 1 WLR 896, 912–13.

[17] [2009] 1 WLR 1988 at [17] (emphasis added). In *Mediterranean Salvage & Towage Ltd v Seamar Trading & Commerce Inc* [2009] 2 Lloyd's Rep 639 at [8] Lord Clarke of Stone-cum-Ebony, MR predicted that Lord Hoffmann's extensive analysis of implied terms in *Attorney General of Belize* 'will soon be as much referred to as his approach to the construction of contracts in *Investors Compensation Scheme v West Bromwich BS* [1998] 1 WLR 896, 912–13.

[18] See *The Moorcock* (1889) 14 PD 64.

[19] See *Shirlaw v Southern Foundries (1926) Ltd* [1939] 2 KB 206, 227 *per* Mackinnon, LJ.

[20] '(1) [The term] must be reasonable and equitable; (2) it must be necessary to give business efficacy to the contract, so that no term will be implied if the contract is effective without it; (3) it must be so obvious that "it goes without saying"; (4) it must be capable of clear expression; (5) it must not contradict any express term of the contract': (1977) 180 CLR 266, 282–3.

[21] [2009] 1 WLR 1988 at [21].

[22] [1937] 3 All ER 759.

a contract under which he would obtain and send to the principal information relating to gold mines and concessions in West Africa and that his services would be remunerated and he would receive a share in the profits. The principal denied such an agreement. The House of Lords held that there was no agreement concerning remuneration. However, there was a contract of employment between the parties, which clearly indicated that the work was not to be done gratuitously, and the agent was therefore entitled to a reasonable remuneration on the implied contract, to be paid on a *quantum meruit*. It may be possible to interpret *Way v Latilla* in two different ways: *Way v Latilla* was either a case in which a term was to be implied that payment would be made on a *quantum meruit* basis because the express contract contemplated payment for services but did not contain an express term as to such payment, or a case in which there was no express contract between the parties but their dealings gave rise to an implied contract to pay on a *quantum meruit* basis.[23] In either eventuality, the consequence was that the House found that the agent was to receive a reasonable remuneration which the court fixed at £5,000, a rough-and-ready figure it inferred from what Lord Wright termed 'the communings of the parties while the business was going on'.[24]

### Restitutionary claims

**9.09**  Even in the absence of a contract, an agent may be entitled to remuneration on the basis of a *quantum meruit*. By way of illustration, in *William Lacey (Hounslow) Ltd v Davis*, between January 1951 and June 1952, WL, a firm of builders, which had been led to believe that in due course they would receive a contract, at the request of D's surveyors, and at not inconsiderable effort, provided a series of estimates regarding repair of D's war-damaged premises. D sold the property in July 1952 and WL claimed remuneration on a *quantum meruit*. Barry, J held that the work carried out by WL, at D's request, was not work a builder would customarily perform gratuitously, but had been done in a belief, mutual to both sides, that WL would eventually receive the contract for rebuilding the premises. Barry, J, therefore, implied a promise by D to pay reasonable remuneration to WL in respect of such work.[25] As Greer, LJ explained in *Craven-Ellis v Canons Ltd*:

> The obligation [to pay reasonable remuneration] is imposed by law in all cases where the acts are purported to be done on the faith of an agreement which is supposed to be but is not a binding contract between the parties.[26]

---

[23] See *Berkeley Community Villages Ltd v Pullen* [2007] 3 EGLR 101 at [102] *per* Morgan, J.
[24] [1937] 3 All ER 759, 766.
[25] [1957] 1 WLR 932.
[26] [1936] 2 KB 403, 411–12.

Even if remuneration has not been contractually agreed, if an agent can show that his services have been accepted by a principal on this basis, it is open to the court to award remuneration on a *quantum meruit.*

### Effective cause

In order to become entitled to commission, a term may be implied into the con- **9.10** tract that the agent must have been the 'effective cause' of the transaction. The requirement that the agent was the 'effective cause' demands that the agent's intervention must not have been merely incidental to the transaction, but that it must have been directly instrumental in bringing about the desired result: namely, a concluded contract between principal and third party.[27] This involves a question of causation, and will be a determination of fact in each individual case. In the majority of instances, 'effective cause' is unlikely to be an issue: it will be obvious that the agent has brought about a particular result, as instructed. However, in cases where the chain of causation is more difficult to discern—notably, where more than one intermediary may have contributed to bringing principal and third party into direct relations,[28] where other events may have intervened, or simply where considerable time may have elapsed—'effective cause' comes into its own, serving primarily as a means of avoiding that a principal has to pay commission to more than one party.

#### *The origins of the effective cause requirement*

Lord Neuberger of Abbotsbury has pointed out that the implication of an 'ef- **9.11** fective cause' term in an agency contract occurred for the first time in Henn Collins, MR's judgment in the 'relatively briefly reported case',[29] *Millar Son & Co v Radford.*[30] In *Millar* an agent had received instructions to find a purchaser or a tenant for the principal's property. The agent found a tenant and was paid his commission. Fifteen months later the tenant purchased the property, whereupon the agent, who in the meantime had had no further dealings with the property, claimed an additional commission for having found the party who became the ultimate purchaser. The Court of Appeal rejected the agent's claim, stating that it was not enough for the agent to show that he had been the *causa sine qua non* in the transaction; the agent had actually to show that he had been the 'effective cause' in bringing about the sale.

---

[27] *Aliter*, the agent must have been 'the primary or originating influence' of the contract between principal and third party: *Gibb v Bennett* (1906) 14 SLT 64, 67 *per* Lord Johnston.

[28] Eg, *John D Wood & Co v Dantata* [1987] 2 EGLR 23, where two rival agents had each contributed in different ways to the sale of a substantial property, but where, as Nourse, LJ stressed, the court's job was to determine which was actually *the* effective cause in bringing about the sale.

[29] *Foxtons Ltd v Bicknell* [2008] 2 EGLR 23 at [18].

[30] (1903) 19 TLR 575.

**9.12** 'Effective cause' terms will be implied quite readily into estate agency contracts, which typically are unilateral agreements that do not bind the agent to do anything and where only the accomplishment of the prescribed task—very frequently, the sale of a property—will activate the agent's right to claim agreed commission. Nevertheless, if there is a question as to whether such a term ought to be implied into any given contract, conventional contractual principles governing the implication of terms apply.[31] Lord Neuberger reviewed the authorities in *Foxtons Ltd v Bicknell*, suggesting that six principles inform the implication of effective cause terms into agency agreements:

- First, the term is very readily implied, especially in a residential consumer context, unless the provisions of the particular contract or the facts of the particular case negative it.
- Secondly, the main reason for implying an effective cause term is to minimize the risk of a seller having to pay two commissions.
- Thirdly, although the courts normally refer to '*the* effective cause', it is not entirely clear if the true test is whether the agent was '*an* effective cause' or '*the* effective cause' of the relevant transaction.[32]
- Fourthly, whether an agent was the effective cause turns very much on the facts of the particular case.[33]
- Fifthly, while two commissions are to be avoided, there will be (rare) cases where the terms of the relevant contracts and the facts compel such a result.[34]
- Sixthly, where the term is implied, the burden is on the agent seeking payment of commission to establish that he was the effective cause.[35]

**9.13** Determining whether an agent has been the effective cause in a transaction is by no means straightforward in all cases. In *Gibb v Bennett*,[36] for example, an agent found a potential buyer, M, whom he introduced to the principal, who was seeking to sell a public house. M sought finance from W. Negotiations with M fell through, but W subsequently bid successfully for the pub. The Scots Outer House held that the transaction with W had been brought about by the actions of the agent 'in a sufficiently direct manner to entitle him to his commission'.[37] As Lord Johnston put it, in this instance 'the agent was the primary or originating

---

[31] *Luxor (Eastbourne) v Cooper* [1941] AC 108, 119 *per* Viscount Simon.

[32] See further para **9.17**.

[33] 'Cases … must vary infinitely on the same facts, and questions of causation can give rise to endless argument': *Chesterfield & Co v Zahid* [1989] *2* EGLR 24, 26 *per* Garland, J.

[34] Very occasionally, two agents may each be held to be entitled to commission. See *Lordsgate Properties Ltd v Balcombe* [1985] 1 EGLR 20, where two estate agents were simultaneously employed by the principal on different terms, both of which came to be fulfilled.

[35] [2008] 2 EGLR 23 at [20]. See also *MSM Consulting Ltd v United Republic of Tanzania* [2009] EWHC 121 (QB); (2009) 123 Con LR 154 at [125]–[136] *per* Christopher Clarke, J.

[36] (1906) 14 SLT 64.

[37] *Ibid* at 66.

influence' of the sale.[38] In contrast, in *Coles v Enoch*[39] C agreed to find a tenant for E's empty shop, which was ripe for conversion into a pin-table arcade. C telephoned A, whose conversation was overheard by W. W asked A where the shop was situated, but A deliberately gave a vague answer. W discovered the shop's location and ultimately acquired the shop as a pin-table arcade. Scott LJ admitted that this case fell near the line. However, since C had to accept what A, his 'sub-agent', did just as if he had done it himself, C had not achieved the result which the commission contract contemplated:

> [C] stopped short of being the direct or efficient cause of W taking that shop. The fact that [A] did not give the address must be interpreted as a deliberate act falling short of what was essential to bring [C] within the terms under which he would be entitled to commission under the oral contract.[40]

Although it is often stated that it will be a question of fact in each and every case **9.14** whether or not a particular agent was the 'effective cause' in a given transaction, from time to time it is sought to increase this requirement and to demand the agent's direct instrumentality in the achievement of the desired end. In *Berezovsky and Petersham Holdings Ltd v Edmiston & Co Ltd*,[41] for example, E & Co claimed commission on the sale of a luxury yacht, the 'Darius', to the Al Futtaim family. The claimants unsuccessfully argued that in the context of the super yacht market, if a broker introduces the eventual buyer to the seller but is not used as a channel for at least some of the ensuing negotiations, he is not an effective cause of the sale. Although E & Co had originally introduced the Al Futtaims to the vendor, B, the Al Futtaims did not negotiate the price of the yacht with the brokers who made the initial introduction, E & Co. Individuals who can afford super yachts, it was contended, are few and far between. Their identities, however, can be easily ascertained through the annual *Forbes* list or the *Sunday Times* 'rich list'. A broker has to do more to earn commission than simply circularize particulars of the yacht to those whose names appear on such lists. He must 'bring the potential buyer into the transaction', in particular by 'eliciting' an offer from him. Field, J, rejecting this argument, first acknowledged that there exists no authoritative definition of 'effective cause' before quoting Jacobs, J's words in *LJ Hooker Ltd v WJ Adams Estates Pty Ltd* to the effect that:

> 'Effective cause' means more than simply 'cause'. The inquiry is whether the actions of the agent really brought about the relation of buyer and seller and it is seldom conclusive that there were other events which could each be described as a cause of the ensuing sale.[42]

---

[38] *Ibid* at 67.
[39] [1939] 3 All ER 327.
[40] *Ibid* at 328.
[41] [2011] 1 Lloyd's Rep 419.
[42] (1977) 138 CLR 52, 86.

In Field, J's view:

> [I]t is open to a broker operating in the super yacht market to establish that he was the effective cause of the eventual sale notwithstanding that the eventual buyer whom he alerted to the availability of the vessel chooses not to negotiate through the introducing broker. Whether the introducing broker was indeed the effective cause of the sale will depend on the facts of the individual case.[43]

*Considerable delay*

9.15 The fact that there has been considerable delay between the acts performed by the agent and the accomplishment of the desired result will not necessarily mean that the agent was not the 'effective cause' of the contract ultimately concluded between principal and third party. In *Nahum v Royal Holloway & Bedford College*,[44] for instance, N, at an agreed rate of commission, was instructed by the College to 'introduce' purchasers for three of its valuable paintings—a Turner, a Gainsborough, and a Constable. Having found a buyer (K) for the Gainsborough, N was impeded by K's agent from negotiating freely with K to persuade him also to purchase the Constable. N, therefore, was less directly involved in negotiating the sale of the Constable. When, after a lengthy delay, K did actually purchase the Constable, N claimed commission on that sale too. The Court of Appeal held that one had to look at what precisely the contract required of the agent. In this case, the notion of 'introducing' buyers conveyed a causative element of bringing a purchaser to the transaction. N had to establish that it was his actions that had really brought about the relation of buyer and seller between the College and K. There was evidence that, even though K's agent had endeavoured to cut N out of the transaction, N nevertheless had made the initial introduction and had then continued to encourage K through his agent. In consequence, on these facts the trial judge had been entitled to find that N had indeed been the effective cause in the sale of the Constable.

*Dismissal of agent*

9.16 The fact that an agent has been dismissed prior to the accomplishment of his mandate will not necessarily mean that his intervention was not the effective cause of the transaction. In *Harding Maughan Hambly Ltd v Compagnie Européenne de Courtage d' Assurances et de Réassurances SA*,[45] a sub-broker in a chain of brokers sued its principal, another sub-broker, for commission which it claimed was due because the claimant had succeeded in the feat of placing a political risks insurance largely in the London market on behalf of an ultimate client. Although the claimant sub-broker had been dismissed before the deal was finally completed, Rix, J found that the claimant had performed the most important part of what it had contracted to

---

[43] [2011] 1 Lloyd's Rep 419 at [41]. Cf *Allan v Leo Lines Ltd* [1957] 1 Lloyd's Rep 127.
[44] [1999] EMLR 252.
[45] [2000] 1 Lloyd's Rep 316.

do, and to the extent that it had not done anything else, it was prevented from doing so by its immediate principal.

Is the proper question whether the agent was 'the' effective cause or simply 'an' **9.17** effective cause of the transaction? Rix, J pondered this question, later posed in Lord Neuberger's third principle, in *Harding Maughan Hambly Ltd v Compagnie Européenne de Courtage d'Assurances et de Réassurances SA*.[46] In that case, whilst accepting that in most instances 'the effective cause' represented orthodoxy, Rix, J pointed out:

> Where ... as frequently occurs in insurance broking, numerous brokers are involved in chain, ... the test cannot be simply that of *the* effective cause. That is so even if the acts of all sub-brokers are attributed to any broker higher in the chain: in such a case it would only be where the last sub-broker was the effective cause that all of the other brokers higher in chain could earn their commission ... [S]uch a rule would not seem to me to do adequate justice to the complexities of the situation. Thus some of the brokers may be producing brokers and some placing brokers, and their roles, responsibilities and functions may be very different.[47]

Rix, J saw appeal in the American Law Institute's formulation of the test: 'an agent is an "effective cause" ... when his efforts have been sufficiently important in achieving a result for the accomplishment of which the principal has promised to pay him, so that it is just that the principal should pay the promised compensation to him.'[48] Although this approach possibly imports a certain circularity into the inquiry, he claimed: 'It articulates the thought that the decision on causation is a matter of common sense informed by its context and designed to produce a just result.'[49] Whether or not the proper requirement is that the agent must have been 'the effective cause' or merely 'an effective cause' in the transaction, the dispute is somewhat sterile. The tendency of the courts is to say that this question will only become live in those unusual cases where two agents have agreements under which they will be entitled to commission if they both perform the relevant task.[50]

### *Effective cause requirement overridden by terms of contract*

The terms of a particular contract may override any implication that the agent must **9.18** have been the effective cause of a particular transaction. In *County Homesearch Co*

---

[46] *Ibid.*

[47] [2000] 1 Lloyd's Rep 316, 334. In broad terms, a 'producing broker' is the broker directly responsible to an insured party for placement of the insurance. A 'placing broker' is a sub-broker who may be employed by a producing broker to place a risk, say, if the latter is based overseas or if the sub-broker happens to possess some specific skill or has particular experience within a specialized insurance market.

[48] *Second Restatement of Agency*, 1958, para 448.

[49] [2000] 1 Lloyd's Rep 316, 335.

[50] *Nahum v Royal Holloway and Bedford New College* [1999] EMLR 252, 261 *per* Waller, LJ. Cp *LJ Hooker Ltd v WJ Adams Estates Pty Ltd* (1977) 138 CLR 52 at [23] *per* Barwick, CJ.

*(Thames & Chilterns) Ltd v Cowham*,[51] for example, an agent claimed a sizeable commission, having contracted to assist C to acquire a property. Clause 4 of the contract stated that the agent would be 'deemed to have introduced a property to [C] if [C has] either received the particulars of the property from ourselves directly or indirectly or from any of the firms of estate agents with whom we have regular contact, etc.' C bought a property which had appeared on a list the agent had sent to him and which the agent had mentioned in a telephone conversation. C, however, maintained that the property had in fact been brought to his attention by his own planning consultant and that the agent's actions had not been the effective cause. Longmore, LJ acknowledged that normally the law would imply a term into a contract to the effect that commission would become payable only if the agent was the effective cause of the transaction. In this case, however, the express term was plainly inconsistent with such an implication: in clause 4 the notion of deemed introductions suggested that there might be 'cases where commission is due following a situation where there is no true introduction by [the agent] at all. If even the limited causation inherent in an introduction is unnecessary, it makes no sense to say that nevertheless there must be an effective cause before the agent can recover his commission.'[52]

### The agent's right to earn commission

*In the absence of any express or implied contractual term to the contrary, an agent possesses no right to earn his commission*

**9.19**  Although this issue occurs most commonly in the particular context of estate agency, a question arises: Is a principal under any obligation not to prevent his agent from earning commission? The courts have held that an agent may only sue his principal for damages to compensate for having been deprived of an opportunity to earn commission if an express or implied term in the agency contract forbids the principal from impeding the agent from earning that commission.

**9.20**  In the case of estate agents, in *Luxor (Eastbourne) Ltd v Cooper*[53] the House of Lords categorically refused to introduce an implied term into estate agency contracts depriving sellers of their power to prevent their agents from earning their commission. Vendors had employed an estate agent to find a purchaser for their four cinemas. The vendors agreed that if he introduced a party who purchased the property for not less than £185,000, the agent would receive a commission of £10,000, upon completion. The agent duly introduced a potential purchaser prepared to pay

---

[51] [2008] 1 WLR 909. See also *Glentree Estates Ltd v Favermead Ltd* [2010] EWCA Civ 1473; [2011] 1 EGLR 23.

[52] [2008] 1 WLR 909 at [19]. See also *Edmond de Rothschild Securities Ltd (UK) Ltd v Exillon Energy plc* [2014] EWHC 2165 (Comm); [2014] 5 Costs LR 749.

[53] [1941] AC 108.

£185,000 for the cinemas, 'subject to contract'. The vendors, however, withdrew from negotiations. The agent sued the vendors for damages, claiming that the latter's withdrawal from negotiations had deprived him of the opportunity to earn commission. The House unanimously held that in order to give the contract business efficacy, it was unnecessary to imply a term whereby the principal undertook not to deprive the agent of the opportunity to earn commission. Quite simply, if an agent is promised a commission only if he brings about a sale, there is no room for an implied term that the principal will not dispose of the property himself or through other channels or otherwise act so as to prevent the agent earning his commission.[54]

Similar considerations apply in the case of other forms of agency. In *L French &* **9.21** *Co Ltd v Leeston Shipping Co Ltd*,[55] for example, shipbrokers successfully effected an eighteen-month time charter between charterers and shipowners. It had been agreed that the brokers would be paid two-and-a-half per cent commission on hire paid under the charterparty. After four months, the owners sold the vessel to the charterers and hire ceased to be payable. The brokers thereupon sued the owners for damages equivalent to the commission they would have earned over the remaining fourteen months of the charterparty. The House of Lords rejected the claim, declining to imply a term into the broking agreement whereby the shipowners agreed not to put an end to the charterparty by selling the ship to the charterers. In the words of Lord Buckmaster:

> There is no need whatever in the present case for the introduction of any such term. The contract works perfectly well without any such words being implied, and, if it were intended on the part of the shipbroker to provide for the cessation of the commission which he earned owing to the avoidance of the charterparty, he ought to have arranged for that in express terms between himself and the shipowner.[56]

Again, in *Marcan Shipping (London) Ltd v Polish SS Co The Manifest Lipowy*,[57] shipbrokers unsuccessfully argued that sellers of a ship had broken an implied term of their brokerage agreement according to which they would not deprive the brokers of their opportunity to earn commission in the agreed amount by

---

[54] The House thereby endorsed Scrutton, LJ's dissenting judgment in *Trollope & Sons v Martyn Bros* [1934] 2 KB 436, 444, where he famously said that the view that one must imply a term that a principal shall not 'without just cause' prevent his agent from earning his commission 'seems to make the subsidiary matter, the remuneration of the agent who is to obtain a contract of sale, as of more importance than the sale itself, which without breach of any contract with the purchaser has not been completed or materialised. It does not seem to me that a vendor taking an attitude towards the purchaser which by his contract he is entitled to adopt, if he gives no reason why he so acts except that it is in the bond, is acting arbitrarily and therefore in some unspecified default. Every man who receives and refuses without giving a reason an offer which he is not bound to accept, may be said to act arbitrarily, but I cannot understand why he is in default.'

[55] [1922] 1 AC 451.

[56] *Ibid* at 454–5.

[57] [1989] 2 Lloyd's Rep 138.

breaching their contract of sale with the buyers. The parties' contract provided that the shipbrokers were only entitled to commission once the sale of the ship had been completed by delivery and that their commission was to be deducted from the purchase price. Nothing in the agreement suggested that it was intended to remunerate the brokers if, owing to the sellers' default, no sale ever took place and no money was handed over from which commission might be deducted. Indeed, the contract, as made, was wholly workable without the implication of a term. As Bingham, LJ explained:

> It is by no means obvious … that the sellers would have intended to pay nearly a quarter of a million dollars in hard currency to the other party's agents even if, albeit through their own fault, they never received any proceeds of the sale of the vessel. As for the agents, the fact that they did not agree the term expressly must throw doubt on the proposition that they intended it, because this eventuality cannot be one they never thought of.[58]

**9.22**  Most unusually, the Court of Appeal was prepared to imply a term under which a principal was not allowed to deprive his agent of agreed commission in *Alpha Trading Ltd v Dunnshaw-Patten Ltd.*[59] D-P agreed to pay commission to the agents, A, for having introduced them to M, to whom they agreed to sell a large quantity of cement. A claimed that D-P had wrongfully refused to perform their contract with M, thereby breaching their agency contract. A's claim for £25,000 was based on two alternative grounds: either A was owed commission, or D-P had breached an implied term of its contract with A according to which D-P would perform their contract with M and do nothing to prevent A from earning its commission. The Court of Appeal upheld Mocatta J's award of £25,000 plus interest, deciding that D-P had broken an implied term of the agency contract by breaching its contract with M. Because the sole reason for non-performance of the contract was that D-P was either unwilling or unable to perform it, the Court felt it right to imply a term into the agency contract to the effect that D-P would not fail to perform their contract with the buyers so as to deprive the plaintiffs of their remuneration under that agency contract. The Court was strongly influenced by the fact that D-P was in breach of an enforceable contract with M, a circumstance which enabled it to distinguish other cases where, as has been seen, courts will typically decline to imply such terms into agency agreements. In this case, the Court was especially anxious that principals ought not to be free to resile from their obligations to agents once the latter had performed their agencies. In Lawton, LJ's memorable words:

> The life of an agent in commerce is a precarious one. He is like the groom who takes a horse to the water-trough. He may get his principal to the negotiating table but when he gets him there he can do nothing to make him sign, any more than the groom can

---

[58]  *Ibid* at 144.
[59]  [1981] QB 290. See JW Carter, *The Life of an Agent in Commerce is a Precarious One* (1982) 45 MLR 220.

make a horse drink ... Once the signing has been done, the agent is in a different position altogether, because by that time the principal has accepted the benefit of the agent's work. In those circumstances, he ought not to be allowed to resile from his obligations to the agent ... [T]he whole relationship of principal and agent depends upon the principal accepting his obligations to the agent once the agent has done his work and the principal has accepted the benefit of it.[60]

*Preventing an agent from earning commission and agreements in restraint of trade*

Whilst a principal will not incur liability for preventing an agent from earning his commission unless the contract between the parties expressly or by necessary implication wears such a construction, after an agency has terminated a principal may not further restrain a former agent from earning his living as an agent if the parties' agreement is in restraint of trade. A covenant in restraint of trade is void. Courts will only enforce such a covenant, restricting an agent's ability to work, to the extent that the restriction is reasonable.[61] As Jack, J explained in *Tullett Prebon plc v BGC Brokers LP*, in this context a reasonable restraint means: **9.23**

[T]he court will consider whether it is reasonable in the interests of the parties and whether it is reasonable in the interests of the public. In modern times the emphasis is on the former. If the restraint is greater than is necessary to give adequate protection to the party claiming its benefit, it will not be reasonable between the parties. The party seeking enforcement must show a 'protectable interest'. That will often be his trade connection with customers with whom the employee has been dealing. It may be confidential information held by the employee. The court will not enforce a covenant where the employer's object is simply to prevent lawful competition by the ex-employee.[62]

Similar considerations apply whether the covenant prevents the former agent from working outright or whether the restraint takes the form of 'garden leave'.[63] Equally, the law does not differentiate between a covenant that prevents a person from exercising his chosen calling and a covenant that deprives someone of a reward should he fail to honour an undertaking not to work. In *Marshall v NM Financial Management Ltd*,[64] for example, a principal agreed to pay commission **9.24**

---

[60] [1981] QB 290, 308.

[61] *Nordenfelt v Maxim Nordenfelt Guns & Ammunition Co* [1894] AC 535, esp at p 557 *per* Lord Ashbourne: 'I do not know that there is a single reported case, whose facts are clearly known, where a covenant in general restraint of trade, clearly reasonable in itself and only affording a fair protection to the parties, has been held to be void.'

[62] [2010] IRLR 648 at [219].

[63] 'An employer gives proper notice of termination to his employee, tells the employee that he need not work until the termination date and gives him the wages attributable to the notice period in a lump sum. In this case (commonly call "garden leave")': *Clinton v Revenue and Customs Commissioners* [2010] STI 487 at [13(1)]. '[T]he court should be careful not to grant interlocutory relief to enforce a garden leave clause to any greater extent than would be covered by a justifiable covenant in restraint of trade previously entered into by an employee': *William Hill Organisation Ltd v Tucker* [1999] ICR 291, 301–2 *per* Morritt, J. See also *SG & R Valuation Service Co v Boudrais* [2008] IRLR 770.

[64] [1995] 1 WLR 1461.

for one year to his commission agent provided that the latter did not within that year become an independent intermediary or work for a competitor. This was held to amount to a restriction in restraint of trade which could not be justified as in reasonable protection of the principal's trade interest. Jonathan Sumption, QC stated:

> I do not think that there can be any doubt that [this provision] is a restraint of trade. It [has] been well established since the decision of the Court of Appeal in *Wyatt v Kreglinger and Fernau*[65] that there is no relevant difference between a contract that a person will not carry on a particular trade and a contract that if he does not do so he will receive some benefit to which he would not otherwise be entitled. Proviso (i) is a financial incentive to the agent not to carry on business in the specified fields. It is therefore unlawful unless it is justified as being reasonable in the interests of the parties and in that of the public.[66]

As Rimer, J explained in *Peninsula Business Services v Sweeney*, 'that condition amounted to … a condition restricting the former agent's liberty to carry on his trade in such manner and with whom he might choose.'[67]

### Remuneration of commercial agents under the Commercial Agents Directive

#### *The obligation to act dutifully and in good faith*

9.25    A commercial agent under the Regulations is owed a number of duties by his principal, the most significant being a right to be remunerated. Before turning to the right to remuneration, however, it should first be noted that reg 4(1) of the Commercial Agents (Council Directive) Regulations 1993 imposes an overarching obligation on the principal to 'act dutifully and in good faith' towards his commercial agent. It is not permissible to derogate from this obligation (reg 5(1)), but 'the law applicable to the contract shall govern the consequence of breach of the rights and obligations under reg … 4' (reg 5(2)). Regulation 4(2) specifies in particular that the obligation to 'act dutifully and in good faith' entails that the principal must supply the commercial agent with necessary documentation relating to the goods concerned (reg 4(2)(a)) and must:

> obtain for his commercial agent the information necessary for the performance of the agency contract, and in particular notify his commercial agent within a reasonable period once he anticipates that the volume of commercial transactions will be

---

[65] [1933] 1 KB 793. In *Wyatt v Kreglinger*, assuming that there was one, the contract would have been void as in restraint of trade even though it contained no express covenant under which the former employee agreed in the future not to work in the wool trade but only a stipulation that if he did so he would forfeit a pension.

[66] [1995] 1 WLR 1461, 1465. The judge's finding was not challenged when the case subsequently came before the Court of Appeal: see [1997] 1 WLR 1527.

[67] [2004] IRLR 49 at [41].

significantly lower than that which the commercial agent could normally have expected (reg 4(2)(b)).

The court reflected on the meaning of the concept, unfamiliar to English law, of **9.26** acting dutifully and in good faith in *Vick v Vogle-Gapes Ltd*.[68] It was suggested that the content of this obligation is 'at least as wide as the obligation implied on the part of both an employer and an employee in a contract of employment to act towards the other with mutual trust and confidence.'[69] The content of an employer's obligation of good faith under English law was considered by the House of Lords in *Malik v BCCI SA*,[70] which concluded that an employer must not, without reasonable and proper cause, conduct itself in a manner calculated and likely to destroy or seriously damage the relationship of confidence and trust between employer and employee. Breach of this duty requires a deliberate, rather than an inadvertent act of the employer, and is to be judged objectively.[71] In *Vick v Vogle-Gapes Ltd* the judge adopted this approach and held that the principal had had reasonable and proper cause to take the decision to reduce his commercial agent's territory, in view of the downward spiral in the agent's sales figures, his failure to merchandise and to adjust to modern technology, and his general truculent attitude.

### Remuneration

A commercial agent is presumed to be entitled to remuneration, even if his con- **9.27** tract has made no provision for payment of commission. Normally, an agreement between a principal and a commercial agent could be expected to provide for an agreed rate of commission. As has been seen, English law will only very rarely imply a term granting an agent remuneration where the contract is silent. If, however, the agent is a 'commercial agent' within the meaning of reg 1(2) of the Commercial Agents (Council Directive) Regulations 1993, reg 6(1) makes special provision for his remuneration if his agreement is silent on the matter of 'commission':[72]

> In the absence of any agreement as to remuneration between the parties, a commercial agent shall be entitled to the remuneration that commercial agents appointed for

---

[68] [2006] EWHC 1665 (TCC).

[69] *Ibid* at [85]. In *Simpson v Grant & Bowman Ltd* [2006] Eu LR 933 the court depicted good faith as demanding that a balance be struck between the needs of the agent and the business needs of the principal. Good faith, it was suggested, did not require parity of treatment between the principal's various agents. Nor was it necessary to show malice or bad faith in order to establish a breach of the duty. Finally, unless it was sufficiently serious, a principal's breach of his obligation to act dutifully and in good faith would not automatically constitute a repudiatory breach of contract.

[70] [1998] AC 20.

[71] 'If conduct objectively considered is likely to cause serious damage to the relationship between employer and employee a breach of the implied obligation may arise': [1998] AC 20, 47 *per* Lord Steyn.

[72] Reg 2 provides that ' "commission" means any part of the remuneration of a commercial agent which varies with the number or value of business transactions.' Cp *Rathbone Bros Plc v Novae Corporate Underwriting* [2014] Lloyd's Rep IR 203 at [44]–[45] *per* Burton, J.

the goods forming the subject of his agency contract are customarily allowed in the place where he carries on his activities and, if there is no such customary practice, a commercial agent shall be entitled to reasonable remuneration taking into account all the aspects of the transaction.

In contrast to English law, the Regulations presume that the parties intended that, throughout the duration of the agency, the agent would receive the rate of commission customary for the type of goods in which the agent has been dealing. Moreover, in the absence of any agreed customary rate of remuneration, the court is to award 'reasonable remuneration taking into account all the aspects of the transaction.'

*For which transactions is the commercial agent entitled to receive remuneration?*

**9.28** Regulation 7 specifies those transactions performed by a commercial agent during the period covered by the agency contract which are to be remunerated. It provides:

(1) A commercial agent shall be entitled to commission on commercial transactions concluded during the period covered by the agency contract—
   (a) where the transaction has been concluded as a result of his action; or
   (b) where the transaction is concluded with a third party whom he has previously acquired as a customer for transactions of the same kind.
(2) A commercial agent shall also be entitled to commission on transactions concluded during the period covered by the agency contract where he has an exclusive right to a specific geographical area or to a specific group of customers and where the transaction has been entered into with a customer belonging to that area or group.

*What is meant by 'where the transaction has been concluded as a result of his action'?*

**9.29** It was seen that at common law an agent's entitlement to commission is normally dependent upon his having been the effective cause of the transaction. The expression in reg 7(1)(a), 'where the transaction has been concluded as a result of his action', invites comparison with the common-law notion of 'effective cause', as both formulations demand that the agent must have been in some sense instrumental in bringing about a desired result. The two tests are not necessarily identical, but it is obvious that in each case a clear causative link has to be demonstrated between the commercial agent's intervention and the successful selling, purchasing, or negotiation of sales and purchases on behalf of the principal. Even if, in practice, both tests are prone to lead to the same result, it is probably best not to gloss the language or to supplant the wording employed in the Directive with a concept of the common law which the Directive never set out to replicate.

**9.30** Regulation 7(1)(b) indicates that an agent has a continuing interest in customers whom he has acquired for his principal in the course of his activities. He will also be entitled to claim commission on any other transactions of the same kind into which his principal and these customers may enter during the currency of the agency contract.

*What is meant by 'transactions concluded during the period covered by the agency contract where he has an exclusive right to a specific geographical area or to a specific group of customers'?*

According to reg 7(2), the agent is entitled to commission on transactions con-   **9.31**
cluded during the currency of his agreement:

> where he has an exclusive right to a specific geographical area or to a specific group of customers and where the transaction has been entered into with a customer belonging to that area or group.

One question this provision poses is whether an entitlement to commission can arise without the necessity for any action on the part of the agent. Although this issue has not arisen directly, decisions of the European Court of Justice on a broadly similar provision suggest the likely answer.[73] In *Kontogeorgas v Kartonpak*, for example, it was held that where an agent was entrusted with a specific geographical area, he was entitled to commission on transactions concluded with customers belonging to that area, even if those transactions were concluded without any action on his part.[74] In *Kontogeorgas* the principal had sold goods directly to customers within the agent's geographical area. The agent was nevertheless held to be entitled to commission.

In *Chevassus-Marche v Groupe Danone*,[75] where the French *Cour de cassation* sought   **9.32**
a preliminary ruling from the European Court of Justice, the situation was even starker: Was a commercial agent entitled to commission on transactions effected without the intervention of either the agent or the principal? Groupe Danone's predecessor in title had employed C-M as its exclusive agent to represent its various subsidiaries, who sold beer and spirits, within the specific geographical area of the islands of Mayotte and La Réunion. His contract having been terminated, *inter alia*, C-M sought commission on purchases made by two companies established in his geographical area. Groupe Danone refused to pay on the ground that the purchases had been made from central buying offices or dealers in metropolitan France, outside the control of Groupe Danone and its subsidiaries and without any

---

[73] Article 7(2) of the Commercial Agents Directive, Directive 86/653/EEC, required Member States to subscribe to one of two alternative formulations. The Greek and French references discussed in this section both concerned the commercial agent's entitlement to commission 'where he is entrusted with a specific geographical area or group of customers', whereas England opted for situations 'where [the agent] has an exclusive right to a specific geographical area or group of customers'. The difference in wording looks unlikely to affect interpretation of the Regulations in this regard.

[74] [1996] ECR I-6643, para 19.

[75] Case C-19/07; [2008] 1 Lloyd's Rep 475.

action on the part of C-M. The Cour de Cassation put the following question to the European Court:

> Is art. 7(2) ... to be interpreted as meaning that a commercial agent entrusted with a specific geographical area is entitled to commission where a commercial transaction between a third party and a customer belonging to that area has been concluded without any action, either direct or indirect, on the principal's part?

Looking at art 7(2) in isolation, the provision only refers to 'transactions concluded during the period covered by the agency agreement'.[76] There is no express requirement that either the agent or the principal should have contributed directly or indirectly to the conclusion of the transaction. The European Court, however, said that art 7(2) ought not to be read in this way. Article 10, which sets out when commission becomes due, needs also to be taken into account. According to art 10, commission becomes due as soon as and to the extent either that:

(a) the principal has executed the transaction; or
(b) the principal should, according to his agreement with the third party, have executed the transaction; or
(c) the third party has executed the transaction.[77]

Further, art 10(2) provides that commission becomes due, at latest, when that third party has executed his part of the transaction or should have done so 'if the principal had executed his part of the transaction'. The European Court noted that 'in each instance, the presence of the principal in the transactions for which the commercial agent can claim commission is indispensable.'[78] Moreover, such a reading of the Directive is reinforced by art 11(1), which provides that the right to commission can only be extinguished:

> if and to the extent that
> (a) it is established that the contract between the third party and the principal will not be executed; and
> (b) that fact is due to a reason for which the principal is not to blame.[79]

The fact that the sole ground of extinguishment of the agent's right to commission makes express reference to the principal 'emphasises the importance of his role for the existence of the right to commission'.[80] Consequently, the agent can only claim commission on the basis of a transaction to the extent that the principal acted, directly or indirectly, in the conclusion of that transaction. The principal's action may be what the Court describes as 'of a legal nature'—for instance, the principal

---

[76] The English Regulations similarly refer to 'commercial transactions concluded during the period of the agency contract'.
[77] This wording has also been incorporated into the English Regulations, reg 10(1).
[78] [2008] 1 Lloyd's Rep 475 at [19].
[79] The wording of the English Regulation, reg 11(1), is identical.
[80] [2008] 1 Lloyd's Rep 475 at [20].

acting through the intermediary of a representative—or 'of a factual nature'. In the absence of such action, the commercial agent is not entitled to commission. Given the similarity of the wording, it is submitted that the European Court's ruling on the French rendering of art 7(2) in *Chevassus-Marche v Group Danone* is also applicable to interpretation of reg 7(2) of the English Regulations.

### *Transactions concluded after termination of agency*

A commercial agent is entitled to commission on transactions concluded within a **9.33** reasonable period after termination of his agency contract. Regulation 8 provides:

> Subject to reg. 9 below, a commercial agent shall be entitled to commission on commercial transactions concluded after the agency contract has terminated if—
> (a) the transaction is mainly attributable to his efforts during the period covered by the agency contract and if the transaction was entered into within a reasonable period after that contract terminated; or
> (b) in accordance with the conditions mentioned in reg. 7 above, the order of the third party reached the principal or the commercial agent before the agency contract terminated.

Thus, according to reg 8(a), so long as the agent can show both that a transaction was entered into within a reasonable period after termination of his agency contract and that it was 'mainly attributable to his efforts', he will be entitled to commission.[81]

As with the expression in reg 7(1)(a), 'transaction ... concluded as a result of his **9.34** action',[82] the question has arisen as to the exact relationship between the notion of a transaction 'mainly attributable to [the agent's] efforts' under reg 8 and the notion of a transaction of which the agent was 'the effective cause' at common law. In *Tigana Ltd v Decoro Ltd*, Davis, J was inclined to think that it was best not to assume that the two expressions were freely interchangeable:

> It is ... clear that the phrase 'mainly attributable' connotes a causative link between the efforts of the commercial agent and the conclusion of the transaction (albeit after the agency contract has terminated). One might perhaps see an analogy with the familiar English legal phrase 'effective cause': but it is perhaps better not to gloss the words actually used in reg. 8(a).[83]

Subsequently, however, in *PJ Pipe & Valve Co Ltd v Audco India Ltd* Fulford, J **9.35** observed:

> In my judgment there is no discernible difference, certainly as applied to the facts in this case, between the two tests: 'mainly attributable' and 'the effective cause.'[84]

---

[81] *Smith v Reliance Water Controls Ltd* [2004] EWHC 1016 (QB).
[82] See para **9.29**.
[83] [2003] Eu LR 189 at [54].
[84] *Ibid* at [120]. See, eg, *Cureton v Mark Insulations Ltd* [2006] EWHC 2279 (QB) at [33] *per* Bean, J.

**9.36**  The relationship, then, remains mysterious. Under reg 8(a) it will be equally necessary to determine what amounts to 'a reasonable period after the contract terminated'. In one case, *Tigana Ltd v Decoro Ltd*, where an agent was responsible for procuring orders for leather furniture in the UK for a Hong Kong manufacturer, Davis, J gave reasons for concluding that in that particular case a reasonable period was nine months.[85] 'A reasonable period', however, will vary widely from case to case. In *Vick v Vogle Gapes Ltd*, for example, the judge considered that one month was 'a reasonable period' in the context of one particular contract,[86] whereas in *Smith v Reliance Water Controls Ltd*, although the court did not ultimately have to decide the matter, six months was suggested as a reasonable period.[87]

*Provision for apportionment of commission between new and previous commercial agents*

**9.37**  Regulation 9 regulates a situation that can arise where one commercial agent claims commission under reg 7, and commission is also due to a previous commercial agent under reg 8. In such situations reg 9 provides:

(1)  A commercial agent shall not be entitled to the commission referred to in reg 7 above if that commission is payable, by virtue of reg 8 above, to the previous commercial agent, unless it is equitable because of the circumstances for the commission to be shared between the commercial agents.

(2)  The principal shall be liable for any sum due under para (1) above to the person entitled to it in accordance with that paragraph, and any sum which the other commercial agent receives to which he is not entitled shall be refunded to the principal.

Claims for commission by a previous commercial agent under reg 8 will normally take priority. But there may be situations in which the principal's new agent is entitled to a share in that commission. In apportioning commission between new and previous commercial agents under reg 9, it is entirely for the court to determine what is 'equitable' in the particular circumstances.

*When the agent's commission falls due and by what date payment must have been made*

**9.38**  Regulation 10 states when the agent's commission becomes due. Depending on the type of transaction, it will be due when either the principal or the third party has executed the transaction brought about through the agent's efforts or, in the event of non-performance by the principal, when the latter 'should, according to his

---

[85]  [2003] Eu LR 189 at [65].
[86]  [2006] EWHC 1665 (TCC) at [131] *per* HHJ Seymour, QC.
[87]  [2004] EWHC 1016 (QB).

agreement with the third party, have executed the transaction' (reg 10(1)(b)). The parties are at liberty to vary these conditions. However, reg 10(2), from which the parties may not derogate (reg 10(4)), goes on to specify the very latest point at which commission will become due:

> Commission shall become due at the latest when the third party has executed his part of the transaction or should have done so if the principal had executed his part of the transaction, as he should have.

Regulation 10(3), which is also non-derogable, provides that 'commission shall be paid not later than on the last day of the month following the quarter in which it became due', and also supplies a scheme for determining the dates on which those quarter days fall:

> The commission shall be paid not later than on the last day of the month following the quarter in which it became due, and, for the purposes of these Regulations, unless otherwise agreed between the parties, the first quarter period shall run from the date the agency contract takes effect, and subsequent periods shall run from that date in the third month thereafter or the beginning of the fourth month, whichever is the sooner.

### *Extinguishment of the agent's right to commission*

**9.39** Regulation 11(1), from which the parties may not derogate to the detriment of the agent (reg 11(3)), curtails the circumstances in which the agent's right to commission can be extinguished. It provides:

> The right to commission can be extinguished only if and to the extent that—
> (a)  it is established that the contract between the third party and the principal will not be executed; and
> (b)  that fact is due to a reason for which the principal is not to blame.

In short, emphasizing that unless the agency contract provides otherwise commission is payable only upon performance of the relevant transaction,[88] commission ceases to be payable only if the transaction remained unperformed for reasons unattributable to the principal.

### *Periodic supply of information as to commission due and right of inspection of principal's books*

**9.40** In order to reinforce the agent's rights in respect of remuneration, reg 12(1) requires the principal to supply his agent with periodic statements of commission owed. Alongside any other rights the agent may have to inspect his principal's books, reg 12(2) also entitles the agent to demand 'all the information (and in particular an extract from the books) which is available to his principal and

---

[88]  See further reg 10; para **9.38**

which he needs in order to check the amount of the commission due to him.'
Regulation 12(3) stipulates that 'any agreement to derogate from paragraphs (1)
and (2) above shall be void.'

## The Agent's Right to an Indemnity

**9.41** Every agent is entitled:

(a)  to be reimbursed expenses he has incurred in performance of his agency, and
(b)  to be indemnified for losses and liabilities he has incurred in performing that
agency.

If the agency is governed by a contract—as most agencies in the commercial sphere
inevitably are—these entitlements will derive from either express or implied terms
of the agency contract. As Hobhouse, J pointed out, 'The implication only arises as
a matter of law in the absence of some express agreement.'[89]

**9.42** The right to indemnity, however, may be excluded by the terms of the contract. For
instance, in the case of *del credere* agency, where the agent customarily charges a
higher rate of commission in exchange for his agreement to indemnify the principal
in respect of the performance of the persons with whom he deals,[90] the principal
will be under no obligation to reimburse the agent if third parties fail to pay sums
due under their contracts.

**9.43** In those uncommon cases where the agency is not governed by contract, either
because the agency is gratuitous or because for some reason the contract with the
principal is not valid, the agent's right to an indemnity will found in quasi-contract.
The agent's indemnity will arise here only if it can be shown that the payment made
by the agent was one that the agent was compelled to make, that the principal bore
ultimate liability for the sum in question, and that the principal obtained a benefit
from the agent's payment. The operation of this principle is exemplified by *Brook's
Wharf and Bull Wharf Ltd v Goodman Bros.*[91] A consignment of furs had been stolen
from a bonded warehouse. The consignor was held liable to indemnify the bonded
warehouseman in respect of customs duty the latter had had to pay on the furs by
statute owing to the goods having been taken out of the warehouse without due

---

[89]  *Islamic Republic of Iran Shipping Lines v Zannis Compania Naviera SA ('The Tzelepi')* [1991] 2
Lloyd's Rep 265, 270.
[90]  *Associated British Ports v Ferryways NV* [2008] 2 Lloyd's Rep 353 at [63] *per* Field, J. Because
the main object of the agent's charging higher commission is in respect of his employment generally
and not in respect of his liability to his principal as a surety, *del credere agency* is not founded on a
promise falling within s 4 of the Statute of Frauds 1677; it is a contract of indemnity, not a contract
of guarantee. See further *Pitt v Jones* [2008] QB 706 esp at [34]–[38] *per* Smith, LJ; and para **1.07**.
[91]  [1937] 1 KB 534.

entry. Lord Wright, MR applied the principle laid down by Cockburn CJ in *Moule v Garrett* to the effect that:

> Where the plaintiff has been compelled by law to pay, or, being compellable by law, has paid money which the defendant was ultimately liable to pay, so that the latter obtains the benefit of the payment by the discharge of his liability; under such circumstances the defendant is held indebted to the plaintiff in the amount.[92]

The principal is under a general duty to indemnify the agent in respect of all liabilities incurred whilst acting within the scope of his actual, implied, or customary authority. Provided that an agent's acts fall within the scope of his authority, he may claim an indemnity from his principal. In *Re Famatina Development Corporation*[93] a consulting engineer, O, who was employed by his company to visit Argentina and report back on the financial potential of various properties, made serious allegations concerning transactions effected by the company's managing director, P. P sued O for libel and slander. The action proceeded to the House of Lords, where it was eventually dismissed with costs when P failed to comply with an order for security for the costs of a new trial. Most of O's costs proved irrecoverable as P was outside the jurisdiction. O, therefore, sought to prove for them in the liquidation of the company. The Court of Appeal held that because O's duties were far wider than those of a normal consulting engineer, and all that he had done had been in pursuance of his duties as agent for the company, O fell within the well-settled rule that an agent has a right against his principal, founded upon an implied contract, to be indemnified against all losses and liabilities, and to be reimbursed all expenses incurred by him in the execution of his authority. Similarly, in *PSA Transport Ltd v Newton, Lansdowne & Co Ltd*[94] PSA, forwarding agents, had been engaged by N at an agreed fee to inspect and trans-ship to Poland parcels of Palmyra fibre that had been discharged in London. Solely owing to N's delay in giving PSA its instructions, rather than being transferred by lighter for immediate transhipment, the consignment was discharged to the quayside, thereby incurring inward port dues. The Port of London Authority refused to release the goods until the various port charges and wharfage charges were paid. PSA paid these dues and then sought to recover the sums it had disbursed from N. N contested the additional payment. As Sellers, J remarked, '[T]here is no defence to this action and never was.'[95] Because the inward port charges had accrued solely by reason of N's dilatoriness, and would not have been incurred if the matter had been carried out merely by way of collection without the goods being landed on the quay, such disbursements were the liability of N, for whom PSA were acting PSA were therefore entitled to recover these additional sums from N.

**9.44**

---

[92] (1872) LR 7 Ex 101, 104.
[93] [1914] 2 Ch 271.
[94] [1956] 1 Lloyd's Rep 121.
[95] *Ibid.*

*Liabilities incurred by agent under trade custom recoverable from principal*

**9.45**   Provided that the custom is found to be reasonable, liabilities incurred by an agent
arising out of the operation of a trade custom will be recoverable from the principal.
In *Anglo Overseas Transport Ltd v Titan Industrial Corp (UK) Ltd* [96] evidence was
adduced abundantly satisfying the court that in the London freight market it was a
reasonable, if not wholly necessary custom that if a forwarding agent booked space
on board a ship for his principal's goods and that space was not taken up, he would
stand personally liable to the shipowner in respect of that dead freight. Space reserved
by the agents was left unfilled owing to late delivery of the goods. Barry, J held that it
'cannot be ... questioned, that [the agents] are entitled to be indemnified against the
expenses to which they have been put in connection with this transaction.'[97] Again,
in *Bayliffe v Butterworth*,[98] where the court adjudged that the principal was aware
of the relevant custom, the Court of Exchequer held that a principal was liable to
indemnify his broker, B, for sums he had paid to another broker, F, on the Liverpool
Stock Exchange in respect of some scrip shares he had been employed to sell but on
whose delivery the principal had defaulted. F, in consequence, went into the market
to purchase the relevant shares and charged B the difference in price. According
to custom, brokers were answerable to each other for engagements entered into
between them on behalf of third parties, and for this reason B satisfied F's demand.
The principal was therefore held liable to indemnify his broker, B.

*The principal's obligation to indemnify his agent may extend beyond things for
which the principal himself would be personally liable*

**9.46**   The agent may also claim for expenses and liabilities that he, the agent, personally
incurs in the performance of his agency. Thus, in *Adams v Morgan & Co Ltd*,[99]
where the seller of a business had carried it on from the date of the contract until
the date of completion on the purchaser's account, and a clause in the contract of
sale expressly provided for him to receive an indemnity, the seller was entitled to
be indemnified in respect of super tax he had been obliged to pay even though the
principal was a company and therefore not itself liable to super tax.

---

[96] [1959] 2 Lloyd's Rep 152.

[97] *Ibid* at 160.

[98] (1847) 1 Exch 425. Scrip shares, with which this case is concerned, are shares that a company
issues free to its existing shareholders in direct proportion to their existing shareholdings. Nowadays,
it is more often known as a capitalization issue, and is intended to rectify any imbalance between
the company's reserves and its share capital, particularly if the company has been trading successfully
over a period of time.

[99] [1924] 1 KB 751. Cp *Re Hollebone's Agreement* [1959] 1 WLR 536: here, the transaction was as
between principal and principal, and the liability of the purchasers of a wine and spirit business could
not be regarded as extending to tax on profit which the vendor made, not as agent but as principal,
and which he was entitled to retain for himself. In *Adams* the agent's tax liability was assessed on profits for which he was accountable to the principal as agent, whereas in *Hollebone* the vendor was not
accountable to the purchasers for the profit which he had made on the sale to them of the business.

*The principal is not bound to indemnify the agent in respect of liabilities incurred outside the scope of his authority*

In *Islamic Republic of Iran Shipping Lines v Zannis Compania Naviera SA ('The* **9.47** *Tzelepi')*[100] shipowners instructed charterers to effect a war risks insurance on a ship that was to sail into a war zone on the same terms as another named ship. The owners claimed that the charterers had failed to comply with their instructions and had insured the hull and machinery at 1 per cent of $3m instead of $2m, and each member of the crew for $2,100 instead of $500, as requested. Hobhouse, J held that the charterers were entitled to be indemnified in respect of any liabilities incurred and sums disbursed in performance of their agency in accordance with the instructions and authority they had been given by their principal. As it turned out, the owners were mistaken as to the value of the hull and the charterers could recoup their expenses in that respect since they had effected the insurance on identical terms to those obtained for the other ship. However, as regards the crew, the evidence plainly showed that the owners had not agreed to pay more than $500 *per capita* in respect of crew cover. The charterers, therefore, were not entitled to recover the excess over the $500 per capita from the owners. Similar considerations applied in *Barron v Fitzgerald*,[101] where a principal instructed B and S, to whom he owed money, to effect an insurance on his life for seven years in their two names in order to secure the debt. Contrary to instructions, B and S effected the insurance not only in their names but also in the name of a third person, S, who had subsequently joined their firm. The court held that since the principal had not granted B and S authority to take out an insurance in three names, he was not liable to indemnify them in respect of the premiums they had paid.

*Liabilities which agent has a strong moral duty to settle*

The agent is entitled to be indemnified by the principal not only in respect of dis- **9.48** bursements the agent is legally liable to make in the performance of his agency but also for liabilities which he has a strong moral duty to settle. In *Rhodes v Fielder, Jones and Harrison*[102] a country solicitor instructed London solicitors to act for him in an appeal in the House of Lords in which he was acting. The London agents briefed two leading counsel, but after the delivery of briefs the country solicitor revoked the London agents' authority to pay the fees on the briefs. The London agents felt that they had no choice but to pay counsel, and then recouped themselves out of monies of the country solicitor which they held. The country solicitor sought to recover the monies retained by the London agents. The court determined that even though counsel could not sue the London agents for their fees, if the agents failed to pay

---

[100] [1991] 2 Lloyd's Rep 265.
[101] (1840) 6 Bing NC 201.
[102] (1919) 89 LJKB 15.

them 'they would be behaving in a way which would unquestionably place them in a position.' Therefore, they had 'made themselves responsible as honourable members of their profession for the payment of these fees' and the country solicitor had not been entitled to revoke their authority to pay counsel.

*An agent may not claim an indemnity in respect of expenses and liabilities incurred through his own fault*

**9.49** In *Lewis v Samuel*[103] a solicitor who had agreed to pursue a perjury prosecution on the defendant's behalf, undertaking 'not to charge ... full costs ... except the money out of pocket', conducted the case negligently. In consequence, the prosecution failed. The court held that sums disbursed by the solicitor were not recoverable from the defendant. In similar fashion, in *Lage v Siemens Bros & Co Ltd*[104] a ship's master incurred a fine in Rio de Janeiro because a quantity of cable wire he was carrying was not discharged or passed through Customs in the usual way. Under Brazilian law the ship's agent became liable for this fine because the ship left port without the master having paid it. The ship's agent paid the fine and then sought reimbursement from the principal. Mackinnon, J held that an agent could not claim an indemnity if his liability arose by reason of his failure to discharge with reasonable diligence his duties as agent. In the event, the court concluded that the agent had failed to exercise reasonable diligence after the fine was imposed: had he promptly acquired an account of what had happened and tendered the necessary documents to support that account, in Mackinnon, J's estimation, he would have been able to obtain remission of the fine.

**9.50** A distinction may be drawn between cases where the agent is negligent towards his principal and cases where the agent is negligent towards a third party. In *Linklaters v HSBC Bank plc*[105] a cheque payable to Linklaters for legal fees, drawn on HSBC, was stolen from Linklaters' mailroom and came into the hands of a Spanish bank, BPE. BPE sent a remittance letter to HSBC instructing it to make payment. Linklaters' claims in conversion against HSBC and BPE were settled. Following the settlement, one issue that arose between the parties was that HSBC, as BPE's agent for collection, having cleared the cheque and settled Linklaters' claim, sought an indemnity against BPE in respect of its liability to Linklaters. Gross, J considered statements made by Rix, J in *Middle Temple v Lloyds Bank plc*,[106] where he had applied the proposition:

> An agent for collection which had not breached any duty to its correspondent bank was entitled to the benefit of an implied indemnity, unless it had acted in bad faith,

---

[103] (1846) 8 QB 685.
[104] (1932) 42 Ll L Rep 252.
[105] [2003] 2 Lloyd's Rep 545.
[106] [1999] 1 All ER (Comm) 193.

or in a way which it knew to be unlawful or was manifestly unlawful, or had acted outside its authority.[107]

In *Middle Temple* Rix, J had stated:

> [T]here is an important distinction to be made between the case where the agent is in breach of some duty *vis-à-vis* the party which requests him to act, and the case where the agent is in breach of some duty to a third party. In the former case there is good reason to think that the implied indemnity cannot be intended to cover the agent's default *vis-à-vis* the requesting party ... Where, however, the negligence is *vis-à-vis* a third party, ... I do not see why the implied indemnity should not operate, since *ex hypothesi*, the agent can only be liable in a case of negligence.[108]

Gross, J's conclusion in *Linklaters* was that such a distinction was precluded neither by principle nor authority.[109]

*An agent is not entitled to an indemnity in respect of transactions which he knows, or must be taken to know, are illegal*

In *Re Parker*[110] a candidate employed an election sub-agent, a solicitor, who made **9.51** illegal payments to canvassers contrary to the Corrupt Practices legislation. It was held that because the payments were illegal, the sub-agent was not entitled to be reimbursed these expenses. In contrast, if the agent is unaware of the illegality of the transaction, he will be entitled to an indemnity. Thus, in *Adamson v Jarvis*[111] an auctioneer was instructed to sell valuable cattle, goods, and chattels. Only after the items had been sold and the proceeds of sale handed over to the principal did it emerge that the principal had no right to sell the goods. The true owner compelled the auctioneer to pay him the value of the goods that had been wrongfully sold. Best, CJ held that 'the rule that wrong-doers cannot have redress or contribution against each other is confined to cases where the person seeking redress must be presumed to have known that he was doing an unlawful act.'[112] Therefore, since in this case the transaction was not *ex facie* illegal and the principal had no notice of the principal's lack of title, the auctioneer was held entitled to be reimbursed the cost of the goods.

## The Agent's Lien

In order to facilitate recovery by the agent of sums owed to him by the principal, the **9.52** law grants the agent a possessory lien on the goods and chattels of his principal in

---

[107] *Ibid* at 194.
[108] *Ibid* at 234.
[109] [2003] 2 Lloyd's Rep 545 at [37].
[110] (1882) LR 21 ChD 408.
[111] (1827) 4 Bing 66.
[112] *Ibid* at 73.

respect of all claims arising out of his employment as agent.[113] A lien can be of considerable utility. The lien covers both the agent's remuneration and his indemnity:

> It is clear that an agent's lien extends not only to sums due to him by way of his own remuneration but also to liabilities properly incurred by him in the course of his agency.[114]

Diplock, LJ pointed out in *Tappenden v Artus* that 'the common law remedy of possessory lien, like other remedies such as abatement of nuisance, self-defence or ejection of trespassers to land, is one of self-help.'[115]

**9.53** A lien merely confers on the agent the right to possess the principal's goods or documents. As the court ruled in *West of England Bank v Batchelor*,[116] a case in which a solicitor asserted a lien over a client's life insurance policy in respect of that client's bill of costs, the solicitor was under no obligation to give notice to the insurance company as against a subsequent assignee because the solicitor had no right against the fund itself; he merely had a right to embarrass anyone who attempted to claim the fund:

> What is the nature of a solicitor's lien? It is merely a passive right, a right to hold the piece of paper or the piece of parchment, as the case may be, until he is paid. In this case it gives the solicitor no right against the fund, but merely a right to embarrass the person who claims the fund by the non-production of the piece of paper.[117]

Although it might appear that the agent's right to obstruct the principal in order to secure payment of sums due to him cannot be exactly squared with the agent's general fiduciary duties to the principal,[118] as Mustill J noted in *The Borag*:

> [T]he exercise by the agent of remedies over his principal's goods is not ruled out merely because an agent is under a general obligation not to prefer his own interests to that of his principal—as witness the fact that the law recognises the right of an agent to enforce his claims for remuneration and indemnity by exercising a lien over his principal's goods.[119]

---

[113] Since a lien consists in a right to retain possession, liens do not extend to intangibles. Thus, in *Your Response Ltd v Datateam Business Media Ltd* [2014] 3 WLR 887 a database management company could not claim a lien over a publishing company's records which it had contracted to hold and maintain. Moore-Bick, LJ displayed sympathy for the view expressed in Green and Randall, *The Tort of Conversion* (2009: Hart Publishing, Oxford) that the general bar on 'possession' of all intangibles, particularly digitalized materials, required to be reviewed (at [27]). All three members of the Court of Appeal, however, considered that this was too bold a step for a court to contemplate, Davis, LJ noting that 'the law of unintended consequences is no part of the law of England and Wales' (at [39]).

[114] *Fraser v Equitorial Shipping Co Ltd and Equitorial Lines Ltd. The Ijaola* [1979] 1 Lloyd's Rep 103, 116 *per* Lloyd, J.

[115] [1964] 2 QB 185, 195. See also *Compania Financiera 'Soleada' SA v Hamoor Tanker Corporation Inc. The Borag* [1980] 1 Lloyd's Rep 111, 122 *per* Mustill, J.

[116] (1882) 51 LJCh 199.

[117] *Ibid* at 200 *per* Fry, J.

[118] See paras **8.15–8.75**.

[119] [1980] 1 Lloyd's Rep 111, 122.

A person claiming a lien must either claim it for a definite amount or give the owner **9.54**
of the goods under lien particulars from which he himself can calculate the amount
for which a lien is due. The owner must then, in the absence of express agreement,
tender an amount equivalent to the value of the lien. If he does not, unless excused,
he has no answer to a claim of lien.[120]

### General liens and particular liens

English law has traditionally drawn a distinction between general liens and par-  **9.55**
ticular liens. A general lien confers on the agent the right to retain the principal's
goods until the general balance of the account between principal and agent is settled. A particular lien, however, only entitles the agent to retain possession of his
principal's goods until money owed to him by the principal on those particular
goods has been paid over. On the whole, the law views general liens with considerable suspicion,[121] and courts are more generally disposed to recognize particular
liens. Nevertheless, by the terms of their contract or by recognized custom, parties
may acquire general liens. By way of an example, the Road Haulage Association
Conditions of Carriage 1998 and Road Haulage Association Conditions of Storage
1998 provide for both general and particular liens in their standard terms. They
state that a carrier/contractor shall have a general lien against the customer, where
the customer is the owner of the consignment, for any monies whatever due from
the customer to the carrier/contractor. Where, however, the customer is not the
owner of the consignment, the carrier/contractor shall have a particular lien against
the owner, allowing the carrier/contractor to retain possession, but not to dispose of, the consignment against monies due from the customer in respect of the
consignment.[122] At other times, the courts recognize that certain classes of merchants or financiers are entitled to a general lien by custom.[123] Thus, in *Re Spectrum
Plus Ltd (in liquidation)*[124] Lord Nicholls of Birkenhead declared the established
truth that:

> A banker has a general lien over all bills, notes and negotiable Instruments belonging
> to the customer which his customer may have deposited with him in security of the
> customer's indebtedness to the bank.

---

[120] See Scrutton, LJ's judgment in *Albemarle Supply Co Ltd v Hind & Co* [1928] 1 KB 307, esp
at p 318.

[121] See, eg, *Bock v Gorrissen* (1860) 2 De GF&J 434, 443 *per* Lord Campbell, LC: 'The law of
England does not favour general liens, and I apprehend that a general lien can only be claimed as
arising from dealings in a particular trade or line of business, such as wharfingers, factors and bankers,
in which the custom of a general lien has been judicially proved and acknowledged, or upon express
evidence being given that, according to the established custom in some other trade or line of business,
a general lien is claimed and allowed.'

[122] See, eg, *T Comedy (UK) Ltd v Easy Managed Transport Ltd* [2007] 2 Lloyd's Rep 397.

[123] 'It is well settled that a general lien can only exist as a common-law right arising from general
usage': *Tellrite Ltd v London Confirmers Ltd* [1962] 1 Lloyd's Rep 236, 239 *per* Elwes, J.

[124] [2005] 2 AC 680.

His Lordship went on to say:

> But a lien is a right to retain possession of property that belongs to someone else, and the banker has no lien over funds which, when deposited in its account by the customer, become his own property.[125]

Some liens—for example a solicitor's lien for costs[126]—have been recognized by statute.[127]

*Parties are at liberty to exclude the operation of a lien by an express term in their contract*

**9.56**  Alternatively, by necessary implication, the nature of a particular transaction may obviously show that a lien was not contemplated by the parties. Hence, as Lord Scott of Foscote noted in *Yeomans Row Management Ltd v Cobbe*,[128] the risky, speculative property development contract into which the parties proposed entering 'would plainly have excluded reliance on a vendor's lien.'[129] In *Re Bowes, Earl of Strathmore v Vane*,[130] too, by necessary implication the terms of the parties' agreement excluded a banker's general lien. A customer deposited a life assurance policy with his bankers, accompanied by a memorandum of charge indicating that it was to secure overdrafts not exceeding £4,000. It was held that the memorandum served to displace the banker's general lien as the terms of the agreement were inconsistent

---

[125] *Ibid* at [60]. See also *Brandao v Barnett* (1846) 12 Cl&Fin 787, 805 *per* Lord Campbell: 'the general lien of bankers is part of the law-merchant, and is to be judicially noticed—like the negotiability of bills of exchange, or the days of grace allowed for their payment.' Other species of agent, such as factors, solicitors, and stockbrokers, have variously been held to have general liens. However, confirming houses have been held not to be mercantile agents within the meaning of the Factors Act 1889 entitled to a general lien (*Tellrite Ltd v London Confirmers Ltd* [1962] 1 Lloyd's Rep 236).

[126] The courts have for long protected the solicitor's lien for unpaid costs. As Kekewich, J observed in *Groom v Cheesewright* [1895] 1 Ch 730, 732: 'It appears to me to be only common justice that when a solicitor has expended his brains and time and resources in working for a client, he should be paid out of the produce of his industry and skill.' More recently, Scarman, J affirmed that 'it is the policy of the law' to protect the solicitor's lien: *In the estate of Fuld (decd) (No 4)* [1968] P 727, 736.

[127] See County Court Act 1984, s 72, discussed recently in *Revenue & Customs Commissioners v Xicom Systems Ltd* [2008] STC 3492. The solicitor's lien has a long ancestry and is well illustrated by *Loescher v Dean* [1950] 1 Ch 491, where a purchaser obtained an order for specific performance instructing the vendor, D, to convey the property to L on the latter's paying a stated sum. L paid that sum to D's solicitors, who paid it into their client account. L then served a garnishee order nisi on D's solicitors in respect of L's costs against D. The solicitors, who had not rendered a bill of costs to their client, took out a summons for a charging order on the sum paid by L. Harman, J noted that the money was not entrusted to the solicitors for any specific purpose, but was paid to them in the ordinary course of business as solicitors of their client. They received it as the client's agent. Therefore, upon receipt of the money the solicitors had a lien over it for his unpaid costs and that therefore a creditor could not attach it (pp 495–6). See also *Irwin Mitchell v Revenue & Customs Prosecution Office* [2009] 1 Cr App R 22, esp at [25]ff.

[128] [2008] 1 WLR 1752.

[129] *Ibid* at [7].

[130] (1886) 33 ChD 586.

with the banker's right to retain the policy as security for the settlement of the general balance of the customer's account.

Parties often try to claim that they hold a lien over another's goods or documents, attracted by the leverage it gives them to compel the settlement of liabilities. However, such claims frequently fail. Thus, in *Chellaram v Butlers*,[131] in the absence of a custom or specific agreement, Megaw, LJ declined to hold that where owners of goods had sent them to a company for shipment to Africa, which in turn had sent them on to the defendants, when the company went into liquidation, the defendants became entitled to a lien as against the owners: **9.57**

> There is no custom giving persons in the position of the defendants a general lien—certainly not a general lien against the owners of the goods in respect of someone else's debts unrelated to the particular goods.[132]

### Acquisition of the agent's lien

Assuming that a right of lien has not been expressly or impliedly excluded by the terms of the parties' contract, an agent will only have a lien over his principal's property if he has come into possession of the principal's goods lawfully and in his capacity as agent. **9.58**

#### *An agent only enjoys a lien if he is in possession of the principal's goods*

In many cases, this will signify that the goods are in the agent's actual physical possession. As Burrough, J said in *Taylor v Robinson*, a case concerning a factor's unsuccessful claim of a possessory lien, 'It is incumbent on factors who claim a lien, to prove their possession of the property on which the lien is claimed. Possession is matter of fact.'[133] However, the court will also recognize the agent's right if the latter has only constructive possession. In *Bryans v Nix*[134] a carrier was employed to convey a cargo of oats to the principal's agent in Dublin. The carrier was handed documents 'In care for and to be shipped to the agents in Liverpool', clearly indicating that the carrier held the oats for the agent. Parke, B treated the agent as having constructive possession of the goods, and hence as possessing a lien over them, from the moment the principal handed the goods over to the carrier.[135] Again, in *McCombie v Davies*,[136] where a broker had pledged tobacco belonging to his principal, Lord Ellenborough, CJ made clear that it was the opinion of the entire court that a lien would not be lost where someone 'delivers over the actual possession of **9.59**

---

[131] [1978] 2 Lloyd's Rep 412.
[132] *Ibid* at 415. See also *Pendragon Plc v Walon Ltd* [2005] EWHC 1082 (QB).
[133] (1818) 8 Taunt 648, 653.
[134] (1839) 4 M&W 775.
[135] *Ibid* esp at 791.
[136] (1805) 7 East 5.

goods, on which he has the lien, to that other, with notice of his lien, and appoints that other as his servant to keep possession of the goods for him'.[137]

*An agent must have acquired possession of his principal's goods by lawful means*

**9.60**   In *Taylor v Robinson*[138] M instructed his factor to purchase a quantity of Quebec staves. By agreement, the staves would be stored on the seller's premises, M paying rent to the seller. In due course, the seller asked the factor to remove M's staves, which the factor did without M's authorization. In response to the factor's claim that he possessed a lien on the staves, Park, J commented: 'I never remember to have met with a case more destitute of facts to authorize the supposition, that the possession was in the factor.'[139] The principal retained possession of the goods throughout and, by removing them the factor had acted unlawfully and could not thereby acquire a lien over the staves. In similar fashion in *Nichols v Clent*,[140] following the shipper's bankruptcy, it was held that the fact that a carrier at the shipper's order had given possession of certain sacks of flour to the factor did not operate to give the factor a lien as against the shipper's assignees, even though the goods had been shipped on the factor's account, and the factor had accepted bills on the faith of it:

> [T]hough the law is quite clear that when a factor obtains possession of goods consigned to him, he has a lien for his general balance, yet it is as clear that he must obtain actual possession of the goods, for that is essentially necessary and indispensable.[141]

*The agent must have acquired possession of the goods in his capacity as agent*

**9.61**   If the agent acquires the goods in some other capacity—for instance, the principal has simply deposited the goods or chattel with the agent for safekeeping—the agent will not have gained possession of them as agent and will not be entitled to a lien over them.[142] Moreover, the lien an agent enjoys over the principal's goods will only extend to claims against the principal arising out of the contract of agency under which the agent came to possess the goods in question. In *Dixon v Stansfield*[143] a factor who regularly sold goods on his principal's behalf on one occasion acted as an insurance broker for him, effecting an insurance of a ship's cargo. The factor was held not to be entitled to claim a lien on the insurance policy over the monies owed to him by the principal in his general capacity as factor. The agent's lien only allows

---

[137]  *Ibid* at 8.
[138]  (1818) 8 Taunt 648.
[139]  *Ibid* at 652.
[140]  (1817) 3 Price 547.
[141]  *Ibid* at 567 *per* Graham, B.
[142]  Eg, *Muir v Fleming* (1822) Dow & Ry NP 29, where a policy of insurance was left in the hands of an agent, merely for safe custody.
[143]  (1850) 10 CB 398.

him to retain goods and chattels in order to secure payment of sums due under the agency agreement to which those particular goods relate. Similarly, in *Houghton v Matthews*,[144] M, a factor, sold a quantity of logwood and fustic belonging to G in his own name to J. J, without having paid for the logwood and fustic, sent M a parcel of indigo to sell for him, never having employed M as a factor before. J subsequently became bankrupt. J's assignees claimed the indigo that J had sent to M, which still remained unsold, tendering the charges upon those goods. M refused to deliver up the indigo, claiming a lien upon it for the price of the logwood and fustic he had previously sold to J, since G still owed him money. The court held that the factor had no lien on J's goods as the factor's claims against J had arisen prior to his having been employed as J's agent.

### The scope of the agent's lien

The agent's lien will normally extend to all sums owed in connection with the rel- **9.62** evant transaction, even if the agent only has possession of a portion of the goods. In *Fraser v Equitorial Shipping Co Ltd and Equitorial Lines Ltd. The Ijaola*[145] shipowners employed F, a consulting engineer, as their agent to effect repairs on the engines of a ship which at that time was anchored in Lagos, Nigeria. F flew out to Lagos with a team of engineers but failed to gain entry to Nigeria as they were without visas. They gained entry at a later attempt, began work but encountered various difficulties. F and the owners were in dispute over the estimated cost of the work. Eventually, the owners said that they would find someone else who was cheaper, and requested that F hand over the ship's main bearings which F had sent to Scotland to be re-metalled. The shipowners owed F money for work that had been carried out and F asserted a lien by indicating that the bearings would be available to the owners as soon as the outstanding monies had been settled. One question that arose, once it was determined that a consulting engineer acting as agent was entitled to a lien, was whether the lien F was exercising over the bearings extended only to charges he could levy against the owners in respect of the bearings or whether the lien extended to the whole of F's services in respect of the ship. Lloyd, J concluded:

> Just as a solicitor must be able to exercise a lien for his charges in a case on such papers as he has in his possession, even though there are other papers in the case of which he never had possession, or of which he had lost possession, so also [F] is entitled to exercise a lien on a part of the vessel which admittedly was in his possession in respect of his work on the vessel as a whole.

For good measure, Lloyd, J added:

> Similarly, to take another example, a car repairer could exercise a lien on the spare tyre for work carried out on the engine.[146]

---

[144] (1803) 3 Bos & P 485.
[145] [1979] 1 Lloyd's Rep 103.
[146] *Ibid* at 115–16.

**9.63**   Once a lien attaches, it is valid not only against the principal but also against third parties who subsequently acquire title or rights in the goods. As was seen in *West of England Bank v Batchelor*,[147] the agent's lien on his principal's insurance policy was not defeated when the principal assigned that policy to a third party. In the same way, agents' liens have variously been held to withstand their principals' insolvency[148] or bankruptcy.[149] Nevertheless, an agent cannot acquire greater rights than were enjoyed by the principal himself when the lien first attached. Therefore, the agent's lien normally takes effect subject to any existing rights or equities of third parties already held at the moment when the lien first came into being. In *Peat v Clayton*,[150] for instance, the owner of shares in a company executed an assignment of all his property to P, as trustees for his creditors, but refused to hand over the certificates. P served the company with notice of the assignment. The debtor then, through his brokers, sold the shares on the Stock Exchange, executed a transfer, and received the purchase money. Notwithstanding the notice, the company at first entered the purchaser's name on the register, but later removed it and refused to issue certificates. At the purchaser's request, the brokers provided her with other shares in the company, and then claimed to be entitled to the shares sold on behalf of the debtor. Joyce, J, however, held that any lien to which the brokers might have been entitled was only upon the debtor's interest, which was subject to P's rights under the deed of assignment.

### An Agent cannot create a lien beyond his own interest

**9.64**   'It is a general principle of the law of agency that no one can create a lien beyond his own interest.'[151] This means that if a lien has been created over a principal's goods, if the principal subsequently disposes of those goods in some way, the lien is frozen at the sum due at that time. There is no requirement that the holder of the lien need have notice of any such disposition. In *Eide UK Ltd v Lowndes Lambert Group Ltd*[152] the Court of Appeal held that whilst the Marine Insurance Act 1906, s 53(2)

---

[147] (1882) 51 LJCh 199; para **9.53**.

[148] *Re Capital Fire Insurance Association* (1883) 24 ChD 408, 420 *per* Cotton, LJ ('His lien, which was good before the winding-up commenced, is not interfered with by the winding-up order').

[149] *Robson v Kemp* (1802) 4 Esp 233, 236 *per* Lord Ellenborough, CJ.

[150] [1906] 1 Ch 659.

[151] *Eide UK Ltd v Lowndes Lambert Group Ltd* [1999] QB 199, 213 *per* Phillips, LJ. See also, *Masponsy Hermano v Mildred, Goyeneche & Co* (1882) 9 QBD 530; (1883) 8 App Cas 874. That is, unless statute has made special provision. Thus, the Factors Act 1889, s 7(1) extends special protection to consignees of goods: 'Where the owner of goods has given possession of the goods to another person for the purpose of consignment or sale, or has shipped the goods in the name of another person, and the consignee of the goods has not had notice that such person is not the owner of the goods, the consignee shall, in respect of advances made to or for the use of such person, have the same lien on the goods as if such person were the owner of the goods, and may transfer any such lien to another person.' And under the general principles of negotiability, the Bills of Exchange Act 1882, ss 27(3) and 29 impose a special regime.

[152] [1999] QB 199, 213.

gave a broker a lien on a policy of marine insurance in respect of any balance on any insurance account due to him from a policyholder with whom he had dealt as principal, thereby entitling the broker to apply claims proceeds collected under the policy in discharge of the debt protected by the lien, the Act did not in terms extend to insurances placed on behalf of both the broker and other interests because he did not then deal 'as a principal', as required by the 1906 legislation. In *Eide* it was held that since no one could create a lien beyond his own interest, s 53(2) did not create such a lien over a policy of composite insurance where an assured had placed insurance on behalf of himself and his co-assured so that each could sue on his own interest. Therefore, the brokers, who had collected claims from underwriters, who had paid them into a mixed bank account, and who asserted a general lien seeking to retain the entirety of the proceeds in part satisfaction of the operators' outstanding liabilities to them on an unrelated insurance account, were held to have no right to retain the proceeds recovered on behalf of the bank under the policies in diminution of the debts owed to the brokers by the operators in respect of other insurance business placed by them.

## Loss of the agent's lien

### Extinguishment by settlement

In the normal course of events, a lien is extinguished once the principal has tendered to the agent all sums owing by way of compensation or indemnity. **9.65**

In addition to the sum required to discharge the principal's indebtedness, does the agent's lien also include an entitlement to expenses for costs incurred in enforcing and exercising the lien? The storage costs necessitated by exercise of the lien might be a good example. To answer this question, it is necessary to distinguish between different classes of lienholders. Broadly speaking, *Somes v British Empire Shipping Co*[153] established that an artificer's lien (that is, a lien held by someone who employs his labour and skill repairing or improving another's goods and who holds such lien solely in respect of the cost of his labour) will not normally comprehend a right to claim the expenses of enforcing or exercising the lien. If expenses are to be claimed by the artificer, such a claim has to found either in a contractual provision or in damages for breach of contract. From this, it naturally follows that the agent cannot hold a lien for such expenses, unless of course the contract with the principal so provides. However, there is no overriding principle of law applicable to all liens according to which, subject to any contractual term to the contrary, the expenses of retaining possession of goods in the exercise of a lien are not recoverable from their owner. Indeed, such a principle would make very little sense in many commercial contexts. As Sir Bernard Rix pointed out in *Metall Market OOO v Vitorio Shipping* **9.66**

---

[153] (1860) HL Cas 338.

*Co Ltd*, it is 'difficult ... to fit the complexities of a contract of carriage by sea into the ... simplicity of a straightforward common-law artificer's lien of pure self-help uncomplicated by contractual terms or implications.'[154] More specifically, in the context of *Metall Market OOO*, a shipping case concerned with general average, he stressed that shipping is performed on the basis that time is money and that a ship is a floating and travelling warehouse for which cargo has to pay either in the form of agreed freight or hire, or by way of damages for any breach of contract. Because, in the event of a ship being delayed, say, by the cargo owner's failure to arrange timely discharge, the contractual arrangement between the parties contemplated that the cargo owner would compensate either by means of the liquidated damages in the form of demurrage, or by means of general damages for detention, the contractual context immediately distinguished this situation from that of the artificer's lien, considered by the House of Lords in *Somes*. Sir Bernard Rix also made the point that the artificer's lien fails to take into account some obvious commercial realities:

> Where the lienor cannot pay, the lien is worthless, because it does not bring with it a right of either expenses or sale; and where the lienor will not pay, [the lienholder] can blackmail the lienor with the expense of retention: even though he could choose, if he wished, to obtain the release of his chattel by giving adequate security for the lienee's claim (and nowadays by a payment into court).[155]

### An agent may waive his right of lien

**9.67**  If the agent expressly waives his right of lien, if he conducts himself in a manner that suggests an intention to abandon the lien, or if his conduct is inconsistent with the lien's continued existence, the courts will treat the lien as extinguished. The test of waiver is objective,[156] which is said to allow for situations where both parties, lienor and lienee, positively intend that existing rights will be unaffected by the taking of security or where it is made plain that the rights of lien are reserved.[157] In *Weeks v Goode*[158] an agent held a lien on his principal's lease. The latter demanded its return. The agent refused to return the lease on grounds quite unconnected with the existence of a lien. Because it was adjudged inconsistent with the continued existence of the lien, the agent's behaviour was construed as a waiver of his right to retain possession of the lease. Similarly, in *Forth v Simpson*,[159] whilst the court was prepared to concede that a racehorse trainer might have a lien over the horse he trained, if the owner could send the horse to run at any race he chose, and select the jockey, the

---

[154]  [2014] QB 760 at [109].

[155]  *Ibid*, at [123].

[156]  See *Clifford Harris & Co v Solland International Ltd* [2005] 2 All ER 334 at [38]–[40], where it was held that the principle applies to liens held by solicitors. In the case of solicitors, inconsistency is as essential as in the case of other lienholders, but is also somewhat more readily to be found owing to the solicitor's duty to explain matters to his client.

[157]  *Metall Market OOO v Vitorio Sipping Co Ltd* [2014] QB 760 at [45] *per* Sir Bernard Rix.

[158]  (1859) 6 CBNS 367.

[159]  (1849) 13 QB 680.

trainer had no continuing right of possession, and, consequently, no lien. To take a more recent example, in *Hatton v Car Maintenance Co Ltd*[160] the owner of a car contracted to pay a company an agreed sum so that her car, when in London, would be kept at the company's garage and be maintained. When the owner was in London or elsewhere she took the car out as and when she pleased. Because she owed the company money under the agreement, the company took possession of the car, claiming a lien on it for the amount due. Although the court held that no lien came into being as the company only maintained the car—had it been a repairer, it would have been entitled to a lien—Sargant, J went on to say:

> [E]ven if [the company] had such a lien originally, that lien would be lost by virtue of the arrangement under which the owner was to be at liberty to take the car away, and did take the car away, as and when she pleased. The existence of a lien seems to me to be inconsistent with an arrangement under which the article is from time to time taken entirely out of the possession and control of the contractor.[161]

### *Parting with possession of the principal's goods or chattels in a manner inconsistent with continuance of the lien*

An agent may lose his lien by parting with possession of the principal's goods or chattels in a manner inconsistent with continuance of the lien. If the agent is tricked into parting with possession or if the goods are unlawfully removed from his possession, his lien remains unaffected. Also, as we have seen, the agent's lien is not lost merely because the agent instructs another party to hold the principal's goods for him.[162] For this reason, were the agent to return possession of the goods to the principal in order that the latter might sell them and pay the agent out of the money raised, by analogy with the law governing pledge, the lien is not lost until extinguished by settlement:

**9.68**

> There can be no doubt the pledgee might hand back to the pledgor as his agent for the purpose of sale, as was done in this case, the goods he had pledged, without in the slightest degree diminishing the full force and effect of his security.[163]

### The lien of sub-agents

### *A sub-agent cannot acquire a lien over the principal's goods if its grant falls outside the agent's actual or apparent authority*

A sub-agent may acquire a lien over the principal's goods and chattels, but the rights of a sub-agent differ from those enjoyed by agents. Notably, if the delegation of the agent's authority is unauthorized—that is, does not fall within the actual or

**9.69**

---

[160] [1915] 1 Ch 621.

[161] *Ibid* at 624.

[162] See *McCombie v Davies* (1805) 7 East 5; para **9.59**.

[163] *North Western Bank Ltd v John Poynter, Son, & Macdonalds* [1895] AC 56, 68 *per* Lord Herschell, LC.

apparent authority of the agent—the sub-agent cannot acquire a lien over the principal's property. In *Solly v Rathbone*,[164] the leading authority, a principal consigned timber to its factor. Because he could not afford to pay freight and duties, the factor delegated the task to the defendant sub-agent, without the assent of his principal. The sub-agent performed the task. The factor then became bankrupt, having first informed the sub-agent that the timber belonged to the principal. The sub-agent proceeded to sell the goods in order to recoup the cost of freight and duties. The court held that the sub-agent was aware that the timber did not belong to the factor and that he was not entitled to a lien on the principal's goods. More recently, in *Chellaram & Sons (London) Ltd v Butlers Warehousing & Distribution Ltd*[165] AFCL, a firm of 'operators'—ie, intermediaries responsible for shipping goods overseas—customarily subcontracted storage, containing and packing of goods to a warehousing company, B. AFCL customarily granted B a lien over all goods stored in respect of storage monies owed by AFCL. AFCL stored goods purchased by an Indian company, C, prior to shipping them to India. C was unaware that AFCL subcontracted this work. Indeed, it was found that any implication that C had contemplated and intended that AFCL would give this work out to B would have been 'wholly inconsistent with reality'. Contemplation or intention was, in the view of the court, 'the minimum which is requisite if [B] are to hold [C] bound by the lien which is asserted'.[166]

### Sub-agent's rights of lien

**9.70** If the agent has actual or apparent authority to grant a lien in favour of the sub-agent, the sub-agent has identical rights of lien against the principal as he would have had against the agent, had the latter in fact been owner of the goods. In *Fisher v Smith*[167] a sub-agent effected an insurance and retained possession of the policy until his liabilities were met. As Lord Penzance explained, in this instance:

> [The owner] knew that [the sub-agent] had been employed for the purpose of effecting the policy, and [the sub-agent] knew that he was effecting the policy, not for [the agent] but for [the owner]. It was, therefore, a perfectly well understood transaction; the principal … had employed the local agent, the local agent had employed the agent at Liverpool, that agent thoroughly understanding for whom he was acting, and the principal thoroughly understanding that the local agent was acting for him. Under these circumstances it appears to me that the ordinary rule of law, that a lien would arise in favour of the broker who held in his hands the policy, could not but be applicable to this case. It is precisely the same as if there had been no intermediate agent at all, and as if [the owner] had written direct to the sub-agent to ask him to open a policy for him. Having opened that policy, and having got possession of it, he

---

[164] (1814) 2 M&S 298.
[165] [1978] 2 Lloyd's Rep 412.
[166] [1978] 2 Lloyd's Rep 412, 417 *per* Megaw, LJ.
[167] (1878) LR 4 App Cas 1.

was not liable to give it up to his principal until he had received the premium, which he had either paid or become liable to pay, in respect of it ... [I]t appears to me that ... the case does not admit of argument.[168]

The sub-agent's lien, however, even if authorized, does not extend to securing the general balance of account as between agent and sub-agent. In *Mildred, Goyeneche & Co v Maspons*[169] London merchants arranged marine insurance for a cargo of tobacco consigned by shipping agents in Havana. The London merchants were aware that the agents in Havana were acting for an unnamed principal. A total loss occurred and the London merchants received the policy monies, but before receipt had notice that the monies were claimed by the principals in Havana. The London merchants unsuccessfully attempted to retain the monies in order to secure the settlement of their general account with the Havana shipping agents.

If the principal remains concealed from the sub-agent, the sub-agent may exercise against the principal the lien which he would have possessed against the agent, had the latter in fact been the owner of the goods. Thus, in *Mann v Forrester*[170] it was held that insurance brokers, who effected a policy without notice that it was not on account of the person from whom they received the order, had a lien upon it for their general balance due from him. Because the principal's existence was concealed at the time they performed the sub-agency, the lien was not defeated even after the sub-agent had notice of the existence of the principal. Again, in *Montagu v Forwood*[171] M, who acted as agents for cargo owners, employed B as their agents to collect from underwriters contributions in respect of a general average loss. B, not being brokers, employed F, who were Lloyd's brokers, to collect the money, which they did. At the time when F received the money, B owed F money. F believed that B were the principals in the transaction, and nothing in the circumstances would have led F to suppose otherwise. The court held that F were entitled to stand in the position in which they would have stood if B had really been principals. In consequence, F were entitled to set off against M's demand for the underwriter contributions the debt due to them from B. **9.71**

---

[168] *Ibid* at 8.
[169] (1883) 8 App Cas 874.
[170] (1814) 4 Camp 60.
[171] [1893] 2 QB 350.

# 10

## LEGAL RELATIONS BETWEEN
## PRINCIPAL AND THIRD PARTY

The primary purpose of agency is to bring principal and third party into direct **10.01**
contractual relations. This chapter will consider how and when these relations
are created. In the first section, disclosed agency will be considered — that is,
situations in which the third party is aware of the existence of a principal,
whether that principal is identified or not. The second section deals with the
more anomalous situation, where the agent acts for a principal whose very existence is concealed from the third party. Finally, the third section explores two
exceptions to the principle, *nemo dat quod non habet*: the doctrine of apparent
ownership, and the provisions of the Factors Act 1889 which permit mercantile agents to make unauthorized dispositions of their principal's property to
third parties.

## Disclosed Agency

### Rights and liabilities of disclosed principals

*Where the existence of the principal has been disclosed to the third party,*
*the principal may both sue and be sued by the third party*

**10.02**  Disclosed agency, for these purposes, may take several forms: the principal may be truly 'a disclosed principal'—that is, his identity may actually have been revealed to the third party; or he may be 'an unnamed principal'—that is, the third party may be aware of the principal's existence but unaware of his exact identity; or finally, the principal may have ratified an unauthorized act performed by the 'agent' in the principal's name. The disclosed principal's right to sue and be sued on transactions effected on his behalf is at the very root of agency, whose primary purpose is to bring principal and third party into direct contractual relations with one another.

*Determining whether or not the principal can sue and be sued will often be a matter*
*of construing the scope of the agent's authority*

**10.03**  Leaving aside cases where the principal ratifies an agent's unauthorized acts, if the agent has acted within authority the principal is bound by the agent's acts. As an example of a court having to construe the precise ambit of an agent's actual authority, in *Camillo Tank Steamship Co Ltd v Alexandria Engineering Works*[1] a principal authorized his agent to verify repairs carried out on a vessel in the port of Alexandria and to 'approve' the repairers' bill, which the agent did. A dispute arose over the price of the work and the court was required to consider whether the agent's authority to 'approve' the bill signified that the agent actually enjoyed the power to agree the debt on behalf of the principal. The House of Lords held that the term 'approve' did indeed mean that the agent had the power to agree the debt on behalf of the principal and that it was 'the same as if the owner himself had been on the spot ... and had signed the accounts as [the agent] did.'[2] In consequence, the principal could not evade liability to the third party. In contrast, if an agent is acting outside the scope of his authority, and his acts have not been ratified, the principal can neither sue nor be sued on the contract. In *Comerford v Britannic Assurance Co Ltd*[3] a superintendent working in an insurance company's branch office had negotiated an insurance policy which a wife took out on the life of her husband. A policy endorsement stated that certain sums would be paid out in each of the first five years of cover, up to a maximum of £150. The superintendent, however, told the

---

[1]  (1921) 9 Ll L Rep 307.
[2]  *Ibid* at 319.
[3]  (1908) 24 TLR 593.

wife that £150 would become payable at any time within those first five years in the event of her husband's dying as a result of an accident. Two years into the policy, the husband accidentally drowned. Bray, J held that only £75 was payable under the written terms of the contract as the superintendent did not possess authority to vary the terms of the company's insurance policies.

It was seen in an earlier chapter that a principal will be bound by the acts of his **10.04** agent if the latter is found to have been acting within his apparent authority.[4] If it can be shown, however, that the third party had notice of the agent's lack of authority, the principal will not be bound by acts the agent performs purportedly on his behalf. In *Jordan v Norton*[5] a father wrote to a third party from whom his son was to buy a mare indicating that the horse had to be accompanied by a warranty that she was 'sound, and quiet in harness'. The son took delivery of the mare at the appointed place but did not receive the desired warranty from the vendor. The court held that the father was entitled to repudiate the transaction as the third party had been distinctly informed that the son was authorized to receive the mare only if a warranty were given that the mare was 'quiet in harness'. There is a similar outcome if the third party has constructive notice of the agent's lack of authority. In *Jacobs v Morris*[6] an agent, purporting to act under a power of attorney executed by a principal in Australia, on the security of bills drawn on that principal obtained from a third party an unauthorized loan of £4,000, which he dishonestly appropriated. The power of attorney did not authorize the agent to take out loans. The agent had presented the power of attorney to the third party but the latter did not trouble to read it, being satisfied with the agent's assurances. The Court of Appeal held that owing to its neglect in failing to observe standard business precautions when lending money, the third party was constructively fixed with full notice of the terms of the power of attorney. In the words of Cozens Hardy, LJ, in these circumstances 'it would not be just to hold the [principal] liable for an act done by his attorney beyond the scope of his authority in favour of [the third party], who knew the limits of the authority.'[7]

### Special cases

*Negotiable instruments.* Owing to the fact that they are negotiable and therefore **10.05** likely to come into the hands of parties who will be unaware of the circumstances of their creation, special rules apply to signatories of negotiable instruments, such as bills of exchange, promissory notes, and cheques. Section 23 of the Bills of Exchange Act 1882 states as a general principle:

---

[4] See **chapter 4**.
[5] (1838) 4 M&W 155.
[6] [1902] 1 Ch 816.
[7] *Ibid* at 834.

> No person is liable as drawer, indorser, or acceptor of a bill who has not signed it as such ...

This principle, which entails that a principal will only incur liability on a negotiable instrument on which his signature appears, is qualified by s 91(1), which provides:

> Where, by this Act, any instrument or writing is required to be signed by any person it is not necessary that he should sign it with his own hand, but it is sufficient if his signature is written thereon by some other person by or under his authority.

Therefore, it will be sufficient that some other person, acting by or under his authority, writes the principal's signature on the document. Hence, the principal will be bound if the agent, acting within the scope of his authority, signs the instrument with the principal's name. However, in so doing the agent must make clear that he is signing the instrument only in his capacity as agent. Section 26 lays down:

> (1) Where a person signs a bill as drawer, indorser, or acceptor, and adds words to his signature, indicating that he signs for or on behalf of a principal, or in a representative character, he is not personally liable thereon; but the mere addition to his signature of words describing him as an agent, or as filling a representative character, does not exempt him from personal liability.[8]
> (2) In determining whether a signature on a bill is that of the principal or that of the agent by whose hand it is written, the construction most favourable to the validity of the instrument shall be adopted.[9]

By virtue of s 25 of the 1882 Act, a signature by procuration operates as notice that the agent has but a limited authority to sign, and such signature will only bind the principal if the agent, in so signing, was acting within the actual limits of his authority.

**10.06**  *Deeds.* It is the rule that a principal cannot sue or be sued on a deed *inter partes* unless he is named as a party to it and it is executed in his name. In *Re International Contract Co Pickering's Claim*[10] a managing director, who was authorized to enter into contracts on behalf of the company, entered into an agreement with P, whereby, in consideration of certain assignments, he bound himself to pay P a sum of money. The company was not mentioned in the deed. Despite the fact that the directors had taken part in the negotiations, and that P knew that the agreement was made on behalf and for the benefit of the company, P was held not to be entitled to claim against the company under the deed. Again, in *Schack v Anthony*[11] a ship's master

---

[8]  Cf *Polhill v Walter* (1832) 3 B&Ald 114.
[9]  Cf *Britannia Electric Lamp Works Ltd v D Mandler & Co Ltd and D Mandler* [1939] 2 KB 129, 136 *per* Branson, J.
[10]  (1871) LR 6 Ch App 525.
[11]  (1813) 1 M&S 573.

entered into a charterparty by deed in his own name 'as agent for owners'. Since they were not named as parties to the deed, the owners were not permitted to sue on the contract.

The rule that only named signatories may sue and be sued on a deed is subject to **10.07** a small number of significant exceptions. First, if the agent who executes a deed does so as trustee for the principal, equity will permit the principal to sue on the contract.[12] Secondly, under s 7(1) of the Powers of Attorney Act 1971, where an agent is appointed under a power of attorney, provided that he is acting within the scope of his authority, the agent may execute a deed in his own name and the principal may sue and be sued on that deed. Thirdly, under s 56(1) of the Law of Property Act 1925:

> A person may take an immediate or other interest in land or other property, or the benefit of any condition, right of entry, covenant or agreement over or respecting land or other property, although he may not be named as a party to the conveyance or other instrument.[13]

The effect of this provision is that, even though the principal's agent was in fact party to the deed, the principal may acquire an interest in land under the instrument and may sue on the deed. Finally, it remains to be noted that under the Contracts (Rights of Third Parties) Act 1999 a person who is not a party to a contract may in his own right enforce a term of the contract if the contract expressly provides that he may, or the term purports to confer a benefit on him.[14]

### Liabilities of agents and disclosed principals where the agent has undertaken personal liability

In cases where an agent has undertaken personal liability on his principal's contract, **10.08** the third party may look to either principal or agent for settlement of any claims on the contract: there is considerable authority suggesting that once the third party has obtained judgment against the agent, he may no longer proceed against the principal. Although an agent does not normally acquire rights or incur liabilities under his principal's contract with the third party, an agent may contract in such a way as to make himself a party to the contract which he has brought about between principal

---

[12] Eg, *Harmer v Armstrong* [1934] Ch 65, where it was held that as all the parties to the agreement were before the court, the fact that the agreement was under seal did not prevent the plaintiffs from enforcing it, when the defendant, having been found to be agent and trustee, was willing that the agreement should be carried out: 'under the principle of equity the contract is always enforced in the name of and for the benefit of the trustee' (p 95).

[13] As Sir Guenther Treitel memorably remarked of this provision, 'It is not easy to retain the attention of an audience while lecturing on s 56(1) of the Law of Property Act 1925': *Some Landmarks of Twentieth Century Contract Law* (2002: Oxford, Clarendon Press) p 94.

[14] For more detailed treatment of this statute, see Treitel, *The Law of Contract* (2015: London, Sweet & Maxwell) 14th ed, by Peel, ch 14.

and third party, thereby rendering himself personally liable on that contract. As May, LJ observed in *Foxtons Ltd v Thesleff*:[15]

> As to the point that the first defendant should not be liable because he was agent to the disclosed principal, this would, of course, normally be the position in law. But there is no principle of law which says that parties may not contract on the explicit basis that the agent also is liable ...[16]

**10.09**  Wright, J enumerated various ways in which the agent may render himself personally liable in *Montgomerie v UK Mutual SS Association Ltd*, on the one hand, noting that an agent may be added as a party to the contract 'if he has so contracted, and is appointed as the party to be sued' and, on the other, observing that the principal may be excluded as a party from engagements entered into by his agent—for example, in the case of deeds *inter partes*.[17] In the former class of situation, where both principal and agent are potentially liable to the third party on the contract, the question arises: whom of the two is the third party entitled to hold liable? The classical answer to this question was to be found in Scrutton, LJ's judgment in *Debenham's Ltd v Perkins*,[18] in which it was indicated that the general rule is one of alternative liability, requiring the third party to choose whether to hold the principal or the agent liable:

> When an agent acts for a disclosed principal, it may be that the agent makes himself or herself personally liable as well as the principal. But in such a case the person with whom the contract is made may not get judgment against both. He may get judgment against the principal or he may get judgment against the agent who is liable as principal ...[19]

Significantly, Scrutton, LJ went on to indicate that this was a matter of the third party choosing whether to hold either principal or agent liable on the contract. However:

> once [the third party] has got judgment against either the principal or the agent who has the liability of the principal, he cannot then proceed against the other party who might be liable on the contract if proceedings had been taken against him or her first.[20]

Scrutton, LJ added:

> This is sometimes explained by the doctrine of election and sometimes by the doctrine that when one has merged a contract in a judgment, one can have only one judgment, and, having merged the contract in the judgment, one cannot

---

[15] [2005] EWCA Civ 514.
[16] *Ibid* at [28].
[17] [1891] 1 QB 370, 371–2.
[18] [1925] All ER Rep 234; (1925) 133 LT 252.
[19] *Ibid* at 237.
[20] *Ibid* at 237.

use the contract to get a second judgment. It is unnecessary to consider which is right.[21]

Several propositions need to be considered. First, there is the assumption that when- **10.10** ever an agent undertakes personal liability on his principal's contract with the third party, that liability will be alternative. That is to say, the natural interpretation of the contract will be that the parties intended that the third party would have to elect whether to look to the principal or to the agent for satisfaction. Obviously, if a contract expressly stipulates that principal and agent are to be liable jointly or jointly and severally with the principal, or if that were the proper objective construc- tion of the parties' agreement, the contract must be so read. In *Middle East Tankers & Freighters Bunker Services SA v Abu Dhabi Container Lines PJSC*,[22] for example, where *pro forma* invoices stipulated that 'such agent shall be jointly and severally liable with the buyer(s) as a principal and not as agent for the due and proper per- formance of the agreement', it was held that these words were without ambiguity[23] and effectively rendered the agent a 'buyer' by assuming the obligations of the buyer. In general, however, the law assumes alternative liability.

Secondly, there is the question whether, as outlined in Scrutton, LJ's judgment in **10.11** *Debenham's Ltd v Perkins*, the doctrines of merger of actions or of election adequately explain why a third party who has obtained a judgment against either principal or agent which remains unsatisfied may not then proceed against the other party. In truth, neither explanation affords convincing justification for the rule. The doctrine of merger of actions once sounded in the notion that 'the contract is merged in the judgment, and therefore the cause of action on the contract is gone.'[24] Given that the Civil Liability (Contribution) Act 1978, s 3 has abolished English law's rule that judgment obtained against one party jointly liable on a debt automatically releases the other from that liability by providing:

> Judgment recovered against any person liable in respect of any debt or damage shall not be a bar to an action, or to the continuance of an action, against any other person who is (apart from any such bar) jointly liable with him in respect of the same debt or damage.

It seems incongruous to persist in applying this reasoning today to disclosed agency. The alternative explanation, that the third party is called upon to make an election whether to look to either the principal or the agent, is also unrealistic—notably, because it is difficult to conceive that a third party, aware that both principal and agent have undertaken liability to him, would have opted for alternative, rather than

---

[21] *Ibid* at 237.
[22] [2002] 2 Lloyd's Rep 643.
[23] *Ibid* at 649–50 *per* HHJ Dean, QC.
[24] *Moore v Flanagan* [1920] 1 KB 919, 925 *per* Scrutton, LJ.

some form of joint, liability.[25] Moreover, as will be seen, a New Zealand decision, *LC Fowler & Sons Ltd v St Stephens College Board of Governors*,[26] has cast doubt on the conventional application of the doctrine of election in the context of undisclosed agency.[27] *Ex hypothesi* one might anticipate that similar scepticism could attach to even greater effect to election in cases of disclosed agency.

**10.12**    Despite the powerful reservations that have been voiced, however, the concept of alternative liabilities is deeply engrained in English agency cases. Both the House of Lords[28] and the Privy Council[29] have sanctified the approach, and Atkin, LJ even claimed that the rule was 'founded on good sense.'[30] Most recently, the Court of Appeal, in *Barrington v Lee*,[31] expressed approval of the statement in *Bowstead on Agency* to the effect that:

> Where an agent enters into a contract on such terms that he is personally liable thereon, and a judgment is obtained against him on the contract, the judgment, although unsatisfied, is, so long as it subsists, a bar to any proceedings against the principal, disclosed or undisclosed, on the contract.[32]

Thus, disregarding any misgivings concerning the rationale underlying the doctrine, as matters currently stand, the law probably is that a third party must elect whether to look to the disclosed principal or the agent for satisfaction of his claims against them. Once the third party has obtained judgment against one or other, unless the judgment has been set aside—for instance, on the ground that the original judgment was delivered in error or is for some reason a nullity[33]—the third party is debarred from looking to the other party if the judgment ultimately remains unsatisfied. In this sense, the third party is required to make an election.

**10.13**    In order to hold that an election has taken place a court must be able to conclude that the third party, in full knowledge of the facts,[34] has unequivocally displayed by

---

[25] These questions are addressed in detail in *Bowstead & Reynolds on Agency* (2014: London, Sweet & Maxwell) 20th ed, by Watts, paras 8-115ff. See also Reynolds, *Election Distributed* (1970) 86 LQR 318.

[26] [1991] 3 NZLR 304.

[27] See para **10.64**.

[28] *Morel Bros & Co Ltd v Earl of Westmorland* [1904] AC 11, 14 *per* Lord Halsbury, LC: 'The plaintiffs might have sued either the agent or the principal ... The result was that the plaintiffs got judgment against the agent. They cannot get judgment against the principal also. It is an alternative remedy; it cannot be made available against the two.'

[29] *RMKRM (a firm) v MRMVL (a firm)* [1926] AC 761, 770–1 *per* Lord Atkinson.

[30] [1920] 1 KB 919, 928.

[31] [1972] 1 QB 326, 343 *per* Edmund Davies, LJ.

[32] (1968: London, Sweet & Maxwell) 13th ed, by Reynolds and Davenport, p 289.

[33] For example, in *Lang Transport Ltd v Plus Factor International Trucking Co* (1997) 143 DLR (4th) 672 a majority of the Ontario Court of Appeal set aside a default judgment, which was a nullity, thereby allowing the third party to bring an action against an undisclosed principal. See also *Crossline Carriers Inc v Selkirk Specialty Wood Ltd*, 2004 ABPC 147 (Provincial Court of Alberta), a case of disclosed agency.

[34] *Pyxis Special Shipping Co Ltd v Dritsas & Kaglis Bros Ltd (The Scaplake)* [1978] 2 Lloyd's Rep 380, esp at p 385 *per* Mocatta, J; *Kammins Ballrooms Co Ltd v Zenith Investments (Torquay) Ltd*

his words or conduct the intention henceforth to look exclusively to either agent or disclosed principal for satisfaction of his claim. In *Barrington v Lee*[35] Stephenson, LJ declared that *Priestly v Fernie*[36] was 'clear authority for the proposition laid down in *Bowstead*', quoted in the preceding paragraph.[37] In *Priestly* the master of a ship, K, had signed a bill of lading in his own name in respect of a consignment of gas retorts. On the ground that the goods had not been delivered to Melbourne in the condition recorded in the bill, the consignee, the secretary of the Melbourne Gas Company, successfully brought an action against the master. The master was imprisoned and later declared bankrupt. The consignee thereupon sued the shipowners for whom the master had been acting. Bramwell, B, delivering the judgment of the court, held that the consignee, having successfully obtained judgment against the agent, could not then sue the owners even though the judgment against the agent remained unsatisfied:

> Where the agent, having made a contract in his own name, has been sued on it to final judgment, there can be no doubt that no second action would be maintainable against the principal. The very expression that where a contract is so made the contractee has an election to sue agent or principal, supposes he can only sue one of them, that is to say, sue to judgment.[38]

*Priestly v Fernie* would indicate that suing the agent or the disclosed principal to **10.14** final judgment will be interpreted as an unequivocal election on the part of the third party. Indeed, such a conclusion is further borne out by remarks made in *Chestertons (a firm) v Barone*,[39] where, having quoted Russell, LJ's remarks in *Clarkson Booker v Andjel*, a case of undisclosed agency, to the effect that:

> the external acts of the plaintiff must lead to the conclusion, as a matter of fact, that the plaintiff has settled to a choice involving abandonment of his option to enforce his right against one party.[40]

May, LJ articulated the following view:

> For my part, I think it is difficult to think of facts where a plaintiff is claiming against both principal and agent, the agent having acted originally on behalf of the principal

---

[1971] AC 850, 883 *per* Lord Diplock: 'If [a person] has knowledge of the facts which give rise in law to these alternative rights and acts in a manner which is consistent only with his having chosen to rely on one of them, the law holds him to his choice even though he was unaware that this would be the legal esconce of what he did. He is sometimes said to have "waived" the alternative right, as for instance a right to forfeit a lease or to rescind a contract of sale for wrongful repudiation or breach of condition; but this is better categorized as "election" rather than as "waiver".'

[35] [1972] 1 QB 326.

[36] (1863) 3 H&C 977.

[37] [1972] 1 QB 326, 347. See para **10.12**.

[38] (1863) 3 H&C 977, 983–4. Burton, J was provoked to declare: 'it has always seemed to me that the nineteenth-century cases of election (eg *Priestly v Fearney* ...) constitute a wholly unfair historical anomaly, which I see no need or justification to extend': *Antonio Gramsci Shipping Corp v Stepanos* [2011] 1 Lloyd's Rep 647 at [28].

[39] [1987] 1 EGLR 15.

[40] [1964] 2 QB 775, 795.

undisclosed, where an election can be shown without legal proceedings having been started. However, I would not like to be thought to be saying that in exceptional circumstances such a situation could not arise. It seems to me, however, that the clearest evidence of an election is at least the commencement of proceedings by the plaintiff against one or other of the two relevant parties.[41]

**10.15** *Priestly v Fernie* is often contrasted with *Calder v Dobell*,[42] where a broker, who had originally been employed to purchase cotton from the third party in his own name, revealed his principal's identity before concluding the contract. The bought and sold notes that passed between the broker and the seller named the broker as the purchaser, as did the invoice for the cotton. The seller called upon the broker to pay for the cotton and threatened him with legal proceedings, to no avail. Having failed to extract payment from the broker, the seller proceeded to bring a suit against the principal. It was held that the insertion of the broker's name in the contract, even though the principal was known at the time, and the subsequent demands made upon the broker for payment, did not necessarily amount to an election on the part of the plaintiffs to give exclusive credit to the broker.

**10.16** As Bovill, CJ pointed out in *Calder v Dobell*, 'election must be a matter of fact'[43] in each individual case. In *Calder v Dobell* itself, the principal's claim that the third party seller had made an election to look exclusively to the broker was contradicted by the fact that at the time of entering in to the contract the seller had expressly refused to trust to the broker's credit, thereby forcing the latter to reveal the identity of his principal. Additionally, the court considered that the simple demand for payment also was 'an equivocal act':[44]

> [T]he evidence relied on to shew an election was extremely slight, especially where the only action brought was brought against the principal.[45]

### Settlement with the agent of a disclosed principal

**10.17** In disclosed agencies, principal and third party cannot normally obtain a good discharge of their respective liabilities by settling with the agent. Because in the case of disclosed agency direct contractual relations are established between principal and third party, the agent normally drops out of the transaction and ceases to affect the others' legal relations. This means that, in ordinary circumstances, (i) the third party can only acquire a good discharge of his obligations from the principal, and

---

[41] [1987] 1 EGLR 15.
[42] (1871) LR 6 CP 486.
[43] *Ibid* at 491.
[44] *Ibid* at 491.
[45] *Ibid* at 492 *per* Bovill, CJ. The decision of Bovill, CJ and his colleagues was later upheld in the Court of Exchequer Chamber.

(ii) *e contra* the principal can only obtain a good discharge of his obligations by settling with the third party. Payments made to the agent, therefore, will not normally serve to discharge principal or third party from their contractual liabilities to one another. This principle is subject to some exceptions.

*When the third party has led the principal to think his liability*
*has been discharged by the agent*

The principal may obtain a good discharge by settling with his agent if the third **10.18** party has led the principal to think that his liability to the third party has already been discharged by the agent. Such situations will arise comparatively rarely. In *Wyatt v Marquis of Hertford*,[46] however, a principal owed money to a third party for work performed on his estate. The third party elected to take a security from the agent—a draft on the agent's bank, but issued the agent with a receipt as though he had received payment. Payment on the draft was refused and the third party sought to recover the debt from the principal. It was held that if the principal did not realize what his agent had done and, concluding from the receipt that his agent had settled the sum he owed to the third party, dealt differently with his agent on the faith of such receipt, the principal would be treated as discharged, even though the security taken by the third party failed. In short, the third party would be estopped from denying that, as between the principal and himself, the obligation had been discharged.

This estoppel will arise if, as in *Wyatt*, the third party has misled the principal into **10.19** believing that his obligation to the third party has been discharged by the agent. An estoppel has also been held to arise where the third party does something indicating that he intends to look exclusively to the credit of the agent. In *Smith v Ferrand*,[47] for example, waiving its right to immediate payment in cash from monies specifically deposited for this purpose, a third party chose instead to take a bill at three months accepted by a stranger. The bill was later dishonoured. It was decided that because the third party had waived its right to immediate payment, and had elected to take the security, it had to bear the loss occasioned through its own default.

A number of the older authorities suggested that such cases proceeded on a slightly **10.20** different footing—namely, the potential injustice inflicted on a principal who, having once settled with his agent, was then required to settle a second time with the third party In *Heald v Kenworthy*,[48] for instance, Parke, B had declared:

> If the conduct of the seller would make it unjust for him to call upon the buyer for the money; as for example, where the principal is induced by the conduct of the

---

[46] (1802) 3 East 147.
[47] (1827) 7 B&C 19.
[48] (1855) 10 Exch 739.

seller to pay his agent the money on the faith that the agent and seller have come to a settlement on the matter, or if any representation to that effect is made by the seller either by words or conduct, the seller cannot afterwards throw off the mask and sue the principal. It would be unjust for him to do so.[49]

This broader rationale has now been abandoned and, notably since *Irvine & Co v Watson & Sons*,[50] the courts prefer to explain such cases on the basis of estoppel rather than on the inequitable treatment of the principal.[51] In *Irvine* an agent had purchased casks of oil on behalf of principals. The terms of the contract were 'cash on or before delivery'. The sellers did not insist on payment before delivering the oil. After delivery, the principal, who assumed that the agent had already paid the sellers, paid the purchase price over to the agent. The agent stopped payment and the sellers duly sued the principal. The Court of Appeal held that the sellers would only have been precluded from suing the principal for the price if, prior to his having paid the agent, they had by their conduct induced the defendants to believe that they had already been paid by the agent. In the absence of an invariable custom to such effect, the sellers' mere omission to insist on prepayment was not thought to be conduct such as would reasonably induce such belief. The principle, as formulated subsequently by Sir George Jessel, MR, is:

> If the [principal] has been misled by the [third party], either by his words or by his conduct, to believe that which is not true, so that his position is altered, the [third party] cannot be heard to deny the truth of what he has thus led the [principal] to believe.[52]

**10.21** One circumstance that may sometimes give rise to such estoppel is where the third party delays in asserting his right to payment by the principal. In *Irvine & Co v Watson & Sons* Brett, LJ did say that on the facts the seller's non-insistence on prepayment did not amount, of itself, to laches.[53] Similarly, in *Davison v Donaldson*[54] the Court of Appeal held that a claim for payment of the price of ship's stores acquired by an agent three years previously could be maintained against the principal, who had settled with the agent three months, and again two years, after their acquisition. As Bowen, LJ pointed out, echoing a passage of the judgment he had delivered in *Irvine & Co v Watson & Sons*:[55]

> I do not say that in very special circumstances mere delay may not amount to misrepresentation: it may be conduct misleading the [principal]. But that can only be when

---

[49] *Ibid* at 746. See also *per* Alderson, B at pp 747–8: 'Where a creditor by his conduct induces the debtor to pay a third party, and thereby alters his debtor's position, it would be unjust to call upon the debtor to pay the amount of the debt to the creditor.'

[50] (1880) LR 5 QBD 414.

[51] Eg, *ibid* at 421 *per* Brett, LJ.

[52] *Davison v Donaldson* (1882) LR 9 QBD 623, 627.

[53] (1880) LR 5 QBD 414, 421.

[54] (1882) LR 9 QBD 623.

[55] (1879) LR 5 QBD 102, 107–8: 'if a delay has intervened which may reasonably lead the principal to infer that the seller no longer requires to look to the principal's credit, such a delay

there is something in the original contract, or in the conduct of the parties, which renders the delay misleading.[56]

These principles, according to which a principal on occasion may settle with his **10.22** agent and thereby obtain a good discharge of his liability to the third party, only apply in cases where the principal is disclosed; that is, where the third party is aware of the principal's identity or where the principal has been disclosed but remains unnamed. As we will see, owing to the fact that the third party will be oblivious of the principal's existence and will therefore be looking exclusively to the credit of the agent, estoppel does not sit comfortably with cases where the principal's existence is undisclosed.[57]

### *When the third party can obtain a good discharge of his liability to the principal by settling with the agent*

Owing to the fact that the agent of a disclosed principal brings the third party and **10.23** his principal into direct contractual relations, unless the principal has conferred special authority on the agent to receive payment on the principal's behalf, the third party can only obtain a good discharge of his obligations by settling with the principal. By the same virtue, a third party cannot normally set off sums owed to him by the agent against what he owes to the principal.

In *Butwick v Grant*[58] a tradesman gave an agent, C, an order for sixty-four **10.24** sports coats. The tradesman was aware that C was likely to have been acting as an agent. The wholesaler, for whom C had been working, duly dispatched the coats to the tradesman along with an invoice bearing the wholesaler's name. The tradesman settled with the agent, C, who failed to hand these monies over to the wholesaler. The wholesaler then sought to recover the sums owed from the tradesman. Since it is clear law that an agent authorized to sell does not, as a necessary legal corollary, have authority to receive payment,[59] the wholesaler continued to be entitled to be reimbursed the cost of the coats by the tradesman. As Sankey, J pointed out, it would have been a different matter if it could have been shown that C enjoyed authority to receive payment on the wholesaler's behalf:

> In an action by the seller of goods against the buyer for the price it would be open to the buyer who had paid the seller's agent to show, and in the absence of any reason to

---

for example as leads to the inference that the debt is paid by the agent, or to the inference that though the debt is not paid the seller elects to abandon his recourse to the principal and to look to the agent alone.'

[56] (1882) LR 9 QBD 623, 631.

[57] See paras **10.71–10.72**.

[58] [1924] 2 KB 483. In *Linck, Moeller & Co v Jameson & Co* (1885) 2 TLR 206 the court declined to infer that the agent had power to receive payment even though in one previous sale the principal had authorized him to receive payment.

[59] See notably *Drakeford v Piercy* (1866) 7 B&S 517, 522 *per* Lush, J.

the contrary he would be entitled to succeed on showing, either that the agent had actual authority to receive payment, or that he had ostensible authority to receive payment, or that he had a customary authority by reason of the fact that the payment was made to him in the ordinary course of the business of agencies of the kind in question.[60]

10.25   An agent, of course, may be expressly or impliedly authorized to receive payment on behalf of the principal, or may have apparent authority to do so.[61] Alternatively, if the agent receives payment without authority, it is open to the principal to ratify the agent's unauthorized act—for instance, by receiving from the agent the sums paid by the third party to the agent.

10.26   If an agent is authorized to receive payment on his principal's behalf, the third party will be entitled to gain a good discharge by paying the agent. As *International Sponge Importers Ltd v Andrew Watt & Sons*[62] shows, in such cases it may be necessary to inquire what the third party ought reasonably to have concluded the agent's authority to be. The principal in that case had intended to authorize the agent exclusively to receive payment for parcels of sponge she sold by crossed cheques made payable to the principal. After dealing with the agent for several years, the third party made out two cheques to the agent and paid one invoice by handing cash over to the agent. The agent made off with this money. Even though customers were informed, *inter alia*, 'Cheques to be crossed "London and Joint Stock Bank—account payees", "All cheques to be made payable to International Sponge Importers, Ltd", and "No receipt valid unless on the firm" printed form to be attached hereto', the House of Lords considered that these printed intimations on customers' invoices, restricting the method by which the agent was to be paid, did not constitute a sufficiently plain declaration that no ready-money trade was done by the principal, and that agents were prohibited from receiving money in exchange for goods delivered. 'Such a prohibition', declared Lord Shaw of Dunfermline, 'should not be lightly inferred'.[63] In contrast, where the instruction is clear, the third party must comply with the principal's restrictions. In *The Netherholme, Glen Holme and Rydal Holme*[64] insurance brokers were authorized by their principal to settle a claim with insurers and to receive payment in cash in accordance with the recognized custom. Contrary to their express instructions, the brokers took a bill of exchange at three months in payment of a general account,

---

[60] [1924] 2 KB 483, 489–90.

[61] Such authority may be a general authority to receive payments or simply to receive payment in a particular transaction.

[62] [1911] AC 279.

[63] *Ibid* at 288.

[64] *Hine Bros v Steamship Insurance Syndicate Ltd, The Netherholme, Glen Holme and Rydal Holme* (1895) 11 TLR 224.

including the principal's claim. The bill was discounted and the insurers paid the brokers, who later became insolvent. The principal, who had not been paid the settled insurance claim, sought the sums still owed to it by the insurers. The Court of Appeal held that the principal had not authorized the brokers to take the bill; indeed, payment by bill of exchange was contrary to recognized business custom, and even when discounted it did not constitute a payment to the insured.[65]

# Undisclosed Agency

### General principles affecting undisclosed agency

A third party who negotiates a contract with an agent may be kept completely in the **10.27** dark that the agent is in fact acting for a principal and the third party may believe that the agent with whom he is negotiating is actually the real principal in the transaction. This may happen because the principal has deliberately sought to remain concealed from the third party. It may arise because no one thought or chose to disclose his existence to the third party—for instance, if a particular agent always or invariably transacts business on behalf of principals in his own name. Alternatively, the agency may remain undisclosed because the agent has reason to prevent giving the third party direct access to his principal—wishing not to see the middleman cut out. Moreover, the third party is under no duty to inquire whether the other contracting party may be acting as agent for another. Nor do the courts resort to constructive notice in this context. The law requires actual notice that the agent is acting for another in order to exclude the doctrine of the undisclosed principal.[66] Otherwise, in the words of Jacob, J:

> Whenever any agent acts for an undisclosed principal he is, to the outside world, the principal. The outside world treats him as a principal and is entitled to treat him as a principal. Whether he has a private arrangement with someone else is no business of the outside world as far as its dealings with him are concerned.[67]

Contrary to what might have been anticipated, however, when the agent acts in his own name concealing the fact that he is acting on behalf of another, the undisclosed principal is permitted to intervene on his agent's contract.[68]

---

[65] Similarly, in *Williams v Evans* (1866) LR 1 QB 3 52 it was held that an auctioneer, authorized to sell goods provided that purchasers paid a deposit at once and the rest of the purchase money on or before delivery of the goods, had no authority to receive payment by a bill of exchange. A payment made by bill of exchange would not discharge the purchaser.

[66] *Greer v Downs Supply Co* [1927] 2 KB 28.

[67] *Oystertec plc v Barker* [2003] RPC 29 at [5].

[68] See R Munday, 'The Undisclosed Principal in Commercial Law' (2012), European Journal of Commercial Contract Law 43.

*The principal may make his existence known*

**10.28** The undisclosed principal may choose to make his existence known to the third party at any time and may intervene on the contract that the third party might otherwise have assumed had been made exclusively with the agent. In short, in the case of written contracts parol evidence may be given proving that, contrary to appearances, the principal is a party to the transaction into which the agent and the third party have entered. Similarly, in the case of oral contracts evidence may be adduced to show who was the true principal in the transaction. An undisclosed principal's right to take over the rights and obligations of his agent's contract and to sue—and, in addition, once his existence comes to the attention of the third party, to be sued by the latter—is one of the most unusual rules of the law of agency, if not of English law as a whole. The rules surrounding the undisclosed principal have variously been said to be 'anomalous'[69] and 'inconsistent with the elementary doctrines of the law of contract',[70] and as having 'no exact counterpart in civil law'.[71] Viewed historically, one explanation for the existence of a rule, which now appears odd to us, may be that the doctrine of the undisclosed principal emerged in the eighteenth century in cases where the principals of factors were permitted to intervene when the factor became bankrupt before many of the major contractual principles, such as privity and the objective approach to contract, had established themselves. What we now see as out of the ordinary, in all likelihood, would have appeared less so in earlier times.

**10.29** The courts typically justify the doctrine on grounds of commercial convenience. In the words of Lord Lindley in *Keighley, Maxsted & Co v Durant*:

> The explanation of the doctrine that an undisclosed principal can sue and be sued on a contract made in the name of another person with his authority is, that the contract is in truth, although not in form, that of the undisclosed principal

---

[69] Eg, *Keighley, Maxsted & Co v Durant* [1901] AC 240, 261 *per* Lord Lindley; *Welsh Development Agency v Export Finance Co Ltd* [1992] BCC 270, 290 *per* Dillon, LJ and at p 298 *per* Ralph Gibson, LJ.

[70] Pollock (1887) 3 LQR 359.

[71] *Western Digital Corp v British Airways plc* [2000] EWCA Civ 153 at [43] *per* Mance, LJ. The passage continues: 'The concept of an undisclosed principal has, it seems, no exact counterpart in civil law, although a similar result may often be achievable by other routes (see *Bowstead & Reynolds on Agency* 16th ed, paras 1-018 and 8-070; Zimmerman, *The Law of Obligations* ch 2, § II, Agency). A note of caution appears appropriate in respect of any such generalization, since (a) we were, understandably, not given the benefit of any comparative law material in this area and (b) as Lord Bingham of Cornhill CJ, speaking extra-judicially, has recently recalled, "the civil law as found in (say) France, Germany, Italy, Spain or The Netherlands is no more uniform than the common law as found in (say) England, the United States, Canada and Australia" ("A New Common Law for Europe", published as one of The Clifford Chance Millennium Lectures, and in turn citing Cappelliti [*sic*], *New Perspectives for a Common Law of Europe* (1978)).' A comparatist would probably want to re-point most of these propositions.

himself. Both the principal and the authority exist when the contract is made; and the person who makes it for him is only the instrument by which the principal acts. In allowing him to sue and be sued upon it, effect is given, so far as he is concerned, to what is true in fact, although that truth may not have been known to the other contracting party.

[A]s a contract is constituted by the concurrence of two or more persons and by their agreement to the same terms, there is an anomaly in holding one person bound to another of whom he knows nothing and with whom he did not, in fact, intend to contract. But middlemen, through whom contracts are made, are common and useful in business transactions, and in the great mass of contracts it is a matter of in-difference to either party whether there is an undisclosed principal or not. If he exists it is, to say the least, extremely convenient that he should be able to sue and be sued as a principal, and he is only allowed to do so upon terms which exclude injustice.[72]

The courts sometimes employ the term 'undisclosed principal' quite loosely. **10.30** They may speak of a principal who is 'undisclosed' when they mean that the principal's identity, but not his existence, has been concealed from the third party (an 'unnamed principal')—as, for example, when the principal may be one of a class of persons referred to generically in the agent's dealings with the third party but has not been specifically identified. For purposes of legal analysis, an undisclosed principal needs to be distinguished from an unnamed principal. As Rix, LJ correctly noted, 'the law relating to the liability of an agent of an unidentified principal is somewhat different from the law relating to an agent of an undisclosed principal.'[73] Thus, depending upon the construction the court puts upon the agreement, an agent who concludes a contract on behalf of an unnamed principal, whether orally or in writing, may well incur no liability and acquire no rights under the contract made with the third party.[74]

[I]t may be that, even though a person is known to be acting as an agent, it is to be inferred that the other party does not rely on the credit of the prin-cipal but is looking to the agent, for example if the identity of the principal is not disclosed. On the other hand, the circumstances may show that even if the identity of the principal is not known, the other party is nevertheless content to look to the credit of the principal whoever he may be.[75]

More generally, the question whether the agent for an unnamed principal has en-gaged his personal liability on a written contract he has entered into with the third party will depend upon the manner in which he has signed the contract. Typically, an agent who signs a contract in his own name without qualification will be pre-sumed personally liable, unless his personal liability has been excluded by words

---

[72] [1901] AC 240, 261–2.
[73] *Cumbria Roofing Ltd v Athersmith* [2005] EWCA Civ 1098 at [19].
[74] *N & J Vlassopulos Ltd v Ney Shipping Ltd. 'The Santa Carina'* [1977] 1 Lloyd's Rep 478.
[75] *Cifal Groupe SA v Meridian Securities (UK) Ltd* [2013] EWHC 3553 (Comm) at [88] *per* Males, J.

which make clear that he is acting in his capacity as an agent.[76] In the case of oral contracts, however, a different principle applies:

> [W]hen one is dealing with an oral contract, the law is plain ... [I]t is a question of fact in each case whether it was intended ... that the agent should or should not be personally liable ... The question is always, what did these parties agree? There cannot in these circumstances be any question of presumption because if there were a presumption that would put the onus of proof upon [agents] to prove that they were not personally liable. It is for [the third party] to prove those facts from which an inference must be drawn on a balance of probabilities that the [agents] are personally liable notwithstanding that the [third party] knew that the [agents] were contracting as agents.[77]

**10.31** The parties' agreements do not always make it clear in which capacity the agent is acting, whether as an unnamed principal or as an undisclosed principal. In *Nueva Fortuna Corporation v Tata Ltd ('The Nea Tyhi')*,[78] for example, two actions were brought alleging that the defendant, Tata Ltd, was liable to the claimant owners of two vessels on the basis that it was either the undisclosed principal or the joint venture partner and thus co-principal, of the time charterer of those vessels. Although he found it unnecessary to reach a concluded view on the nature of the agency, Rix, J did remark that:

> A particular difficulty which arises is whether, had I found in favour of the plaintiffs' main case, Tata should be regarded as an undisclosed principal, a disclosed principal, or an unnamed albeit disclosed principal; and if any of those, whether as a joint venture partner or as the real principal; and if a partner as well as an undisclosed principal, whether the liability is to be viewed as alternative *(qua* undisclosed principal) or joint *(qua* partner) only in which latter case would s. 3 of the [Civil Liabilities (Contribution) Act, 1978] seem to apply ...[79]

In contrast, if, as occurred in *Boston Fruit Co v British & Foreign Marine Ins Co*,[80] insurance brokers make a contract in their own name and in the names of 'all and every other person or persons to whom the subject matter does, may, or shall pertain', the brokers will clearly be acting as unnamed, not as undisclosed principals.

**10.32** Whether undisclosed or simply unidentified, if the principal's right to intervene and take the benefit of the contract is disputed, it is clear that what will count 'is the authority and intention of the person in whose name the contract is made'.[81]

---

[76] See *post* paras **12.07**ff.
[77] *N & J Vlassopulos Ltd v Ney Shipping Ltd. 'The Santa Carina'* [1977] 1 Lloyd's Rep 478, 484 *per* Roskill, LJ.
[78] [1999] 2 Lloyd's Rep 497.
[79] *Ibid* at 534.
[80] [1905] 1 KB 637. Cp *TTMI Sarl v Statoil ASA* [2011] 2 Lloyd's Rep 220 at [37] *per* Beatson, J.
[81] *Talbot Underwriting Ltd v Nausch Hogan & Murray Inc. The Jascon 5* [2006] Lloyd's Rep I.R 531 *per* Moore-Bick, LJ at [26].

Thus, in *The Jascon 5* it was the position of the party named in the contract (*sc.* Sempra Energy) rather than the authority and intention of the placing broker that was

> determinative in deciding whether or not a person who claims to be an undisclosed principal ... can take the benefit of the contract ... Since the principal is, by definition, undisclosed or unidentified, as the case may be, it is the intention of the party to the contract and his authority to act for that principal, when concluding the contract through his subagents, which matters.[82]

### *The fundamental principles underlying undisclosed agency*

The fundamental principles underpinning this area of English law were set out by Lord Lloyd of Berwick in the Board's opinion in *Siu Yin Kwan v Eastern Insurance Co Ltd*: **10.33**

> For present purposes the law can be summarised shortly. (1) An undisclosed principal may sue and be sued on a contract made by an agent on his behalf, acting within the scope of his actual authority. (2) In entering into the contract, the agent must intend to act on the principal's behalf. (3) The agent of an undisclosed principal may also sue and be sued on the contract. (4) Any defence which the third party may have against the agent is available against his principal. (5) The terms of the contract may, expressly or by implication, exclude the principal's right to sue, and his liability to be sued. The contract itself, or the circumstances surrounding the contract, may show that the agent is the true and only principal.[83]

This passage is very frequently quoted, and is taken as an authoritative statement of the relevant principles.

The strength of the rule whereby an undisclosed principal is generally entitled to sue and be sued on contracts made on his behalf by his agent can be gauged from an oft-quoted passage in Diplock, LJ's judgment in *Teheran-Europe Co Ltd v ST Belton (Tractors) Ltd*, in which he declared: **10.34**

> Where an agent has ... actual authority and enters into a contract with another party intending to do so on behalf of his principal, it matters not whether he discloses to the other party the identity of his principal, *or even that he is contracting on behalf of a principal at all*, if the other party is willing or leads the agent to believe that he is willing to treat as a party to the contract anyone on whose behalf the agent may have been authorised to contract. In the case of an ordinary commercial contract such willingness of the other party may be assumed by the agent unless either the other party manifests his unwillingness or there are other circumstances which should lead the agent to realise that the other party was not so willing.[84]

---

[82] [2005] 2 CLC 868 at [57] *per* Cooke, J. See also *TTMI Sarl v Statoil ASA* [2011] 2 Lloyd's Rep 220 at [35]–[38] *per* Beatson, J.

[83] [1994] 2 AC 199, 207.

[84] [1968] 2 QB 545, 555 (emphasis added).

The prevalence of the doctrine is also evident from the fact that when s 14(5) of the Sale of Goods Act 1979 provides that the various implied terms relating to fitness for purpose 'apply to a sale by a person who in the course of a business is acting as agent for another', the House of Lords has held that a third party may be entitled to sue either the agent or the undisclosed principal for breaches of these implied terms. In other words, because the language of the 1979 legislation does not exclude the operation of the rules affecting undisclosed principals, it is to be assumed that they have been incorporated.[85] It has similarly been acknowledged in *P & O Nedlloyd BV and Utaniko Ltd v Dampskibsselskabet AF, 1912, Aktieselskab* that claims might be made under the Carriage of Goods by Sea Act 1992 by undisclosed principals of lawful holders of bills of lading. However, the normal incidents of undisclosed agency must still be satisfied. In *Nedlloyd*, whilst it was the case that under the statute rights transferred to certain banks were held by those banks as agents for the respondents, as Mance, LJ pointed out, 'they are seeking to "intervene" by pursuing contractual rights under a contract which they made on their own behalf ... This is a situation outside the scope of the English law of contract and agency.'[86] Not all statutes, however, necessarily admit of this interpretation. The Law of Property (Miscellaneous Provisions) Act 1989, s 2, for example, requires that in the case of sales of real property all terms expressly agreed by the parties must be in writing.[87] It has been argued that s 2 excludes the intervention of an undisclosed principal. Whilst recognizing that the question is vexed, David Richards, J, in *Government of Sierra Leone v Davenport*,[88] in the absence of full argument, declined to take a firm position on this issue.

### Proof of the agent's intention

**10.35**  The agent is required both to have actual authority to act on behalf of the undisclosed principal and to have entered into the contract with the third party

---

[85] *Boyter v Thomson* [1995] 2 AC 628. See further Brown (1996) 112 LQR 225. *E contrario*, occasionally the normal rule for undisclosed agency has been modified by legislation. Thus, for the purposes of VAT, s 47(2A) of the Value Added Tax Act 1994 provides that, 'Where, in the case of any supply of goods to which subs (1) does not apply, goods are supplied through an agent who acts in his own name, the supply shall be treated both as a supply to the agent and as a supply by the agent.' This deeming provision, a statutory fiction, is claimed to make 'pragmatic sense in the context of VAT', at least in relation to input deduction, because 'but for the fiction, the agent would be unable to claim an input deduction because he would not own the goods purchased, albeit that the VAT invoice would have been in his name where a valid VAT invoice had been issued. Equally the principal would be in the reverse position of owning the goods but of not having a VAT invoice in his name': *Scandico Ltd. v HMRC* [2015] UKFTT 36 (TC); [2015] SFTD 364 at [77]. Cp *Gold Standard Telecom Ltd v HMRC* [2014] UKFTT 577; [2014] STI 2254 (TC). It might be noted that there is a far more serious question lurking within, namely, whether s 47(2A) correctly applies Arts 14.1 and 14.2.(c) of the EU Sixth VAT Directive (77/388/EEC): see, eg, *Express Medicare Ltd v HMRC* [2001] BVC 2152; [2000] V& DR 377 at [46]; *Scandico Ltd, supra* at [132].

[86] [2003] 1 Lloyd's Rep 239 at [18]. See also *Scottish & Newcastle Int'l Ltd v Othon Ghalanos Ltd* [2008] 1 Lloyd's Rep 462 at [34] *per* Lord Mance.

[87] 'A contract for the sale or other disposition of an interest in land can only be made in writing and only by incorporating all the terms which the parties have expressly agreed in one document or, where contracts are exchanged, in each.'

[88] [2003] EWHC 2769 (Ch) at [69]–[70].

intending to do so on behalf of that principal. A third party, or even the agent himself, may dispute that the latter was in fact acting for the principal at the moment of contracting. In such cases, what proof exactly needs to be adduced in order to show that the agent intended to act on behalf of the undisclosed principal? Colman, J considered this issue in *National Oilwell (UK) Ltd v Davy Offshore Ltd*, an insurance case which required the court to express a view as to how intention to enter into a policy of insurance on behalf of other parties might be demonstrated. The judge said:

> Evidence as to whether in any particular case the principal assured or other contracting party did have the requisite intention may be provided by the terms of the policy itself, by the terms of any contract between the principal assured or other contracting party and the alleged co-assured or by any other admissible material showing what was subjectively intended by the principal assured.[89]

This passage would suggest that the relevant intention may be proved subjectively. One reason for this subjective requirement, it has been argued, is that, if one recalls the five principles Lord Lloyd laid down in *Siu Yin Kwan v Eastern Insurance Co Ltd*,[90] were it otherwise the second principle, which states that 'in entering into the contract, the agent must intend to act on the principal's behalf,' would add nothing to the first, which merely requires that in order for the undisclosed principal to enjoy a right to intervene on the contract entered into by the agent, the latter must have been acting within the scope of his actual authority.[91]

The correctness of Colman, J's ruling—which, strictly speaking, concerned unidentified rather than undisclosed principals—has since been seriously doubted in *Magellan Spirit*, where it was argued that the agent's subjective intention to act on an undisclosed principal's behalf was determinative.[92] Leggatt, J pointed out: **10.36**

> It is one thing to infringe the objective principle—as the doctrine of undisclosed principal undoubtedly does—by allowing the existence of contractual rights and obligations to depend on an intention which is not communicated to the other contracting party. But it would go a step further, and would give rise to wholly unacceptable uncertainty, if such rights and obligations were to depend on a purely private intention of the supposed agent which was not even communicated to the supposed principal before the contract was made.[93]

On the authorities, whether or not there was an undisclosed principal should not depend on the state of mind of the supposed agent at the time of contracting, but on whether the supposed agent had communicated to the supposed principal an

---

[89] [1993] 2 Lloyd's Rep 582, 597. See also *Lai Wo Heung v Cheung Kong Fur Pty Co Ltd* [2004] 1 HKLRD 959, and *Bowstead & Reynolds on Agency* (2014) 20th ed, para 8-072, n 399.

[90] See para **10.33**.

[91] *Rolls Royce Power Engineering plc v Ricardo Consulting Engineers Ltd* [2004] 2 All ER (Comm) 129 at [52] *per* HHJ Richard Seymour, QC.

[92] *Magellan Spirit ApS v Vitol SA. Magellan Spirit* [2016] EWHC 454 (Comm) at [19].

[93] *Ibid* at [17].

intention to contract on his behalf. Such a view is consistent with *dicta* in the House of Lords' decision in *Keighley Maxsted & Co v Durant* to the effect that there is a difference between an agency existing at the date of the contract which is susceptible of proof and an intention locked up in the mind of the contractor,[94] and a passage in Lord Pearson's speech in *Garnac Grain Co Inc v HMF Faure & Fairclough Ltd* where he said:

> The relationship of principal and agent can only be established by the consent of the principal and the agent. They will be held to have consented if they have agreed to what amounts in law to such a relationship, even if they do not recognise it themselves and even if they have professed to disclaim it ... *But the consent must have been given by each of them, either expressly or by implication from their words and conduct.*[95]

For Leggatt, J, Lord Pearson's declaration that an undisclosed principal is unable to ratify a contract made without authority even if the person who entered into the contract subjectively intended to act on the supposed principal's behalf, is 'conclusive of the test to be applied',[96] and to be preferred to Colman's *obiter* pronouncement in *National Oilwell (UK) Ltd v Davy Offshore Ltd*.

### The principal may only intervene on contracts made by the agent acting within the scope of his actual authority

**10.37** It is axiomatic that evidence will only be admitted to show that, when negotiating the contract with the third party in his own name, the agent was in fact operating within the scope of his actual authority on behalf on an undisclosed principal. More specifically, because the third party will have been unaware of the existence of the principal, it cannot be claimed that the agent enjoyed apparent authority to transact business on the principal's behalf.[97] Similarly, if the agent did not possess actual authority at the time of entering into the contract with the third party, no matter what the agent's secret intentions may have been, it is not open to the putative principal to ratify the transaction. In the case of disclosed agency the third party has been informed from the outset that the 'agent' is acting for another, and ratification effectively comes to fulfil his expectations. As Lord Lindley observed in *Keighley, Maxsted & Co v Durant*:

> The doctrine of ratification as hitherto applied in this country to contracts has always, I believe, in fact given effect in substance to the real intentions of both contracting parties at the time of the contract, as shewn by their language or conduct. It has never

---

[94] [1901] AC 240, 256 *per* Lord Shand, and 247 *per* Lord M'Naghten.

[95] [1968] AC 1130, 1137 (emphasis added). See also *Yukong Line Ltd of Korea v Rendsburg Investments Corp of Liberia. The 'Rialto'* [1998] 1 WLR 294, 303 *per* Toulson, J.

[96] [2016] EWHC 454 (Comm) at [20].

[97] This statement is subject to an unconventional cluster of cases, deriving from *Watteau v Fenwick* [1893] 1 QB 346, in which an agent of a concealed principal is sometimes held to have usual authority to act on his behalf and to bind him to transactions into which the agent has been expressly forbidden to enter. See paras **10.76–10.83**.

yet been extended to other cases. The decision appealed from extends it very materially, and I can find no warrant or necessity for the extension.[98]

These conditions are absent in the case of undisclosed agency.

In *Keighley, Maxsted & Co v Durant* an agent, R, acting beyond his authority, purchased a consignment of wheat from a third party, D. R made the contract in his own name. Unknown to D, R intended to make the purchase in the joint names of KM and himself. The following day KM's manager agreed with R to take the wheat on joint account. Subsequently, when KM and R failed to take delivery D was forced to resell the wheat at a loss. He sued KM and R for the money he had lost on the transaction. The issue was whether KM's manager had successfully ratified R's unauthorized act, thereby rendering KM liable on the contract made between R and D. The House of Lords held that a party cannot ratify a contract made on his behalf without authority if, at the time of making it, the would-be agent did not profess to be acting on behalf of the former. As Lord Macnaghten explained, normally only persons who are parties to a contract, acting either by themselves or by an authorized agent, can sue or be sued on the contract. Ratification constitutes 'the most remarkable exception' to this general rule. The doctrine of ratification, it will be recalled,[99] was once described by Tindal, CJ in *Wilson v Tumman* as follows:

**10.38**

> That an act done, for another, by a person, *not assuming to act for himself,* but for such other person, though without any precedent authority whatever, becomes the act of the principal, if subsequently ratified by him, is the known and well-established rule of law. In that case the principal is bound by the act, whether it be for his detriment or his advantage, and whether it be founded on a tort or on a contract, to the same effect as by, and with all the consequences which follow from, the same act done by his previous authority.[100]

By this 'wholesome and convenient fiction' a party who ratifies another's act performed in his name 'is deemed to be, though in fact he was not, a party to the contract'. Ratification, however, does not extend to cases where the would-be agent 'keeps his intention locked up in his own breast'. Civil obligations in English law, as Lord Macnaghten explained in *Keighley, Maxsted*, 'are not to be created by, or founded upon, undisclosed intentions'.[101] Moreover, this applies even if in the particular case in hand no injustice would result were effect given to the undisclosed intentions of that would-be agent. Dillon, LJ stated matters crisply in *Welsh Development Agency v Export Finance Co Ltd*:

> Now it is clear law that the doctrine of subsequent ratification, in the law of agency, only applies where the contracting party has expressly made a contract as agent for another. It does not apply where the contracting party has ostensibly made a contract

---

[98] [1901] AC 240, 263.
[99] See **chapter 6**.
[100] (1843) 6 Man&G 236, 242 (emphasis added).
[101] [1901] AC 240, 247.

as principal, without any hint of agency. For the doctrine of the undisclosed principal to apply, therefore, the authority of the agent to bind the undisclosed principal must exist at the time when the agent made the contract, ostensibly as principal. Only if that is so will the undisclosed principal be able to step in and enforce the contract against the other contracting party. So much is clear law.[102]

### Where the undisclosed principal may not intervene on the agent's contract

**10.39**  Whilst English law recognizes that in most situations a concealed, undisclosed principal can sue or be sued on contracts his agent has made on his behalf, in a number of exceptional circumstances the principal will not be allowed to do so. Collectively, such situations would fulfil Lord Lindley's assurance in *Keighley, Maxsted & Co v Durant* that an undisclosed principal 'is only allowed to do so upon terms which exclude injustice'.[103] Broadly speaking, the principal may not intervene on his agent's contract in the following situations, each of which will be considered in turn:

(i) if an express term of the contract made between the agent and the third party indicates that it was not intended that an undisclosed principal might intervene on the contract;

(ii) if, by implication, the terms of the contract into which the agent and the third party have entered indicate that the intervention of an undisclosed principal is excluded;[104] and

(iii) if the agent's identity is of especial importance to the extent that it shows that the third party wished specifically to contract with the agent, to the exclusion of other parties.

*Where the express terms of the contract made between the agent and the third party exclude the intervention of the undisclosed principal*

**10.40**  If the agent has expressly undertaken that he is not acting for another party, it seems obvious that an undisclosed principal will be debarred from taking over the agent's contract.[105] Although the Court of Appeal considered that it was unnecessary to the

---

[102] [1992] BCC 270, 277. See also *Novasen SA v Alimenta SA* [2011] 1 Lloyd's Rep 390 at [48] per HHJ Mackie, QC.

[103] [1901] AC 240, 262.

[104] 'There is no question that parol evidence is admissible to prove that the plaintiff in an action is the real principal to a contract; but it is also well established law that a person cannot claim to be a principal to a contract, if this would be inconsistent with the terms of the contract itself': *Dunlop Pneumatic Tyre Co v Selfridge & Co Ltd* [1915] AC 847, 867 *per* Lord Parmoor.

[105] '[T]he terms of the standard form B contract of the London Metal Exchange, which governs the transactions sued upon, preclude any suggestion of agency. These terms unambiguously specified that the contract is between "ourselves and yourselves as principals" and the words which follow— "we alone being liable to you for its performance"—cannot reasonably be construed as importing that the words "as principals" refer only to the "ourselves" (the brokers) and not also to the "yourselves" (the ITC). [Counsel's] further submission that "as principals" does not mean "as sole principals" was described by Kerr, LJ as commercially implausible. With that I agree': *JH Rayner (Mincing Lane) Ltd v DTI* [1990] 2 AC 418, 516 *per* Lord Oliver of Aylmerton.

decision,[106] at first instance in *Foster v Action Aviation Ltd* Hamblen J referred to the widely accepted principle that where an agent contracts for a named principal, no other principal may intervene on that contract.[107]

More generally, in the words of McNair, J:                                              **10.41**

> It is clear law ... that a person who has concluded a contract in his own name may prove by parol evidence that he was acting for an undisclosed principal unless he has contracted in such terms as to show that he was the real and only principal, and ... it [is] really a question of construction of the particular contract which determine[s] whether parol evidence [is] admissible to prove that some person other than the party named in the written contract [is], in fact, the true principal.[108]

Sometimes there will be some feature of the agent's contract that excludes the possibility of a principal's intervention. In *UK Mutual Steamship Assurance Association v Nevill*,[109] for example, T, the managing part-owner of a vessel, joined a mutual insurance association, insuring the ship under the rules of the association. Both the policy and the association's own articles stipulated that only members could be made liable to pay rateable contributions. T became bankrupt and the association sought to collect contributions due from T from the defendant, N, who was also part-owner of the relevant vessel but not a member of the association. The Court of Appeal held that N could not be made liable for T's contributions because the express terms of the agreement required that only members of the association could incur these liabilities. As Lord Esher, MR explained:

> If a person could be an undisclosed principal with regard to such a policy, it would really make him an undisclosed member ... I do not think there can be such an undisclosed member or partner so far as the other members are concerned. If it were so, then the making of such a policy as this would make the alleged undisclosed principal of the person effecting it an associate with the members of the association without their knowledge and consent. I do not think this can be so ... [T]o make him so, it would be necessary to say that he is a member of the association to which he is wholly undisclosed and unknown.[110]

### *Where, by implication, the terms of the contract between agent and third party exclude the intervention of the undisclosed principal*

More often, the terms of the contract made between the agent and the third party    **10.42**
may impliedly exclude the intervention of the undisclosed principal. This tends to

---

[106] *Foster v Action Aviation Ltd* [2014] EWCA Civ 1368 *per* Longmore, LJ.

[107] [2013] EWHC 2439 (Comm) at [135]–[136]; *Phillips v Duke of Bucks* (1683) 1 Vern 227. See, eg, *Chitty on Contracts* (2015: London, Sweet & Maxwell) 32nd edn, vol II at para 31-066 and *Bowstead and Reynolds on Agency* (2014) 20th ed, para 8-079, where it is also suggested that there is no reason why a purported undisclosed principal might not also resist a third party's claim against him in such circumstances on the ground that the contract is one that excludes his intervention.

[108] *Finzel, Berry & Co v Eastcheap Fried Fruit Co* [1962] 1 Lloyd's Rep 370, 375.

[109] (1887) 19 QBD 110.

[110] *Ibid* at 117.

follow from the way in which the agent's role is described in the written contract. In *Humble v Hunter*[111] an agent, who had entered into a charterparty with the defendant on behalf of an undisclosed principal, had signed the contract 'C.J. Humble, owner of the good ship or vessel called the Ann'. When the principal subsequently sought to intervene on the charterparty, the court held that since the agent had described himself as the owner of the ship, he had to be taken to have contracted as the sole principal in the transaction. Parol evidence, therefore, was not admissible in contradiction of the appearance created in the contract and to show that in reality the agent had entered into the contract on behalf of another party. One member of the court, Patteson, J, did express the view that had the agent described himself in more ambiguous terms—say, merely as 'the contracting party'—evidence would have been admissible to show who was in fact the true principal in the transaction.[112]

**10.43** *Humble v Hunter* is authority for the proposition that 'the assertion of title to the subject-matter of the contract'[113] will render inadmissible any parol evidence that contradicts the written terms of the contract. However, it probably represents a broader principle that the undisclosed principal's intervention is excluded whenever the agent can be shown impliedly to have contracted as the sole principal in the transaction. Certainly, if the agent contracts as 'owner' or 'proprietor',[114] the principal tends to be debarred from intervening on his agent's contract. In many instances, however, the courts have allowed parol evidence to be adduced because the description of the agent's role is not inconsistent with the agent acting on behalf of another. Thus, in *Danziger v Thomson*, the fact that the agent was referred to as the 'tenant' in a tenancy agreement did not prevent his principal from intervening on the contract. As Lawrence, J pointed out, 'The description "tenant" does not imply that the person so described is not acting as an agent or nominee ... [T]he description "tenant" no more negatives agency than would the description "contracting party".'[115]

**10.44** Viscount Haldane sought to instil order in the case law in *F Drughorn Ltd v Rederiaktiebolaget Trans-Atlantic*.[116] An agent, acting for an undisclosed principal, had described himself as the 'charterer' of a vessel in his contract with a third party. Did this description exclude the intervention of the principal? Viscount Haldane drew a distinction between two classes of case. On the one hand, there were cases like *Humble v Hunter* in which the agent effectively asserted title to property, and

---

[111] (1848) 12 QB 310.
[112] (1848) 17 LJ(NS)QB 350, 352.
[113] *Ibid* at 366, *per* Wightman, J.
[114] *Formby v Formby Bros* (1910) 102 LT 116.
[115] [1944] KB 654, 657.
[116] [1919] AC 203.

where it became a term of the contract that the agent contracted as owner of that property. In these cases it was not permissible to contradict the contractual terms by introducing parol evidence to show that another party was actually the real owner. On the other, there were cases where the description affected by the agent was not inconsistent with the intervention of an undisclosed principal:

> [T]he term 'charterer' is a very different term from the term 'owner' or the term 'proprietor'. A charterer may be and *prima facie* is merely entering into a contract. A charterparty is not a lease—it is a chattel that is being dealt with, a chattel that is essentially a mere subject of contract; and although rights of ownership or rights akin to ownership may be given under it *prima facie* it is a contract for the hiring or use of the vessel. Under these circumstances it is in accordance with ordinary business common-sense and custom that charterers should be able to contract as agents for undisclosed principals who may come in and take the benefit of the charterparty.[117]

The *Drughorn* case has considerably reduced the influence of *Humble v Hunter*. **10.45** Indeed, in *Epps v Rothnie*[118] Scott, LJ even suggested that the House of Lords in *Drughorn* might have overruled *Humble v Hunter*. Although this is not the case, certainly only in exceptional circumstances will an undisclosed principal's right to intervene on his agent's contract be held inconsistent with the terms of the written contract; possibly, this may only arise in cases where the agent has affected the clear role of owner of property which is the subject of the contract. Such a view is supported by Morris, J's decision in *O/Y Wasa SS Co Ltd v Newspaper Pulp and Wood Export Ltd*[119] where agents had described themselves in a charterparty as 'the disponent owners' and signed the contract as 'disponents'. The case presented obvious parallels with *Humble v Hunter*. Morris, J, however, considered this particular description 'somewhat vague' and capable of covering someone who could dispose of a ship without being the actual owner.[120] Whilst the Finnish undisclosed principals were allowed to intervene in this case, every contract has to be construed individually to determine whether the terms do or do not exclude the undisclosed principal's intervention. In *The Astyanax*, for example, the agent again used the description 'disponent owner'. The Court of Appeal accepted that this designation was 'in itself neutral', but held that the surrounding circumstances and the course of negotiations between the parties:

> clearly show that the intention was that [the agent] would conclude a time charter with the registered owners and that it was on this basis that he was described in the sub-voyage charter as 'disponent owner'. This was inconsistent with his

---

[117] *Ibid* at 207.
[118] [1945] KB 562.
[119] (1949) 82 Ll L Rep 936.
[120] *Ibid* at 954. See *Navig8 Inc v South Vigour Shipping Inc* [2015] 1 Lloyd's Rep 436 at [98] *per* Teare, J: 'the present case is another example of the phrase disponent owner being used in that, admittedly rare and unusual, sense of a manager of a vessel.'

contracting in the capacity of a mere agent on behalf of the registered owners, with the result that they cannot contend that they were in fact his undisclosed principals.[121]

More recently, in *Ferryways NV v Associated British Ports*,[122] a case in which a port owner/operator denied liability to F for payments following the death of an employee of A for which ABP was liable, Teare, J held that the words 'as the employers' did not exclude the intervention of the undisclosed principal as 'there is no express provision that [A] is the only person to have the rights and obligations of an employer under the contract of employment.'

**10.46**  Occasionally, the omission of a party's name from a contract may be highly significant. A court may construe the omission of a would-be principal's name, by necessary implication, to mean that the intervention of a particular undisclosed principal is excluded. This situation, in some sort, resembles the statutory canon of construction, *inclusio unius est exclusio alterius*. It must be stressed, however, that this type of situation will be unusual: the mere fact that a would-be principal's name does not appear in the contract, whereas other principals are specifically named, will not automatically signify that the former is not entitled to be treated as an undisclosed principal. As Moore-Bick, LJ pointed out in *Talbot Underwriting Ltd v Nausch, Hogan & Murray Inc*:

> The mere identification, whether by name or description, of certain persons as assureds cannot be sufficient of itself to demonstrate an unwillingness on the part of the insurer to contract with any other person. If it were otherwise, the principles [of undisclosed agency] would have no application at all to contracts of insurance.[123]

It will always be a matter of examining the specific case to determine what inferences are justified. In *Talbot Underwriting*, having analysed the facts, Moore-Bick, LJ concluded that the omission of the would-be principal's name was in fact significant, not neutral. The case concerned a policy of insurance effected on a ship entering a shipyard for completion work. Whilst other companies within the same group as the owner, and even joint venturers, were referred to expressly in the agreement, rather like the dog that did nothing in the night-time in Sir Arthur Conan Doyle's *Silver Blaze*,[124] the omission of the shipyard and its sub-contractors from the list of assured parties was said to be 'striking, particularly when it is borne in mind that

---

[121]  See *Asty Maritime Co Ltd v Rocco Giuseppe & Figli, SNC. The Astyanax* [1985] 2 Lloyd's Rep 109, 114 *per* Kerr, LJ.

[122]  [2008] 1 Lloyd's Rep 639, esp at [56].

[123]  [2006] 2 Lloyd's Rep 195 at [27]. For discussion of unnamed and undisclosed agency principles in the particular context of insurance, see F Reynolds, 'Some Agency Problems in Insurance Law' in F Rose (ed), *Consensus ad Idem: Essays in the Law of Contract in Honour of Guenter Treitel* (1996: London, Sweet & Maxwell) pp 77ff.

[124]  *The Memoirs of Sherlock Holmes* (1894: London, George Newnes).

their inclusion as co-assureds would have a significant effect on the insurers' rights of subrogation and therefore on the risk.'[125] The Court of Appeal interpreted the omission as a positive indication that the insurers were not willing to contract with the shipyard or its subcontractors. By implication, therefore, the terms of the contract excluded any right on the part of the shipyard to sue on it as an undisclosed principal.

More normally, a party will be entitled to sue on a contract as an undisclosed princi- **10.47** pal even though the policy identifies a broad class of co-assured. It is all a matter of proving the agent's authority and intention at the time of the contract. In *National Oilwell (UK) Ltd v Davy Offshore Ltd*[126] DOL, as principal contractor for the construction of a North Sea floating oil production system, entered into a contract with NOW for the supply of a wellhead completion system. DOL obtained insurance on the works in which the assureds were identified as Davy Corporation plc (its parent company) and its 'parent and/or subsidiary and/or affiliated and/or associated and/or interrelated companies', all of whom were described in the agreement as 'Principal Assureds'. The policy was also expressed to include as assureds other companies and firms 'with whom the Assured(s) ... have entered into agreement(s) and/or contract(s) in connection with the subject matter of this Insurance and/or any works activities, preparations etc. connected therewith', who were described generically as 'Other Assureds'. NOW, being an unidentified member of a class of persons described in the policy as 'Other Assureds', the case raised the question of the means by which a person who is not named as a co-assured but who falls within a class of unnamed persons, all of whom are described as assureds for their respective interests, can become bound to the insurers on any terms of the contract. Colman, J declared:

> [W]here at the time when the contract of insurance was made the principal assured or other contracting party had express or implied actual authority to enter into that contract so as to bind some other party as co-assured and intended so to bind that party, the latter may sue on the policy as the undisclosed principal and co-assured regardless of whether the policy described a class of co-assured of which he was or became a member.[127]

As Cooke, J later emphasized in *North Atlantic Insurance Co Ltd v Nationwide General Insurance Co Ltd*,[128] where it is necessary to ascertain the identity of a principal with whom the other party knows it is contracting but who remains unidentified on the face of the contract, it is necessary to resort to the intention of the agent at the time of making the contract.

---

[125] [2006] 2 Lloyd's Rep 195 at [35].
[126] [1993] 2 Lloyd's Rep 582.
[127] [1993] 2 Lloyd's Rep 582, 596.
[128] [2003] 2 CLC 731.

**10.48**    A similar point arose in *O' Kane v Jones The Martin P.*[129] The owners of 'The Martin P', NS, employed another company, ABC Maritime AG, to act as manager of the vessel. ABC was responsible for arranging insurances. Insurance on the vessel's hull and machinery was placed in London under a slip policy which described the assured as 'ABC Maritime as managers and/or affiliated and/or associated companies for their respective rights and interests'. NS subsequently sought to claim under the policy as undisclosed principals. The underwriters, however, maintained that the description of the assured in the slip precluded it from doing so, their contention being that the only persons who could be assureds were ABC itself and companies to which it had some corporate relationship. This did not include NS, with which its relationship was purely contractual. The Deputy Judge rejected that argument both on the ground that the description of the assured in that case was not such as to exclude the right of a third party to enforce the contract as an undisclosed principal and also on the additional ground that NS and ABC could be regarded as affiliated or associated companies within the meaning of the slip. As Moore-Bick, LJ was later to comment:

> Insofar as the case decides that the identification of the assured by reference to a class of persons who are to be covered for their respective interests will not necessarily preclude the intervention of an undisclosed principal, I would agree with it, but I do not think that it can be treated as authority for any wider proposition. In each case the question whether the insurers have demonstrated an unwillingness to contract with anyone other than the persons identified in the policy has to be answered by reference to the terms of the contract and the circumstances surrounding it.[130]

*Where the personality of the agent is a matter of importance to the third party*

**10.49**    Although the general principle holds that parol evidence will normally be admissible to prove that, contrary to appearances, a contract was made on behalf of an undisclosed principal, the courts refuse to allow the undisclosed principal to intervene on the agent's contract in cases where the personality of the agent or the principal is an especially relevant factor. Broadly, this means that the principal will not be entitled to take the advantage of or sue on contracts in which the third party clearly intended to contract with the agent, and with no one else. The courts have sometimes refused to permit the undisclosed principal to intervene where the third party's contract with the agent is one which the former entered into relying entirely upon the agent's personal skill or solvency.

**10.50**    Obviously, if he has concluded a personal contract, such as an agreement to paint a portrait, write a book, or employ Bob Marley as a musician,[131] an undisclosed

---

[129] [2004] 1 Lloyd's Rep 389.
[130] *Talbot Underwriting Ltd v Nausch, Hogan & Murray Inc* [2006] CLC 1138 at [34].
[131] *Barrett v Universal-Island Records Ltd* [2006] EMLR 21 at [233] *per* Lewison, J.

principal will not be allowed to substitute himself for the agent whose services were contracted for. The Privy Council was required to consider exactly what counts as a personal contract in *Siu Yin Kwan v Eastern Insurance Co Ltd ('The Osprey').*[132] The claims of the estates of two seamen killed in a typhoon remained unsatisfied following the winding up of the business of their employer, A, against whom judgment had previously been obtained. The estates next sued A's insurer. The relevant insurance had been taken out by A's agent, R, a firm of shipping agents. The insurance document referred to 'your [R's] employees', but also referred to *The Osprey*, a ship that the insurers knew R did not own. The Board held, firstly, that no term in the insurance contract expressly excluded the right of an undisclosed principal to intervene. But secondly, it determined that the contract of insurance was not a personal contract for the purposes of the law of agency. Whereas in the case of an assignment, a species of transaction with which undisclosed agency is often compared, an insurance has been treated as a personal contract, in the context of agency there is authority to suggest that provided that all the material facts have been disclosed an undisclosed principal is entitled to intervene on a marine insurance contract.[133] Assignment and undisclosed agency may be differentiated because in the case of the assignment of the benefit of an insurance the transfer may be to anyone and the scale of the risk therefore becomes uncertain: assignment necessarily involves a change from a known to an unknown risk. In the case of undisclosed agency, Lord Lloyd considered that the insurer's risk would remain unaltered provided that all matters relevant to the risk had been correctly stated at the time of contracting. In this particular case the insurer's objection was technical and more or less devoid of merit: although the Board was bound by a finding of fact that the insurers had dealt with R as principal, in truth they had been aware that R acted as agents, that R had acted for the now insolvent employer A, and that the crew of *The Osprey* would not have been R's employees. At one point in his opinion Lord Lloyd proposed that the key to determining whether the undisclosed principal can intervene is whether or not the insurers would have been willing to contract on the same terms with the real principal. It is unclear whether this is the true rationale of *The Osprey* or whether the explanation of this case resides in the fact that insurers already enjoy so much protection, thanks to their assured's duty of disclosure, that they require no further protection against the intervention of an undisclosed principal.

---

[132] [1994] 1 All ER 213.

[133] See *Browning v Provincial Insurance Co of Canada* (1873) LR 5 PC 263, 272–3 *per* Sir Montague E Smith: 'By the law of England, speaking generally, an undisclosed principal may sue and be sued upon mercantile contracts made by his agent in his own name, subject to any defences or equities which without notice may exist against the agent ... There seems no sufficient ground for making a distinction in the case of marine policies of insurance, especially when, having regard to the ordinary course of business, it must be known they are commonly made by agents.'

**10.51**   The exception that would deny the undisclosed principal the right to intervene on his agent's contracts extends beyond personal contracts, *stricto sensu*. In *Greer v Downs Supply Co* a third party contracted with an agent solely as a means of securing a set-off, which would settle a debt owed to him by the agent. The Court of Appeal held that the agent's undisclosed principal, who subsequently sought to intervene on the contract, was not entitled to intervene on the contract and to sue the third party. As Scrutton, LJ explained, because the third party had contracted with the agent for reasons personal to the agent and these reasons had induced him to contract with the agent to the exclusion of the principal or, indeed, anyone else, the undisclosed principal would not be allowed to sue on the agent's contract.[134] Similarly, in *Collins v Associated Greyhound Racecourses Ltd*[135] it was held that an undisclosed principal was not entitled to rely on an agent's application for shares on the terms of a prospectus and memorandum and articles of association as, under the terms of the transaction, the company was entitled to consider the personality of the applicant before deciding to accept the application.[136]

*Where the personality of the undisclosed principal is of particular importance to the third party*

**10.52**   Just as in *Greer v Downs Supply*, a third party may have specific positive reasons for wishing to contract with the agent to the exclusion of all others, conversely the third party may have strong reasons for not wishing to conclude a contract with the hidden principal. Given that concealment of the existence and identity of the true principal lies at the root of undisclosed agency, it is not surprising that the third party's right to fend off the principal's intervention is restricted. The normal position is that an undisclosed principal cannot be prevented from intervening on his agent's contract merely because the third party would not have contracted had he in fact known that the agent was representing the principal. In *Dyster v Randall & Sons*[137] the plaintiff employed an agent to negotiate a purchase for him precisely because he knew that the vendor would not have agreed under any circumstances to sell certain plots of land to him. Upon discovering that the agent had secretly been working on behalf of the plaintiff, the vendor sought to resist specific performance

---

134   [1927] 2 KB 28, 35.

135   [1930] Ch 1.

136   Scottish courts have held that this personal element may be present in cases where, owing to the complexity of the transaction, it can be inferred that the contract was to be treated as *delectus personae*. In *Karl Construction Ltd v Palisades Property plc* [2002] ScotCS 350 at [8] Lord Drummond Young accepted that, in the absence of special circumstances, an undisclosed principal would not be permitted to intervene on 'a building contract involving complex work', which would 'be personal to the contracting parties ... particularly if detailed administrative or management work is called for, or if elements of design are involved.' See also *Mooney v Keys* [2012] NICh 23 at [26] *per* Deeny, J.

137   [1926] Ch 932.

of the contract on the ground that the agent had deceived him. Lawrence, J ordered specific performance: this was not a personal contract and the identity of the real purchaser was not a material ingredient:

> [M]ere non-disclosure as to the person actually entitled to the benefit of a contract for the sale of real estate does not amount to misrepresentation, even though the contracting party knows that, if the disclosure were made, the other party would not enter into the contract.[138]

As the latter passage suggests, the situation may be altered if the agent has mis- **10.53** represented the identity of the true principal. In *Archer v Stone*[139] the third party particularly inquired of the agent whether he was acting for a certain S. The agent, untruthfully, denied that he was acting on behalf of S. When the agent subsequently sought specific performance of the contract, North, J held that since the agent's misrepresentation, which he termed 'a lie appurtenant', induced the third party to contract with him, specific performance would be refused:

> If [the agent] tells a lie relating to any part of the contract or its subject-matter, which induces another person to contract to deal with his property in a way which he would not do if he knew the truth, the man who tells the lie cannot enforce the contract.[140]

These cases would indicate that, unless the contract is a personal contract, the prin- **10.54** cipal will only be debarred from intervening if the agent has expressly denied that he is acting on that principal's behalf. There is, however, some authority to the effect that if a third party can show that he would never have agreed to contract with the true principal, he can resist the intervention of the undisclosed principal even though no positive misrepresentation has been made to the third party. In *Said v Butt*[141] S, the managing director of a theatre, had made certain unfounded charges concerning ticket sales at B's theatre and was in consequence *persona non grata* at B's establishment. S, wishing to attend a first-night performance of a play at B's theatre but having twice been refused a ticket when he applied for one in his own name, employed an agent to purchase a ticket on S's behalf in the agent's own name. On the first night S was ejected from the theatre[142] and later claimed damages against B for wrongfully and maliciously procuring the theatre company to break a contract made with S. McCardie, J appears to have proceeded upon the unconventional assumption that in cases of undisclosed agency the contract is made between the

---

[138] *Ibid* at 939.
[139] (1898) 78 LT 34.
[140] *Ibid* at 35.
[141] [1920] 3 KB 497.
[142] Such spats do break out in artistic circles. Not so long ago, the critic and museums consultant, Julian Spalding, had to be smuggled into Damien Hirst's retrospective exhibition of 'Con Art' at the Tate Modern, being *persona non grata* having previously described that artist as a 'money-hungry charlatan' and a 'talentless conman': *Daily Mail*, 7 April 2012.

principal and the third party. Relying upon a passage in Fry's *Specific Performance* to the effect that:

> where one person is deceived as to the real person with whom he is contracting, and that deception either induces the contract or renders its terms more beneficial to the deceiving party, or more onerous to the deceived, or where it occasions any other loss or inconvenience to the deceived party, there the contract cannot be enforced against him ...

the judge held that the contract was affected by mistake as to the identity of the contracting party and that S's action therefore failed. This construction is open to serious question. It is normally taken as axiomatic that in the first instance a third party's contract is with the agent, not with the undisclosed principal. If McCardie, J had proceeded upon this basis, the question that he would have posed would have been whether this particular contract with the agent was of such a personal nature as to exclude the intervention of the undisclosed principal. It is certainly arguable that a first-night performance, that can make or break a new play, is 'an event of great importance' and that the management will only dispose of tickets to those whom it specially selects. However, in this case there was nothing to suggest that B had placed positive reliance upon the character of the purchaser of the ticket. It was only later that B placed negative reliance upon the fact that the agent was not acting on behalf of S. Strictly speaking, this was not a personal contract where the third party placed special reliance upon the skill, solvency, or indeed character of the agent. Although the reasoning in *Said v Butt* is difficult to support, it is nevertheless taken as authority for the proposition that if a contract is one in which some personal consideration forms a material ingredient—in McCardie, J's words, if the personal element is 'strikingly present'[143]—the undisclosed principal will not be permitted to intervene on the agent's contract.[144] Lord Millett endorsed this reading of the case in *Shogun Finance Ltd v Hudson (FC)*,[145] where he noted that the evidence in *Said v Butt* showed that a first night is a special event with characteristics of its own, and that first-night tickets are only given or sold to persons whom the management selects and wishes to favour. Although Lord Millett thought that McCardie, J had been in error to treat *Said v Butt* as a case of a contract between principal and third party that was void for mistake—not least because the agent who had bought the ticket could have used it to gain admission himself, nevertheless the result was unobjectionable because the case exemplified:

> the rule that an undisclosed principal cannot intervene where the nature of the contract shows that the contract was intended to be with the agent personally ... The evidence showed that tickets for a first night are not transferable, from which it follows

---

[143] [1920] 3 KB 497, 503.
[144] Eg, *Dyster v Randall* [1926] Ch 932, 939.
[145] [2004] 1 AC 919.

that they are incapable of being bought for an undisclosed principal; so that even on its own terms the contract could not be enforced by the plaintiff.[146]

Hitherto, the cases have concerned agents who were acting on behalf of undisclosed **10.55** principals whom the third parties considered particularly undesirable. If it can be established that the person with whom the third party negotiated a contract was not in fact an agent, but was acting as a principal in his own right, then it would seem that the restrictions on the true beneficiary of the contract's power to intervene may be circumvented. In *Nash v Dix*[147] a committee of Roman Catholics was interested in acquiring a Congregationalist chapel in order to use the building for Roman Catholic worship. Following earlier unsuccessful overtures, the would-be purchasers were keenly aware that the vendor did not desire to sell to them. The Catholic interests therefore entered into an arrangement whereby the plaintiff would purchase the chapel and then re-sell it to the Catholic committee at £100 profit. North, J was prepared to find, in the rather special circumstances obtaining in this case, that the plaintiff was not the committee's agent but was buying the chapel for himself with a view to re-sale at a profit:

> The fact that [the plaintiff] knew that the defendants would have been reluctant to sell to a person who was buying as agent for the Roman Catholics, did not touch the case if he were buying, not as agent for the Roman Catholics, but on his own account.[148]

Lawrence, J, in *Dyster v Randall & Sons*, did later opine that even if an agency had **10.56** been established in this case, the court would have arrived at the same conclusion.[149] Whilst such a view may be reconciled with the decision in *Dyster* that, in the absence of misrepresentation, the identity of the purchaser of property is immaterial, it is more difficult to see how the personality of one person attending a theatre's first night in *Said v Butt* is more obviously material to a third party than the sale of a consecrated site to a rival religious order. In any event, North, J did add that, had the purchaser of the chapel misrepresented his position and informed the vendors that their chapel was not destined to find its way into the hands of the Roman Catholic committee, the case would have been altered and specific performance would have been refused.[150]

*Preventing the third party from suing the undisclosed principal on contracts in which the personal element forms a material ingredient*

The previous paragraphs have considered in what circumstances a third party can **10.57** resist the intervention of the undisclosed principal on the grounds that it is in some

---

[146] *Ibid* at [88].
[147] (1898) 78 LT 445.
[148] *Ibid* at 448.
[149] [1926] Ch 932, 939.
[150] (1898) 78 LT 445, 449.

extreme way undesirable. The question may also arise as to whether the converse is also true. Can the undisclosed principal, if his existence and identity become known to the third party, resist the latter's suit on the ground that because the third party would never have agreed to contract with the principal, had he been aware of the true facts, that third party is equally debarred from looking to the principal to settle his claims. In short, is the third party's contract personal to the agent in this sense too? The courts have not yet formally pronounced on this matter. To hold that such a defence is available to the principal would create a legal symmetry. However, as Lord Steyn once remarked: 'the pursuit of logical symmetry is not the ultimate goal of law.'[151]

10.58　It is suggested that a distinction needs to be drawn between the case of an undisclosed principal seeking to take advantage of a situation in which the third party had the strongest reasons for not entering into a contract with him and the case of an undisclosed principal who may furnish an additional source of liability for a third party who was induced to contract with the agent in circumstances where, had the third party been fully apprised of the facts, he would in all likelihood not have entered into the contract. In the former case, we have seen that the law considers it unjust to enforce contracts against third parties who had strong personal reasons for not contracting with the undisclosed principal or who were misled into doing so by false representations made by the agent. In the latter case, the unfairness is less apparent. For example, if a third party has sold goods to an agent who was secretly purchasing on behalf of an undisclosed principal for whom he actually denied that he was acting,[152] if the agent becomes insolvent or refuses to pay for the goods, there is some justice in holding that, should he so desire, the third party should be permitted to turn to the principal for payment. The principal was responsible for setting events in train, and in that sense is not blameless. It is not an especially attractive argument to allow a principal to resist the third party's claim on the ground that, had the third party not deliberately been kept in ignorance of the true situation, he would never have contracted with or delivered goods up to an agent who, contrary to what he had misrepresented, was covertly acting in league with the principal.

### Legal effects of undisclosed agency

*Legal effects turn on whether principal's identity comes to be revealed*

10.59　The legal effects of undisclosed agency depend upon whether or not the principal's identity becomes revealed. So long as the third party remains unaware of the

---

[151] *Mills v R* [1995] 3 All ER 865, 874. Lord Steyn might almost have been echoing Jorge Luis Borges' sentiment, 'Reality favours symmetries and slight anachronisms': 'The South' in *Ficciones* (1962: Grove Press, trans. Anthony Bonner).

[152] See *Archer v Stone* (1898) 78 LT 34.

principal's existence the contract continues to bind agent and third party.[153] Once the principal intervenes on the contract and sues or settles with the third party, however, the agent's right to sue on the contract is lost. Similarly, once the third party becomes aware of the existence of an undisclosed principal, the former is said to dispose of a right of election enabling him to choose whether to look to the agent or to the principal for satisfaction of obligations owed to him under the contract made with the agent. In either eventuality, whether the principal chooses to intervene on the contract or the third party elects to look to the principal in preference to the agent, the principal comes to supplant the agent and acquires rights and liabilities that closely resemble those of a disclosed principal.

### *Third party's right of election whether to look to the agent or to the principal*

Upon discovering the existence of an undisclosed principal the third party dis- **10.60** poses of a right of election whether to look to the agent or to the principal. Until the principal chooses to reveal himself or the third party learns of the principal's existence and identity, the correlative rights and duties under the contract operate as between agent and third party. Once the principal is discovered, however, the third party acquires the right to choose whether to look to the agent or to the principal to satisfy the obligations owed to him under the contract. This is referred to as the third party's right of election. In the words of Sir John Knox in *Muldoon v Wood*:

> The well established law relating to undisclosed principals gives a third party who enters into a contract with a person who has authority from an undisclosed principal but does not reveal it a choice between suing the agent with whom he or she makes the contract and the subsequently disclosed principal.[154]

After the third party, in possession of all the relevant facts, has made his elec- **10.61** tion, and has determined unequivocally to look to either agent or principal to the exclusion of the other, the third party will not permitted thereafter to change his mind and look to the other party for satisfaction. Clearly, it will be critical to identify what exactly the courts find amounts to an unequivocal election. In the early case of *Thomson v Davenport* Lord Tenterden, CJ took the general rule to be:

> that if a person sells goods (supposing that at the time he is dealing with a principal), but afterwards discovers that that the person with whom he has been dealing is not

---

[153] An intriguing question pursued by Tan, *Undisclosed Agency and Damages* [2013] JBL 799 is whether, in case of breach of contract by the third party, the agent for an undisclosed principal who sues that third party is entitled to a full measure of damages. Tan suggests that the loss for which the agent can claim 'will be based on objective measures rather than the actual loss suffered by the principal', this right being founded upon 'the implied contract entered into between the third party and the principal' under which it is 'implicit … that the agent has the authority to do all such things as are necessary to enforce the contract on the principal's behalf' (pp 800 and 816).

[154] [1998] EWCA Civ 588.

the principal in the transaction, but an agent for a third person, though he may in the mean time have debited the agent with it, he may afterwards recover the amount from the real principal ...[155]

Clearly, billing the agent or simply requesting payment in ignorance of the true state of affairs will not amount to an elective act. However, once the third party is fully apprised of the facts, at what point do the courts hold that the third party is irrevocably committed to looking to either agent or principal?

**10.62** In *Clarkson, Booker Ltd v Andjel*[156] an agent failed to pay for some airline tickets which he had booked through the claimant company without informing it that he was acting on behalf of a principal. When it became aware of the true state of affairs, the company wrote to both agent and principal requesting payment, before serving a writ on the principal. Upon subsequently learning that the principal was insolvent, the claimant abandoned these proceedings and set about suing the agent instead. On behalf of the agent it was argued that the commencement of proceedings against the principal amounted to an unequivocal election on the claimant's part which thereafter prevented the claimant from looking to the agent for satisfaction. In the Court of Appeal Russell, LJ considered that the court had to decide whether the election had 'crystallized' the claimant's rights. This point is reached when:

> the external acts of the third party must lead to the conclusion, as a matter of fact, that the third party has settled to a choice involving abandonment of his option to enforce his right against one party.[157]

Although the Court felt that this case fell close to the line, it held that the claimant's service of a writ on the principal did not amount to an unequivocal act indicating an intention to look exclusively to the principal. Russell, LJ did say, however, that since the service of a writ against either agent or principal, something those parties will ignore at their peril, constitutes the first stage in the legal enforcement of rights, such service 'points significantly towards a decision to exonerate the other'. In appropriate circumstances, therefore, something short of final judgment could suffice to demonstrate the third party's unequivocal decision.[158] If, however, the third party had issued a writ simultaneously against the other party, had expressly informed the other party that he was not abandoning his alternative claim or had in some way let it be known that the other party 'might be looked to for liability

---

[155] (1829) B&C 78, 86.
[156] [1964] 2 QB 775.
[157] *Ibid* at 795.
[158] 'I have no doubt that in a given case this may be shown without [the third party's] proceeding to the length of obtaining judgment; indeed, if judgment is obtained against either principal or agent, this is more than election, though frequently referred to as election; the judgment supersedes the contractual right against either, and if obtained against the agent precludes action against the

on the contract', Russell, LJ considered that a court would not hold that the third party had made a final election thereby abandoning his alternative source of contractual liability.[159]

Although not strictly necessary to the decision, in *Kendall v Hamilton* Lord Cairns, LC declared:　　**10.63**

> [W]here an agent contracts in his own name for an undisclosed principal, the person with whom he contracts may sue the agent, or he may sue the principal, but if he sues the agent and recovers judgment, he cannot afterwards sue the principal, even although the judgment does not result in satisfaction of the debt.[160]

Such a rule was said to serve a number of ends. A third party was given the right to continue to hold the agent liable because it would otherwise be unfair for someone who had seen, known, dealt with and given credit to the agent to be made to sue the principal against his will. Conversely, it would be unjust to prevent a third party creditor, on discovering the principal who in reality had taken the benefit of the transaction, from suing that principal if he wished so to do. That said, Lord Cairns was also concerned lest a principal be vexed by multiple suits:

> [I]f an action were brought and judgment recovered against the agent, he, the agent, would have a right of action for indemnity against his principal, while, if the principal were liable also to be sued, he would be vexed with a double action. Farther than this, if actions could be brought and judgments recovered, first against the agent and afterwards against the principal, you would have two judgments in existence for the same debt or cause of action; they might not necessarily be for the same amounts, and there might be recoveries had, or liens and charges created, by means of both, and there would be no mode, upon the face of the judgments, or by any means short of a fresh proceeding, of shewing that the two judgments were really for the same debt or cause of action; and that satisfaction of one was, or would be, satisfaction of both.[161]

Thus, it would appear that once the third party has obtained judgment against one or other of the parties, the right of election is exhausted and no further action can be brought.

English courts do not fully agree upon the theoretical basis underlying the doctrine　　**10.64**
of election. In a thoughtful judgment, in *LC Fowler & Sons Ltd v St Stephens College Board of Governors*,[162] however, a New Zealand judge, Thomas, J, re-examined the basis of the doctrine afresh. He argued that election ought to be viewed as 'an

---

principal even if the plaintiff was ignorant of his existence, and therefore unable to elect': [1964] 2 QB 775, 795.

　[159] [1964] 2 QB 775, 796.
　[160] (1879) 4 App Cas 504, 514. See further *Priestly v Fernie* (1865) 3 H&C 977.
　[161] (1879) 4 App Cas 504, 514–15.
　[162] [1991] 3 NZLR 304.

instance of waiver (or estoppel or release)' and that the normal incidents of waiver should attend the third party's election. The latter's decision not to sue one or other of the parties must therefore be deliberate and unequivocal and based on a full knowledge of all the relevant facts.[163] Waiver, then:

> may range from explicit assurances to a party that he or she will not be sued to the implication to be drawn from the [third party's] conduct where it is inconsistent with the maintenance of the right to sue that party. In such cases the right to sue has been abandoned.[164]

This means both that an election does not require the third party to have sued either agent or principal to final judgment and that, contrary to what some cases might suggest, the fact that the third party has obtained final judgment against one or other of the parties does not conclusively establish that an election has taken place. Thomas, J's analysis of the doctrine of election was deployed before the English Commercial Court in *The Nea Tyhi*,[165] but because that case did not raise those issues directly, Rix, J expressed no view on Thomas, J's judgment in the *LC Fowler* case. It is not at all improbable that when eventually an English court next has to confront this issue Thomas, J's analysis will prevail.

*The undisclosed principal intervenes on the agent's contract subject to defences and equities which, without notice, may exist against the agent*

**10.65** Because in the case of undisclosed agency the contract is concluded in the first instance between agent and third party, the general rule is that, if the undisclosed principal chooses to intervene, he does so subject to all equities and defences with which the third party could have met an action brought by the agent. It would simply be unfair to permit the principal to intervene if the third party were not allowed to set up against him any defences with which he could meet the agent's claim. As Sir Montague Smith declared in *Browning v Provincial Insurance Co of Canada*:

> By the law of England, speaking generally, an undisclosed principal may sue and be sued upon mercantile contracts made by his agent in his own name, subject to any defences or equities which without notice may exist against the agent.[166]

The third party may only set up such defences or equities provided that they have accrued prior to his having actual notice of the principal's existence. Lord Denman put matters succinctly when he said that the third party is 'entitled to be placed in the same situation, at the time of the disclosure of the real principal, as if the agent had been the contracting party.'[167]

---

[163] See *Clarkson Booker Ltd v Andjel* [1964] 2 QB 775, 792–3 *per* Willmer, LJ.
[164] [1991] 3 NZLR 304, 308.
[165] [1999] 2 Lloyd's Rep 497.
[166] (1873) LR 5 PC 263, 272.
[167] *Sims v Bond* (1833) 5 B&Ald 389, 393. *E contra*, 'The rule which allows a person who deals with an agent not known to be such to set off against his principal any debt due from the agent to

This principle is well settled. In *Rabone v Williams*[168] a third party successfully   **10.66**
claimed a right of set-off against an undisclosed principal who intervened on his
agent's contract. A factor had sold goods to the defendant, who owed money to
the factor on another account. In holding that the principal took over the factor's
contract subject to this counterclaim, Lord Mansfield, CJ said:

> Where a factor, dealing for a principal but concealing that principal, delivers goods
> in his own name, the person contracting with him has a right to consider him to all
> intents and purposes as the principal; and though the real principal may appear and
> bring an action upon that contract against the purchaser of the goods, yet that pur-
> chaser may set off any claim he may have against the factor in answer to the demand
> of the principal. This has long been settled.

In principle, these statements of the law would lead to the conclusion that when-   **10.67**
ever a right of set-off against the agent accrues to a third party before he has
actual knowledge of the principal's existence, the third party will automatically
be allowed to set off these sums against any claim brought by the undisclosed
principal. To this extent, the position of the third party would be broadly akin to
that of an assignee of a chose in action, who takes the chose subject to all those
equities that have priority over the right of the assignor. In the case of undisclosed agency, however, somewhat surprisingly there is House of Lords authority
that would seek to restrict a third party's right of set-off to cases where the principal's conduct has raised an estoppel. In *Cooke & Sons v Eshelby*[169] brokers sold
two parcels of cotton to a third party without disclosing that they were acting
as agents. The third party was aware that the brokers sometimes dealt on their
own account and sometimes acted for other parties. In the case of this particular
transaction, the third party was held to have no particular belief as to whether
they were acting as agents or principals. When the undisclosed principal revealed
himself and sued the third party for the purchase price of the cotton, it was held
that the latter could not set off against the principal's claim other monies owed
to him by the brokers. In his speech Lord Watson suggested that it would not
be sufficient to justify a set-off simply to show that the agent had acted in his
own name:

---

the person so dealing with him, is well settled ... but it is equally well settled that this rule does not
apply where the person dealing with the agent knows him to have a principal, although the name of
the principal may not be disclosed': *Masponsy Hermano v Mildred, Goyeneche & Co* (1882) 9 QBD
530, 544 *per* Lindley, LJ.

[168] (1785) 7 TR 360n. See also *Semenza v Brinsley* (1865) 18 CB(NS) 467, 477 *per* Willes,
J: 'In order to make a valid defence within the rule above stated, it is obvious that the plea should
shew that the contract was made by a person whom the plaintiff had intrusted with the possession of the goods, that that person sold them as his own goods in his own name as principal,
with the authority of the plaintiff, that the defendant dealt with him as and believed him to be
the principal in the transaction, and that before the defendant was undeceived in that respect the
set-off accrued.'

[169] (1887) 12 App Cas 271.

[I]t must also be shewn that the agent was enabled to appear as the real contracting party by the conduct, or by the authority, express or implied, of the principal. The rule thus explained is intelligible and just ... it rests upon the doctrine of estoppel. It would be inconsistent with fair dealing that a latent principal should by his own act or omission lead a purchaser to rely upon a right of set-off against the agent as the real seller, and should nevertheless be permitted to intervene and deprive the purchaser of that right at the very time when it had become necessary for his protection.[170]

In this case, because the third party was unable to establish that the principal's conduct had induced him to believe that the agent was selling on his own account, no right of set-off accrued. More particularly, the House held that a broker who effected a sale in his own name with an intimation, express or implied, that he was possibly selling as an agent, did not sell the goods as his own, and in such a case the purchaser would have no reasonable grounds for believing that the agent was the real party with whom he had contracted.

**10.68** The precise significance of Lord Watson's remarks is not easy to gauge. On its facts, the decision in *Cooke & Sons v Eshelby* is unobjectionable. The court found that the third party was aware of the risk that a principal might intervene on the agent's contract. This emerges clearly from Lord Halsbury, LC's speech, which gave prominence to the question of how the evidence was to be assessed in these situations:

> The selling in his own name by a broker is only one fact, and by no means a conclusive fact, from which, in the absence of other circumstances, it might be inferred that he was selling his own goods. Upon the facts proved or admitted in this case the fact of selling in the broker's name was neither calculated to induce nor did in fact induce that belief.[171]

In principle, it would seem mistaken to place emphasis on a concealed principal's conduct because it would entail that the third party's right of set-off is dependent upon a representation emanating from a principal of whose very existence he is blithely ignorant. In all cases of undisclosed agency, in a sense, the agent is held out by the principal as the true principal in the transaction. Since there always will be an implicit representation from the mere situation of undisclosed agency, it can only create confusion to have further recourse to representations and notions of estoppel. Significantly, in *Cooke & Sons v Eshelby* one member of the House of Lords did express certain reservations. Lord Fitzgerald admitted to having 'some hesitation in accepting the view that the decisions rest on the doctrine of estoppel', adding that 'estoppel *in pais* involves considerations not necessarily applicable to the case before

---

[170] *Ibid* at 278–9.
[171] *Ibid* at 276.

us.'[172] The better view, it is suggested, is that estoppel has no part to play in determining the state of the undisclosed principal's rights as and when he intervenes on his agent's contract. The contract, in the first instance, is made between third party and agent, and the third party simply enjoys a right of set-off in all cases where he had no actual notice of the principal's existence.[173]

### Settlement

*Where the third party settles with the agent of an undisclosed principal*

Since the undisclosed principal allows his agent to appear to the third party as the true principal in the transaction, so long as the principal has not intervened on the contract and the third party remains ignorant of his existence the third party may settle with the agent and obtain a good discharge of his obligations. This means that by settling with the agent, the third party will acquire a complete defence to actions the principal may subsequently bring on the contract. In *Coates v Lewes*[174] the plaintiffs employed an agent to sell linseed oil on their behalf, fully aware that the agent always acted in his own name. The defendant purchased oil from the agent and paid the agent. The plaintiffs later sought to sue the defendant for the purchase price. Lord Ellenborough, CJ held that because the plaintiffs had authorized the agent to deal with the oil as though he were the true principal in the transaction, the defendant's payment to the agent prior to discovering the existence of the undisclosed principal was binding upon the latter.

**10.69**

*Where the undisclosed principal settles with the agent*

Where the principal is disclosed, it has been held that he may obtain a good discharge of his obligations to the third party by making payment to the agent if he can show that the third party has done something to induce him to settle with the agent. This will require proof that the third party has so conducted himself as to lead the principal to believe that agent and third party have come to a settlement.[175] This situation might arise where the third party has delayed asserting his rights against the disclosed principal or where the transaction effected between the agent and the third party is dressed up in such a way that the principal might be deceived into believing that his agent and the third party have come to a settlement.[176] Such a

**10.70**

---

[172] *Ibid* at 282–3. Without wishing to commit himself to any particular principled explanation of the rule, Lord Fitzgerald confined himself to noting that the concealed principal had done nothing in this case wilfully to mislead the third party into thinking that the agents were the owners of the cotton or authorized to sell them as their own.

[173] See further F Reynolds, *Practical Problems of the Undisclosed Principal Doctrine* (1983) 36 CLP 119; R Derham, *Set-Off and Agency* [1985] CLJ 384.

[174] (1808) 1 Camp 444.

[175] *Heald v Kenworthy* (1855) 10 Exch 739, 746 *per* Parke, B.

[176] Eg, *Wyatt v Marquis of Hertford* (1802) 3 East 147.

situation effectively gives rise to an estoppel, preventing the third party from deny-ing no such settlement has occurred. Does a similar principle apply in the case of undisclosed agency? Since the third party will be unaware of the undisclosed prin-cipal's very existence, one would have thought that estoppel had no role to play in undisclosed agency and that even if, for example, the third party had inordinately delayed seeking payment from the agent, the principal would not be permitted to assert that this amounted to a representation directed to him entitling him there-upon to settle with his agent.

**10.71**  In *Armstrong v Stokes*,[177] however, Blackburn, J would appear to have suggested that a similar principle does in fact apply in the case of undisclosed agency. Commission agents, who sometimes acted as agents and sometimes acted on their own account, had purchased goods from the plaintiff without disclosing that they were acting for a principal. Before the plaintiff had learned of his existence, the principal paid the purchase price to his agents, who subsequently found them-selves unable to pay the plaintiff. Blackburn held that this payment discharged the principal of his obligation to the plaintiff. His reason for so holding was that to make the principal pay twice over for the goods would have imposed 'intolerable hardship'.[178]

**10.72**  It is difficult to justify the proposition that a third party can no longer look to the undisclosed principal once the latter has chosen to settle with his agent. Bramwell, LJ, in *Irvine & Co v Watson & Sons*,[179] was later to describe *Armstrong v Stokes* as 'a very remarkable case'[180] decided on its own particular facts. It is improbable that *Armstrong v Stokes* would be followed today. The simple fact is that the undisclosed principal cannot claim to have been induced to settle with his agent by a representa-tion held out to him by someone who is unaware of his existence. Given that the principal has either created this situation by choosing to remain concealed from the third party behind the cloak of the agent or has been aware that the agent pro-posed to act on his behalf in this way, it is equally difficult to see why at the end of the day the third party should suffer if the principal takes it into his head to settle with his agent. The 'intolerable hardship' to which Blackburn, J alluded looks to be self-inflicted. It seems preferable, therefore, to treat the state of accounts between the undisclosed principal and the agent as immaterial and to hold that settlement with the agent will not discharge the undisclosed principal of his obligations to the third party.

---

[177]  (1872) LR 7 QB 598.

[178]  *Ibid* at 610: '[I]f the rigid rule thus laid down were to be applied to those who were only dis-covered to be principals after they had fairly paid the price to those whom the vendor believed to be the principals, and to whom alone the vendor gave credit, it would produce intolerable hardship.'

[179]  (1880) 5 QBD 414. See further F Reynolds, *Practical Problems of the Undisclosed Principal Doctrine* (1983) CLP 119.

[180]  (1880) 5 QBD 414, 417.

## Undisclosed principals and deeds

The principal may neither sue nor be sued on a deed *inter partes*, unless he is de- **10.73** scribed as a party to the deed and it is also executed in his name. In *Re International Contract Co. Pickering's Claim*[181] a principal, whose agent executed a contract under seal without naming the principal in the document, could not be sued on the contract by the third party. Indeed, owing to the strictness of the rules governing deeds, such is the case even if the deed is expressed as having been executed on the principal's behalf. In *Schack v Anthony*[182] owners of a ship were held not to be entitled to sue for freight on a contract under seal executed by the ship's master 'as agent for the owners'. In order to confer rights and liabilities upon the principal, the signature on the deed will often conform to the formula 'P, by A his attorney', making quite clear that the deed is being executed in the principal's name. In practice, it will be seen that executing a contract under seal can to all intents exclude the intervention of an undisclosed principal.

The conventional rule concerning deeds can be bypassed in certain circumstances. If **10.74** the agent, when signing a deed in his own name, is acting as trustee for the principal, it has been held that if the trustee declines to bring an action the beneficiary (ie, the principal) can sue in his place, joining the trustee as co-defendant. In *Harmer v Armstrong*[183] an undisclosed agent agreed by contract under seal to purchase the copyright in a number of periodicals from a third party. The agent was acting as both agent and trustee for himself and the principal. The agency and the trust having been established to the satisfaction of the court, the principal was both granted a declaration affirming that there was an agency and a trusteeship and also accorded specific performance of the contract. Further, s 56 of the Law of Property Act 1925 permits someone to take various interests and benefits in land even though not named as a party to the conveyance or sealed instrument. The Contracts (Rights of Third Parties) Act 1999, too, allows those who are not actual parties to enforce terms of a contract if it makes express provision for this and the term purports to confer a benefit on that person.

The most frequent commercial exception to the conventional rules regarding par- **10.75** ties to deeds concerns powers of attorney executed under the Powers of Attorney Act 1971, s 7(1).[184] This provision now lays down:

> The donee of a power of attorney may, if he thinks fit—
> (a) execute any instrument with his own signature and, where sealing is required, with his own seal, ...

---

[181] (1871) LR 6 Ch App 525.
[182] (1813) 1 M&S 573.
[183] [1934] Ch 65.
[184] As amended by the Law of Property (Miscellaneous Provisions) Act 1989.

by the authority of the donor of the power; and any document executed ... in that manner shall be as effective as if executed or done by the donee with the signature and seal ... of the donor of the power.

In all save the four exceptional situations mentioned above, a deed will serve to prevent the undisclosed principal from asserting rights or assuming responsibilities under that instrument.

### *Watteau v Fenwick*: cases in which an undisclosed 'principal' incurs liability for prohibited acts falling within his agent's usual authority

**10.76**  There exists a small but problematic cluster of cases that are sometimes treated as falling within the law of agency—and, more particularly, as being allied to undisclosed agency. Although these authorities may not be commercially significant, being concerned in the main with that waning commercial force, the unincorporated one-man business, they do pose an intriguing intellectual puzzle. One question is whether, despite what the judgments say, they are cases actually involving the law of agency at all. If they are, where do they fit within the wider scheme of things? The leading authority, *Watteau v Fenwick*,[185] appears to predicate that whenever a 'principal', whose existence is concealed from third parties, seeks to restrict the usual authority of his 'agent', third parties are not bound by this limitation of authority but may assume that the 'agent' possesses all the authority usually enjoyed by an individual exercising that role or calling.

**10.77**  In *Watteau v Fenwick*[186] H managed F's beer house. F's existence remained concealed from the public: the premises' licence had been taken out in H's name, and H's name was painted above the door of the beer house. F forbade H to purchase any goods for the business except bottled ales and mineral waters; all other goods for the business had to be supplied by F. In contravention of his instructions, for several years H bought cigars and Bovril on credit from W for use in the business. Upon learning that F in fact owned the business, W decided to bring an action against F for the cost of the products that H had acquired from them on credit without F's authority. Lord Coleridge, CJ at one point did view the case as one involving an undisclosed principal.[187] In the judgment of the court, however, delivered by Wills, J, the operative principle was said to be:

> Once it is established that the defendant was the real principal, the ordinary doctrine as to principal and agent applies—that the principal is liable for all the acts of the agent which are *within the authority usually confided to an agent of that character,*

---

[185]  [1893] 1 QB 346.

[186]  *Ibid.*

[187]  'Cannot you, in such a case, sue the undisclosed principal on discovering him?' [1893] 1 QB 346, 347 (*in arguendo*).

notwithstanding limitations, as between the principal and the agent, put upon that authority.[188]

F was therefore held liable for the unauthorized purchases made by H, on the ground that an agent in H's position would usually be authorized to purchase supplies for a beer house.[189]

It would be difficult to criticize the justness of the court's ruling. By placing H in **10.78** a position where third parties would assume that H was the owner of the business, it is wholly appropriate that F can be held liable for purchases that typically would be made by someone managing his own business. Why should innocent third parties be placed at a disadvantage merely because the owner of a business chooses to lie concealed behind a manager? It hardly seems wrong to hold the hidden owner liable, given that the purchases have benefited his business, albeit they were ordered by a manager to whom the supplier gave exclusive credit. *Watteau v Fenwick*, however, does raise very considerable conceptual difficulties, which were discussed by the court. The problem lies in identifying the source of the manager's authority to bind his 'principal' to unauthorized contracts. Notably, it was argued that apparent authority would not apply in this situation because, if third parties were unaware of the existence of a 'principal', there could be no holding out, *aliter* no representation.[190] W never regarded H as an agent. Wills, J rejected this point, declaring that were the principal not bound in these circumstances:

> in every case of undisclosed principal, or at least in every case where the fact of there being a principal was undisclosed, the secret limitation of authority would prevail and defeat the action of the person dealing with the agent and then discovering that he was an agent and had a principal.[191]

This does not quite meet the point. The rightfulness of a solution does not necessarily equate with conceptual orthodoxy. Nor could the situation presented in *Watteau v Fenwick* be comfortably integrated into the doctrine of the undisclosed principal.[192] It is an unassailable feature of the anomalous rules governing this

---

[188] [1893] 1 QB 346, 348–9 (emphasis added).

[189] This situation may be contrasted with the case of a 'tied' house. Where, as in *Daun v Simmins* (1879) 41 LT 783, an agent is employed to manage a house that third parties could be taken to know was only entitled to acquire provisions from a given supplier, third parties in the trade could not hold the principal liable for the agent's unauthorized purchases. This case, however, differs from *Watteau v Fenwick* in two significant respects: first, the existence of the *agency* was known to the third party who sold spirits to the agent; and secondly, the supplier, as a professional operating within that trade, should have been aware of the restriction on the agent's purchasing authority.

[190] See discussion of the agent's apparent authority, **chapter 4**.

[191] [1893] 1 QB 346, 349.

[192] See paras **10.27–10.74**.

species of agency that the undisclosed agent must have been acting within his actual authority. The signal feature in *Watteau v Fenwick* was that, even if his 'principal' was undisclosed, H's acts were in fact unauthorized.

**10.79**  *Watteau v Fenwick* was followed shortly afterwards by *Kinahan & Co Ltd v Parry*.[193] Here, a third party sought to recover the price of some whisky supplied to a hotel. As in the previous case, the hotel was run by a manager who, to all intents, appeared to be the owner of the business. The manager had express instructions from the true owners only to buy spirits from a particular supplier. The manager ignored this injunction and purchased whisky on credit from the plaintiff. Although the decision was subsequently reversed on other grounds,[194] Lord Coleridge, CJ simply declared that in these circumstances the supplier was 'entitled ... to sue the real principal when disclosed, notwithstanding any limitations on the authority given to the agent by the principal.'[195]

**10.80**  Bingham, J, in *Rhodian River Shipping Co SA and Rhodian Sailor Shipping Co SA v Halla Maritime Corporation. The Rhodian River and Rhodian Sailor*,[196] before whom *Watteau v Fenwick* had been cited, described the authority as 'a somewhat puzzling case', confessing that the argument advanced on appeal, that the owner could be liable only if the manager had or was held out as having authority, appeared in principle correct.[197] Bingham, J did cautiously advance one suggestion:

> The true ratio of [*Watteau v Fenwick*] is not altogether easy to perceive, and certainly the case does not appear to have sired a line of authority, but the case perhaps reflects an undeveloped doctrine that an undisclosed principal should be vicariously liable on contracts made by an agent where they are contracts which a person would ordinarily make in the position which the principal has allowed the agent to assume (see *Edmunds v Bushell and Jones* (1865) LR 1 QB 97, relied on by the court in *Watteau v Fenwick*, and *Bowstead on Agency*, 14th ed, p 72).[198]

However, his Lordship immediately added, 'I would myself be extremely wary of applying this doctrine, *if it exists.*'[199]

**10.81**  *Watteau v Fenwick* has been strongly criticized in many, but not all academic writings.[200] The case has been rejected virtually out of hand in at least one

---

[193] [1910] 2 KB 389.
[194] See [1911] 1 KB 459.
[195] [1910] 2 KB 389, 394.
[196] [1984] 1 Lloyd's Rep 373.
[197] [1984] 1 Lloyd's Rep 373, 378.
[198] *Ibid* at 379.
[199] *Ibid* at 379 (emphasis added).
[200] Eg, Pollock (1893) 9 LQR 111; JA Hornby, *The Usual Authority of an Agent* [1961] CLJ 239, 246; J Collier [1985] CLJ 363; GHL Fridman, *The Demise of Watteau v Fenwick* (1991) 70 Can Bar Rev 329.

common-law jurisdiction,[201] and doubted in another.[202] True, attempts have been made to justify the decision variously by invoking an extended doctrine of apparent ownership[203] or by drawing a broad analogy with vicarious liability.[204] But these re-interpretations have not been widely endorsed. Most recently, it has been argued that *Watteau v Fenwick* can be justified on orthodox legal principles 'provided one gets away from the idea that the law of agency has anything to do with it'.[205] The 'tentative' hypothesis is that what F can be said to have represented was that H and the owner of the beer house (whoever that might have been) were one and the same person:

> By putting someone in charge of their business in such a way that he seemed to be the proprietor of it, they gave W the impression that they, as owners of the hotel, were not a distinct legal entity from the person W did business with … There is no doubt that this representation was relied on (since it is inconceivable that W would have contracted with H personally had they known he was a mere manager). If so, F should not later have been allowed to resile from it and assert their separate identity, and hence were rightly held liable on the contract.[206]

This is claimed to offer 'a neat way of reconciling *Watteau v Fenwick* with orthodoxy',[207] in addition to providing an explanation of other puzzling cases, such as *Edmunds v Bushell and Jones*[208]—a decision cited with approval by the court in *Watteau v Fenwick*.

In *Edmunds v Bushell and Jones*,[209] J, a Luton-based straw-hat dealer, also had a **10.82** branch in London. B managed J's London business under the name of 'Bushell & Co'. Drawing and accepting bills of exchange would have been a normal incident of running such a business. However, whereas B had authority from J to draw cheques in the name of Bushell & Co for the purposes of the business, he had no authority to draw or accept bills. Contrary to instructions, B accepted a number of bills in the name Bushell & Co. The court held that the principal could be made liable on the bill, which had come into the hands of an indorsee, E, who took it without knowing that B had limited authority preventing him from doing what would be usual by

---

[201] *Sign-O-Lite Plastics Ltd v Metropolitan Life Insurance Co* (1990) 73 DLR (4th) 541, where Wood, J declared, 'It is astonishing that, after all these years, an authority of such doubtful origin, and of such unanimously unfavourable reputation, should still be exhibiting signs of life and disturbing the peace of mind of trial judges. It is surely time to end any uncertainty which may linger as to its proper place in the law of agency.' See also *McLaughlin v Gentles* (1919) 51 DLR 383.

[202] *International Paper Co v Spicer* (1906) 4 CLR 739, 763 *per* Isaacs, J.

[203] See M Conant, *The Objective Theory of Agency: Apparent Authority and the Estoppel of Apparent Ownership* (1968) 47 Neb L Rev 678, 687–8.

[204] See G Treitel, *The Law of Contract* (2011: London, Sweet & Maxwell, ed. Peel) 13th ed, §16-029.

[205] AM Tettenborn, *Agents, Business Owners and Estoppel* [1998] CLJ 274, 278.

[206] [1998] CLJ 274, 279, invoking the authority of *Lease Management Services Ltd v Purnell* (1994) 13 TrLR 337.

[207] [1998] CLJ 274, 280.

[208] (1865) LR 1 QB 97.

[209] (1865) LR 1 QB 97.

one who appeared to be the owner of a business. Cockburn, CJ, who confusingly referred to this as an instance of 'apparent authority',[210] held that the case fell within:

> the well-established principle, that if a person employs another as an agent in a character which involves a particular authority, he cannot by a secret reservation divest him of that authority.[211]

Shee, J expressed the principle slightly differently:

> The natural inference when a person allows an agent to carry on a particular business as an ostensible principal, is that be clothes him with every authority incidental to a principal in the business.[212]

Clearly, the decision to hold J liable in *Edmunds v Bushell and Jones* cannot be founded upon apparent authority: owing to the fact that E was unaware of J's existence, he could not claim to have relied upon any representation by J as to the extent of B's authority.

**10.83** The true basis for decisions like *Watteau v Fenwick* has not been finally resolved. Tettenborn's attractive argument, to the effect that this group of cases can be explained on the basis of a representation that the owners of the hotel were one and the same legal entity as the person with whom the third party did business, is at odds with the courts, which either side-step the issue or evince polite scepticism. The better view, it is suggested, is that *Watteau v Fenwick* is a decision which, despite the terms in which it was delivered, does not in truth concern the law of agency.

## Unauthorized Dispositions of Property by the Agent

**10.84** The law of agency, as has been seen, is largely concerned with contractual questions. However, property aspects of the subject cannot be neglected. Since the purpose of the contracts formed between principal and agent will involve transfers of property, this section will address some of the peculiar rules affecting transfer of title to property in the special context of the law of agency. In the main, these rules concern unauthorized dispositions of the principal's property by the agent.

**10.85** In the majority of cases, the agent's ability to transfer good title in the principal's property to third parties will hinge upon the scope of the agent's authority. If the principal has expressly or impliedly authorized the agent to carry out a transaction, or if the transfer of title falls within the agent's apparent authority, then the agent is capable of transferring good title to the third party. If, however, the agent lacks the necessary authority, unauthorized dispositions will tend to fall foul of the general

---

[210] *Ibid* at 99. As did Mellor, J, p 100.
[211] *Ibid* at 99.
[212] *Ibid* at 100.

principle of property law, embodied in the maxim *nemo dat quod non habet*. No one can give a better title than he himself has.

The principle, *nemo dat quod non habet*, can be quite unforgiving. In *RH Willis & Son (A Firm) v British Car Auctions Ltd*,[213] for example, in considering the scope of the rule that an auctioneer, no matter how innocent, is liable to the true owner in conversion where he sells under the hammer goods to which the seller has no title, Lord Denning, MR said *of nemo dat*:   **10.86**

> In answering that question in cases such as this, the common law has always acted on the maxim *nemo dat quod non habet*. It has protected the property rights of the true owner. It has enforced them strictly as against anyone who deals with the goods inconsistently with the dominion of the true owner. Even though the true owner may have been very negligent and the defendant may have acted in complete innocence, nevertheless the common law held him liable in conversion. Both the 'innocent acquirer' and the 'innocent handler' have been hit hard. That state of the law has often been criticised. It has been proposed that the law should protect a person who buys goods or handles them in good faith without notice of any adverse title, at any rate where the claimant by his own negligence or otherwise has largely contributed to the outcome. Such proposals have however been effectively blocked by the decisions of the House of Lords in the last century ... to which I may add the decision of this court in *Central Newbury Car Auctions Ltd v Unity Finance Ltd* [1957] 1 QB 371.[214]

Lord Denning did acknowledge that the harshness of the principle had occasionally been mitigated by statute, but in general confessed that in other situations the only way in which innocent acquirers or handlers have been able to protect themselves is by insurance.

Almost 30 years previously Denning, LJ had reflected upon *nemo dat* in *Bishopsgate Motor Finance Corp Ltd v Transport Brakes Ltd*,[215] declaring:   **10.87**

> In the development of our law, two principles have striven for mastery. The first is for the protection of property: no one can give a better title than he himself possesses. The second is for the protection of commercial transactions: the person who takes in good faith and for value without notice should get a good title. The first principle has held sway for a long time, but it has been modified by the common law itself and by statute so as to meet the needs of our own times.[216]

Broadly, in two situations an agent may pass a better title than he in fact possesses. First, the doctrine of apparent ownership may intervene in order to enable an innocent third party in specified circumstances to acquire a good title in property that the agent lacks authority to transfer. This doctrine, which is also embodied in s 21 of the Sales of Goods Act 1979, is 'confined to situations in which the owner   **10.88**

---

[213] [1978] 1 WLR 438.
[214] *Ibid* at 441–2.
[215] [1949] 1 KB 322.
[216] *Ibid* at 336–7.

of a chattel has clothed a third party with the *indicia* of ownership.'[217] Second, the Factors Act 1889 protects third parties who deal with 'mercantile agents', as defined in the statute, permitting mercantile agents to transfer good title in their principals' goods even though they possess no express authority to do so.

### The doctrine of apparent ownership

**10.89** The doctrine of apparent ownership intervenes whenever an owner clothes another party with the *indicia* of title to his property—for instance, by handing over to the recipient a document of title—so as to suggest to third parties that the recipient is in fact the owner. In such cases the true owner will be estopped from denying the recipient's apparent title. The reason for the doctrine is not far to seek. As Ashhurst, J explained in *Lickbarrow v Mason*,[218] a case in which an unpaid seller of goods was estopped from exercising his right of stoppage *in transitu* because he had endorsed over the bill of lading to the purchaser, thereby enabling the latter to represent himself as the owner of the goods and so to deceive an innocent third party:

> We may lay it down as a broad general principle, that, wherever one of two innocent persons must suffer by the acts of a third, he who has enabled such third person to occasion the loss must sustain it.[219]

Merely handing a chattel over to another will not suffice to trigger the doctrine. A court will need to be persuaded that the true owner has actually invested the recipient with the *indicia* of ownership. Lord Lindley, in *Farquharson Bros & Co v King & Co*, commented that Ashhurst, J's pronouncement in *Lickbarrow v Mason* was 'far too wide', needed considerable qualification, and that the word 'enable' introduced an element of error.[220]

**10.90** In the course of discussing the doctrine of the undisclosed principal, the case of *Watteau v Fenwick*,[221] and the decisions that have flowed from it, showed that a principal who remains concealed cannot become liable for the acts of his agent under the doctrine of apparent authority. Nevertheless, a concealed principal, who secretly restricts the authority of the manager of his business, may incur liability to third parties for the reason that he has caused the agent to appear to third parties as the owner of property entrusted to him.[222] This is part of a broader notion according

---

[217] *Papamichael v National Westminster Bank plc* [2003] 1 Lloyd's Rep 341 at [258] *per* HHJ Chambers, QC.
[218] (1787) 2 TR 63.
[219] *Ibid* at 70.
[220] [1902] AC 325, 343. Lord Halsbury famously observed in the same case: 'in one sense every-man who sells a pistol or a dagger "enables" an intending murderer to commit a crime; but is he, in selling a pistol or a dagger to some person who comes to buy in his shop, acting in breach of any duty?' ([1902] AC 325, 332).
[221] [1893] 1 QB 346.
[222] See paras **10.76–10.83**.

to which a principal who clothes his agent with the *indicia* of title, enabling that agent to appear to the world to be the owner of the principal's goods or property, is bound by dispositions of that property made to third parties who claim to have taken title from the agent.

The concept of apparent ownership extends far beyond the bounds of the law of **10.91** agency. Notably, s 21(1) of the Sale of Goods Act 1979 provides:

> Subject to this Act, where goods are sold by a person who is not their owner, and who does not sell them under the authority or with the consent of the owner, the buyer acquires no better title to the goods than the seller had, unless the owner of the goods is by his conduct precluded from denying the seller's authority to sell.

Our concern will be to determine when a principal will be considered to have conferred the *indicia* of ownership on his agent, leading to the former being estopped from the denying of the latter's title to dispose of the principal's property. The case law, it has to be said, is not capable of entirely rational analysis. However, what emerges from it is that proof will be required of more than the simple fact that the principal has handed his property over to the agent.

To take a leading example, in *Central Newbury Car Auctions Ltd v Unity Finance* **10.92** *Ltd* [223] motor dealers agreed to sell a second-hand Morris car on hire-purchase to a personable stranger who gave the name of C. Contrary to the dealers' agreement with the hire-purchase company, C was handed the car together with the registration book, which happened not to have been signed by the previous owner, A, from whom the dealers had acquired the car at auction. Giving the name of A, C then sold the Morris to a garage, together with a registration book purportedly bearing A's signature. The garage sold the car to the first defendants, another hire-purchase company, which let it out to the second defendants. The motor dealers who had originally sold the car to C sued the defendants for conversion. The defendants replied that under the doctrine of apparent ownership the dealers were estopped from denying C's authority to sell the car since they had permitted C to take possession of the car and registration book without having made any or any sufficient inquiries. The majority of the Court of Appeal seized upon the circumstance that a motor car's registration book is not a document of title, and actually contained on its face the warning that the person registered therein might not be the legal owner of the car which it accompanies. By entrusting the car to C along with a document clearly stating that it did not prove legal ownership, the motor dealers were not making any representation that C was entitled to deal with the car as his own, so as to estop them from asserting their own title. The registration book's primary purpose is to identify who is liable to pay the road fund licence tax in respect of the vehicle, not to provide

---

[223] [1957] 1 QB 371.

evidence of ownership.[224] Thus, Hodson and Morris, LJJ considered that in these circumstances the motor dealers had not given C the means to represent himself as the owner of the Morris car; in fact, they had handed C a document which stated the precise opposite.[225]

**10.93**    In contrast, in *Rimmer v Webster*,[226] R, having delivered a mortgage bond to a broker, H, to sell, was induced by the dishonest broker to execute deeds of transfer in the requisite statutory form acknowledging that they had been made in consideration of payments of £1500 and £500 respectively made by H to R. H then borrowed £1000 from W and executed a formal sub-mortgage of the bond to W, producing the transfers as proof of title. This sub-mortgage was not registered. H made off with the money, and R sought retransfer of the bond, free from the mortgage to W. Farwell, J refused to order the re-transfer employing both the concept of apparent authority and the doctrine of apparent ownership. On the one hand, he held that where an owner of property gives all the *indicia* of title to another person with the intention that he should deal with the property, the principles of agency apply, and any limit which he has imposed on his agent's dealing cannot be enforced against an innocent purchaser or mortgagee from the agent, who has no notice of the limit. Because in this case R had acknowledged that H had paid full consideration for the bond, R was thereby estopped from asserting his equitable title to the bond:

> [I]t was the unnecessary transfer of the legal title to H that enabled him to deal with the bond as owner ... The gist of the case is that the real owner has invested the dishonest vendor or mortgagor with all the *indicia* of title as absolute owner for the purpose of enabling him to deal with the property, although in a limited way only; whether the trust was to sell only, or to mortgage only, is immaterial, if the mortgagee or purchaser had no notice of the existence of any trust at all.[227]

On the other hand, Farwell, J also held that this case fell within the principle of 'pure estoppel' laid down by Ashhurst, J in *Lickbarrow v Mason*:

> If the owner of property clothes a third person with the apparent ownership ... not merely by transferring it to him, but also by acknowledging that the transferee has paid him the consideration for it, he is estopped from asserting his title as against a person to whom such third party has disposed of the property, and who took it in good faith and for value ... In this case the plaintiff transferred the whole legal title to [H] for the purpose of enabling him to sell; and he executed a transfer which stated that [H] had paid him the consideration, and he was fully aware of this.[228]

---

[224] *Ibid* at 388.

[225] *Ibid* at 391 and 398. Denning, LJ dissented: he agreed that there was no estoppel by representation, but contended that the motor dealers were estopped by their conduct from denying C's capacity to pass title in the car since they had intended to part with the car and, additionally, had armed C with the car and registration book thereby enabling him to dispose of the car.

[226] [1902] 2 Ch 163.

[227] *Ibid* at 173.

[228] *Ibid* at 173 and 174. See also *Rice v Rice* (1853) 2 Drew 73.

Again, in *Eastern Distributors Ltd v Goldring*,[229] the Court of Appeal determined    **10.94**
that M, the owner of a Bedford van, had dealt with his vehicle in such manner
as to allow C, a dealer, to appear to third parties as its true owner. In order to
raise sufficient funds to put down a deposit on a new motor car M had entered
into a fraudulent agreement with C which conveyed the impression that M was
purchasing the van from C on hire-purchase. Because the finance company, to
which the applications for finance were made, declined to approve the purchase
of the new car but agreed to finance the purchase of the van, the contemplated
fraud never took place. C only had authority from M to proceed if both transactions were approved by the finance company. C nevertheless went through
with the hire-purchase transaction on the van. C later informed M that the
whole transaction had been cancelled. M, therefore, made no payments under
the hire-purchase agreement, and eventually purported to sell the van to G. At
all times prior to that sale the van had remained in M's possession. The finance
company claimed the return of the van from G. In the court's view, M had
clearly 'armed' C with documents that enabled him to represent to the finance
company that he was the owner of the van and had the right to sell it. For this
reason the case fell within the apparent ownership provision, s 21 of the Sale of
Goods Act 1893 (now 1979), and M was precluded from denying C's authority
to sell.[230]

Although it is plain that the cases all turn on their specific facts, what emerges is that    **10.95**
courts will not apply the doctrine of apparent ownership merely because a principal/
owner has handed goods over to the agent/recipient. Further acts are required that
actually invest the agent with the trappings of ownership, thereby permitting the
agent/recipient to effect dispositions of the principal/owner's property, to all intents
appearing to innocent third parties to be the true owner.

Finally, Devlin, J made a further telling point in *Eastern Distributors Ltd v Goldring*.    **10.96**
Observing that courts often spoke of the apparent ownership doctrine in terms of
estoppel,[231] Devlin, J pointed out that in truth the doctrine does not resemble a
conventional case of estoppel:

> [I]t differs from what is sometimes called 'equitable estoppel' in this vital respect, that
> the effect of its application is to transfer a real title and not merely a metaphorical
> title by estoppel.[232]

---

[229] [1957] 2 QB 600.

[230] Salmon, LJ later distinguished the decision in *Eastern Distributors* in *Mercantile Credit Co Ltd
v Hamblin* [1965] 2 QB 242 on the grounds that in *Hamblin* the owner had neither given the dealer
authority to complete hire-purchase documents on the owner's behalf nor expressly agreed to the
dealer making misrepresentations to the finance house. Cf *Campbell Discount Co Ltd v Gall* [1961]
1 QB 431.

[231] Eg, *Lowther v Harris* [1927] 1 KB 393.

[232] [1957] 2 QB 600, 611.

In this sense, apparent ownership operates as a true exception to the principle of *nemo dat quod non habet*.

### Sales, pledges or other dispositions of goods by mercantile agents under the Factors Act 1889

**10.97**　The Factors Act 1889 confers upon a 'mercantile agent', as defined in the Act, power to transfer a good title in his principal's goods even though he lacks express authority to do so. The 1889 Act is the most recent in a succession of statutes in which Parliament, initially to the evident disbelief of the courts, sought to afford added protection to third parties in their dealings with this class of agent. As Denning, LJ explained in *Pearson v Rose & Young Ltd*:[233]

> In the early days of the common law the governing principle of our law of property was that no person could give a better title than he himself had. But the needs of commerce have led to a progressive modification of this principle so as to protect innocent purchasers. The way that Parliament has done it in the case of mercantile agents is this ... Parliament has not protected the true owner, if he has himself consented to a mercantile agent having possession of them: because, by leaving them in the agent's possession, he has clothed the agent with apparent authority to sell them; and he should not therefore be allowed to claim them back from an innocent purchaser.[234]

*Who qualifies as a 'mercantile agent' under the Factors Act 1889?*

**10.98**　The term 'mercantile agent' is defined in s 1(1) of the 1889 Act as follows:

> The expression 'mercantile agent' shall mean a mercantile agent having in the customary course of his business as such agent authority either to sell goods, or to consign goods for the purpose of sale, or to buy goods, or to raise money on the security of goods.

It will be observed that the Act's title is something of a misnomer. The statute is not concerned solely with regulating the activities of the traditional commercial factor, who was defined at common law as a selling agent whose normal business was to sell or otherwise dispose of goods whose possession was entrusted to him by the principal.[235] It covers a much wider class of agents. There is no requirement that a 'mercantile agent' need fall within an established class of agent, such as brokers and factors. A mere employee or servant will fall outside the definition.[236] However,

---

[233]　[1951] 1KB 275.

[234]　*Ibid* at 286–7.

[235]　*Baring v Corrie* (1818) 2 B&Ald 137, 143 *per* Abbott, CJ. 'The usual characteristics of a factor are these: He is an agent entrusted with the possession of goods of several principals, or sometimes only one principal, for the purpose of sale in his own name without disclosing the name of his principal, and he is remunerated by a commission': *Rolls Razor Ltd v Cox* [1967] 1 QB 552, 568 *per* Lord Denning, MR.

[236]　As did the lawyer of an exiled Russian noble who, as a personal favour, agreed to sell his client's pearl necklace: *Budberg v Jerwood* (1934) 51 TLR 99.

provided that he acts 'in the customary course of his business', a party acting as agent in a single, isolated transaction may qualify as a mercantile agent. In *Lowther v Harris*,[237] for example, an art dealer, employed on a single occasion to sell a tapestry, fraudulently acquired possession of it from the owner and proceeded to sell it to an innocent third party. The dealer was held to be a mercantile agent under the Act, and the innocent purchaser was not liable in conversion, even though the dealer acted for only one principal,[238] had limited authority, and acting as agent was not his general occupation.

The statutory definition has been held to apply to disparate commercial relation- **10.99** ships. Moreover, the courts insist that they will look to the reality of the parties' relationship, not simply accept the language the parties have employed in their agreement.[239] The definition has been held to cover 'stocking plans', for instance. In *St Margaret's Trusts v Castle*[240] a finance company entered into a 'stocking agreement' with a car dealership in the form of an ordinary hire-purchase agreement. There was a clause prohibiting the dealer from selling vehicles until he had discharged debts due under the agreement. When a dishonest dealer sold to a *bona fide* purchaser, ignorant of the relationship between the finance company and the dealer, the former claimed that the dealer was unable to give good title by reason of the clause in the hire-purchase agreement. The Court of Appeal held that, looking at the reality of the transaction, the dealer was a mercantile agent under the Factors Act 1889 and could pass a good title to the *bona fide* purchaser.

The definition provisions demonstrate clearly that the Factors Act 1889 was intended **10.100** to confer protection on third parties who deal *bona fide* with mercantile agents acting without authority in a very wide range of circumstances. Thus, whereas 'goods' are defined in s 1(3) as comprising 'wares and merchandise', a 'document of title' includes:

> any bill of lading, dock warrant, warehouse-keeper's certificate, and warrant or order for the delivery of goods, and any other document used in the ordinary course of business as proof of the possession or control of goods, or authorising or purporting to authorise, either by endorsement or by delivery, the possessor of the document to transfer or receive goods thereby represented. (s 1(4))

The Act also gives a generous meaning to the term 'pledge', so as to encompass:

> any contract pledging, or giving a lien or security on, goods, whether in consideration of an original advance or of any further or continuing advance or of any pecuniary liability[241] (s 1(5))

---

237 [1927] 1 KB 393.
238 See *Weiner v Harris* [1910] 1 KB 285.
239 *Ibid.*
240 [1964] CLY 1685.
241 In *Waddington & Sons v Neale & Sons* (1907) 96 LT 786, where owners consigned goods to H, a mercantile agent, for sale on their behalf for cash or on the hire system, it was held that

and deems a pledge of documents of title to be a pledge of the goods (s 3).

*Powers of mercantile agents with respect to disposition of goods*

**10.101**   The most significant powers possessed by a party who qualifies as a 'mercantile agent' under s 1(1) are conferred by s 2(1), which provides:

> Where a mercantile agent is, with the consent of the owner, in possession of goods or of the documents of title to goods, any sale, pledge, or other disposition of the goods, made by him when acting in the ordinary course of business of a mercantile agent, shall, subject to the provisions of this Act, be as valid as if he were expressly authorised by the owner of the goods to make the same; provided that the person taking under the disposition acts in good faith, and has not at the time of the disposition notice that the person making the disposition has not authority to make the same.

*Owner must have confided the goods or documents to the agent in his capacity as mercantile agent*

**10.102**   Section 2(1) requires that the mercantile agent has possession of the goods or of documents of title relating to such goods and, furthermore, must have acquired possession of them in his capacity as mercantile agent. Thus, in *Staffs Motor Guarantee Ltd v British Wagon Co Ltd*[242] a car dealer, H, and a finance company, B, entered into a transaction whereby H sold his lorry to B, who then let the lorry back to H on hire-purchase. H, who was in possession of the lorry, fraudulently sold it to S, who was unaware of the true position. When H fell in arrears in respect of payments due to B under the hire-purchase agreement, B repossessed the lorry. Thereafter S sued B, claiming delivery up of the lorry or damages for its detention. S sought to argue that, because H was a mercantile agent within the meaning of s 1(1) of the 1889 Act, he had successfully passed a good title to S even though he in fact possessed no authority to do so. MacKinnon, LJ rejected this contention, stating:

> Because one happens to entrust his goods to a man who is in other respects a mercantile agent, but with whom he is dealing not as a mercantile agent but in a different capacity, I do not think that it is open to a third party who buys the goods from that man to say that they were in his possession as a mercantile agent and that therefore he had power to sell them to a purchaser and so give him a good title to them. The claimant must be able to assert not only that the goods were in the man's possession as a mercantile agent, but also that they were entrusted by the owner to him as a mercantile agent.[243]

---

when H in turn sent the goods to auctioneers for sale by auction, obtaining from them an advance upon the goods in contemplation of their sale, that did not constitute a 'pledge' within s 2(1) of the Act.

[242]   [1934] 2 KB 305.
[243]   *Ibid* at 313.

Here, H was not in possession of the lorry as a 'mercantile agent', but as a bailee. Therefore, H's sale of the lorry to S was not rendered valid as against the defendants by s 2(1) of the Factors Act.

**10.103** Adopting a point made by Channell J in *Oppenheimer v Frazer & Wyatt*,[244] MacKinnon, LJ stressed that under s 2(1) it is the consent of the owner of the goods to the possession of them by the mercantile agent *qua* mercantile agent that is 'the important part of the matter'. Indeed, Chapman, J was later to ridicule the contrary view in a judgment delivered on assize in *Astley Industrial Trust Ltd v Miller*:[245]

> [I]f I take my car into the local garage to have a puncture repaired ..., I would be at the risk of the garage not only purporting to sell it, but actually passing good title if, besides carrying out repairs and servicing for customers, they professed the business of buying and selling motor cars ... This would seem a startling conclusion. Or to go further to extremes: if my next-door neighbour (being in fact a motor dealer) came to me and said, 'My car has to go into dock for a fortnight. You are going on a cruise for your holidays. Would you, as a friend, lend me your car while you are away?' If, as one neighbour to another, I yielded to his importunity, I would, according to counsel's argument, be at risk of losing my car, merely because he happened to be a motor dealer, if he decided to flog it to some fly-by-night. At such a conclusion one's commonsense revolts.[246]

*The mercantile agent must have received the goods or documents 'with the consent of the owner'*

**10.104** This requirement will normally be easily satisfied if it can be shown that the owner handed the goods or documents over to the agent with a view to the agent's selling, pledging or otherwise disposing of them on behalf of the owner. Problems arise, however, if, for example, the owner has confided goods to an agent for some other purpose and the latter then fraudulently sells them to an innocent purchaser. In *Pearson v Rose & Young Ltd*[247] an owner handed his automobile over to a car dealer to see what offers could be obtained for it as and when he took delivery of a new car, ordered through the agent. The dealer obtained the registration book from the car's owner by a subterfuge, and the same day sold the car, along with its registration book, to an innocent third party. In answer to the third party's claim that he had not actually consented to the agent's having possession of the car, it was argued that the agent's fraudulent intentions did not frustrate the owner's consent. The Court of Appeal invoked the words of Scrutton, LJ in *Folkes v King*:[248]

---

[244] [1907] 2 KB 50.
[245] [1968] 2 All ER 36.
[246] *Ibid* at 40. See also *Pearson v Rose & Young Ltd* [1950] 2 All ER 1027, 1033 *per* Denning, LJ; *Stadium Finance Ltd v Robins* [1962] 2 All ER 633, 638 *per* Willmer, LJ.
[247] [1951] 1 KB 275.
[248] [1923] KB 282.

[W]here there is agreement on the person and the true owner intends to give him possession, it does not seem to me that the fact that the person apparently agreeing to accept an agency really means to disregard the agency, and act for his own benefit, destroys the consent of the true owner under the Factors Act. That Act intended to protect a purchaser in good faith carrying out an ordinary mercantile transaction with a person in the position of a mercantile agent. It does not do so completely, for it requires the purchaser to prove that the goods were in possession of the mercantile agent 'with the consent of the owner'. But it does not require the purchaser in addition to prove that the mercantile agent agreed both openly and secretly, ostensibly and really, to the terms on which the owner transferred possession to the mercantile agent. It appears to me to be enough to show that the true owner did intentionally deposit in the hands of the mercantile agent the goods in question.[249]

Denning, LJ considered that it was sufficient that the owner had consented to the agent's having possession of the goods for some purpose connected with his business as a mercantile agent. The Act demanded that emphasis be placed on the conduct of the owner in conferring possession upon the agent rather than upon the owner's exact state of mind when he did so:

That means that the owner must consent to the agent having them for a purpose which is in some way or other connected with his business as a mercantile agent. It may not actually be for sale. It may be for display or to get offers, or merely to put in his showroom; but there must be a consent to something of that kind before the owner can be deprived of his goods.[250]

**10.105** The term 'owner' is not necessarily restricted to someone who actually enjoys true rights of ownership, but stretches to a party without whose agreement the true owner could not dispose of the goods. In *Lloyds Bank Ltd v Bank of America National Trust and Savings Association*[251] a bank, L, had advanced money to S, receiving in exchange documents relating to goods which conferred on L an immediate right of sale. L handed the documents to S to sell the goods, S having signed trust receipts that constituted them trustees for L. S, unknown to L, pledged the documents with the defendant bank, A, which acted in good faith. When S went into liquidation, L sued A for the return of the documents or damages for their detention or conversion. The Court of Appeal held that because L were effectively 'owners' of the goods represented by the documents within s 2(1) of the Factors Act 1889, to the extent that they could authorize their sale, and because S were mercantile agents within

---

[249] *Ibid* at 305. Thus, in *Gray v Smith* [2014] 2 All ER (Comm) 359 at [124], once Cooke, J had found that the purported mercantile agent was in fact the legal owner of the multi-million-pound McLaren racing car in dispute, it necessarily followed that s 2(1) of the Factors Act 1889 had no application in passing property to a *bona fide* third party purchaser. Cp *Belvoir Finance Co Ltd v Harold G Cole & Co Ltd* [1969] 1 WLR 1877, where Donaldson, J held that because a car dealer only held cars subject to the hire-purchase agreements it could not be established that they were in possession of the cars with the consent of the plaintiffs under s 2(1) of the Act.

[250] [1951] 1 KB 275, 288 *per* Denning, LJ.

[251] [1938] 2 KB 147.

the terms of the statutory definition, S's pledge of documents to A in the ordinary course of their business was valid. For good measure, the court added that, even had L not had an immediate power of sale, the result would have been the same, as in those circumstances L and S would together have been the 'owners'.

*The mercantile agent must have disposed of the goods 'when acting in the ordinary business of a mercantile agent'*

The courts have considered this requirement in a number of cases. Notably, in **10.106** *Oppenheimer v Attenborough & Son*[252] the Court of Appeal had to decide whether the words, 'when acting in the ordinary business of a mercantile agent', are to be read as applying to mercantile agents generally or whether the customary practices of the specific trade or profession in which the relevant agent engages are to be taken into account. In *Oppenheimer*, O handed diamonds over to S, a diamond broker of his acquaintance, to show to potential purchasers. Contrary to instructions, S pledged the diamonds with pawnbrokers, A, for an advance of money to himself, sending a note to O to the effect that the diamonds were sold. This happened more than once before S's dishonesty was discovered. A was aware that it was unheard of for diamond brokers to be employed to pledge diamonds entrusted to them. When O sued A to recover the parcels of diamonds, the latter claimed that, although unauthorized, S's pledges were valid under s 2(1) of the Factors Act. The central question for the Court of Appeal was whether it could be said that a disposition, which was not customary within a particular commercial *milieu*, could nevertheless be said to have been effected by a mercantile agent 'when acting in the ordinary business of a mercantile agent'. The Court determined that when authority is conferred on someone who qualifies as a mercantile agent under the Act and who is in possession of goods with the consent of the owner, the authority to pledge the goods when acting in the ordinary course of business of a mercantile agent, is a general authority given to every mercantile agent, and is not restricted by the existence in any particular trade of a custom that a mercantile agent employed in that trade to sell goods has no authority to pledge them. As Buckley, LJ explained:

> The plaintiff's argument involves our reading there 'of such mercantile agent,' or 'of a mercantile agent in such a trade as that in which he carries on business.' I do not think that is the meaning of the expression. I think it means, 'acting in such a way as a mercantile agent acting in the ordinary course of business of a mercantile agent would act'; that is to say, within business hours, at a proper place of business, and in other respects in the ordinary way in which a mercantile agent would act, so that there is nothing to lead the pledgee to suppose that anything wrong is being done, or to give him notice that the disposition is one which the mercantile agent had no authority to make.[253]

---

[252] [1908] 1 KB 221.
[253] [1908] 1 KB 221, 230–1.

**10.107**   The Act serves to protect third parties who have dealt with the mercantile agent whenever the latter has conducted himself in the manner in which such an agent might generally be expected to act. This may require proof. In *Newtons of Wembley Ltd v Williams*[254] for instance, B bought a car from a mercantile agent in Warren Street for cash. Evidence having been adduced to show that 'in this somewhat unusual market' it was the established practice to conduct cash sales of second-hand cars, the Court of Appeal concluded that the sale to B had been made in the ordinary course of business of a mercantile agent.[255] On the other hand, in *Lloyds & Scottish Finance Ltd v Williamson*[256] Salmon, LJ seemed prepared to accept that an agent who instructed the purchaser of a motor car to pay the purchase price over to a creditor to whom he owed money was intrinsically an unusual transaction which might not have been within the ordinary course of business.[257]

*When a mercantile agent's unauthorized disposition will be treated as valid*

**10.108**   A mercantile agent's unauthorized disposition will be treated as valid provided that the third party 'has not at the time of the disposition notice that the person making the disposition has not authority to make the same.' It is for the third party to prove that he acted in good faith. Although actual notice is frequently required in commercial transactions, the absence of good faith may be inferred from the circumstances. In *Janesich v George Attenborough & Son*,[258] for instance, Hamilton, J suggested that a pledge at an unusual rate of interest could provide evidence for an inference that the pledgee had notice that the pledgor/mercantile agent lacked the necessary authority to effect the pledge. Similarly, in *Pearson v Rose & Young Ltd*,[259] whilst acknowledging that a vehicle log-book is not a document of title, merely 'the best evidence of title', Denning, LJ strongly indicated that without it a mercantile agent could not dispose of an automobile in the ordinary business of a mercantile agent and *ex hypothesi* a purchaser could not acquire the car in good faith.[260]

**10.109**   The Act's requirements are somewhat technical, and the courts interpret them fairly literally. Unless all the requirements discussed above are satisfied, s 2(1) will not therefore serve to validate an otherwise unauthorized transaction. As the majority of the Court of Appeal's decision in *Beverley Acceptances Ltd v Oakley*[261] reminds us, even if one can show the presence of an owner and a mercantile agent, and that agent can be shown to have had possession of the goods, s 2(1) contemplates that

---

[254] [1965] 1 QB 560.
[255] *Ibid* at 575.
[256] [1965] 1 WLR 404.
[257] *Ibid* at 410–11.
[258] (1910) 102 LT 605, 606.
[259] [1951] 1 KB 275, 289.
[260] See esp pp 289–90. Some would doubt, however, whether possession of the log-book should in fact be relevant to the purchaser's good faith.
[261] [1982] RTR 417.

the 'possession' to which the owner has consented and the 'disposition' by the agent have to be simultaneous in order for the agent's unauthorized act to be treated as valid. *Beverley Acceptances*, however, did produce a sharp division of opinion within the Court of Appeal over how liberally the Factors Act ought to be interpreted. Whereas Donaldson and Slade, JJ were content to take the wording of the statute at face value, Lord Denning, MR took a more commodious view, noting that the law increasingly required owners to take responsibility for their actions and, more particularly, held them liable if their fault resulted in an innocent third party being deceived:[262]

> Such a duty arises by statute in cases under the Factors Acts. It also arises in modern times in the course of the development of our commercial law. The old maxim— *nemo dat quod non habet*—no longer prevails. It has been replaced by the modern principle which gives protection to a person who takes in good faith and for value without notice … This means that we need no longer interpret the Factors Acts by the letter. We can go by the spirit which lies behind them. Modern law has made them a particular application of general principle.[263]

The courts have not chosen to follow Lord Denning, MR's audacious lead when construing the Factors Act 1889.

---

[262] Eg, *Mercantile Credit Co Ltd v Hamblin* [1965] 2 QB 242, 275 *per* Pearson, LJ.

[263] [1982] RTR 417, 426. In *Pearson v Rose & Young Ltd* [1951] 1 KB 275, at p 290 Denning, LJ had already indicated that, as he read the statute, 'the legislature intended the courts to make every reasonable presumption in favour of the innocent purchaser.'

# 11

# THE TORTIOUS LIABILITIES
# OF PRINCIPAL AND AGENT

Both principal and agent may incur personal liability for torts they commit. **11.01** Additionally, because an agent may also technically be the employee of his principal, the liabilities of principals for the torts of their agents overlap to a considerable degree with the liability of an employer for the torts of his employee. The interrelationship between these two heads of liability is not always easy to delineate. The important question is, in what precise circumstances will a principal be held liable for tortious acts of his agent that harm third parties?

## The Personal Liability of the Agent in Tort

### An agent will be personally liable for torts committed that inflict damage or loss on a third party

As in the case of employees, an agent is personally liable for torts he commits in the **11.02** course of his agency that occasion damage to a third party, irrespective of whether the agent was acting within or outside his principal's authority. In *Standard Chartered Bank v Pakistan National Shipping Corp (Nos 2 and 4)*[1] a managing director, M,

---

[1] [2003] 1 AC 959.

agreed with the seller's shipping agent and the shipowners to issue a bill of lading which was falsely dated so as to appear to comply with the condition of credit that the goods be shipped by a certain date. The House of Lords held that M could not evade personal liability for fraud simply because he had acted within the scope of his employment and was committing the fraud on behalf of his employer. In this case M was being sued for his own fraud and, once all the elements of the tort were established against him, he was liable for the loss that the claimant had incurred as a consequence. Lord Hoffmann emphasized: 'No one can escape liability for his fraud by saying: "I wish to make it clear that I am committing this fraud on behalf of someone else and I am not to be personally liable." '[2] Lord Rodger of Earlsferry, too, made clear that it is no defence to claim to have been acting tortiously on behalf of another:

> My Lords, the maxim *culpa tenet suos auctores* may not be the end, but it is the beginning of wisdom in these matters. Where someone commits a tortious act, he at least will be liable for the consequences; whether others are liable also depends on the circumstances.[3]

**11.03** On occasion, an employee or agent may not be held personally liable for actions which otherwise might carry tortious liability. For instance, the agent or employee may have been acting on the instructions of a superior, who may well be liable instead. Mackinnon, LJ furnished an example in *Gold v Essex County Council*:[4]

> The master will not be liable for the act of his servant if he is only doing, without personal negligence, that which he is directed to do ['under the control of some third party']. An example is when a captain by command of the commodore goes at eight knots in a dense fog. His employer is not liable for a resulting collision, since the servant is not negligent, and if anyone is negligent it is the commodore for whose acts the shipowner is not liable.[5]

---

[2] *Ibid* at at [22].

[3] *Ibid* at [40]. See also *Barclay Pharmaceuticals Ltd v Waypharm LP* [2012] EWHC 306 (Comm), esp at [243]–[244] *per* Gloster, J.

[4] [1942] 2 KB 293.

[5] *Ibid* at 305. In some sort, this situation in tort is distantly akin to the doctrine of 'ministerial receipt' that an agent may invoke when sued by a third party, say, for money paid over to the agent by mistake and received by the latter on the principal's behalf. Millett, LJ defined ministerial receipt in *Portman BS v Hamlyn Taylor Neck* [1998] PNLR 664, at 669: 'The general rule is that money paid (e.g. by mistake) to an agent who has accounted to his principal without notice of the claim cannot be recovered from the agent but only from the principal ... At common law the agent recipient is regarded as a mere conduit for the money, which is treated as paid to the principal, not to the agent. The doctrine is therefore not so much a defence as a means of identifying the proper party to be sued. It does not, for example, avail the agent of an undisclosed principal.' In the banking context, where ministerial receipt is most often encountered, the critical point occurs when the crediting of funds can no longer be reversed. The authorities, however, may not be finally settled upon the question when exactly this point is reached in the various types of banking transaction: see, eg, *Jones v Churcher* [2009] 2 Lloyd's Rep 94 esp at [69]–[78] *per* HHJ Havelock-Allan, QC.

Equally, as has already been noted, in some cases an otherwise wrongful act of the agent may be rendered lawful by the subsequent ratification of his actions by the principal.[6]

## Common Forms of Tortious Liability affecting Agency

### Negligent misstatement

Most commonly, an agent's tortious liability will flow from a negligent misstate- **11.04** ment. Although an agent may commit a wide range of torts, owing to the fact that his main task is to bring principal and agent into direct relations, the agent's torts typically involve the making of false representations to third parties. Most frequently, this can give rise to liability either (i) under the rule originally laid down in *Hedley Byrne & Co Ltd v Heller & Partners*,[7] (ii) under the tort of deceit, or (iii) if a contract has been concluded and the agent is a party to the contract,[8] also under the provisions of the Misrepresentation Act 1967.

### *Liability under* Hedley Byrne

In *Hedley Byrne & Co Ltd v Heller & Partners* the House of Lords resolved that 'if **11.05** someone possessed of a special skill undertakes, quite irrespective of contract, to apply that skill for the assistance of another person who relies upon such skill, a duty of care will arise.'[9] It made no difference that words, rather than actions, were the means whereby economic damage resulted. If, within a particular sphere of economic activity:

> a person is so placed that others could reasonably rely upon his judgment or his skill or upon his ability to make careful inquiry, a person takes it upon himself to give information or advice to, or allows his information or advice to be passed on to, another person who, as he knows or should know, will place reliance upon it, then a duty of care will arise.[10]

An assumption of responsibility by the defendant, then, was integral to liability **11.06** for negligently caused economic loss under *Hedley Byrne*.[11] Deciding when an

---

[6] See, eg, *Buron v Denman* (1848) 2 Exch 167; para **6.03**.
[7] [1964] AC 465.
[8] See esp paras **10.08–10.15**.
[9] [1964] AC 465, 502–3 *per* Lord Morris of Borth-y-Gest.
[10] *Ibid* at 503 *per* Lord Morris of Borth-y-Gest.
[11] The test of whether a party has assumed responsibility for his words is objective and does not depend upon the subjective state of mind or intention of claimant or defendant: *Williams v Natural Life Health Foods Ltd* [1998] 1 WLR 830, 836 *per* Lord Steyn. It might be added that, according to Arden, LJ in *Precis (521) plc v William M Mercer Ltd* [2005] PNLR 511 at [24], the precise limits of the concept of assumption of responsibility are still in a state of development and there is no exhaustive list of guiding principles to help a court determine when an assumption of responsibility arises.

assumption of responsibility has actually taken place has never been easy to determine. The courts have regard to all the circumstances. In *BCCI (Overseas) Ltd v Price Waterhouse (No 2)*[12] Sir Brian Neill derived assistance by enumerating the following potentially relevant factors: the precise relationship between adviser and advisee; the precise circumstances in which the information relied upon came into existence; the precise circumstances in which that information was communicated, considering the purpose or purposes of the communication both as seen by the adviser and as seen by the advisee, the degree of reliance which the adviser intended or should reasonably have anticipated would be placed on its accuracy and the reliance in fact placed on it; the presence or absence of other advisers; and the opportunity for disclaimers. Subsequent courts have made use of this list.[13]

**11.07**  Liability for economic loss under *Hedley Byrne* may be avoided, for instance, if the defendant's advice is delivered on an informal occasion or if an adequate disclaimer accompanies it.[14] Such circumstances serve to counter any claim of a voluntary assumption of responsibility.

**11.08**  The original *Hedley Byrne* principle has undergone persistent refinement. Courts have variously applied three different tests in determining liability in negligence for pure financial loss. These tests were summarized by Lord Bingham of Cornhill in *Commissioners of Customs and Excise v Barclays Bank plc*:[15]

> *The first* is whether the defendant assumed responsibility for what he said and did *vis-à-vis* the claimant, or is to be treated by the law as having done so. The *second* is commonly known as the threefold test: whether loss to the claimant was a reasonably foreseeable consequence of what the defendant did or failed to do; whether the relationship between the parties was one of sufficient proximity; and whether in all the circumstances it is fair, just and reasonable to impose a duty of care on the defendant towards the claimant ... *Third* is the incremental test, ... approved by Lord Bridge of Harwich in *Caparo Industries plc v Dickman*,[16] that:
>
> > It is preferable ... that the law should develop novel categories of negligence incrementally and by analogy with established categories, rather than by a massive extension of a *prima facie* duty of care restrained only by indefinable considerations which ought to negative, or to reduce or limit the scope of the duty or the class of person to whom it is owed.[17]

---

[12] [1998] PNLR 564, 587–8.

[13] Eg, *Precis (521) plc v William M Mercer Ltd* [2005] PNLR 511 at [24] *per* Arden, LJ.

[14] Eg, *Hedley Byrne & Co Ltd v Heller & Partners Ltd* [1964] AC 465, 492 *per* Lord Reid.

[15] [2007] 1 AC 181.

[16] [1990] 2 AC 605, 618.

[17] [2007] 1 AC 181 at [4]. These principles were helpfully reviewed by Lord Clarke of Stow-cum-Ebony, MR in *Patchett v Swimming Pool & Allied Trades Association Ltd* [2010] 2 All ER (Comm), 138 at [12]–[23]. See also Watts, *Principals' Tortious Liability for Agents' Negligent Statements—Is 'Authority' Necessary?* (2012) 128 LQR 260, 274: '[U]ntil someone comes up with a *principled* and workable alternative ... judges should continue to treat an assumption of responsibility as the foundation of liability for negligent statements.'

That said, it would be idle to pretend that the three tests provide straightforward **11.09** answers to the question whether or not, in a novel situation, a party owes a duty of care.[18] As Lord Bridge of Harwich made clear in *Caparo*, the various concepts are incapable of precise definition such as would give them utility as practical tests:

> [They] amount in effect to little more than convenient labels to attach to the features of different specific situations which, on a detailed examination of all the circumstances, the law recognises pragmatically as giving rise to a duty of care of a given scope. Whilst recognising, of course, the importance of the underlying general principles common to the whole field of negligence, I think the law has now moved in the direction of attaching greater significance to the more traditional categorisation of distinct and recognisable situations as guides to the existence, the scope and the limits of the varied duties of care which the law imposes.[19]

The concepts have been variously described as 'a blunt instrument' and mere 'labels … commonly used by lawyers [to] help steer the mind through the task in hand', even if they do amount to 'progress of a sort.'[20] Proximity, it is acknowledged, operates primarily as a 'control mechanism'[21] avoiding the risk of 'liability in an indeterminate amount for an indeterminate time to an indeterminate class'[22] for negligently caused economic loss. In practice, the three tests of liability overlap and are not to be applied in isolation to one another.[23]

Notably, following the decision of the House of Lords in *Caparo Industries plc v* **11.10** *Dickman*,[24] the existence of a *Hedley Byrne* duty of care was to be conditional upon the third party establishing not merely the necessary degree of 'proximity'—or what Lord Atkin famously termed the duty owed by a 'neighbour' in law,[25] but also upon the court being satisfied that the imposition of that duty was 'fair, just and reasonable.'[26] This approach informed Sir Donald Nicholls V-C's judgment in *Gran Gelato Ltd v Richcliff (Group) Ltd*.[27] A solicitor wrongly informed a prospective purchaser of the underlease of a basement that, to the lessor's knowledge, no interests affecting

---

[18] *Commissioners of Customs and Excise v Barclays Bank plc* [2007] 1 AC 181 at [6] *per* Lord Bingham of Cornhill.

[19] [1990] 2 AC 605, 618.

[20] *Commissioners of Customs and Excise v Barclays Bank plc* [2007] 1 AC 181 at [71] *per* Lord Walker of Gestingthorpe.

[21] *Caparo Industries plc v Dickman* [1990] 2 AC 605, 620–1 *per* Lord Bridge of Harwich.

[22] See *Ultramares Corporation v Touche*, 174 NE 441, 444 (1931) *per* Cardozo, CJ.

[23] *Commissioners of Customs and Excise v Barclays Bank plc* [2007] 1 AC 181 at [6].

[24] *Caparo Industries plc v Dickman* [1990] 2 AC 605.

[25] *M'Alister (or Donoghue) (Pauper) v Stevenson* [1932] AC 562, 580 *per* Lord Atkin.

[26] *Caparo Industries plc v Dickman* [1990] 2 AC 605, 617–18 *per* Lord Bridge of Harwich: 'What emerges is that, in addition to the foreseeability of damage, necessary ingredients in any situation giving rise to a duty of care are that there should exist between the party owing the duty and the party to whom it is owed a relationship characterised by the law as one of "proximity" or "neighbourhood" and that the situation should be one in which the court considers it fair, just and reasonable that the law should impose a duty of a given scope upon the one party for the benefit of the other.'

[27] [1992] Ch 560.

superior leasehold titles would inhibit the tenant's enjoyment of the property. The parties agreed that the principal was liable to the purchaser for his agent's misstatement. However, owing to the fact that it was questionable whether the lessor would be in a position to satisfy any substantial judgment debt, the question confronting the court was whether the solicitor, acting for the seller of an interest in property, owed a duty of care to the buyer when responding to the latter's preliminary inquiries. The Vice-Chancellor held that in normal conveyancing transactions a solicitor, acting as the agent of the vendor, did not owe a separate duty of care to the purchaser. More particularly, he argued that whilst there was no difficulty in establishing the necessary degree of proximity and reliance, it was sufficient that the law provides the buyer with a remedy against the seller if answers to the latter's inquiries are given without due care. As it happens, the law does in fact supply such a remedy because in the ordinary way the vendor's solicitor has implied authority to answer on his behalf the traditional pre-contract inquiries made on behalf of the buyer, and also because, finally:

> [I]n the field of negligent misrepresentation caution should be exercised before the law takes the step of concluding, in any particular context, that an agent acting within the scope of his authority on behalf of a known principal, himself owes to third parties a duty of care independent of the duty of care he owes to his principal. There will be cases where it is fair, just and reasonable that there should be such a duty. But, in general, in a case where the principal himself owes a duty of care to the third party, the existence of a further duty of care, owed by the agent to the third party, is not necessary for the reasonable protection of the latter.[28]

**11.11** As emerges from the extract from Sir Donald Nicholls, V-C's judgment quoted in the preceding paragraph, the additional requirement that the imposition of a duty of care be 'fair, just and reasonable' does not signify that agents will inevitably escape liability for negligent misstatement. In *Smith v Eric S Bush (a firm)*,[29] for example, liability was imposed because a mortgagor would have been left without a remedy against the vendor of property had he not been allowed to sue the surveyor and valuer. In Sir Donald Nicholls, V-C's words:

> Good reason, therefore, should exist before the law imposes a duty when the agent already owes to his principal a duty which covers the same ground and the principal is responsible to the third party for his agent's shortcomings.[30]

---

[28] *Ibid* at 570. Thus, in *Kingspan Environmental Ltd v Borealis A/S and Borealis UK Ltd* [2012] EWHC 1147 (Comm), since liability for negligent statements made on behalf of a disclosed principal rests on the principal and not the agent, Christopher Clarke, J was not prepared to find that the agent could be taken to have assumed a responsibility of its own separate from that of its principal. Not only was there no evidence to suggest to the third party that the agent had assumed this liability expressly. It could also be said: 'There is nothing special about the position of Borealis UK as a commercial agent in the present case to give rise to a duty. The agent has no liability under the contract and it would be anomalous if that which could not be achieved in contract could, nevertheless, be achieved in tort. I do not regard it as a sufficient reason for imposing the duty that any claim against [the principal] is subject to contractual limitations. If anything the fact that the imposition of a tortious duty would circumvent the limitations is a reason not to impose one' (at [514]).

[29] [1990] 1 AC 831.

[30] *Gran Gelato Ltd v Richcliff (Group) Ltd* [1992] Ch 560, 571.

More recently, however, in *Henderson v Merrett Syndicates Ltd*[31] the House of Lords **11.12** admitted the possibility both of situations in which the 'fair, just and reasonable' requirement could be dispensed with and of concurrent liability in the agent in both tort and contract. In *Henderson* Lloyd's had incurred vast insurance liabilities following an unprecedented series of natural disasters in the United States. Lloyd's called upon its syndicates of names to indemnify them for these losses. The names, in turn, brought suit against the underwriting agents who ran the syndicates for negligent mismanagement of the investment fund, and against sub-agents retained by their agents. In *Henderson* the sub-agents were held liable in tort. Lord Goff of Chieveley suggested that, although use of the concept of 'assumption of respon- sibility' as a means of determining when a duty of care for economic loss caused by negligence arose and for limiting the range of potential claimants has been criticized,[32] in the kind of situation present in *Henderson* 'there seems no reason why recourse should not be had to the concept' of assumption of responsibility. Lord Goff continued:

> Furthermore, especially in a context concerned with a liability which may arise under a contract or in a situation 'equivalent to contract,' it must be expected that an objective test will be applied when asking the question whether, in a particular case, responsibility should be held to have been assumed by the defendant to the plaintiff.[33]

Moreover, unlike other situations in which *Hedley Byrne* liability or a duty of care is in question, 'there should be no need to embark upon any further enquiry whether it is "fair, just and reasonable" to impose liability for economic loss.'[34]

Neuberger, LJ carefully reviewed Lord Goff's speech in *Henderson* in *Riyad Bank* **11.13** *v AHLI United Bank*.[35] His analysis, as later explained by HHJ Stephen Davies in *Robinson v PE Jones (Contractors) Ltd*, ran as follows:

> [T]he correct principle ... is that there may be concurrent liability in cases involving a direct contract for the provision of advice between A and B, not that there will be concurrent liability in all such cases save where the contractual context is inconsistent with such liability.... [A] concurrent duty of care in tort may arise from a contractual relationship, which itself may be a general relationship or a specific relationship, in circumstances where:
> (a) One party has a special skill (an expression which has a broad meaning, extend- ing to cases where he has a special knowledge); and
> (b) That party agrees to perform services (which are not limited to the provision of information and advice, nor to the performance of professional services), in

---

[31] [1994] 2 AC 145.
[32] Eg, *Smith v Eric S Bush (a firm), Harris v Wyre Forest DC* [1989] 2 All ER 514, 536 *per* Lord Griffiths; *Caparo Industries plc v Dickman* [1980] 1 All ER 568, 582–3 *per* Lord Roskill.
[33] [1994] 2 AC 145, 181.
[34] *Ibid* at 181.
[35] [2006] 2 Lloyd's Rep 292, esp at [47].

circumstances where there is an express or implied obligation to exercise reasonable care and skill whilst providing those services.

(c) Considered objectively, those circumstances disclose both an assumption of responsibility by that party to the other for the performance of those services, and reliance by the other party.

(d) The contractual relationship is not inconsistent with the duty.[36]

**11.14** In *Henderson* the House of Lords allowed claims in both contract and tort, permitting some of the names to claim in tort, thereby avoiding the three-year limitation period within which an action must be brought in contract.[37] Arguably, this blurs the distinction between the two species of liability:

> [A]n assumption of responsibility ... may give rise to a tortious duty of care irrespective of whether there is a contractual relationship between the parties, and in consequence, unless his contract precludes him from doing so, the plaintiff, who has available to him concurrent remedies in contract and tort, may choose that remedy that appears to him to be the most advantageous.[38]

If the correct circumstances are present, it would appear that an agent liable to the third party in contract may also be concurrently liable in tort, and the third party will have the option whether to hold the former liable in contract or tort, whichever chances to be more advantageous to the third party.

**11.15** *Hedley Byrne* liability eludes crisp definition. In *Caparo Industries plc v Dickman*, however, Lord Oliver of Aylmerton did deliver the following useful, if tentative, summary of the *Hedley Byrne* principles:

> What can be deduced from the *Hedley Byrne* case, therefore, is that the necessary relationship between the maker of a statement or giver of advice ('the adviser') and the recipient who acts in reliance upon it ('the advisee') may typically be held to exist where
> (1) the advice is required for a purpose, whether particularly specified or generally described, which is made known, either actually or inferentially, to the adviser at the time when the advice is given;
> (2) the adviser knows, either actually or inferentially, that his advice will be communicated to the advisee, either specifically or as a member of an ascertainable class, in order that it should be used by the advisee for that purpose;
> (3) it is known either actually or inferentially, that the advice so communicated is likely to be acted upon by the advisee for that purpose without independent inquiry; and
> (4) it is so acted upon by the advisee to his detriment.

---

[36] [2010] EWHC 102 (TCC); [2010] TCLR 3 at [56].

[37] In so doing, the House of Lords disregarded Lord Scarman's foreboding in *Tai Hing Cotton Mill Ltd v Liu Chong Hing Bank Ltd* [1986] AC 80 that 'there is nothing advantageous to the law's development in searching for a liability in tort where the parties are in a contractual relationship.'

[38] [1995] 2 AC 145, 194 *per* Lord Goff of Chieveley.

That is not, of course, to suggest that these conditions are either conclusive or exclusive, but merely that the actual decision in the case does not warrant any broader propositions.[39]

*Liability in deceit*

As Lord Bramwell explained in *Derry v Peek*,[40] adapting a definition originally proposed in the Court of Appeal by Cotton, LJ, the tort of deceit is committed whenever a person makes a statement to be acted on by others which is false, and which is known by him to be false, or is made by him recklessly, or without care whether it is true or false, '[f]or a man who makes a statement without care and regard for its truth or falsity commits a fraud. He is a rogue.'[41]  **11.16**

It is notorious that courts will not readily assume that a fraud has been perpetrated. **11.17** They often point out that '[f]raud is a serious allegation and therefore the cogency of the evidence required to discharge the burden of proof must reflect the seriousness of the charge.'[42] Certainly, where a serious allegation of dishonesty had been made, a court will set out from the premiss that it is inherently improbable that such an act occurred; cogent evidence will be required to persuade the court that fraud has actually taken place.[43] As Lord Nicholls of Birkenhead observed in *Re H*:

> The balance of probability standard means that a court is satisfied an event occurred if the court considers that, on the evidence, the occurrence of the event was more likely than not. When assessing the probabilities the court will have in mind as a factor, to whatever extent is appropriate in the particular case, that the more serious the allegation the less likely it is that the event occurred and, hence, the stronger should be the evidence before the court concludes that the allegation is established on the balance of probability. Fraud is usually less likely than negligence ... Although the result is much the same, this does not mean that where a serious allegation is in issue the standard of proof required is higher. It means only that the inherent probability or improbability of an event is itself a matter to be taken into account when weighing the probabilities and deciding whether, on balance, the event occurred. The more improbable the event, the stronger must be the evidence that it did occur before, on the balance of probability, its occurrence will be established.[44]

*Liability under the Misrepresentation Act 1967*

If a false representation has induced the third party to enter into a contract, **11.18** liability for contractual misrepresentation may also arise. Liability under the

---

[39] [1990] 2 AC 605, 638.

[40] (1889) LR 14 App Cas 337.

[41] *Ibid* at 350.

[42] *Maersk Sealand v Far East Trading Côte d'Ivoire* [2004] EWHC 2929 (Comm) at [8] *per* Nigel Teare, QC.

[43] Eg, *LPMG Ltd v Stapleford Commercials Ltd* [2006] EWHC 3753 (Ch) at [85]ff *per* HHJ Williams, QC.

[44] [1996] AC 563, 586.

Misrepresentation Act 1967, s 2(1) for negligent misrepresentation will in the majority of cases exclusively concern the liability of the principal as only the latter will be party to the contract. As Mustill, J pointed out in *The Skopas*, there would be no sense in imposing an additional liability on an agent who is not a party to the contract he has negotiated on the principal's behalf.[45] However, if the agent has contracted in such a manner as to engage his personal liability under the contract, he becomes 'another party thereto' within the terms of s 2(1) and may be liable in damages to the third party for what is loosely termed 'negligent misrepresentation' inducing the contract. Owing to the peculiar phraseology of s 2(1)[46] the measure of damages in negligent misrepresentation, where the defendant is unable to prove on a balance of probabilities that 'he had reasonable ground to believe and did believe up to the time the contract was made the facts represented were true', is identical to the measure of damages in the case of fraud:[47] namely, 'all the actual damage directly flowing from [ie, caused by] entering into the transaction.'[48]

## The Tortious Liability of the Principal

### A principal is personally liable for torts which he has authorized his agent to commit

**11.19**  Not surprisingly, if a principal personally authorizes, orders, or ratifies his agent's tortious act, that principal will be personally liable. It is as though he had personally committed the tort.[49] The states of mind of principal and agent, however, need not be identical. The principal may act deceitfully through an innocent agent. Rolfe, B, in *Cornfoot v Fowke*[50]—a case in which an agent sold a house which, unknown to the purchaser who had been assured that nothing was wrong with the house, stood next door to a brothel—indicated that the principal's liability in deceit could be

---

[45] *Resolute Maritime Inc v Nippon Karji Kyokai. The Skopas* [1983] 1 Lloyd's Rep 431, 433.

[46] '... if the person making the misrepresentation would be liable to damages in respect thereof had the misrepresentation been made fraudulently, *that person shall be so liable ...*' (emphasis added).

[47] *Royscot Trust Ltd v Rogerson* [1991] 2 QB 297. This construction of the provision has attracted considerable critical comment: eg, R Hooley (1991) 107 LQR 547; I Brown and A Chandler [1992] LMCLQ 40. It even appears to have had a distorting effect, echoing the courts' reluctance to find fraud proven. In *Avon Insurance plc v Swire Fraser Ltd* [2000] 1 All ER (Comm) 573, esp at p 633, Rix, J observed of s 2(1): 'Since that is the law which binds me, it ought in my view to follow that, where there is room for an exercise of judgement, *a misrepresentation should not too easily be found.*'

[48] *Doyle v Olby* [1969] 2 QB 158, 167 *per* Lord Denning, MR. See further *Smith v New Court Securities* [1997] AC 254, 266–7 *per* Lord Browne-Wilkinson; *4EngLtd v Harper* [2009] Ch 91 at [54]–[55] *per* David Richards, J; *Parabola Investments Ltd v Browallia Cal Ltd* [2009] 2 All ER (Comm) 589 at [180]ff *per* Flaux, J.

[49] See, eg, *Monaghan v Taylor* (1886) 2 TLR 685.

[50] (1840) 6 M&W 358.

wider than that of his agent, encompassing situations where, for instance, a principal acquiesces in a false representation by omitting to enlighten the agent as to the true state of affairs:

> If the [principal], knowing of the nuisance, expressly authorized [his agent] to state that it did not exist, or to make any statement of similar import; or if he purposely employed an agent, ignorant of the truth, in order that such agent might innocently make a false statement believing it to be true, and might so deceive the party with whom he was dealing, in either of these cases he would be guilty of a fraud.[51]

Conversely, if the principal innocently utters a false statement, even if the agent happens to know the true facts, the principal will not be liable for deceit. Both parties' states of mind will need to be examined. As Devlin, J said in *Armstrong v Strain*:[52]

> You may add knowledge to knowledge, or, as Slesser, LJ put it, state of mind to state of mind. But you cannot add an innocent state of mind to an innocent state of mind and get as a result a dishonest state of mind.[53]

### A principal is vicariously liable for torts committed by his agent in the course of employment

If the agent is also the employee/servant of his principal, according to standard **11.20** tortious principles the principal will be vicariously liable for the torts of his agent if they were committed in the course of his employment.[54] The House of Lords reviewed when a servant could be said to be acting within the course of his employment in *Dubai Aluminium Co Ltd v Salaam*.[55] In that case both Lord Nicholls and Lord Millett stressed that vicarious liability rests on an underlying legal policy that recognizes that carrying on a business enterprise necessarily involves risks to others. Lord Millett asserted, 'vicarious liability is a loss-distribution device based

---

[51] *Ibid* at 370. See also *Occidental Worldwide Investment Corp v Skibs A/s Avanti, Skibs A/s Glarona, Skibs A/s Navalis. The Sibven and the Sibotre* [1976] 1 Lloyd's Rep 293, esp at p 321 *per* Kerr, J. Had the agent been aware of the deceit, he too would have been liable, and principal and agent would have been liable as joint tortfeasors.

[52] (1951) 51 TLR 856.

[53] *Ibid* at 872.

[54] As recently as 2004, in *Bernard v Att Gen of Jamaica* [2005] IRLR 398 at [21]–[23], Lord Steyn may well have warned that vicarious liability is a principle of strict liability that needs to be kept within clear limits and that is 'not infinitely extendable'. However, whilst the relationship that gives rise to vicarious liability will in the great majority of cases be that of an employer and an employee operating under a contract of employment, in *Various Claimants v Catholic Child Welfare Society* [2012] 3 WLR 1319 the Supreme Court has held that where a relationship between the parties wears many of the elements—and certainly all the essential elements—of the relationship between employer and employee, the relationship between the parties (*in specie*, Christian lay brothers and the institute to which they belonged) may be one capable of giving rise to vicarious liability. See also *E v Province of Our Lady of Charity* [2013] 2 WLR 958.

[55] [2003] 2 AC 366. See also Lord Steyn's speech in *Lister v Hensley Hall Ltd* [2002] 1 AC 215 at [28], where he adopted the seemingly laxer notion that employers were to be held liable if 'it would be fair and just to hold the employers vicariously liable.'

on social and economic policy'. Lord Nicholls, with whom three of the other Law Lords concurred, emphasized that, for that reason, liability for agents should not be strictly confined to acts done with the employer's authority. Authority not being the touchstone, the best general test is that the wrongful conduct must be so closely connected with acts the employee was authorized to do that the wrongful conduct may fairly and properly be regarded as done by the employee in the course of the employee's employment.[56] Lords Millett and Nicholls considered that, although it has its limitations, Salmond's general approach remains useful:

> Take a case where an employee does an act of a type for which he is employed but, perhaps through a misplaced excess of zeal, he does so dishonestly. He seeks to pro-mote his employer's interests, in the sphere in which he is employed, but using dis-honest means. Not surprisingly, the courts have held that in such a case the employer may be liable to the injured third party just as much as in a case where the employee acted negligently. Whether done negligently or dishonestly the wrongful act com-prised a wrongful and unauthorised mode of doing an act authorised by the em-ployer, in the oft-repeated language of the 'Salmond' formulation: see Salmond, *Law of Torts* (1907) 1st ed, p 83. As Willes J said, in *Barwick v English Joint Stock Bank*:[57] 'It is true, [the master] has not authorised the particular act, but he has put the agent in his place to do that class of acts, and he must be answerable for the manner in which the agent has conducted himself in doing the business which it was the act of his master to place him in.'[58]

On the other hand, if the agent's wrongful conduct is remote from the acts the employee was authorized to perform, the principal will not be held liable. In *Richards v West Middlesex Waterworks Co*,[59] for example, a landlord was not held liable for an unauthorized assault committed by his bailiff in the course of levying a distress.

---

[56] [2003] 2 AC 366 at [23]. This test, according to which one asks whether the employee's tort is so closely connected with his employment that it would be just to hold the employer liable, has recently been endorsed by the Supreme Court in *Mohamud v WM Morrison Supermarkets plc* [2016] UKSC 11. See also *Northampton Regional Livestock Centre Co Ltd v Cowling* [2016] PNLR 5 (part-nership held liable where one partner at all material times did what he had been authorised to do 'albeit in a misguided fashion', but simultaneously furthered both his own interest and that of the partnership).

[57] (1867) LR 2 Ex 259, 266.

[58] [2003] 2 AC 366 at [30] *per* Lord Nicholls. '[T]he conduct for which the employer is sought to be held liable must be so closely connected with acts the employee was authorised to do that the wrongful conduct may fairly and properly be regarded as done by the employee in the course of the employee's employment': *Playboy Club London Ltd v Banca Nazionale Del Lavoro SpA* [2015] LLR 171 at [37] *per* HHJ Mackie. These issues have been ventillated by Etherton, LJ in *Kevin So v HSBC Bank plc* [2009] EWCA Civ 296; [2009] 1 CLC 503 and by Sir Anthony Clarke, MR in *Gravil v Carroll* [2008] ICR 1222. Detailed treatment of vicarious liability is beyond the scope of a general study of agency law and the reader is referred to such specialized texts as *Clerk & Lindsell on Torts* (2014: London, Sweet & Maxwell) 21st ed. However, see Watts' commentary on *So v HSBC: Principals' Tortious Liability for Agents' Negligent Statements—Is 'Authority' Necessary?* (2012) 128 LQR 260.

[59] (1885) 15 QBD 660, 663 *per* Lord Coleridge, CJ: 'it was no part of the duty of the bailiff or his man, who were only authorized to levy the rate due to the company, to commit an assault upon

In the case of torts involving representations, when considering the case of an agent **11.21** who is an employee, the outer bounds of the employee's course of employment are dictated by the scope of the agent's apparent authority. As was seen in *Lloyd v Grace Smith & Co*,[60] a principal will even be liable for the fraud of his agent, if acting within the scope of his authority, irrespective of whether or not the fraud was committed for the benefit of the principal. Indeed, in the Court of Appeal in *Armagas Ltd v Mundogas Ltd. The Ocean Frost*[61] Dunn, LJ opined:

> It may be that in theory a person can act in the course of his employment but beyond the scope of his authority. But [the decided cases] all show that in cases of fraud the parameters of the course of the employment are set by the scope of the ostensible authority.[62]

Certainly, if the agent acts fraudulently within the scope of his actual or appar- **11.22** ent authority, the principal will incur liability for the agent's deceit. In *Briess v Woolley*,[63] in the course of selling shares in a company the managing director, acting without the knowledge of the company's shareholders, made fraudulent representations concerning the company's production figures. It having been established that the shareholders had expressly authorized the sale of shares, the House of Lords held the latter liable for their agent's fraud. In *Briess v Woolley*, unusually, the representation was made by the managing director before the other shareholders appointed him to act on their behalf. The House of Lords held on the facts that, given the continuing effect of pre-contractual misrepresentations, if the managing director 'has in the meantime been appointed agent with authority to make representations for the purpose of inducing a contract he, in his capacity as agent, is by his conduct repeating the misrepresentations previously made by him', both agent and principal will be liable to third parties for the fraudulent misrepresentation originally made by the agent before commencement of the agency.[64] This selfsame principle, holding that both principal and agent might acquire not just liability but also rights in such circumstances, was adopted by the Supreme Court in *Cramaso LLP v Ogilvie-Grant*,[65] a Scots case concerned with *Hedley Byrne* liability for a negligent misrepresentation. The defenders had made a false representation concerning the adequacy of grouse stocks on a moor they wished to lease out. The representation was originally made to E before the latter formed a limited liability

---

the plaintiff.' Whether the same decision would be reached today in light of a case like *Mohamud v WM Morrison Supermarkets plc* [2016] UKSC 11, where the employer was held liable for the actions of a petrol station employee who had launched an unprovoked attack on someone inquiring about printing facilities, is debatable.

[60] [1912] AC 716. See para **1.24**.
[61] [1986] AC 717.
[62] *Ibid* at 751. See also at pp 766–8 *per* Stephenson, LJ.
[63] [1954] AC 333.
[64] *Ibid* at 34 *per* Lord Tucker.
[65] [2014] 2 WLR 317.

partnership, which continued negotiations and ultimately entered into the lease. As Lord Reed, JSC explained,

> the change in the identity of the prospective contracting party did not affect the continuing nature of its representation, or the defenders' continuing responsibility for its accuracy ... [T]he representation ... remained operative in the mind of [E] after he began to act in the capacity of an agent of the pursuer up until the time when the lease was executed on behalf of the pursuer. The pursuer was thus induced to enter into the contract by that representation.[66]

**11.23** In contrast, if the third party has been made aware that the agent lacks authority to make representations, any representations he makes will be treated as outside the scope of the agent's authority. In *Collins v Howell-Jones*[67] C claimed a reduction in the contract price on the purchase of a property on the ground of an innocent misrepresentation made by H-J's agents, B. The misrepresentation concerned an error as to the original height of a demolished building on the site, which would have meant that the two-storey development contemplated by C would no longer be possible. The agents' particulars of sale had referred to the plans and stated that the vendors and agents gave no representations or warranty in relation to the property. Waller, LJ, applying the principle laid down in *Overbrooke Estates Ltd v Glencombe Properties Ltd*,[68] held:

> [I]f express authority specifically forbids any representation being made, then any representation in fact made is outside the authority given ... The principal announces to those who are dealing with his agent what are the limits of that agent's authority. In this particular case the misrepresentation was not contained in the actual particulars of sale, ...[69]

### Contribution between principal and agent and indemnity between master and servant

**11.24** Finally, as in the case of master and servant, when the principal is liable for the tortious acts of his agent, technically principal and agent are joint tortfeasors and enjoy rights of contribution against one another under the Civil Liability (Contribution) Act 1978. Also, where the agent is a servant, the principal may have a right to seek an indemnity from his servant for the damage the latter has occasioned his master, even if in practice such indemnities tend not to be enforced.[70]

**11.25** Principal and agent may incur liability as joint tortfeasors. According to classical doctrine, such liability will arise where the principal has *either* procured the commission of the tort by the agent *or* where the principal has participated with the agent

---

[66] *Ibid* at [30].
[67] [1981] 2 EGLR 108.
[68] [1974] 1 WLR 1335. See para **4.41**.
[69] [1981] 2 EGLR 108, 109.
[70] *Lister v Romford Ice & Cold Storage Co* [1957] AC 555.

(the primary tortfeasor) in a common design relating to that tort. The concepts of 'procurement' and 'common design' overlap to a considerable degree.[71] Indeed, procurement has sometimes been treated as no more than a subset of common design,[72] and Lord Hoffmann went so far as to indicate that only common design matters:

> The test for such liability in English law is whether the acts were done pursuant to a common design so that the secondary party has made the act his own.[73]

In *Unilever plc v Gillette (UK) Ltd* Mustill, LJ mulled over what might be meant by **11.26** 'common design', concluding:

> I use the words 'common design' because they are readily to hand, but there are other expressions in the cases, such as 'concerted action' or 'agreed on common action' which will serve just as well. The words are not to be construed as if they formed part of a statute. They all convey the same idea. This idea does not, as it seems to me, call for any finding that the secondary party has explicitly mapped out a plan with the primary offender. Their tacit agreement will be sufficient. Nor, as it seems to me, is there any need for a common design to infringe. It is enough if the parties combine to secure the doing of acts which in the event prove to be infringements.[74]

Mustill, LJ's expression, 'tacit agreement', perhaps needs to be treated with a degree of circumspection.[75]

The Supreme Court, in 2015, had an opportunity to review common design in the **11.27** field of joint tortious liability in *Sea Shepherd UK v Fish & Fish Ltd*.[76] The Justices disagreed over the outcome of the case, three of the five concluding that there was no joint liability by reason of application of the *de minimis* principle. However, the Justices did agree when it came to identifying the principles that govern joint liability. In the words of Lord Toulson:

> [I]t is not enough to show that D did acts which facilitated P's commission of the tort. D will be jointly liable with P if they combined to do or secure the doing of acts which constituted a tort. This requires proof of two elements. D must have acted in a way which furthered the commission of the tort by P; and D must have done so in pursuance of a common design to do or secure the doing of the acts which constituted the tort. I do not consider it necessary or desirable to gloss the principle further.[77]

Therefore, three conditions must be satisfied. *First*, the defendant must have assisted the commission of an act by the primary tortfeasor; *secondly*, the assistance

---

[71] See, eg, *Twentieth Century Fox Film Corp v Newzbin Ltd* [2010] FSR 21 at [103] *per* Kitchin J.

[72] *CBS Songs Ltd v Amstrad Consumer Electronics plc* [1988] AC 1013, 1058 *per* Lord Templeman. E contra, *Unilever plc v Gillette (UK) Ltd* [1989] RPC 20, p. 608 *per* Mustill, LJ.

[73] *SABAF SpA v Meneghetti SpA* [2005] RPC 10 at [40]. See also *Sea Shepherd UK v Fish & Fish Ltd* [2015] 2 WLR 694.

[74] [1989] RPC 20, p. 609.

[75] Eg, *L'Oréal SA v eBay International AG* [2009] RPC 21 at [369]–[382] *per* Arnold, J.

[76] [2015] 2 WLR 694.

[77] *Ibid* at [21].

must have been pursuant to a common design on the part of the defendant and the primary tortfeasor that the act be committed; and, *thirdly*, the act must constitute a tort as against the claimant.[78]

**11.28**  Additionally, Lord Sumption, whose analysis all other members of the Court accepted, identified two limiting features relevant to the scope of joint liability. The first relates to a joint tortfeasor's intent:

> Intent in the law of tort is commonly relevant as a control mechanism limiting the ambit of a person's obligation to safeguard the rights of others, where this would constrict his freedom to engage in activities which are otherwise lawful ... What the authorities ... demonstrate is that the additional element which is required to establish liability, over and above mere knowledge that an otherwise lawful act will assist the tort, is a shared intention that it should do so.[79]

The second limiting feature identified by Lord Sumption is a requirement of active co-operation:

> The required limitation on the scope of liability is achieved by the combination of active co-operation and commonality of intention. It is encapsulated in Scrutton, LJ's distinction between concerted action to a common end and independent action to a similar end, and between either of these things and mere knowledge of the consequences of one's acts.[80]

**11.29**  Questions of joint liability have frequently arisen in the context of intellectual property torts. In such cases, the co-operation of the alleged joint infringer must go beyond merely assisting, even knowingly assisting, the primary defendant to carry out the relevant act.[81] If the alleged tortfeasor does more than facilitate the infringement, but does something actively to induce, incite, or persuade the primary infringer to carry it out, this will amount to joint tortfeasance by reason of both procurement and common design.[82] It will be necessary to show that some act has been performed in furtherance of the common design.[83] As Judge Hacon recently held:

> [I]n order to establish joint liability for infringement of an intellectual property right, the alleged joint tortfeasor must have done something more than having knowingly (and even profitably) facilitated the infringements.[84]

---

[78]  *Ibid* at [55] *per* Lord Neuberger.

[79]  *Ibid* at [44].

[80]  *Ibid* at [44]. The reference is to Scrutton, LJ's judgment in *The Koursk* [1924] P 140, 156.

[81]  See *Crédit Lyonnais Bank Nederland NV v ECGD* [1998] 1 Lloyd's Rep. 19, 46 *per* Hobhouse, LJ.

[82]  *CBS Songs Ltd v Amstrad Consumer Electronics plc* [1988] AC 1013, 1058 *per* Lord Templeman.

[83]  *Unilever plc v Chefaro Proprietaries Ltd* [1994] FSR 135, 138 *per* Glidewell, LJ. Thus, in one case involving online trading, the mere offer of a marketplace in the knowledge that it would be used by certain parties as a channel for selling infringing goods was insufficient: *L'Oréal SA v eBay International AG* [2009] RPC 21. However, in a case where websites were structured in such a way as to promote acts of infringement and in fact render them inevitable, joint liability was established: *Twentieth Century Fox Film Corp v Newzbin Ltd* [2010] FSR 21.

[84]  *Vertical Leisure Ltd v Poleplus Ltd* [2015] EWHC 841 (IPEC) at [35].

The required state of mind of the party will vary according to the nature of the tort in question. Thus, in the case of torts of strict liability, such as patent infringement, neither party need have been aware of the unlawfulness of their acts. In contrast, in the case of torts of which knowledge is a constituent element, the knowledge of the parties will be relevant to the establishment of joint tortfeasance.[85]

---

[85] See *Vestergaard Frandsen A/S v Bestnet Europe Ltd* [2013] RPC 33 at [36]–[37].

# 12

# LEGAL RELATIONS BETWEEN AGENT AND THIRD PARTY

## Liability of Agents to Third Parties on their Principals' Contracts

An agent acting for a disclosed principal (named or unnamed) normally can neither **12.01**
sue nor be sued by the third party on contracts he has concluded on behalf of that
principal. In cases of disclosed agency, the object is to bring principal and third party
into direct contractual relations. At this point the agent customarily drops out of the
transaction, neither acquiring rights against the third party nor incurring liability
to the third party. As Wright, J made crystal clear in *Montgomerie v UK Mutual SS
Association Ltd*:

> There is no doubt whatever as to the general rule as regards an agent, that where a
> person contracts as agent for a principal, the contract is the contract of the principal
> and not that of the agent; and, *prima facie*, at common law the only person who may
> sue is the principal and the only person who can be sued is the principal.[1]

---

[1] [1891] 1 QB 370, 371. As Lord Scarman showed in his speech in *Yeung Kai Yung v Hongkong
and Shanghai Banking Corp* [1981] AC 787, 795, when set against the backdrop of the law of contract this self-same proposition can be formulated as an exception to the general rule of contractual
liability: 'The true principle of law is that a person is liable for his engagements ... even though he
is acting for another, unless he can show that by the law of agency he is held to have expressly or
impliedly negatived his personal liability.'

**12.02**  In *Wakefield v Duckworth & Co*[2] a third party unsuccessfully sought to hold an agent for a disclosed principal personally liable. D, who was a member of the defendant firm of solicitors, ordered photographs from W, a photographer, for the purposes of litigation in which the solicitors were acting for a client charged with manslaughter. W, knowing why the solicitors required the photographs, nevertheless debited them with the price of the photographs in his books and sought to hold the solicitors personally liable for the price of the photographs. W's claim failed as the solicitors were *prima facie* agents acting on behalf of a principal. Whilst recognizing that there did exist 'certain exceptional cases' in which an agent can render himself personally liable, Lord Coleridge, J noted:

> There is no question that the plaintiff knew that the defendants were solicitors acting on behalf of a client, and that being so, apart from any other considerations, they were agents acting on behalf of a principal. *Prima facie* in such a contract the plaintiff would have to have recourse to the principal and not the agent.[3]

Again in *Royle v Busby & Son*,[4] in the course of their work, the solicitors of a judgment creditor lodged a writ of *fieri facias* at the office of the sheriff, with a request for execution. The solicitors, however, did not select any particular bailiff to execute the writ. The sheriff therefore employed one of his own officers to execute the writ. The sheriff's officer subsequently brought an action against the solicitors to recover his fees. The Court of Appeal held that unless the sheriff's officer could show an express or implied undertaking by the solicitors that they would be personally liable for the fees, no claim would lie since they were merely acting as agents for the judgment creditor. As Lord Selborne, LC pointed out:

> There is no reasonable ground on which it can be implied that the solicitor, who, in the proper and ordinary course of his duty to his client, simply delivers a writ to the sheriff for execution, thereby enters into a personal contract to pay such fees.[5]

**12.03**  In contrast, in *Fawkes v Lamb*[6] an agent attempted to sue on his principal's contract. F, a broker, had some rum for sale. F entered into a contract with L, handing over a sale note that stated: 'L, …—I have this day bought in my own name for your account of T 259 puncheons of Cuba rum, sold at 1s 9d per gallon ….—F, broker.' Part of the purchase price was afterwards paid to T. F then brought an action against L for the residue of the price, which failed. Although F had used the words 'in my own name', these words were held to have been

---

[2] [1915] 1 KB 218.
[3] *Ibid* at 220.
[4] (1880) LR 6 QBD 171.
[5] *Ibid* at 174.
[6] (1861) 31 LJQB 98.

inserted in the sale note simply to indicate that F was liable to the seller. The action for the balance of the price ought to have been brought by T, the principal in the transaction.

### An agent can exceptionally acquire rights and incur liabilities under his principal's contract

An agent can exceptionally acquire rights and incur liabilities under his principal's **12.04** contract either under the terms of the contract he has concluded on the principal's behalf, or under a collateral contract. In *Teheran-Europe Co Ltd v ST Belton (Tractors) Ltd*,[7] in what has been dubbed 'a classic analysis',[8] Donaldson, J set out the different ways in which an agent can contract on behalf of a principal, including those in which exceptionally he may acquire rights and incur liabilities under his principal's contract, either in addition to the principal (see (b) below) or in place of the principal (see (c) below):

> An agent can conclude a contract on behalf of his principal in one of three ways:
> (a) *By creating privity of contract between the third party and his principal without himself becoming a party to the contract.* The principal need not be named but the contract must show clearly that the agent was acting as such. Familiar examples are contracts made by X as agents and signed by X, the signature being claused 'as agents only.' The consequence of such an arrangement is that the third party can only sue, and be sued by, the principal.
> (b) *By creating privity of contract between the third party and his principal, whilst also himself becoming a party to the contract.* The consequence of this arrangement is that the third party has an option whether to sue the agent or the principal, although this is of little practical value if he does not know of the principal's existence. Equally the third party is liable to be sued either by the agent or by the principal. Where both agent and principal are privy to the contract, questions of election can arise ...
> (c) *By creating privity of contract between himself and the third party, but no such privity between the third party and his principal.* In other words, in relation to the third party he is a principal, but in relation to his principal he is an agent. The consequence of this arrangement is that the only person who can sue the third party or be sued by him is the agent.[9]

In each individual case it will be necessary to construe the terms of the contract in order to determine which particular configuration of liability applies to that particular agreement.

---

[7] [1968] 2 QB 53.
[8] *Innovatis Investment Fund Ltd v Ejder Group Ltd* [2010] EWHC 1850 (Ch) at [56] *per* Norris, J.
[9] [1968] 2 QB 53, 59–60. In the third category of situation enumerated by Donaldson, J, although the principal will not be in direct legal relations with the third party, as between principal and agent certain incidents of agency may still apply: notably, the agent may be entitled to commission and to an indemnity.

## Contracts under which the Agent is held to have undertaken Personal Liability

**12.05** There exist a number of exceptions to the general rule that an agent does not customarily acquire rights or incur liabilities under his principal's contract. Thus, as was seen in an earlier chapter,[10] if an agent acts for an undisclosed principal, the contract is initially made between the third party and the agent. True, the undisclosed principal may intervene and take over his agent's contract. Similarly, if the principal's existence becomes known, the third party may choose to treat the principal as his co-contractant. However, in the first instance—and, it may well be, throughout the life of the contract—the agent will be treated as the principal in the transaction. Nor is the agent of an undisclosed principal able to evade liability to the third party by pointing out that in reality he was only acting as agent for an undisclosed principal. In *Saxon v Blake*[11] a solicitor purchased a freehold in his own name. When later he sought to resist the performance of the contract on the ground that he had acted as the mere agent of a client, Sir John Romilly, MR held that the solicitor was bound to perform the contract.

**12.06** More generally, however, an agent may expressly agree to incur personal liability, and may also acquire rights, under contracts he makes with third parties. If, under the terms of the contract, the agent is made a party to the contract, the courts will give effect to the contract. It is a matter of construing the terms of the contract and identifying the precise nature of the personal liability undertaken by the agent. In *The Swan*[12] Brandon, J set out the relevant guiding principles:

> Where A contracts with B on behalf of a disclosed principal C, the question whether both A and C are liable on the contract or only C depends on the intention of the parties. That intention is to be gathered from (1) the nature of the contract, (2) its terms and (3) the surrounding circumstances ... The intention for which the Court looks is an objective intention of both parties, based on what two reasonable businessmen making a contract of that nature, in those terms and in those surrounding circumstances, must be taken to have intended.[13]

It has been noted that in English law, where an agent's personal liability is engaged, there is a strong presumption that the parties will have contracted for alternative

---

[10] See **chapter 10**.
[11] (1861) 29 Beav 438.
[12] [1968] 1 Lloyd's Rep 5.
[13] *Ibid* at 12. In *Killen v Horseworld Ltd* [2011] EWHC 1600 (QB), esp at [48] Cox, J adopted the words of *Bowstead & Reynolds on Agency*, 16th ed, para 9-005: 'As in all matters of formation of contract, the test is objective. The rules can be most easily articulated in relation to written contracts where the use of a particular form of words may constitute an agent a contracting party though it is on the underlying facts doubtful whether he intended to become such.'

liability.[14] However, it is possible that the agent will have contracted so as to be either solely liable or jointly or jointly and severally liable. In each case it will be a matter of determining the intentions of the parties. As Luxmoore, LJ observed in *International Railway Co v Niagara Parks Commission*:

> There is nothing to prevent an agent from entering into a contract on the basis that he is himself to be liable to perform it as well as his principal.[15]

Indeed, it is arguable that in more recent times the courts have shown themselves less averse than in the past to contemplate the possibility that the parties intended both principal and agent to be liable under the contract.[16]

### An agent who signs a contract in his own name will be considered to have contracted personally

Unless a contrary intention appears elsewhere in the document, an agent who signs a contract in his own name, without qualification, will be considered to have contracted personally. It has been noted by Rix, LJ that 'the way in which a party named in a contract signs that contract may be of particular strength in the overall question of whether he is a party to that contract with personal liability under it.'[17] This is borne out in many of the cases. In *Parker v Winlow*[18] a charterparty was expressed to be made 'between Captain P, of the good ship *Celerity*, and W, agent for E. W. & Son', to whom the ship was to be addressed. Because W had signed the memorandum without restriction, the court held that W incurred personal liability as charterer. As Lord Campbell, CJ pointed out, the mere fact

**12.07**

---

[14] See, eg, *Debenham's Ltd v Perkins* [1925] All ER Rep 234, 237 *per* Scrutton, LJ, discussed at paras **10.09–10.12**.

[15] [1941] AC 328, 342.

[16] Eg, *Teheran-Europe Co Ltd v ST Belton (Tractors) Ltd* [1968] 2 QB 545, 558 *per* Diplock, LJ. See further F Reynolds, *Personal Liability of an Agent* (1969) 85 LQR 92; F Reynolds, *Agency: Theory and Practice* (1978) 94 LQR 224.

[17] *Internaut Shipping GmbH v Fercometal Sarl. The Elikon* [2003] 2 Lloyd's Rep 430 at [46]. In some cases the contracting party may have been misdescribed. Although parol evidence may be admissible to assist in resolving the contracting party's true identity, as Jackson, LJ noted in *Muneer Hamid (t/a Hamid Properties) v Francis Bradshaw Partnership* [2013] EWCA Civ 470 at [57(iv)], 'Where the issue is whether a party signed a document as principal or as agent for someone else, there is no automatic relaxation of the parol evidence rule. The person who signed is the contracting party unless (i) the document makes clear that he signed as agent for a sufficiently identified principal or as the officer of a sufficiently identified company, or (ii) extrinsic evidence establishes that both parties knew that he was signing as agent or company officer.' The expression 'sufficiently identified', the judge added, includes cases in which there has been 'an inconsequential misdescription of the entity on behalf of whom the individual was signing', as in *Badgerhill Properties Ltd v Cottrell* [1991] BCC 463 where a company director signed on behalf of his company, whose name was misspelled at the foot of the document as 'Badgerhill Property Ltd' owing to a printer's error. See also *Surrey (UK) Ltd v Mazandaran Wood & Paper Industries* [2014] EWHC 3165 (Comm) at [12]–[17] *per* Eder J.

[18] (1857) 7 E&B 942. This case was approved by Rix, LJ in *Internaut Shipping GmbH v Fercometal Sarl. The Elikon* [2003] 2 Lloyd's Rep 430 at [48].

that W had described himself as an agent did not operate to exclude his personal liability:

> I can have no doubt myself that [W] is personally liable. He makes the contract, using apt words to shew that he contracts; and the only ground suggested for rebutting his personal liability is that he says he is agent for another: but he may well contract and pledge his personal liability, though he is agent for another. If he had signed the contract as 'by procuration for E W & Son', he might have exempted himself from liability; but on principle ... an agent is liable personally if he is the contracting party; and he may be so though he names his principal.[19]

What, then, is required in order for the agent to escape personal liability on contracts he concludes on the principal's behalf? Crompton, J perhaps expressed the principle most clearly:

> Mere words of description attached to the name of a contractor, such as are used here, saying he is agent for another, cannot limit his liability as contractor. A man, though agent, may very well intend to bind himself; and he does bind himself if he contracts without restrictive words to shew that he does not do so personally. It is important that mercantile men should understand that, if they mean to exclude personal recourse against themselves on contracts which they sign, they must use restrictive words, as if they sign '*per* procuration', or use some other words to express that they are not to be personally liable.[20]

### The agent who employs words of restriction plainly showing that he is signing the contract in a purely representative capacity will not incur personal liability

**12.08**  If the agent employs words of restriction, whether in the body of the contract or appended to his signature, that plainly show that the agent is signing the contract in a purely representative capacity, he will not incur personal liability on his principal's contract. In contrast to *Parker v Winlow*, in *Gadd v Houghton*[21] Liverpool fruit brokers issued a sold note to a fruit merchant that read, 'We have this day sold to you on account of James Morand & Co., Valencia, 2000 cases Valencia oranges, of the brand James Morand & Co., at 12s. 9d. *per* case free on board ...' The brokers signed the note without qualification. The oranges were not delivered, and the purchaser brought an action against the brokers for non-delivery. The Court of Appeal held the words 'on account of James Morand & Co.' showed an intention to make the principals, and not the brokers, liable upon the contract. James, LJ expressed the view:

> When a man says that he is making a contract 'on account of' some one else, it seems to me that he uses the very strongest terms the English language affords to shew that he is not binding himself, but is binding his principal.[22]

---

[19] (1857) 7 E&B 942, 947. 'W says that he is agent for EW & Sons; but that is not enough to rebut the inference of personal liability arising from the rest of the contract': *per* Erle, J at p 948.

[20] (1857) 7 E&B 942, 949.

[21] (1876) 1 ExD 357.

[22] *Ibid* at 359.

The judge added that the expression 'as agents', appended to an agent's signature, ought to be given similar effect and not be treated as simply words of description. Nor does it matter whether the agent's disclaimer of liability occurs in the body of the contract or is appended to his signature. As Mellish, LJ noted:

> I can see no difference between a man writing 'I, A. B., as agent for C. D., have sold to you,' and signing 'A. B.'; and his writing, 'I have sold to you' and signing 'A. B. for C. D. the seller.' When the signature comes at the end you apply it to everything which occurs throughout the contract.[23]

What is clear is that there must be sufficient evidence to displace what Scrutton, LJ termed 'the strong *prima facie* presumption that a person who says he has bought and signs his own name to the document without qualification is contracting personally'[24] and 'it does not matter whether the qualification of his liability, if he be only an agent, is found only in the body of the document or whether it is found in words added after the signature.'[25]

Although *Parker v Winlow* and *Gadd v Houghton* demonstrate that the courts will **12.09** require clear words indicating that the agent was contracting solely in a representative capacity, it is important to note that the fact that a specific form of words has served to exclude the agent's personal liability in a particular case does not signify that the identical phrasing will be similarly construed in another case. As Staughton, LJ pointed out in *Punjab National Bank v de Boinville*,[26] when counsel argued that the wording of the contract before the court was not dissimilar to that successfully deployed by the brokers in *Gadd v Houghton*, 'a decision on similar but different words used by a fruit broker is scarcely any authority for the meaning of words used in an insurance contract in 1983.'[27] This point is made with great force by Megaw, LJ in *Tudor Marine Ltd v Tradax Export SA. The Virgo*, where he declared:

> We were referred to many other cases ... I do not think that much help is to be obtained from them, beyond the broad principle that you must look at the contract as a whole in relation to the particular provisions of the particular contract that may be relevant. Contracts are infinitely various in subject-matter, content, word and form—and, indeed, in surrounding circumstances. At least one of the authorities, *Brandt v Morris*,[28] appears to show that surrounding circumstances may be of importance in this context. Words and phrases cannot sensibly be assessed in the abstract: for their significance—even words like 'agent', or 'on account of', or 'for account of'—may vary with their context ... I do not, therefore, propose to lengthen this judgment further by seeking to analyse the cases that have been cited to us,

---

23 *Ibid* at 360. *Digby Brown & Co v Lyall* 1995 SLT 932, 934 *per* Lord Cullen.
24 *HO Brandt & Co v HN Morris & Co* [1917] 2 KB 794, 797.
25 *Lester v Balfour Williamson* [1953] 2 QB 168, 175 *per* Goddard, LJ.
26 [1992] 1 Lloyd's Rep 7.
27 *Ibid* at 31. See also the remarks of Hobhouse, J at p 12.
28 [1917] 2 KB 794.

or to steer a passage between, for example, the Scylla *of Gadd v Houghton* and the Charybdis of *Brandt v Morris*. I suspect that, in truth, that is a dangerous channel only if the important differences in the wording of the contract in the two particular cases are ignored.[29]

**12.10**  The House of Lords reviewed this issue thoroughly in *Universal Steam Navigation Co Ltd v James Mckelvie and Co*.[30] Agents had signed a charterparty for the hire of a steamer, 'For and on behalf of James McKelvie & Co. (as Agents), J.A. McKelvie.' Along with several other provisions imposing obligations on the 'charterers', the charterparty made provision for payment by the 'charterers' of demurrage on the occurrence of certain events. At the time of signature, the shipowners were aware that James McKelvie & Co was acting for other persons. Nevertheless, the shipowners sued the agents for demurrage, arguing that the agents had made themselves personally liable on the agreement by describing themselves as 'charterers' throughout the entire body of the document. The House of Lords determined that, having signed as agents, James McKelvie & Co were not liable as principals to pay demurrage, notwithstanding that they were described as 'charterers' in the body of the charterparty. Viscount Cave, LC considered that, despite their having described themselves as charterers in the body of the contract, the words appended to their signature, 'as Agents', showed plainly that they did not intend to bind themselves personally to the terms of the contract:

> If the respondents had signed the charterparty without qualification, they would of course have been personally liable to the shipowners; but by adding to their signature the words 'as agents' they indicated clearly that they were signing only as agents for others and had no intention of being personally bound as principals. I can imagine no other purpose for which these words could have been added; and unless they had that meaning, they appear to me to have no sense or meaning at all.[31]

Lord Shaw of Dunfermline, too, considered that appending the word 'agents' to the signature of a party to a mercantile contract was, in all cases, the dominant factor in resolving whether a party signed as principal or agent. Lord Shaw conceded that:

> [A] highly improbable and conjectural case (in which this dominating factor might be overcome by other parts of the contract) may by an effort of the imagination be figured, but, apart from that, the appending of the word 'agent' to the signature is a conclusive assertion of agency, and a conclusive rejection of the responsibility

---

[29]  [1976] 2 Lloyd's Rep 135, 145–6. 'In their ordinary and natural meaning the words "on behalf of" import agency, which is how the courts have ordinarily construed them': *Plevin v Paragon Personal Finance Ltd* [2014] 1 WLR 4222 at [30] *per* Lord Sumption.

[30]  [1923] AC 492.

[31]  *Ibid* at 495.

of a principal, and is and must be accepted in that twofold sense by the other contracting party.[32]

It will be seen that in order that an agent who puts his signature to a contract **12.11** avoids incurring personal liability under it, the words the agent appends to his signature must not simply be words of description, describing his profession or business, but must qualify the capacity in which he signs the contract. In *Sika Contracts Ltd v BL Gill and Closeglen Properties Ltd*[33] a chartered civil engineer engaged a building contractor to repair some beams at the second defendant's premises. Although it was apparent that the engineer was performing his professional function as consulting engineer, there was no mention of the second defendant in the contract. The second defendant having gone into liquidation, the engineer was called upon to pay for the completed work. The engineer claimed that he had only acted as the agent of the second defendants. Kerr, J held that, as a matter of construction, since in this case the engineer had signed the letter of acceptance in his own name, merely adding the words 'chartered civil engineer' after the signature, and had not added any words qualifying the capacity in which he contracted thereby showing that he was contracting as agent for another, the building contractor was perfectly entitled to say that he had relied upon the credit of the engineer. Kerr, J acknowledged that it would have been unusual to find someone in the defendant's situation adding words qualifying the capacity in which he was acting:

> It would have been open to him (though I accept that it would have been unusual) to have added to his signature and to the words 'Chartered Civil Engineer' words such as 'as agent only', or even, 'acting for building owner' ... I appreciate that this is not commonly done. But whether or not it is done may be crucial.[34]

The law, then, is relatively unforgiving: a court is most unlikely to conclude that merely because it is uncommon for a particular category of person to assume personal contractual liability, in the absence of any clear expression to the contrary the parties' intention was that the agent would not be liable on that contract.

In *The Swan* Brandon, J sought to summarize what courts will tend to treat as a clear **12.12** indication that it was not intended that the agent was to assume personal liability under the principal's contract:

> Where it is stated in the contract that a person makes it 'as agent for' or 'on account of', or 'on behalf of', or simply 'for', a principal, or where words of that kind are added after such person's signature, he is not personally liable ...

---

[32] *Ibid* at 499.
[33] (1978) 9 BLR 11.
[34] *Ibid* at 18.

Where such words are not used but the person is merely stated to be an agent, or the word 'agent' is just added after his signature, the result is uncertain, because it is not clear whether the word is used as a qualification or a description ... In general it would seem that in such a case the person does not avoid personal liability, although there may be exceptions to this general rule depending on the other terms of the contract or the surrounding circumstances.[35]

### An agent may not adduce parol evidence to contradict the terms of the written contract

**12.13**  An agent may not adduce parol evidence to contradict the terms of the written contract in order to show that, contrary to the written terms, it was not intended that he should incur personal liability under the contract. In *Higgins v Senior*[36] commission agents agreed to sell 1,000 tons of iron to the claimants, who were iron merchants. The sold note was signed, 'John Senior & Son. William Senior.' The iron was never delivered and the claimants sued the agents for non-delivery. The sold note bore no mention that the agents were acting on behalf of the Varteg Iron Co. The agents, however, sought to adduce other evidence, notably in the form of correspondence passing between the parties, showing that in reality they had contracted as agents and that the claimants knew that it was not intended that the agents assume personal liability on this contract. In the view of Parke, B:

> [T]o allow evidence to be given that the party who appears on the face of the instrument to be personally a contracting party, is not such, would be to allow parol evidence to contradict the written agreement; which cannot be done.[37]

### Evidence may be adduced to show that parties additional to the agent were to be liable under the contract

**12.14**  Provided that it does not contradict the express terms of the contract imposing personal liability on the agent, evidence may be adduced to show that it was intended that parties additional to the agent were to be liable under the contract. In *Higgins v Senior* Parke, B recognized that evidence might be admitted to show that the contracting parties were also acting as agents for others when they entered into the contract. This would be the case where agents were acting for unnamed principals. Such evidence 'in no way contradicts the written agreement':

> It does not deny that it is binding on those whom, on the face of it, it purports to bind; but shews that it also binds another, by reason that the act of the agent,

---

[35] [1968] 1 Lloyd's Rep 5, 13. See also *Ignazio Messina & Co v Polskie Linie Oceaniczne* [1995] 2 Lloyd's Rep 566, 571 *per* Clarke, J.
[36] (1841) 8 M&W 834.
[37] *Ibid* at 844.

in signing the agreement, in pursuance of his authority, is in law the act of the principal.[38]

**Parol evidence may be adduced to show that an agent who appears not to have been a party to the contract did in fact engage his personal liability**

Sometimes parol evidence may be adduced to show that an agent who appears not **12.15** to have been a party to the contract did in fact engage his personal liability. Several authorities illustrate the proposition that even though a written contract appears not to contemplate the personal liability of the agent, a custom of the relevant trade holds that, in addition to the principal, the agent is also personally liable. In *Hutchinson v Tatham*,[39] for example, agents acting for Lyons chartered a ship to carry a cargo of currants from the Ionian Islands, stating in the charterparty that they were acting as 'agents to merchants' but without disclosing the principal's name. The shipowners sued the agents and were able to show that by trade usage if the name of the principal was not disclosed within a reasonable time of signing the charterparty, the agents themselves became personally liable on the contract. As Bovill, CJ explained:

> There is nothing unreasonable in such a custom, ... With respect to many branches of trade of a speculative character, where contracts are made through a broker to take advantage of the rise and fall of the markets, it may be all important that the names of the real principals should not be disclosed. In such cases, if the opposite party cannot obtain the name of the principal, no one can be responsible to him but the broker. If the custom does exist, its only effect is to add a term to the contract, and to make the contract, which, *primâ facie*, is that of the principal, likewise bind the agent personally in a particular event.[40]

Shipping agents supply a classical example of a profession where a similar custom has regularly been held to obtain. As Salmon, LJ stressed in *Perishables Transport Company Ltd v N Spyropoulos (London) Ltd*,[41] a case concerned with air transport's equivalent of shipping agents:

> It is quite plain that air agents (if that is the right appellation) are in the same position as shipping agents: if they arrange for the shipment or air passage, even although they disclose that they are doing so for a principal, even for a named principal, they incur a personal liability to the shipping company or the air company for the freight. This

---

[38] *Ibid* at 844.

[39] (1873) LR 8 CP 482.

[40] *Ibid* at 485–6. Brett, J insisted that because the agent's liability was dependent upon the agent not revealing his principal's identity within a reasonable time, the custom did not contradict the written contract: p 487. In the view of Grove, J, evidence of the custom was not 'irreconcileable with the written contract ... It is not attempted to shew that the defendants' principals would not, *prima facie*, and, in most cases, be liable as the principals, and not the defendants; but that, in a certain particular contingency, the defendants might themselves be personally liable. This does not seem to me so inconsistent and irreconcileable with the contract as to amount to a contradiction or variation beyond what is admissible': p 488.

[41] [1964] 2 Lloyd's Rep 379.

has been so for many years in shipping; it has been so for quite a long time so far as air transport is concerned.[42]

## Contracts under which the Agent may be assumed to have undertaken Personal Liability

### Agents of unnamed principals

*The fact that the principal is unnamed may play a significant part in determining the respective rights and liabilities of the parties*

**12.16** When considering the liability of the agent for an unnamed principal, where the act of the agency is disclosed but the identity of the principal remains concealed, the fact that the principal is unnamed may play a significant part in determining the respective rights and liabilities of the parties. In *Benton v Campbell, Parker & Co Ltd*,[43] for example, Salter, J was clear that in the absence of any contrary intention, the agent for an unnamed principal incurs personal liability on the principal's contract alongside the principal:

> Where an agent purports to make a contract for a principal, disclosing the fact that he is acting as an agent, but not naming his principal, the rule is that, unless a contrary intention appears, he makes himself personally liable on the authorized contract. It is presumed that the other party is unwilling to contract solely with an unknown man. He is willing to contract with an unknown man, and does so, but only if the agent will make himself personally liable, if called on, to perform the contract which he arranges for his principal. The agent is presumed to agree.[44]

This assumption, however, has not been endorsed in other cases. In *The Osprey*,[45] for instance, Lord Lloyd of Berwick at one point spoke of 'the beneficial assumption in commercial cases'[46] that an undisclosed principal has a right to intervene on his agent's contract. Lord Lloyd was actually adverting to Diplock, LJ's influential judgment in *Teheran-Europe Co Ltd v ST Belton (Tractors) Ltd*,[47] which appears to state that if the third party is prepared, or leads the agent to believe that he is content, to deal with whomsoever turns out to be the principal, the unnamed principal is to be treated as a party to the contract and it is not inevitably the case that the agent will be taken to have assumed personal liability on the contract alongside the principal:

> Where an agent ... enters into a contract with another party intending to do so on behalf of his principal, it matters not whether he discloses to the other party the

---

[42] *Ibid* at 382.
[43] [1925] 2 KB 410.
[44] *Ibid* at 414.
[45] *Siu Yin Kwan v Eastern Insurance Co Ltd. The Osprey* [1994] 2 AC 199.
[46] *Ibid* at 209.
[47] [1968] 2 QB 545.

identity of his principal, or even that he is contracting on behalf of a principal at all, if the other party is willing or leads the agent to believe that he is willing to treat as a party to the contract anyone on whose behalf the agent may have been authorised to contract. In the case of an ordinary commercial contract such willingness of the other party may be assumed by the agent unless either the other party manifests his unwillingness or there are other circumstances which should lead the agent to realise that the other party was not so willing.[48]

However, as with other situations we have examined, it is a matter of construing the particular contract in light of all relevant circumstances, one of which will be the fact that at the time of contracting the third party was ignorant of the principal's identity. The terms of the contract may indicate that the agent was meant to undertake personal liability. In *The Frost Express*[49] the Court of Appeal determined that it was clear from the fact that the agent had signed the charterparty without qualification that it was liable as a principal under the chartering contract. Moreover, even if the agent was known by third parties to be contracting as a pool manager on behalf of other owners and disponent owners, it had plainly undertaken an obligation as principal to provide one or another of the vessels available to it.[50] On the other hand, in *The Santa Carina*,[51] where the third party was aware that the defendant brokers supplied bunkers to a ship at Penang as agents, the Court of Appeal held that the onus lay with the third party to adduce evidence from which the court might deduce that the brokers were intended to be personally liable on the contract, notwithstanding that they were known to the third party to be acting in the capacity of agents.[52]

**12.17**

## Agents of foreign principals

### Agents acting for foreign principals

There used once to be a strong presumption that where a home agent contracted with a third party on behalf of a foreign principal, the intention was that the agent was to be personally liable on the contract. As the court observed in the early eighteenth-century case, *Gonzales v Sladen*:

**12.18**

> But where a factor to one beyond the seas buys or sells goods for the person to whom he is factor, an action will lie against him or for him in his own name; for the credit will be presumed to be given to him in the first case, and in the last the promise will be presumed to be made to him, and rather so, as it is so much for the benefit of trade.[53]

---

[48] *Ibid* at 555.
[49] *Seatrade Groningen BV v Geest Industries Ltd. The Frost Express* [1996] 2 Lloyd's Rep 375.
[50] *Ibid* at 379–80.
[51] *N&J Vlassopoulos Ltd v Ney Shipping Ltd. The Santa Carina* [1977] 1 Lloyd's Rep 478.
[52] See further F Reynolds, *Practical Problems of the Undisclosed Principal* (1983) 36 CLP 119.
[53] Cited in *Buller's Introduction to the Law relative to Trials at Nisi Prius* (1788: London, Hugh Gaine) 5th ed, p 130.

The broad rationale was that in such circumstances a third party would elect to trust to the home agent's financial standing rather than to that of a foreign principal, whose creditworthiness might be something of an unknown quantity. Nor, according to Blackburn, J in *Die Elbinger AG für Fabrication von Eisenbahn Materiel v Claye*,[54] did the foreign principal necessarily authorize the agent to bring him into direct contractual relations with the home third party:

> I take it that the usage of trade, established for many years, has been that it is understood that the foreign constituent has not authorized the merchants to pledge his credit to the contract, to establish privity between him and the home supplier. On the other hand, the home supplier, knowing that to be the usage, unless there is something in the bargain shewing the intention to be otherwise, does not trust the foreigner, and so does not make the foreigner responsible to him, and does not make himself responsible to the foreigner.[55]

The presumption of fact fixing the agent with personal liability, which was occasionally stated even more strongly—'we are justified in treating it as a matter of law, and saying that, in the absence of an express authority to that effect, the commissions agent cannot pledge his foreign constituent's credit'[56]— reflected the problems posed when great distances might separate principal and third party, when communications were slow and unreliable, and when information about foreign merchants' creditworthiness might be hard to come by.

12.19  The presumption did not entirely exclude the possibility that it was intended to create direct relations between foreign principal and third party. If it could be shown that the parties had evinced such contrary intention, privity of contract would be held to have been established between principal and third party. Similarly, if it appeared that it was not intended to bring foreign principal and third party into direct relations, the courts would give effect to the parties' wishes. The doctrine, then, only applied in cases where the parties' intentions were open to doubt.

*Decline in importance of foreign principal presumption*

12.20  In more recent times the strength of the presumption has markedly declined in importance. International trade carries less risk than once it did. Although some twentieth-century cases still referred to the continuing existence of

---

[54] *Die Elbinger Actien-Gesellschaft für Fabrication von Eisenbahn Materiel v Claye* (1873) LR 8 QB 313.

[55] (1873) LR 8 QB 313, 317. As Diplock, LJ subsequently pointed out in *Teheran-Europe Co Ltd v ST Belton (Tractors) Ltd* [1968] 2 QB 545, 558, 'Blackburn, J was really dealing with two usages which he considered (for the suggestion came from him, not from counsel) were current in 1873.'

[56] *Armstrong v Stokes* (1872) LR 7 QB 598, 605 *per* Blackburn, J.

a presumption,[57] as early as 1917 in *HO Brandt & Co v HN Morris & Co*[58] Scrutton, LJ had recognized that it was on the wane:

> The other fact which I take into account is that [the principals] are foreigners, and while I think that one cannot at the present day attach the importance which used to be attached forty or fifty years ago to the fact that the supposed principal is a foreigner, it is still a matter to be taken into account in deciding whether the person said to be an English agent has or has not made himself personally liable.[59]

More recently still, the courts have ceased to speak of a presumption and prefer to say that the foreign character of the principal is just one factor to be taken into account when construing the parties' intentions.[60] Bray, J had already adopted this approach in *Miller, Gibb & Co v Smith & Tyrer Ltd*:[61]

> [T]he true view is, whether the foreign principal is a buyer or a seller, that the facts that the principal is a foreigner and that the agent has not disclosed his name are ... circumstances to be considered, and when the facts are doubtful or, in the case of a verbal contract, in dispute, or when there is a written contract the terms of which are ambiguous, they are of some importance; but when there is a written contract the terms of which are unambiguous they are of no importance, and it is not true to say that there is a presumption of fact or law that the agent for the foreign principal is personally liable.[62]

Today, the fact that the principal is foreign will often be treated by the court as **12.21** only a minor consideration. Obviously, if the principal is resident in a particularly unstable jurisdiction where the political environment is highly volatile, where the banking system is not to be trusted, or where communications and transport system are not at all reliable, the foreign character of the principal may loom large. However, in the case of most modern states it is unlikely that this factor will weigh heavily, if at all. In *Teheran-Europe Co Ltd v ST Belton (Tractors) Ltd (No 1)*[63] a Persian company, trading in Teheran as importers, bought machinery in England through an English intermediary. The agent purchased twelve machines from the defendants without revealing the identity of the foreign principal, but did indicate that descriptive literature was required for advertising purposes in Iran and that it was acting for 'clients'. The importer

---

[57] Eg, *Rusholme & Bolton & Roberts Hadfield Ltd v SG Read & Co (London) Ltd* [1955] 1 WLR 146, 150 *per* Pearce, J; *Cox (t/a Port of Richborough) v Sorrell* [1960] 1 Lloyd's Rep 471, 478 *per* Pilcher, J.

[58] [1917] 2 KB 784.

[59] *Ibid* at 796.

[60] Eg, *Maritime Stores Ltd v HP Marshall & Co Ltd* [1963] 1 Lloyd's Rep 602, 608 *per* Roskill, J; *Anglo-African Shipping Co of New York v J Mortner Ltd* [1962] 1 Lloyd's Rep 610, 617 *per* Sellers, LJ.

[61] [1917] 2 KB 141.

[62] *Ibid* at 162–3.

[63] [1968] 2 QB 545.

sued the seller over the poor quality of the machines, and the seller argued that, as an 'undisclosed' foreign principal,[64] the importer had no right to sue on the contract, which had been concluded solely with the agent. The foreign principal, it would appear, was in reality an unnamed principal. No matter how he was designated, the Court of Appeal held that nothing in the contract displaced the ordinary rule that an undisclosed principal could sue and be sued, nor was there now any usage of trade which precluded the extension of the rule to the case of an undisclosed foreign principal. For Lord Denning, MR '[t]he fact that the principal is a foreigner is an element to be thrown into the scale on construction, but that is all.'[65] Diplock, LJ considered the matter in greater detail. He doubted whether the first usage to which Blackburn, J had referred in *Elbinger v Claye*[66] had ever existed and declared that the reason for the second had now ceased to exist,[67] concluding:

> [T]he fact that the principal is a foreigner is one of the circumstances to be taken into account in determining whether or not the other party to the contract was willing, or led the agent to believe that he was willing, to treat as a party to the contract the agent's principal, and, if he was so willing, whether the mutual intention of the other party and the agent was that the agent should be personally entitled to sue and liable to be sued on the contract as well as his principal.[68]

Foreignness, however, is only one of many factors that may need to be considered in determining whether privity has been established between third party and foreign principal. Its weight may be 'minimal, particularly in a case … where … no credit is extended by the other party to the principal.' The factor may be more significant in settling whether the mutual intention of the third party and the agent was that the agent should be personally liable to be sued, in addition to the principal, especially if the third party has extended credit to the foreign principal.[69]

## Special Cases: Deeds and Negotiable Instruments

**12.22**  In addition to cases where the agent has subscribed to a contract in such a way as to indicate that he was to undertake personal liability, as has been mentioned already special rules also apply in the case of deeds and negotiable instruments signed by the agent.

---

[64] Lord Denning, MR, eg, said: 'I think it was correct for the defendants in the issue to describe the Persian company as "undisclosed foreign principals." Their identity was not disclosed. Their existence as principals was not disclosed': [1968] 2 QB 545, 553.

[65] [1968] 2 QB 545, 553.

[66] (1873) LR 8 QB 313: see para **12.18**.

[67] See para **12.18**.

[68] [1968] 2 QB 545, 559.

[69] *Ibid* at 559. See further Munday, 'A Legal History of the Factor' (1977) 6 Anglo-American LR 221, 235–42.

**An agent incurs personal liability on contracts executed under seal**

It is a firm rule governing the execution of deeds that even if a party describes him- **12.23** self as acting for another, he will be personally liable on a deed which he executes in his own name. Thus, in *Hancock v Hodgson*[70] the directors of a mine company contracted by deed to purchase a mine for £4,500. The purchase price was to be paid within twelve months out of monies to be raised by the company. The deed also provided that the directors should be allowed six months' additional time, in case the bankers of the company should not within those twelve months have received sufficient deposits from subscribers to enable the directors to make payment from those funds. Even though the deed expressly stated that the directors were acting on behalf of the company, at the expiry of the eighteen months they were held personally liable on the deed which they had signed. As the court remarked in the earlier case of *Appleton v Binks*:

> There [is] nothing unusual or inconsistent in the nature of the thing, that one should covenant to another that a third person should do a certain thing, as that he should go to Rome. The party to whom the covenant is made may prefer the security of the covenantor to that of the principal.[71]

**An agent incurs personal liability if he signs a bill of exchange, promissory note or cheque without indicating that he is signing solely as agent**

As long ago as 1816 Lord Ellenborough, CJ declared that 'unless [a person who **12.24** puts his name to a bill of exchange] says plainly, "I am the mere scribe", he becomes liable.'[72] Section 26(1) of the Bills of Exchange Act 1882 enshrines these sentiments, providing that anyone who signs a bill, in whatever capacity, indicating that he is acting on behalf of a principal or in a representative capacity will not be personally liable on that bill; mere words of description, however, will not suffice.[73]

# Rights that the Agent acquires under the Principal's Contract

### Whether or not the agent enjoys the right to sue on the contract is a question of construction

The rules governing the rights an agent may acquire under contracts concluded **12.25** on his principal's behalf largely follow an identical pattern to those affecting the agent's liability, discussed above. Normally, therefore, an agent will acquire no

---

[70] (1827) 4 Bing 269.
[71] (1804) 5 East 148, 149.
[72] *Leadbitter v Farrow* (1816) 5 M&W 345, 349.
[73] See para **10.05**.

rights under his principal's contract and will not be entitled to sue the third party. In *Fairlie v Fenton*,[74] for example, a broker, signed and delivered to the defendants a bought note for cotton in which it was indicated that he was acting for a named principal, and to which the word 'broker' was added after his signature. When the broker sued the purchaser for non-acceptance of the cotton, it was held that he was not a contracting party and was not entitled to sue the third party. In Kelly, CB's view:

> [A broker] may ... frame a contract in such a way as to make himself a party to it and entitled to sue, but when he contracts in the ordinary form, describing and signing himself as a broker, and naming his principal, no action is maintainable by him.[75]

By the same token in *Repetto v Millar's Karri and Jarrah Forests Ltd*,[76] having construed the terms of the charterparty and the relevant bill of lading which had to be read as one, Bigham, J held that a ship's master, who had signed bills of lading as agent of the shipowner, was not entitled to sue the charterers for freight under the bills, not being a party to the contract.

**12.26**    In contrast, where it appears from the terms of the agreement that the intention was that the agent was to enjoy rights under the contract, the agent will be entitled to sue. In *Short v Spackman*[77] brokers bought whale oil from the defendant on behalf of H in their own names. However, the purchaser was informed that there was an unnamed principal. The brokers then, with H's authority, agreed to sell whale oil, which remained undelivered. When he learned of the second contract, H told the brokers that he was renouncing the entire transaction. The brokers accepted H's repudiation. The defendant refused to deliver the oil, and the brokers sued him for damages. The court held that as both bought and sold notes indicated that the brokers had contracted personally with the defendants, they were entitled to sue on the contract for non-delivery. Moreover, the brokers' right to sue was not at all prejudiced by the fact that the principal had repudiated the contract: 'the plaintiffs appear as the principals. The rest of the facts are *dehors* the present question.'[78]

### Agents for undisclosed principals

**12.27**    It has been seen that the agent for an undisclosed principal, being in the first instance a contracting party, is entitled to sue the third party on his principal's contract

---

[74] (1870) LR 5 Exch 169.
[75] *Ibid* at 171.
[76] [1901] 2 KB 306.
[77] (1831) 2 B&Ald 962.
[78] *Ibid* at 965 *per* Lord Tenterden, CJ.

as and until the principal decides to reveal himself and to intervene on and take over the contract.[79]

### Agents possessing special property in or holding a lien over the subject matter of the contract

Certain classes of agent have traditionally been permitted to sue third parties on the **12.28** ground either that they possess a 'special property' in the subject matter of the contract or that they possess a lien over it.[80] Auctioneers, for example, are said to have a special interest in the sales they make and have the right to sue the highest bidder for the purchase price. Salter, J explained this phenomenon in *Benton v Campbell, Parker and Co Ltd*:

> The auctioneer sues for the price by virtue of his special property and his lien, and also, in most cases, by virtue of his contract with the buyer, that the price shall be paid into his hands, and not by virtue of the contract of sale.[81]

Although at one time it was common to explain the auctioneer's right to sue for the price in terms of the 'special property' he has in goods confided to him for sale, it is now accepted that his right more properly derives from a collateral contract into which he and the highest bidder have entered at the moment that the goods are knocked down to the latter.[82] As Lord Denning, MR commented in a later case, the consequence is that:

> Under this [collateral] contract, the purchaser cannot avoid his liability to the auctioneer by paying the vendor direct without telling the auctioneer. If he does so, the auctioneer can make the purchaser pay him the full price again, even though it means that the purchaser pays twice over ...[83]

Factors, too, have for long been held entitled to sue third parties on contracts they **12.29** have concluded as agents.[84] The factor's right has often been explained in terms of the lien he possesses over the goods committed to him for sale. However, since a factor, by virtue of his being a factor, is authorized to deal with his principal's goods in his own name and has possession of them, his right to sue would today more likely be justified on the basis of the true construction of the factor's contract with the third party.

---

[79] See para **10.27**.

[80] Liens are discussed at paras **9.52–9.70**.

[81] [1925] 2 KB 410, 416.

[82] See further *Bowstead & Reynolds on Agency* (2014: London, Sweet & Maxwell) 20th ed, by Watts, paras 9-009 and 9-023.

[83] *Chelmsford Auctions Ltd v Poole* [1973] QB 542, 549.

[84] See, eg, *Drinkwater v Goodwin* (1775) 1 Cowp 251, 255–6 *per* Lord Mansfield, CJ: 'We think that a factor who receives cloths, and is authorised to sell them in his own name, but makes the buyer debtor to himself; though he is not answerable for the debts, yet he has a right to receive the money: his receipt is a discharge to the buyer; and he has a right to bring an action against him, to compel the payment ...'

## Rights of the Agent who in Reality acts for himself

**A person who masquerades as agent for a named principal will not necessarily be allowed to reveal himself as the true principal in the transaction**

**12.30**   May an agent who purports to contract on behalf of a named principal but who in fact is the real principal in the transaction acquire rights against a third party? The orthodox answer might appear to be, No. Unless the contract indicates otherwise, an agent who acts for a named principal normally drops out of the transaction and a contract is only formed between principal and third party. The latter's intention was to contract with the named principal, not with the agent. Thus in *Bickerton v Burrell* [85] the claimant brought an action seeking the return of a deposit respecting a ground rent acquired at auction 'for C Richardson'. The auctioneer objected that the proper person to bring the action was the named principal, C Richardson. The claimant thereupon sought to show that Mrs C Richardson, his housekeeper, was not in reality the principal and that she had no interest whatever in the purchase of the ground rent. The claimant, as the true principal, asserted that he had the right to sue the auctioneer. The court rejected his claim, Lord Ellenborough, CJ declaring:

> where a man assigns to himself the character of agent to another whom he names, I am not aware that the law will permit him to shift his situation, and to declare himself the principal, and the other to be a mere creature of straw.[86]

**12.31**   However, if the third party suffers no prejudice by the 'agent's' subterfuge, the latter may be recognized to have rights against the 'third party'. Certain members of the court in *Bickerton v Burrell* did indicate that the claimant might have been allowed to sue, had he first undeceived the auctioneer before bringing his action.[87] In *Rayner v Grote* [88] the court adopted this suggestion. In *Rayner* the claimant had concluded a contract in writing for the sale of goods in which he described himself as the agent of A. After the buyer had accepted and paid part of the purchase price, he learned that the claimant was himself the real principal in the transaction, and not A's agent. Although in this particular case the court held that the claimant could sue in his own name for the non-acceptance of and non-payment of the residue of the purchase price as the purchaser's affirmation of the contract showed that he was not prejudiced by the agent revealing himself to be the true principal in the transaction, Alderson, B reasoned:

> In many such cases, such as, for instance, the case of contracts in which the skill or solvency of the person who is named as the principal may reasonably be considered

---

[85] (1816) 15 M&W 383.
[86] *Ibid* at 386.
[87] Eg, *per* Abbott, J at p 391, and *per* Holroyd, J at pp 391–2.
[88] (1846) 15 M&W 359.

as a material ingredient in the contract, it is clear that the agent cannot then shew himself to be the real principal, and sue in his own name; and perhaps it may be fairly urged that this, in all executory contracts, if wholly unperformed, or if partly performed without the knowledge of who is the real principal, may be the general rule.[89]

In *Rayner v Grote* the contract had been part performed, and the part performance had been accepted by defendants in the full knowledge that the claimant was not an agent, but the real principal. Alderson, B took the view that, unlike *Bickerton v Burrell*, the distinguishing feature in *Rayner* was that before the action was brought the defendants knew that the claimant was the principal in the transaction.[90]

If, however, it can be shown that the third party did rely on the skill and solvency **12.32** of the person named by the 'agent' as principal, the agent will not be permitted to take over the contract as principal. Thus, in *The Remco*[91] the court refused to allow an agent to enforce a charterparty against the defendant shipowners on the ground that it was evident that the owners considered the identity of the charterers important. The agent had falsely represented to the shipowners who his principal was, and the evidence showed that they took an interest in who was to be responsible for payment of freight and, further, that they would not have concluded the contract had they been aware that in reality the agent was the true principal in the transaction.

This cluster of cases is not especially easy to justify.[92] Although they are unlikely to **12.33** wreak great injustice, not only are the authorities difficult to square with orthodox agency principles, they also seem at odds with a parol evidence rule which, in the case of contracts reduced to writing, would forbid the adduction of evidence contradicting the express, written terms of the contract.[93]

The courts may more readily permit an 'agent' who affects to contract on behalf of a **12.34** principal whom he does not name to reveal subsequently that in fact he, the 'agent',

---

[89] *Ibid* at 365.

[90] See also *Braymist v Wise Finance Co Ltd* [2002] Ch 273 at [60]ff *per* Arden, LJ. It has been suggested that such cases may be better explained on the basis of novation: *Bowstead & Reynolds on Agency* (2014: London, Sweet & Maxwell) 20th ed, by Watts, para 9-094.

[91] *Gewa Chartering BW v Remco Shipping Lines Ltd. The Remco* [1984] 2 Lloyd's Rep 205.

[92] If these cases are difficult to justify, even more puzzling is *Fraser v Thames TV* [1984] QB 44, where Hirst, J held that a party pretending to conclude a contract as agent might subsequently reveal that he was in fact acting as an additional principal in the transaction and be joined as a co-claimant in any action brought by the original principal against the third party. Hirst, J's decision is criticized by Tettenborn at [1983] CLJ 211.

[93] See para **12.13**. The force of the latter point is unaffected by Jackson, LJ's recent remarks on the diminishing scope of the parol evidence rule in *Muneer Hamid v Francis Bradshaw Partnership* [2013] BLR 447at [47]: 'There are a number of exceptions to the parol evidence rule and these have increased in recent years. This may in part be due to the increasing ease and speed with which documents can be created and dispatched. The temptations of the keyboard, the "cut and paste" facility and the mouse cannot always be resisted.'

was the true principal in the transaction. In this situation it can be argued that, by agreeing to contract with whomsoever the 'agent' may happen to be acting for, the third party has signified a lack of interest in the identity of the principal. This appears to be borne out by *Schmalz v Avery*,[94] where an agent, who was signatory to a charterparty on behalf of an unidentified principal, was permitted to reveal himself as the real principal and to sue on the charter: it appeared that it was of no particular significance to the third party with whom he contracted. However, the fact the third party is indifferent to the party with whom he may have contracted does not necessarily entail that he is content to contract with the 'agent' who, by acting as agent, may have conveyed the impression that he was not in the running to assume the character of principal. Even in the context of what purports to be an unnamed agency, an 'agent' who turns out to have been acting in his own behalf occupies 'a somewhat curious position'.[95] One would like to think that if the contract contained some general indication of the character of the unnamed principal and the 'agent' did not meet that description, the 'agent' would not be permitted to take over the transaction and adopt the contract as his own. Similarly, if there were evidence that the third party would positively not have contracted had the true position been known, it might be anticipated that the agent's intervention would thereby be excluded. In the latter situation, however, *Harper & Co v Vigers Bros*[96] suggests that even when such evidence is adduced, the courts may still allow the agent to show that he was in fact the unnamed principal and to take the benefit of the contract. The purported agent had signed a charterparty 'as agent for owner'. Even the third party's evidence that he would not have contracted with the agent did not deter the court from holding that the agent was entitled to sue on the disputed charterparty.[97]

---

[94] (1851) 16 QB 655, 662 *per* Patteson, J.

[95] *Harper & Co v Vigers Bros* [1909] 2 KB 549, 561 *per* Pickford, J.

[96] [1909] 2 KB 549.

[97] Perhaps to preserve the decencies, the purported agent, although successful, was refused his costs.

# 13

## TERMINATION OF AGENCY

This chapter will consider both how agencies come to be terminated, and the effects **13.01** of termination of agency. In the ordinary course of events, as between principal and agent, an agency will come to an end because the parties so wish it—for example, the task confided to the agent has been accomplished, the parties mutually agree to terminate their relationship, or the agreed duration of the agency has elapsed. As was seen in an earlier chapter,[1] however, the fact that an agent's actual authority has been restricted or terminated will not automatically mean that that agent's acts may not continue to bind the principal *vis-à-vis* third parties if the latter do not have notice of the agent's lack of authority.

As a general rule, parties whose legal relations derive from agreement are at liberty **13.02** to release one another from their obligations. Certain agencies, however, are treated as irrevocable, and cannot be freely revoked. An agency may also be terminated by operation of law, independently of the will of the parties—for example, if the contract between principal and agent is frustrated or if the principal loses legal capacity, say, through death or supervening mental incapacity. As regards the effects

---

[1] See **chapter 4**.

of termination, the rules that obtain at common law to reimburse agents whose agencies have been wrongfully terminated are entirely distinct from those that apply to commercial agents operating under the Commercial Agents (Council Directive) Regulations 1993. The two species of liability will therefore be treated separately.

## Termination by Act of the Parties

**13.03**  Agency terminates if the agency has expired either because the agreed period of the agency has run its course, because an event upon which termination of the agency was made contingent by the parties has occurred, or because the agent has accomplished his allotted task. The parties will often have agreed in advance the duration of the agency, although just occasionally a trade custom may impose an expiry date. In *Dickenson v Lilwal*,[2] for instance, in the absence of special authority to the contrary, it was found that by a custom of the Irish provision trade, in the absence of special authority to the contrary a broker's authority to sell his principal's goods expired with the day on which the authority was given.

### Revocable agencies

**13.04**  Where the parties' agency relationship derives from agreement, it is open to the parties to agree between themselves to terminate the agency prematurely by voluntary discharge of their relationship. Similarly, an agency may be terminated by either party giving reasonable notice of an intention to do so. In the absence of agreement, if the agency derives from contract—as it invariably will—and the principal unilaterally revokes the agreement, he may be liable to the agent in damages for breach of contract. The agent will be unable to compel the principal to continue to employ him under the contract as a court will not specifically enforce a personal contract.[3]

### *Revocation of agency*

**13.05**  As between principal and agent, unless the agency is an irrevocable agency,[4] revocation of the agency by either party brings the actual authority of the agent to an immediate end. Revocation must normally be drawn to the attention of the other party. As Lord Wilberforce stated in *Heatons Transport (St Helens) Ltd v TGWU*:

> To be effective in law a withdrawal or curtailment of an existing actual authority of an agent must be communicated by the principal to the agent in terms which the

---

[2]  (1815) 1 Stark 128.

[3]  These principles were recently affirmed by Lord Sumption in *Bailey v Angove's Pty Ltd* [2016] UKSC 47, [6]. An agent cannot compel his continued employment by means of an injunction (*Warren v Mendy* [1989] 1 WLR 853), although 'there is no inflexible principle precluding negative injunctive relief which prevents activity outside the contract contrary to its terms' (*Lauritzencool AB v Lady Navigation Inc* [2005] 1 WLR 3686 at [20] per Mance, LJ).

[4]  See paras **13.06–13.16**.

agent would reasonably understand as forbidding him to do that which he had previously been authorised to do on the principal's behalf.[5]

Occasionally, revocation may be inferred from the conduct of the parties. However, as Arden, J stressed in *Re E (Enduring Power of Attorney)*, where, in the absence of clear proof of the mother's intentions, execution of a fresh enduring power of attorney was held not to have revoked an earlier power:

> The general law of agency ... shows that to amount to revocation by conduct, the conduct must be inconsistent with the continuation of the agency ... [T]his ... means more than that the conduct should be reasonably understood as amounting to revocation. To be inconsistent, it must be unambiguous in its effect.[6]

### Irrevocable agencies

*Not all agencies are freely revocable*

If the agent or a third party has some particular interest in the agency's performance, **13.06** the law may treat such agencies as irrevocable. Statute has also intervened both to create a form of agency that survives the principal's loss of capacity—the lasting power of attorney (formerly, the enduring power of attorney)[7]—and to protect specific classes of third party in the event of insolvency.

**(i) Where the agent's authority is 'coupled with an interest', at common law the agency** **13.07** **will be treated as irrevocable**   If principal and agent have entered into an agreement whose underlying purpose, whether express or implied, is to secure or protect an interest of the agent, at common law such an agency is treated as irrevocable. Irrevocability in this context means that the principal may only revoke the agency with the agreement of the agent. As Lord Sumption recently explained in *Bailey v Angove's Pty Ltd*:

> The exception applies if two conditions are satisfied. First, there must be an agreement that the agent's authority shall be irrevocable. Secondly, the authority must be given to secure an interest of the agent, being either a proprietary interest (for example a power of attorney given to enable the holder of an equitable interest to perfect it) or a liability (generally in debt) owed to him personally. In these cases, the agent's authority is irrevocable while the interest subsists.[8]

In *Gaussen v Morton*[9] JL became liable to F for £231 owed to F by JL's son. In order **13.08** to satisfy this liability, JL conferred upon F a power of attorney entitling the latter to sell certain of JL's premises and to receive the purchase price. F sold the property for

---

[5] [1973] AC 15, 100.

[6] [2001] Ch 364, 373.

[7] 'Lasting powers of attorney' were introduced on 1 October 2007 by the Mental Capacity Act 2005 to replace 'enduring powers of attorney'. Enduring powers of attorney, executed before 1 October 2007 under the Enduring Powers of Attorney Act 1985, remain valid.

[8] [2016] UKSC 47 at [7]. See also *Smart v Sandars* (1848) 2 CB 895, 917-18 *per* Wilde CJ; *Clerk v Laurie* (1857) 2 H&N 199, 200 per Williams J.

[9] (1830) 10 B&C 731.

£105, and received £20 from the purchaser by way of deposit. JL then purported to revoke the power of attorney. Lord Tenterden, CJ held that it was not open to JL to revoke the power of attorney as 'it was not a simple authority to sell and surrender the premises, but an authority coupled with an interest.'[10] The underlying object of F's power of attorney was clearly to secure JL's liability and to provide a means of satisfying that liability.

**13.09** An agency will only be treated as irrevocable if its explicit object is to secure some particular interest or to confer some particular benefit on the agent. Thus, in *Carmichael's case*, the donor of a power, for valuable consideration, conferred upon the donee authority to apply for the shares in a company which the donee was promoting for the purpose of purchasing his own property from him. It was held that the donor could not revoke that authority before the benefit was reaped.[11] Again, in *Spooner v Sandilands*[12] a donor had charged his lands with certain debts due, and to accrue due, to the donees. He granted the donees possession of those properties and put them in receipt of the rents and profits with the express design of enabling the donees to discharge his liability out of those receipts. The donor was not allowed to eject the donees before their debts were paid. More recently, Colman, J has explained why the principal is prevented from revoking his agent's authority as follows:

> [T]here cannot be any conceptual basis for confining irrevocability of the authority of the agent in cases where the purpose of the authority is to secure his money interest. In the authorities under discussion the purpose of preventing the revocation of the agent's authority is that the perpetuation is necessary to provide the agent with a means which is under his control of ensuring that some obligation of his principal for the benefit of the agent is performed. The inability of the principal to withdraw authority is what ensures that the principal will not be able to avoid satisfying his contractual obligations.[13]

**13.10** The sole fact that an agent will suffer prejudice or lose commission if his agency is revoked of itself will not suffice to render an agency irrevocable. In *Frith v Frith*[14] an executrix and her sons had granted possession of properties to an estate manager for a period of seven years under a power of attorney. When she purported to revoke the power of attorney eleven months after its execution, the executrix was met with the manager's claim that the power was irrevocable. Lord Atkinson held that the power was revocable: the power of attorney merely appointed the manager

---

[10] *Ibid* at 734.
[11] *Re Hannan's Empress Gold Mining & Development Co. Carmichael's case* [1896] 2 Ch 643.
[12] (1842) 1 Y&C Ch 390.
[13] *Society of Lloyd's v Leigh* [1997] CLC 759, 773–4. See also *Bailey v Angove's Pty Ltd*, supra, at [8]: 'Where the parties agree that the agent is to have a personal financial interest in the performance of his agency, over and above the receipt of his remuneration, his duty of loyalty is to that extent compromised. The reason for declining to enforce his right to act for the principal therefore falls away.
[14] [1906] AC 254.

at a salary and contained no reference to any special interest created by his guarantee, and was not intended to 'subserve' or to be dependent on the continuance of such interest:

> It cannot be contended that the ordinary case of an agent or manager employed for pecuniary reward in the shape of a fixed salary comes within this exception, though his employment confers a benefit upon him.[15]

**(ii) Powers of attorney given as security**   Section 4(1) of the Powers of Attorney   **13.11**
Act 1971 makes provision for the irrevocability of powers of attorney executed in order to provide security for certain interests of the donee. To a significant degree, this provision overlaps with the common-law concept of an authority coupled with an interest, discussed above. Provided that the power has been duly executed and is expressed to be irrevocable:

> (1) Where a power of attorney is expressed to be irrevocable and is given to secure—
>   (a) a proprietary interest of the donee of the power; or
>   (b) the performance of an obligation owed to the donee, then, so long as the donee has that interest or the obligation remains undischarged, the power shall not be revoked—
>     (i) by the donor without the consent of the donee; or
>     (ii) by the death, incapacity or bankruptcy of the donor or, if the donor is a body corporate, by its winding up or dissolution.

**(iii) Lasting powers of attorney and enduring powers of attorney**   According   **13.12**
to orthodox agency principles, an agency terminates when the principal ceases to enjoy legal capacity. In order to allow attorneys to continue to act on behalf of individuals who, through age or infirmity, come to lose their legal capacity, Parliament first created an enduring power of attorney (EPA) under the Enduring Powers of Attorney Act 1985. The EPA enabled donors, whilst still of sound mind, to provide for the future when such might no longer be the case.[16] As part of a review of the law regulating those lacking mental capacity, and more particularly to prevent against abuses to which the EPA was supposedly subject, the EPA has since been replaced by a more wide-ranging device, the lasting power of attorney (LPA). As of 1 October 2007, under the Mental Capacity Act 2005 it has been possible to execute an LPA, under which an individual may appoint an attorney, or attorneys, to look after his property and financial affairs (a Property and Affairs LPA) and also to make health and personal welfare decisions (a Personal Welfare LPA) at some future date when the donor may have

---

[15] *Ibid* at 260. Similarly, in *Taplin v Florence* (1851) 10 CB 744 it was held to be clear that, even though he might have a special property in the goods to be sold, 'an auctioneer who is employed to sell goods upon the premises of a third party, has no such interest in the goods as will make the licence to enter the premises for the purpose of selling the goods irrevocable' (p 764).

[16] The essential features of EPAs are helpfully enumerated and discussed in *Re J (Enduring Power of Attorney)* [2009] EWHC 436 (Ch) at [6]ff *per* Lewison, J.

ceased to possess the capacity to make these decisions for himself.[17] Section 9(1) defines the LPA:

> (1) A lasting power of attorney is a power of attorney under which the donor ('P') confers on the donee (or donees) authority to make decisions about all or any of the following—
> (a) P's personal welfare or specified matters concerning P's personal welfare, and
> (b) P's property and affairs or specified matters concerning P's property and affairs, and which includes authority to make such decisions in circumstances where P no longer has capacity.

**13.13**   Section 10 lays down who may be appointed as a donee of an LPA and states that, if more than one donee is appointed, the instrument may prescribe that they may act jointly, jointly and severally, or jointly in respect of some matters and jointly and severally in respect of others.[18] Donees, duly appointed, may take decisions affecting the personal welfare, property, affairs and various other specified matters of persons who lack mental capacity, in the sense that they are unable to make a decision for themselves in relation to a particular matter because of an impairment of, or a disturbance in the functioning of, the mind or brain.[19] Decisions taken by donees on behalf of donors must comply with the general principles laid out in s 1 of the Act.[20] They must also be taken in the best interests of the donor,[21] as defined in detail in s 4 of the Act. EPAs created under the Enduring Powers of Attorney Act 1985 remain valid, and the 2005 Act makes provision for their integration into the new scheme.[22]

**13.14**   (iv) **'Executed authority'**   A further group of cases is sometimes placed under the general heading of irrevocable agencies. These cases arise when an agent has commenced performance of his agency and, during its currency, incurred liabilities on behalf of the principal for which the principal is liable to indemnify him. The agent, however, proceeds to satisfy those liabilities only after the principal has purported to terminate the agency. Courts have tended to speak of such agencies as being 'irrevocable'. More generally, an agent's authority is also sometimes said to be irrevocable in circumstances where he has incurred a personal liability to a third party in respect of which he would be entitled to reimbursement or an indemnity from the principal. Some judicial statements have been quite sweeping. Thus Wilde,

---

[17] See further S Cretney and D Lush, *Lasting and Enduring Powers of Attorney* (2013: Bristol, Jordan Publishing Ltd) 7th ed; C Ward, *Lasting Powers of Attorney: A Practical Guide* (2011: London, The Law Society) 2nd ed.

[18] Mental Capacity Act 2005, s 10(4).

[19] Lack of mental capacity is defined in s 2 of the 2005 Act, whilst inability to take decisions is defined in s 3. Detailed provision regulating LPAs is to be found primarily in ss 9–14.

[20] Notably, a donor is not to be treated as unable to make a decision unless all practicable steps to help him to do so have been taken without success, and he is not to be treated as unable to make a decision merely because he makes an unwise decision (Mental Capacity Act 2005, s 1(3) and (4)).

[21] Mental Capacity Act 2005, s 1(5).

[22] See esp Mental Capacity Act 2005, Sch 4.

B, in *Chappell v Bray*, asserted that 'an authority cannot be revoked if it has passed an interest and been executed.'[23]

In the leading authority, *Read v Anderson*,[24] A had instructed R, a turf commission **13.15** agent, to place bets on his behalf but in R's name on various horse races. A was aware that R would thereby become personally liable to the bookmakers with whom bets were laid. When A repudiated his liability to R for lost bets, R sued A for the relevant sums. A argued, *inter alia*, that the bets were unenforceable wagers, that he had not authorized R to pay them and that, even if he had, that authority had been revoked before payment was actually made. At first instance Hawkins, J held that if one employs an agent to place bets in his own name on behalf of a principal, that impliedly carries with it an authority to pay the bet if lost, and on the placing of the bet that authority becomes irrevocable. This conclusion was supported both on the ground that this case fell within the general ambit of an authority coupled with an interest,[25] and also on the ground that 'if one man employs another to do a legal act, which in the ordinary course of things will involve the agent in obligations pecuniary or otherwise, a contract on the part of the employer to indemnify his agent is implied by law.'[26] On appeal, the Court of Appeal upheld this ruling.[27] Brett, MR, who dissented, said:

> The question is whether the law will imply an undertaking by the [principal], that he will not revoke the [agent's] authority to pay bets which have been lost. If a principal employs an agent to perform an act, and if upon revocation of the authority the agent will be by law exposed to loss or suffering, the authority cannot be revoked.[28]

Bowen and Fry, LJJ similarly considered:

> It will not be denied that if a principal employs an agent to do something which by law involves the agent in a legal liability, the principal cannot draw back and leave the agent to bear the liability at his own expense.[29]

In this case R had placed himself in a position of pecuniary difficulty at the request of A, who had impliedly contracted to indemnify R from the consequences which would ensue in the ordinary course of his business from the step which he had taken.

In *Temple Legal Protection Ltd v QBE Insurance (Europe) Ltd*[30] Moore-Bick, LJ sub- **13.16** sequently reflected on the true status of this group of cases. He first noted that two

---

[23] (1860) 6 H&N 145, 152.
[24] (1882) 10 QBD 100; aff'd (1884) 13 QBD 779.
[25] (1882) 10 QBD 100, 107.
[26] *Ibid* at 108.
[27] As Wilson, LJ pointed out in *Fahad al Tamimi v Khodari* [2009] EWCA Civ 1109; [2009] CTLC 288 at [21], within a decade *Read v Anderson* had been reversed by statute: see Gaming Act 1892, s 1.
[28] (1884) 13 QBD 779, 781.
[29] *Ibid* at 783.
[30] [2009] 1 CLC 553.

rather different principles emerge from these passages, one relating to the revocability of authority, the other relating to an agent's right to be indemnified by his principal in respect of any liability incurred to third parties in exercise of that authority. In answer to the argument that *Read v Anderson* is authority for the proposition that an agent's authority cannot be revoked if he would suffer loss or other prejudice in consequence, Moore-Bick, LJ adopted the explanation proposed by *Bowstead & Reynolds*[31] according to which:

> [*Read v Anderson*] and others like it, are not concerned with revocation of the agent's authority in the sense of his power to affect the legal position of the principal but to authority in the context of the rule that the right to reimbursement and indemnity does not extend to unauthorised acts.[32]

The distinction, it was said, would matter, say, if a principal were willing and able to indemnify the agent against any loss flowing from the revocation of his authority, but was unwilling to allow the agent to take action on his behalf so as to avoid the loss. It must be understood, therefore, that such agencies are 'irrevocable' in a highly peculiar sense, and essentially involve cases that recognize that, despite the principal's purported revocation of the agency, the agent retains a contractual (or, possibly, a restitutionary) claim for sums due from the principal owing to the fact the obligations were incurred during the currency of the parties' agreement.

## Termination by Operation of Law

**13.17** An agency can be terminated not only by the conscious act of the parties, but also automatically and independently of the will of the parties by operation of law. Termination by operation of law can arise in four principal ways.

### Agency is terminated by the death of the principal or the agent

**13.18** Since agency is considered to be a personal contract, where the identity of the parties is of capital importance, an agent's obligations do not pass to his executors. In the same way the principal's death automatically terminates agency. In *Campanari v Woodburn*[33] an agent, C, agreed to sell a picture on behalf of W, for which service he was to be paid £100 once the painting was sold. C attempted to make a sale but before he succeeded in so doing, W died. Unaware of W's death, the agent proceeded to sell the picture. W's administratrix 'confirmed' the sale but refused to pay £100 to C. Although the court held that C was entitled to recover reasonable expenses incurred in endeavouring to execute the authority on a *quantum meruit*,

---

[31] *Bowstead & Reynolds on Agency* (2006: London, Sweet & Maxwell) 18th ed, para 10-010.
[32] [2009] 1 CLC 553 at [59].
[33] (1854) 15 CB 400.

C was not entitled to the £100 commission since the agency had been terminated automatically upon W's death.

## Mental incapacity

Supervening mental incapacity, in sense of an inability to comprehend the nature **13.19** and character of the acts that he is called upon to do,[34] terminates agency. Mental incapacity means that the agent is unable to continue to act, whilst the principal's mental incapacity brings agency to an end because 'where such a change occurs as to the principal that he can no longer act for himself, the agent whom he has appointed can no longer act for him.'[35]

The automatic termination of the agent's authority occasioned by the principal's **13.20** loss of mental capacity needs to be distinguished from the status of any underlying contract between principal and agent, at least in the case of solicitors' retainers. It had once been held by a Senior Costs Judge that where a principal lost capacity so that he was no longer able to give instructions in person, the contract of retainer was at that point frustrated.[36] In *Blankley v Central Manchester & Manchester Children's University Hospitals NHS Trust*,[37] however, a solicitor had been engaged to act for her principal under a conditional fee agreement (CFA). The client suffered anoxic brain damage and lost mental capacity. Phillips, J, in a judgment that subsequently received the most emphatic support in the Court of Appeal,[38] distinguished between the agent's actual authority, which according to earlier case law is automatically terminated by the principal's insanity,[39] and the termination of the underlying contract, a matter which had not been considered by the courts in *Drew v Nunn*[40] and *Yonge v Toynbee*.[41] Phillips, J declared:

> [T]he intervening incapacity of a party does not frustrate or otherwise terminate a solicitor's retainer. Whilst such incapacity does have the effect of removing the authority of the solicitor to act on behalf of the party lacking capacity for the duration of that incapacity, such authority can be restored when a deputy is appointed and provides instructions to the solicitors in that capacity, or otherwise if and when the claimant regains capacity. There is no reason, as a matter of authority or legal principle, why an inability to instruct solicitors in the intervening period (which may be quite short) should be taken to have the effect of immediately ending a solicitor's retainer.[42]

---

[34] *Boughton v Knight* (1873) LR 3 P&D 64, 72 *per* Sir James Hannen.
[35] *Drew v Nunn* (1879) LR 4 QBD 661, 666 *per* Brett, LJ.
[36] *Findley v Barrington Jones* [2009] EWHC 90130 (Costs).
[37] [2014] 1 WLR 2683.
[38] [2015] 1 WLR 4307 at [41].
[39] *Drew v Nunn* (1879) 4 QBD 661, 666 *per* Brett, LJ.
[40] In any case, in *Drew v Nunn* there was no question of a contract between the husband and wife.
[41] See further Treitel, *Frustration and Force Majeure* (2014: Sweet & Maxwell) 3rd ed, para 4-023.
[42] [2015] 1 WLR 4307 at [4].

The judge applied the classical statements of Lord Radcliffe in *Davis Contractors Ltd. v Fareham Urban District Council* to the effect that

> frustration occurs whenever the law recognises that without default of either party a contractual obligation has become incapable of being performed because the circumstances in which performance is called for would render it a thing radically different from that which was undertaken by the contract. *Non haec in foedera veni*. It was not this that I promised to do,[43]

and of Lord Reid in the same case to the effect that:

> The question is whether the contract which they did make is, on its true construction, wide enough to apply to the new situation: if it is not, then it is at an end.[44]

**13.21**  Phillips, J gave the following reasons for declining to hold the CFA contract between solicitor and client had been frustrated:

- *First*, whilst the giving of instructions and the consequent authority of a solicitor to act on behalf of a client according to those instructions is certainly central to the contract in question, the manner and capacity in which those instructions is given is not. The supervening inability of a party to give instructions personally, with the likelihood (if not the certainty) that a deputy will be appointed, does not change the nature of the contract of retainer, radically or even significantly ...
- *Second*, the obligation to provide such instructions is express in the CFA and would in any event be implied, from which it follows that an inability to provide such instructions cannot be said to be a matter not dealt with by the contract ...
- *Third*, even if any delay caused by supervening incapacity was not within the scope of the contractual terms, it is clear that [in the normal course of events] mere delay does not frustrate a contract ...
- *Fourth*, in cases such as the present [where the solicitor was acting for a client who had undergone a suction termination and laparoscopic sterilisation which had not gone according to plan], the possibility that the client will at some point lose mental capacity is plainly a matter which was within the reasonable contemplation of the parties ...
- *Fifth*, far from being unjust to hold the parties to their literal bargain, it would plainly give rise to an unjust and unreasonable result to treat a retainer as terminated by reason of what may be a fleeting period of incapacity ...
- *Sixth*, it is established that supervening incapacity of an employee does not necessarily frustrate a contract of employment, despite the personal nature of that contract ... In deciding whether the employment is frustrated by such incapacity, the court will consider the nature and likely duration of the incapacity, the prospects of recovery and whether performance of the contractual duties would

---

[43] [1956] AC 696, 729.
[44] *Ibid* at 721.

be either impossible or radically different. A client's role in a contract of retainer is far less personal than a contract of employment and can readily be assumed by a deputy, further indicating that incapacity does not in itself frustrate such a contract.[45]

Before the Court of Appeal, in *Blankley*, it was again urged that that the claimant's **13.22** supervening incapacity caused the CFA to be terminated by reason of frustration because the agreement was a personal contract between solicitor and client and the claimant could no longer give instructions to the solicitor. The contract therefore became incapable of performance. Richards, LJ, who was doubtful that a CFA even required instructions to be given by the client personally, was persuaded that

> [T]he parties must have contemplated in the particular circumstances of this case that the claimant might suffer from a further period of incapacity in which she would be unable to give instructions personally but they could be given by a litigation friend or a receiver/deputy or on her behalf ... The fact that supervening incapacity prevented the claimant from giving instructions personally did not render the contract of retainer impossible of performance; it simply gave rise to a short period of delay pending appointment of a receiver/deputy who could continue the conduct of the proceedings on the claimant's behalf and give instructions to the solicitors for that purpose.[46]

In any event, even if the claimant was under an obligation to give instructions personally and was unable to comply with that obligation by reason of her supervening incapacity, the terms of this CFA contract catered expressly for these consequences.

It should be said that the issue of the effect of incapacity on agency is in an uncertain **13.23** state. Baroness Hale, in *Dunhill v Burgin (Nos 1 and 2)*, has described this area of law as 'in a state of some confusion'.[47] In *Blankley v Central Manchester and Manchester Children's University Hospitals NHS Trust* Richards, LJ similarly referred to the potentially unfair and unsatisfactory consequences of the principle in *Yonge v Toynbee*. In particular, he observed that if one was considering the position afresh,

> one might at least expect the principle to be qualified so that:
> (i) the solicitor retains authority to act so long as he is unaware of the incapacity and
> (ii) he retains authority to take necessary steps in consequence of the incapacity, including an application to the court for the appointment of a deputy and/or litigation friend, when he does become aware of it. It might also be preferable to talk in terms of 'suspension' rather than 'termination' of authority, on the basis that the solicitor's authority is restored if the client regains capacity or a litigation friend is appointed to continue the litigation on the client's behalf.[48]

---

[45] [2014] 1 WLR 2683 at [38]–[43].
[46] [2015] 1 WLR 4307 at [38].
[47] [2014] 1 WLR 933 at [31].
[48] [2015] 1 WLR 4307 at [36].

**13.24** Whereas the automatic character of termination in the case of supervening mental capacity is likely to occasion little injustice as between principal and agent, the case may be altered where third parties, unaware of his supervening infirmity, contract with an agent whose principal has become mentally incapable. Although the agent will have lost his actual authority to act on behalf of the principal, the doctrine of apparent authority may afford third parties continued protection. In *Drew v Nunn*[49] a husband held out his wife as his agent with authority to act for him and to pledge his credit. After the husband became insane the wife ordered goods from a tradesman who was unaware of the husband's mental incapacity. The husband subsequently recovered his reason and refused to pay for the goods. The appeal stood over for a prolonged period in order to allow Brett, LJ time 'to ascertain whether it can be determined upon some clear principle'. The law, the judge concluded, 'stands upon a very unsatisfactory footing'.[50] Brett, LJ rejected the husband's contention that his wife's authority had automatically terminated upon his becoming insane on the ground that:

> where one of two persons both innocent must suffer by the wrongful act of a third person, that person making the representation which, as between the two, was the original cause of the mischief, must be the sufferer and must bear the loss.[51]

Whilst the concept of the failure of someone who lacks mental capacity to warn third parties that his agent has been deprived of authority to act is difficult to swallow, the ruling has been taken to mean that even though the agent's actual authority is terminated by supervening mental incapacity, the agent may continue to have apparent authority to bind the principal until the third party is made aware of the agent's lack of authority.

**13.25** As an alternative, the third party may be entitled to turn to the agent for breach of his warranty of authority.[52] In *Yonge v Toynbee*[53] solicitors employed by a client to conduct legal proceedings on his behalf, unaware that their client had become of unsound mind, continued to represent him. The suitor, who had incurred legal costs as a result of the solicitors' actions, sought to recover his costs from the solicitors on the ground that they had acted without authority. The Court of Appeal held that, by taking it upon themselves to act for the defendant in the action, the solicitors had thereby impliedly warranted that they had authority to do so, and therefore were liable personally to pay the plaintiff's legal costs. As Willes, J had pointed out in *Collen v Wright*:

> The fact that the professed agent honestly thinks that he has authority affects the moral character of his act; but his moral innocence, so far as the person whom

---

[49] (1879) LR 4 QBD 661.
[50] *Ibid* at 664–5.
[51] *Ibid* at 667–8.
[52] See **chapter 7**.
[53] [1910] 1 KB 215.

he has induced to contract is concerned, in no way aids such person or alleviates the inconvenience and damage which he sustains. The obligation arising in such a case is well expressed by saying that a person professing to contract as agent for another, impliedly, if not expressly, undertakes to or promises the person who enters into such contract, upon the faith of the professed agent being duly authorized, that the authority which he professes to have does in point of fact exist.[54]

It is recognized that the doctrine represented by *Yonge v Toynbee* can operate un-   **13.26**
fairly on agents. For this reason, s 5 of the Powers of Attorney Act 1971 provides protection for both donees of powers of attorneys and third parties in the event of a power being revoked. Section 5(1), for instance, provides the agent with protection if he has acted unaware that his authority has been revoked:

> A donee of a power of attorney who acts in pursuance of the power at a time when it has been revoked shall not, by reason of the revocation, incur any liability (either to the donor or to any other person) if at that time he did not know that the power had been revoked.

Section 5(2), similarly, provides relief for third parties:

> Where a power of attorney has been revoked and a person, without knowledge of the revocation, deals with the donee of the power, the transaction between them shall, in favour of that person, be as valid as if the power had then been in existence.

The lasting power of attorney, the instrument that replaces the enduring power of attorney, by providing a form of agency that survives the principal's mental incapacity also avoids this potentially harsh rule.

## Insolvency

In general, a principal's bankruptcy will automatically terminate agency since   **13.27**
bankruptcy amounts to a legal incapacity. Similarly, an agency may terminate upon the agent's becoming personally insolvent, although this may depend upon the terms of the parties' agreement.[55] Certain agencies, however, such as lasting powers of attorney, are automatically revoked by the donee's/agent's bankruptcy.[56]

Does an agent's ceasing business automatically terminate agency? If either principal   **13.28**
or agent is a body corporate, winding-up or dissolution of either party will automatically terminate the agency.[57] Thus, in *Pacific and General Insurance Co Ltd v Hazell*[58]

---

[54] (1857) 8 E&B 647, 657.
[55] See, eg, *Elliot v Turquand* (1881) 7 App Cas 79 where an agent was allowed a right of set-off in respect of mutual dealing between principal and agent prior to the agent's receiving notice of the principal's act of bankruptcy.
[56] Mental Capacity Act 2005, s 13(3) and (4).
[57] *Salton v New Beeston Cycle Co* [1900] 1 Ch 43 (dissolution of company).
[58] [1997] BCC 400.

Moore-Bick, J held that the appointment of a provisional liquidator automatically revoked the authority of agents appointed to act on behalf of the company by or under the authority of its directors. The ruling reflects the well-established proposition that an agent's authority ceases when his principal becomes incapable of acting on his own behalf. From time to time it is suggested that the range of situations where an agency is automatically terminated ought to be extended. Longmore, J reviewed the question in *Triffit Nurseries v Salads Etcetera Ltd.*[59] He pointed out that, in the absence of agreement, agency is usually terminated only by death, insanity or bankruptcy on the part of an agent who is an individual and the equivalent of death (*viz.* dissolution) on the part of a corporation. He then conceded that it remains unclear whether the actual commencement of a winding-up or the appointment of a receiver automatically has the effect of determining a company's authority to act. However, what does appear from the authorities is that there exist no grounds for believing that a mere cessation of business on the part of the agent determines the agency contract:

> [T]here is no suggestion in the books or the authorities that a cessation of the business of an agent constitutes an automatic termination of the agency relationship.[60]

The very uncertainty of the concept 'cessation of business',[61] Longmore, J considered, militated against adding this to the list of circumstances in which an agency automatically terminated.[62]

### Frustration

**13.29**  Where the agreement between principal and agent is embodied in a contract, the contract may be frustrated by intervening events that either render performance impossible or illegal, or that frustrate the contractual venture converting performance into something radically different from what the parties originally contemplated.[63] By way of example, in *Marshall v Glanvill*[64] M was appointed regional agent by G, a firm of drapers, under an agreement terminable by six months' notice on either side. On 12 July 1916, when his exemption from military service expired, M enlisted in the Royal Flying Corps, although had he waited four further days M would have been conscripted into the forces by virtue of the Military Service Acts. M thereupon sued G for six months' commission by way of damages for dismissal. McCardie,

---

[59] [1999] 1 Lloyd's Rep 697.

[60] *Ibid* at 700.

[61] See, eg, *Theophile v Solicitor-General* [1950] AC 186, 201ff *per* Lord Porter.

[62] The subject of insolvency and agency is too complex to be treated in full in a general text. For more detailed treatment the reader is directed to I Fletcher, *The Law of Insolvency* (2014: London, Sweet & Maxwell) 4th ed.

[63] *Davis Contractors Ltd v Fareham UDC* [1956] AC 696, 729 *per* Lord Radcliffe. On discharge by frustration, see generally *Chitty on Contracts* (2015: London, Sweet & Maxwell) 32nd ed, by H Beale.

[64] [1917] 2 KB 87.

J held that since performance of the contract had been rendered unlawful by the Military Service Acts, the contract between G and M had been frustrated and no commission was due to M.

## Termination under the Commercial Agents (Council Directive) Regulations 1993

The Commercial Agents (Council Directive) Regulations 1993 make special pro-    **13.30**
vision for termination of commercial agency contracts in respect of minimum periods of notice, the circumstances permitting immediate termination of the agreement, and the indemnity or compensation that may become payable to the commercial agent following 'termination' of his agency. The regime govern-ing commercial agents must be considered separately from the rules that obtain at common law.

### Minimum periods of notice

Regulation 15(1) states that if an agency contract has been concluded for an indefi-    **13.31**
nite period, either the principal or the agent is at liberty to terminate the agreement provided that due notice has been given. The minimum periods of notice, which vary according to the duration of the agency, are laid down in reg 15(2):

> The period of notice shall be—
> (a)  1 month for the first year of the contract;
> (b)  2 months for the second year commenced;
> (c)  3 months for the third year commenced and for the subsequent years.[65]

Although the parties are forbidden to agree any shorter periods of notice (reg 15(2)), it is open to them to agree longer periods of notice. However, if they do agree longer minimum periods, reg 15(3) stipulates, 'the period of notice to be observed by the principal must not be shorter than that to be observed by the commercial agent.'

Because reg 14 provides that an agency contract which begins life as a fixed-term    **13.32**
contract will be deemed to have been converted into an agency contract for an indefinite period if both parties continue to perform it after the expiry of the fixed period, reg 15(5) lays down that the minimum period of notice must be taken into account in respect of both manifestations of the agreement:

> The provisions of this regulation shall also apply to an agency contract for a fixed period where it is converted under regulation 14 above into an agency contract for an indefinite period subject to the proviso that the earlier fixed period must be taken into account in the calculation of the period of notice.

---

[65] Regulation 15(4) states that 'unless otherwise agreed by the parties, the end of the period of notice must coincide with the end of a calendar month.'

**Circumstances permitting immediate termination of the agency agreement**

**13.33** Regulation 16 allows for immediate termination of an agency agreement in defined circumstances:

> These Regulations shall not affect the application of any enactment or rule of law which provides for the immediate termination of the agency contract—
> (a) because of the failure of one party to carry out all or part of his obligations under that contract; or
> (b) where exceptional circumstances arise.

As Briggs, J pointed out in *Crane v Sky-In-Home Ltd*, in determining to what the phrase 'any enactment or rule of law' may refer, '[t]he obvious candidate in English law is the doctrine of repudiatory breach.'[66]

**The meaning of 'termination' under the Regulations**

**13.34** Although in the context of giving notice of 'termination', the term is used in its orthodox sense, as we shall see 'termination' bears more than one meaning in the Regulations. Notably, in the context of indemnity or compensation that may become due to the agent, in *Light v Ty Europ Ltd*[67] the Court of Appeal has held that 'terminate' in reg 17 covers not only cases where a principal has put an end to the agency but also the case of an agency that has simply run its course.[68]

# The Effects of Termination

**The effects of termination at common law**

**13.35** If a principal terminates his agent's agency, rights which have accrued prior to termination will survive: the agent will therefore be entitled to claim commission he has earned on transactions concluded on the principal's behalf prior to the agency being brought to an end. If the termination amounts to a breach of contract, termination may give rise to a right to compensation in the form of damages at common law.[69]

*After the principal has revoked the agent's actual authority, the latter may continue to have apparent authority to represent the principal*

**13.36** As regards third parties, if the principal is held to have made a representation that the agent possesses authority to act for him and revocation of the agent's authority

---

[66] [2007] 2 All ER (Comm) 599 at [84]. See discussion at paras **13.71–13.72**.
[67] [2004] 1 Lloyd's Rep 693.
[68] See further, paras **13.51–13.53**.
[69] If the agency is gratuitous, contractual damages will not be payable although the agent may have restitutionary entitlements against the principal.

has not been brought to the attention of third parties, even after revocation of his actual authority the agent may continue to be capable of binding the principal by virtue of apparent authority.[70] In *Trueman v Loder*[71] it was well known in the mercantile community that for a number of years the defendant, a St Petersburg merchant, had employed H as his London agent. The defendant revoked H's authority, but H proceeded to sell tallow to the claimant, purportedly on behalf of the defendant. No tallow was ever delivered. Lord Denman, CJ held that because the claimant was unaware of the revocation of the agent's authority, the defendant was liable for non-delivery of the tallow. Similarly, in *Curlewis v Birkbeck*,[72] where, unaware that the authority of a horse dealer—authorized to sell in his own name, to sell and to receive the purchase price of a principal's horses—had been revoked, a third party had paid the purchase price over to the horse dealer, it was held that unless the purchaser had been notified of the revocation his payment was good as against the principal.

### After revocation the agent may be entitled to be compensated in respect of lost commission

After termination, principal and agent will be entitled to proceed against one an-    **13.37**
other in respect of claims which arose before termination. Occasionally, however, depending upon the construction of the agency agreement, an agent may be entitled to claim from the principal sums representing commission the agent would have earned had the agency not been prematurely terminated. In most cases, however, such compensation will not have been contemplated by the contract. In *Rhodes v Forwood*,[73] for example, a colliery owner employed an agent for a seven-year period to sell all coal that the owner chose to send to Liverpool. After four years the owner sold the mine and the agent sued for the resulting loss of commission. The House of Lords rejected the agent's claim on the ground that the agreement did not bind the colliery owner to keep his colliery, or to do more than employ the agent in the sale of such coals as he sent to Liverpool. There was no term, express or implied, that the agreement should absolutely continue for the full seven years. In the words of Lord Penzance:

> Upon such an agreement as that, surely, unless there is some special term in the contract that the principal shall continue to carry on business, it cannot for a moment be implied as a matter of obligation on his part that, whether the business is a profitable one or not, and whether for his own sake he wishes to carry it on or not, he shall be bound to carry it on for the benefit of the agent, and the commission that he may receive.[74]

---

[70] *Willis Faber & Co Ltd v Joyce* (1911) 104 LT 576.
[71] (1840) 11 Ad&El 589.
[72] (1863) 3 F&F 894.
[73] (1876) LR 1 App Cas 256.
[74] *Ibid* at 272.

**13.38**   In every case, however, it will be a matter of construing the terms of the individual contract. As Lord O'Hagan stressed in *Rhodes v Forwood*:

> As in most cases of the kind, we are little assisted by authorities. Judicial decision on one contract can rarely help us to the understanding of another.[75]

Nevertheless, 'in some cases it may be necessary to give effect to a transaction, that the law should supply a stipulation not wilfully to put an end to a business.'[76] Thus, in *Turner v Goldsmith*[77] G, a shirt manufacturer agreed to employ T as agent, canvasser, and traveller on a specified commission for a period of five years. T was employed to sell 'any shirts or other good manufactured by G'. After approximately two years, G's factory was destroyed by fire. G did not resume business, and ceased to employ T, who successfully sued for breach of contract. Because the contract neither specifically referred to the factory nor required that the shirts actually had to be manufactured by G (the contract referred to goods 'manufactured or sold by the defendant as should from time to time be forwarded or submitted by sample or pattern to T'), the Court of Appeal held that it was not impossible for G to carry on business in articles of the kinds mentioned in the agreement, refusing to imply a term that the continuance of the contract was conditional upon the continued existence of the factory.[78]

### The effects of termination under the Commercial Agents (Council Directive) Regulations 1993

*Intervention by the Court of Justice to protect commercial agents*

**13.39**   The Court of Justice of the European Communities has intervened more than once to ensure that those who qualify as commercial agents are not deprived of the various protections conferred on them under the Council Directive. In *Bellone v Yokohama SpA*,[79] for instance, the CJEC (First Chamber) determined that the Directive precludes a national rule making the validity of an agency contract conditional upon the commercial agent being entered in the appropriate register. In *Ingmar GB Ltd v Eaton Leonard Technologies Inc*,[80] too, the Fifth Chamber concluded that harmonization and the elimination of restrictions on the carrying on

---

[75] *Ibid* at 275. See also the forcible views of Carnwath, LJ in *Cel Group Ltd v Nedlloyd Lines UK Ltd* [2004] 1 Lloyd's Rep 381 at [23]–[27].

[76] *Hamlyn & Co v Wood & Co* [1891] 2 QB 488, 493 *per* Bowen, LJ. Similarly, in order to give a contract business efficacy a court may be compelled to imply a term under which, throughout the duration of the contract, the principal is bound to give the agent a reasonable amount of work to enable him to earn that which the parties must be taken to have contemplated: *Bauman v Hulton Press Ltd* [1952] 2 All ER 1121.

[77] [1891] 1 QB 544.

[78] *Ibid* at 550 *per* Lindley, LJ. See also *Alpha Trading Ltd v Dunnshaw-Patten Ltd* [1981] QB 290.

[79] [1998] 3 CMLR 975.

[80] [2001] 1 CMLR 9, esp at [23]–[26].

of the activities of a commercial agent are so important that a principal established outside the Community, whose agent operated within the Community, was not free to elect to evade the application of the Directive by a contractual clause providing for the application of the law of a non-member State. As Waller, LJ pointed out in *AMB Imballaggi Plastici SRL v Pacflex Ltd*, echoing sentiments often expressed in CJEC decisions:

> The object of the Directive and the Regulations was to provide a scheme to protect commercial agents from unscrupulous principals by providing for compensation at the termination of commercial agency whether the termination was rightful or wrongful.[81]

To this end, regs 17 and 18 make generous financial provision for commercial agents following termination of their agencies. Such compensation may take the form of either an 'indemnity' or 'compensation', both terms being defined in the Regulations.

*Choice-of-law clauses and the proper law of the commercial agency contract*

Since the declared objective of the Commercial Agents Directive is to promote 'the **13.40** proper functioning of the common market', it is recognized that at all costs provisions governing freedom of establishment and the operation of undistorted competition in the internal market must be observed throughout the Community. More specifically, as the Fifth Chamber of the CJEC emphasized in *Ingmar GB Ltd v Eaton Leonard Technologies Inc*:

> [I]t is essential for the Community legal order that a principal established in a non-member country, whose commercial agent carries on his activity within the Community, cannot evade those provisions by the simple expedient of a choice-of-law clause. The purpose served by the provisions in question requires that they be applied where the situation is closely connected with the Community, in particular where the commercial agent carries on his activity in the territory of a Member State, irrespective of the law by which the parties intended the contract to be governed.[82]

Whereas the CJEC has made clear that the provisions of the Directive cannot be evaded by the simple expedient of inserting a choice-of-law clause into a contract to oust the jurisdiction of the courts of member states, it is perhaps less apparent what is the resulting proper law of the contract in cases where a commercial agent, operating within Member States under an agreement that claims to be governed by the law

---

[81] [1999] CLC 1391, 1392. See further *Ingmar GB Ltd v Eaton Leonard Technologies Inc* [2001] 1 CMLR 9 at [20] (CJEC, 5th chamber); *Honyvem Informazioni Commerciali Srl v De Zotti*, Case C-465/05 [2006] ECRI-2879 at [19] (CJEC, 1st chamber). The Regulations' compensation provisions have been described as 'their principal feature': *Berry v Laytons* [2009] EWHC 1591 (QB); [2009] ECC 34 at [13] *per* Sharp, J.

[82] [2001] 1 CMLR 9 at [25].

of a non-Member State, nevertheless lodges a claim against his principal under one of the non-derogable provisions of the Directive.

**13.41** In *Fern Computer Consultancy Ltd v Intergraph Cadworx & Analysis Solutions Inc* [83] the claimant agreed to act as agent, fulfilling the role of a commercial agent under the 1993 Regulations, for two Texas software companies, procuring business for them in a territory that included Western Europe. The contract expressly specified that in all respects the parties' relations were to be governed by Texas law. Following the defendant's termination of the contract, the agent obtained leave of a Master to serve a claim under the Commercial Agents Directive out of jurisdiction on the basis that the contract was in truth 'governed by English law' under the Civil Procedure Rules.[84] The agent had successfully argued before the Master that in *Accentuate Ltd v Asigra Inc*[85] Tugendhat, J had previously applied the reasoning in *Ingmar GB Ltd v Eaton Leonard Technologies Inc* and held that an arbitration clause, specifying that the parties' contract was governed by Ontario and Canadian law, was overridden by the mandatory provisions of EU law. Any contractual choice of law which had the effect of depriving a commercial agent of compensation due under the Regulations, it had been said, would fall foul of the mandatory nature of reg 17 or 18, which by virtue of reg 19 are non-derogable.

**13.42** In *Fern Computer Consultancy*, however, a case which raised similar issues, Mann, J disagreed with Tugendhat, J's reasoning in *Accentuate* to the effect that, in the words of the gateway created in Appendix 6B, para 3.1(6)(c) to CPR Part 6, service out of jurisdiction was permissible whenever 'the contract … is governed by English law'. Palpably, the Fern contract was not 'governed by English law': the contract unambiguously stated that it was governed by the law of Texas. Mann, J rejected both grounds on which it might otherwise have been asserted that such an agency contract, despite its choice-of-law clause, was nevertheless governed by English law. First, he did not consider it realistic to contend that the Regulations require the implication into the contract of a term governed by English law. Not only do the Regulations not express themselves as giving rise to any such implication;[86] CPR only requires that the claim be 'in respect of a contract where the contract … is governed by English law'. In any case, the insertion of such an implied term would also produce the odd result that any term implied would have become part of a Texan-law contract and would be as much governed by Texas law as the rest of the contract. Nor, secondly, did Mann, J favour a second argument propounded by the agent that his claim under the Regulations, which undoubtedly did sound in English law, equated with contract for purposes of the rule:

---

[83] [2015] 1 Lloyd's Rep 1.
[84] See CPR Part 6, *Practice Direction 6B–Service out of the Jurisdiction*, para 3.3(6)(c).
[85] [2009] 2 Lloyd's Rep 599.
[86] [2015] 1 Lloyd's Rep 1 at [36].

The Regulations do not affect the proper law of the contract. There will be various aspects of the contract that have nothing to do with the Regulations and there is no reason that they should not survive, subject to Texas law. Similarly there are areas of the law in which the Regulations themselves do not purport to intrude—see for example reg 6 which leaves it to the parties, if they wish, to fix remuneration. So the proper law can continue to govern … The Regulations do not render the choice of law clause otiose. English law does not somehow infect the express contractual terms so as to nullify the choice of law clause. The effect of English law, to be applied by the English courts, is confined to the English law Regulations, which bind the parties so far as their subject matter is concerned, because derogating from some of them is forbidden. So far as any provision of Texas law would otherwise override them then to that extent the proper law of the contract does not have full effect, but it can otherwise apply.[87]

The Regulations, then, are not superimposed on any existing contract as an actual **13.43** higher or parallel contract:[88] 'they acknowledge the existence of the contract to which they relate as a separate legal concept (see, eg, regs 1(3)(a) and 5(2)) and override it to the extent that there are frequent bars on derogation from the Regulations.'[89] In *Fern Computer Consultancy*, therefore, since the contract was not one governed by English law, service out of jurisdiction was impermissible under the CPR gateway:

The claim is undoubtedly one governed by English law, but it is not a claim under a contract and so cannot be brought as such. The gateway requires an English law contract, not an English law claim, and the Regulations do not qualify in that respect.[90]

Nor could the claimant rely upon CPR Practice Direction 6B, para 3.1(7) which permits service out of jurisdiction where 'a claim is made in respect of a breach of contract committed within the jurisdiction.' Whilst it is true that compensation under the Regulations would be payable to the agent in England, this claim could not be said to arise 'in respect of' a breach of contract. The contract had been performed and terminated. That performance and termination was what gives rise to a separate statutory entitlement; it is not a claim in respect of a breach of contract.

---

[87] *Ibid* at [34].

[88] See *Lonsdale v Howard & Hallam Ltd* [2007] 1 WLR 2055 at [3]–[4] *per* Lord Hoffmann.

[89] [2015] 1 Lloyd's Rep 1 at [38].

[90] *Ibid* at [40]. Nor was Mann, J eventually seduced by the argument that the principles set out in *Pfeiffer v Deutsches Rotes Kreuz* [2005] 1 CMLR 44 ought to apply and the word 'contract' be given a generous interpretation in order to achieve the result envisaged by the Directive and to comply with the duty imposed by Article 10 EC to take all appropriate measures, whether general or particular, in order to ensure that fulfilment of that obligation is binding on all authorities of Member States, including the courts: 'The principles in *Pfeiffer* might be brought to bear if there are provisions of national law which would otherwise undermine the operation of the Regulations themselves and frustrate one or more of their provisions. However, the particular gateway paragraph under consideration is not such a provision. It does not purport to affect how the Regulations work. It is merely one of the jurisdictional provisions which govern whether the English court will assume jurisdiction. The obligation on a member state to implement the Directive, and to adjust its substantive laws accordingly, does not require a forced construction of this (or any) particular jurisdictional provision' (at [42]).

Moreover, a failure by the principals to pay would be a breach of obligation under the Regulations, but not a breach of contract.[91]

**13.44**  Mann, J acknowledged that this state of affairs created an impasse and was unsatisfactory in that even though the Regulations seek to impose obligations in respect of commercial agents operating within the Member States, if service out of jurisdiction is not permissible under CPR, for all practical purposes, the Regulations will not be enforceable in a non-Member State whose law is the subject of a choice-of-law clause. The judge did speculate that in such circumstances, in so far as a failure to pay compensation under the Regulations following termination of an agent's contract derives from a breach of statutory duty, for purposes of service out of jurisdiction, it might be possible to treat an agent's claim 'conceptually' as a tort if the damage is suffered by the agent within jurisdiction.[92] Alternatively, it might be possible to contend that the claim is made 'under an enactment which allows proceedings to be brought and those proceedings are not covered by any of the other grounds referred to in CPR Practice Direction 6B, para 3.1'.[93] However, in the final analysis, confronted with the fact that it was improbable that a Texas court would give effect to the Regulations and unlikely that the defendant would acquiesce in its doing so, Mann, J concluded that English courts offered the appropriate forum in which to bring these proceedings. After all, the agent's main activity was here; the agent was an English corporation; it was to be paid here; the claim was under a 'public law mandatory order'; the claimant's witnesses were here; and its documents were here.[94] As Tugendhat, J had declared in *Accentuate*:

> The decision in [*Ingmar GB Ltd v Eaton Leonard Technologies*] requires this court to give effect to the mandatory provisions of EU law, notwithstanding any expression to the contrary on the part of the contracting parties.[95]

In order to give primacy to the commercial agent's claim under the Regulations, Mann, J felt justified in overriding the choice-of-law clause and in determining that an English court was the proper place to resolve the dispute given that it was not clear that a Texas court would give effect to the Regulations at all, and that it was also clear that the defendant was going to say that it should not do so.

*Rights conferred under regs 17 and 18 are non-derogable*

**13.45**  Regulation 19 reinforces the protection regs 17 and 18 afford to commercial agents by providing:

> The parties may not derogate from regulations 17 and 18 to the detriment of the commercial agent before the agency contract expires.

---

[91]  *Ibid* at [46].
[92]  *Ibid* at [55]. See CPR Practice Direction 6B, para 3.1(9)(a), which provides that 'a claim is made in tort where damage was sustained within the jurisdiction.'
[93]  [2015] 1 Lloyd's Rep 1 at [57]. See CPR Practice Direction 6B, para 3.1(20).
[94]  *Ibid* at [123].
[95]  [2009] 2 Lloyd's Rep 599 at [88].

*Indemnity or compensation?*

Regulation 17(1) offers two alternative forms of financial protection for the com-    **13.46**
mercial agent whose agency has terminated, either 'indemnity' or 'compensation':

> This regulation has effect for the purpose of ensuring that the commercial agent is,
> after termination of the agency contract, indemnified in accordance with paragraphs
> (3) to (5) below or compensated for damage in accordance with paragraphs (6) and
> (7) below.

Unlike other European jurisdictions which have selected one regime or the
other when they implemented the Directive, the United Kingdom adopted a
more complex approach opting for both, thereby allowing the parties freedom
to choose in their agreements whether an 'indemnity' or 'compensation' would
become due following termination of the commercial agency. Indeed, com-
plicating matters further, the Department of Trade and Industry, as was explained in Guidance Notes to the Regulations, stated that nothing prevented
parties from electing indemnity for certain eventualities and compensation for
others within the same contract. In *Page v Combined Shipping and Trading Co
Ltd* [96] Staughton, LJ observed that harmonization sought under the European
Regulations was intended to let 'people compete—in the popular *cliché* of
today—on a level playing field'. In view of the UK's decision to leave both
compensation and indemnity available to the parties, Davis, J in *Tigana Ltd v
Decoro Ltd* [97] aptly remarked:

> The UK, however, has compounded the compromise, as it were, by providing for
> both. Thus, if the overall policy is that parties compete on a level playing field …
> parties, in the context of reg 17 and depending on whether the indemnity system
> or compensation system applies, could be said to be competing on different football
> pitches.[98]

Regulation 17(2) places the sole restriction on the parties' freedom to choose be    **13.47**
tween indemnity and compensation by prescribing:

> Except where the agency contract otherwise provides, the commercial agent shall be
> entitled to be compensated rather than indemnified.

As *Crane v Sky-In-Home Ltd* illustrates, this means that where the principal
has unsuccessfully sought to exclude liability for both compensation and indemnity and the contract necessarily provides for neither, by default the agent
upon termination will be entitled to compensation.[99] It will have to be shown
that the contract actually does 'provide otherwise'. Thus, in *Shearman v Hunter*

---

[96] [1996] CLC 1952; [1997] 3 All ER 656.
[97] [2003] EWHC 23 (QB); [2003] ECC 23.
[98] *Ibid* at [85].
[99] [2007] 2 All ER (Comm) 599 at [93]. Appeal was unsuccessfully taken against Briggs, J's judgment on procedural grounds: see [2008] EWCA Civ 978.

*Boot Ltd*,[100] the court refused to accept as valid an agreement under whose terms it was not clear at the time the agreement was concluded which system was to prevail. The contract merely provided that whichever system turned out to be cheapest for the principal was to apply. As the court noted, 'The clause does not give the agent, in a real sense, the "*Entitlement*" (as it is described in the heading to the Regulation) to either compensation or, alternatively, indemnity.'[101] A similar contractual situation arose in *Brand Studio Ltd v St John Knits Inc*.[102] However, in this case, Teare, J was able to sever the offending portion of the disputed contractual clause, employing the criteria set out in *Sadler v Imperial Life Assurance*,[103] according to which the remaining unchanged wording had to be supported by adequate consideration and the remaining text did not fundamentally alter the character of the parties' contract, and held that the agent was entitled to an indemnity from the principal following termination of his contract.

*Ought English courts to interpret 'indemnity' and 'compensation' in light of their French and German precursors?*

**13.48** Although 'indemnity' and 'compensation', as defined in the Regulations, are inspired by German and French legal counterparts respectively, ought English courts to interpret the regimes which are available to parties under the English Regulations in light of their French and German precursors? In *Lonsdale v Howard & Hallam Ltd*[104] Lord Hoffmann commented upon the origins of the two terms 'indemnity' and 'compensation':

> The words 'indemnity' and 'compensation' are not very illuminating in marking the distinction between these two rights. They are both ways of dealing with the unfairness which it was thought might arise if the termination of the agency leaves the agent worse off and the principal better off than if the agency had continued. It appears that the right under article 17(2), which the draftsman has chosen to label 'indemnity', is derived from German law and is now contained in s. 89b of the *Handelsgesetzbuch*. The right to 'compensation' under article 17(3) is derived from French law and is now contained in art 12 of the *loi n° 91-593 du 25 juin 1991 relative aux rapports entre les agents commerciaux et leurs mandants*. The two systems can plainly lead to different results, so that, on this point at any rate, the extent of the coordination achieved by the Directive is modest.[105]

---

[100] [2014] 1 All ER (Comm) 689.
[101] *Ibid* at [25].
[102] [2016] 1 Lloyd's Rep 179. This approach has not met with universal approval: Harris (2015) 159(48) SJ 27; Belgrove & Padfield (2016) 166 NLJ 16 (Comm Law Update).
[103] [1988] IRLR 388.
[104] *Lonsdale (t/a Lonsdale Agencies) v Howard & Hallam Ltd (Winemakers' Federation of Australia Inc intervening)* [2007] 1 WLR 2055.
[105] [2007] 1 WLR 2055 at [5]. More recently, in *Berry v Laytons* [2009] EWHC 1591 (QB); [2009] ECC 34 at [14], having noted that in Germany, upon termination of a commercial *agency*, the agent became entitled to 'an equitable payment', known as an 'indemnity', whereas in France the

At first, it had been widely assumed that because the origins of these two institu-  **13.49**
tions lay in German and French law, the terms 'indemnity' and 'compensation' were
meant to be given equivalent meanings to those they possessed in those foreign
systems.[106] Elias, J, however, called this approach into question in *Bell Electric Ltd v
Aweco Appliance Systems GmbH & Co KG*:

> I will not enter the debate as to whether or not the courts in England and Wales
> ought to apply the principles of French Law in determining compensation, save
> to observe that it does seem to me that they are plainly not obliged to do so as a
> result of European Union law itself. This is because the community legal order
> should not be assumed in general to have intended to define concepts by reference
> to the law of one or more national legal system unless there is an express provision
> to that effect.[107]

The House of Lords subsequently endorsed this view in *Lonsdale v Howard &
Hallam Ltd*,[108] holding that, when computing 'compensation' payable under reg
17(6), for example, English courts are not obliged to adopt the French method
of calculating the value of an agency following termination. The CJEC itself had
already made clear:

> [A]lthough the system established by art. 17 of the Directive is mandatory and
> prescribes a framework ... it does not give any detailed indications as regards the
> method of calculation of the indemnity for termination of contract ... Therefore ...
> within the framework prescribed by art. 17(2) of the Directive, the Member States
> enjoy a margin of discretion which they may exercise....[109]

Because the way in which individual states implement the Directive is a matter
for national judgement, the House of Lords in *Lonsdale* concluded that in operating these concepts account may be taken of the, sometimes very, different
market conditions under which commercial agencies operate in France and in
England.[110]

---

courts awarded 'compensation,' Sharp, J has also made the point that the two regimes operate differently, and can lead in any particular case to different results.

[106] See, eg, *Moore v Piretta Pta Ltd* [1998] CLC 992, 994 *per* John Mitting, QC: 'It is apparent
from the preamble that the primary purpose of the Directive is the harmonisation of community
law by requiring all member states to introduce rights and duties similar to those already subsisting in at least two of the member states of the Community, the Federal Republic of Germany and
France.' See also *King v T Tunnock Ltd* [2000] EuLR 531; *Ingmar GB Ltd v Eaton Leonard Inc*
[2001] CLC 1825.

[107] [2002] CLC 1246 at [56].

[108] [2007] 1 WLR 2055.

[109] *Honeyvem Informazioni Commerciali Srl v de Zotti*, Case C-465/04; [2006] ECR I-02879, at
[34]–[36]. See also *Ingmar GB Ltd v Eaton Leonard Technologies Inc*, Case C-381/98; [2000] ECR
I-9305 at [21].

[110] [2007] 1 WLR 2055, esp at [18]. This approach has been criticized by Saintier [2007] JBL
90–8, who—mistakenly, I suggest—inquires whether the *Lonsdale* approach does not pay 'too much
regard to existing common law principles'.

*What is meant by the concept of 'termination' in regs 17 and 18?*

**13.50**  Regulation 17(1) lays down that a commercial agent may be indemnified or compensated 'after *termination* of the agency contract'.[111] Regulation 18 restricts this right by providing that indemnity and compensation are not payable if 'the principal has *terminated* the agency contract' or if 'the commercial agent has *himself terminated* the agency contract'.[112] Although the word 'terminate' appears both in reg 17 ('termination') and in reg 18 ('terminated'), in *Cooper v Pure Fishing (UK) Ltd*[113] Tuckey, LJ reiterated a point made in earlier cases, that the word does not bear the same meaning in the two regulations.

*The meaning of 'termination' under reg 17*

**13.51**  Regulation 17(8) expressly provides that a commercial agent's entitlement to an indemnity or to compensation 'shall also arise where the agency contract is terminated as a result of the death of the commercial agent'. However, in *Light v Ty Europe Ltd*[114] the Court of Appeal decided that 'terminate' in reg 17 also covers the case of an agency that has simply run its course—that is, reg 17 entitles a commercial agent to compensation even when his agency has terminated through pure effluxion of time. The Court of Appeal approved Davis, J's judgment in *Tigana Ltd v Decoro Ltd*,[115] in which the judge had held that the word 'termination' in reg 17 was employed in an intransitive sense and meant no more than 'come to an end'. As Tuckey, LJ noted in *Light v Ty Europe Ltd*:

> A purposive construction reinforced this view since there could be no policy or purpose for excluding contracts which expire by effluxion of time in Regulations designed to protect commercial agents.[116]

Had it been the intention of the Regulations to exclude a contract that expired by mere effluxion of time, they could have made this explicit. Agents on single fixed-term contracts that come to an end are not therefore to be denied compensation as a matter of principle. The compensation provisions, it needed to be remembered, derived from proprietary remedies developed in some civil law jurisdictions, where compensation was payable not only on the basis that the agent had suffered loss, but also on the basis that the agent's efforts had

---

[111]  Emphasis added.
[112]  Regulation 18(a) and (b) (emphasis added).
[113]  [2004] 2 Lloyd's Rep 518.
[114]  [2004] 1 Lloyd's Rep 693.
[115]  [2003] Eur LR 189.
[116]  [2004] 1 Lloyd's Rep 693 at [32].

provided benefit to the principal.[117] Thus, Lightman, J concluded in *Light v Ty Europe Ltd*:

> ... [Regulation] 17 [is] apt to provide for payment of compensation where the agency agreement between the principal and the commercial agent expired automatically at the end of a fixed period because:
>
> (1) the characteristic of a commercial agent entitled to the protection of the Directive is ... that his services rendered during the period of his agency agreement will continue to produce profits for his principal after his agency agreement has terminated; and
>
> (2) it is the purpose of ... in particular art 17 ... to secure that, unless (as provided in art 18) the principal has terminated the agency agreement because of default by the commercial agent or the agent has himself terminated the agency agreement without justification, the commercial agent shall have a share of these post-termination profits.

The word 'terminate' in the context of the Directive is therefore apt to include the situation where an agency contract expires by effluxion of time.[118]

### The meaning of 'termination' under reg 18

Regulation 18 prescribes the circumstances in which indemnity and compensation will not be due to the agent: namely, either when the principal has terminated the agency contract because of default attributable to the commercial agent or when the commercial agent has himself terminated the agency. As Tuckey, LJ explained in *Cooper v Pure Fishing (UK) Ltd*,[119] in reg 18(a) the word 'terminated' requires to be read in the context of the entire paragraph, which reads: 'the principal has terminated the agency contract because of a default attributable to the commercial agent ...' This being so:

**13.52**

> Read as a whole the natural meaning of these words is that the principal has done something unilaterally which brings the contract to an end and that his reason for doing so is some default on the part of the agent which justifies summary termination— in other words, because the agent has committed some serious breach of the contract which entitles the principal to bring it to an end ... I do not see how this analysis of

---

[117] *Ibid* at [35]. Tuckey, LJ also invoked reg 17(7)(a), which deems damage to have occurred if termination '(a) deprive[s] the commercial agent of the commission which proper performance of the agency contract would have procured for him whilst providing his principal with substantial benefits linked to the activities of the commercial agent' (at [35]).

[118] *Ibid* at [46]. Lightman, J reinforced the argument: 'It is sufficient for this purpose to refer to art 20.2 which provides that a restraint of trade clause shall be valid for not more than two years after termination of the agency contract. The term "termination" in this Article must plainly include expiration by effluxion of time. This conclusion may place a premium on a principal, when sufficient grounds exist, terminating an agency contract on grounds of default as provided for in art 18 prior to expiration of the agreement by effluxion of time rather than allowing the agency contract to run its full course.'

[119] [2004] 2 Lloyd's Rep 518.

what reg. 18(a) apparently says can possibly be applied to a termination which occurs when a contract comes to an end simply by effluxion of time.[120]

Where a contract of agency expires by pure effluxion of time, therefore, a principal will not have 'terminated' the agency contract within the meaning of reg 18 and compensation may continue to be due to the agent.

### Indemnity and compensation

*How is an agent's 'indemnity' calculated under reg 17(3) and (4)?*

13.53 Regulation 17 provides for an indemnity in the following terms:

> (3) Subject to paragraph (9) and to regulation 18 below, the commercial agent shall be entitled to an indemnity if and to the extent that—
> (a) he has brought the principal new customers or has significantly increased the volume of business with existing customers and the principal continues to derive substantial benefits from the business with such customers; and
> (b) the payment of this indemnity is equitable having regard to all the circumstances and, in particular, the commission lost by the commercial agent on the business transacted with such customers.
> (4) The amount of the indemnity shall not exceed a figure equivalent to an indemnity for one year calculated from the commercial agent's average annual remuneration over the preceding five years and if the contract goes back less than five years the indemnity shall be calculated on the average for the period in question.

13.54 It is tolerably clear that the indemnity is intended to indemnify the agent to the extent that he has contributed to the expansion of the principal's business and the latter continues to benefit there from. Lord Hoffmann stressed this aspect of the commercial agent's entitlement to an indemnity in *Lonsdale*:

> It is a condition of the indemnity that the agent should have 'brought the principal new customers or … significantly increased the volume of business with existing customers' and that the principal 'continues to derive substantial benefits from the business with such customers': art 17(3)(a). It follows that in a case such as the present, in which the principal went out of business and therefore derived no benefit from the customers introduced by the agent, no indemnity will be payable.[121]

*Indemnity and damages*

13.55 If an agent is awarded an indemnity following termination of his contract, reg 17(5) further provides:

> The grant of an indemnity as mentioned above shall not prevent the commercial agent from seeking damages.

---

[120]  *Ibid* at [15].
[121]  [2007] 1 WLR 2055 at [20].

This is necessitated by the nature of the indemnity. The 'damages' referred to would be damages in the normal course of events payable to an agent by his principal under domestic law for breach of contract (which would include the principal's failure to pay commission due).

### How is 'compensation' calculated under reg 17(6) and (7)?

Regulation 17 entitles a commercial agent to recover sums representing damage he **13.56** has suffered in consequence of termination of his relations with the principal. The provision lays down that such damage is 'deemed to occur particularly', but not exclusively, in certain circumstances. The Regulation reads:

(6) Subject to paragraph (9) and to regulation 18 below, the commercial agent shall be entitled to compensation for the damage he suffers as a result of the termination of his relations with his principal.

(7) For the purpose of these Regulations such damage shall be deemed to occur particularly when the termination takes place in either or both of the following circumstances, namely circumstances which—

(a) deprive the commercial agent of the commission which proper performance of the agency contract would have procured for him whilst providing his principal with substantial benefits linked to the activities of the commercial agent; or

(b) have not enabled the commercial agent to amortize the costs and expenses that he had incurred in the performance of the agency contract on the advice of his principal.

In *Vick v Vogle-Gapes Ltd* HHJ Seymour, QC remarked upon the 'curious' draft- **13.57** ing of reg 17(7), which deems damage to have occurred in one of two alternative scenarios.[122] From this, it was to be assumed that it is to this deemed damage that the entitlement to compensation in reg 17(6) relates:

The compensatable damage is thus either loss of the commission which proper performance of the agency contract would have procured or unamortized costs incurred on the advice of the principal.[123]

Loss of the commission which proper performance of the agency contract would have procured, however, can only be recovered under reg 17(7)(a) if and to the extent that the principal has received 'substantial benefits linked to the activities of the commercial agent'. Thus, if no such substantial benefits have accrued to the principal, there is no damage for which to compensate. On the other hand, if the agent's performance has yielded substantial benefits, no matter how large or small, full compensation for loss of commission is payable. As regards the second type of deemed damage under reg 17(7)(b), where termination has occurred in

---

[122] [2006] EWHC 1665 (TCC) at [124].
[123] *Ibid* at [125].

'circumstances which … have not enabled the commercial agent to amortize the costs and expenses', it has been suggested:

> The second type of compensatable damage seems, in effect, to be that which would have been appropriate if the principal had warranted to the commercial agent that he would amortize the costs which he was advised to incur.[124]

**13.58**  In *Lonsdale v Howard & Hallam Ltd*[125] the House of Lords was required to consider how compensation is to be calculated under reg 17. In *Lonsdale* L had sued his principal, H, a shoe manufacturer, whose products L had sold to shoe shops between 1990 and 2003. In 2003 H, whose business was in steep decline, ceased trading, having terminated L's agency by reasonable notice. It was agreed that L was owed compensation under reg 17(6); the dispute concerned the amount due. H paid £7,500, but L claimed £19,670—being the equivalent of two years' gross commission averaged over the last five years of his agency, less the amount already received. In 1997–98 L's gross commission had been almost £17,000, but by 2002–03 it had slumped to £9,621. The judge, taking into account that at the date of termination of the agency H's business had been in serious decline, awarded L £5,000, a decision subsequently upheld by the Court of Appeal.

**13.59**  On appeal to the House of Lords, it was argued that since 'compensation' was inspired by an institution of French commercial agency, the practice of the French courts ought to be followed. The Regulations, the argument ran, require that an agent be compensated for 'the damage he suffers as a result of the termination of his relations with the principal'. In making this calculation, French law's 'elegant theory' is that the agent is regarded as having had a share in the goodwill of the principal's business, which he has assisted in building up. Their relationship, therefore, is treated as having existed for their common benefit. Since the agent has acquired a share in the goodwill—an asset the principal retains after the termination of the agency—the agent is held entitled to compensation. In calculating compensation, French law values 'the income stream which the agency would have generated', had it continued, and the common practice is for French courts to value agencies at twice the average annual gross commission over the previous three years—although they retain discretion to award less if the agent's loss in fact was less. UK courts would not therefore be acting inconsistently with the Directive were they to calculate compensation by reference to the value of the agency on the assumption that it had continued 'because, as a matter of common sense, that is what will matter to the hypothetical purchaser'—namely, the amount which the agent could reasonably expect to receive for the right to stand in his shoes, to continue to perform the duties of the agency and to receive the commission which he would have received.

---

[124] *Ibid* at [125]. The judge commented: 'All of this seems very alien and not to possess any obvious logical foundation.'

[125] [2007] 1 WLR 2055.

Lord Hoffmann rejected this approach, noting that because it is open to States to **13.60** implement the Council Directive in such a way as to take account of the different market conditions under which commercial agencies operate in different jurisdictions, the principles that govern French compensation have no application in the UK:

> It would appear that in France agencies do change hands and that it is common for the premium charged on such a transaction to be twice the gross commission. Whether the judicial practice of estimating the value of the agency at twice gross commission is based upon this fact of French economic life or whether vendors of agency businesses are able to charge such a premium because the purchaser knows that he will be able to recover that amount, either from the next purchaser or from the principal on termination of the agency, is unclear ... There does seem to be evidence that some principals demand payment of an estimated twice gross commission in return for the grant of a commercial agency (even if they have to lend the agent the money) because they know that they will have to return this amount to the agent on termination. At any rate, whatever the origins of the practice, it would appear that twice gross commission is often the real value of an agency in France because that is what you could sell it for in the market.... *There is no such market in England.*[126]

The difference between French and English practice, therefore, resides not in those countries' respective courts applying different rules of law but in different market conditions.[127]

In calculating compensation due under reg 17, Lord Hoffmann approved the for- **13.61** mula employed by Judge Bowers in *Barrett McKenzie v Escada*, who had said:

> [O]ne is valuing the agency and its connections that have been established by the agent at the time of or immediately before termination, and it is really a question of compensating for the notional value of that agency in the open market ...[128]

The value of an agency will depend upon the circumstances actually obtaining at the time of termination. Notably, these will include the agent's earning prospects and what people would have been prepared to pay for the agent's services. Lord Hoffmann was critical of the approach adopted by the court in *Smith, Bailey Palmer v Howard & Hallam Ltd*,[129] where it had been assumed that the entire goodwill of

---

[126] *Ibid* at [18] (emphasis added).

[127] '[I]t comes as no surprise that any valuation evidence used to support a claim for compensation is likely to deal in hypothetical terms with what a willing purchaser might be prepared to pay on various assumptions including that the contract of agency is assignable but without being able to produce evidence of comparable transactions to suggest the estimate of value': *Nigel Fryer Joiner Services Ltd v Ian Firth Hardware Ltd* [2008] 2 Lloyd's Rep 108 at [56] *per* Patten, J.

[128] [2001] Eu LR 567. Lord Hoffmann did express one small reservation concerning the judge's use of the word 'notional': 'All that is notional is the assumption that the agency was available to be bought and sold at the relevant date. What it would fetch depends upon circumstances as they existed in the real world at the time: what the earnings prospects of the agency were and what people would have been willing to pay for similar businesses at the time' (at [28]).

[129] [2006] Eu LR 578.

the company had been attributable to the sales and marketing endeavours of the agent, and where the court had made no allowance for the fact that the principal might have made a good product. The court had also made:

> no allowance ... for the fact that the commission, which is treated as the measure of the proprietary interest of the agents in the assets of the company, is what the agents were actually paid for their services. On this theory, the advertising agents should have acquired an interest proportionate to what they were paid.[130]

Finally, Lord Hoffmann took issue with the judge's approach because the valuation was based entirely on cost rather than what anyone would actually have paid for the agency.

**13.62** In *Lonsdale* Lord Hoffmann, speaking for the whole House, approved the trial judge's approach to reg 17(3). At first instance HHJ Harris, QC had said:

> If it is kept in mind that the damage for which the agent is to be compensated consists in the loss of the value or goodwill he can be said to have possessed in the agency, then it can be seen that valuation ought to be reasonably straightforward. Small businesses of all kinds are daily being bought and sold, and a major element in the composition of their price will be a valuation of goodwill.[131]

Turning to the specific case, Judge Harris had declared:

> The value of that agency, the commercial value is what someone would pay for it ... This was an agency producing a modest and falling income in a steadily deteriorating environment. There is no evidence that anyone would have paid anything to buy it ... I am strongly tempted to find that no damage has been established ... But perhaps that conclusion, though I regard it as logical, is a little over-rigorous given that the defendant has already made a payment. Doing the best I can, I find that the appropriate figure for compensation is one of £5,000.

This conclusion was subsequently endorsed by Moore-Bick, LJ in the Court of Appeal,[132] and ultimately by the House of Lords.[133]

**13.63** Similarly, in *Warren t/a On-Line Cartons and Print v Drukkerij Flack BV*,[134] it was unsuccessfully argued that, following his retirement, an English commercial agent's agency, in which he had acted on behalf of a Dutch printed cardboard manufacturer, was valueless. The Court of Appeal was critical of the first-instance judge who appeared to have assumed not only the existence of Lord Hoffmann's 'hypothetical

---

130 [2007] 1 WLR 2055 at [31].
131 *Ibid* at [18].
132 [2006] 1 WLR 1281 esp at [53]–[54].
133 [2007] 1 WLR 2055 at [34]. For a further example of a court's efforts to assess the value of an agency, see *Alan Ramsay Sales & Marketing Ltd v Typhoo Tea Ltd* [2016] EWHC 486 (Comm) at [88]ff *per* Flaux, J.
134 [2015] 1 Lloyd's Rep 111.

purchaser' but also that the latter would have been prepared to pay something for the agency:

> All that Lord Hoffmann meant by referring to the 'hypothetical purchaser' was that for the purpose of deciding what value (if any) an agency has one has to assume the existence of someone who is prepared to buy. In one sense, of course, if a hypothetical purchaser would not be prepared to pay anything, it is odd to refer to him as a 'purchaser' at all. But for the purpose of making a valuation one always does assume a hypothetical purchaser. It does not mean that one also assumes that there is a price he will pay. The argument that the agency is in fact valueless does have to be addressed, if it is raised.[135]

Longmore, LJ nevertheless went on to hold that the agent had shown on a balance of probabilities that the agency did have a value of some kind. Therefore, it was for the principal 'to show on the evidence that the agency was in fact valueless ... The court would have to be persuaded that the evidence points to no other conclusion'.[136] In this particular case, the agent's claim did not fail merely because the agent could not point to an identifiable purchaser who would have been prepared to take the agency on at a price.[137] Nor was there strong evidence suggesting that after the agent's retirement the agency would disappear as his principal would in future deal directly with the third party.

**13.64** Compensation under reg 17, therefore, is to be calculated by reference to the value of the agency on the assumption that it had continued, mainly taking into account the agent's right to commission. The value of an agency will depend upon the circumstances which actually existed at the time of termination, including what its earning prospects were and what people might have been prepared to pay for it. In *Lonsdale* itself the court had been correct to take into account the fact that L's agency had been producing a modest and falling income in a steadily deteriorating environment and that there was no evidence that anyone would have paid anything for the agency.

### The need for expert valuation evidence

**13.65** Because the approved measure of 'compensation' is the cost of acquiring the goodwill, in *Lonsdale* the question was raised whether it was essential to obtain expert valuation evidence. Lord Hoffmann shared concerns at the cost of having to produce such evidence. However, his Lordship considered that since comparable businesses

---

[135] *Ibid* at [14].

[136] *Ibid* at [15].

[137] Longmore, LJ declined to accept that an agent's failure to point to an identifiable purchaser who would have been prepared to take over the agency could constitute evidence sufficient to enable a court to declare an agency valueless. However, 'if there had been evidence of a sustained effort to sell which had failed for reasons connected with the agency itself, that would be a matter which a judge would, no doubt, take into account' (at [17]).

are regularly bought and sold, in the majority of cases parties will choose not to bring the matter to court: with the benefit of advice about the going rate for such businesses, it ought not to be difficult for the parties to agree amongst themselves on an appropriate valuation. Nevertheless, if the matter is litigated, the court will need to be informed about standard methods for valuing such businesses. This was not done in *Lonsdale*, where:

> the judge was simply invited to pluck a figure out of the air from across the Channel and rightly refused to do so. Nothing is more likely to cause uncertainty and promote litigation than a lottery system under which judges are invited to choose figures at random.[138]

Lord Hoffmann did suggest that over course of time it might be possible for courts to take judicial notice of such matters in the more straightforward situations where an agency which has continued for some time and the net commission figures are relatively stable. But if the case was not of a standard variety, adjustments needed to be made where, as in *Lonsdale*, the market was in decline or had dried up altogether.

*The court is not obliged to accept experts' valuation*

**13.66**  It will obviously be of great assistance to the court, whenever expert valuers are employed by the parties, if the experts can agree a valuation. However, even if the experts are agreed, the judge is not obliged slavishly to accept their joint valuation. In *McQuillan v McCormick*,[139] for example, following last-minute negotiations, the parties' experts agreed a value for the agency relationship which, ostensibly, they arrived at as Lord Hoffmann had directed in *Lonsdale*. HHJ Behrens, however, considered that they had overestimated their valuation primarily because they had taken too little account of the risk of termination:

> Mr McCormick's Licence ... contains in clause 9 rights of termination by the license owner. Under clause 9.3 the license owner had the right to terminate on one year's notice if the orders did not amount to €300,000 in a calendar year. Under clause 9.4 there was a right to renegotiate every year. If no agreement could be reached the agreement continued for a further 12 months and then terminates. It is thus realistically arguable that the agreement is in fact terminable on a year's notice ... If the contract between Mr McCormick and Pandora A/S comes to an end then there will be no income stream. In that event it is clear from Lord Hoffmann's speech that it is of no value.[140]

*Placing a value on an agency where the agent has induced his clientele to defect to another supplier*

**13.67**  In *Lonsdale* Lord Hoffmann offered his views on another matter that did not arise directly from the case. If the agent can transfer the goodwill he has created

---

[138] [2007] 1 WLR 2055 at [35].
[139] [2010] EWHC 112 (QB); [2011] ECC 18.
[140] *Ibid* at [165] and [167].

with customers to another principal—the example given was that of an agent who persuaded supermarkets that had been buying the produce of one winery to transfer their custom to another winery—the former principal would not retain the goodwill which the agent had created and, it was said, it would be unfair to have to pay compensation on the basis that the agent had gone out of business. In the view of Lord Hoffmann, this was not problematical. It would simply affect the price someone would hypothetically be prepared to pay for the agency:

> If the situation in real life is that the hypothetical purchaser would be in competition with the former agent and could not have any assurance that the customers would continue to trade with him, that would affect the amount he was prepared to pay. If it appeared that all the customers were likely to defect to the former agent (or, for that matter, to someone else), he would be unlikely to be prepared to pay much for the agency.[141]

Although the court is concerned with what would have appeared likely at the date of termination and not what actually happened afterwards, it cannot be required to shut its eyes to what actually happened. This may provide evidence of what the parties were likely to have expected to happen.[142]

### Loss of agent's entitlement to indemnity or compensation for damage

*Loss of the commercial agent's right to indemnity and remuneration*

The Regulations require a commercial agent to act with comparative expedition if **13.68** it is proposed to claim an indemnity or compensation following termination of the agency. Regulation 17(9) provides:

> The commercial agent shall lose his entitlement to the indemnity or compensation for damage ... if within one year following termination of his agency contract he has not notified his principal that he intends pursuing his entitlement.[143]

However, because in the words of reg 19, 'the parties may not derogate from regulation 17... to the detriment of the commercial agent before the agency contract expires', it is open to the parties to allow the agent greater latitude in their agreement.

The operative dates may not be easy to establish. In *Claramoda Ltd v Zoomphase Ltd* **13.69** *(t/a Jenny Packham)*[144] Simon, J was required to fix the date upon which an agency terminated and from which time began to run. The task was especially difficult

---

[141] *Ibid* at [38].

[142] *Ibid* at [39].

[143] Eg, *Berry v Laytons* [2009] EWHC 1591 (QB); [2009] ECC 34 at [47], which involved a professional negligence action brought against solicitors concerning advice they gave in respect of reg 17(9).

[144] [2010] 1 All ER (Comm) 830.

owing to a lack of written contractual material. This meant that the judge had to rely heavily on oral evidence and inferences derived from the parties' conduct. There was also the pronouncedly seasonal nature of the parties' business (the fashion trade) to be considered, as well as the fact that much of the parties' business was conducted by telephone and few documents were generated. In the event, Simon, J concluded that notice had been given within the required twelve-month period because, although no further sales were made, there was evidence showing the commercial agent's continuing authority to negotiate (in the broad sense identified by Morritt, LJ in *Parks v Esso Petroleum Ltd*[145]). Indeed, 'although reg 2(1) defines the role of a commercial agent by reference to a continuing authority to negotiate, the agency contract dos not necessarily terminate when the agent ceases to negotiate sales.'[146] The agent's continuing after-sales activities on behalf of the principal also indicated that the agency had not finally terminated.[147]

**13.70** (i) **The entitlement to indemnity and compensation is lost if the principal has terminated the agency owing to a default attributable to the commercial agent**   Regulation 18(a) excludes the agent's entitlement to an indemnity or to compensation where:

> the principal has terminated the agency contract because of default attributable to the commercial agent which would justify immediate termination of the agency contract pursuant to regulation 16 ...

Regulation 16, in turn, provides:

> These Regulations shall not affect the application of any enactment or rule of law which provides for the immediate termination of the agency contract—
> (a)   because of the failure of one party to carry out all or part of his obligations under that contract; or
> (b)   where exceptional circumstances arise.

**13.71** In *Crane v Sky In-Home Ltd*[148] counsel for the principal had contended that the words 'any ... rule of law' in reg 16 could include English contract law, and that a clause in the agency agreement entitling a party to terminate the contract forthwith when the other party either committed irremediable, persistent or recurring breaches of the agreement, or remediable breaches which were not remedied within seven days of notice of the breach, therefore meant that the injured party might terminate the agreement pursuant to reg 16 whenever termination was permissible under the contract. Briggs, J, however, rejected this general argument on the ground that it would enable parties to evade the requirements of Part IV of the Regulations, which govern conclusion and termination of commercial agency

---

[145]   (2000) Eu LR 25; see para **1.45**.
[146]   [2010] 1 All ER (Comm) 830 at [43].
[147]   *Ibid* at [44].
[148]   [2007] 2 All ER (Comm) 599.

agreements, by providing that any contractual breach might justify termination. In the view of Briggs, J:

> [T]he expression 'any enactment or rule of law' points to a provision of the applicable law which justifies immediate termination regardless of the terms of the contract. The obvious candidate in English law is the doctrine of repudiatory breach.[149]

Determining whether a repudiatory breach has taken place is 'highly fact-sensi-  **13.72**
tive', a circumstance that renders comparison between cases 'of limited value'.[150] Nevertheless, by way of illustration, in *Crocs Europe BV v Anderson et al (t/a Spectrum Agencies)*[151] an employee of the agent, employed to sell the principal's footwear, had posted derogatory comments, broadly aping Star Wars themes, mocking the principal's business on an internet website. A link to the website was emailed both to other employees and to third parties, including UK customers and distributors in other markets. Did this breach of various duties imposed under the Regulations (notably, the duty to act dutifully and in good faith)[152] or of fiduciary duties (notably, the duty of loyalty)[153] amount to a repudiatory breach of contract entitling the principal to terminate the agency, thereby precluding any claim to compensation under reg 17? Mummery, LJ rejected the principal's arguments that reg 3 creates an implied condition, breach of which will automatically terminate the agency contract, or that the Regulations contemplate an automatic right to terminate in the event of breach of any of the various statutory duties they impose.[154] He also dismissed the proposition that the agent's breach of fiduciary duty led to a similar outcome:

(a) [N]or all duties owed within a fiduciary relationship ... are properly classified as fiduciary duties (the duty to obey instructions and the duty of skill and care being examples of non-fiduciary duties); and

(b) not all breaches of duty owed by a fiduciary and properly classified as fiduciary (the duty of fidelity and loyalty being the prime example of a fiduciary duty) either automatically or necessarily repudiate the contract.[155]

---

[149] *Ibid* at [84].

[150] *Eminence Property Developments Ltd v Heaney* [2011] 2 All ER (Comm) 223 at [62] *per* Etherton, LJ. In order to bring the contract to an end, the innocent party must have accepted the repudiation because 'an unaccepted repudiation is a thing writ in water: it confers no legal rights of any sort or kind' (*Howard v Pickford Tool Co Ltd* [1951] 1 KB 417, 421 *per* Asquith, LJ). Although an innocent party's failure to perform the contract may be treated as acceptance, simple acquiescence will not. The innocent party who, in full knowledge of the circumstances, continues to perform the contract or, in some other way, unequivocally indicates that he is waiving the breach, will be taken to have affirmed the contract. The innocent party has to elect one course or the other within a reasonable time (*Stocznia Gdanska SA v Latvian Shipping Co (No 2)* [2002] 2 Lloyd's Rep 436 at [87] *per* Rix LJ).

[151] [2013] 1 Lloyd's Rep 1.

[152] See para **8.76**.

[153] See paras **8.19ff**.

[154] [2013] 1 Lloyd's Rep 1 at [45] and [46].

[155] *Ibid* at [47]. As HHJ Simon Brown, QC remarked in *Gledhill v Bentley Designs (UK) Ltd* [2011] 1 Lloyd's Rep 270 at [7]–[8], in the analogous setting of a contract of employment, 'abusive language by an employee towards his ... employer may amount to a repudiatory breach of contract

Breaches of fiduciary duty, therefore, are capable of producing other consequences than simple termination of the fiduciary relationship, depending not only on 'the nature of the duty owed, but also on the factual circumstances in which the particular breach occurred and the intentions of the parties, as expressed or inferred, in relation to the contract'.[156] Thus, the question to be considered was: How serious, in all the circumstances, was the claimant's conduct in connection with the internet posting? The Court of Appeal thereupon upheld the trial judge's decision that, albeit a breach of contract by the agent, it did not go to the root of the agency relationship, being more a one-off incident involving no bad faith on the agent's part, not presenting a real risk of harm to the principal by dissemination to the world at large and, when viewed objectively, not connoting an intention to abandon or to refuse to perform the commercial agency contract.[157]

**13.73** According to *Crane*, a principal is not required to show that he actually did terminate the contract with immediate effect in a manner justified by an enactment or rule of law. Regulation 18(a) allows the principal to terminate otherwise than summarily or by acceptance of an anticipatory breach provided that at that moment the principal had a right to terminate immediately within the meaning of reg 16—that is, by the acceptance of a repudiatory breach.[158] Thus, in *Crane*, C's agency was terminated because his default fell within the ambit of reg 18(a). C had deliberately and persistently passed off his extended warranty service as that of the Sky group. This amounted to a continuing and serious breach of his duty of fidelity to Sky In-Home Service Ltd. The person responsible for termination of the agreement on the latter's behalf correctly believed that C had continued in that course of conduct, and had terminated the agreement for that reason. The fact that the person responsible had made no further enquiries, which would merely have demonstrated the truth of that belief, was neither here or there. Nor was that person's decision to take the risk-free course of giving fourteen days' notice rather handing out a summary notice.

**13.74** Regulation 18(a) is more restrictive than the common law. At common law, it is well established that when dismissing a servant or agent an employer is entitled to

---

depending on the circumstances. Words spoken in the heat of the moment may not always lead to a conclusion that they are such that the relationship cannot continue: *Wilson v Racher* [1974] ICR 428; but in the content and the context of what is said and done may amount to a repudiatory breach: *Pepper v Webb* [1969] 1 WLR 514. An apology may lead to the conclusion that the conduct is not repudiatory but this is likely to be only the position where the words were spoken in heat and haste and the apology is heartfelt and sincere: *Charles Letts & Co v Howard* [1976] IRLR 248.'

[156] [2013] 1 Lloyd's Rep 1 at [48].

[157] Bean, J, who observed that in his view the *Crocs* case fell 'quite close to the borderline' (at [64]), stated that the majority of obligations in an employment contract will be innominate terms, analogous to the seaworthiness clause analysed by Diplock, LJ in *Hong Kong Fir Shipping Co v Kawasaki Kisen Kaisha* [1962] 2 QB 26, and not akin to a maritime time clause such as was present in *Bunge Corporation (New York) v Tradax Export SA* [1981] 1 WLR 711: unlike time clauses, not all employees' duties under contracts of employment will inevitably be of the essence.

[158] [2007] 2 All ER (Comm) 599 at [85].

rely upon breaches of the contract by the agent which would have justified immediate dismissal but which were not known to the employer at the time.[159] Regulation 18(a), however, refers to the principal terminating the agency contract 'because of default attributable to the commercial agent which would justify immediate termination of the agency contract.' In order to bring himself within reg 18(a), a principal must show:

(a) that he terminated the agency agreement on grounds of default by the commercial agent that constituted a repudiation by him of the contract; and

(b) that the existence of repudiatory conduct on the part of the agent would not assist the principal if that was not the reason actually relied upon for his termination of the contract.

Therefore, whenever reg 18(a) is invoked the court must inquire into whether any of the commercial agent's alleged breaches of contract were repudiatory and which, if any, was the actual reason for the termination of the agreement.[160] By way of example, in *Nigel Fryer Joinery Services Ltd v Ian Firth Hardware Ltd* F was in breach of his agreement with IFH in two respects: F had failed to submit weekly reports to IFH, as agreed in the contract, and F was acting for other concerns rather than working exclusively for IFH, as promised. F's failure to file reports, even after warnings from IFH, demonstrated that this was considered an important term in their contract and IFH was 'entitled ... to treat it as a repudiation by [F] of the agency agreement'.[161] Similarly, F's unauthorized pursuit of outside activities and his failure to disclose them were also held to amount to repudiatory conduct.[162] Patten, J next considered whether IFH had actually relied upon either of these repudiatory breaches as the reason for terminating F's agency. Particularly in light of F's letter of dismissal, which referred to F's outside activities and his continuing 'lack of performance', Patten, J concluded that IFH were entitled to rely upon reg 18(a) and that F was not entitled to compensation under reg 17.

**(ii) Subject to two exceptions, the entitlement to indemnity or compensation is lost if the agent has himself terminated the agency contract** Regulation 18(b) provides that an agent loses his entitlement to indemnity or compensation if 'the commercial agent has himself terminated the agency contract.' However, this is subject to two important exceptions. First, if the commercial agent is justified in terminating the agency 'by circumstances attributable to the principal', he retains his entitlement (reg 18(b)(i)). Second, if the commercial agent cannot reasonably

**13.75**

---

[159] Eg, *Cyril Leonard v Simo Securities Trust Ltd* [1971] 3 All ER 1313. In relation to reg 17, see *Volvo Car Germany GmbH v Autohof Weidensdorf GmbH* (case C-203/09) [2011] 1 All ER (Comm) 906.

[160] See *Nigel Fryer Joiner Services Ltd v Ian Firth Hardware Ltd* [2008] 2 Lloyd's Rep 108 at [22] *per* Patten, J.

[161] *Ibid* at [42].

[162] *Ibid* at [47].

be required to continue his activities 'on grounds of ... age, infirmity or illness', the fact that the agent has himself terminated the agency will not deprive him of his entitlement to indemnity or compensation.

**13.76** **(iii) The entitlement to indemnity and compensation is lost when, with the principal's agreement, the commercial agent assigns his rights and duties under the agency contract** Finally, if the principal agrees to the commercial agent's assigning his rights and duties under the agency contract, the commercial agent will lose his entitlement to indemnity or compensation (reg 18(c)).

## Commercial Agents and Restraint of Trade Clauses

**13.77** Following termination of their agreement, the principal may wish to protect his position by imposing restrictions on the agent's freedom to compete with his former employer. Regulation 20 of the Commercial Agents (Council Directive) Regulations 1993 provides that contractual clauses in restraint of trade may be treated as valid subject to three conditions:

- The clause must have been concluded in writing (reg 20(1)(a));
- The clause must relate 'to the geographical area or the group of customers and the geographical area entrusted to the commercial agent and to the kind of goods covered by his agency under the contract' (reg 20(1)(b)); and
- The clause must not be valid for more than two years (reg 20(2)).

Finally, reg 20(3) stipulates that it does not affect any legislation or rule of law imposing other restrictions on the validity or enforceability of restraint of trade clauses or which enables a court to reduce the obligations on the parties resulting from such clauses. Thus, domestic rules affecting clauses in restraint of trade will also apply.[163]

**13.78** English law on restrictive practices embodies the proposition stated by Lord Macnaghten in *Nordenfelt v Maxim Nordenfelt Guns and Ammunition Co Ltd* that:

> The public have an interest in every person's carrying on his trade freely: so has the individual. All interference with individual liberty of action in trading, and all restraints of trade of themselves, if there is nothing more, are contrary to public policy ...[164]

Clauses in contracts impeding individuals' right to ply their trade, therefore, will only be enforced provided that they can be shown to be reasonable. This requirement, which emerged in cases involving contracts of employment, is frequently said to lead to a three-stage test.[165] *First,* the court must decide what the covenant

---

[163] See further paras **1.12–1.14**.
[164] [1894] AC 535, 564.
[165] Eg, *TFS Derivatives Ltd v Simon Morgan* [2005] IRLR 246.

means when properly construed. This may mean that if a clause is susceptible of two meanings, one which leads to the conclusion that the covenant constitutes an unreasonable restraint on trade and the other that it is not, the latter interpretation is to be preferred.[166] *Secondly*, the court will consider whether the former principal/employer has demonstrated on the evidence that he has legitimate business interests requiring protection in relation to the agent/employee's employment. The principal may not restrict the agent's freedom to work post-termination just because that is what he wishes to do. In order to show that the restraint is reasonable, the principal may be able to point to such things as, say, the need to protect his customer contacts, to protect confidential commercial information[167] or to maintain the integrity or stability of the workforce. *Thirdly*, once the existence of legitimate protectable interests has been established, the covenant must be shown to be no wider than is reasonably necessary for the protection of those interests. Reasonable necessity is to be assessed from the perspective of reasonable persons in the position of the parties as at the date of the contract, having regard to the contractual provisions as a whole and to the factual matrix to which the contract would then realistically have been expected to apply.[168] The practice followed within an industry or terms found in similar contracts employed within a particular industry may be a relevant consideration.

Irwin, J applied these principles to a commercial agency contract in *BCM Group plc v Visualmark Ltd*,[169] where, for the first time, an English court was required to consider the enforceability of a post-termination restrictive covenant in an agency agreement. The clause in question provided that following termination of the parties' agreement: **13.79**

> Within a period of two years thereafter [Visualmark] will not thereafter canvass, approach or solicit the custom of (in respect of any business which competes for the business of [BCM] as at the date of such termination) any person firm or company who has, during the period of one year prior to termination been a customer of [BCM].

In determining the reasonableness of this term, and more particularly its duration, Irwin, J observed that an agent, who is less closely tied to his principal than an employee is to his employer, ought not to be subject to more onerous restrictive covenants than an employee.[170] In this case, he held, the BCM could be said to be protecting a legitimate business interest, namely its interest in maintaining the business and contacts established by Visualmark. Nor was the period of two years too long in the circumstances, bearing in mind that it did not infringe reg 20(2) of the

---

[166] *BCM Group plc v Visualmark Ltd* [2006] EWHC 1831 (QB).
[167] Eg, *Extec Screens & Crushers Ltd v Rice* [2007] EWHC 1043 (QB).
[168] *TFS Derivatives Ltd v Simon Morgan* [2005] IRLR 246 at [37] *per* Cox, J.
[169] [2006] EWHC 1831 (QB).
[170] *Ibid* at [56].

Commercial Agents (Council Directive) Regulations 1993.[171] The clause was nevertheless too widely drawn in that it applied to any of BCM Group plc's customers, regardless as to whether Visualmark had actually had any dealings with the customer concerned. In short, Visualmark had no means of identifying with which customers it had or had not had previous dealings on behalf of BCM. Furthermore, such persons could not be said to be the customers which were 'entrusted to' Visualmark for the purposes of reg 20(1)(b) of the 1993 Regulations.[172]

**13.80**   Once a contractual clause has been found to be in restraint of trade, the judge finally has to consider whether the clause can be read down or subject to severance in order that a reduced portion of the clause might remain enforceable. Because the courts may not make contracts for the parties, Irwin, J, citing the decision of the Court of Session in *Hinton & Higgs (UK) Ltd v Murphy*,[173] stated that he could proceed 'by deletion only':

> If the law can cut out a part of what was agreed but leave a comprehensible and working agreed text which is enforceable, then the law is really saying that what is not unenforceable was nevertheless agreed in comprehensible terms between the parties and can stand. That is the process by which the blue pencil operates. What the court will not generally do, save in very exceptional circumstances, is to say, in effect, what you chose falls away but the law will rewrite for you, retrospectively, obligations you never agreed.[174]

In the event, Irwin, J concluded that the clause could not be saved 'by deletion only'.

---

[171] Irwin, J did, however, point out that the maximum two-year period allowed for under the Regulations would not always be appropriate in all cases: *ibid* at [46].

[172] 'It seems to me impossible ... to strain the meaning of the term 'entrusted' as far as [counsel] seeks to do. Customers who were handled by employed sales staff, working from [BCM's] headquarters, and who had no dealings whatever with ... Visualmark ... can in no sense be said to be entrusted to him': *ibid* at [51]. Cp *Herbert Morris Ltd v Saxelby* [1916] AC 688; *GW Plowman & Son Ltd v Ash* [1964] 1 WLR 568.

[173] 1989 SLT 450, 452 *per* Lord Devaird.

[174] [2006] EWHC 1831 (QB) at [61].

# INDEX